DRAMA
for Students

DRAMA
for Students

**Presenting Analysis, Context and Criticism on
Commonly Studied Dramas**

Volume 8

David Galens, Editor

Detroit
New York
San Francisco
London
Boston
Woodbridge, CT

National Advisory Board

Drama for Students

Staff

Editorial: David M. Galens, *Editor*. Andrea Henry, Mark Milne, and Kathleen Wilson, *Contributing Editors*. James Draper, *Managing Editor*. David Galens, *"For Students" Line Coordinator*.

Research: Victoria B. Cariappa, *Research Manager*. Andrew Guy Malonis, Barbara McNeil, Gary J. Oudersluys, Maureen Richards, and Cheryl L. Warnock, *Research Specialists*. Patricia Tsune Ballard, Wendy K. Festerling, Tamara C. Nott, Tracie A. Richardson, Corrine A. Stocker, and Robert Whaley, *Research Associates*. Phyllis J. Blackman, Tim Lehnerer, and Patricia L. Love, *Research Assistants*.

Permissions: Maria Franklin, *Permissions Manager*. Kimberly F. Smilay, *Permissions Specialist*. Kelly A. Quin, *Permissions Associate*. Sandra K. Gore, *Permissions Assistant*.

Graphic Services: Randy Bassett, *Image Database Supervisor*. Robert Duncan and Michael Logusz, *Imaging Specialists*. Pamela A. Reed, *Imaging Coordinator*. Gary Leach, *Macintosh Artist*.

Product Design: Cynthia Baldwin, *Product Design Manager*. Cover Design: Michelle DiMercurio, *Art Director*. Page Design: Pamela A. E. Galbreath, *Senior Art Director*.

Copyright Notice

Table of Contents

The Study of Drama

We study drama in order to learn what meaning others have made of life, to comprehend what it takes to produce a work of art, and to glean some understanding of ourselves. Drama produces in a separate, aesthetic world, a moment of being for the audience to experience, while maintaining the detachment of a reflective observer.

Drama is a representational art, a visible and audible narrative presenting virtual, fictional characters within a virtual, fictional universe. Dramatic realizations may pretend to approximate reality or else stubbornly defy, distort, and deform reality into an artistic statement. From this separate universe that is obviously not ''real life'' we expect a valid reflection upon reality, yet drama never is mistaken for reality—the methods of theater are integral to its form and meaning. Theater is art, and art's appeal lies in its ability both to approximate life and to depart from it. By presenting its distorted version of life to our consciousness, art gives us a new perspective and appreciation of reality. Although, to some extent, all aesthetic experiences perform this service, theater does it most effectively by creating a separate, cohesive universe that freely acknowledges its status as an art form.

And what is the purpose of the aesthetic universe of drama? The potential answers to such a question are nearly as many and varied as there are plays written, performed, and enjoyed. Dramatic texts can be problems posed, answers asserted, or moments portrayed. Dramas (tragedies as well as comedies) may serve strictly ''to ease the anguish of a torturing hour'' (as stated in William Shakespeare's *A Midsummer Night's Dream*)—to divert and entertain—or aspire to move the viewer to action with social issues. Whether to entertain or to instruct, affirm or influence, pacify or shock, dramatic art wraps us in the spell of its imaginary world for the length of the work and then dispenses us back to the real world, entertained, purged, as Aristotle said, of pity and fear, and edified—or at least weary enough to sleep peacefully.

It is commonly thought that theater, being an art of performance, must be experienced—that is, seen—in order to be appreciated fully. However, to view a production of a dramatic text is to be limited to a single interpretation of that text—all other interpretations are for the moment closed off, inaccessible. In the process of producing a play, the director, stage designer, and performers interpret and transform the script into a work of art that always departs in some measure from the author's original conception. Novelist and critic Umberto Eco, in his *The Role of the Reader: Explorations in the Semiotics of Texts,* explained, ''In short, we can say that every performance offers us a complete and satisfying version of the work, but at the same time makes it incomplete for us, because it cannot simultaneously give all the other artistic solutions which the work may admit.''

Thus Laurence Olivier's coldly formal and neurotic film presentation of Shakespeare's *Hamlet* (in which he played the title character as well as directed) shows marked differences from subsequent adaptations. While Olivier's Hamlet is clearly entangled in a Freudian relationship with his mother, Gertrude, he would be incapable of shushing her with the impassioned kiss that Mel Gibson's mercurial Hamlet (in director Franco Zeffirelli's 1990 film) does. Although each of the performances rings true to Shakespeare's text, each is also a mutually exclusive work of art. Also important to consider are the time periods in which each of these films were produced: Olivier made his film in 1948, a time in which overt references to sexuality (especially incest) were frowned upon. Gibson and Zeffirelli made their film in a culture more relaxed and comfortable with these issues. Just as actors and directors can influence the presentation of drama, so too can the time period of the production affect what the audience will see.

A play script is an open text from which an infinity of specific realizations may be derived. Dramatic scripts that are more open to interpretive creativity (such as those of Ntozake Shange and Tomson Highway) actually require the creative improvisation of the production troupe in order to complete the text. Even the most prescriptive scripts (those of Neil Simon, Lillian Hellman, and Robert Bolt, for example), can never fully control the actualization of live performance, and circumstantial events, including the attitude and receptivity of the audience, make every performance a unique event. Thus, while it is important to view a production of a dramatic piece, if one wants to understand a drama fully it is equally important to read the original dramatic text.

The reader of a dramatic text or script is not limited by either the specific interpretation of a given production or by the unstoppable action of a moving spectacle. The reader of a dramatic text may discover the nuances of the play's language, struc-ture, and events at their own pace. Yet studied alone, the author's blueprint for artistic production does not tell the whole story of a play's life and significance. One also needs to assess the play's critical reviews to discover how it resonated to cultural themes at the time of its debut and how the shifting tides of cultural interest have revised its interpretation and impact on audiences. And to do this, one needs to know a little about the culture of the times which produced the play as well as the author who penned it.

Drama for Students supplies this material in a useful compendium for the student of dramatic theater. Covering a range of dramatic works that span from the fifth century B.C. to the 1990s, this book focuses on significant theatrical works whose themes and form transcend the uncertainty of dramatic fads. These are plays that have proven to be both memorable and teachable. *Drama for Students* seeks to enhance appreciation of these dramatic texts by providing scholarly materials written with the secondary and college/university student in mind. It provides for each play a concise summary of the plot and characters as well as a detailed explanation of its themes and techniques. In addition, background material on the historical context of the play, its critical reception, and the author's life help the student to understand the work's position in the chronicle of dramatic history. For each play entry a new work of scholarly criticism is also included, as well as segments of other significant critical works for handy reference. A thorough bibliography provides a starting point for further research.

These inaugural two volumes offer comprehensive educational resources for students of drama. *Drama for Students* is a vital book for dramatic interpretation and a valuable addition to any reference library.

Source: Eco, Umberto, *The Role of the Reader: Explorations in the Semiotics of Texts,* Indiana University Press, 1979.

Carole L. Hamilton
Author and Instructor of English
Cary Academy
Cary, North Carolina

Introduction

Purpose of Drama for Students

The purpose of *Drama for Students* (*DfS*) is to provide readers with a guide to understanding, enjoying, and studying dramas by giving them easy access to information about the work. Part of Gale's "For Students" literature line, *DfS* is specifically designed to meet the curricular needs of high school and undergraduate college students and their teachers, as well as the interests of general readers and researchers considering specific plays. While each volume contains entries on "classic" dramas frequently studied in classrooms, there are also entries containing hard-to-find information on contemporary plays, including works by multicultural, international, and women playwrights.

The information covered in each entry includes an introduction to the play and the work's author; a plot summary, to help readers unravel and understand the events in a drama; descriptions of important characters, including explanation of a given character's role in the drama as well as discussion about that character's relationship to other characters in the play; analysis of important themes in the drama; and an explanation of important literary techniques and movements as they are demonstrated in the play.

In addition to this material, which helps the readers analyze the play itself, students are also provided with important information on the literary and historical background informing each work.

This includes a historical context essay, a box comparing the time or place the drama was written to modern Western culture, a critical overview essay, and excerpts from critical essays on the play. A unique feature of *DfS* is a specially commissioned overview essay on each drama by an academic expert, targeted toward the student reader.

To further aid the student in studying and enjoying each play, information on media adaptations is provided, as well as reading suggestions for works of fiction and nonfiction on similar themes and topics. Classroom aids include ideas for research papers and lists of critical sources that provide additional material on each drama.

Selection Criteria

The titles for each volume of *DfS* were selected by surveying numerous sources on teaching literature and analyzing course curricula for various school districts. Some of the sources surveyed included: literature anthologies; *Reading Lists for College-Bound Students: The Books Most Recommended by America's Top Colleges;* textbooks on teaching dramas; a College Board survey of plays commonly studied in high schools; a National Council of Teachers of English (NCTE) survey of plays commonly studied in high schools; St. James Press's *International Dictionary of Theatre;* and Arthur Applebee's 1993 study *Literature in the Secondary School: Studies of Curriculum and Instruction in the United States.*

Input was also solicited from our expert advisory board (both experienced educators specializing in English), as well as educators from various areas. From these discussions, it was determined that each volume should have a mix of ''classic'' dramas (those works commonly taught in literature classes) and contemporary dramas for which information is often hard to find. Because of the interest in expanding the canon of literature, an emphasis was also placed on including works by international, multicultural, and women playwrights. Our advisory board members—current high school teachers—helped pare down the list for each volume. If a work was not selected for the present volume, it was often noted as a possibility for a future volume. As always, the editor welcomes suggestions for titles to be included in future volumes.

How Each Entry Is Organized

Each entry, or chapter, in *DfS* focuses on one play. Each entry heading lists the full name of the play, the author's name, and the date of the play's first production or publication. The following elements are contained in each entry:

- **Introduction:** a brief overview of the drama which provides information about its first appearance, its literary standing, any controversies surrounding the work, and major conflicts or themes within the work.

- **Author Biography:** this section includes basic facts about the author's life, and focuses on events and times in the author's life that inspired the drama in question.

- **Plot Summary:** a description of the major events in the play, with interpretation of how these events help articulate the play's themes. Subheads demarcate the plays' various acts or scenes.

- **Characters:** an alphabetical listing of major characters in the play. Each character name is followed by a brief to an extensive description of the character's role in the plays, as well as discussion of the character's actions, relationships, and possible motivation.

  Characters are listed alphabetically by last name. If a character is unnamed—for instance, the Stage Manager in *Our Town*—the character is listed as ''The Stage Manager'' and alphabetized as ''Stage Manager.'' If a character's first name is the only one given, the name will appear alphabetically by the name.

Variant names are also included for each character. Thus, the nickname ''Babe'' would head the listing for a character in *Crimes of the Heart,* but below that listing would be her less-mentioned married name ''Rebecca Botrelle.''

- **Themes:** a thorough overview of how the major topics, themes, and issues are addressed within the play. Each theme discussed appears in a separate subhead, and is easily accessed through the boldface entries in the Subject/Theme Index.

- **Style:** this section addresses important style elements of the drama, such as setting, point of view, and narration; important literary devices used, such as imagery, foreshadowing, symbolism; and, if applicable, genres to which the work might have belonged, such as Gothicism or Romanticism. Literary terms are explained within the entry, but can also be found in the Glossary.

- **Historical and Cultural Context:** This section outlines the social, political, and cultural climate *in which the author lived and the play was created.* This section may include descriptions of related historical events, pertinent aspects of daily life in the culture, and the artistic and literary sensibilities of the time in which the work was written. If the play is a historical work, information regarding the time in which the play is set is also included. Each section is broken down with helpful subheads.

- **Critical Overview:** this section provides background on the critical reputation of the play, including bannings or any other public controversies surrounding the work. For older plays, this section includes a history of how the drama was first received and how perceptions of it may have changed over the years; for more recent plays, direct quotes from early reviews may also be included.

- **For Further Study:** an alphabetical list of other critical sources which may prove useful for the student. Includes full bibliographical information and a brief annotation.

- **Sources:** an alphabetical list of critical material quoted in the entry, with full bibliographical information.

- **Criticism:** an essay commissioned by *DfS* which specifically deals with the play and is written specifically for the student audience, as well as excerpts from previously published criticism on the work.

In addition, each entry contains the following highlighted sections, set separate from the main text:

- **Media Adaptations:** a list of important film and television adaptations of the play, including source information. The list may also include such variations on the work as audio recordings, musical adaptations, and other stage interpretations.

- **Compare and Contrast Box:** an "at-a-glance" comparison of the cultural and historical differences between the author's time and culture and late twentieth-century Western culture. This box includes pertinent parallels between the major scientific, political, and cultural movements of the time or place the drama was written, the time or place the play was set (if a historical work), and modern Western culture. Works written after the mid-1970s may not have this box.

- **What Do I Read Next?:** a list of works that might complement the featured play or serve as a contrast to it. This includes works by the same author and others, works of fiction and nonfiction, and works from various genres, cultures, and eras.

- **Study Questions:** a list of potential study questions or research topics dealing with the play. This section includes questions related to other disciplines the student may be studying, such as American history, world history, science, math, government, business, geography, economics, psychology, etc.

Other Features

DfS includes "The Study of Drama," a foreword by Carole Hamilton, an educator and author who specializes in dramatic works. This essay examines the basis for drama in societies and what drives people to study such work. Hamilton also discusses how *Drama for Students* can help teachers show students how to enrich their own reading/viewing experiences.

A Cumulative Author/Title Index lists the authors and titles covered in each volume of the *DfS* series.

A Cumulative Nationality/Ethnicity Index breaks down the authors and titles covered in each volume of the *DfS* series by nationality and ethnicity.

A Subject/Theme Index, specific to each volume, provides easy reference for users who may be studying a particular subject or theme rather than a single work. Significant subjects from events to broad themes are included, and the entries pointing to the specific theme discussions in each entry are indicated in **boldface.**

Each entry has several illustrations, including photos of the author, stills from stage productions, and stills from film adaptations.

Citing Drama for Students

When writing papers, students who quote directly from any volume of *Drama for Students* may use the following general forms. These examples are based on MLA style; teachers may request that students adhere to a different style, so the following examples may be adapted as needed.

When citing text from *DfS* that is not attributed to a particular author (i.e., the Themes, Style, Historical Context sections, etc.), the following format should be used in the bibliography section:

> "Our Town," *Drama for Students.* Ed. David Galens and Lynn Spampinato. Vol. 1. Farmington Hills: Gale, 1997. 8–9.

When quoting the specially commissioned essay from *DfS* (usually the first piece under the "Criticism" subhead), the following format should be used:

> Fiero, John. Essay on "Twilight: Los Angeles, 1992." *Drama for Students.* Ed. David Galens and Lynn Spampinato. Vol. 1. Farmington Hills: Gale, 1997. 8–9.

When quoting a journal or newspaper essay that is reprinted in a volume of *DfS*, the following form may be used:

> Rich, Frank. "Theatre: A Mamet Play, 'Glengarry Glen Ross'." *New York Theatre Critics' Review* Vol. 45, No. 4 (March 5, 1984), 5–7; excerpted and reprinted in *Drama for Students,* Vol. 1, ed. David Galens and Lynn Spampinato (Farmington Hills: Gale, 1997), pp. 61–64.

When quoting material reprinted from a book that appears in a volume of *DfS,* the following form may be used:

> Kerr, Walter. "The Miracle Worker," in *The Theatre in Spite of Itself* (Simon & Schuster, 1963, 255–57; excerpted and reprinted in *Drama for Students,* Vol. 1, ed. Dave Galens and Lynn Spampinato (Farmington Hills: Gale, 1997), pp. 59–61.

We Welcome Your Suggestions

The editor of *Drama for Students* welcomes your comments and ideas. Readers who wish to suggest dramas to appear in future volumes, or who have other suggestions, are cordially invited to contact the editor. You may contact the editor via

E-mail at: **david.galens@gale.com.** Or write to the
editor at:

David Galens, *Drama for Students*
The Gale Group
27500 Drake Rd.
Farmington Hills, MI 48331-3535

Literary Chronology

c. 496 B.C.: Sophocles is born in Colonus Hippiu, part of what is now Athens, Greece.

c. 450 B.C.: Sophocles composes *The Ajax.*

c. 406 B.C.: Sophocles dies in Athens.

1828: Henrik Ibsen is born in Skien, Norway, on March 20.

1854: Oscar Wilde is born Oscar Fingal O'Flahertie Wills Wilde on October 16 in Dublin, Ireland.

1873: Alfred Jarry is born in Laval, France, on September 8.

1876: Ibsen adapts his prose work *Peer Gynt* for the stage.

1882: Susan Glaspell is born in Davenport, Iowa, on July 1.

1893: *Salome* is published in France and England following two years of controversy surrounding the work; the play is published with drawings by Aubrey Beardsley; the play is finally produced for the stage in France in 1896 and in England in 1905.

1896: Jarry's *Ubu Roi* debuts to considerable controversy on December 11 in Paris, France.

1900: Having lived in shame and exile, Oscar Wilde dies in France (where he had assumed the pseudonym Sebastien Melmoth) on November 30.

1906: Following several strokes and years of ill health, Henrik Ibsen dies on May 23.

1907: Following years of substance abuse and a descent into mental illness, Alfred Jarry dies in a charity hospital in Paris, France, on November 1.

1911: Terrence Rattigan is born on June 10 in London, England.

1913: William Inge is born on May 3 in Independence, Kansas.

1915: Arthur Miller is born on October 17 in New York City.

1916: *Trifles* debuts.

1920: Alice Childress is born on October 12 in Charleston, South Carolina.

1928: Edward Albee is born.

1934: Edward Bond is born in Holloway, North London.

1937: Tom Stoppard is born Tomas Straussler in Czechoslovakia on July 3.

1938: John Guare is born on February 5 in New York City.

1939: Charles Fuller is born in Philadelphia on March 5.

1940: David Rabe is born on March 10 in Dubuque, Iowa.

1947: *All My Sons* debuts at the Coronet Theatre in New York City on January 29.

1948: *The Browning Version* debuts at London's Phoenix Theatre on September 8; it debuts in New York City the following year.

1948: Susan Glaspell dies.

1955: *Bus Stop* opens on Broadway on March 2.

1955: *Trouble in Mind* debuts at the Greenwich Mews Theatre in New York City on November 5.

1965: Bond's controversial play *Saved* is produced on November 3 at the Royal Court Theatre in London as a private club production in order to avoid the censorship of the Lord Chamberlain.

1971: *House of Blue Leaves* opens Off-Broadway on February 10.

1973: William Inge dies from carbon monoxide inhalation; the death is ruled a suicide.

1976: *Streamers* debuts at the Long Wharf Theatre in New Haven, Connecticut, on January 30.

1977: Terrence Rattigan dies of bone cancer on November 30.

1981: *A Soldier's Play* debuts at the Negro Ensemble Theatre on November 20.

1982: *The Real Thing* is produced in London's West End; the successful production moves to New York City two years later.

1991: Albee's *Three Tall Women* is first produced.

1994: Alice Childress dies of cancer in New York City on August 14.

Acknowledgments

The editors wish to thank the copyright holders of the excerpted criticism included in this volume and the permissions managers of many book and magazine publishing companies for assisting us in securing reproduction rights. We are also grateful to the staffs of the Detroit Public Library, the Library of Congress, the University of Detroit Mercy Library, Wayne State University Purdy/Kresge Library Complex, and the University of Michigan Libraries for making their resources available to us. Following is a list of the copyright holders who have granted us permission to reproduce material in this volume of *DfS*. Every effort has been made to trace copyright, but if omissions have been made, please let us know.

COPYRIGHTED EXCERPTS IN *DfS*, VOLUME 8, WERE REPRODUCED FROM THE FOLLOWING PERIODICALS:

Classical Journal, v. 61, December, 1965. Reproduced by permission of the publisher.—*Commonweal,* v. LXII, April 8, 1955. Copyright © 1955 Commonweal Publishing Co., Inc. Reproduced by permission of Commonweal Foundation.—*The Explicator,* v. 42, Fall, 1983; v. 44, Spring, 1986; v. 45, Fall, 1986; v. 53, Summer, 1995; v. 55, Winter, 1997. Copyright © 1983, 1986, 1995, 1997 by Helen Dwight Reid Educational Foundation. All reproduced with permission of the Helen Dwight Reid Educational Foundation, published by Heldref Publications, 1319 18th Street, NW, Washington,

DC 20036-1802.—*The Hudson Review,* v. XXXV, Autumn, 1982. Copyright © 1982 by The Hudson Review, Inc. Reproduced by permission.—*Literature/Film Quarterly,* v. 17, 1989. © Copyright 1989 Salisbury State University. All rights reserved. Reproduced by permission.—*Maclean's Magazine,* v. 102, July 24, 1989. © 1992 by Maclean's Magazine. Reproduced by permission.—*Modern Drama,* v. 7, May, 1964; v. XV, May, 1972; v. XXXV, September, 1992. Copyright © 1964, 1972, 1992 University of Toronto, Graduate Centre for Study of Drama. All reproduced by permission.—*The Nation,* New York, v. 178, May 29, 1954; v. 234, January 23, 1982; v. 242, June 7, 1986; v. 258, March 14, 1994. Copyright 1954, (c) 1982, 1986, 1994 The Nation magazine/ The Nation Company, Inc. All reproduced by permission.—*The New Republic,* v. 142, February 1, 1960; v. 109, January 30, 1984. © 1960, 1984 The New Republic, Inc. Both reproduced by permission of *The New Republic.*—*The New Yorker,* v. LII, May 3, 1976; v. 62, March 31, 1986. © 1976, 1986 by The New Yorker Magazine, Inc. All rights reserved. Both reproduced by permission.—*New York,* Magazine, v. 9, May 10, 1976; v. 17, January 16, 1984; v. 19, March 31, 1986; v. 22, April 24, 1989. Copyright © 1976, 1984, 1986, 1989 PRIMEDIA Magazine Corporation. All rights reserved. All reproduced with the permission of *New York* Magazine.—*Theater,* v. XVII, Summer/Fall, 1987. Copyright © 1987 by Theater. Reproduced by permission of Duke University Press.—*Theatre Journal,* v. 44, May, 1992. © 1992, University and College Theatre Association of the American Theatre Association. Reproduced by permission of The Johns Hopkins University Press.—*The Times Literary Supplement,* October 23, 1992. © The Times Supplements Limited 1992. Reproduced from *The Times Literary Supplement* by permission.

COPYRIGHTED EXCERPTS IN *DFS,* VOLUME 8, WERE REPRODUCED FROM THE FOLLOWING BOOKS:

Brown-Guillory, Elizabeth. From *Their Place on the Stage: Black Women Playwrights in America.* Greenwood Press, 1988. Copyright © 1988 by Elizabeth Brown-Guillory. All rights reserved. Reproduced by permission of Greenwood Publishing Group, Inc., Westport, CT.

PHOTOGRAPHS AND ILLUSTRATIONS APPEARING IN *DFS,* VOLUME 8, WERE RECEIVED FROM THE FOLLOWING SOURCES:

Albee, Edward, photograph. The Library of Congress.—Bond, Edward, photograph by Jerry Bauer. © Jerry Bauer. Reproduced by permission.—Childress, Alice, photograph by Jerry Bauer. © Jerry Bauer. Reproduced by permission.—From a movie still of *Bus Stop* by William Inge, Directed by Joshua Logan, with Marilyn Monroe as Cherie and Don Murray as Beauregard "Beau" Decker, 1956, photograph. Archive Photos, Inc. Reproduced by permission.—From a movie still of *Salome's Last Dance* based on the play by Oscar Wilde, Directed by Ken Russell, with Stratford Johns as Herod/Alfred Taylor and Glenda Jackson as Herodias/Lady Alice, 1988, photograph. Archive Photos, Inc. Reproduced by permission.—From a movie still of *Streamers* by David Rabe, Directed by Robert Altman, with Mitchell Lichenstein as Richie and Michael Wright as Carlyle, United Artists, 1983, photograph. UNITED ARTISTS. Courtesy of The Kobal Collection. Reproduced by permission.—From a movie still of *Streamers* by David Rabe, Directed by Robert Altman, with Michael Wright as Carlyle, United Artists, 1983, United Artists, 1983, photograph. UNITED ARTISTS. Courtesy of The Kobal Collection. Reproduced by permission.—From a movie still of *The Browning Version* by Terrence Rattigan, Directed by Mike Figgis, with Albert Finney as Andrew Crocker-Harris and Greta Scacchi as Laura Crocker-Harris, Paramount Pictures 1994, photograph by Clive Coote. Reuters/Archive Photos, Inc. Reproduced by permission.—

From a theatre production of Arthur Miller's *All My Sons* Directed by Irving Reis, with Edward G. Robinson as Joe Keller, Burt Lancaster as Chris Keller and , Universal Pictures, Inc. 1948, photograph. UNIVERSAL. Courtesy of The Kobal Collection. Reproduced by permission.—From a theatre production of Arthur Miller's *All My Sons* Directed by Irving Reis, with Edward G. Robinson as Joe Keller and Howard Duff as George Deever, Universal Pictures, Inc. 1948, photograph. UNIVERSAL. Courtesy of The Kobal Collection. Reproduced by permission.—From a theatre production of *Peer Gynt* by Henrik Ibsen, with (l-r) Derek Jacob and Nigel Hawthorne, RSC/The Other Place, June, 1982, photograph. (c) Donald Cooper/Photostage. Reproduced by permission.—From a theatre production of *Peer Gynt* by Henrik Ibsen, with Derek Jacob, RSC/The Other Place, June, 1982, photograph. (c) Donald Cooper/Photostage. Reproduced by permission.—From a theatre production of *Saved* by Edward Bond, Royal Court, London, December, 1984, photograph. (c) Donald Cooper/Photostage. Reproduced by permission.—From a theatre production of *Saved* by Edward Bond, Royal Court, London, 1969, photograph. (c) Donald Cooper/Photostage. Reproduced by permission.—From a theatre production of *The House of Blue Leaves* by John Guare, with (l-r) Helen Lederer as Bunny, Nichola McAuliffe as Bananas and Denis Quilley as Artie, Lilian Bayliss Theatre, London, October 24, 1988, photograph. (c) Donald Cooper/Photostage. Reproduced by permission.—From a theatre production of *The Real Thing* by Tom Stoppard, with Roger Rees as Henry and Felicity Kendal as Annie, Strand Theatre, 1982, photograph. (c) Donald Cooper/Photostage. Reproduced by permission.—From a theatre production of *The Real Thing* by Tom Stoppard, with Jennifer Ehle as Annie and Stephen Dillane as Henry, Donmar Warehouse, February 6, 1999, photograph. © Donald Cooper/Photostage. Reproduced by permission.—From a theatre production of *Three Tall Women* by Edward Albee, with (front, clockwise) Samantha Bond, Sara Kestelman and Maggie Smith, Wyndham's, September, 1995, photograph. © Donald Cooper/Photostage. Reproduced by permission.—From a theatre production of *Ubu Roi* by Alfred Jarry, with (l-r) Charlie Drake, Claire Davenport and Roy Barraclough, Jeanetta Codrane Theatre, March 31, 1980, photograph. © Donald Cooper/Photostage. Reproduced by permission.—From a theatre production of *Ubu Roi* by Alfred Jarry, with Luis Alberto Soto as Pa Ubu and Christine Entwisle as Ma Ubu, Young Vic Studio, July 22, 1998, photograph. © Donald Cooper/Photostage. Reproduced by permission.—Fuller, Charles, photograph. AP/Wide World, Inc. Reproduced by permission.—Glaspell, Susan, photograph. AP/WIDE WORLD PHOTOS. Reproduced by permission.—Guare, John, photograph. Jerry Bauer. Reproduced by permission.—Ibsen, Henrik, photograph. The Library of Congress.—Inge, William R., photograph. The Library of Congress.—Jarry, Alfred, drawing by F. A. Cazalz, 1897, photograph. Corbis-Bettmann. Reproduced by permission.—Miller, Arthur, photograph. The Library of Congress.—Rabe, David, photograph. AP/Wide World Photos. Reproduced by permission.—Rattigan, Sir Terence, age 60, 1971, photograph. AP/Wide World Photos. Reproduced by permission.—Sophocles, photograph of a illustration. Archive Photos, Inc. Reproduced by permission.—Stoppard, Tom, photograph. AP/Wide World Photos. Reproduced by permission.—Wilde, Oscar, photograph. The Library of Congress.

Contributors

Terry Browne: Affiliated with the School of Performing Arts at the State University of New York, Geneseo. Entry on *Saved.*

Clare Cross: Doctoral candidate, University of Michigan, Ann Arbor. Entry on *Salome.*

John Fiero: Professor Emeritus of Drama and Playwriting, University of Southwestern Louisiana. Entries on *All My Sons* and *Streamers.*

Lane A. Glenn: Author, educator, director, and actor, Lansing, Michigan. Entries on *Three Tall Women* and *Trifles.*

Helena Ifeka: Doctoral candidate, Columbia University, and freelance author. Entries on *The Philadelphia Story* and *The Real Thing.*

Sheri Metzger: Freelance writer and Ph.D., Albuquerque, NM. Entries on *Ajax, Bus Stop, Peer Gynt* and *A Soldier's Play.*

Annette Petrusso: Freelance author and screenwriter, Austin, TX. Entries on *The Browning Version, House of Blue Leaves,* and *Trouble in Mind.*

William Wiles: Educator and free-lance author, Rutland, Vermont. Entry on *Ubu Roi.*

Ajax

SOPHOCLES

444 B.C.

Ajax is the earliest of Sophocles's surviving plays. It is thought that the play's first performance took place about 444 B.C., but the exact date is not certain and might have been a few years earlier or later.

The hero of the play, Ajax, illustrates the uncompromising nature of the noble warrior; yet at the same time, he also represents the failings of excess pride, or hubris. Ajax believes that he deserves the armor of Achilles, and he is unable to accept that another warrior has been chosen as more worthy. His pride will not permit him to see the strength of Odysseus, nor will it allow Ajax to recognize his own limitations.

Ajax is a great hero, but he is rigidly defined as the old-fashioned hero—uncompromising and unable to recognize his own weaknesses. It is his rejection of help from the goddess Athena that sets the stage for this tragedy. Athena's gloating punishment of Ajax also presents the gods in a less favorable way than earlier plays, such as Aeschylus's *Oresteia,* which portrays the gods as wise protectors rather than vengeful deities.

Sophocles's source was probably Homer, who depicted Ajax as obstinate to the point of stupidity in *The Iliad.* Both Ajax and Odysseus fought bravery with Achilles, and it took both warriors to retrieve Achilles's body after his death. Both men were honorable, but the Greek commanders voted that Achilles's armor should be awarded to Odysseus.

This act provides the impetus for Ajax's actions, which take place just prior to the opening of Sophocles's play.

AUTHOR BIOGRAPHY

Sophocles was born in Colonus Hippiu, now a part of Athens, c. 496 B.C. He was the son of Sophillus, an armor manufacturer. Little is known of his youth, except that he is thought to have received a traditional aristocratic education. Sophocles married and was elected to high military office, although he was not interested in the military life.

His dates of birth and death closely correspond to the beginning and end of the Golden Age of Athens (480-404 B.C.). This was a period in which the city reached political and cultural supremacy in the Greek world. In 468 B.C., he entered the drama competition at the Great Dionysia, a festival to celebrate the god Dionysus. As part of the festival, four plays were performed and judged. Sophocles defeated Aeschylus, then the preeminent dramatic poet in Greece, and won the competition; unfortunately, his winning play, *Triptolemos,* has since been lost. Sophocles later won the first prize more than twenty times and the second prize many more times. It is said that he never won less than second prize in any competition.

Sophocles lived to be ninety, and during his long life he is believed to have composed more than one hundred and twenty-three plays; unfortunately, only seven are known to have survived in their entirety. Of these seven, *Ajax* is the earliest composition, having been written in about 450 B.C.

Other surviving dramas include *Antigone* (c. 442 B.C.), *Ichneutai* (c. 440 B.C.), *Trakhiniai* (c. 440-430 B.C.), *Oedipus Rex* (c. 430-426 B.C.), *Electra* (c. 425-410 B.C.), *Philoctetes* (409 B.C.), and *Oedipus at Colonus* (c. 404 B.C.). This last play was presented posthumously in 401 B.C. by Sophocles's grandson.

Sophocles is responsible for several theatrical innovations that changed Greek drama. Among these modifications was the focus on individual characters and individual tragedy. In addition, he created a greater realism on stage by introducing scene paintings and more elaborate masks to the usually austere stage. The most important innovation was the addition of a third actor. Prior to Sophocles, two actors played all the roles, with the chorus to comment upon and fill in the missing pieces. The addition of a third actor permitted more complex dialogue and moved the focus from the chorus to the actors, thus changing the drama to a more character-driven format.

Sophocles was able to create exceptional and complex characters, heroes and heroines who were often afflicted with a fatal flaw. Rather than being ideal, his characters embodied a realistic humanity; they often struggled with their own weaknesses and limitations. Sophocles's impact on Greek drama and the literature that follows cannot be overestimated. He is considered to be one of the great figures in world literature.

PLOT SUMMARY

Scene I

The play opens with Athena telling Odysseus that Ajax slaughtered all the captured sheep and cows during the previous night because Odysseus was given the shield of Achilles, an honor Ajax felt he deserved instead. Athena explains that she cast a spell over Ajax so that he thought the animals were Greek warriors; Ajax thought he was killing his fellow soldiers. Meanwhile, Ajax has recovered his wits and is shocked and ashamed at his actions.

The Chorus enters and underscores how low this great warrior has been brought by fate and the actions of the gods. Tecmessa, Ajax's captive and the mother of his child, enters and relates the details surrounding Ajax's attack on the sheep. She also tells of his profound grief and pain when he realized what he had done.

In a lengthy monologue, Ajax bemoans his family honor. He contends that he deserved the honor of Achilles's arms. Instead, the prize unfairly went to Odysseus. Ajax's grief derives not from his homicidal impulse to kill Agamemnon or Odysseus, but that Athena fooled him into killing sheep. Worse, he believes that the other warriors are laughing at him.

Ajax speaks of suicide, and Tecmessa argues that he must not kill himself. She maintains that she needs him and so does his son. She also points to his mother's grief and his father's love, and Ajax responds by asking that his son be brought to him.

After Ajax and Tecmessa leave the stage, a soldier enters and describes the arrival of Ajax's brother, Teucer. He has entered the camp to the jeers and insults of soldiers who call him the brother of a madman. He was also warned by a prophet to keep Ajax inside all day, but he has arrived too late to prevent Ajax from leaving. The prophet has predicted that Athena's rage will be spent by nightfall, and that unless Ajax is kept inside for the day, he will die.

The prophet asserts that humans aim too high and that men should not look to be as great as the gods. This was Ajax's mistake, and this is why the gods are punishing him. The scene ends with Tecmessa asking that everyone go in search of Ajax and save him.

Scene II

Ajax enters, alone. He puts his sword in the sand, hilt first, and asks Zeus to send messengers to inform his brother of his death. Ajax is afraid that his enemies will learn of his death first and his body will be desecrated. Ajax also asks that his death be avenged, and after expressing concern for his mother and father, Ajax falls upon his sword and commits suicide.

The Chorus enters, looking for Ajax, but Tecmessa finds him and emits a loud wailing sound of grief. The Chorus and Tecmessa lament for Ajax's life, now lost. Teucer enters and he, too, is grief-stricken at his brother's death. Teucer orders that his nephew be brought so that he can be protected from Ajax's enemies, who might seek to harm the child. Teucer expresses concern that their father will blame him for having allowed Ajax to die in such a manner.

Menelaus enters and orders that Ajax's body be left to rot where it fell and that no honor be given to the warrior in death. Menelaus decrees that Ajax's rotting body will serve as a lesson to any soldier who thinks to raise a hand against him. The Chorus warns that there must be respect for the dead, but Teucer interrupts in anger and reminds Menelaus that he had no authority over Ajax when he was alive and certainly not when he is dead. Teucer will bury his brother because the law of the gods demands it.

The argument between Teucer and Menelaus continues, with both men calling each other names and insulting one another. The conflict ends when Menelaus and his men leave. In a few moments, Tecmessa and her child enter for a final farewell with Ajax. Teucer leaves to dig a grave, but hurries back accompanied by Agamemnon. Agamemnon is angry and insults Teucer and Ajax.

An illustration of Sophocles

The Chorus calls for compromise, but Teucer reminds Agamemnon of the times that Ajax saved his life and fought beside him in terrific battles. Teucer also reminds Agamemnon of the honorable lineage of Ajax's family.

Odysseus enters, complaining that he could hear Menelaus and Agamemnon yelling across the camp. Acting as the voice of reason, Odysseus asserts that Ajax deserves the honor. Not to bury him would do serious dishonor to the gods. Agamemnon disagrees and argues with Odysseus that to bury Ajax would make Menelaus and Agamemnon appear weak.

Agamemnon finally agrees to a burial, but only out of friendship with Odysseus. Teucer thanks Odysseus for his help, but asks that the burial be left to family and Ajax's soldiers; Ajax would not have wanted Odysseus to touch his body. As the men begin to prepare the body for burial, the play ends.

CHARACTERS

Agamemnon

Agamemnon is a great Greek warrior. He appears after Ajax's suicide to support Menelaus's decree that Ajax not be buried. He and Teucer argue bitterly, and he also argues with Odysseus. Finally out of friendship with Odysseus, Agamemnon permits Ajax to be buried.

Ajax

A courageous Greek warrior, Ajax feels that he has been disrespected when he is passed over for the shield of Achilles. In his grief and disappointment he tries to sneak into the tents of the other Greek warriors and slay them. Casting a spell, Athena causes him to think that he has captured Odysseus and that he will torture him, but in reality he has killed sheep and cattle. When the spell wears off and he recovers his wits, Ajax is deeply shamed and kills himself to save face and family honor.

It becomes clear that the gods are punishing Ajax because he has rejected their help. When Athena attempted to help Ajax during battle, he rebuffed her, stating that the gods should help lesser men.

Athena

The daughter of the god Zeus, Athena is the goddess of war. It is she who creates the illusion that Ajax is killing Agamemnon and Menelaus; in reality, he is slaying sheep and cattle. She is punishing Ajax for his rejection of her help.

Chorus

The Chorus sings sections of the play. Their purpose is to explain events or actions and to provide commentary on the events that are occurring. During their first appearance they blame the gods for having brought such a great warrior—Ajax—so low.

Comprised of Ajax's soldiers, the Chorus laments his death and sympathizes with Tecmessa's grief. When Menelaus and Agamemnon refuse Ajax's burial, the Chorus reminds them of the gods' insistence on observing the proper burial rights. They also provide the voice of reason and compromise.

Eurysaces

The son of Ajax and Tecmessa, Eurysaces is a small child. He is taken to Ajax in an emotional farewell scene and again to help prepare his father's body for burial.

Menelaus

Another great Athenian warrior, Menelaus appears after Ajax dies and refuses permission to have him buried. He argues with Teucer until he finally leaves to get Agamemnon's help.

Odysseus

Odysseus is a great warrior. He is given the arms of Achilles, much to Ajax's chagrin. When Ajax's murder of the sheep is revealed, Odysseus is initially angry; yet when he learns that Ajax has lost his mind, he feels great pity for him.

When Agamemnon refuses to allow Ajax's burial, Odysseus is the calm voice of reason who reminds those present that Ajax was a great warrior and that he deserves to be honored with a proper burial. Odysseus emerges as a strong, thoughtful leader.

Soldier

The unnamed soldier brings news of Teucer's arrival as well as the prophet's warning.

Tecmessa

Tecmessa is Ajax's Phrygian captive and the mother of his son. She loves him very much and grieves at the madness that has overtaken him. It is Tecmessa who describes to the Chorus and the listening audience the details of Ajax's madness during the night. She begs Ajax not to kill himself, pointing out that her future will be at great risk. After his suicide, she is the one who finds Ajax's body.

Teucer

Teucer is Ajax's brother. As he rides into camp he is insulted and attacked by soldiers who call his brother a madman. He learns from a prophet that if Ajax remains inside until nightfall, Athena's rage will end and Ajax will live; in a panic, he sends a soldier ahead to warn Ajax in an attempt to save his brother's life.

Teucer grieves for his brother and is concerned that his father will blame him for his brother's death. He also risks his own career in arguing with Menelaus and Agamemnon over the burial of Ajax. Teucer proves himself brave and honorable. When Odysseus agrees with his argument, Teucer is appreciative and thanks Odysseus for his help. He prepares his brother's body for honorable burial.

THEMES

Anger and Hatred

The action of the play is driven by Ajax's vengeful anger as he turns on Odysseus, Menelaus, and Agamemnon after Odysseus is voted Achilles's armor. The hatred once meant for his enemies is now directed on these three warriors, and Ajax sets out to murder them in their sleep. The interference of Athena spares their lives, but his intended victims learn of how near they came to death and turn their fury on Ajax.

After Ajax's suicide, Menelaus and Agamemnon are so filled with hate that they would willingly offend the gods and leave Ajax's body to rot in the open. Only Odysseus's levelheaded calm prevents anger from ruining more lives.

Choice and Fate

Ajax believes that he is in control of his destiny. He thinks that his strength and reputation as a warrior should govern his fate, but he is really a pawn in the hands of the gods. When Ajax rejects Athena's help, declaring that he needs no assistance from the gods, he seals his doom. It is the gods who determine if Ajax is honored, and while men may vote on the disposition of Achilles's armor, Athena leaves little doubt that she had a hand in that decision.

When Ajax would take revenge upon Odysseus, Menelaus, and Agamemnon, it is Athena who saves their lives. Ajax believes he is murdering his former colleagues, but Athena has cast a spell so that he is really murdering a herd of sheep.

Although Ajax is unaware of Athena's interference, it is she who leads him toward suicide. As the prophet foretold, if Ajax remains inside for this day, Athena's anger would dissipate and he would survive. Yet she makes sure that he recovers his senses and leaves his dwelling to view his shame; thus, she sets into motion Ajax's final scene, his death.

Gods and Man

In the Judeo-Christian tradition, God is a forgiving and beneficent creator. Man views his relationship with God in a cause-and-effect manner, in which good deeds and faith are rewarded with God's grace.

The Greeks had a different relationship with their gods. For instance, instead of one all-powerful

TOPICS FOR FURTHER STUDY

- Discuss the relationship between man and the gods as portrayed in *Ajax*.

- What do the speeches in *Ajax* suggest about the heroic ideal?

- Research fifth century Greek society. What is the role of women in this society? Is Tecmessa correct in being concerned about her future?

- Both *Ajax* and *Antigone* deal with the issue of the proper burial of dead bodies, but in *Ajax*, Odysseus is able to modify Agamemnon's anger and peace is restored. Consider how Creon reacts to similar advice in *Antigone* and compare the way these two plays deal with a similar problem.

- Research the role of early Greek drama in Greek life. What lessons would fifth-century Greek men learn from this play?

god, there were many gods; man's relationship with these deities was marked by the arbitrary nature of each god. Whether or not a man was good, honest, or brave had no bearing on how the gods treated him. Instead, it depended on the whims of the gods themselves. If the gods were warring amongst themselves, they would quite likely inflict some revenge upon men, rather than on the offending deity.

This very arbitrary nature of the gods meant that men could not determine their own fates, nor could they even assume responsibility for their own behavior. There were no rules to live by, because the gods behaved on impulse. Moreover, the gods often had favorites and scapegoats amongst the mortal population, and they didn't hesitate to punish those that displeased them. Obviously this created a very precarious and dangerous world.

The effects of the capricious behavior of the gods are clearly seen when Ajax is destroyed because he rejects Athena's help. Ajax has too much confidence in his own ability and not enough respect for Athena's strength, and this means that he is doomed. He has no warning of her anger and no way of placating it.

Pride

Excessive pride—also known as hubris—leads to Ajax's downfall. His first mistake is in rejecting the help of the gods. According to Greek life, his life, his destiny, and his successes are all determined by the gods; when he rejects Athena's help, her pride is offended, and she decides that Ajax's boast that he needs no help from any god means he must be destroyed. When Achilles's armor is given to Odysseus, Ajax's pride is what leads him to seek revenge.

Unfortunately, he is so blinded by his pride that he is unable to see that Odysseus is as strong and deserving as he is. Odysseus has qualities that Ajax lacks, such as the ability to solve conflict without weapons. However, Ajax's arrogance does not permit him to accept that he is deficient in the qualities that make Odysseus a great leader.

Finally, it is pride that leads Ajax to kill himself. He is shamed before the other Greek warriors and cannot live with that shame. He perceives his only recourse as suicide.

Strength and Weakness

Ajax is a strong and brave warrior. In fact, he is known as Ajax the Great because of his excellence. Yet the problem is he views himself as perfect. Ajax believes that he exemplifies the best of heroic man, but he forgets that heroism is more than just exhibiting bravery. It also involves making good choices, compromise, and the ability to recognize and compensate for his weaknesses.

Ajax is lacking in these areas. The very strengths that he exhibits in battle—leadership of men, physical strength, and prowess with his weapons—are incomplete without these other abilities. A hero needs modesty and the strength to compromise; he also needs to realize that accepting another man's competence does not diminish his own.

STYLE

Chorus

In ancient Greek drama, a chorus consists of a group of actors who interpret and comment on the play's action and themes, most often singing or chanting their lines. Initially the chorus had an important role in drama, as it does in *Ajax,* but eventually its role diminished. As a result, the chorus became little more than commentary between acts. Modern theater rarely uses a chorus.

Drama

A drama is often defined as any work designed to be presented on the stage. It consists of a story, action, and actors portraying characters. Historically, drama can also consist of tragedy, comedy, religious pageant, and spectacle. In modern times, drama explores serious topics and themes but does not achieve the same level as tragedy. *Ajax* is traditional Greek drama, and as such, provides important lessons for men about their relationship with the gods.

Genre

Genres are a way of categorizing literature. Genre is a French term that means ''kind'' or ''type.'' Genre can refer to both the category of literature such as tragedy, comedy, epic, poetry, or pastoral. It can also include modern forms of literature such as drama, novels, or short stories. This term can also refer to types of literature such as mystery, science fiction, comedy, or romance. *Ajax* is a Greek tragedy.

Plot

Plot refers to the pattern of events. Generally plots should have a beginning, middle, and conclusion—but they may also sometimes be a series of episodes connected together. Basically, the plot provides the author with the means to explore themes. Students are often confused between the two terms; but themes explore ideas, and plots simply relate what happens in a very obvious manner. Thus the plot of *Ajax* is what happens to Ajax after he chooses to seek revenge upon Odysseus, Menelaus, and Agamemnon. The theme of the play is how excessive pride and vanity can lead to a man's destruction.

Scene

Traditionally, a scene is a subdivision of an act and consists of continuous action of a time and place. However, Sophocles is not using acts, and so two scenes divide the action, which is separated by only a few hours at most.

Setting

The time and place of the play is called the setting. The elements of setting may include geographic location, physical or mental environments, prevailing cultural attitudes, or the historical time in which the action takes place. The primary location for *Ajax* is the battle for Troy, with the initial setting outside Ajax's tent. In the second scene, the setting moves to a nearby beach and the action spans a day.

Tragic Flaw

In tragedy, this is the mechanism that brings about the destruction of the hero. While Ajax is brave, strong, and heroic, he also suffers from excessive pride. This flaw angers Athena and provokes her revenge upon Ajax.

HISTORICAL CONTEXT

In the fifth century B.C., life in Greece was characterized by warfare and epic battles. For many years Greece struggled to expand its empire, and it was inevitable that conflict would result. Athens enjoyed her first great military triumph at the Battle of Marathon in 491 B.C., when legend has it, some 20,000 Greeks defeated the 100,000 man Persian army. The numbers were probably much lower, but the odds were definitely against the Greeks, who proved that superior discipline and courage were stronger than sheer numbers.

This was the first major defeat for the Persian army, whose strength and reputation actually scared and intimidated many Greek soldiers. This victory would inspire the story of a courier who ran to Athens with news of the victory but then fell dead of exhaustion upon his arrival, thus inspiring the idea of 26-mile marathon races, which endures to modern times.

Within ten years, the tables would turn. The Persian army—then more than two million men—would score a huge victory, pushing the Greek army into retreat. The Persians sacked Athens, but within a month, the Greeks once again got the upper hand, and in a decisive naval victory, more than 1000 Persian ships were sunk. Within a year, the Persian invasions stopped completely, and Greece once again entered a peaceful period known as the Golden Age of Greece.

These are the battles that form a backdrop to Sophocles's childhood. These historical events are filled with heroic men and great leaders, tremendous odds and great victories, and function as the source material for much of Greek theater.

Greek drama needed these larger-than-life heroes, since real life did not seem to provide material for heroic drama. Historically, there are many complaints about Greek tradesmen, who were well known for short-changing their customers and lying about their goods. Many politicians were also thought to be dishonest, and bribery was a common way of transacting government. Therefore, heroic warriors and brave leaders offered the role models and excitement many Greek citizens needed for their entertainment.

For many Greek citizens, life revolved around not offending the gods; unfortunately, there were no hard, set rules for this. Therefore, much controversy arose from what was offensive to the gods. The Greeks used oracles and dreams to figure this out, and eventually there were certain behaviors that were established as necessary, such as extending hospitality to a traveler or not violating an oath. Generally, gods were not interested in petty thievery, primarily because Greek political life involved bribery, corruption, and lying. Moreover, gods were also not interested in more serious crimes, except for murder.

The disposal of dead bodies was deemed important. Corpses were thought to cast a bad aura upon both victim and murderer; besides, it was a public health concern. It was especially important to deal with corpses in a correct and ritualized manner, regardless of the cause of death. Not to do so could result in serious divine punishment, hence Odysseus's reminders to Agamemnon that Ajax's body must be given proper burial.

The precarious relationship between gods and humans is the basis for a number of plays during that time. Plays were performed once a year at the festival of Dionysus. Three playwrights were chosen to present four plays, three tragedies and one comedy. These plays were performed during daylight, in outdoor theaters that often held as many as 14,000 spectators. All actors were men, and until Sophocles, there were only two actors and the chorus. Sophocles introduced the third actor, which permitted more complex plays to be presented. Although there was little scenery—in fact, often none—the actors wore elaborate masks.

In addition to the competition between playwrights, the lead actors also competed for awards.

COMPARE
&
CONTRAST

- c. 445 B.C.: Architecture and art make Athens preeminent in the world and lead to the designation of the Golden Age of Greece.

  Today: Greece remains a favorite tourist destination, as thousands of people journey each year to visit the Temple of Poseidon, Delphi, and the Parthenon, which was rebuilt after the Persians sacked Athens.

- c. 445 B.C.: 25-35% of the population of Greece are slaves, many of whom work in the silver mines.

  Today: Slavery has long since ended, but Greece is now dealing with severe poverty and a shrinking economic base.

- c. 445 B.C.: The Greeks triumph over the Persians and stave off the invasion of their country.

  Today: Greek politics has been preoccupied with military coups and conflict with neighboring Turkey since the end of World War II.

- c. 445 B.C.: The Greek historian, Herodotus, provides some of the earliest and most thorough histories of Greece. He will later be known as the ''father of history.''

Today: History now unfolds on television and in newspapers everyday. The future role of historians will have to accommodate the overwhelming proliferation of material now available.

- c. 445 B.C.: Destroyed by the Persians, the rebuilding of the Acropolis begins. It will take fifteen years to finish the job.

  Today: The Parthenon, situated on the Acropolis and overlooking Athens, is still a favorite destination for tourists.

- c. 445 B.C.: Festival games, a tradition of competitiveness begun nearly three hundred years earlier, continue in Greece. By the 5th century, their ritual meaning—they were originally held at funerals—has been lost.

  Today: The Olympic Games, a reminder of the former competitiveness of the Greeks, were revived in the late 19th century. Today, they are often imbued with political agendas that detract from the spectacle and celebration.

Playwrights probably did not receive much compensation for the writing, staging, and directorial duties that occupied them, and all of the best known playwrights, including Sophocles, Aeschylus, and Euripides also held military or political posts. These plays fulfilled an important function, since they illustrated moral issues important to early Greeks. Ajax's situation would have provided an important lesson to the audience.

CRITICAL OVERVIEW

There is almost no information regarding the reaction of fifth-century Greek audiences to *Ajax*. Sopho-

cles was a popular playwright, and his plays would undoubtedly have been eagerly awaited. The fact that he was awarded a prize also signals the play's reception.

There are many reasons why the plays of Sophocles were so popular and why their popularity continues. One reason was his deft ability to reinterpret the ancient myths through exploration of the individual. In this, the earliest of his surviving plays, Ajax is presented as a flawed, yet heroic figure. His suffering is compelling and functions as the focus of the play.

Ajax is also unique because Ajax dies on stage. Traditionally in Greek tragedy, the action occurs offstage. Battles are fought and deaths do occur, but the audience learns of these events through the chorus, whose role it is to relate to the audience these offstage incidents.

Without the kind of action that modern audiences have come to expect, Greek audiences relied upon the power of language to create drama. Even before the development of drama, Greeks relied upon oral epics to provide much of their entertainment. The very stories that Sophocles drew upon for source material were rich in characters, battles, and spectacle, and their progression from oral tales to stage productions brought much excitement into the lives of the Greeks.

These stage productions were eagerly anticipated and drew huge crowds of upward to 14,000 people. Audiences were accustomed to sitting all day on hard stone benches, but even so, these plays had to be capable of holding the audience's attention. The grandeur of ancient myths, with their exciting heroes and battles, provided an important escape from the routine nature of Greek life. They also served to inspire Greeks by reminding them of the greatness of heroic leaders. This was especially important in the years following the great Persian-Greek wars.

Ajax is still performed occasionally, as it was during the fall 1997 State Theatre of Northern Greece season. The American National Theatre also staged a production in June and July of 1986. In this latter production, Sophocles's play was moved into modern dress and staged as an American drama.

The setting of this production was sometime in the near future after America has just won a great victory in Latin America. The director, Peter Sellers, uses a courtroom and a trial as the means to explore this Greek tragedy. Ajax uses sign language, translated by a member of the chorus, to tell his story. He is covered in blood and communicates in ''slashing, spattering signs,'' and according to the reviewer, W. D. King, the effect is that of ''estrangement.'' The cast is clothed in military uniforms, and they hold rank as according to modern military custom.

King is more of an observer than a reviewer, and he relates the actions on stage as a witness, mostly without critical analysis of the action. Ajax emerges as pathetic, as he does in the original play on which this modern adaptation is based. But by using the setting of a courtroom, *Ajax* becomes more centered on questions of responsibility.

With Athena as judge, her role in this tragedy seems amplified. As King observes, ''She seats herself at the judge's table, and at once the feeling that there is a higher force in the world, beyond human understanding, and of ambiguous moral substance, takes hold.'' This modern production of Sophocles's tragedy illustrates that these dramas still have a place in modern theater. Critics agree that there is a timeless quality in Ajax's emotional breakdown that transcends time and resonates with modern audiences.

CRITICISM

Sheri E. Metzger

Metzger is a Ph.D., specializing in literature and drama at the University of New Mexico. In this essay, she discusses how Renaissance humanism and the heroic nature of the epic form sustains the modern appeal of Sophocles's drama.

No doubt students might think that there is little reason to read Sophocles, or plays such as *Ajax*. In fact, students might consider the mythic warriors of Greek epic and drama outdated or even unimportant as the twentieth century nears its end. This was how many people viewed Greek drama for hundreds of years following the end of the Golden Age of Greece. Yet in thirteenth century Italy, a new movement that came to be called humanism resurrected classical Greek texts, including drama, and found that there was a place for these ancient heroes in educating young men.

At that time, it was the goal of every young man of aristocratic birth to serve his country. The idea behind humanism was to prepare a young man for his new role in civic life, and ethics was an important feature of this new emphasis on education. Classical Latin and Greek became crucial elements of a gentleman's education, while each country's vernacular language became the language of the peasant class. Within two hundred years, knowledge of classical Greek would become an essential attribute of an educated man.

With the adoption of these languages, the literature soon followed, and this included Greek drama. Greek drama taught important lessons about loyalty, heroism, and religion. From these plays young men learned about leadership and responsibility. Young gentlemen also learned that heroism was more than bravery on the battlefield. They learned

WHAT DO I READ NEXT?

- *Oedipus Rex,* a drama written by Sophocles (c. 430-426 B.C.), is the story of one man's attempts to escape his fate. It is the dramatist's best-known play.

- *Antigone,* also by Sophocles (c. 441 B.C.), focuses on the problems of excessive pride and stubbornness. Like *Ajax,* this play emphasizes the importance of the ritualized practice of burial of the dead.

- Sophocles's *Electra* (c. 425-410 B.C.) examines the family tragedy that surrounds the death of Agamemnon.

- *Prometheus Bound,* by Aeschylus (c. 490 B.C.), is the story of how Prometheus is punished for disobeying Zeus.

---

from Ajax that heroism coupled with excessive pride would lead to disaster. Heroism brought with it responsibility and the need for compromise.

Young men also learned that great heroes like Odysseus were heroic not just because they were brave and won many battles, but because they did what was expected of them. Odysseus was heroic because he could put aside his anger at Ajax and do what he knew to be the right thing. Odysseus also knew that Ajax had offended the gods, and that he too would offend the gods if Ajax were to be denied burial. From Odysseus, young men learned about the correct relationship between man and god. These models for gentlemanly behavior became an important reason to study classical literature.

Humanism also emphasized intellectual autonomy and individual expression. Sophocles's plays focused on these attributes. He created heroes whose need to express their individuality became the centerpiece of drama. In his book on Greek drama, J. Michael Walton contends that Sophocles created a "world of unusual personal detail, a world in which a small object or a human gesture can define a man's estate." The world portrayed on stage ceased to be huge, with mythic heroes who were larger than life.

In *Ajax,* the audience perceives a protagonist in profound pain. Walton maintains that the audience sees is not the "stoicism of mankind but the pain to which he is heir." The audience cannot help but react to this individual suffering.

Clearly, as Walton notes, Sophocles is able to engage the audience's sympathy for the individual. This became increasingly important as the world grew larger and more complex, and was as true of the fledgling scientific world of the Renaissance as it is today.

The Renaissance humanist was willing to accept the responsibility of governing that accompanied intellectual autonomy. Here, too, the Greek model proved important. Greek heroes exemplified responsibility to their gods and to the men who fought beside them. Ajax's tragedy was in betraying those with whom he fought: Odysseus, Agamemnon, and Menelaus. His shame is twofold—deriving from the mistaken slaughter of animals and his madness that turned such terrible anger on his allies.

In her discussion on the use of debate and conflict in Sophoclean tragedy, Jacqueline de Romilly states that there is a contrast in *Ajax* between "an aristocratic ethic based on honor and a more humane ethic based on obligations to individuals." This obligation to the individual is seen in Odysseus's championing of Ajax's burial rights. Odysseus clearly understands the god's directive that bodies must be buried, but his reasons go beyond that. Although he abhors Ajax's actions, Odysseus acknowledges that Ajax was a great warrior who fought bravely for their causes:

"Deny him burial and trample justice! I loathed him, more than any other Greek in camp. I detested all he was—and still I say he was the bravest man I ever saw, except for Achilles, the best and bravest who ever came to Troy. Admit it! Justice demands! If you shame him you smear God's law. Hate him or love him, he was an honorable man; you owe him honor.''

In the ensuing argument with Agamemnon, Odysseus contends that Ajax deserves respect. In the end, as both Agamemnon and Odysseus agree, this is fulfilling obligations and providing the honors rightfully bestowed upon an honorable man. Doing what was right, what benefited the individual man, was a crucial part of Odysseus's decision.

Honesty and the search for truth were also important elements of the humanist movement, and they were important to defining the strengths of the individual. Ajax chooses to die alone, separate from family and the men who still follow him. He commits suicide. This is not the expected death for a great hero—Ajax is in great pain and thinks that he can redeem his honor only through taking his own life. In her essay on the feminine in Greek drama, Froma I. Zeitlin argues that Ajax's suicide is a woman's way of dying but that Ajax appropriates a woman's death and makes it masculine:

''Suicide is a solution in tragedy normally reserved only for women—and what we are given to witness is this convention borrowed for a man's version of it. He [Ajax] dies a heroic death, then, in the women's way, a whetted will penetrated by a whetted weapon, befitting . . . the curious ambiguities of this most masculine hero.''

Zeitlin asserts that although Ajax briefly considers Tecmessa's pleas, to continue living would feminize his will and deepen his shame. Ajax is embracing the only recourse left to an honorable man, hoping to restore his family's honor. He deceives his family and the chorus, convincing them that he is recovering and the danger has passed.

There is a temptation to label Ajax's words as lies, heaping more dishonor on a man already dishonored. But Ajax is a complex man, and as Zeitlin suggests, Ajax ''seems to have arrived at the kind of tragic knowledge we recognize as intrinsically true to the genre.'' This is because, as Zeitlin argues, although ''deceit and intrigue are condemned in women, they are also seen as natural to her sphere of operations and the dictates of her nature.''

Thus, since Ajax has chosen to die in the manner of women, that he first deceives those around him means that he is employing, as Zeitlin

> AJAX IS ALMOST SETTING A PRECEDENT FOR THE TWENTIETH-CENTURY ANTI-HERO. THE MODERN HERO IS PREPARED TO DO THE RIGHT THING, TO REBEL AGAINST A CONTROLLING GOVERNMENT WHEN IT IS WRONG"

notes, a ''feminine strategy enlisted in the service of restoring an unequivocal manliness he can only achieve . . . by dying the manly death . . . in the woman's way.'' The audience is left with the knowledge that Ajax took the only choice still left to him, the choice to die. For Ajax, truth lies in his acceptance of his actions.

Medieval Christianity taught that obedience was more important than individualism, but humanism stressed just the opposite. If individualism was identified with arrogance, the study of classical Greek pointed to individualism as the mark of the strong, virtuous man—one who saw good deeds, not as the way to get into heaven, but as the way to create a better world.

This individualism is not with problems, as the complexity of Ajax illustrates. The opening ceremonies of the festival in which Sophocles presented his plays included honoring the children of Greece's war victims. Simon Goldhill states that this ceremony affirms the connection between these young men and the city that has been responsible for their education. It was a moment of civic pride, and combined with the remainder of the ceremonies, it provided an important civic occasion.

Yet as these ceremonies affirm the importance of the city, the tragedies themselves affirm the importance of the individual. This tension, this ambiguity in the hero, provides for a realistic depiction. This is not a remote hero without fault; this is a hero who is capable of mistakes.

As Goldhill observes, ''the negative example of Ajax is touched with a certain glory. It is an essential dynamic of Sophocles's tragedy that Ajax should seem both an outstanding hero and also unacceptable in society. The hero does not simply *reverse* the norms of what it means to fit into society but *makes a problem of* such integration.''

Ajax is almost setting a precedent for the twentieth-century anti-hero. The modern hero is prepared to do the right thing, to rebel against a controlling government when it is wrong. Athena's role as god is not unlike the authority of modern government. She establishes laws and expects exact obedience, and she does not expect to be challenged. Ajax does challenge authority; but as Goldhill points out, Ajax, although managing to transgress what is expected of him, ''achieves his greatness, his superhuman status, precisely by such transgression.''

Ajax is first and foremost an individual. He wants to be in control of his destiny, and although not flawless, he proves that he is heroic in coming to terms with those faults. The Greek tragic hero was an important model for the autonomy and individual expression that humanists embraced, and it became an important element in creating the Renaissance man who would build the foundation of the modern world. Humanism's resurrection of Greek drama created a profound change in the way Renaissance men approached society and religion, and this has carried over into the twentieth century.

Source: Sheri E. Metzger, for *Drama for Students,* Gale, 2000.

J. Michael Walton

Walton provides an overview of Sophocles's play, identifying the major characters and plot motivations.

After the death of Achilles in the war against Troy, the Greek hero's arms were awarded to Odysseus rather than to Ajax who believed he had deserved them. Intent on revenge for the slight, Ajax is diverted from his purpose by the goddess Athena who drives him mad so that he kills and tortures sheep and cattle, seeing them as his Greek enemies. When he returns to sanity, shame at what he has done impels him to commit suicide. Odysseus pleads with Agamemnon and Menelaus for Ajax to be treated with the respect due to a hero and eventually wins his point.

Ajax is the only Sophocles play, with the arguable exception of *Philoctetes,* in which a god or goddess appears. Traditionally a devout man. Sophocles proposes a theological standpoint which is more complex than it is sometimes painted. Ajax may have been planning a dire revenge against his former friends, when he believes himself cheated of

his due, but the way in which the goddess Athena gloats over the state to which she has reduced him looks forward to the savage Dionysus of Euripides' *Bacchae* rather than back to the wise patron-goddess of Athens who solves the problems in Aeschylus' *Oresteia.*

Applying modern standards to a Greek attitude towards friends and enemies is, of course, risky. Turning the other cheek would have seemed as contrary to the nature of the Greek hero as turning his back. Nevertheless, there is in *Ajax* a sense of moral argument which suggests that man is progressing beyond the simple rules of programmed response. Odysseus is not only the soldier who defeated Ajax in the award of arms but is also traditionally a crafty and untrustworthy man whose eye is always to the main chance. So he appears in Sophocles's later play *Philoctetes,* where his machinations to persuade the eponymous hero to go to Troy are so Machiavellian as to be self-defeating. In *Ajax* this is the sort of man Athena is expecting when she invites Odysseus to witness Ajax' humiliation. Instead of pleasure at the downfall of an enemy, Odysseus shows himself instinctively compassionate.

The tone of the play is established in the first scene. All the later characters to appear reveal predictable attitudes. Ajax' half-brother, Teucer, defends him as best he may, but he is only half-hero as well as half-brother. Tecmessa, mother of Ajax' son Eurysaces, is loyal and loving but utterly without influence in such a male world. Agamemnon and Menelaus, respectively commander-in-chief of the Greek forces at Troy, and husband of Helen, the cause of the war, are angry savages for whom the only response to what Ajax has done is the ultimate insult: deprivation of burial. Odysseus stands up to them and wins for Ajax the honour due to what the man was when he was a friend, not what he became when thwarted and deranged. If the play's moral dimension is its paramount feature, there is little sense of *Ajax* degenerating into a tract. The appearance of Athena in the prologue is literally above the action where Odysseus cannot see her. Such an awareness of stage space, a principal factor of Sophocles' stagecraft in all his surviving plays, is given an unusual twist in the handling of both location and chorus.

Changes of scene are rare in surviving Greek tragedy and appear to have become more so, with tragedy moving towards realism at the same time as comedy, in the hands of Aristophanes, moves to a world of fantasy where anything can happen anywhere. The initial setting of *Ajax* is outside Ajax's tent, over which Athena appears (presumably, in the original production, with the help of the stage-crane). After Athena has departed and Ajax has returned to sanity, his sailors, who form the chorus, and Tecmessa with his baby attempt to save him from despair at the carnage he has perpetrated. For a time it seems that they have been successful. Ajax emerges from his tent calm and apparently reconciled to what he has done. He departs for the beach to cleanse himself.

News arrives that this is to prove a crucial day in Ajax's fortunes and the chorus and Tecmessa leave the scene to look for him. Ajax now appears at the sea-shore and carefully prepares his own death, before falling on the sword given to him in battle by the Trojan Hector. The sense of isolation is emphasised both by the place where the action is now unfolding and by the absence of the chorus who habitually accompany on-stage action, from their first entrance through to a play's conclusion. Physical use of the resources of the Athenian theatre and the expectations of the audience are consciously manipulated by Sophocles to draw attention to the man's loneliness and to the unusual sight on the Greek stage of someone committing suicide.

Ajax is a touching play and a heartening one for ending on a note of hope, if not reconciliation. Life may present atrocities and heroes may perpetrate them, but a case can be made for human decency which allows some rules and some rights for even the major sinner.

Source: J. Michael Walton. ''Ajax'' in *The International Dictionary of Theatre,* Volume 1: *Plays,* edited by Mark Hawkins-Dady, St. James Press, 1992, pp. 7–8.

W. Edward Brown

In the following essay, Brown compares and contrasts the tangential subject matter in the writings of Sophocles and Homer.

Modern critics have proposed a number of interpretations of the nature of the tragedy in Sophocles' *Ajax,* without perhaps completely exhausting the subject. The present paper is no more than an attempt to add slightly to this material by focusing attention on what seems to be an overlooked element in the drama, that is, the implicit contrast between the title character and the Homeric Hector.

Without attempting to go more fully into the question, I shall say at the outset that in general it

> *AJAX* IS A TOUCHING PLAY AND A HEARTENING ONE FOR ENDING ON A NOTE OF HOPE, IF NOT RECONCILIATION"

seems to me that the *Ajax,* in its ''diptych'' structure, is preeminently a study in contrasts, as has been usually recognized, and that the contrast between the enemies Ajax and Odysseus is the most important and striking of these. This contrast is first and most drastically shown in the prologue, which juxtaposes the savage vengefulness of Ajax with Odysseus' canny moderation and pity for the misfortunes even of an enemy. This contrast is carried through the play in the ironic disparity between the distorted image of Odysseus held by Ajax and shared by Tecmessa and the chorus, and the magnanimous reality, as it appears in the prologue and the final episode. Subsidiary contrasts are those between Teucer, a lesser Ajax, and the contemptible Atridae, and between the human characters of Odyssesus and Ajax and the ruthless divinity Athena.

Another contrast, however, is implicit, I believe, in the characterization of Ajax in his relations with his wife and his infant son. It is impossible, I think, to read Tecmessa's speech of expostulation to Ajax bent on suicide, without being immediately reminded of the colloquy between Hector and Andromache in *Iliad* 6.407–65: there is the same plea that the rest of the wife's family being dead, the husband is all in all; the same vivid picture of the wife's captivity in a hostile land; the same imagined taunt—''this was the wife of a hero who was once the mightiest, and see how she has fallen''; the same pleading to the warrior not to leave his son a helpless orphan. Is this a mere chance echo, Sophocles' homage to the poet who had exhausted the pathetic possibilities in the fate of a dead warrior's family? If there were no other evidence, this might be. But is it chance that the sword with which Ajax kills himself is Hector's sword? He says of it bitterly in his speech of deception to the chorus: ''For ever since I received this in my hand from Hector, the gift of my worst enemy, I have never yet had anything good from the Achaeans. True is that proverb of mortals, that an enemy's gifts are no gifts, and the reverse of helpful.'' And in his last

> " *AJAX,* IS PREEMINENTLY A
> STUDY IN CONTRASTS, AS HAS BEEN
> USUALLY RECOGNIZED, AND THE
> CONTRAST BETWEEN THE ENEMIES
> AJAX AND ODYSSEUS IS THE MOST-
> IMPORTANT AND STRIKING OF
> THESE."

soliloquy, Ajax addresses the sword as it stands braced in the Trojan ground to be his killer, as "the gift of Hector, that man who of all my guest-friends was most hated by me, the most detested to look upon." And finally, when Teucer uncovers his brother's body and recognizes the sword, he calls attention to the fatality of the gift exchange between Ajax and Hector (*Iliad* 7.303–5): "You see how it was destined that in time Hector, though dead, should destroy you? Consider, in God's name, the chances of two mortals: Hector, bound to the chariot rail by the belt he received from this man, was torn continually until he breathed out his life; and this man, with the gift he received from the other, has perished in a leap of death." It is hard to pass over the persistent appearance of the Hector theme as a chance irrelevance.

But if there is an intentional coupling here of Ajax and his dead enemy, what does Sophocles mean by it? Without explicitly pointing out the contrast, he seems to be letting the hearer form his own conclusions on two sorts of heroic conduct. Granting that Odysseus, the cool calculator who reasons out his pity for his mad enemy by saying "I think as much of my own fate as of his," is no warrior, and that the contrast here is one between the "exceptional" and the "ordinary" man, it is necessary to the full appreciation of Ajax's tragedy that he also be contrasted with a warrior of unquestioned stature. This contrast is afforded by the omnipresent figure of Hector. The soldier who received with gentleness and pity his wife's tearful pleas to spare his life and not make her a widow and his son an orphan, and the comfort that "no man shall send me to Hades against my fate," stands ghostlike in the background as Ajax with callous brutality brushes aside his wife and child and pre-

pares to compass his own death. And when that consummation of his desires has been accomplished, and Teucer moralizes over the silver-studded sword and purple belt which had been the instruments of both men's fates, the audience cannot but remember that Hector had died bravely in battle, fighting an unequal fight in defense of wife and child and parents and city, while Ajax had deliberately deceived his friends and destroyed himself as a useless sacrifice to his concept of honor.

The tragedy of Ajax cannot properly be explained by applying the classical *hybris* formula. This, formula implies that there is a norm of conduct valid for all men, deviation from which brings down the wrath of the gods upon the offender. It may be appropriate to explain some of Aeschylus' tragedies by the concept of *hybris,* but not those of Sophocles. The tragedy of *Ajax,* as of *The Trachinian Women,* lies precisely in the fact that certain individuals, like Ajax and Heracles, are, by the very nature with which they have been endowed, at variance with the standards of conduct that apply to normal men. Neither a religious nor a moral consideration is involved here. Certain conduct is inevitable in the "exceptional man," his nature being what it is; and this conduct inevitably also results in destruction for himself and misery for his loved ones. The very fact of being such an exceptional man is therefore tragic, but the tragedy is not the punishment of heaven for overstepping the bounds. The gods of Sophocles are merely conventional names for the sum of "the way things are."

The figure of Athena in the *Ajax* and the enmity of the goddess for the hero cannot be taken, I believe, in any personal sense, nor is undue importance to be attached to the "guilt" of Ajax in the words of Calchas as reported by the messenger. . . . In the first of these passages a statement is made which perhaps most clearly formulates the tragedy of Ajax, if correctly interpreted: "For, said the seer, exceptional and profitless beings fall at the gods' hands into grievous misfortunes—all who, being engendered after the fashion of men, have thoughts that are not of human pattern." This seems to be no more than a mere statement of fact, without moral implications. . . .

But Hector too was a warrior, as valiant and devoted to duty as Ajax. The difference lay in Hector's . . . acceptance of the limitations of human power and the obligation of human living, which his enemy rejected. The contrast is glaringly apparent in the scene with Tecmessa in which Ajax contemptuously brushes aside the claims of family as against those of honor; it is apparent also in the words which Ajax addresses to his infant son: ''Child, may you be more fortunate than your father, but in other respects like him; so you will prove no coward.'' Hector prays for the babe Astyanax: ''Zeus and you other gods, grant that this child of mine may be distinguished among the Trojans, as am I, and as great in strength, and may he reign with power over Ilion. And some day may one say of him: 'He is far braver than his father''' (*Iliad* 6.476–9). The one prays that his son may be better than he, the other that he may be his equal in everything but luck—a difference that speaks volumes of Ajax's unbridled egotism. And yet the comparison between Hector and Ajax is made explicit in Sophocles' play only in Teucer's contrast of the gifts exchanged—and these were the cause of death for the one as for the other. Hector, who goes to his last battle with the prayer that he may lie under mounded earth before he hears the cry of Andromache being dragged to captivity, and Ajax, who invokes the vengeance of the Furies upon the Atridae and their whole army for the death that he is about to inflict on himself, are alike in this—death is the end for both.

Does this mean that Sophocles views the careers of both men as moral equivalents—''the paths of glory lead but to the grave''? If this is so, then it is indeed futile to look for any meaning—or indeed any tragedy—in the play. It is inconceivable, however, that all a great poet could say on such a theme should be reducible to such banal and irrelevant pessimism. Nor would it ever occur to one of Sophocles' contemporaries to imagine that this was so. The hero who dies at his own hand because of a nature that cannot bend itself to conform to human norms is tragic; but not the hero who dies, as a soldier should, in defending his city and his people. Such a man's fate is happy in Greek eyes; Solon's anecdote of Tellus the Athenian (Herodotus 1.30) is evidence enough without citing Tyrtaeus, alien in time and place; and Hector's fate for the fifth-century Athenian must have had much the same aura as the dead whom Pericles eulogizes (Thucydides 2.42), who ''endured the brunt of battle with their bodies, and in the briefest moment of time, at the summit of their fortune, were taken not out of fear, but away from fame.''

But the dead, however different in the mode of their death, must be buried. The ending of the *Ajax* often been criticized, as destructive of the play's unity, as blatantly anticlimactic, even as mere padding. These criticisms are, I believe, absurdly un-

just, and possible only as long as the mistaken notion is held that the play is ''about Ajax,'' and nothing more. It is ''about'' human life, and Ajax and Odysseus and Teucer and the Atridae—and I believe Hector—are all symbols through whom the poet may voice his thoughts on this subject. It is sometimes said that Ajax is ''rehabilitated'' in the second half of the play; so he is—as a human being. The whole importance of the contrast so pointedly made between Odysseus' magnanimity and the vindictiveness of the Atridae lies in this. When Agamemnon queries: ''You urge me then to permit the burial of this corpse?'' Odysseus replies simply: ''I do; for I myself shall come to this.'' Whatever its conduct in life, this ''profitless body'' had been a human being, and resentment may not humanly be carried beyond death.

And here we have the last implied comparison with Hector: his body too his enemy had outraged and left unburied, until with appeals to their common humanity his old father had persuaded the vengeful Achilles to relinquish the corpse and let it be given to the fire. Odysseus plays the part of Priam here, with none of his pathos and grandeur, to be sure, but with basically the same argument: we are all mortal. The play ends with the parallelism between Ajax and Hector complete, the contrast sharply drawn between the hero and his two enemies: Odysseus, his polar opposite, the man of craft and intellect and cold blood; and Hector, the warrior so strangely like him, whose ''human mindedness'' as surely as Ajax's ''inhuman mindedness'' terminates in the grave that is the common lot of all humans.

Source: W. Edward Brown. ''Sophocles's Ajax and Homer's Hector'' in *Classical Journal,* Vol. 61, no. 3, December, 1965, pp. 118–21.

SOURCES

Goldhill, Simon. ''The Great Dionysia and Civic Ideology,'' in *Nothing to Do With Dionysos? Athenian Drama in Its Social Context,* edited by John J. Winkler and Froma I. Zeitlin, Princeton University Press, 1992, pp. 97-129.

King, W. D. ''Nailed to a Circus of Blood; *Ajax* at the American National Theatre,'' *Theatre* Vol. 18, No. 1, Fall-Winter, 1986, pp. 6-15.

Romilly, Jacqueline de. ''Drama in the Second Half of the Fifth Century: Sophocles, Euripides, and Aristophanes,'' in

A Short History of Greek Literature, translated by Lillian Doherty, University of Chicago Press, 1985, pp. 66-89.

Walton, J. Michael. *The Greek Sense of Theatre: Tragedy Reviewed,* Methuen, 1984.

Zeitlin, Froma I. "Playing the Other: Theatre, Theatricality, and the Feminine in Greek Drama," in *Nothing to Do With Dionysos? Athenian Drama in Its Social Context,* edited by John J. Winkler and Froma I. Zeitlin, Princeton University Press, 1992, pp. 63-96.

FURTHER READING

Ashby, Clifford. *Classical Greek Theatre: New Views of an Old Subject,* University of Iowa Press, 1999.
> An examination of Greek theater based on architectural evidence. The author has traveled extensively and examined many of the remaining sites in Greece, Southern Italy, and the Balkans.

Gressler, Thomas H. *Greek Theatre in the 1980s,* McFarland & Company, 1989.
> A study of modern Greek theater in which the author focuses on social and cultural influences of drama, discusses the history of theater, and provides a look at productions and the restoration of theaters.

Griffith, R. Drew. *The Theatre of Apollo: Divine Justice and Sophocles's Oedipus the King,* McGill Queens University Press, 1996.
> This is a reinterpretation of Sophocles's play that explores Apollo's role in bringing about this tragedy. It also attempts to recreate the play's original staging.

Rehm, Rush. *Greek Tragic Theatre,* Routledge, 1994.
> Discusses performances of several plays and encourages readers to consider the context in which the plays were performed.

Walton, J. Michael. *Living Greek Theatre,* Greenwood, 1987.
> Focuses on the staging and performance of Greek drama. The author attempts to integrate classical and modern theater, while providing a great deal of information about a number of the most important plays from this period.

Wise, Jennifer. *Dionynsus Writes: The Invention of Theatre in Ancient Greece,* Cornell University Press, 1998.
> Discusses the relationship between literature and drama by examining the influences of a newly emerging literary world on drama.

Zelenak, Michael X. *Gender and Politics in Greek Tragedy,* Peter Lang, 1998.
> This book offers some insight into the status of women in Greek culture and provides interesting analysis of many women characters from Greek drama.

All My Sons

ARTHUR MILLER

1947

All My Sons, Arthur Miller's first commercially successful play, opened at the Coronet Theatre in New York on January 29, 1947. It ran for 328 performances and garnered important critical acclaim for the dramatist, winning the prestigious New York Drama Critics' Circle Award.

Miller's earlier play, *The Man Who Had All the Luck* (1944), had not done well and had quickly closed; therefore, at the time *All My Sons* opened, Miller's reputation as a writer was based almost solely on *Focus* (1945), his lauded novel about anti-Semitism.

All My Sons is now regarded as the first of Miller's major plays. The work also greatly helped the career of Elia Kazan, who had first won accolades for his direction of Thornton Wilder's *The Skin of Our Teeth* in 1942 and after directing *All My Sons* would continue to work with the plays of both Miller and Tennessee Williams to produce both legendary stage productions and important films.

In *All My Sons* Miller evidenced the strong influence of both Henrik Ibsen and Greek tragedy, developing a ''formula'' that he would brilliantly exploit in his next play, *Death of a Salesman* (1949), which many regard as his finest work.

AUTHOR BIOGRAPHY

Arthur Miller was born on October 17, 1915, in New York City. He spent his early years in comfortable circumstances, until his father, Isidore, a prosperous manufacturer, lost his wealth in the economic devastation of the Great Depression. After completing high school, Miller had to take a job in a Manhattan warehouse.

He had not been much of a student, but after reading Dostoevsky's great novel *The Brothers Karamazov* he decided that he was destined to become a writer. He had trouble getting into college but was eventually accepted at the University of Michigan, where he began his apprenticeship as a writer and won several student awards for his work.

After college he returned to New York and worked briefly as a radio script writer, then tried his hand at writing for the stage commercially. His first Broadway play, *The Man Who Had All the Luck* (1944), closed after only four performances, but it did win a Theater Guild award and revealed the young writer's potential.

He had more success with *Focus* (1945), a novel dealing with anti-Semitism. In fact, at the time he wrote *All My Sons* (1947), his first dramatic hit, he was better known as a writer of fiction than as a playwright.

All My Sons established Miller's standing as a bright and extremely talented dramatist. The play had a good run and won Miller his first New York Drama Critics' Circle Award. Even the least favorable commentators recognized the playwright's great promise.

Miller followed *All My Sons* with three of his most critically and commercially successful plays: *Death of Salesman* (1949), *The Crucible* (1953), and *A View from the Bridge* (1955). In these works, Miller attempted to show that tragedy could be written about ordinary people struggling to maintain personal dignity at critical moments in their lives. With these plays, Miller joined Eugene O'Neill and Tennessee Williams in what in the post-World War II years was generally recognized as the great triumvirate of the American theater.

Miller, a political leftist, gained some notoriety in the 1950s when he refused to cooperate with the House Un-American Activities Committee and was held in contempt of Congress. From this experience he found thematic material for one of his most famous and controversial plays, *The Crucible,* which focuses on the Salem Witch Trials of 1692.

After the 1955 production of *A View from the Bridge,* Miller took a nine-year hiatus from playwriting. In the interim, Miller married and divorced the famous actress, Marilyn Monroe. He did adapt one of his stories, *The Misfits* as a screen vehicle for his celebrated wife but did not complete another Broadway play until 1964, when both *After the Fall* and *Incident at Vichy* were produced. The former play, considered Miller's most experimental play, is also his darkest work, with many autobiographical parallels.

His last Broadway success was *The Price,* produced in 1968. After his next play, *The Creation of the World and Other Business* (1972), failed on Broadway, Miller stopped premiering works in New York. He continued to write plays, and enjoyed some success, but nothing that matched that of his earliest works. Many of his later plays were short one-act plays and works comprised of sketches or vignettes.

His greatest triumphs remain *Death of a Salesman* and *The Crucible.* Both have been revived with great success. In 1999, for example, the New York production of *Death of a Salesman* garnered four Tony awards, including one for best revival and one for best direction. At the age of eighty-four, Miller was also presented with a special, lifetime achievement award for his great contributions to the American theater.

PLOT SUMMARY

Act One

The play opens on a Sunday morning in August and is set in the back yard of the Keller home, located on the outskirts of an unidentified American town, a couple of years after the end of World War II. Joe Keller, who has been reading classified ads in a newspaper, banters pleasantly with his neighbors, Dr. Jim Bayliss and Frank Lubey. He explains that the apple tree had split in half during the night.

It is a source of some concern, for the tree is a memorial for Joe's son, Larry, and its destruction might upset Joe's wife, Kate. Frank refers to it as Larry's tree and notes that August is Larry's birth month. He plans to cast Larry's horoscope, to see if the date on which he was reported missing in action was a favorable or unfavorable day for him.

The men ask after the Kellers' visitor, Ann, the daughter of Joe's former partner, Steve Deever, who once lived in the house now owned by the Baylisses. Sue, Jim's wife, arrives and sends Jim home to talk on the phone with a patient. She is followed by Frank's wife, Lydia, who reports a problem with a toaster.

Joe's son, Chris, comes from the house, and a neighborhood boy, Bert, darts into the yard. Joe amuses Bert in a role-playing game in which Bert is learning to be a police deputy under Joe's authority. He has shown Bert a gun and they pretend that the basement of the house is actually a jail.

After the others leave, Joe and Chris talk about the tree and the fact that Kate was outside when it fell. She has never stopped hoping that Larry will return, still alive. Her failure to accept his death is a major obstacle for Chris, who hopes to marry Ann. Kate can only think of Ann as Larry's girl, and she can not accept a marriage of Chris and Ann without first accepting her son's death. Chris's proposed solution, much to his father's chagrin, is to leave the Keller home and business unless his father helps him make Kate accept Larry's death.

Kate enters and muses over the significance of the fallen tree and Ann's arrival. She also speaks of a dream in which she saw Larry and expresses her belief that the memorial tree should never have been planted. Exasperated, Chris talks of trying to forget Larry. She sends him off to get an aspirin, then tries to wring from Joe an explanation for Ann's visit. She also discloses that if she were to lose faith in her belief that Larry was alive, she would kill herself.

Chris returns with Ann, and a tense confrontation almost immediately begins. Ann pointedly rejects Kate's hope that Larry is still alive. She also divulges that she is unwilling to forgive her father, now in jail, as Joe once was, convicted of providing the Army Air Force with 121 defective cracked cylinder heads. The parts were used in the engines of P-40 fighter planes, twenty-one of which crashed.

Joe, who was later exonerated, attempts to defend his former partner as a confused, somewhat inept "little man" caught in a situation that he did not fully fathom. Ann is unmoved and holds her father responsible for Larry's death. Yet Kate knows

Arthur Miller at his writing desk

the truth: Joe ordered his partner to weld the cracked cylinder heads and hide the defect.

After Joe and Kate leave, Chris confesses his love to Ann, and she ardently confirms her own for him. She is mystified by his long delay in disclosing his feelings, and he explains that it took him a long time to shake free from a guilt he felt for his survival in the war. They are interrupted when Ann is told that her brother, George, is on the phone.

As she exits, Joe and Chris discuss the fact that George is in Columbus, visiting his father in jail. Ann is heard talking on the phone, trying to mollify her angry brother, while Joe speculates as to the possibility that George and Ann may be trying to open the criminal case again. Chris placates Joe, who shrugs off his concern and begins talking of Chris's future and telling him that he will help Chris and Ann make Kate accept their marriage. Ann then comes out to tell them that George is coming to visit that same evening.

Act Two

It is late afternoon on the same day. Kate enters to find Chris sawing up the fallen apple tree. After telling Chris that Joe is sleeping, she asks Chris to tell Ann to go home with George. She is afraid that

Steve Deever's hatred for Joe has infected his children, and she wants them both to leave.

When Ann appears, Kate returns to the house. Ann wants Chris to tell his mother about their marriage plans, and he promises to do so that evening. As he leaves, Sue enters, looking for her husband. She and Ann discuss Ann's marriage plans. Sue encourages her to move away after her marriage. She is bitter towards Chris, who, as Jim's friend, has tried to convince him to pursue work in medical research, a luxury that the Baylisses can not afford.

When Ann defends Chris, Sue suggests that Chris is a phony, given the fact that Chris has greatly benefited from Joe's ruthless and unethical business practices. She also tells Ann that everyone knows that Joe was as guilty as Steve Deever and merely ''pulled a fast one to get out of jail.''

When Chris returns, Sue goes in the house to see if she can calm Kate down. Ann tells Chris that Sue hates him, and that the people of the community believe that Joe should be in jail. Chris believes in his father's innocence and tells her that he can not put any stock in what the neighbors believe.

Joining them in the backyard, Joe tells the young lovers that he wants to find George a good local job, and then announces that he even wants to hire Steve Deever when he is released from prison. Chris is adamantly opposed, believing that Deever had wrongly implicated his father, and he does not want Joe to give him a job. Joe exits.

Having picked up George at the train station, Jim Bayliss enters quickly from the driveway. Jim warns Chris that George has ''blood in his eye,'' and that Chris should not let him come into the Keller yard. However, Chris welcomes George as a friend, but from George's surly behavior it is soon clear that he is angry.

As a result of visiting his father, he is convinced that Joe knew about the cracked cylinder heads but ordered Deever to ship them anyway, and he is now intent on stopping Ann from marrying Chris. He presents his father's account of the day the cracked cylinder heads were made, but Chris, believing in his father's innocence, tries to make him leave rather than confront Joe and upset his mother.

The tense situation is defused when Kate and Lydia enter the yard. After some amiable recollec-tions are exchanged, Joe enters and asserts that Steve Deever only blames Joe because Steve, un-able to face his faults, could never own up to his mistakes. George seems almost at ease, but when Kate makes a critical blunder, inadvertently disclos-ing that Joe had not been ill in fifteen years, George is once again upset. Joe's alibi was that he had been home with pneumonia when the defective parts were doctored up and shipped out by Deever; George realizes that Joe's alibi was a lie.

Frank Lubey enters with Larry Keller's horo-scope, which speculates that Larry is still alive. Kate wants Ann to leave with George and has even packed her bag. Chris tries to make his mother see that Larry is dead, but Kate, knowing the truth about the defective parts, insists that he must be alive. Otherwise, she believes that Joe is responsible for his death.

Finally realizing the truth, Chris angrily con-fronts his father, who lamely tries to defend his actions as ''business.'' Chris, profoundly hurt and disillusioned, beats furiously on his father's shoulders.

Act Three

It is 2:00 AM of the following morning. Alone, Kate waits for Chris to return. Jim joins her and asks what has happened; he then reveals that he has known about her husband's guilt for some time. He contends that he hopes that Chris will go off to find himself before returning.

Jim exits just as Joe comes in. Kate tells him that Jim knows the truth. Meanwhile, he is con-cerned about Ann, who has stayed in her room since Chris left. He talks, too, of needing Chris's forgive-ness and his intent to take his own life should he not get it.

Ann enters and hesitantly gives Kate a letter that she had received from Larry after Joe and her father were convicted. Chris returns and tells his father that he cannot forgive him. Ann takes the letter from Kate and gives it to Chris, who reads it aloud.

Composed just before Larry's death, it tells of his plan to take his own life in shame over what his father had done. It suddenly becomes clear to Joe that Larry believed that all the fighter pilots who perished in combat were Joe's sons. He then with-draws into the house, and Chris confirms his plan to turn Joe over to the authorities.

Burt Lancaster as Chris and Edward G. Robinson as Joe Keller in a scene from the film adaptation

Suddenly, a shot is heard from the house. Chris enters the house, presumably to find his father's body. He returns to his mother's arms, dismayed and crying, and she tells him to forget what has happened and live his life.

CHARACTERS

Annie

See Ann Deever

Dr. Jim Bayliss

Jim Bayliss is a close friend of Chris Keller. He and his wife Sue bought the house formerly owned by Steve Deever and his family; this makes him a neighbor of the Kellers. Although Jim suspects that Joe is as guilty as his former partner is, he likes the Keller family. He even tries to protect Joe from a confrontation with George Deever.

Sue Bayliss

Sue Bayliss, Jim's wife, reveals that the town knows the truth about Joe Keller, and, unlike her husband, she basically dislikes the family. However, her animus is largely directed against Chris, not Joe. She believes that he knows his father is guilty and has profited from the situation. As a result, she deems him a phony, and she deeply resents his friendship with her husband.

Bert

Bert is a neighborhood boy. He plays with Joe in the beginning of the play, pretending to be a policeman. Bert's gullibility provides a comic counterpoint to the more serious gullibility of Joe's son, Chris, who believes in his father's innocence. Joe has also shown Bert the gun with which, at the end, he kills himself.

Ann Deever

Ann is the attractive daughter of Steve Deever, Joe's former partner. She is visiting the Kellers for the first time since her boyfriend, Larry Keller, was reported missing in action. She has been invited by Chris; they are in love, much to the consternation of Kate, Chris's mother.

Ann believes that her father is guilty and has refused to visit him in jail. She is perhaps blinded by her love for Chris, whom she plans to marry.

MEDIA ADAPTATIONS

- *All My Sons* was adapted as a film in 1948. Chester Erskine wrote the screenplay. Directed by Irving Reis, the cast included Edward G. Robinson as Joe Keller, Burt Lancaster as Chris, Mady Christians as Kate, Louisa Horton as Ann Deever, and Howard Duff as George Deever. The film is available on videocassette.

- The play was also produced as a television play in 1955 and again in 1987. The 1955 version featured Albert Dekker, Patrick McGoohan, and Betta St. John in its cast. It is not, however, extant. The 1987 version, directed by John Power, was a television special produced by the Corporation for Public Broadcasting. It featured Joan Allen, Zeljko Ivanek, Michael Learned, Joanna Miles, Aidan Quinn, Alan Scarfe, Marlow Vella, and James Whitmore. It is not currently available on videocassette.

However, she carries what is in fact a suicide letter that Larry wrote to her before his final mission. Deeply shamed by his father's conviction, Larry disclosed his inability to live with the fact of his father's crime. When Kate continues to refuse to believe that Larry is dead and tries to prevent her marriage to Chris, Ann is forced to show her the letter. With the Larry's final thoughts revealed, Chris is forced to face his father's guilt.

George Deever

George is Steve Deever's son and brother to Ann Deever. He is a lawyer and a threat to Joe Keller, who fears that he might try to reopen the case that put Joe and his father in prison. After visiting his father in jail, he confronts Joe. George is convinced that Joe destroyed his father and was the real instigator of the crime. When he discovers that Ann is in love with Chris, he tries to persuade her to leave with him.

Kate's kindness almost placates him, and he even seems ready to accept Joe's version of what

happened; but Kate inadvertently reveals that Joe was not sick when the defective parts were shipped and thereby confirms what his father had told George. He storms off before Chris is forced to face the truth and Joe commits suicide.

Chris Keller

Chris, at age thirty-two, is Joe and Kate Keller's surviving son. He is in love with Ann Deever, the former girlfriend of his deceased brother, Larry. He invites Ann to visit the Keller home so that he might propose to her.

A veteran of World War II, Chris now works for his father, Joe. Since being exonerated and released from prison, Joe has built a very successful company. Chris believes that his father is innocent, as he feels was proved at the pardon hearing before Joe's release. An idealist, he has a very strong sense of justice and responsibility, and he bears a residual guilt for surviving the war when many of his friends died.

He also believes that one should be guided by the noblest principles, and he tries to encourage his friend, Jim Bayliss, to leave his medical practice to pursue a higher calling in medical research. His influence angers Jim's wife, Sue, who believes that Joe is guilty and that Chris is a hypocrite.

Although his love for his father blinds him to the truth, when Joe's guilt is finally revealed, he believes that he has no choice but to see to it that his father is returned to prison.

Joe Keller

The Keller family patriarch, Joe is a self-made businessman who started out as a semi-skilled laborer and worked his way up in the business world to become a successful manufacturer. He owns a factory, where he employs his surviving son, Chris.

Initially, Joe seems like a very genial, good-natured man, almost like a surrogate grandfather to the neighborhood kids. He is very outgoing with his neighbors, and has a disarming tendency to engage in some self-deprecation, noting, among other things, that he is not well educated or as articulate as those around him. It is partly a pose, however, for he actually prides himself on his business acumen. His business means a great deal to him, almost as much as his family.

Unfortunately, Joe has sacrificed quite a bit for such success. During the war, he ordered his partner, Steve Deever, to cover cracks in some airplane-engine parts, disguise the welds, and send them on to be used in fighter planes, causing the death of twenty-one pilots. Although convicted, Joe put the blame on Steve and got out of prison.

When the truth is revealed about Larry's death, Joe is at first unwilling to face the responsibility. Finally realizing the consequences of his actions and his limited course of action, he commits suicide.

Kate Keller

Kate is Joe's wife and the mother of Chris. Although her older son, Larry, was reported missing in action during World War II, she hopes that he has survived and will eventually return home. She hopes for this not only because she loves her son, but also because she knows the truth about Joe: he ordered his partner Steve to cover the cracks in the cylinder heads that eventually resulted in the death of several American fighter pilots. Although Larry never flew a P-40 fighter, Kate believes that Joe must be held accountable as his murderer. She is finally forced to face Larry's death when confronted with the letter that he sent to Ann Deever announcing his impending suicide.

Her motives are hidden from Chris, who earnestly wants her to face the fact of Larry's death and move on with life. He wants to marry Larry's former girl friend, Ann Deever, but he knows he will not be able to obtain his mother's blessing as long as she continues to hold on to her unrealistic conviction that Larry is still alive.

Kate is a sympathetic character. She is kind and motherly, but the truth of her husband's guilt tortures her. As the pressure mounts, she develops physical symptoms of her inner agony. At the end, after Joe shoots himself, she tells Chris to live—something she had not been able to do since the death of her other son.

Frank Lubey

Frank Lubey is Lydia's husband. A haberdasher, he is perceived as flighty and socially inept. Gracious, intelligent, and attractive, Lydia makes him seem rather silly by comparison. Frank, always missing each draft call-up by being a year too old, did not go to war. He married Lydia when George Deever, her former beau, did not return to his hometown from the war.

Frank's foolishness extends to his belief in astrology, which would be harmless enough were it not for the fact that he keeps Kate's hopes of Larry's survival alive with his insistence that Larry's horoscope could reveal the truth.

Lydia Lubey

Lydia is Frank's wife. She is a charming, very pretty woman of twenty-seven, described by Miller as a "robust laughing girl." Before George went off to war, she was his girlfriend; when he did not return home after his father was imprisoned, she married Frank, a dull alternative. When George does come to confront the Kellers with his father's accusations, he is reminded of everything he lost. He also knows that Lydia deserved better than she got.

Mother

See Kate Keller

THEMES

American Dream

In a sense, *All My Sons* is a critical investigation of the quest to achieve material comfort and an improved social status through hard work and determination. In the Horatio Alger myth, even a disadvantaged, impoverished young man can attain wealth and prestige through personal fortitude, moral integrity, and untiring industry. Joe Keller is that sort of self-made man, one who made his way from blue-collar worker to factory owner. However, Joe sacrifices his integrity to materialism, and he makes a reprehensible decision that sends American pilots to their deaths, something he is finally forced to face.

Atonement and Forgiveness

Paradoxically, Joe Keller's suicide at the end of *All My Sons* is both an act of atonement and an escape from guilt. It stems from Joe's realization that there can be no real forgiveness for what he had done. The alternative is confession and imprisonment. Death offers Joe another alternative.

Forgiveness must come from Kate and Chris. The letter written by Larry reveals that he deliberately destroyed himself during the war, profoundly shamed by his father's brief imprisonment for fraud and profiteering. It is a devastating irony that Joe's initial attempt to do right by his family—resulting in fraud and the deaths of twenty-one fighter pilots—leads to destruction of his world.

TOPICS FOR FURTHER STUDY

- Research the problem of profiteering during both World War II and the Cold War. Was it a prevalent phenomenon? What forms did it take (e.g., cost overruns, ridiculous pricing, fraudulent claims)? Describe the worst case you can find from your research.

- Trace the influence of either Henrik Ibsen or Anton Chekhov on *All My Sons.*

- Investigate Miller's role in the investigations of the House Un-American Activities Committee (HUAC), including his contempt conviction and eventual exoneration. Do you agree with Miller's position? Give reasons for your answer.

- Determine the influence of the politics of the left, including socialism and communism, on the American theater and cinema during the 1930s and 1940s.

Choices and Consequences

All My Sons employs a pattern that is fundamental to most tragedies. Protagonists in tragedy must, in some degree, be held accountable for their actions. When faced with a moral dilemma, they often make a wrong choice. Joe, at a critical moment, elected to place his family's finances above the lives of courageous American soldiers.

The revelations that lead up to Joe's tragic recognition of guilt and his suicide, the final consequences of his choice, are essential to *All My Sons.* There is a sense of *anake,* or tragic necessity, that moves the work along towards its inevitable moment of truth and awful but final retribution.

Death

The key in the tragic arc of *All My Sons* is Kate Keller's refusal to accept the death of her son, Larry. Initially, prone to false hopes, it seems that she is in denial; finally, it is revealed that her need to believe that Larry is alive allows her to avoid the terrible consequences of her husband's deeds. She realizes

that if Larry is dead, then Joe is responsible for his death—something Larry himself confirmed in his letter to Ann. All along, Kate knew her husband's guilt but desperately avoided it, knowing that it would destroy her family.

Duty and Responsibility

Joe Keller's sense of duty and responsibility is to the material comfort of his family and the success of his business. At a weak moment, under pressure, he puts these values ahead of what should clearly have been a higher duty, his obligation to human life. His fear of losing lucrative government contracts—essentially his greed—blinded him to the murder he was committing.

Ethics

Joe's decision to send defective parts is not merely a result of skewed values, it is a serious breach of ethics. Joe does not fully comprehend how serious a breach it is. To him, success is more important than anything else, including human life and the good of his country. By setting up this ethical situation, Miller clearly questions the implications of a value system that puts material success above moral responsibilities to others.

Guilt and Innocence

In *All My Sons,* there are hints that Joe is troubled by his guilt—even before his eventual suicide. His suspicions of Ann and George Deever reveal his fears of being forced to face the truth. Even when he attempts to atone for his guilt by helping his former partner, Steve Deever as well as Deever's son, George, his offer seems rather lame given the enormity of his guilt. There is no way he can atone for the deaths of the American fighter pilots, however, something that he finally realizes.

Punishment

Joe's death at the end of *All My Sons* is paradoxically both punishment and escape. In one sense, Joe can do no less than pay for his crime with his life. It is not an empty gesture. It is made abundantly clear from the play's beginning that Joe is a man who is full of life and cherishes his roles as both husband and father.

When the truth comes out, Joe has to face not only a return to prison but also the alienation of his remaining son and the destruction his family. Death offers the only escape from that pain. It may also be seen as a sacrificial act, one which saves Joe's son, Chris, from further humiliation.

Revenge

Fueled by his anger over Joe's guilt, George Deever comes to the Keller's house seeking revenge and retribution. He is a major catalyst and intensifies the emotional tension of the play. For a moment, Kate's friendliness and warmth placate him. When, towards the end of the second act, Kate inadvertently confirms the probable truth of his father's accusations, George's anger returns. Joe is then forced to reveal his fraudulent and deceitful actions.

STYLE

Climax

All My Sons has a very traditional dramatic structure, with carefully orchestrated action that reaches a climax. Although it may be argued that each act has its own climax, with a particularly powerful one in the second act, the final climax occurs in the last act, when Joe finally realizes that he was responsible for the deaths of the American fighter pilots, his "sons."

Conflict

Tension in drama evolves from conflict. In fact, conflict is virtually mandatory in what is termed the dramatic moment, whether in a play or in fiction. A good play generally evinces a sense of a deepening conflict that heightens the emotional tension as the play works towards its climactic moment. Conflict arises as a character strives toward a goal and is met by an obstacle to that goal.

The key conflict in *All My Sons* develops as a result of Chris's desire to marry Ann Deever. Standing in the way of his desire is his mother's ability to block the marriage; she opposes the union because she cannot accept the death of her son, Larry. If she accepts his death, then she must also face Joe's role in it.

Ironically, Chris tries to enlist his father's help in this matter. On account of his love for Ann, Chris pushes his family into facing truths that have tragic and destructive consequences.

Exposition

Exposition in drama is often more of a problem than it is for writers of fiction. Somehow, information about past events and relationships must be conveyed to an audience so that the action in the present can be fully understood. Because *All My Sons* is a realistic play in which all the action occurs on the day in which the family crisis is met and tragically resolved, Miller has few options for revealing Joe's fraudulent past. The action strictly adheres to a normal chronological order, allowing nothing like a flashback or the hallucinatory reveries of the main character so brilliantly used by Miller in his next play, *Death of Salesman*.

Miller's chief device is the reunion, the introduction of a character who needs to be told what has transpired since that character's former estrangement. That character is Ann Deever; inadvertently, she opens old wounds because of her familial relationship with Joe's former partner, Larry. She also bears the truth of Larry's death in a letter that he had written to her. In this way she is like the messenger of Greek tragedy whose task it is to bear in the pain of truth that will force the tragic recognition in the main character.

Foreshadowing

Foreshadowings of an impending disaster appear in the first act of *All My Sons*. The memorial apple tree planted for Larry is destroyed during a storm in the early morning hours, suggesting a dark force that has the power to destroy the Keller family.

Kate's response to the tree's felling at first seems odd. She says that it should never have been planted in the first place. However, it is soon learned that she has desperately held on to the hope that Larry, reported missing in action during the war, is still alive. That she suffers from the emotional burden of her hope is revealed by her sleeplessness and physical pain.

In its way, even Joe's role-playing game is a foreshadowing. Playing with Bert, they pretend that the Keller home is a jail. This game suggests that Keller views his home as a kind of jail. On account of what he has done, he can not really be free.

Even the play's setting foreshadows events. The backyard of the Kellers is pleasant and, initially, a happy place; but it is also rather insular, hidden from its neighbors by the poplar trees that grow on both sides. The trees stand like sentinels, protecting Joe from the suspicions of his neighbors, most of whom believe that he was at least as guilty as Steve Deever.

Realism

All My Sons strictly adheres to the tenets of realistic drama as first put in practice by such early modern playwrights as Henrik Ibsen and Anton Chekhov. Fundamental to such drama is faithfulness to real life in both character and action. Characters speak and act very much like real people. Nothing happens that could not happen in reality.

However, like the realism of most plays in the Ibsen tradition, the realism of *All My Sons* is of a selective variety, deliberately controlled to advance a particular thesis. Matters are rather conveniently drawn to a climactic head on a single day with the visit of the two Deever siblings, a coincidence that is nevertheless wholly within the realm of plausibility.

Setting

The setting of *All My Sons,* the Keller's backyard in a small Midwestern town shortly after World War II, has a significant role in the play. The setting suggests comfort and isolation from the community. Isolation is necessary because the townspeople suspect the truth about Joe, that he did what he had been convicted of doing during the war. Yet because he is so successful and provides jobs in the community, they do not openly reproach him for it.

Destructive forces threaten the setting. Nature first invades, destroying the apple tree planted in memory of Larry. It is followed by the "messengers," Ann and George. At the end of the play, the yard is engulfed in the darkness of night, the destructive truth that leaves Kate and Chris alone in the grim aftermath of Joe's suicide.

Thesis

All My Sons is a thesis play that focuses on a problem that Arthur Miller believed was eating at the fabric of American democracy: material greed. Miller's protagonist, Joe Keller, is an affable and pleasant man with a strong sense of family loyalty, but his values have been shaped by a prevalent American belief that human success and worth can best be measured by how many things a person owns.

Joe believes that his son's love is based on material concerns. The fact that Chris wants Joe to atone for his crime finally forces him to recognize his guilt.

Tragic Flaw

Joe lets a love of materialism and fear cloud his moral compass. He sets in motion events that have tragic consequences. Joe fears failure in business, as if, somehow, failure would threaten the love and respect of his family. Under pressure, that fear leads him to make an ill-considered decision to put the lives of American pilots at risk by disguising cracked cylinder heads and shipping them to assembly plants.

Unities

In addition to being a realistic play, *All My Sons* has some characteristics of classical drama, notably an adherence to the so-called dramatic unities of time, place, and action. First, it basically observes the Aristotelian notion that the action should all occur within a twenty-four-hour time period. The action opens in the morning and ends in the early hours on the morning of the next day.

Second, the action all occurs in one locale, the backyard of the Keller home. Third, although the action is not continuous, within each of the three acts the action is continuous, and the three acts are arranged chronologically, as is the standard practice in most realistic plays. Breaks between acts are in part used to indicate the passage of time in the play's action.

HISTORICAL CONTEXT

In March of 1947, President Harry S. Truman presented the Truman Doctrine to the U. S. Congress. The Truman Doctrine was an anti-Communist declaration that would shape American foreign policy for over four decades. With the Cold War heating up, fears of an international communist conspiracy were rapidly growing. The Truman Doctrine was meant to alleviate some of those very fears.

The now infamous House Un-American Activities Committee (HUAC) began its very visible investigations of alleged communist influence in Hollywood, resulting in the jailing and blacklisting of witnesses who refused to cooperate with investigators. The FBI, meanwhile, looked for evidence of communist infiltration in America; for example, they concluded that Frank Capra's classic Christmas film, *It's a Wonderful Life,* was little more than insidious communist propaganda.

To counter the growing spread of communism in Eastern Europe and Asia, the United States took

COMPARE & CONTRAST

- **1940s:** In the aftermath of World War II, the industrialized world divided into two armed superpowers: the Soviet bloc of communist nations and the Western democracies. In the West, the threat of communism led to suspicion and paranoia at the highest levels of government. Nuclear war seemed imminent.

    Today: The threat of a nuclear war between the Soviet Union and United States dissipated with the economic and political collapse of the Soviet Union in the 1980s. Instead, the threat of terrorism reigns as well as the growing nuclear capabilities of rogue states such as Pakistan, India, Iran, and Iraq.

- **1940s:** The Nuremberg Trials for war crimes and atrocities, which began soon after World War II, continued into 1949. The trials resulted in the imprisonment or execution of many high-ranking Nazis, particularly those involved in the running the concentration camps, which exterminated millions of victims.

    Today: Reaction to genocide in several countries has led to a new call for tribunals to indict and condemn war criminals. A notable example of a modern war criminal is Serbian president Slobodan Milosevic, who in 1999 was charged with the mass murder of ethnic Albanians and indicted by the World Court. Such ''ethnic cleansing'' has also occurred in other states, including Iraq, Burundi, and Rwanda.

- **1940s:** In the wake of World War II, concerns about wartime profiteering and unethical practices were widespread. In the 1950s such concerns would eventually compel President Dwight D. Eisenhower to warn America about what he called ''the industrial-military complex.'' War profits also took the form of stealing the assets of the war's victims.

    Today: In light of charges by several Jewish families that Swiss banks cooperated with Nazis during World War II and expropriated gold stolen from war victims, the whole issue of wartime profiteering has once more emerged. New concerns have emerged over the role some American industrialists may have played in the rise of Germany's military in the 1930s.

- **1940s:** Professional sports, with some rare exceptions (boxing, for example) were largely segregated. It was not until 1947 that the color line in Major League baseball was broken when Jackie Robinson joined the Brooklyn Dodgers of the National League. Until that time, African Americans could play only in the segregated Negro League.

    Today: African Americans successfully compete in professional sports that seemed almost the exclusive domain of white athletes, notably tennis and golf.

---

positive steps to help rebuild the war-torn countries of both its allies and its former enemies, including Germany and Japan. On June 5, 1947, Secretary of State George Marshall announced his plan for the economic recovery of Europe. With the Brussels Treaty of March 17, 1948, the Western European Union, the forerunner of the North Atlantic Treaty Organization (NATO), was formed.

Meanwhile, King Michael of Romania abdicated, bringing another European country into the Soviet bloc. India and Pakistan were granted independence from Great Britain. In that same year, Mother Teresa left her Loreto order to move into the slums of Calcutta to establish her first school.

In Roswell, New Mexico, in July, 1947, there was a rash of UFO sightings and the reported crash of an alien space ship, the basis for what many still consider a lame government cover-up of the truth. Also that summer, Jackie Robinson, the first African American baseball player to play in the Major

Leagues, had joined the Brooklyn Dodgers and was on his way to winning the National League Rookie of the Year award.

In cinema, Elia Kazan, the director of *All My Sons,* won an Oscar for his direction of *Gentlemen's Agreement,* a film about anti-Semitism. Chuck Yeager became the first human to break the sound barrier in October, 1947. Breaking a different kind of barrier, Bell Telephone Laboratories introduced the transistor, the first important Postwar breakthrough in the evolution of microelectronics, fundamental in the development of the post-industrial, information-age technology of the late twentieth century.

CRITICAL OVERVIEW

All My Sons was Arthur Miller's first successful play on Broadway. In hindsight, it may seem that the work lacks the great imaginative force of his next play, *Death of Salesman* (1949), still widely regarded as his masterpiece, but in *All My Sons* Miller certainly showed that he could both use dialogue very well and construct a riveting drama in the tradition of social realism.

Miller was fortunate to have as his director Elia Kazan, whose mercurial career was then rapidly rising, and an excellent cast, headed by Ed Begley as Joe Keller, Beth Merrill as Kate, Arthur Kennedy as Chris, Lois Wheeler as Ann Deever, and Karl Malden as her brother, George. In most reviews, the quality of the production was recognized and applauded. The play chalked up a run of 328 performances and garnered the New York Drama Critics' Circle Award. It was an impressive achievement for a new and virtually unknown playwright.

The work did not receive uniform raves, but it did win the approval of some influential critics, notably Brooks Atkinson of the *The New York Times,* the city's most distinguished newspaper. In his autobiography, *Timebends* Miller says "it was Brooks Atkinson's campaign for *All My Sons* that was responsible for its long run and my recognition as a playwright."

Among other things, Atkinson defended the play against those who took umbrage with Miller's depiction of an American businessman as one who puts material comfort and success above moral responsibility. For Atkinson, the play was "the most talented work by a new author in some time," and though he recognized the important contribution of Kazan and the cast to the play's power, he credited Miller with devising a "pitiless analysis of characters that gathers momentum all evening and concludes with both logic and dramatic impact."

Most reviewers recognized Miller's great promise even while finding flaws in the work. For Joseph Wood Krutch, the plot of the drama was "almost too neat." "The pieces," Krutch argued, "fit together with the artificial, interlocking perfection of a jig-saw puzzle, and toward the end one begins to feel a little uncomfortable to find all the implicit ironies so patly illustrated and poetic justice working with such mechanical perfection." Moreover, Krutch took issue with Miller's "warm respect for all the leftist pieties" and complained that the playwright's "intellectual convictions" are "more stereotyped than his dramatic imagination."

That Miller imposed a classical structure on a social problem play in the tradition of Henrik Ibsen and Anton Chekhov was recognized by his reviewers, whether leftist in sympathies, like Atkinson, or conservative, like Krutch. The influence of both Ibsen and Chekhov is noted by John Mason Brown, who views Dr. Bayliss as a Chekhovian interloper, and in the "spiritual stripteasing" of his main character, the use of symbolism, and his digging into the past to reveal the present and "rush forward to a new climax" the abiding and persistent influence of Ibsen.

To some critics, *All My Sons* also reflected the influence of classical tragedy. In the play, Kappo Phelan wrote, Miller "attempted and delivered a tragedy," and the play is, in fact, the playwright's first successful attempt to create what he would later call "a tragedy of the common man." There are clear parallels to such Sophoclean tragedies as *Oedipus Rex,* both in structure and technique.

Both leftist ideology and the classical influence would keep *All My Sons* in the limelight until *Death of a Salesman* replaced it as the cynosure of critical attention. With that play, Miller came as close as any playwright before or since to demonstrate the validity of his assertion that tragedy is possible in a modern, egalitarian democracy. For that play, as well as *The Crucible* and *View from the Bridge, All My Sons* provided a firm foundation in both its theme of guilt and expiation and its tragic elements and structure.

CRITICISM

John W. Fiero

Fiero is a Ph.D., now retired, who formerly taught drama and playwriting at the University of Southwestern Louisiana and is now a freelance writer and consultant. In this essay he considers All My Sons *as Miller's first attempt to write what he would call a tragedy of the common man, comparing it with Sophocles's great tragedy,* Oedipus Rex.

Writing in 1929, almost two full decades before *All My Sons* opened on Broadway, critic Joseph Wood Krutch wrote a celebrated essay entitled "The Tragic Fallacy." His thesis was that modern audiences could not fully participate in the experience of tragedy because the tragic spirit, so vital and alive in the past, had simply stopped haunting the human landscape. Modern man no longer had tragedy's requisite belief, if not in God or some other power greater than man, then at least in man.

Tragedy, opined Krutch, depended on what he termed the "tragic fallacy," the "assumption which man so readily makes that something outside his own being, some 'spirit not himself'—be it God, Nature, or that still vaguer thing called a Moral Order—joins him in the emphasis which he places upon this or that and confirms him in his feelings that his passions and his opinions are important." Because of the "universally modern incapacity to conceive man as noble," Krutch maintained that dramatists could no longer create tragedies, only "those distressing modern works sometimes called by its [tragedy's] name," works that, rather than celebrate a "triumph over despair" while exhibiting a "confidence in the value of human life," simply depicted man's haplessness and insignificance.

For Krutch, modern man's diminished stature makes a character like Oswald Alving of Ibsen's *Ghosts* a far more "relevant" character than Shakespeare's Hamlet. Krutch essentially indicts his contemporaries for allowing the tragic light to fade from the universe.

Arthur Miller, as he makes clear in his early plays *All My Sons, Death of a Salesman, The Crucible,* and *A View from the Bridge,* was unwilling to admit that the light was gone. For him, a tragic consciousness still existed, even in the most ordinary sort of people. As he wrote in his piece called "Tragedy and the Common Man," he believed that "the tragic feeling is evoked in us when we are in the presence of a character who is ready to lay down his life, if need be, to secure one thing his sense of personal dignity."

Moreover, Miller claimed, "the common man is as apt a subject for tragedy in its highest sense as kings were," a heretical view for those critics whose definition of tragedy was largely delimited by Aristotle's *Poetics.*

Orrin Klapp, pondering what he called Americans' "armor against tragic experience," found a partial explanation for it in the "actual shrinkage in the stature of the heroes being presented," a reduction in human significance that made it almost impossible "to see them as having the dignity necessary to be tragic."

For Miller, nobility of soul is not contingent upon rank at all; it rather rests on an individual's moral integrity and, at the last, a willingness to face the consequence of a fateful decision and shoulder its attendant guilt.

All My Sons was Miller's first attempt to write such a tragedy of the common man, and although with *Death of a Salesman,* his next play, he made almost a quantum leap forward in technique, in the former work he created a prototype for all his common-man, familial tragedies, including the latter. In it he welded features of classical tragedy to the realistic thesis play in the tradition of Ibsen, maintaining a surface verisimilitude while advancing a plot designed in accordance with the logic of causality and plausible human motives.

Academically at least, Sophocles seems to haunt *All My Sons.* As more than one critic has noted, the parallels between Miller's play and the Greek tragedian's masterpiece, *Oedipus Rex,* are readily apparent. W. Arthur Boggs maintains, for example, that like *Oedipus Rex,* Miller's play is a "tragedy of recognition."

There is, of course, one major and obvious difference: the works do not share a commensurate tragic scope. The *hamartia* of Oedipus, the killing of his father, has consequences not just for his family but for the entire city state of Thebes; Keller's *hamartia,* his transgression against a clear moral imperative, has primary consequences, at least among the living, only for his family and close associates.

However, both Oedipus and Joe Keller are patriarchs. Both are asked to solve a problem, which, unknowingly or unconsciously, they have themselves created. And both must confront the

WHAT DO I READ NEXT?

- Aristotle's *Poetics* offers a descriptive definition of ancient Greek tragedy. For some theorists, it is the ultimate critical authority on the nature of tragedy.

- Eugene O'Neill, in *Long Day's Journey into Night* (1956), comes as close as Miller does to writing a modern, family tragedy.

- An important sociological study, *The Lonely Crowd* (1969), by David Reisman, suggests that modern America has lost the capacity for guilt (necessary to tragedy).

- *Culture of Narcissism: American Life in an Age of Diminishing Expectations* (1991, revised edition), by Christopher Lasch, a more recent look at American culture, examines the changing cultural landscape.

- Stuart D. Brandes's study, *Warhogs: A History of War Profits in America* (1997), is a thorough history of wartime profiteering in the United States, both before and since World War II.

---

truth, shoulder their terrible guilt, and respond by inflicting punishment upon themselves—Oedipus by blinding himself and exiling himself from Thebes, and Joe Keller by taking his own life.

Oedipus Rex and *All My Sons* share a similar pattern and structure, a common tragic rhythm. As Robert Hogan notes, both works involve "the revelation of a criminal whose crimes has occurred years earlier" and which has become "the crux of the present action." In other words, both plays deal with untying the knot of a devastating and destructive truth that has been the source of a sickness that cannot be cured until it is recognized and faced by the protagonist. The sickness in *Oedipus Rex,* a plague, afflicts the entire community of Thebes; in *All My Sons,* it takes the form of a family's failure to deal with the death of a son.

Furthermore, both *Oedipus Rex* and *All My Sons* deal with the transgression of one or more universal taboos and thus have strong moral focus. In the former, Oedipus violates taboos against incest and parricide; in the later, Joe Keller "kills" his son, Larry, and his spiritual sons, the twenty-one fighter pilots who die as a result of his actions.

Oedipus must first discover the truth of what he has done, while Joe must own up to the consequences of what he knows he has done and accept

responsibility and guilt. Both protagonists in some sense lack knowledge, sharing a blindness to truth that is only cured when their ignorance, in a tragic recognition or epiphany, is sloughed off and they finally see clearly for the first time—even as their understanding destroys them. Ironically, their insight is the necessary recompense without which tragedy has no positive meaning and no power to elate rather than simply depress an audience.

Oedipus Rex comes from an age that accepted one premise alien to the modern mind: the victimization of "innocent" offspring used against their parents as instruments of divine justice. It is Oedipus's unavoidable destiny that he should murder his father and marry his mother, atoning for their affront to the gods. A raw deal, perhaps, but Oedipus, who learns of his fate from the Oracle at Delphi as a young man, tries to defy the will of the gods by averting his fate. Not knowing that he is only the foster child of the king and queen of Corinth, he flees that city and, ironically, runs headlong into his fate. His defiance and resulting conviction that he has escaped his fate are evidence of his tragic flaw, his *hubris,* which, paradoxically, is also the source of his greatness.

Although Miller could hardly incorporate such a view of divine justice into *All My Sons,* he employs a modern parallel of sorts. Joe's actions

A scene from the film adaptation of All My Sons

victimize his innocent sons, Larry and Chris, both of whom have ethical principles that could never condone what their father has done.

Joe also shares some of Oedipus's pride and arrogance. After leaving Corinth, Oedipus had struggled to regain the princely stature he sacrificed in his attempt to escape his divinely-ordained fate. By virtue of his strength, he survives a fateful encounter on the road, unwittingly committing parricide, and, through his intelligence, he solves the riddle of the Sphinx, becoming king of Thebes and unwittingly marrying Joscasta, his own mother.

As depicted by Sophocles, he repeatedly displays pride in his accomplishments, his rise to the throne of Thebes by merit rather than influence, and displays almost paranoid suspicions towards his uncle and brother-in-law, Creon, who, he believes, is jealous and resents him. In his mocking of the blind prophet, Tiresias, who, he suspects, is part of Creon's conspiracy to usurp the throne, he is nearly blasphemous in his arrogance.

Joe Keller is also a proud man. Through hard work, he has made his way up in the world, from semi-skilled laborer to factory owner and become one of the richest men in town. He is confident in Chris's faith and trust in him and cares little about what neighbors like Sue Bayliss believe about his culpability in the matter of the cracked cylinder heads.

However, his equanimity and affability dissolve with the arrival of Ann Deever, and then her brother, George. Like Oedipus, Joe suspects the motives of others. He mistrusts Ann, daughter to a man he left in prison to pay for what was his own crime. The Deevers, ghosts from the past, are a threat to Joe, not just because of what their father might have told them but because they can and do force a familial showdown, something that Joe has assiduously avoided. Ann and Chris want to marry, but they will not as long as Kate Keller clings to her hope that Larry Keller is still alive. If she must accept Larry's death, then she will hold Joe responsible for it, something that neither Kate nor Joe can face.

The Deevers are like the Sophoclean messengers who bear fateful information. They confirm that Joe ordered the welding of the cracked cylinder heads and that he was the cause of his son's death. Ann even bears a letter from Larry, in which, shamed by his father, Larry confides that he is setting out on a suicidal mission.

George, on the other hand, is an interesting parallel to the messenger from Corinth in *Oedipus*

OEDIPUS REX AND *ALL MY SONS* SHARE A SIMILAR PATTERN AND STRUCTURE, A COMMON TRAGIC RHYTHM"

Rex, the one who comes to announce the deaths of the king and queen of that city, temporarily allaying Oedipus's fears and, thereby, briefly turning the tide against the tragic direction of the play. There is a similar reversal in *All My Sons,* when George, disarmed by the amiability of Kate Keller, begins to accept Joe's account of his father as a weak man, the one who made the sole decision to send on the defective airplane parts. Only when Kate inadvertently lets slip the fact that Joe was not sick on the fateful day does George begin to confront Joe again.

The influence of classical tragedy on *All My Sons* also resonates in other ways. For example, the idea of destiny or fate is introduced by Frank Lubey, the amateur and inept astrologer. He tries to convince Kate that there is hope that Larry is still alive because the day he was lost in action was, according to his horoscope, a propitious and fortunate day for him. There is also the virtual observance of the unities of time, place, and, to a degree, action, and a set that suggests the standard *skene* of Greek tragedy.

For some of the critics of the play, Miller seemed to be crowding such devices of tragedy into the somewhat unreceptive frame of realistic drama, jamming them into a confused situation made more confused by their inclusion or, as in the case of the letter in Ann's possession, making them a bit too convenient and coincidental to pass muster as a device suited to the probability demanded by realism. To Boggs, for example, *All My Sons* lacks the precision and simple and direct focus of *Oedipus Rex* and, therefore, fails.

Still, *All My Sons* is the first effort by one of America's major post-World War II dramatists, albeit unconsciously, to contest Krutch's thesis of the impossibility of modern tragedy. Although in *All My Sons* he may not have succeeded according to critics, he at least succeeded in raising expectations. In fact, many commentators came to believe that the playwright was just one work shy of a

masterpiece, which, two years later, graced the American theater in the guise of *Death of a Salesman.*

Source: John W. Fiero, for *Drama for Students,* Gale, 2000.

Arvin R. Wells

Wells discusses the merits of Miller's play as a work of social thesis, but the critic also contends that the play offers a greater wealth of themes than that simple assessment—including the playwright's probing insights into human nature.

Looked at superficially, Arthur Miller's *All My Sons* may appear to be simply a social thesis play. Such classification—a valid one if severely qualified—is suggested both by the timeliness of the story and by the presence of considerable overt social criticism. The story itself is obviously calculated to engage the so-called social conscience. Stated in the simplest terms, the play dramatizes the process by which Joe Keller, a small manufacturer, is forced to accept individual social responsibility and, consequently, to accept his personal guilt for having sold, on one occasion during World War II, fatally defective airplane parts to the government.

However, while this bare-bone synopsis is essentially accurate, it does, in fact, do violence to the actual complexity of the play. In his well-known essay "Tragedy and the Common Man," Miller comments,

> Our lack of tragedy may be partially accounted for by the turn which modern literature has taken toward the purely psychiatric, or purely sociological. . . . From neither of these views can tragedy derive, simply because neither represents a balanced concept of life.

What is reflected here is Miller's own careful avoidance of the "purely" this or that. And it might similarly be said that no satisfactory understanding of Miller's *All My Sons* may be derived from a criticism which commits itself to a "purely" or even predominantly sociological or psychiatric view. The sociological view is particularly limiting in that it carries with it the temptation to approach the dramatic action from the level of broad socio-cultural generalizations and, consequently, to oversimplify character and action and, stumbling among subtleties of characterization, to accuse the playwright of a confusion of values which belongs appropriately to the characters in their situations.

Actually, like most of Miller's plays, *All My Sons* demands of the reader an awareness of the deviousness of human motivation, an understanding of the way in which a man's best qualities may be involved in his worst actions and cheapest ideas, and, in general, a peculiarly fine perception of cause and effect. Nowhere is it suggested that the social realities and attitudes that are brought within the critical focus of the play can be honestly considered outside of some such context of human aspirations and weaknesses as is provided by the play; and nowhere is it suggested that the characters are or can be judged strictly on the basis of some simple social ethic or ideal that might be deduced from the action. The characters do not simply reflect the values and attitudes of a particular society; they use those values and attitudes in their attempt to realize themselves. And it is these characteristics that give *All My Sons,* and other Miller plays, a density of texture so much greater than that of the typical social thesis play, which seeks not only to direct but to facilitate ethical judgments upon matters of topical importance.

For most of us there is no difficulty in assenting to the abstract proposition which Chris puts to his mother at the end of the play:

> You can be better! Once and for all you can know now that the whole earth comes through those fences; there's a universe outside and you're responsible to it.

And there is no problem either in giving general intellectual assent to the morality of brotherhood for which Chris speaks. There is, however, considerable difficulty in assenting to the actual situation at the end of the play, in accepting it as a simple triumph of right over wrong. For the play in its entirety makes clear that Joe Keller has committed his crimes not out of cowardice, callousness, or pure self-interest, but out of a too-exclusive regard for real though limited values, and that Chris, the idealist, is far from acting disinterestedly as he harrows his father to repentance.

Joe Keller is a successful small manufacturer, but he is also "a man whose judgment must be dredged out of experience and a peasant-like common sense." Like many uneducated, self-made men, he has no capacity for abstract considerations; whatever is not personal or at least immediate has no reality for him. He has the peasant's insular loyalty to family which excludes more generalized responsibility to society at large or to mankind in general. At the moment of decision, when his business seemed threatened, the question for him was not basically one of profit and loss; what concerned him was a conflict of responsibilities—his responsibility to his family, particularly his sons to whom the business was to be a legacy of security and joy, versus his responsibility to the unknown men, en-

> **BECAUSE IT FORCES UPON THE READER AN AWARENESS OF THE INTRICACIES OF HUMAN MOTIVATION AND OF HUMAN RELATIONSHIPS, *ALL MY SONS* LEAVES A DUAL IMPRESSION: THE ACTION AFFIRMS THE THEME OF THE INDIVIDUAL'S RESPONSIBILITY TO HUMANITY, BUT, AT THE SAME TIME, IT SUGGESTS THAT THE STANDPOINT OF EVEN SO FINE AN IDEAL IS NOT AN ALTOGETHER ADEQUATE ONE FROM WHICH TO EVALUATE HUMAN BEINGS"**

gaged in the social action of war, who might as a remote consequence suffer for his dishonesty. For such a man as Joe Keller such a conflict could scarcely exist and, given its existence, could have only one probable resolution.

When the worst imaginable consequence follows—twenty-two pilots killed in Australia—Keller is nonetheless able to presume upon his innocence as established before the law. For in his ethical insularity—an insularity stressed in the play by the hedged-in backyard setting—he is safe from any serious assault of conscience so long as he can believe that the family is the most important thing and that what is done in the name of the family has its own justification. Yet, he is not perfectly secure within his sanctuary. His apparently thick skin has its sensitive spots: in his unwillingness to oppose his wife's unhealthy refusal to accept her son Larry's death, in his protest against Ann Deever's rejection of her father, in his insistence that he does not believe in "crucifying a man," and in his insistence that Chris should use what he, the father, has earned, "with joy ... without shame ... with joy," he betrays a deep-seated fear. His appeal on behalf of Herb Deever (Act I) is in fact, partly a covert appeal on his own behalf, an appeal for merciful understanding called forth by the shocked realization that some considerations may override and even destroy the ties of family upon which his own security rests.

It is Chris Keller who, in reaching out for love and a life of his own, first undermines and then destroys this security altogether. Chris has brought out of the war an idealistic morality of brotherhood based on what he has seen of mutual self-sacrifice among the men whom he commanded. But he has not survived the war unwounded; he bears a still festering psychological wound, a sense of inadequacy and guilt. He has survived to enjoy the fruits of a wartime economy, and he fears that in enjoying them he becomes unworthy, condemned by his own idealism. Even his love for Ann Deever, the sweetheart of his dead brother, has seemed to him a guilty desire to take advantage of the dead to whom he somehow owes his life.

As the play opens, however, he has decided to assert himself, to claim the things in life and the position in life which he feels should rightfully be his, and as the initial step he has invited Ann to his family home. His decision brings him into immediate conflict with his mother, Kate Keller, who looks upon the possible marriage between Chris and Ann as a public confirmation of Larry's death. At first Joe Keller seems only peripherally involved in this conflict; his attempt to evade Chris's demand that Kate be forced to accept Larry's death carries only ambiguous suggestions of insecurity. However, at the end of Act II, Kate, emotionally exhausted by the fruitless effort to use George Deever's accusations as a means of driving out Ann, and opposed for the first time by the declared disbelief of both husband and son, breaks down and reveals the actual basis of her refusal: if Chris lets Larry go, then he must let his father go as well. What is revealed here is that Kate is fundamentally like her husband; only what is personal or immediate is real for her. If Larry is alive, then, in a sense, the war has no reality, and Joe's crimes do not mean anything; their consequences are merely distant echoes in an unreal world. But if Larry is dead, then the war is real, and Joe is guilty of murder, even, by an act of association, guilty of murdering his own son. Her own desperate need to reject Larry's death against all odds and upon whatever flimsy scrap of hope has been the reflex of her need to defend her relation to her husband against whatever in herself might be outraged by the truth about him. Actually, however, Kate has "an overwhelming capacity for love" and an ultimate commitment to the living which makes it possible for her to "let Larry go" and rise again to the defense of her husband at the end. It is Larry living not Larry dead that she clings to, and she does this because to admit his death would make both life and love more difficult. Moreover, as is generally true of Miller's important women, Kate's final loyalty is to her husband; to him as a living, substantial being, she, like Linda in *Death of a Salesman,* has made an irrevocable commitment in love and sympathy which no knowledge *about* him can destroy.

Chris, on the other hand, is incapable of any such surrender of the letter of morality in the name of love or mercy; he cannot, as his father would have him, "see it human." At the rise of the curtain in Act II, Chris is seen dragging away the remains of Larry's memorial tree. The action is clearly symbolic; Chris, because of his own needs, has determined to free the family of the shadow of self-deception and guilt cast over it by the memory of Larry, to let in the light of truth. Yet, when the light comes, he is less able to bear it than the others. Ann, in the hope of love and marriage, rejects the seeds of hatred and remorse which her brother, George, offers her, and Kate sacrifices the dead son to the living father. But Chris has too much at stake; his life must vindicate the deaths of those who died in the war, which means that he must maintain an ideal image of himself or else be overwhelmed by his own sense of guilt. Because he is closely identified with his father, his necessary sense of personal dignity and worthiness depends upon his belief in the ideal image of his father; consequently, he can only accept the father's exposure as a personal defeat.

It becomes clear in the exchange between Chris and George Deever (Act II) that Chris has suspected his father but has suppressed his suspicions because he could not face the consequences—the condemnation of the father, whom he loves, and the condemnation of himself as polluted by sharing in the illicit spoils of war. Yet, this is precisely what the exposure of Joe Keller forces upon him, and Joe's arguments in self-defense—that he had expected the defective parts to be rejected, that what he did was done for the family, that business is business and none of it is "clean"—all shatter upon the hard shell of Chris's idealism not simply because they are, in fact, evasions and irrelevant half-truths, but because they cannot satisfy Chris's conscience. Consequently, even after Larry's suicide letter has finally brought to Joe a realization of his personal responsibility, Chris must go on to insist upon a public act of penance. The father becomes, indeed, a kind of scapegoat for the son; that is, if Joe expiates his crimes through the acceptance of a just punishment, then Chris will be relieved of his own burden of paralyzing guilt. His love of his father and his complicity with his father will then no longer imply his own unworthiness. In insisting that Joe must go to prison, Chris is, in effect, asking Joe to give him back his self-respect, so that he may be free to marry Ann and assume the life which is rightfully his. But Chris's inability to accept his father "as a man" leads Joe to believe that not only have his defenses crumbled but that the whole basis of his life is gone, and he kills himself.

Because it forces upon the reader an awareness of the intricacies of human motivation and of human relationships, *All My Sons* leaves a dual impression: the action affirms the theme of the individual's responsibility to humanity, but, at the same time, it suggests that the standpoint of even so fine an ideal is not an altogether adequate one from which to evaluate human beings, and that a rigid idealism operating in the actual world of men entails suffering and waste, especially when the idealist is hagridden by his own ideals. There is no simple opposition here between those "who know" and those who "must learn," between those who possess the truth and those who have failed to grasp it, between the spiritually well and the spiritually sick. Moreover, the corruption and destruction of a man like Joe Keller, who is struggling to preserve what he conceives to be a just evaluation of himself in the eyes of his son, implies, in the context of the play, a deficiency not only in Keller's character but in the social environment in which he exists. Keller's appeal to the general ethics of the business community—

> If my money's dirty there ain't a clean nickel in the United States. Who worked for nothin' in that war? . . . Did they ship a gun or a truck outa Detroit before they got their price?. . . It's dollars and cents, nickels and dimes; war and peace, it's nickels and dimes, what's clean?

—is irrelevant to his personal defense; yet, it is an indictment of that community nonetheless. For it indicates that the business community failed to provide any substantial values which might have supplemented and counter-balanced Keller's own limited, family-based ethics. From the business community came only the impulse to which Chris also responds when he feels prompted to express his love for Ann by saying, "I'm going to make a fortune for you!"

Furthermore, there is a sense in which Kate's words, "We were all struck by the same lightning," are true; the lightning was the experience of the second World War—a massive social action in which they were all, willy-nilly, involved. It was the war that made it possible for some to profit by the suffering and death of others and that created the special occasion of Joe Keller's temptation, which led in turn to his son Larry's suicide and his wife's morbid obsession. Chris Keller and George Deever brought something positive out of the war—an ideal of brotherhood and a firmer, more broadly based ethic—but George, as he appears in the play, is paying in remorse for the principles that led him to reject his father, and Chris's idealism is poisoned at the source by shame and guilt, which are also products of his war experience and which make it impossible for him to temper justice with mercy either for himself or anyone else.

Source: Arvin R. Wells. "The Living and the Dead in *All My Sons*" in *Modern Drama*, Vol. 7, no. 1, May, 1964, pp. 46–51.

Harold Clurman

One of the most highly regarded drama critics of the twentieth century, Clurman examines All My Sons *in the context of the other plays of 1947, finding that the work "rouses and moves."*

A dramatic critic eminent among dramatic critics recently wrote an article which suggested that plays "about something" were generally duds. The article was either very sly or very stupid. It was very sly insofar as it is unarguable that most plays the premise and sentiment of which we do not accept cannot please us. What was stupid in the article was to isolate "plays about something" into a special category of plays that are topical, political or, in some over-all manner, propaganda. Propaganda in the theatre may be defined as the other fellow's point of view or any position with which we disagree.

All plays are about something, whether or not they have an explicit thesis. *Peter Pan* is as much about something as *Candida*. *Cyrano de Bergerac* is as clear an expression of something as *Bury the Dead*. *The Iceman Cometh* is as much "propaganda" as *Deep Are the Roots*. *St. Joan* is as definitely a preachment as any play ever presented on Fourteenth Street by the old Theatre Union.

The critic's first job is to make clear what a play is about. Many reviewers are signally inept in the performance of this simple duty. The reason for this is that they mistake a play's materials for its meaning. It is as if an art critic were to say that Cézanne's painting is about apples, or to suppose that because religious subjects were used in many classic paint-

> WHAT MAKES THE THEME OF
> *ALL MY SONS* INCREASINGLY
> IMPORTANT IS THAT WE
> CONSTANTLY TALK OF 'SERVICE'
> AND REPEAT OTHER RESIDUAL
> PHRASES FROM THE RELIGIONS WE
> INHERIT WHILE WE ACTUALLY LIVE
> A DAILY LIFE DEVOTED TO THE
> PURSUIT OF POWER OR SUCCESS,
> THE MOST UNQUESTIONED SYMBOL
> OF WHICH IS MONEY"

ings all these paintings were necessarily inspired by religious feeling.

An artist generally finds it convenient to use the material he finds closest at hand. What he says with his material always reveals something personal and distinct that cannot be described comprehensively merely by stating the materials he has employed. One play about a strike may convey some intimate frustration, another may be a lyric outburst of youthful aspiration. A slight comedy like Noel Coward's *Present Laughter* is not so much a play about the affairs of a successful playwright as a demonstration of a state of mind in which contempt and indifference to the world have been accepted as a sort of aristocratic privilege.

In the Simonov comedy *The Whole World Over,* which I directed, the subjects of the housing shortage and the rehabilitation of the veteran are brought into play, but they are not at all the essence of the matter. This comedy is essentially an image of faith and joy in everyday living, told in the folk tradition of those gay and sentimental songs which establish the continuity between what is universal in the spirit of the old and the new Russia.

Another play that has been variously characterized as a war play or as a play about the returned GI or as an attack on war profiteers is Arthur Miller's *All My Sons.* The central character of *All My Sons* is a small businessman who during the war sent out defective airplane parts which he hoped would not be used in actual combat but which he would not recall for fear his army contracts would be canceled and his business and his family ruined as a result. The play presents the gradual disclosure of these facts to the businessman's younger son, a former army officer. The revelation brings with it not only a realization that twenty-one boys were killed as a consequence of the use of the defective material but that the manufacturer's older son—an army pilot—committed suicide because of his father's crime. The younger son tries to make his father and mother understand that nothing—not business necessity nor devotion to family—can mitigate the father's guilt. A man must be responsible not alone to his wife and children but, ultimately, to all men. Failure to act on this fundamental tenet must inevitably lead to crime.

Contrary to what some reviewers have suggested, the author does not exonerate the central character by making the "system" responsible for his guilt. Such an explanation is the cogent but desperate excuse that the guilty man offers, but his son (and the author) emphatically deny his right to use it. There can be no evasion of the burden of individual human responsibility.

The distorted "individualism" of our day that makes the private good of the individual the final criterion for human action is shown to be inhuman and destructive, whereas the true individualism of our early American prophets made the individual responsible to the community. The man who blames society for his betrayal of it is a weakling and a coward. The individual of Arthur Miller's ethic is the guarantor in his own person of society's health. The difference between Arthur Miller's individualist and the believer in "rugged individualism" today is that the latter narrows his sense of self so that it extends no further than the family circle, while the former gives himself the scope of humanity.

What makes the theme of *All My Sons* increasingly important is that we constantly talk of "service" and repeat other residual phrases from the religions we inherit while we actually live a daily life devoted to the pursuit of Power or Success, the most unquestioned symbol of which is money. The real war in modern life is between a memory of morality and the pressure of "practicality." We live in a schizoid society. This is an open secret, but everybody pretends not to see it or condemns as "idealism" any attempt to remedy the condition. To understand that our double standard is a fatal disease is, as a matter of fact, the first step in a realistic attitude toward life. We shall see—at a later point of the present article—that it is this realism which a part of our society at the moment wishes to resist.

Some reviewers complain that the plot of *All My Sons* is too complicated. For a while I failed to understand what was meant by this criticism. Then I realized that the whole aspect of the mother's insistence that her son, reported missing, is alive—her clinging to every prop of belief, including the solace of astrological assurance—was what struck some of the reviewers as irrelevant. This is a misunderstanding that derives from thinking of the play as an exposé of war profiteering.

The war-profiteering aspect of the play, I repeat, represents the play's material, not its meaning. What Arthur Miller is dramatizing is a universal not a local situation. The mother, whose role in the explicit plot of the play is incidental, is the center of the play's meaning. She embodies the status quo or norm of our present-day ethic and behavior pattern. It is on her behalf that the husband has committed his crime. She, as well as what she represents, is his defense. But she cannot consciously accept the consequence of the morality she lives by, for in the end it is a morality that kills her children and even her husband. In order to retain her strength she cannot abandon her position—everything must be done for one's own—and yet it is this position that has destroyed what she hopes to protect. She is a "normal" woman, yet she is sick. She suffers from severe headaches; she is subject to anxiety dreams. She believes in the stars and with fervid complacency maintains that "some superstitions are very nice."

If there is a "villain" in the piece, it is the mother—the kindly, loving mother who wants her brood to be safe and her home undisturbed. When her husband, who believes too slavishly in her doctrine—it is the world's doctrine, and so there can be no fault with it—when her husband breaks down under the logic of her doctrine, which has made him a murderer, she has no better advice than, "Be smart! ..." Yet she, too, is innocent. When her son's friend, the doctor, mumbles: "How many people walking around loose, and they're crazy as coconuts. Money, money, money, money; you say it long enough, it doesn't mean anything. Oh how I'd love to be around when that happens," she answers, "You're so childish, Jim! ..." She is innocent because she cannot understand. Not even in the extremity of her grief does she understand. When her son tells her: "I'm like everybody else now. I'm

practical now. You made me practical," she answers, "But you have to be." To her dying day, she will remain with this her only wisdom, her only conviction.

Her son cries out: "The cats in the alley are practical. The bums who ran away when we were fighting were practical. Only the dead ones weren't practical. But now I'm practical and I spit on myself. I'm going away." This is the essence of the playwright's meaning: "This is the land of the great big dogs. You don't love a man here, you eat him! That's the principle; the only one we live by ... This is a zoo, a zoo! ..." The mother is sorry ... deeply sorry. "What more can we be?" she asks. "You can be better!" her son answers, and it is the dramatist's answer as well.

Arthur Miller's talent is a moral talent with a passionate persistence that resembles that of the New England preacher who fashioned our first American rhetoric. *All My Sons* rouses and moves us even though it lacks the supreme fire of poetic vision. The determined thrust of its author's mind is not yet enough to melt or transfigure us, but in a theatre that has grown slothful it will have to do. Yes, it will do.

Source: Harold Clurman. "Arthur Miller: 1947" in his *Lies Like Truth,* Macmillan, 1958, pp. 64–68.

Peter Fleming

In this review of the original stage production, Fleming assesses Miller's play as a thought-provoking and entertaining theatrical experience.

During the war Joe Keller allowed a batch of defective cylinder heads to be incorporated in the aircraft engines made by his factory. It was a deliberately irresponsible act, but Keller never saw it in that light. To him, because he accepted no responsibilities outside the circle of his own family and his own business, it seemed the prudent, the natural, thing to do; to hold up production by declaring the parts defective might in those frantic urgent times have lost him his Government contract and thus damaged his business and reduced the size of his sons' inheritance. So the cylinder heads went out to the South West Pacific and caused the death of twenty-one pilots to whose number (we learn at the end of the play) must be added Keller's elder son.

All this happened two years before the play begins. Keller has almost lived down the scandal caused by a judicial enquiry at which he contrived to shift the blame on to an associate, who as a consequence is still in gaol. The associate's daughter, Ann, was the sweetheart of Keller's dead son and now wants to marry the brother who survived him. This is opposed both by Mrs. Keller, who insists on believing that Larry, whose death has never been officially confirmed, will turn up again one day, and by Ann's brother, George, who knows that Keller framed their father and has understandably little use for the family. Bit by bit the full measure of Keller's guilt becomes apparent to the other characters, and at last even Keller himself is shocked into the realisation that what he has done amounts, not to an astute though unfortunate trick, but to a major crime against his fellow-men. The burden of this knowledge is more than he can bear, and he shoots himself.

This play—sincere, deft, at times distinguished—is well worth seeing. Its fault is a tendency, not uncommon on the American stage and screen, to moralise a shade too explicitly; but its virtues—good dialogue, confident characterisation and strong situations—more than compensate for the undertone of uplift. Its production by the Company of Four marks an achievement which is painfully rare in London; the cast—only two of whom, I think, are American—manage to give the impression that they all are. They also act very well. Mr. Joseph Calleia makes Keller a man whose past villainies, until in a flash of revelation he acknowledges them as such, cause him only the same sort of mild, embarrassed uneasiness as he might feel if he had a hole in his sock; it is a very good performance, and so is Miss Margalo Gillmore's as his wife. The others do admirably, too, and my only criticism of the production is that the tree, alleged to have been blown down in a storm and much discussed during the first act, had so obviously been the victim of some sharp instrument that distracting and erroneous suspicions of vandalism obtrude themselves.

Source: Peter Fleming. "The Theatre" in the *Spectator*, May 21, 1948, p. 612.

SOURCES

Atkinson, Brooks. "The Play in Review," *New York Times*, January 30, 1947, p. 21.

Atkinson, Brooks. "Welcome Stranger," *New York Times*, February 9, 1947, sec. 2, p. 1.

Boggs, W. Arthur. "Oedipus and *All My Sons*" in the *Personalist*, Vol. 42, 1961, pp. 555-60.

Brown, John Mason. "New Talents and Arthur Miller," *Saturday Review of Literature*, Vol. 30, March 1, 1947, pp. 22-4.

Hewes, Henry. "Introduction" in *Famous American Plays of the 1940s*. Dell Publishing, 1960, p. 15.

Hogan, Robert. *Arthur Miller*, University of Minnesota Press, 1964, p. 17.

Klapp, Orrin E. "Tragedy and the American Climate of Opinion," in *Tragedy: Vision and Form*, edited by Robert W. Corrigan, 2nd edition. Harper & Row, 1981, pp. 252- 62.

Krutch, Joseph Wood. "Drama," *Nation*, Vol. 164, February 15, 1947, pp. 191, 193.

Krutch, Joseph Wood. "The Tragic Fallacy," in *Tragedy: Vision and Form*, edited by Robert W. Corrigan, 2nd edition. Harper & Row, 1981, pp. 227-37.

Miller, Arthur. "Tragedy and the Common Man," in *Tragedy: Vision and Form*, edited by Robert W. Corrigan, 2nd edition. Harper & Row, 1981, pp. 168-70.

Miller, Arthur. *Timebends: A Life*, Grove Press, 1987, p. 138.

Phelan, Kappo. "The Stage and Screen: *All My Sons*," *Commonweal*, Vol. 45, February 14, 1947, pp. 445-46.

FURTHER READING

Adam, Julie. *Versions of Heroism in Modern American Drama: Redefinitions by Miller, Williams, O'Neill and Anderson*, St. Martin's Press, 1991.

Examining and comparing the protagonists of major American playwrights who attempted to write tragedy, Adam finds that their heroism can fit into distinct categories: idealism, martyrdom, self-reflection, and survival.

Gross, Barry. "*All My Sons* and the Larger Context," *Modern Drama*, Vol. 18, 1975, pp. 15-27.

Gross examines Joe Keller and his son Chris in light of Miller's aim to create a play functioning as "legislation," exhibiting a strong social purpose, and examines the generation gap between the father and son.

Hayman, Ronald. *Arthur Miller*, Frederick Ungar Publishing, 1972.

In this brief monograph, Hayman offers a good critical introduction to Miller's earliest plays. Hayman, concludes that Miller's principal concern is with cause and effect.

Hogan, Robert. *Arthur Miller*, University of Minnesota Press, 1964.

A brief work in the pamphlet series on American writers, Hogan's study is a critical overview of Miller's early works up to and including *After the Fall*. It notes the similarity of structure between *All My Sons* and *Oedipus Rex*.

Miller, Arthur. *Timebends: A Life*, Grove Press, 1987.

Miller's autobiography offers insights to all his work written into the 1980s. He offers personal reflections on his plays.

Moss, Leonard. *Arthur Miller,* Twayne Publishers, 1967. Moss examines Miller's "technical resources," his "dialogue styles, narrative conventions, symbolic devices, and structural principles."

Moss, Leonard. "Arthur Miller and the Common Man's Language," *Modern Drama,* 7 (1964), pp. 52-9.

Moss's article explores Miller's tendency to use ordinary speech for the expression of ethical abstractions. It uses *All My Sons* to illustrate some of its points.

Wells, Arvin R. "The Living and the Dead in *All My Sons,*" *Modern Drama,* Vol. 7, 1964, pp. 46-51. This article argues that *All My Sons* and other Miller plays have a "density of texture" that is much greater than that of a "typical social thesis play."

The Browning Version

TERENCE RATTIGAN

1948

The Browning Version is the play that cemented Terence Rattigan's reputation as a serious, mature playwright. It is viewed as one of his best works, and one of the best one-acts ever written. First performed at the Phoenix Theatre, London, England, on September 8, 1948, *The Browning Version* was coupled with another one-act by Rattigan entitled *Harlequinade* under the umbrella name, *Playbill*. This show ran for 245 performances, and Rattigan received the Ellen Terry Award for *The Browning Version,* his second. (The first was won two years earlier for *The Winslow Boy.*)

The Browning Version made its New York debut with *Harlequinade* on October 12, 1949, but only ran for sixty-two performances. While praise from British audiences and critics was nearly universal when the play was performed in England, American critics were generally not as kind to the Broadway version, perhaps due to the subject matter.

The Browning Version concerns the life of Andrew Crocker-Harris, a classics schoolmaster at a British public school. Andrew is disliked by his unfaithful wife Millie, his colleagues, and his students. Rattigan based the character and the story of *The Browning Version* on a classics master he had at school as a student.

The Browning Version is sometimes derided for being too sentimental, but many critics draw a distinction between its sympathetic sentiment and overt sentimentalism. Most critics and scholars be-

lieve that Rattigan's skills as a playwright transcend such problems. Though only a one-act play, *The Browning Version* is a well-crafted and complete psychological study, indicative of his future direction as a playwright.

As John Russell Taylor writes in *The Rise and Fall of the Well-Made Play,* ''*The Browning Version,* as well as being at once Rattigan's tightest and most natural-seeming construction job up then and his most deeply felt play, marks the beginning of his most distinctive and personal drama.''

AUTHOR BIOGRAPHY

Terence Rattigan was born on June 10, 1911, in London, England. His father, William, was a career diplomat, and served in countries such as Turkey and Romania. While his parents lived abroad, Terence and his brother were raised by their grandparents in England. Rattigan was about eleven years old when his parents returned. By that time, he had fallen in love with reading and going to plays. He wrote his first play about the age of ten.

Rattigan was educated at the Harrow School from 1925 until 1930, when he entered Trinity College, Oxford. His experiences at the former, a public school, informed such plays as *The Browning Version.* Although Rattigan was training for the diplomatic core, by the time he reached Oxford, his interest was focused on the stage.

His first play, *First Episode* (1933) was written with Philip Heimann while still attending Oxford. It was a complete failure. Yet this did not deter Rattigan from leaving school and moving to London to become a professional playwright.

He achieved early success with his comedic play *French without Tears* (1934), which did extraordinarily well in London and in several other countries. At the time, the play held the record for the longest-running play in England. It was based on Rattigan's experiences studying French. His next few plays were much less successful, both at home and in New York.

While Rattigan served in the Royal Air Force during World War II, he continued to write plays, producing about one a year until the early 1960s.

Terence Rattigan

His *Flare Path* (1942), a war-themed romantic drama, was well-received in London. Rattigan also began a career writing screenplays with *A Quiet Wedding* (1940). Although his plays were popular with critics and audiences in London, critical acclaim in the United States continued to elude him.

This changed with Rattigan's next two works. *The Winslow Boy* (1946), which concerned the Archer-Shee case in Great Britain, was lauded on both sides of the Atlantic and received several prestigious awards. His reputation as a serious dramatist was cemented with *The Browning Version* (1948), which received a similar critical response.

After 1948 Rattigan's plays garnered mixed critical and commercial success. Such plays as *The Deep Blue Sea* (1952) about a woman's obsessive love for an unworthy man were not well-received.

One of Rattigan's last big successes was *Separate Tables* (1954), which concerns people's loneliness and isolation. By the early 1960s, Rattigan stopped writing for the stage when his ideas about the theater were criticized for being old-fashioned. He focused on writing screenplays and traveling for several years; but he returned to writing for the stage in his final years. His last produced play was *Cause Celebre* (1977), based on the trial of Alama

Rattenbury in 1930s England. Rattigan died of bone cancer on November 30, 1977.

PLOT SUMMARY

The Browning Version opens in the sitting room of the home of Andrew and Millie Crocker-Harris. A young student, John Taplow, knocks at the front door, then lets himself inside. He steals a chocolate from an open box, then uses his walking stick to practice his golf swing.

Frank Hunter, a young schoolmaster, watches Taplow's moves unseen. Finally, he interrupts and gives Taplow pointers on his swing. They converse for a few moments. Taplow has come for his tutoring session with Andrew, although it is the last day of school. The young man is worried, however, that Andrew will not give him his "remove." He plans to study science, which is Hunter's subject.

Taplow does a wicked impersonation of Andrew, which he almost immediately regrets. However, Frank asks him to do it again, then suggests that since Crocker-Harris is rather late, Taplow should go play golf. Taplow is appalled at the suggestion. Despite his problems with Andrew, Taplow does like him and fears him enough to stay. Taplow relates an incident and again mimics Andrew for Frank's benefit. This time, Millie Crocker-Harris appears at the door, and she listens for a moment before coming inside.

Taplow is afraid that Millie has overheard his imitation. Millie informs Taplow that her husband will be tied up at the Bursar's for a while and that he could go, but he decides to wait. Millie sends him on an errand.

Once Taplow is gone, Millie and Frank have a more intimate discussion, and it becomes clear that they are lovers. They make plans for a rendezvous later in the summer. Millie tries to kiss him, but Frank fears they will be caught by her husband. Millie asks Frank if Taplow was imitating her husband when she walked in. When the answer is affirmative, Millie says that it seemed like a rather good one.

Millie discusses her troubled relationship with her husband. She explains that he once aspired to be a headmaster and had more ambition than he has now. After another kiss, Millie tells Hunter about her day. She was saying good-bye to all the wives of the faculty. Andrew is leaving his teaching position, ostensibly due to a heart condition.

Just as Millie and Frank are about to kiss again, Andrew finally arrives. He is somewhat peeved that Millie sent Taplow on an errand. Andrew invites Frank to sit down for a while, and they make small talk. Andrew reveals that his next position is at a school for "backwards" boys. Frank is sympathetic, but Andrew dismisses his concerns.

Taplow returns. After Millie goes to make dinner and Frank leaves, Andrew and Taplow begin their session. Taplow is translating *Agamemnon* from the Greek as he reads, and adds a touch of the dramatic to his interpretation, which Andrew chides him for. But Andrew also tells Taplow that he once wrote a free translation of the play in verse. Their lesson is interrupted by the appearance of the school's headmaster.

The headmaster, Dr. Frobisher, wants to talk to Andrew privately, so Taplow is dismissed. Frobisher informs Andrew that the Gilberts, who will take over the flat, will be dropping by. He also tells Andrew that the school will grant him no pension, because he has only been at the school eighteen years. Andrew asks about an exception to this rule that had been recently made, but Frobisher explains that the circumstances were different.

Furthermore, Frobisher wants Andrew to speak first at the prize ceremony the next day, although he is the most senior staff member and therefore entitled to speak last. The other man is more popular, and involved with the cricket team. Andrew agrees to the change. Millie enters, and after the headmaster takes his leave, she chides Andrew for just accepting, without argument, the denial of his pension.

Their discussion is interrupted by the arrival of the Gilberts. Millie shows Mrs. Gilbert around the flat. Andrew makes conversation with Mr. Gilbert, who informs Andrew that he has heard that Andrew is renowned for his discipline. The headmaster describes Andrew as "The Himmler of the lower fifth."

Andrew is upset by Mr. Gilbert's comments, and he discloses some of his experiences as a teacher to Mr. Gilbert. Confessing that he is a failure as a teacher, Andrew explains that by being funny, a character, he thought that maybe his students would learn something. Yet, as a result, he is extremely disliked by his students and colleagues. Embarrassed at his revelations, Andrew wishes Mr. Gilbert luck with his new position. The couple leave.

Taplow returns. He has come to say farewell, but he brings a gift: a verse translation of *Agamemnon*, authored by Browning. Andrew is deeply touched, especially by the inscription the boy has written. Frank Hunter returns. When Andrew shares the inscription with Frank, he is again overcome with emotion. Frank signals Taplow to leave, which he does after saying his good-byes. Andrew is embarrassed about his display of emotions, and apologizes to Frank. Frank is understanding.

Millie returns to the sitting room. Frank shows her Taplow's gift. Laughing, Millie maintains that the gift was a bribe for Taplow's remove and tells her husband that Taplow was imitating him earlier. Andrew goes to his room for a moment.

As soon as he is gone, Frank tells Millie to take back what she said, or he will tell Andrew that it was a lie. Millie's negative response and vicious attitude compel Frank to end their relationship. Millie does not believe him, but Frank is appalled by her cruelty. He tells Millie to look after Andrew and tries to leave, but she will not let him go. Millie says that Andrew is dead inside and not a man. Frank is revolted by what she is saying.

Andrew returns from his room, and Millie exits. Frank says that Taplow was imitating him, but that Taplow also said that he liked Andrew. Frank believes the gift was genuine and that Andrew should keep it. Andrew claims that the book is not that good anyway, and believes that Taplow is probably spreading the story of Andrew's expression of emotion to his friends right now. Frank does not believe this is true and decides to leave.

Frank advises Andrew to leave Millie, and is appalled to find out that Andrew knows about the affair because Millie told him. Andrew says that he has never been able to satisfy his wife. Again, Frank tries to convince him to leave her. Frank wants to visit him at his new position in September, and insists on getting his new address.

Millie returns, and asks if Frank will stay for dinner. Frank declines and leaves. Millie tells Andrew that Frank will visit her, not him. Andrew does not believe he will visit either of them. He also tells her of his decision to stay for the summer. Millie informs him that she will not be going with him to his new job. When Dr. Frobisher phones, Andrew informs him that he will speak second at the ceremony. After he gets off the phone, he asks Millie to serve dinner. She does so.

CHARACTERS

Andrew Crocker-Harris

Andrew is a gifted classical scholar and unpopular schoolmaster. He has worked at the same school for eighteen years and is leaving for a different, less stressful job in Dorset. It seems that a heart condition is forcing the move. In his eighteen years, Andrew has tried to reach his students by becoming something of a character, which has only increased most students and faculty dislike of him. He also has a reputation for being a strict disciplinarian.

On this, the last day of school, Andrew suffers several indignities. His wife has been having an affair with colleague, Frank Hunter, and Andrew has known about it from the beginning. He has been denied a pension by the school because he has not been there long enough. He has been asked by the headmaster to speak first at a prize-winning ceremony, when he should speak last because of his seniority.

Yet, he is moved by the gift of his pupil, John Taplow. After mentioning to the boy that he wrote his own translation of the play they are working on in Taplow's tutoring session, Taplow buys a similar version of the book and presents it to Andrew as a gift. This affects Andrew deeply until his wife, Millie, undermines his happiness over the gift.

Throughout *The Browning Version* Andrew has taken abuse from his wife without much comment. But, urged on by Frank, he reclaims some of his dignity by insisting on speaking second at the ceremony and deciding to stay there for the summer, no matter what his wife decides to do. As the play ends, Andrew is a stronger man than he was at the beginning.

Millie Crocker-Harris

Millie is the long-suffering wife of Andrew. She dislikes her husband immensely and has been having an affair with Frank Hunter. Although she

MEDIA ADAPTATIONS

- *The Browning Version* was adapted as a film in 1951. Produced by Teddy Baird and directed by Anthony Asquith, the movie stars Michael Redgrave as Andrew, Jean Kent as Millie, and Nigel Patrick as Frank Hunter.

- A made-for-television version was filmed in 1985 in Great Britain. Directed by Michael A. Simpson, it stars Ian Holm as Andrew, Judi Dench as Millie, and Michael Kitchen as Frank.

- Another filmed version was released in 1994. Directed by Mike Figgis, it features Albert Finney as Andrew, Greta Scacchi as Millie, and Matthew Modine as Frank Hunter.

does many of the household chores and social duties expected of her, she resents her husband's lack of success as a schoolmaster.

Millie knows her husband is unpopular, and she does not like it. His professional failings have meant that she has to do many of things a maid would take care of, like cook. Since she is a woman of some means, including a yearly income from her father, being associated with Andrew is a disappointment.

Millie expresses her resentment by undercutting anything Andrew says or does with a mean comment. She errs, however, when she destroys a happy moment for her husband in front of Frank. Millie's cruel attitude compels Frank to end their relationship and take Andrew's side. By the end of the play, Millie has informed Andrew that she will not go with him to his new job. He is indifferent to her decision.

Dr. Frobisher

Dr. Frobisher is the headmaster at the school where Frank Hunter and Andrew Crocker-Harris teach. He is uncomfortable with Andrew but acknowledges his intelligence. Dr. Frobisher is the official who informs Andrew that he will not be granted a pension, and he asks him to speak first, rather than second, at the ceremony.

Peter Gilbert

Peter Gilbert is a new schoolmaster at the school. He is the one who informs Andrew that he is known as "The Himmler of the lower fifth." This knowledge upsets Andrew. Gilbert looks to Andrew for advice on teaching, and Andrew responds with a bold, emotional statement on his shortcomings. Andrew's revelations embarrass Gilbert, but he remains polite.

Frank Hunter

Frank Hunter is a young schoolmaster who teaches science at the same school as Andrew. Unlike Andrew, he is quite popular with his students. Frank has been having an affair with Andrew's wife, Millie, for several months.

Although Frank does not seem to like Andrew, he does feel sorry for him and is always polite to him, unlike Millie. After Taplow gives Andrew the book and Millie tries to ruin her husband's happiness over the gift, Frank sympathizes with Andrew. He breaks off the affair with Millie and tries everything he can think of to protect and help Andrew.

John Taplow

John Taplow is one of Andrew's students. Andrew is tutoring Taplow in classical Greek, and they are translating the play *Agamemnon*. Taplow would rather play golf than be doing extra work on the last day of school and expresses his frustrations to Frank Hunter.

Despite the advice of Millie and Frank, Taplow insists on staying for his session. In a sense, he fears Andrew, because he realizes his future is in Andrew's hands. Yet Taplow also likes Andrew, which he proves when he brings Andrew a verse version of the play they have been working on with a meaningful inscription. Taplow's kindness touches Andrew until Millie ruins it for him.

THEMES

Success and Failure

Throughout *The Browning Version,* the ideas of success and failure are used to define characters.

Andrew Crocker-Harris is considered a failure by everyone, including himself. Andrew's intelligence as a classics scholar is never questioned. Yet because he is unpopular, and perceived as a strict schoolmaster and a bad jokester, he is regarded as a failure.

His marriage is also a failure. Andrew has not met Millie's expectations on any front. This failure is emphasized by her flagrant affairs with other men, including her current lover, Frank Hunter. Thus, Andrew's failings have usurped his wife as well.

In *The Browning Version,* success is equated with popularity and sports. Frank Hunter is a successful schoolmaster because he relates better to the boys and teaches a less demanding subject than the classics. He lets John Taplow mock Andrew without penalty. Hunter also gives Taplow golf tips.

Similarly, one of Andrew's biggest humiliations is when the school's headmaster asks him to speak first at the ceremony the next day, instead of last. The headmaster wants that honor to go to another teacher who is leaving after only a few years. This teacher led the school's cricket team to an important victory and is popular among the students, making him more successful.

Generosity

A few moments of generosity change Andrew's life. The most important event occurs when his student, John Taplow, brings him a copy of Browning's verse translation of *Agamemnon* and inscribes the book. *Agamemnon* is the play Taplow is reading to learn Greek. Taplow's generosity touches Andrew deeply and is the catalyst for change.

Frank Hunter is similarly generous to Crocker-Harris. After initially regarding him with the same disdain as Millie, Hunter sees how deeply moved Andrew is when he receives Taplow's gift. In fact, Millie's spiteful comments prompt Hunter to break off his relationship with her. Hunter's most sincere gesture of friendship occurs when he insists on getting Andrew's address at his new school so he can visit. Hunter has completely changed from insincere lover (of Millie) to generous friend (of Andrew).

Apathy and Passivity/Death and Life

Several times in *The Browning Version,* Andrew refers to himself as dead. Millie also expresses

TOPICS FOR FURTHER STUDY

- Compare and contrast Andrew Crocker-Harris with Willy Loman from Arthur Miller's *Death of a Salesman* (1949). Both characters are trapped in unhappy situations. How do they handle the problems in their lives?

- How could Millie and Andrew have avoided their unhappy situation? Was the end of their marriage inevitable? Discuss how certain actions—better communication, compromise, marriage counseling—could have impacted their relationship.

- Compare and contrast Andrew Crocker-Harris with Mr. Chips, the protagonist of the movie *Goodbye Mr. Chips* (1939). This movie concerns the life of a British schoolmaster, Mr. Chips. How do these characters regard their positions? How does this attitude affect those around them, including students and family?

- Research the psychology of wives who cheat on their husbands. How do Millie's actions fit into your findings? Do you believe Millie and Frank really love each other?

the same opinion about him. This description is confirmed by his extreme passivity, letting Dr. Frobisher deny him a pension without argument. In addition, Andrew barely blinks when his final honor at the school is taken away—speaking last at an important ceremony.

This passivity spills over into his relationship with Millie. With her affairs, she has humiliated him over and over. Their marriage is a war, and he refuses to participate.

This attitude changes several times in the course of *The Browning Version.* When Mr. Gilbert, who will be taking over Andrew's apartment and position at the school, informs Andrew that he is known as the "Himmler of the lower fifth," Andrew is upset. He reveals his feelings to Gilbert, which allows him greater insight into his feelings and

A scene from director Mike Figgis's adaptation of Rattigan's play: Andrew (Albert Finney) helps Millie (Greta Scacchi) with her dress

shortcomings. This acknowledgment is one step on the way to a new life.

Andrew's reaction to Taplow's gift proves that he still does have feelings and does not need to accept his "death" passively. Both of these events lead to action for Andrew. He calls Dr. Frobisher and insists that he speak last at the ceremony. He accepts Hunter's advice of staying there for the summer. He tells his wife that he no longer expects even the most superficial of marriages. By the end of the play, Andrew has been reborn.

STYLE

Three Classical Unities

In *The Browning Version,* Rattigan utilizes the unities for drama, as outlined by Aristotle in *Poetics.* The first unity is setting. The story is confined to one setting, the front room of the Crocker-Harris flat in 1948 at a public school in the southern part of England. The room is "gloomy," but the stage directions also indicate that it "is furnished with chintzy and genteel cheerfulness." By restricting

the actions and intense emotions to this room, the confined nature of Andrew's repressed emotions and feelings and his cloying, damaged marriage are highlighted.

The second and third unities are time and action. The whole of *The Browning Version* takes place in less than one day. Indeed here, the story's timeline is only a few hours, emphasizing the story's intensity and the swiftness of change. The action is linear—there is only one very focused plot line. It concerns Andrew's imminent retirement, the truths revealed by it, and how these truths change him.

Eternal Triangle

Rattigan draws a triangle between three of the major characters in *The Browning Version.* At the head of the triangle is Millie, Andrew's wife. Although she is still married to him, she is in love with a younger man, Frank Hunter. Like Andrew, Hunter is a schoolmaster. Yet compared with the crotchety Andrew, Hunter is popular with the students and his colleagues.

The two men form the other two ends of the triangle, and form a bond, despite (or, perhaps, because of) the affair. The triangle allows Rattigan to explore two kinds of love: sexual desire (Hunter and Millie) versus a "higher love," a relationship based on social and intellectual compatibility.

Rattigan parallels this triangle with another in Aeschylus's *Agamemnon.* This text also concerns a philandering wife who takes a lover while her husband is away at war. She murders her husband upon his return. While Millie does not literally kill Andrew, she has hurt and humiliated him with cruel words and heartless behavior.

Symbolism

The course of *The Browning Version* is changed by two key symbolic acts, both of which involved the young student, Taplow. In the beginning of the play, he arrives for his tutoring session, only to find that Andrew is late. To get rid of the boy temporarily, Millie sends him to the pharmacists to pick up Andrew's heart medicine. He completes this task, which foreshadows his role as catalyst for Andrew's rebirth.

When Taplow brings Andrew a small gift, a verse translation of Aeschylus's *Agamemnon,* it reveals to the old teacher that life can be different, that he is not completely "dead." The fact that Taplow had brought him such a meaningful book, beautifully inscribed, gives Andrew a new perspective on life.

HISTORICAL CONTEXT

When World War II ended in 1945, Great Britain was in complete disarray. The country, as most of Europe, had suffered terribly during the war. Although Germany never invaded Great Britain, the country withstood severe bombings and economic turmoil, the latter of which lasted into the Postwar period. In that environment, the Labour Party was elected to power in 1945, and, for the first time, held control of Parliament. Clement R. Attlee served as Prime Minister.

The British economy was near bankruptcy and running on a deficit. The American Marshall Plan (or European Recovery program) was not enough to stimulate a full economic recovery. A budget was constructed to counteract this problem as much as possible. Under the austerity plan, taxes were increased and governmental costs were cut. The former worked better than the latter, and inflation did decrease.

However, Great Britain had problems increasing productivity, especially in essential industries. It could not meet export commitments or turn a significant profit in industries such as coal. To that end, the Labour government moved to nationalize many industries, including railroads, coal mines, and the Bank of England. The Iron and Steel Nationalization Bill took effect in 1950.

The Attlee-led Labour government took similar measures towards socialization in health care. After being in the works for nearly thirty-five years, the National Health Services Act was implemented in 1948. This act, in combination with the National Insurance Act, gave everyone access to free health care. The acts were somewhat controversial, especially among medical professionals such as doctors and dentists. A compromise was worked out, and when the service became effective, demand outstripped supply. Many people had not received decent medical attention since before the war.

Despite such measures, economic circumstances forced a continuation of rationing of certain items and several new items were added to the ration list. The manufacturing sector was slowly returning to a peacetime economy, however, and the standard of living increased. Bread and shoes were two items that actually ceased to be rationed. There were also a few labor problems, including a fourteen-day dock strike in London that temporarily hurt exports and the economy. Attlee himself had to intervene to end the strike.

Attlee and the Labour Party faced other serious issues. There were investigations into allegations of corruption among several of his ministers and public servants. Great Britain had relinquished control over India in 1947. Ireland moved to separate itself technically from the Commonwealth and became a republic the next year. Burma and Ceylon became independent in 1948. The British mandate in Palestine also came to an end, and Israel became a state. And although World War II was over, the Cold War began as Russia was constructing an Iron Curtain. In 1948, Russia blockaded Berlin, creating more international tension.

COMPARE
&
CONTRAST

- 1948: Prince Charles is born to Princes Elizabeth and Prince Philip. Charles is second-in-line to the throne, held by King George VI, after his mother.

  Today: Prince Charles is first-in-line to the throne after his mother, Queen Elizabeth II. His son, Prince William, is his successor.

- 1948: The Labour Party takes control of the British government. Charles Attlee is Prime Minister. It is the first time Labour has been in control of Parliament.

  Today: The Labour Party is in control of the British government, for the first time in many years. Tony Blair is Prime Minister.

- 1948: The Labour-led government of Great Britain begins to establish a socialized welfare state, including nationally-run industry and national health insurance.

  Today: Much of the legislation creating the socialized welfare state had been dismantled during the administration of Conservative Margaret Thatcher in the 1980s. National health care, however, still exists.

- 1948: As part of the Cold War, Berlin is blockaded by Soviet Russia. Germany is separated into eastern and western sections.

  Today: East and West Germany have been reunited for several years. The Soviet Union has been dissolved, and the Cold War is over.

CRITICAL OVERVIEW

When *The Browning Version* premiered in 1948, British critics were quick to praise Rattigan's achievements. Many recognized how Rattigan had matured as a playwright. A London correspondent of the *New York Times,* W. A. Darlington, asserted, "[The play] might have devolved into sentimentality on the one hand or domestic brawling on the other. It does nothing of the sort, for Rattigan has at call not only the superb craftsmanship . . . but also that sure grasp of character. . . ." When the play premiered in the United States a year later, however, critical response was mixed.

Some critics found much to praise. The anonymous critic of *Newsweek* contended: "By skillful writing, Rattigan has been able to endow this stuffed figure of a scholar with genuine emotion. . . ." Howard Barnes of the *New York Herald Tribune* seconded his colleague. He maintained, "*The Browning Version* is honest and eloquent. . . . [H]e has composed a drama of far more depth and consequence than the subject might imply."

Many American critics applauded certain aspects of *The Browning Version* but were dismissive of others. John Mason Brown of the *Saturday Review of Literature* asserted, "Just why Mr. Rattigan chose to subject his theme to the almost inescapable compressions, hence artificialities, of the one-act mold is hard to understand. An absorbing long-play clearly lurks in his materials. Yet considering the elbow-room and scope he has elected to deny himself, I must admit Mr. Rattigan has down an expert and moving job."

Similarly, Brooks Atkinson of the *New York Times* contended "Grant *The Browning Version* the virtues of expert craftsmanship in both writing and acting, and still a playgoer may suspect that Mr. Rattigan has nothing to say. . . . [T]o me Mr. Rattigan's schoolmaster is pure sentimentality and I cannot grieve over his misfortunes. . . . The sorrow Mr. Rattigan asks us to feel over his failure is maudlin despite the expertness of the play craftsmanship."

Other American reviewers of the original Broadway production were downright hostile. The unnamed critic in *Time* maintains, "As playwrighting, it is not too far from double bilge; Rattigan's study of a defeated schoolmaster is only a shade less routine than his spoofing of ham actors."

In *The New Republic,* Harold Clurman claimed: "I doubt that anywhere in the world but in England and among resolute Anglophiles in America are such portraits taken as probing character studies. They are really salon art with most of the attributes of mature work except reality."

Yet over time, many American critics and scholars adopted the attitude of their British counterparts. They appreciated the depth and careful craftsmanship of *The Browning Version.* Many commentators believed the play aged well. As Frank Rich of the *New York Times* explained, when reviewing a 1982 revival, "The once-tattered reputation of Terence Rattigan has risen so steadily, both in London and New York, since his death in 1977 that critics are no longer needed to plead his cause. As it's now clear, Rattigan's best plays are his best defense—they're almost foolproof." He counted *The Browning Version* amongst his best work.

Reviewing the same revival, John Simon of *New York* wrote, "*The Browning Version* if well done is boulevard drama at its very best and nothing to be ashamed of." Later in the review, Simon claimed, "Crocker-Harris is one of those figures that the theatergoing memory, having once-encountered, can never quite dismiss."

Along the same lines, Walter Kerr of the *New York Times* asserted: "Mr. Richardson [the actor who played Andrew Crocker-Harris in the 1982 revival] doesn't cheat or beg for easy effect. Neither, ever does Mr. Rattigan. When it is time for a fresh discovery or psychological shift of the wind, the discovery is valid, the shift rings true."

Thus *The Browning Version,* which some critics had previously condemned as old-fashioned and dull, was soon regarded as quite the opposite. In her study, *Terence Rattigan,* Susan Rusinko contended, "Rattigan shuns sentimentality as well as theatricality, for he has kept at bay the pity one feels for a victim and gradually substitutes admiration for a contemporary middle-class antihero who lives, and eventually, if in a small way, triumphs over his life of quiet desperation. Like the failed, mediocre characters of some of Browning's dramatic mono-

logues, the Crock belongs to a long tradition of modest, modern heroes."

CRITICISM

A. Petrusso

Petrusso is a freelance writer and screenwriter. In this essay, she discusses how fear affects the actions of the characters in The Browning Version.

Throughout the text of Terence Rattigan's *The Browning Version,* every major character is motivated by a fear. Many of these qualms are directly related to Andrew Crocker-Harris.

For instance, the students and staff of the school are intimidated by Andrew's crusty demeanor and odd ways. Yet the fears of Millie, his wife, are more indirect and complicated. She despises him and their life together and seeks any remedy to the situation, even having affairs with her husband's colleagues.

Andrew's fears are the deepest and most repressed. He hides his humanity behind a shield of stoicism, allowing a fundamental diffidence to rule his life. By examining these fears, the outcome of *The Browning Version* seems rather surprising. It is Andrew who overcomes some of his fears, through an indirect action of his own.

The most blatantly fearful characters in *The Browning Version* are Dr. Frobisher, the Headmaster, and John Taplow, Andrew's student. Throughout the conversation between Frobisher and Andrew in the middle of the play, Frobisher is ill at ease. In fact, he is so apprehensive about talking to Andrew that he consults Millie about how to approach him. (Indeed, he asks if Millie is home before relaying his news and is quite happy to see her at the end when she makes an appearance.)

The problem is who will speak last at the prize-giving ceremony the following day: Andrew, the senior retiree; or Fletcher, a schoolmaster who has only taught for five years, but is popular and heavily involved with the school's cricket team. Andrew agrees to speak first—ostensibly to avoid an anticlimax—yet this situation changes by the end of the play. Frobisher rationalizes his demand to Andrew by arguing, "it's more for your own sake than for mine or Fletcher's. . . ."

WHAT DO I READ NEXT?

- *Tom Brown's Schooldays,* a novel by Thomas Hughes, was published in 1857. The story focuses on a young student's trials and tribulations as a public school student in England.

- Rattigan's play, *The Deep Blue Sea,* was first performed in 1963. It is a thriller, concerning a love triangle similar to one found in *The Browning Version.*

- *Cecily,* a novel by Isabelle Holland, was written in 1967. The story focuses on a proud young teacher at a British girls' school whose lack of compassion towards a misfit student brings disaster to her own romance.

- Written in the fifth or sixth century B.C., *Agamemnon,* is a play written by Aeschylus. It concerns a cheating wife, her lover, and her suffering husband.

- *Vintage Stuff,* a novel by Tom Sharpe, was published in 1982. It follows the adventure of some public school boys and their teachers on vacation in France.

Frobisher is also nervous when he has to tell Andrew that he will not be granted a pension. The stage directions read ''The Headmaster is regarding his nails, as he speaks, studiously avoiding Andrew's gaze.'' Frobisher blames the matter entirely on the board of governors at the school in order to deflect attention away from himself.

Taplow's trepidation is much more personal; as his teacher and tutor, Andrew holds the boy's future in his hands. Taplow does not know yet if he will get his remove. He has come to Andrew's home for his extra work session, though it is the last day of school, because he missed a day the previous week when he was ill.

When Frank Hunter, and later Millie, suggest that Taplow leave because Andrew is late, the boy trembles in fear and does not leave until someone will take the blame for his tardiness. He tells Hunter, ''Oh no, I couldn't cut. Cut the Crock—Crocker-Harris? I shouldn't think it's ever been done the whole time he's been here. God knows what would happen if I did. He'd probably follow me home, or something—.''

Taplow's fears increase when Hunter has him mimic Andrew, and Millie enters. Taplow believes she has overheard and will tell her husband, unaware of Millie's resentment toward Andrew. Later, when Andrew has returned, Millie covers for the boy.

The fear Frank Hunter feels is much different than the other two. Like them, he is attached to the school, a science teacher in the upper fifth form. He seems to have a pleasant relationship with everyone, including Andrew. But Hunter is having an affair with Millie, which makes him fear Andrew. It is not until the end of the play that Hunter learns Andrew has known about it all along; Millie always tells him about her liaisons.

For most of the play, Hunter worries about discovery. When he encourages Taplow to imitate Andrew, he is afraid when someone enters the room. He is relieved to find it is Millie. Similarly, when Millie makes him kiss her, he cuts it short in case Andrew returns home and sees them.

Although it would seem Millie might fear her husband the most of any character, her anxieties are altogether different. Because Millie despises her husband and can abuse him verbally without reprisal, she believes she has some measure of control over him.

What Millie fears is being left alone with Andrew. She needs lovers like Frank, the latest in a long line of lovers, to satisfy her in a way that Andrew cannot or will not. This is the only way she can survive, and she is desperate to keep Frank after he sees her cruelty go too far. She needs his pity desperately.

What Millie also fears, though she does not know it until the end of *The Browning Version*, is losing her control over Andrew. When she has finally lost Andrew—no matter how problematic their relationship is—she has nothing.

The character that seems fearless is Andrew himself. Yet what he fears most is emotional involvement. Andrew's marriage has been on the rocks for many years. It has been easier to let Millie do and say what she will in order to avoid a confrontation. He lets each of her negative comments pass without so much as a raised eyebrow.

Similarly, he makes no effort to be popular—and therefore emotionally involved—among his students or colleagues. While Andrew had ambitions at the beginning of his teaching career—even wanting to be a headmaster someday—his early failure to reach his students and the realization that he was disliked led to his present state. Andrew calls himself a "corpse"—he believes he can't even have emotions anymore.

Yet on the last day of classes, circumstances make Andrew confront his fear. It begins with the extra work session with Taplow. The young man's enthusiasm for *Agamemnon* as a play rather than a Greek text reminds Andrew that he once found pleasure in translating the play freely and in verse. He shares his memory with his student—a faint crack in Andrew's armor.

Andrew is further affected by the appearance of the Gilberts, who will be taking over Crocker-Harris's flat when Mr. Gilbert becomes a schoolmaster there. Without thought, Mr. Gilbert tells Andrew that he is known as "the Himmler of the lower fifth" because his students fear his discipline. This comment wounds Andrew. Andrew confides his failures as a schoolmaster to Gilbert but quickly apologizes for his disclosures: "I cannot for the life of me imagine why I should choose to unburden myself to you—a total stranger—when I have been silent to others for so long."

What caps off Andrew's emotional renaissance is Taplow's gift. The young man gives Andrew a secondhand copy of poet Robert Browning's verse translation of *Agamemnon,* inscribed with the phrase "God from afar look graciously upon a gentle master." The gift moves Andrew so deeply, he shakes and his voice trembles as he tries to speak. He directs the boy to pour him a dose of medicine so he has a moment to sob alone.

> ANDREW'S FEARS ARE THE DEEPEST AND MOST REPRESSED. HE HIDES HIS HUMANITY BEHIND A SHIELD OF STOICISM, ALLOWING A FUNDAMENTAL DIFFIDENCE TO RULE HIS LIFE"

At that moment, Andrew realizes that he has made at least one success with a student and with that bond comes the emotional involvement he has denied for so long. Taplow, too, sees Andrew as more of a person. His fear is gone, and he gets his remove.

Because Millie has had nothing to fear from her husband, her attempts to undermine the meaning of Taplow's gift are quite normal for her. She tells her husband about the imitation Taplow did of him earlier and says that she believes the gift is a bribe for his remove. This forces Andrew to leave the room because he needs a moment to digest what has happened.

But Millie's actions make her fears come true. Hunter sees her vicious nature and ends their relationship. When Andrew returns and Millie leaves, Hunter learns that his fear has been pointless. Andrew has known about the affair all along.

Further, Hunter aids in Andrew's rebirth: he explains that Taplow expressed admiration of him earlier; encourages him to leave Millie; and arranges to visit him at his new position in the fall. Hunter's words cause another rush of emotion. Although Andrew may have been planning to leave Millie anyway by this time, he informs her that they will be going their separate ways, then tells Frobisher that he will speak last at the ceremony.

The three characters who confront their fears—Andrew, Taplow, and Hunter—experience growth and understanding. They are better people for the effort. Those who do not—Millie and Frobisher—find themselves not getting what they want. Andrew Crocker-Harris has made a Lazarus-like recovery.

Source: A. Petrusso, for *Drama for Students,* Gale, 2000.

Richard Foulkes

In this essay, Foulkes provides an overview of Rattigan's play, including brief production histories and notes on the actors who have played the lead role.

The plot of this play focuses on Andrew Crocker-Harris, a classics master at an English public school, who is retiring prematurely because of ill-health, and who is confronted by his wife's infidelity and his failure in his chosen profession. Like much of Rattigan's work, *The Browning Version* is drawn from his own experience; in this case as a pupil at Harrow School. The prototype for Crocker-Harris was one of Rattigan's teachers, Mr. Coke Norris, and the central incident of the pupil, Taplow, presenting Crocker-Harris with a copy of Browning's translation of the *Agamemnon* of Aeschylus is based on fact (although there is some doubt as to whether Rattigan himself was the boy involved). Certainly Taplow's interest in cricket and golf reflect Rattigan's enthusiasm for those games.

The action of *The Browning Version* is set in the Crocker-Harris's sitting-room, replete with a stained-glass door leading to the garden as well as an internal door, concealed by a screen. Appropriately, in view of its classical associations, the play observes the unities of time, place, and action demonstrating Rattigan's renowned craftsmanship at its best. Although the dialogue is characteristically everyday (with Taplow's schoolboy slang) Rattigan imbues Crocker-Harris with a distinctive turn of speech (reflecting his classical education) and an articulateness, enabling him to comment upon his predicament (though not to express his feelings), which are consistent with naturalistic drama.

As the title implies, Rattigan seeks to establish parallels between his play and its classical source, thus Taplow remarks to Frank Hunter, a science master and Muriel Crocker-Harris's current lover: "It's rather a good plot, really, a wife murdering her husband and having a lover and all that. . . ." Of course, Crocker-Harris's fate is not the (literal) blood-bath which awaited Agamemnon on his return from the Trojan War, but Mrs. Crocker-Harris uses the no less deadening battery of psychological warfare as she relentlessly humiliates and degrades her husband. In terms of exploration of character and motive *The Browning Version* is closer to Euripides and his treatment of that other archetypal triangle (Theseus, Phaedra, and Hippolytus) in *Hippolytus* than to Aeschylus's bloody chain of murder and revenge.

The eternal triangle was a favourite formula for Rattigan. Although the central character, torn between two lovers, is usually a woman, it has been suggested that Rattigan on occasion depicted homosexual relationships under the guise of heterosexual ones. For Rattigan, the essence of a triangular relationship was that it enabled him to polarise the conflict between two types of love—on the one hand, the "higher love" (social and intellectual companionship and compatibility) and on the other, merely sexual gratification. Thus Muriel Crocker-Harris is caught between her 18-year-long, increasingly arid, marriage and her passionate affair (one of many) with Frank Hunter, in which she is the helpless and undignified pursuer. Crocker-Harris's classical knowledge facilitates Rattigan's exploration of what Plato in *The Symposium* characterised as "the two Aphrodites . . . common love and the other Heavenly love". He does this with an erudition which makes the following speech central not only to this play but to Rattigan's work as a whole:

> Two kinds of love. Hers and mine. Worlds apart, as I know now, though when I married her I didn't think they were incompatible. In those days I hadn't thought that the kind of love—the love she requires and which I was unable to give her—was so important that it's absence would drive out the other kind of love—the kind of love that I require and which I thought, in my folly, was by far the greater part of love. . . .

Although this exploration of the two loves is the major theme of *The Browning Version,* there are others. Alongside the emotional repression of his marriage Crocker-Harris has sought the popularity of his pupils—"by pandering to their delight in his mannerisms and tricks of speech he has tried to compensate for his lack of natural ability to make himself liked" (Michael Darlow and Gillian Hodson, *Terence Rattigan,* 1979). This might be seen as a reflection of Rattigan's willingness as a dramatist to court popular success in the form of the endorsement of Aunt Edna the "nice, respectable, middle-class, middle-aged, maiden lady", who made her debut as Rattigan's representative playgoer in his Preface to Volume Two of his *Complete Plays* (in which *The Browning Version* appears). Such an identification of author and character would imply a sense of failure on Rattigan's part even at this, the most commercially and critically successful period of his career.

Rattigan was taken to task for flinching from unhappy endings to his plays, preferring to send theatregoers home in a reassured state of mind. *The Deep Blue Sea* is susceptible to this criticism, but not so *The Browning Version.* Rattigan contemplated a tragic outcome (probably Crocker-Harris's death from his heart condition), but instead left his protagonist facing an uncertain future both professionally (at a crammer's) and matrimonially (will Muriel accompany him?). Crocker-Harris does, however, assert his right to make his valedictory speech at the end of the next day's prize-giving. In the film version, Rattigan's old friend Anthony Asquith prevailed upon him to open up the action of the play and to extend it to conclude with Crocker-Harris (Michael Redgrave) making his speech. The film thus finishes on a sentimental, "Mr. Chips" note which betrays the integrity of the original play.

Lasting about 80 minutes in the theatre, *The Browning Version* required a companion piece for which Rattigan provided one of his most ebullient comedies *Harlequinade*, about a performance of *Romeo and Juliet* in a midland town. As a double-bill the two plays provide opportunities for the actors to demonstrate their versatility. Although John Gielgud (rather tactlessly) turned down Rattigan's invitation to create the part of Crocker-Harris it has since become one of the recognised classic roles of the modern stage, drawing fine performances from Eric Portman (1948), Nigel Stock (1976), Alec McCowan (1980), and Paul Eddington (1987).

Source: Richard Foulkes. "*The Browning Version*" in *The International Dictionary of Theatre,* Vol. 1: *Plays,* edited by Mark Hawkins-Dady, St. James Press, 1992, pp. 90–92.

Peter Fleming

Fleming offers praise for The Browning Version, *admiring both the dramatic merits of Rattigan's text and the skill of this particular production.*

Mr. Rattigan offers two longish one-act plays, sharply contrasting in mood and method, and this novel formula for an evening's entertainment is such a complete success that one wonders why nobody ever thought of it before. In *Tonight at 8.30* Mr. Coward's playbill included three short plays, but three is a team just long enough to have a tail, a litter just large enough to have a runt, and it was a virtual certainty that one of them would disappoint, however slightly. Mr. Rattigan does not run the risk of overtaxing either his own or his actors' versatility, and *Playbill* can be commended without reservations.

The first half of it, *The Browning Version,* is a psychological study of great strength and poignance. Crocker-Harris, a classical master at a minor public school, is retiring. For years he has realised that he is

> "LIKE MUCH OF RATTIGAN'S WORK, *THE BROWNING VERSION* IS DRAWN FROM HIS OWN EXPERIENCE"

a failure, but it is only in his last hours at the school which he has served so long that he is shown with a terrible clarity how comprehensively and finally he has failed. A brilliant scholar, imbued as a teacher with the noblest traditions and the highest ideals of his profession, it is as a human being that he has been found wanting. The boys fear him, the other masters despise him, the total lack of regret at his departure threatens to create public embarrassment when he makes his farewell speech at the end-of-term celebrations. His lack of humour and of humanity are handicaps which would in any case have told against him; but it is the evil in his wife's character which has so maimed his soul that he has become wholly incapable of establishing a satisfactory relationship with any of his fellow human beings. Like a dog caught unluckily in a gin, he has lost the capacity to recognise or accept friendliness, to restrain himself from snapping at the hands tentatively stretched out to help him.

His wife has the flat, unemphatic malevolence of a snake. Promiscuously false to him, she makes no bones about giving to the husband who can no longer satisfy her desires full particulars of those who do. But this seems a venal fault compared with her contemptuous and unremitting cruelty, which reaches its climax when one of his pupils unexpectedly brings him a book as a farewell present. The boy's motive is really a sort of casual pity for a rather pathetic old hack whom he vaguely feels to be less objectionable than most people find him; but to the poor man, self-outlawed among his sufferings, this unforeseen and unique piece of evidence that someone has appreciated him seems of a disproportionate importance. His defences, for once, go down, he is deeply touched, he weeps. His wife cannot bear to see him enjoying even this crumb of comfort, imputes to the boy an ulterior motive and thrusts the broken man back into the limbo she has made for him. A colleague who has been her lover revolts at this and applies moral first aid to her victim, so that when the curtain falls we are aware of the embryonic stirrings of a new self-confidence in Crocker-Harris.

Source: Peter Fleming. Review of *The Browning Version* in the *Spectator,* Vol. 181, no. 6273, September 17, 1948, p. 366.

SOURCES

Atkinson, Brooks. "Where Men Are Scoundrels," in *The New York Times,* October 23, 1949, section 2, p. 1.

Barnes, Howard. A review of *The Browning Version,* in *The New York Herald Tribune,* October 13, 1949, p. 254.

Brown, John Mason. "Brush Off Your Shakespeare," in *The Saturday Review of Literature,* November 5, 1949, pp. 26-7.

Clurman, Harold. "Theatre: English Visitation," in *The New Republic,* November 7, 1949, pp. 21-2.

Darlington, W. A. A review of *The Browning Version,* in *The New York Times,* October 10, 1948, section 2, p. 3.

Kerr, Walter. "Tasty Slices of Rattigan and Bagnold," in *The New York Times,* May 9, 1982, Section 2, p. 3.

Newsweek, October 24, 1949, p. 84.

Rattigan, Terence. *The Browning Version,* in *The Collected Plays of Terence Rattigan,* Vol. 2, Hamish Hamilton, 1953, pp. 1-48.

Rich, Frank. "Stage: At Roundabout, 'The Browning Version,'" in *The New York Times,* April 23, 1982, p. C3.

Rusinko, Susan. *Terence Rattigan,* Twayne, 1983.

Simon, John. "Croc Without Tears," in *New York,* May 3, 1982, pp. 71-2.

Taylor, John Russell. *The Rise and Fall of the Well-Made Play,* Hill and Wang, 1967, pp. 146-60.

Time, October 24, 1949, p. 58.

FURTHER READING

Darlow, Michael and Gillian Hodson. *Terence Rattigan: The Man and His Work,* Quartet Books, 1979.
   Critical biography of Rattigan.

Havighurst, Alfred F. *Britain in Transition,* The University of Chicago Press, 1985.
   A history of Great Britain from 1900-1983, including the post-World War II period in which *The Browning Version* takes place.

Hyams, Barry. "The People's Playwright . . . A Chat with Terence Rattigan," in *Theatre Arts,* November, 1956, pp. 20-3.
   In this interview, conducted at the height of Rattigan's success, he explains the concept of "Aunt Edna," his ideal audience member.

Smith, Kay Nolte. "Terence Rattigan," in *The Objectivist,* March, 1971, pp. 9-16.
   A critical analysis of Rattigan's writing. Smith considers his work "artistry."

Wansell, Geoffrey. *Terence Rattigan,* Fourth Estate, 1995.
   This biography covers Rattigan's entire life and writing career.

Bus Stop

WILLIAM INGE

1955

When William Inge's play, *Bus Stop,* opened on Broadway March 2, 1955, it was an immediate commercial and critical success. Based on Inge's earlier one-act play, *People in the Wind, Bus Stop* involves a pair of young lovers and their struggle to find love in the modern world.

Unlike his earlier two plays, *Come Back, Little Sheba* and *Picnic,* this work is not an in-depth study of relationships. Instead, it is considered a superficial romantic comedy. As most critics assert, *Bus Stop* simply lacks the depth of Inge's earlier work.

Inge's focus on the main couple—the nightclub singer, Cherie, and the brash cowboy, Bo—inspired more controversy. As critics complained that the other six characters in the play remain undeveloped and fail to hold the audience's attention or sympathy, Inge reasserted his hope that the audience would be interested in every character. His aim was to portray the full spectrum of romantic relationships, from positive to negative, in his work.

AUTHOR BIOGRAPHY

William Inge was born on May 3, 1913, in Independence, Kansas. He was raised by his mother, Maude; his father was a traveling salesman and was rarely at home. After graduating from the University of Kansas in 1935, Inge attended the George Peabody

William Inge

College for Teachers, but left before completing his graduate program.

After a brief period teaching English at a local high school, Inge returned to college to complete his graduate degree. He also worked as a drama critic, and it was during this period that he met Tennessee Williams, who encouraged him to write drama. Inge completed his first play that year, and with the help of Williams, *Farther Off from Heaven* was produced in 1947.

In 1949, Inge wrote *Come Back, Little Sheba,* which was produced on Broadway in 1950 and earned the George Jean Nathan Award and Theatre Time Award. Three years later, *Picnic* won the Pulitzer Prize in Drama, the Outer Circle Award, the New York Drama Critics Circle Award, and the Donaldson Award.

He had two more hits on Broadway in quick succession: *Bus Stop* and *The Dark at the Top of the Stairs.* After so much early success, his next plays, *A Loss of Roses, Natural Affection,* and *Where's Daddy?* were commercial failures, each closing after only a few performances.

Inge had more success with his first attempt at screenwriting, *Splendor in the Grass,* which received the Academy Award for Best Original Screen-

play in 1961. Following this success, he moved to Los Angeles to concentrate on screenplays, but never repeated his early success.

Inge was deeply affected by negative reviews of his work. He struggled with depression and alcoholism much of his life. Several of his plays focus on the complexity of family relationships and deal with characters who struggle with failed expectations, depression, and addiction. His death in 1973 from carbon monoxide poisoning was ruled a suicide.

PLOT SUMMARY

Act I

As the play opens, Grace and Elma anticipate the arrival of the bus and its passengers at the bus stop. The two women are waitresses at the diner, and as they wait for customers they discuss romance, or the lack of it: Grace has been married, but her husband left her; Elma is single and lonely. The sheriff, Will, comes into the diner and announces that the snowstorm has closed the roads and the bus and its passengers will be stuck at the diner until the road is cleared.

Almost immediately, the bus pulls in to the diner. A young blond woman, Cherie, enters. She is scared and trying to hide from a fellow passenger, Bo. Dr. Lyman and the bus driver, Carl, walk into the diner. It becomes obvious that Grace and Carl are interested in one another, and after a whispered conversation, they contrive reasons to leave and, presumably, meet secretly upstairs in Grace's apartment. Meanwhile, Dr. Lyman is obviously drunk, circumspect, and suspicious.

Eventually, Bo and Virgil enter the diner. Bo believes that he is in love with Cherie; moreover, he has practically kidnapped her with the intent of marrying her. Act I ends with a confrontation between Will and Bo, who learns that Cherie has sought the protection of the sheriff. Bo is shocked to learn that Cherie, or any other woman, might be able to resist his charms.

Act II

Act II opens with Dr. Lyman beginning his seduction of Elma. He arranges to meet her later in Topeka, where she will be attending a symphony. Elma is too innocent to recognize that Dr. Lyman's intentions are less than honorable.

begins to mature into a more sensitive, tender one. On account of his inexperience with women and his insecurity with himself, he does not know how to relate to people. His love for Cherie transforms him: only by losing her does he find the courage to confront his limitations and move forward with his life. Only then does Cherie accept his love.

Friendship

Bo and Virgil's friendship is a strong and long-lasting one. Older by twenty years, Virgil has taken care of Bo since the death of his parents and has become a father figure for the young man. During the course of the play, Virgil tries to restrain Bo, hoping to keep him out of trouble. He provides valuable advice on how Bo should act, especially with Cherie. With Virgil, Bo is able to finally express his loneliness. When Cherie accepts Bo's proposal, Virgil bows out of Bo's life so that he can build a life with Cherie.

Loneliness

Loneliness is an important theme in *Bus Stop* and propels most of the action in the play. In particular, Bo cannot bear the thought of returning to his lonely ranch. For this reason he mistakes his sexual relationship with Cherie for love and later mistakes love for ownership. Yet Bo cannot really love Cherie until he begins to acknowledge the depth of his loneliness and need. When he can really relate to her, with tenderness and caring, the young couple find common ground: their loneliness.

Grace is also motivated by loneliness. She tells Elma that she hates to return to her apartment above the diner alone. Her brief sexual encounters with Carl appear to offer her temporary respite from that emptiness, but it is only for a few hours and then she is alone again. Carl's visits are limited to twenty-minute stops, and while that is enough time for a brief sexual tryst, it is ultimately dissatisfying.

Moral Corruption

More than Grace and Carl's casual sexual relationship or Cherie's checkered history, the most egregious moral corruption in the play takes place between Lyman and Elma. His history of seducing young girls into a sexual relationship is known as pedophilia; in fact, he is fleeing the police for seducing underage girls. When he first enters the diner, Lyman is attracted to Elma and devotes much of the play to arranging a secret meeting. He con-

TOPICS FOR FURTHER STUDY

- After World War II, the U. S. government began an aggressive campaign to build a system of freeways that would link the United States and make travel between cities easier. Investigate the sociological impact of the highway system on rural America. How has life changed for these communities?

- In *Bus Stop,* Bo and Virgil have just participated in the rodeo in Kansas City. Research the impact of rodeos on cowboy life. What rewards do cowboys receive from their participation in these events, other than awards?

- Lyman is an alcoholic who has failed at his career and at several marriages. Investigate the role of alcohol addiction among professionals, such as Lyman, an unemployed college professor. What professions are most affected by this disease?

- Alcoholism and sexuality are important themes in several of Inge's plays. Compare Doc and his pursuit of Marie in *Come Back, Little Sheba* with the relationship of Lyman and Elma in *Bus Stop.*

trives business in Toledo and attempts to seduce her with a romantic scene from *Romeo and Juliet.*

Pride

Bo's identity is largely defined by pride. In fact, his initial appearance underscores this theme as he loudly describes his accomplishments to the people in the diner. His relationship with Cherie is negatively affected by this trait too. When she rejects him, he cannot believe that Cherie might not love him; the very idea is inconceivable. Therefore, he tries to force her to love and accept him.

Moreover, after Bo loses his fight with the sheriff, he is humiliated and unable to apologize to Cherie for his behavior. When Bo is finally able to put aside his pride and tell her that he loves her for who she truly is, he is able to form a bond with Cherie.

STYLE

Act

Dramas are divided into different acts. In Greek plays the drama was usually divided into five acts. This is the formula for most serious drama from the Greeks to the Romans and to later playwrights like William Shakespeare. The five acts denote the structure of dramatic action: exposition, complication, climax, falling action, and catastrophe. This five-act structure was standard until the nineteenth century, when Ibsen combined some of the acts.

Bus Stop is a three-act play. The exposition and complication are combined in the first act when the audience first learns of Cherie's abduction and of Bo's plans for a wedding. The climax occurs in the second act when Bo fights with Will, is arrested, and Cherie learns why Bo feels so committed to her. The catastrophe fails to occur in the third act—*Bus Stop* is comedy, not a drama. If this had been written as drama, Cherie would not have changed her mind and Bo would have boarded the bus, alone and heartbroken.

Audience

The audience is defined as the people for whom a drama is performed. Many authors write with an audience in mind. Inge states in the forward to *Four Plays* that he wanted his audience to observe several different portrayals of love and to be interested in all the characters. This is unusual; in general, authors never tell their audience what reaction they expect.

Character

Characters can range from simple stereotypical figures to more complex multifaceted ones. They may also be defined by personality traits, such as the rogue or the damsel in distress. The actions of the characters drive the play.

Characterization is the process of creating a character, replete with personality traits that help define who he will be and how he will behave in a given situation. For instance, Grace is lonely. The audience knows this because she tells them so on several occasions, but also because as she leaves the stage at the end of the play, her wistful glance reveals how much she dreads the loneliness upstairs.

Setting

The elements of setting may include geographic location, physical or mental environments, prevailing cultural attitudes, or the historical time in which the action takes place. The location for *Bus Stop* is a small diner. All of the action occurs between 1 a.m. and 5 a.m. on a Sunday morning in this same setting. The limited setting forces all the action to occur within a small space and all the characters to interact.

HISTORICAL CONTEXT

Booming 1950s Economy

In the post-World War II years, the nation was economically prosperous. The G.I. Bill provided the means for returning soldiers to get a better education. More importantly, it funded a program whereby each soldier could buy a house. This spurred a boom in new home construction, which led to increased production of all the appliances, furniture, and automobiles. All of this production led to an increase in employment and in the gross national product. With World War II behind them, and extra money to spend and more time to spend it, Americans turned to entertainment in increasing numbers.

Joe DiMaggio and Marilyn Monroe

Bus Stop might very well have been art imitating life. The year before the play's debut on Broadway, Joe DiMaggio married Marilyn Monroe. It was not a marriage between a lonely cowboy and a cabaret singer, but the union between DiMaggio, one of the best athletes of all time, and Marilyn Monroe was almost as unlikely. Accordingly, it became front-page news as the world was captivated by their marriage. In many ways, their union represented a joining of two of the most visible forces of the 1950s: baseball and Hollywood.

Marilyn Monroe was one of the biggest stars of the 1950s. She had appeared nude in the very first issue of a new men's magazine, *Playboy,* in 1953. More than fifty thousand copies of the magazine sold, indicating the strength of her appeal. The role of Cherie in *Bus Stop* seems written for her, and indeed, she starred in the film version of the play when it was released in 1956.

Monroe was popular for her ability to appeal to different audiences. A beautiful woman, she represented sexuality—and therefore attracted so many of the budding teenagers of the fifties. It is little wonder that audiences perceived Monroe's marriage to DiMaggio as unlikely. This star of the New York Yankees represented the benefits of hard work

Marilyn Monroe, as Cherie, and Don Murray, as Bo, in a scene from the film adaptation of Inge's play

CRITICAL OVERVIEW

Bus Stop opened on Broadway March 2, 1955, for the first of 475 performances. If the reviews are any indication, this play was a success with both critics and audiences. Robert Coleman of the *Daily Mirror* summed it up when he advised that *Bus Stop* "should prove a popular terminal for playgoers for months to come." In this "endearing, though deceptively simple, comedy," the audience can find "magical warmth and humor," according to Coleman. In wrapping up his review, Coleman advised readers to make reservations right away, since the play "has heart, compassion, wisdom, and loads of laughs."

Another positive assessment was provided by Walter F. Kerr of the *Herald Review*. While citing the strengths of the cast, Kerr also praised Inge's writing. Kerr stated that, "the fascination of the

and good character. He was a private, quiet man that shunned media attention; she was a vibrant, media-savvy movie star that craved attention.

COMPARE & CONTRAST

- 1955: Walt Disney opened Disneyland in Los Angeles, California. Built for $17 million, the park was so successful that Disney immediately made plans to expand it.

  Today: The Disney Corporation continues to grow. The company is now worth nearly 80 billion dollars and has expanded into film and television, as well as merchandising.

- 1955: Nineteen years after its introduction, the Volkswagen Beetle manufactured its one millionth car.

  Today: The Volkswagen Beetle has been redesigned and reintroduced to the American automobile buyer. It has once again proved popular and successful, as it appeals to a youthful demographic.

- 1955: TV dinners are introduced as an easy and popular alternative for busy housewives.

  Today: Frozen prepared meals are very popular with consumers. Their convenience makes them a popular choice for working parents with little time to make home-cooked meals.

- 1955: The first shopping mall opens in the Detroit area in 1954. By the end of the following year, 1800 new shopping malls open across the country.

  Today: Shopping malls are a common experience in American life. They have become gathering places for teenagers.

- 1955: The United States federal minimum wage is increased from $0.75 to $1 an hour.

  Today: Nearly forty-five years later, the minimum wage has increased by less than $5.

---

funny and very touching evening lies not in its surprises but in its sharp, honest, down-to-earth eye for character." He observed that Inge "has not set out to write an epic, just a warm and sensible little scrap between a couple of stranded, stubborn, appealing people."

A mixed review was offered by Richard Watts, Jr. of the *New York Post,* who stated that "in a day when there is reason to worry about the state of American playwriting, he [Inge] brings to the theatre a kind of warm-hearted compassion, creative vigor, freshness of approach and appreciation of average humanity that can be wonderfully touching and stimulating." Watts deemed *Bus Stop* a "romantic comedy about ordinary people that is at once humorous, simple, steadily entertaining and vastly endearing. It is also splendidly acted."

However, Watts maintained that it lacked "the poignant dramatic sturdiness and the tragic implications that were present in *Come Back, Little Sheba* and *Picnic.* It is unashamedly sentimental in its viewpoint. And I suppose it was written chiefly as entertainment, if you regard that as bad." But Watts clearly did not see entertainment as a bad thing, and noted that Inge's play is "set down with all of Mr. Inge's skill and warmth."

John McClain of the *Journal American* also expressed some reservations about *Bus Stop,* noting that "the whole thing stops dead in the middle of the second act." Yet McClain contended that "*Bus Stop* will be with us as long as the road to The Music Box is open."

There is no hesitation in the review by Brooks Atkinson of *The New York Times.* Atkinson deemed *Bus Stop* "an uproarious comedy that never strays from the truth." He also asserted that "once it gets started it flows naturally and sympathetically through the hearts and hopes of some admirable people."

He was especially complimentary of Inge's writing. Atkinson pointed to the dialogue and stated that there are "some moving conversations about the nature of love and the generosity that makes it possible.'' This, according to the reviewer, was because Inge ''has more than an evening's entertainment in mind. He has ideas and principles . . . [and] he says a number of simple truths that give height and depth to his writing.'' To sum up his review, Atkinson recommended ''both the writing and the acting . . . [as] a memorable achievement.''

The one dissenting voice was that of John Chapman of the *Daily News,* who declared that Inge had ''written a scenario instead of a play.'' He deemed the play as ''make-believe, and not very exciting at that.'' He concluded: ''I couldn't get myself to care very much about the romance between the young cowboy and the slightly soiled lady. I just didn't believe in it—and if one doesn't believe in something it is a scenario and not a play.''

CRITICISM

Sheri E. Metzger,

Metzger is a Ph.D. specializing in literature and drama at the University of New Mexico. In this essay, she discusses the changing perceptions of Inge's romanticism.

In 1955, Americans were watching *I Love Lucy, The Adventures of Ozzie and Harriet, Father Knows Best,* and *Davy Crockett.* In these programs, life was easy; jobs were plentiful, and the American Dream appeared as a tangible reality. It was an idealized image of an America that only existed on television—and on the stage.

In *Bus Stop,* William Inge attempts to create a story that is, according to him, ''a composite picture of varying kinds of love, ranging from the innocent to the depraved.'' This was his intent, as stated in the forward to *Four Plays,* published in 1958. This very sentiment recalls a time in American social history when love and sexuality could be neatly defined and classified. Inge's play was meant for an America defined by picket fences, perfect families, and romantic infatuations that could be resolved in thirty minutes.

It is now clear that the world was not so perfect. The Cold War raged, women were marginalized, and the fight for civil rights was escalating; but for two hours audiences could escape and find solace in a small Midwestern town—even if it was not real.

Inge features three romantic situations in *Bus Stop*—Bo and Cherie, Grace and Carl, and Elma and Lyman. While Inge may have hoped that the audience would find each couple equally interesting, it is clear that Bo and Cherie take center stage. And although they are obviously unsuited for one another, the romantic ideal is that love conquers all.

In the 1950s, television audiences knew that all the differences, problems, and conflicts would be neatly resolved before the last commercial aired. Strong parents, mostly fathers, could set any problem straight. Viewers rarely questioned this formula, and indeed, there was something comforting about its very predictability. Critics who reviewed *Bus Stop* noted that whether Bo and Cherie ended up together was never a question. What held the audience's interest was how the couple would reach the end goal.

In this respect, romantic comedy, whether it appeared on television, film, or theater, provided the same comforting resolution. As Gerald Weales notes, ''it is proper that Cherie and Bo exit together for a Montana ranch where, according to the conventions of the theater, they will live happily ever after.'' This is the ultimate goal of the writer whose plot embraces romantic love.

If, as Inge states, he wanted to portray varying kinds of love, how can Cherie and Bo's romance be classified? Consider that Bo's sole goal in finding a wife is to assuage his loneliness. He barely knows Cherie, never ask if she loves him, and indeed, does not seem to want the answer to that question. Her choice to leave with him appears to be based as much on opportunity and lack of choice, as it is on genuine affection, if in fact, she actually loves him. For most of the play she does not even like him.

Thus, their union at the end of the play is formulaic and unrealistic. It is, however, in keeping with romanticized visions of ideal love, which insists that sex should end in marriage.

Inge's goal of portraying depraved love might be defined by any of the three couples, since at least one member of each pairing also defies the mores of the 1950s. In the puritanical atmosphere of the period, illicit sexuality, as Inge demonstrated in *Come Back, Little Sheba* and *Picnic,* is always cause for public concern. In *Bus Stop,* Cherie admits to a sexual history. She has had many partners, beginning at age fourteen with her cousin and continuing even when she met Bo. That is, in fact, how they

WHAT DO I READ NEXT?

- William Inge's *Picnic* (1953) concerns young love. Although more serious than *Bus Stop,* it is also a comedic look at the vicissitudes of sex and relationships.

- *The Canterbury Tales* (c. 1380), by Geoffrey Chaucer, is a compilation of stories told by travelers to pass the time. It is one of the best-known short story collections of English literature.

- Giovanni Boccaccio's *The Decameron* (c. 1350) is a collection of comedic and often risqué stories told by a group of stranded travelers.

- *The Taming of the Shrew* (c. 1593), by the great English playwright William Shakespeare, is a comedic play that chronicles the efforts of a young man to win the love of a reluctant bride.

- Lanford Wilson's play, *Angels Fall* (1982), focuses on a group of people stranded together in northern New Mexico. This work is a serious examination of how tragedy often motivates change and growth.

---

first got together; the problem for Cherie is that Bo mistakes sex for love.

According to the values of the 1950s, Cherie must love Bo, since she cannot simply walk off insisting that it was only sex—even if it was. She must love him, or she must be provided with a reason for her sexual freedom, as is Grace.

The older, more experienced Grace is as lonely as Bo, but marriage is not the answer. She states that she is only looking for a temporary or momentary encounter. Her denial of marriage as a goal contradicts the accepted premise that unmarried sex should lead to love. In *Picnic* Rosemary's sexual encounter forces a marriage to her seducer. And like Grace, Rosemary, is not a young girl. Grace's acceptance of her occasional need for a man, without marriage, could establish her as a female lead with questionable morals.

But neither Cherie nor Grace, although representing questionable morality in the repressed and repressive 1950s, really fits a depraved definition of love. No doubt Inge meant for Lyman's planned seduction of Elma to be viewed as depraved, as it would have been in 1955.

Elma is, after all, still in high school; therefore, Lyman's flirtation appears quite perverted. Yet this seduction also reveals several ambiguities. Although

Elma's age is never revealed, the audience knows she is still in high school; however, she is old enough to be working in a diner at 1 a.m. on a Sunday morning. Thus, Elma is probably only a year or two younger than Cherie, who is nineteen.

Also, Hollywood films have traditionally presented young women, many just out of school, who become involved in romances with older men. This is the staple of romantic comedies of the 1930s and 1940s.

So what makes the situation between Lyman and Elma depraved? It is the very lack of love. Although Inge is looking to reveal depraved love, Lyman is, as the audience learns in the play's last act, a seducer of young girls. He has a history of loitering outside schools in order to meet them. Lyman's carefully orchestrated seduction of Elma is not love, but in fact a pathological perversion.

Although, she is flattered at the attention of an older, educated man, Elma's naive acceptance of his attentions is based on flirtation and on an innocent misunderstanding of his intent. Elma fails to see Lyman as a "disillusioned eastern intellectual," as Rudolf Erben describes him. Although he has a record of failed relationships and a disastrous career, Lyman glosses over his failures. He describes himself as free from responsibility and ready to explore the world. This is attractive to a small-town girl, whose intelligence and knowledge is alienating to her contemporaries. But it is no more than a flirtation, and when Lyman's history is revealed, Elma is shocked to find that she has been the object of a planned seduction.

In the end, Inge cannot resist saving Lyman from his own cardinal desires. The "play within a play," designed as entertainment but appropriated by Lyman as a means of seduction, provides an epiphany for Lyman, who suddenly realizes that he is no young, romantic Romeo. William E. H. Meyer Jr. observes that Dr. Lyman is "forced to come to terms with his dubious and dark penchant for young girls." The audience is promised that Lyman is about to be reformed of his deviant ways. This resolution is in keeping with the television sitcom model, except that Lyman is the father who resolves all conflict.

As the play concludes, Lyman rejects his past behavior, Grace accepts a twice-weekly sexual tryst in place of love, and Cherie accepts the isolation of a Montana ranch in place of the dance halls of Kansas City. Is any of this love? Or is it the easy resolution that audiences accept? In this sense, the romance between Bo and Cherie fits Inge's stated intent to present innocent love—except that he is truly the innocent participant.

Bus Stop is enjoyable; it is humorous and entertaining, but to a modern audience, jaded by the depravity of television that focuses on sexual crime, violence, and confession, Inge's play is innocent flirtation. Even Lyman appears as only disgusting and not depraved when compared to the criminals encountered on the news. Forty years after *Bus Stop*, Inge reveals himself to be the true innocent romantic.

Source: Sheri E. Metzger, for *Drama for Students,* Gale, 2000.

Richard Hayes

Hayes offers a mostly favorable review of Inge's play, but the critic laments that Bus Stop *lacks the spark of the playwright's earlier works, notably* Picnic *and* Come Back, Little Sheba.

A vaudeville of personality, picturesque and vivid: thus might one suggest the flavor and quality of Mr. William Inge's new play. For in this bleached and seedy café, poised carelessly on a wasteland of snowbound prairies, an American *Symposium* is mounted; it is the nature of love with which Mr. Inge is concerned. The light of his sensibility flickers with active indolence over the theme, catching its many faces of truth; the director, Harold

> " *BUS STOP* IS ENJOYABLE; IT IS HUMOROUS AND ENTERTAINING, BUT TO A MODERN AUDIENCE, JADED BY THE DEPRAVITY OF TELEVISION THAT FOCUSES ON SEXUAL CRIME, VIOLENCE, AND CONFESSION, INGE'S PLAY IS INNOCENT FLIRTATION"

Clurman—with his special talent for modulation—faultlessly places each of these small private epiphanies in a seamless texture of dramatic experience. Everything is common about the raw matter of "Bus Stop" but the taste and feeling with which it has been elevated to human worth. How delicately drawn, indeed—and played with such rightness and exactitude by Phyllis Love—is the young girl, burgeoning uneasily into love; how subtly, too, does Mr. Inge convey the initial stirrings into dignity of his two major characters: the lumpish, not-yet-housebroken cowboy, all bullying rush and bravado, and his soundlessly vapid victim, this night-club hostess with her scrappy and pathetic tags of gentility. The subject could not (in the human sense) be less promising, yet out of such shapeless moral anarchy—only the comic face of which is kept in the foreground—Mr. Inge and Mr. Clurman have extracted the truth of the grotesque, modest and vague, but within its small and limited world, legitimate. And the production bodies forth this accomplishment: with their superbly developed realistic techniques, Kim Stanley and Albert Salmi bring wit and wry tenderness and an interior veracity to these two central roles; indeed, the ensemble performance is a superior illustration of the power and ease with which American players inhabit the theater of realistic conventions. It is superfluous, of course, to note that however gratifying and congenial, this is but one of the major modes of dramatic experience.

Pleasure, then, I have recorded; permit me now a reservation. In a notice of Mr. Inge's earlier "*Picnic*," I observed that his was a talent in which sensibility exceeded the dispositions of the intellect—that is, one in which the power to order and clarify experience was as yet inadequate to the imaginative apprehension of it. Now "*Bus Stop*" would seem to suggest that Mr. Inge has sought to dissolve the impasse by developing a vein of domestic comedy, a genre for which he has most considerable gifts. One may commend the resolution of the problem, yet there has been a concomitant loss: what I miss in "*Bus Stop*" is that numinous sense of personality, a bleakly exquisite poetry of solitude which fleetingly brushes the grey actualities of "*Picnic*" and "*Come Back, Little Sheba.*" The *imaging* here is as secure and lucid as in the earlier plays, but there is, behind it, a diminished pressure of intellectual and emotional energy. Mr. Inge is thus limited in his attempt to deal increasingly with serious experience; to its evaluation, he can bring only standards which, however humane, are ultimately provincial. (Would not, for example, a more penetrating mind have reached to the truth of the essential *disastrousness* of love in America?) Again: a haze of sentimentality obscures those characters which, as it were, sustain the moral weight of the play: the complaisant mistress of the café (a good performance by Elaine Stritch, though excessively mannered), and the alcoholic middle-aged intellectual. Anthony Ross' brilliant control of the latter role mutes its slushy banalities, but surely there is something disturbing symptomatic and how typically American, in the fact that the Socrates of this particular *agape* should be a boozy professor of literature, whose irregular amorous interests have more than occasionally invited the serious attention of the local instruments of law?

Source: Richard Hayes. Review of *Bus Stop* in the *Commonweal,* Vol. LXII, No. 1, April 8, 1995, p. 14.

William E. H. Meyer, Jr.

In the following essay, Meyer compares Inge's view of American ideals, as represented in Bus Stop, *with that of other notable authors. The critic also addresses claims that Inge's play lacks depth, arguing that* Bus Stop *actually offers profound insight into small town America.*

Bus Stop—both the play and the movie—is an attempt to dramatize what is pre-eminently *un*dramatic, *viz.,* the evolution of small-town hyperverbality into American hypervisuality. This shift in sensibility or revolution in "taste" is an extremely difficult phenomenon to depict—the playwright, William Inge, here choosing to employ the more demonstrable theme of love/sexuality in order to express or encompass this New-World evolution. Indeed, so vital but protean and mercurial is this

problem of the shift from ear to eye, from traditional authority to self-reliance, that such well-known anthologists of American culture as Blair, Stewart, Hornberger and Miller, in their *The Literature of the United States,* have missed the contribution of Inge altogether and have dismissed his work as "popular" and "lacking depth." Yet, *Bus Stop* remains a profound portrait of the Emersonian/American "transparent eyeball" in transit—the superseding of "small-town" values for Ishmael's passion "to see the world" or the Stevensesque ephebe's command to rise above any municipality in order to "see the sun again with an ignorant eye." All the characters of *Bus Stop*—from Bo to Grace—are confronted with this American hypervisual *rite de passage,* no matter whether they are "lucky" or "unlucky" in love.

Act 1, then, introduces us to the "bus stop" or small-town restaurant where the hyperverbal small-town crew and also the little band of travelers must confront the wider concerns of hypervisual America—where such clichés as "March comes in like a Lion" or the later-employed famous Shakespearean rhetoric of the Old World must face the New-World "great window" and be still before "the sweeping wind and flying snow." Not for nothing does the curtain rise upon Elma standing and "*looking out the large plate-glass window, awed by the fury of the elements*"; and not for nothing are the first words uttered directed to the play's ensuing dangerous command—"You should come over here and *look out, to see* the way the wind is blowing things all over town" (p. 6, italics mine). Grace, however, prefers to concern herself with the tele-*phone*—not tele-*vision*—and she will be one of those characters destined, at the play's end, to fail to grasp the necessity to transcend local talk via national vision.

The storm itself, of course, represents the awesome and ungovernable power of America itself—what Emerson called "Nature" as he was confronted by the god-like power of the wilderness wherein he felt himself both diminished and aggrandized: "I am nothing; I see all; . . . I am part or parcel of God." Here, Will, the "local" authority or small-town sheriff, can only fume at his own impotence: "A storm like this makes me mad. . . . It's just like all the elements had lost their reason . . . I like to see things in order" (p. 8). In the face of this awesome display of power observed through the "large plate-glass window," all Will can do is fall back upon the above cliché of how "March comes in like a Lion." And all Elma, the young waitress, can do is rely upon parental security: "Nights like this, I'm glad I have a home to go to'' (p. 6). Yet, indeed, in the early lines that Elma speaks—''I shouldn't think anyone would take a trip tonight unless he absolutely *had* to'' (p. 6)—we find the primary thrust or ironic ''theme'' of the drama—the absolutely necessary hypervisual *rite de passage* which every American is forced to make at some point in his or her life. Walt Whitman put it thus: ''You must travel that road for yourself.'' And Emerson clarified the nature of that journey with the reprimand: ''Do we fear lest we should *outsee* nature and God, and drink truth dry!'' (italics mine). Here the passengers and the small-town locals are rendered equals by the storm—by the irrational but ultimately vivifying power of our ''genius in America, with tyrannous eye.''

As I noted above, the quintessential shift from small-town word to American vision is most difficult to ''portray'' and certainly cannot be accomplished by means of any traditional or Aristotelian notions of plot, character or even theme. Thus Inge has chosen the more ''popular'' topic of human love and sexuality in order to ''suggest'' the deeper dilemma going on within the restaurant or what Hemingway called his small café, ''a clean, well-lighted place.'' Here Man and Woman come to act out the ''play within a play,'' the voyeur and exhibitionist coming to terms with the essence of American reality and passion. Here, then, it is most important that the ''love affair'' at the center of the drama be that between Bo and Cherie, between Mr. and Miss America—between two ''beautiful people'' who can represent ''amber waves of grain'' and ''purple mountains' majesty'' or the fruitfulness of our Emersonian ''incomparable materials'' from ''sea to shining sea.'' The sexual encounter between Carl and Grace or the flirtation between Dr. Lyman and Elma are also important as variations on the theme of voyeur and exhibitionist or of genuine and spurious love; but the driving force in the play is the pursuit of seductively-dressed and prettily-blond Cherie by Bo—another Brom Bones in hot pursuit of his buxom Miss America, Katrina Van Tassel. Of course, what Bo has to learn about the actual capture of his ''voluptuous'' hypervisual ideal forms the tension of the second and third acts. But the quest of the Montana rancher for the Ozark beauty is the *sine qua non* of *Bus Stop*—and, indeed, of the whole of American literature, from Cooper's Hawkeye to Vonnegut's more ironic Deadeye Dick. These small-town lovers will have to discover in their romance the more serious problem of the American Dream— of what it means to be either a

> *BUS STOP* WILL HAVE TO BE REREAD—NOT AS 'LACKING DEPTH' BUT AS PROFOUNDLY INDICATING THE SUPERSESSION OF THE SMALL TOWN AND ITS HYPERVERBAL TRADITIONS BY THE BROADER HYPERVISUAL CONCERNS OF WHAT WALT WHITMAN CALLED THE DAZZLING PANORAMA OF 'THESE UNITED STATES'''

spot-lighted Hester Prynne or a spotlighted Miss U.S.A. or even a spot-lighted *chanteuse* under the almost unbearable scrutiny of ''the public gaze.'' It does no good for Cherie to exclaim, ''Is there some place I kin hide?'' (p. 9). For the Woman, there is no escape except into the hypervisual maturity and responsibility of ''America is a poem in our eyes.'' For the Man, there is no conquest except by the self-abnegation which confesses the utter destitution of the ''transparent eyeball'': ''I just never realized . . . a gal might not . . . love me'' (p. 29).

Act 2 begins with the ''courting'' of Elma by Dr. Lyman and also with Dr. Lyman's jaded talk about ''higher education.'' Although this dialogue seems almost too peripheral to the main thrust of the play, this commentary about love and wisdom is really essential to what follows. Here, ideal love is to be neither the seduction of the naively young by the old (''people might not understand''); nor is it to be the simple abduction or rape of the Woman by the Man (''Ya cain't *force* a gal to marry ya,'' p. 33). Somehow there has to be an elevation of love wherein both Man and Woman can feel themselves participating in a destiny transcending ''what ya might call a *sexual* attraction'' (p. 34). Hawthorne called this the long-awaited ''brighter period'' in Male-Female relations: and Emerson called it the ''sublime vision'' that elevates the ''chaste'' soul. Perhaps Father Edward Taylor, the early Puritan divine, summed it up best by indicating the merger of sublime sexuality with divine hypervision when he shouted—''Oh! if his Glory ever kiss thine Eye.'' In Bo, this is the impulse behind his ''most fervent love'' for his Miss America—''Ain't she beautiful, Virge?'' (p. 47)—but an impulsive adoration that must find itself molded by patience and tenderness or by what Bo reveals in confessing to Cherie that ''I jest couldn't kill them 'sweet li'l deers with the sad eyes''' (p. 43). Here Bo is beginning to learn something of the congenial power of what we might call ''The America Religion of Vision.''

Of course, too, the most ''dramatic'' moments of *Bus Stop* come here in Act 2, in the ''floor show'' and in the fight between Bo and Will. When Elma suggests the display of talents, Dr. Lyman erroneously supposes it to be an idea ''straight from Chaucer'' (p. 40). Rather, this is an *American* ''demonstration'' and has as its central purpose the hypervisual display of Cherie in her costume, not the hyperverbal recitation of Shakespeare. Elma and Dr. Lyman may repeat some of the lines from *Romeo and Juliet,* but this only serves to reveal the distance between Shakespearean rhetoric and American vision. Juliet-Elma may well be ''like the sun''; but this is the New-World Revolutionary Light wherein, as Jonathan Edwards noted, the former laws of nature were superseded: ''The Sun shall rise in the West.'' Shakespearean language, with its ''winged messenger of heaven,'' can no longer be the American model and is impotent, like Dr. Lyman, in the face of the New-World ''great window'' and ''great awakening'': Emerson writes—''When I see the daybreak I am not reminded of these Homeric, or Shakespearean, or Miltonic, or Chaucerian, pictures''; nor of ''Pope and Johnson and Addison [who] write *as if they had never seen the face of the country*'' (italics mine). However, Dr. Lyman *is* enough of an ''American Scholar'' to at least realize something of his *aesthetic,* as well as moral, failure in asserting that he can't ''continue this meaningless little act!''—when he realizes that he has betrayed the American Dream and thus his ''name . . . is hateful'' to himself (p. 46).

Bo, of course, as the All-American ''hero,'' immediately senses the falsity of the Shakespearean enactment, culminating in Dr. Lyman's breakdown: ''If thass the way to make love . . . I'm gonna give up'' (p. 46). Instead, Bo attempts to win his Miss America by the only means he knows—by physical battle with the small-town authority, the sheriff. It matters little that he is finally whipped and taken to jail; in fact, this ''humiliation'' of lover *and* artist is necessary to demonstrate to the Woman that the Man's ego is sublimated, at her feet. This spectacle of battle and defeat, in fact, gives the Woman the opportunity to experience the voyeur's role, to feel the power of observation: Cherie tells Bo ''. . . and if I was a man, I'd beat the livin' *daylights* out of ya, and thass what some man's gonna do some day, and when it happens, I hope I'm there to *see*'' (p. 47, italics mine). During the fight itself, Elma, Cherie and Grace all ''*hurry to the window to watch*'' (p. 48). Moreover, in the midst of all this exhibitionism and voyeurism, Dr. Lyman points to the crucial evolution occurring—the aesthetic American Revolution generated by New-World pioneers and ''small-town folk'':

> It takes strong men and women to *love* . . . People big enough to *grow* with their love and live inside a whole, *wide new dimension* (p. 49, final italics mine).

D. H. Lawrence called this the new consciousness arising upon the continent of America and no where else—a cultural upheaval which would cause condescending Europeans (and American critics) to ''*open new eyes*'' (italics mine). Emily Dickinson simply called it our ''new Circumference'' or ''new Equation given''—our ''very Lunacy of Light.'' Dr. Lyman here rightly laments his inability to give his ''most private self to another'' (p. 49); for this ''self'' is none other than the ''transparent eyeball'' and its reduction or elevation of the other to hypervision. The most profound and ironic truth that *Bus Stop* has to offer is Dr. Lyman's assertion that ''I've *nothing* in my heart for a true woman'' (p. 50, italics mine)—the same ''nothing'' that drove James's John Marcher into a loveless existence as ''the man to whom *nothing* was to happen,'' as this voyeur cannot ''love'' but only ''see.'' Unless American hypervision can unite Man and Woman into an idealization wherein *both* feel power and worth—*both* experience ''sexuality'' and ''tenderness''—the only result can be the loneliness which encompasses all the characters, from time to time, in *Bus Stop*. This ''theme,'' of course, as has been insisted upon above, is no easy matter for any playwright or ''word-smith'' to incorporate into either words or what Blair, *et al.,* have called Inge's ''popular drama.'' Hence the ''small town'' with its ''small talk'' must finally find itself without anything to say—what Emerson intuited in declaring that ''speech becomes less and ceases in a nobler silence.'' O Say, then, Can *YOU* See why America has no lyrical Lion or growling Bear as its national symbol—but the ''eagle-eyed'' American Eagle of 6X vision! O Say, Can *YOU* See why the American Liberty Bell ominously cracked upon its first ringing—a breach with the courtly muses of Europe and a disfunction which the hyperverbal English would no doubt have immediately repaired, while the

Americans left the bell in silence and are now quite content merely to go and *view* this national symbol. O Say, Can *YOU* See why the American harbor greets its visitors and immigrants with no chiming ''Big Ben,'' cognizant of lyricality and time— but with the upheld torch of Miss Hypervisual American Liberty and her ''Battle Hymn,'' ''Mine EYES Have SEEN the Glory!''

Act 3, then, finds the small-town restaurant under the vital, but quiet, ''dawn's early light'': Inge directs us to the following—

> *Early morning . . . the storm has cleared, and outside the window we see the slow dawning, creeping above the distant hills, revealing a landscape all in peaceful white* (p. 52).

Bo, addressed by the authority of the sheriff, simply says: ''I don't feel like talkin''' (p. 53). However, when later pressed into ''apologizing'' and musing upon his lonesome homestead, Bo has not forgotten his ''beautiful angel''; he tells Virgil, ''I ain't int'rested in no school marm. . . . I want Cherry'' (p. 57). Although Cherie was a *''chanteuse''* who sang of ''That Old Black Magic'' of Word and Music, her real attraction for Bo is her appealing vision; he tells her, ''You was so purty, and ya seemed so kinda warmhearted and sweet'' (p. 59). In the face of this ''tender'' hypervisual confession and kiss, and in the face of her realization that Bo is offering her the chance to participate in the regenerating of the ''Virgin Land''—Bo tells her that he's ''virgin enough'' for both of them— Cherie can be ''won'' by this adoring Brom Bones of Montana: she encourages him, ''Bo—ya think you really did love me?'' (p. 59). Bo can then fully possess his ''pearl of great price,'' conceived in the spot-light or what Hawthorne called ''A Flood of Sunshine'': Bo holds her *''cautiously, as though holding a precious object that was still a little strange to him''* (p. 60). Even Dr. Lyman is now, in the ''dawn's early light,'' forced to come to terms with his dubious and dark penchant for young girls: he no longer wishes to seduce Elma but engages in the aesthetically and morally elevating experience of having simply enjoyed her presence and friendship—of having *seen* her for what she really is.

From now on, then, all the travelers from this small-town depot will find the road ''clear'' but ''awful slick''—what Robert Frost called the dangerous ''road not taken'' into American hypervisuality. Emerson referred to it as the painful challenge to ''bring the past for judgment into the *thousand-eyed present,* and live ever in a *new day.''* From now on, Cherie will find consolation in lonely

Montana from the fact that her ''love'' has transcended small-town values for American fortitude and adventure. Here, Inge has simply given Bo and Cherie the direction: *''They . . . embrace. All look''* (p. 63)—the only time that *all* the characters have been united in a single meaningful act. In *Moby-Dick,* Melville had expanded this direction via the New-World paradigm: ''I look, you look, he looks; we look, ye look, they look.'' Moreover, from now on, Elma will find her status and self-esteem enhanced by the fact that a man—even a questionable one—has found her beautiful and hypervisually valuable: ''Just think, he wanted to make love to *me''* (p. 66). However, from now on, Virgil and his guitar will be ''left out in the cold''—bereft of that Love which offers the highest American consummation in vision, not music. And, finally, Grace will continue to long for, but not receive, the ''true marriage'' of exhibitionist and voyeur under the aegis of our ''genius in America, with tyrannous eye.'' All she can do is to ''[*cast*] *her eyes tiredly over the establishment''* (p. 67). This is the ''establishment'' of ''America the Hypervisual''—the small-town locus where all American buses must finally stop for illumination, where all hyperverbal midnights of the soul are revivified in the cold, clear and hard-won ''dawn's early light.'' The curtain merely falls on an empty stage awaiting the next convoy of what Emerson called our '' foolish traveling Americans.''

O Say, Can *YOU* See why *Bus Stop* will have to be reread—not as ''lacking depth'' but as profoundly indicating the supersession of the small town and its hyperverbal traditions by the broader hypervisual concerns of what Walt Whitman called the dazzling panorama of ''these United States.''

Source: William E. H. Meyer, Jr. ''*Bus Stop:* American Eye vs. Small-Town Ear'' in *Modern Drama,* Vol. XXXV, no. 3, September, 1992, pp. 444–50.

SOURCES

Atkinson, Brooks. A review of *Bus Stop* in *The New York Times,* March 3, 1955.

Chapman, John. A review of *Bus Stop* in *Daily News,* March 3, 1955.

Coleman, Robert. A review of *Bus Stop* in *Daily Mirror,* March 3, 1955.

Courant, Jane. ''Social and Cultural Prophecy in the Works of William Inge.'' *Studies in American Drama, 1945-Present,* Vol. 6, No. 2, 1991, pp. 135-51.

Erben, Rudolf. ''The Western Holdup Play: The Pilgrimage Continues.'' *Western American Literature,* Vol. 23, No. 4, February, 1989, pp. 311-22.

Kerr, Walter F. A review of *Bus Stop* in *New York Herald Tribune,* March 3, 1955.

McClain, John. A review of *Bus Stop* in *New York Journal American,* March 3, 1955.

Shuman, R. Baird. *William Inge,* Twayne Publishers, 1996.

Watts Jr., Richard. A review of *Bus Stop* in *New York Post,* March 3, 1955.

Weales, Gerald. ''The New Pineros.'' *American Drama Since World War II,* Harcourt Brace Jovanovich, 1962, pp. 40-56.

FURTHER READING

Leeson, Richard M. *William Inge: A Research and Production Sourcebook,* Greenwood Press, 1994.
A critical overview of Inge's plays with information about reviews and critical studies.

McClure, Arthur F. *Memories of Splendor: The Midwestern World of William Inge,* Kansas State Historical Society, 1989.
Contains production information and photographs of Inge and his work.

Shuman, R. Baird. *William Inge,* Twayne Publishers, 1996.
This book is primarily a biography of Inge's work. It also contains a detailed discussion of each of his works.

Voss, Ralph F. *A Life of William Inge: The Strains of Triumph.* University of Kansas Press, 1989.
A critical biography of Inge's life and work.

Wager, Walter. ''William Inge.'' *The Playwrights Speak.* Delacorte Press, 1967.
Wagner presents interviews with several contemporary playwrights. This book presents an opportunity to ''hear'' each writer express his or her thoughts about the art of writing.

The House of Blue Leaves

John Guare's *The House of Blue Leaves* is his most popular and arguably most important play. It is based on the Pope's visit to New York City on October 4, 1965.

Since the debut of *The House of Blue Leaves* Off-Broadway on February 10, 1971, however, critics have been divided over the play's artistic merits. The story focuses on one man's desire for success as a big-time songwriter, which clashes with his demanding, middle-class family life. Some reviewers did not know what to make of the play's mix of black comedy, farce, realistic drama, and social commentary. They maintained that its comedic elements undermined the serious issues of the play.

The critics that praised *The House of Blue Leaves* appreciated Guare's treatment of ideas. They also lauded the manner in which he depicted the dark underside of the American dream, especially his emphasis on the destructive nature of the media on people's dreams and personal lives. Several critics noted the skillful manner in which Guare portrayed the quest for personal success as defined by a shallow value system.

Despite the controversy, the play ran for 337 performances and garnered several prestigious awards for Guare, including the Obie and New York Drama Critics Circle Award for Best American Play. Revived on Broadway in 1986, it won more awards for him, including a Tony. Although critics

JOHN GUARE

1971

were still divided over the value of *The House of Blue Leaves* during the revival, most appreciated the power and insight of Guare's message.

AUTHOR BIOGRAPHY

John Guare was born in New York City, on February 5, 1938. He was the only child of Edward and Helen Claire Guare. Raised in a strict Catholic household, Guare attended mass daily with his mother. His father, Edward, worked in the Wall Street stock exchange as a clerk.

Guare was a voracious reader. He also went to the theater quite often and was fascinated by Broadway musicals. His mother's brother, Billy Grady, was a casting director at MGM studios. In the mid-1940s, Grady was casting a new version of *Huckleberry Finn*. Guare put on a show for him similar to the one described in *The House of Blue Leaves*.

Guare began writing plays at age eleven. After graduating from St. John's Preparatory School in Brooklyn, Guare earned his B.A. from Georgetown in 1960, then his M.F.A. in drama from Yale in 1963. His first play was produced in 1962.

After graduation, Guare served in the Air Force Reserves to avoid the military draft and spent the next several years in Europe. While living abroad, he managed to have a one-act play, *To Wally Pantoni, We Leave a Credenza* (1964), produced in New York City.

In 1965, Guare got the idea for *The House of Blue Leaves* while still in Europe. After a successful staged reading in New York City in 1966, he had numerous offers for production but could not produce a solid second act.

While Guare continued to work on the play, he churned out several successful one-acts, including *Muzeeka* (1967), which won him his first Obie Award. On the basis of these short plays, he was recognized as one of America's best young playwrights.

Yet Guare had a lot of trouble finishing *The House of Blue Leaves*. He returned to Europe for a short time, where he finally wrote a solid draft. When the play was produced Off-Broadway in 1971, it proved to be his first big success and his first successful full-length play.

The House of Blue Leaves garnered numerous awards; yet it also produced much critical controversy over his use of black comedy, farce, and social realism. It is regarded by many critics to be his best play.

After *House of Blue Leaves,* Guare continued to explore the danger of fame while living up to his billing as a great American playwright. In *Marco Polo Sings a Solo* (1973), for example, the main character, an astronaut, tries to live up to the reputation the media has created for him.

Not all Guare's plays were successful, nor did every critic like his dramatic style. His 1979 melodrama, *Bosoms and Neglect,* lasted for only four performances. In the 1980s, after writing the Academy Award-nominated screenplay for *Atlantic City,* Guare wrote a trilogy of Civil War-centered melodramas, which were relatively unsuccessful.

After a successful revival of *The House of Blue Leaves* on Broadway in 1986, Guare produced another of his most successful plays, *Six Degrees of Separation* (1990). He also wrote the screenplay for the film version several years later. He continues to write both for the theater and film.

PLOT SUMMARY

Prologue
The House of Blue Leaves opens on the stage of the El Dorado Bar & Grill. Artie Shaughnessy sits at the piano and sings some of his songs. He is frustrated when he cannot get the house lights turned down and a spotlight to shine on him. His anger grows when the audience does not listen to his singing. He continues, but at the end of the show, when there is no applause, he quickly exits.

Act I
Act I opens late at night in Artie's shabby apartment in Sunnyside, Queens. As Artie sleeps in a sleeping bag on the couch, his seventeen-year-old son Ronnie breaks into the apartment. When the doorbell rings soon after, the fatigue-clad Ronnie runs into his room without being seen.

Artie gets up and answers the door. It is Bunny Flingus, Artie's plump girlfriend. She is extremely excited about seeing the Pope as he passes through

Queens, but Artie does not share her enthusiasm. Bunny figures out that Artie performed during amateur night at the El Dorado and is both angry and supportive. During the exchange, Bananas Shaughnessy, Artie's wife, comes out of her bedroom and watches them for a moment, unseen, before returning to her room.

Artie begs Bunny to cook for him, but she wants him to get dressed so they can watch the Pope. Bananas calls Artie from her room; when she makes an appearance, Bunny hides in the kitchen. Obviously mentally unbalanced, Bananas gets hysterical asking Artie if he hates her and if he will leave her. Artie forces pills down her throat and tells Bananas that he is going to see the Pope. Bananas tells him that she cannot go see the Pope because her fingernails are different lengths.

Though Artie tries to stop her, Bananas goes into the kitchen. She begins to act like an animal. When Bananas finally sees Bunny, she addresses her politely, then scares her. Bunny tells the audience that she wishes Bananas was dead.

Despite Artie's protests, Bunny tells Bananas that Artie is leaving her. She urges Bananas to go to Mexico for a divorce. Artie tells Bananas that he found a hospital for her. Bunny tells Bananas that they are going to California to revive Artie's career as a songwriter using Artie's friend Billy, a famous director.

Bunny demands that Artie call Billy. Artie does so, telling Billy about the situation. When the conversation is over, Bunny is extremely pleased. She leaves. Artie decides to take a shower, and tells Bananas that he is tired of taking care of her.

Bananas recalls the point she started losing touch with reality. This touches Artie, and he asks her to come and see the Pope because a miracle might happen. They watch the Pope on television for a few moments. Artie hugs the television, and Bananas goes back to her room.

Bunny returns, announcing that the Pope has arrived. She goes into the kitchen when Bananas comes out, dressed in mismatched clothes and shoes. Bunny sees them together and becomes angry. They all leave to see the Pope. After they are gone, Ronnie comes out of his room holding a large, gift-wrapped box.

Act II, Scene 1

Ronnie proceeds to build a bomb. As he puts on the clothes of an altar boy, Ronnie describes the first

John Guare

time that he met Billy. Ronnie was so eager to play the part of Huckleberry Finn that he acted like an idiot in front of Billy, and Billy thought he was retarded. Ronnie believes that everyone is laughing at him. His monologue ends when Artie's key is heard in the door. Ronnie retreats to his room with the bomb.

As soon as Artie enters, Corrinna Stroller appears at the door. She is Billy's girlfriend and a former actress. Artie is surprised by her appearance, and when he leaves her for a moment, Corrinna reveals that she is partially deaf and needs hearing aids.

Bunny enters and fawns over Corrinna, telling her about Artie's career. Artie sings a tune. Three nuns appear at the window; it turns out they accidentally got locked onto the roof trying to see the Pope. Despite Bunny's protests, Artie lets the nuns in.

Artie introduces Corrinna and Bananas, and Bunny tries to make Bananas look bad in front of everyone. Bananas confirms the negative impression when she tries to cook brillo pads as hamburgers and burns herself.

Artie begins to sing for Corrinna. Bananas asks him to sing an old song, which he does, and then points out that the song is the same as "White

Christmas.'' Humiliated, he makes Bananas take pills, which turn out to be the transistors for Corrinna's hearing aids. He also calls the mental institution and asks that they take Bananas away.

Finally, Ronnie makes an appearance. He tells his father that he is going to blow up the Pope with his bomb. No one, including Artie, listens to him. Corrinna informs Artie that she is moving to Australia with Billy. She almost leaves before she realizes that she has two tickets for the Pope's mass at Yankee stadium.

The nuns take the tickets. An M.P. makes an appearance, looking to arrest Ronnie for leaving the army without permission. Before Corrinna can leave, Ronnie hands her the gift-wrapped package. A few seconds later, the package explodes and Corrinna and two of the three nuns die.

Act II, Scene 2

Later that day, Artie and Billy watch the Pope's mass on television in the apartment. Billy has come to identify Corrinna's body; he is very upset and sobs over Corrinna and her lost career. Artie tries to comfort him while promoting his own career.

Bananas enters, dressed in an old gown. It is revealed that Billy gave Bananas her nickname. The surviving nun rushes in, upset because she cannot turn off the hot water. Bananas tells Artie that she wants to burn Bunny, who lives downstairs, so that Artie won't like her as much. Bananas appeals to Billy for help. The nun introduces herself to Billy, telling him her friends died in the explosion. This touches Billy, who makes a call to get Ronnie out of jail.

While Billy is on the phone, Bunny returns. He has taken care of Ronnie's situation, but it is revealed that he does not know who blew up Corrinna and the two nuns.

Billy realizes that he has two tickets for Australia and invites Bunny to come with him; she excitedly agrees. The nun tells them how she does not want to return to the convent. Billy gives her money to move into Bunny's apartment and help care for Bananas.

As Billy and Bunny leave, Artie makes one last effort to try his songs to his friend. Billy tells him that his life is with Bananas, not in show business. After they leave, Bananas acts like a dog. Artie chokes her to death.

CHARACTERS

Billy Einhorn

Billy is Artie's childhood best friend. He has also known Bananas for many years and had given her that nickname. Billy is now a famous Hollywood movie director, and he is involved in a romantic relationship with Corrinna. At Bunny's urging, Artie gets Billy to help him revive his career as a movie songwriter, but that fails. When Corrinna dies, Billy convinces Bunny to go to Australia, leaving Artie alone with Bananas.

Bunny Flingus

Bunny is Artie's girlfriend and downstairs neighbor. Thirty-nine years old, she is an amazing cook and supportive of Artie's musical ambitions. Once Bananas is out of the way, she plans on marrying Artie and moving to California with him. She tries to control Artie's life and takes every opportunity to express her jealousy of Bananas. Yet at the first chance she gets—Billy's offer to move to Australia—she dumps Artie for a new, more exciting life.

Little Nun

The Little Nun is one of three nuns who get trapped on the roof of Artie's apartment building after the Pope drives by. She has not yet taken her final vows as a nun and is not enthusiastic about her chosen profession. After two nuns die in the explosion, the Little Nun decides not to return to the convent. Eventually she is hired by Billy to live in Bunny's apartment and take care of Bananas.

Artie Shaughnessy

Artie Shaughnessy is the protagonist of *The House of Blue Leaves.* Frustrated on a number of levels, Artie's life is at a turning point. His marriage to Bananas is empty; because of her mental illness, he feels little more than her caretaker. He has a girlfriend, Bunny, who is selfish and controlling.

He works in a New York zoo taking care of animals, but he is really a frustrated songwriter and singer. He wants to make it big but has done nothing to advance his career. Artie is also concerned about his son, Ronnie, who is in the Army. Like Bananas, Ronnie suffers from severe mental illness and has violent, paranoid fantasies. By the end of the play, Artie feels so helpless and trapped that he kills Bananas.

Bananas Shaughnessy

Bananas is Artie's wife; she has been suffering from mental illness for a long time. In fact, she has not left her apartment for several months. She fears going to a mental hospital and the treatment she would receive. Although ill, she provides lucid and insightful comments at certain moments of the action. Artie kills her at the end of the play.

Ronnie Shaughnessy

Ronnie is the teenage son of Bananas and Artie. He is in the army but has gone absent without leave to return home. His parents are unaware of his presence in the apartment for most of the play.

Suffering from severe mental problems, Ronnie builds a bomb to blow up the Pope. He almost has the opportunity to see the Pope at Yankee Stadium but instead uses his bomb to blow up two nuns and Corrinna Stroller. Ronnie is arrested, but Billy gets him released. Instead of jail, Ronnie will serve two weeks in the brig, then be stationed in Italy.

Corrinna Stroller

Corrinna is a famous actress and the girlfriend of Billy. Partially deaf from an accident that happened on the set of a movie, she has not worked since then. She is a very kind person.

THEMES

Betrayal

Nearly every character in *The House of Blue Leaves* is betrayed by another—or by his or her own desires. Artie suffers from the most severe betrayals. His girlfriend, Bunny Flingus, spends most of the play encouraging, if not pushing, his career. She convinces Artie that Billy Einhorn is the key to his success. At the end of the play, Billy offers Bunny his extra ticket to Australia, and Bunny goes with him. She betrays Artie to ensure that she has a secure future.

Artie is also betrayed by his own dreams for success. These dreams are not based on reality, but on Bunny's ideas, which have been propagated by the mass media.

Artie betrays his wife, Bananas. She suffers from some sort of mental illness, and Artie is her primary caretaker. He has betrayed her by becoming involved with Bunny. Indeed, Bunny and Artie

MEDIA ADAPTATIONS

- *The House of Blue Leaves* was filmed for television in 1987 and appeared on PBS. Directed by Kirk Browning and Jerry Zaks, this version features John Mahoney as Artie, Swoozie Kurtz as Bananas, Christine Baranski as Bunny, and Ben Stiller as Ronnie.

---

intend to marry and move to California, leaving Bananas behind.

Yet Artie's biggest betrayal of Bananas comes at the end of the play. After Bunny has abandoned Artie and his dreams are shattered, Bananas begins to act like a dog again and he strangles her to death. Entrusted to take care of her, he instead kills her. He gains only a false, probably short-lived sense of freedom by committing this act.

Success and Failure: Fame

The House of Blue Leaves features characters who define their success or failure based on the idea of fame. For example, Artie is unhappy with his life because he believes that he should be a famous songwriter. However, he is not particularly gifted. When his chance for success is gone, and his opportunities are limited, he strikes out and kills the focus of his rage, his wife.

Artie's definition of success is defined by Bunny, his girlfriend. She garners these values from movie magazines and television. Her obsession with seeing the Pope has little to do with his religious standing, but that he is a celebrity she can see in person.

The three nuns who appear in Act II share these values. They turn seeing the Pope into an event similar to the experiences of the Beatles in their first trip to the United States.

Bunny's definition of success is also for her own benefit. She wants Artie to be a successful songwriter so that she can have a better life in

TOPICS FOR FURTHER STUDY

- Read August Strindberg's *The Dance of Death* (1901) and Georges Feydeau's *A Flea in Her Ear* (1907)—two plays that inspired Guare while writing *The House of Blue Leaves.* How do these plays and their themes relate to *The House of Blue Leaves*?

- Research absurdist theater, including plays like Eugene Ionesco's *The Chairs.* What aspects of *The House of Blue Leaves* are absurdist? What do these elements add to the play and its meaning?

- How were mentally ill people such as Bananas Shaughnessy treated in the mid-1960s? Is the portrayal of her care at home accurate?

- Research the events of October 4, 1965, the date that the play is set. Include information on the Pope's visit to New York City. What do these events say about society?

California. When Artie's friend, the famous director Billy Einhorn, finally makes an appearance, Bunny realizes that Artie will not get his break.

Realizing that Artie will always be a failure, Bunny latches on to the already successful—and famous—Billy and leaves with him. Ironically, unlike Artie, Bunny is basically successful. She reaches her goal of being involved with someone who is famous and rich but only by betraying her boyfriend.

Violence and Cruelty

There are several violent and cruel acts in *The House of Blue Leaves.* This violence emphasizes the superficial values the characters possess, and how these values negatively affect their actions.

For example, Bunny speaks and acts cruelly to Bananas because she is jealous and controlling. She also believes hurting Bananas will force Artie to become a success. For Bunny, cruelty is an acceptable way to achieve her goal.

Other characters commit violent acts. Ronnie, the disturbed son of Bananas and Artie, is hiding out at home. He has left the army and is building a bomb to blow up the Pope. He believes that everyone thinks he is a nothing. To make himself something—in his sick mind—he will assassinate the Pope.

Ronnie tries to tell his father of his intentions, but Artie does not listen. Ronnie's plans are interrupted when the military police come to arrest him. Instead of the Pope, Ronnie hands the bomb to Corrinna Stroller, a famous actress and Billy's girlfriend. She dies in the explosion, though, ironically, no one seems to know whose bomb it was. The violent quest for fame is not always successful.

STYLE

Setting

The House of the Blues Leaves is a dramatic farce set on October 4, 1965, in New York City. The play opens on the stage of the El Dorado Bar & Grill, a little bar in Queens where Artie plays his songs to an unappreciative audience. The rest of the play takes place in Artie's shabby apartment in Sunnyside, Queens. Like the bar, one of the apartment's focal points is a piano. The apartment is cramped and messy; also, it seems transitory, as if the family has not unpacked for many years.

The fact that most of the action takes place in Artie's apartment underscores the claustrophobic nature of his life. Artie is stuck caring for Bananas and working at the zoo.

Parabasis

Parabasis is defined as characters directly addressing the audience. Nearly every major character in *The House of Blue Leaves* talks to the audience. This makes the audience part of the story; the audience is a participant rather than an observer.

In Act I, Bunny welcomes the audience to her home, though it is really Artie and Banana's home. Artie explains to the audience that he wishes they had more spoons when it comes time to eat. This would allow everyone to share in the meal.

Characters also share their secrets with the audience. Bunny confesses her desire for Banana's death, while Corrinna discusses her deafness. Even minor characters, like Ronnie and the Little Nun,

A scene from a production staged at the Bayliss Theatre in 1988; Bunny (Helen Lederer), Bananas (Nichola McAuliffe), and Artie (Denis Quilley)

recite extended monologues that provide insight into their characters and actions. The use of parabasis also emphasizes how the characters in the play are similar to their audience and, perhaps, share the same fantasy-based values.

Irony

There are many ironic situations in *The House of Blue Leaves*. For example, Artie wants success, partly to keep Bunny happy; Bunny wants him to be successful because that's the only way she figures she will be important in life. Yet Artie fails, and Bunny succeeds by becoming involved with Billy Einhorn, a famous Hollywood director.

Similarly, Bananas is supposed to be crazy and pumped full of medication, yet she often has profound insight into events at hand. Corrinna is deaf because of an explosion/accident on the set of a war movie, and she dies in an explosion from the bomb that Ronnie gave to her. Guare uses irony to underscore the play's themes and add to its black humor.

Animal Imagery/Symbolism

Throughout *The House of Blue Leaves*, numerous references to and imitations of animals appear.

Animals represent purity—the opposite of the superficial values many of the characters possess.

For example, Bananas often acts like an animal. While this may seem crazy, it also symbolizes her virtuous and honest nature in the face of Bunny and Artie's shallow values. Even Billy Einhorn perceives this when he tells Artie that he should be happy with what he has.

Artie is employed at the zoo and apparently has a way with animals. It seems that his life is filled with animals, and he desperately wants to escape them. He tries to do this by strangling Bananas, but this act will probably lead to a prison cell—a cage for humans.

HISTORICAL CONTEXT

The 1970s were a tumultuous time in American history. One major reason for this was the troubled American economy. A worldwide monetary crisis contributed to the devaluation of the American dollar. Economic resources were drained by the war

COMPARE
&
CONTRAST

- 1965: The United States increases its presence in Vietnam; in addition, bombing of North Vietnam intensifies. By the end of the year, there are 180,000 American troops in Vietnam, and antiwar protest begins in the United States.

  1971: The United States begins withdrawing troops from Vietnam. There is widespread antiwar protest. By the end of the year, there are only 140,000 American troops left in Vietnam.

  Today: For the United States, the experience in Vietnam is considered a traumatic event in recent history and serves as a measuring stick for involvement in world conflicts.

- 1965: There are five million color television sets in the United States, but only three networks.

  1971: Television is the dominant cultural force in the United States. There are four networks, including public television, and programming is targeted to specific audiences, like children.

  Today: With the explosion of cable and satellite television, the major television networks face stiff competition from cable networks. Program-

ming is targeted to specific audiences—such as the Golf Channel and the Food Network—and there are several channels dedicated to celebrity worship.

- 1965: Unemployment in the United States is 4.2% and inflation is under control.

  1971: The unemployment and inflation rates rise. The cost of living index increases 15% over the previous year.

  Today: With a booming economy, unemployment and inflation are extremely low.

- 1965: President Lyndon B. Johnson pushes much of his Great Society (anti-poverty) legislation through Congress.

  1971: President Richard M. Nixon dismantles many aspects of the Great Society as the American economy falters.

  Today: Although the American economy is strong, there is resistance to increased social spending. There is a movement to move people off welfare and end dependence on social spending.

---

in Vietnam, as well as the Cold War arms race. An inordinate amount of money was spent by the government to pay for Vietnam, and the national debt ran in the hundreds of billions of dollars.

The American economy suffered from stagflation—rapid inflation and faltering businesses. Between 1970 and 1971, the cost of living increased 15%. In 1971, President Richard M. Nixon took several steps to improve the economy. He ordered a wage, price, and rent freeze for ninety days. Later that year, he signed a bill that ordered a $90 million tax cut. American currency was also taken off the gold standard.

These efforts were not completely successful, in part because of the demands of the Vietnam War. As a result, Nixon curbed American involvement in

Vietnam in 1971. U.S. troops were gradually withdrawn, and by the end of the year, only 140,000 U.S. troops remained in Vietnam.

Because of the failing economy, many social programs of the 1960s, remnants of former President Lyndon B. Johnson's "Great Society," were dismantled. Some taxpayers felt these programs were draining the economy. Yet with the deterioration of the economy and the elimination of many of these programs, there came an increasing difference between rich and poor. Moreover, there was an increase in unemployment and more people on welfare.

The reaction to these challenges varied: some people became politically apathetic; others demanded full protection under the law. Consumer activist

Ralph Nader and his Center for the Study of Responsive Law collected public funds in 1971 to challenge the food industry as well as automakers and the aviation industry. Consumer complaints and concerns were addressed by the federal, local, and state governments. Even the television industry had to adjust to new regulatory demands. Parents demanded better television programming for children.

As far as entertainment, television was the most popular form in the early 1970s, especially situation comedies and detective shows. Yet television brought the Vietnam War into living rooms, so that Americans could see footage of the military action. As a result, more people joined the antiwar movement.

There were few new ideas in mainstream film, theater, and art; instead, the real artistic power in the early 1970s was in underground theater and film. Avant-garde art thrived and led to experimentation with other genres, such as film, theater, and television.

The early 1970s did see the emergence of several successful female singer-songwriters, such as Carol King and Carly Simon. There were many changes for women in American society in general. In 1971 a group of women successfully sued *Time* magazine for sexual discrimination. Similarly, the Civil Service Commission banned gender-based job designations. The women's liberation movement and feminism became powerful, though controversial, forces in society.

CRITICAL OVERVIEW

Since its first production in 1971, *The House of Blue Leaves* has been a controversial work. This controversy stems from that fact that Guare blends several, seemingly contradictory elements: black comedy and farce with drama.

For example, Henry Hewes in the *Saturday Review of Literature* maintained "John Guare's Off-Broadway hit *The House of Blue Leaves* . . . outrageously yet responsibly depicts the doomed career of Artie Shaughnessy. . . ." Later in the same review, Hewes contended, "Guare's comic facility is inextricable from an utter and moving emotional sincerity."

Hewes is representative of critics who perceive *The House of Blue Leaves* as a unique balance of

these elements. Indeed, he concluded his review by asserting that "its delights are so great and its vision so essentially true that I find myself valuing it more highly than any new play this season."

Others critics appreciated the balance that Guare attempts to maintain but contended that he fails in one or more elements. Harold Clurman in *The Nation* asserted, "John Guare's most striking talent is for savage farce. . . . Still, the play remains unfulfilled. . . ." Clurman continued: "[S]omething disturbs it. That 'something' . . . causes Guare to inject elements of cruel sorrow into the proceedings. There is nothing at all mirthful about the madness of Artie's wife nor in the play's final moments when he strangles her."

Clive Barnes of *The New York Times* explained: "His play would have been better—and perhaps even funnier—had it been about something lending itself to more formulation than despair. There is a predictability and, at the same time, shapelessness of plot that is, in the ultimate count, unworthy of the macabre zaniness of the writing."

Edith Oliver identified the problem for many of the critics. She contended, "Actually, this play could be considered a whole series of shock treatments, and often I was as horrified at myself for laughing (which I did a lot) as I was at what I saw and heard on the stage."

Other contemporary critics found no merit to Guare's work. Julius Novick of *The New York Times* maintained, "Some of Mr. Guare's comic conceits are in themselves somewhat lame, but the essential problem is that the farce and the agony seem to violate each other instead of reinforcing each other." Novick concluded, "The author's attitude towards the human misery he has created often seems trivial and exploitative: let's go to Bedlam and laugh at all the funny lunatics."

The controversy raged once again when a revival of the *The House of Blue Leaves* opened on Broadway fifteen years later. William A. Henry III is typical when he contended, "Guare's satire may seem a bit less fresh and daring than it did 15 years ago, if only because it has spawned so many imitators, but in the joyous and all but flawless revival at the Lincoln Center, his jokes break up audiences as dizzyingly as ever. So do the wrenching emotional scenes of a boldly tragicomic plot."

Michael Malone of *The Nation* concurred. He claimed, "*Blue Leaves* is dark and full of diamonds. . . . It's a marvelous, maniacal tragicomedy, full of waggish merriment, razor sharp in its mordant wit but never cutting out the hearts of its characters, or turning away from their keen aches.''

Other critics, such as Leo Sauvage of *The New Leader* and Robert Brustein of *The New Republic*, were not as amused by the situations or the set-up. Brustein asserted, ''*The House of Blue Leaves* is black comedy sense through rose-colored glasses. It ends with a shock. . . . But it's tough to accept a tragic climax after having been encouraged all night to regard murder, madness, physical affliction, adultery, and assassination as occasions for gags.'' Brustein compared the plot of the play to a television sitcom, an ironic touch considering the role television plays in *The House of Blue Leaves*.

CRITICISM

A. Petrusso

Petrusso is a freelance writer and screenwriter. In this essay, she discusses the spectrum of women's morality in The House of Blue Leaves, *and how this relates to the play's larger purpose.*

Much of the critical attention paid to John Guare's *The House of Blue Leaves* focuses on the character of Artie Shaughnessy. Artie desperately wants to escape his life in Queens and longs for fame. Unfortunately, he is unrealistic about his life and his chances for success.

Although many critics note that Bunny Flingus, his mistress, pushes Artie to revive his career and that Bananas Shaughnessy, his wife, impedes Artie's efforts, the spectrum of female characters is rarely analyzed on its own. Each of the female characters, two major (Bunny and Bananas) and two minor (Corrinna Stroller and the Little Nun), works to a specific end.

Bunny and Bananas are opposite ends of the spectrum. Bunny's life is defined by media-driven fantasy. Bananas is most in touch with reality, though she is suffering with mentally illness. Corrinna and the Little Nun fit in between them. Corrinna is the movie star; the Little Nun is oppressed by the reality of her chosen profession and is only freed from it because of the death of her two nun companions. This essay explores each female character and

determines their role in the moral tug-of-war of the play.

One of the biggest ironies in *The House of Blue Leaves* is the fact that Bananas Shaughnessy seems crazy, yet speaks profound, sometimes moral insights into play's events. Her words may seem like ravings, but they are discerning and often insightful.

For example, Bananas knows that her husband is having an affair. She silently observes Bunny and Artie together in the beginning of Act I for a few moments. When she announces her presence, she knows that Artie is tired of dealing with her. She yells things like ''You hate my looks—my face—my clothes—you hate me,'' then a few seconds later she states, ''I know you love me.'' While this may sound contradictory, it is also true. Artie does both hate her and love her. He wants to be free, yet he worries about her well-being.

Bananas tries to bring her husband back to reality in unusual ways. She acts like a dog a couple of times, but as she points out, ''I like being animals. You know why? I never heard of a famous animal. Oh, a couple of Lassies—an occasional Trigger—but, by and large, animals weren't meant to be famous.'' She explains this to her husband because she wants him to stay with her and retain his job as a zookeeper.

Bananas does not like fame, essentially because after one encounter with celebrity in Manhattan, she became the butt of a joke broadcast on national television. She knows the reality of fame; in particular, the humiliation and hurt it can bring.

Bananas also has a sharp ear, which she uses to discourage her husband. When Artie ''auditions'' for Corrinna, Bananas requests one of his old songs, ''I Love You So I Keep Dreaming.'' After a few lines, she demands that he play ''White Christmas.'' She points out, and the stage directions confirm, that they are the same song.

This embarrasses Artie but demonstrates that Bananas has some fight left in her. She wants to hold on to her husband, and while this action ends up angering him, it is one of the only ways she can accomplish her goal. This action drives him to explore ways of finally getting rid of her so he can pursue his career and his mistress.

In the next scene, Bananas tries to burn Bunny by letting hot water seep into Bunny's downstairs apartment. Although this particular action fails, Bananas ultimately gets her way. When Bunny

WHAT DO I READ NEXT?

- Guare's play, *Marco Polo Sings a Solo,* was first performed in 1973. The play, like *The House of Blue Leaves*, also deals with aspects of fame. The main character, a well-known astronaut, wants to be the hero the media has made him out to be.

- *Waiting for Godot,* an absurdist play by Samuel Beckett, was written in 1954. The play focuses on two men waiting for a friend and discussing the meaning of life.

- *How to be a Mogul: For Those Who Know the Best Things in Life are Things* is a nonfiction book published by Diane Hartford in 1986. Hartford shares antidotes about successful people.

- A black comedy that chronicles a tragic family situation, *And Miss Reardon Drinks a Little,* is a play by Paul Zindels. It was first performed in 1971.

---

decides to live with Billy in Australia, Bananas lets her take the copper pot she admires. She knows she has won. Yet Artie cannot take this defeat and eventually kills Bananas at the end of the play.

Bunny is the opposite of Bananas. Bunny is focused on one thing: attaching herself to someone famous and successful. Bunny tells Artie at one point, "Billy will get your songs in movies. It's not too late to start. With me behind you!"

All of Bunny's values are formed by television and magazines. For example, Bunny views the Pope's visit as not a religious or cultural event, but as pure entertainment, like the opening of a movie or a play. At one point she excitedly exclaims, "I haven't seen so many people, Artie, so excited since the premiere of *Cleopatra*. It's that big." The fact that Artie might get his sheet music blessed or that Bunny could read the passing as kind of a blessing on her relationship with Artie is only secondary.

Bunny uses the same faulty logic in her treatment of Bananas, her rival. As soon as Bananas makes an appearance, Bunny begins to taunt her. She tries to convince Bananas to go to Mexico for a quickie divorce, but Artie points out that Bananas can barely leave the house.

Bunny also accuses Bananas of faking her illness, based on what she has learned from films. She tells Bananas, "I know these sick wives. I've seen a dozen like you in the movies. . . . You live in wheelchairs just to hold your husband and the

minute your husband's out of the room, you're hopped out of your wheel chair doing the Charleston and making a general spectacle of yourself."

A short time later, Bunny compares Bananas's fear of shock treatments to something she read in a movie magazine about an actress's desperate need for curlers. Bunny makes such belittling comments throughout the play to humiliate Bananas in front of Artie.

Bunny tries to control Artie. She gets angry when she learns that he performed the night before at the El Dorado amateur night. Later, she is dismissive of his job at the zoo, accusing him of being "afraid" of success until she came along.

But Bunny's attempts to control the situation ultimately fail. She ignores the fact that Artie still has some feelings for his wife, and that Bananas is a bit more intelligent than she thinks. Bunny only sees her goal—being kept by a successful man—and does not perceive the complete situation.

Bunny ends up getting what she wants in an unexpected way. The Hollywood director, Billy Einhorn, steals her away with promise of two years in Australia and a glamorous lifestyle. Her departure leaves Artie humiliated and without emotional support and ultimately leads to him murdering his wife.

While Bunny inhabits one end of the moral spectrum, and Bananas the other, Corrinna Stroller

> "AT THE PLAY'S CORE, GUARE IS REALLY EXPLORING HOW HUMANS DISREGARD EACH OTHER AND THEIR FEELINGS AND HOW ISOLATED HUMANS ARE FROM EACH OTHER"

and the Little Nun exist in the middle. They are more balanced people, but each represent different things.

Corrinna represents what happens when dreams come true; she is a successful actress and Billy's girlfriend. In the one movie she has appeared in, *Warmonger,* she lost her hearing because of an accident on the set. A sweet, polite woman, she seems to have handled success and tragedy very well. Unfortunately, Corrinna ends up having her hearing aid transistors disappear and dying in an explosion.

The Little Nun represents reality; a confused, unhappy young woman, she is one of three nuns that get stuck on the roof trying to get a good view of the Pope. She suffers at the hands of her sisters, because they treat her like a child. When she sees peanut butter, a food they are not allowed to have in the convent, she becomes excited. While she wants the peanut butter, the other nuns express their excitement over beer and color television.

Like Bunny, the Little Nun is influenced by the media. She claims to have watched the movie *The Sound of Music* thirty-one times and attributes much of her religious calling to that cinematic representation of the sisterhood.

After she manages to secure the tickets to the Pope's mass in Yankee Stadium, she is told to return home by her companions. This action actually saves the Little Nun's life, as the other two nuns die in the explosion. She realizes that her life as a nun is unsatisfying. Billy hires her to take care of Bananas and live in Bunny's old apartment.

Guare has maintained that the main theme of *The House of Blue Leaves* is humiliation. As this essay has shown, each of the female characters in the play are humiliated in one way or another, and,

in the case of Bunny and Bananas, humiliate others. The moral spectrum that they represent is broad and divergent, but it determines the extent of their humiliation and ability to humiliate. Guare's focus on the quest for fame is just a means to an end.

At the play's core, Guare is really exploring how humans disregard each other and their feelings and how isolated humans are from each other. Artie's humiliations are related to his individual relationships with these women, from the crazy Bananas to the nun who will take Bunny's apartment and care for his wife. These humiliations drive him to murder his wife and open up the possibility for a whole new set of humiliations in prison.

Source: A. Petrusso, in an essay for *Drama for Students,* Gale, 2000.

Michael Malone

Malone reviews a 1986 production of Guare's play, finding that the play's irreverence and subversion are more readily accepted by today's mainstream theatregoers than when House of Blue Leaves *debuted in 1971.*

There is standing room only at *The House of Blue Leaves* these days. John Guare's black comedy about a Queen's songwriting zookeeper, his pathetically disturbed wife and preposterously complacent mistress is now enjoying a well-deserved successful revival in a brilliantly staged production at New York City's Vivian Beaumont Theater, which has itself been recently revived from darkness. *Blue Leaves* is the discovery of the season, the new hot ticket, although the play is neither new nor previously neglected. Sixteen years ago, *Blue Leaves* won the New York and Los Angeles Drama Critics Circle awards; since then, college, community and stock theaters have frequently performed it. But this year it has received eight Tony nominations, including one for the best play of 1986. To be eligible, a play need only have never been previously produced ''on Broadway,'' which means of course that, with any luck, one of these days Aristophanes or Beaumont and Fletcher could grab the gold statue.

This ruling puts *Blue Leaves* in competition with Michael Frayn's *Benefactors* (already recipient of the New York Drama Critics Circle Award for Best Foreign Play), and with Athol Fugard's *Bloodknot* (a revival, now closed), but not with Joe Orton's *Loot* or O'Neill's *The Iceman Cometh,* both of which are nominated for less prestigious Tony's as Best Reproductions. That *Blue Leaves* is no less a revival than these three, and no more on Broadway than Sam Shepard's *A Lie of the Mind* (recipient of the Drama Critics Circle Award for Best Play, but excluded from Tony consideration) has caused some flapdoodle among theater critics, whose dismay at the illogic of the Tony committee reveals a touching idealism that borders on the prelapsarian. Why should they expect prizes in the arts to be any more reasonable than prizes on *Let's Make a Deal?* Why, with theater attendance and box-office income so low, with only thirty-three openings this season (the lowest in Broadway history), should we do anything but rejoice at every good play, newborn or resurrected, that succeeds in getting itself soundly "clapper-clawed by the vulgar"?

In a way, *Blue Leaves* is about prizes, about yearning for them. Its characters are all dreamers; they dream of fame and of the famous. They want what the famous have: laurel and loot, stardust and a place in the sun. This unending American dream (American tragedy)—that we all could have been, should have been, contenders for the only spot there is, the number-one spot—brings Artie Shaughnessy to the El Dorado Bar Amateur Night as the play opens, to sing his heart out ("I wrote all these songs. Words and the music") in hopes of a blue spotlight. In the clichés of his lyrics we hear that dream. "I'm looking for Something." "I'm here with bells on. Ring! Ring! Ring!"

Then, on the Beaumont stage, behind the Shaughnessys' humdrum Queens apartment crammed with its tawdry gewgaws and totems of fame, in rhythm with the blare of Strauss's "Thus Spake Zarathustra" (better known perhaps as the soundtrack from *2001,* or as Elvis Presley's concert theme song), the glittering lights of Manhattan's skyline appear. The audience laughs; no doubt we're supposed to. But those bright towers of big-time success are as near and as far from Artie Shaughnessy in Queens as they were from Willy Loman in Brooklyn. As Guare has written about this play and its genesis in his Catholic boyhood in Queens, "How do you run away to your dreams when you're already there?" He holds his characters' failed aspirations and their absurd worship of celebrity up to a lampooning, madcap mockery that some have called cruel, but his contempt is reserved for the culture, not the creatures who have fed on its junk food of TV and tabloids. Indeed, the sadness of *Blue Leaves* centers, by Guare's account, on the cruelty of our national dream of success: "Everyone in the play is constantly being humiliated by their dreams, their lives, their wants, their best parts. . . . I'm not interested so

> "THE SADNESS OF *BLUE LEAVES* CENTERS, BY GUARE'S ACCOUNT, ON THE CRUELTY OF OUR NATIONAL DREAM OF SUCCESS"

much in how people survive as in how they avoid humiliation . . . avoiding humiliation is the core of tragedy and comedy and probably of our lives." For the truth is that Artie Shaughnessy is never going to win prizes, any more than Chekhov's three sisters are ever going to get to Moscow, any more than Williams's crippled Laura will ever find a gentleman caller or Willy Loman ever follow his brother Ben into the jungle that's "dark but full of diamonds" and walk out a rich man.

Blue Leaves is dark and full of diamonds, and I hope it wins all the prizes it can. It's a marvelous, maniacal tragicomedy, full of waggish merriment, razor sharp in its mordant wit but never cutting out the hearts of its characters, or turning away from their keen aches. Here, as in plays like *Landscape of the Body* and *Bosoms and Neglect* (also revived this season), Guare has the nimbleness to run up and down the scaffold of gallows humor, cap and bells on his head, the comic sock on one foot, the tragic buskin on the other, without tripping into either burlesque or bathos. According to him, the impetus for this tightroping came from seeing Laurence Olivier perform in *Dance of Death* and *A Flea in Her Ear* on successive nights. "Why," he decided, "shouldn't Strindberg and Feydeau get married [or] at least live together, and *The House of Blue Leaves* be their child?" To help him keep his balance, Guare has been blessed by strong direction from Jerry Zaks, wonderful sets and lighting by Tony Walton and Paul Gallo, and, most of all, by consummate acting from his cast, particularly Swoosie Kurtz as the fantastical wife and Stockard Channing as the garrulous mistress. The performances of both women are extraordinary—exquisitely evolved, perfectly sustained and played together in a duet of comic counterpoint that is dazzling to watch.

Blue Leaves takes place on a day in 1965 when the Pope drove through Queens on his way to the United Nations to help stop the war in Vietnam. (On that actual day, Guare—in an irony worthy of his drama—had finally achieved his nun teachers' dream of touring the Vatican.) While crowds gather on the sidewalks, more excited than they've been since the premiere of *Cleopatra,* Artie (played with great charm by John Mahoney) dreams of his son, a recruit bound for Vietnam, becoming Pope and making his dad Saint in Charge of Hymn-Writing. Bunny, Artie's deliciously tacky mistress, a strutting compendium of hackneyed sentiments and Dale Carnegie optimism, urges him to wake up, to go get his songs blessed by the Pope, go get his wife put in a mental institution and, most emphatically, to get the two of them to Billy, Artie's old friend, a movie big shot in California. There they will have a new life where dreams can come true. Then and only then will she cook for him; until they're legally wed, he will have to content himself with sex, and with looking at photos of her dishes in a scrapbook hidden under the couch.

The scrapbook is hidden there from Bananas, Artie's mentally disturbed wife, who wanders eerily through the house she has been too frightened to leave since her suicide attempt several months ago. Its windows are now barred by an iron gate, because, like the mother in Guare's *Bosoms and Neglect,* like the mother in O'Neil's *Long Day's Journey,* like the mothers and wives in so many American plays and in so much of American life, Bananas bears the psychic burden of her family's failures; she feels the pain, screams the truth and for doing so has to be sedated with pills or sent away to an institution, the house of blue leaves (the leaves were really bluebirds that flew off and left the boughs bare). Through the luminous sensitivity of Swoosie Kurtz's portrayal, Bananas transcends the pathos of her delusions and stands at the play's center, quiet as grief, heartbreaking as honesty. She moves quietly in and out of Guare's hilarious, absurdist parade of deaf starlets, monstrous moguls, terrorist sons and a trio of madcap nuns who roar on stage like the Marx brothers in habits. Bananas stands there with the lucidity of madness and asks us to laugh and cry with her at all their—all our—lost dreams. Artie cannot escape her truth even by destroying her. Nor can we, no more than dreamer Tom in *The Glass Menagerie* (fled to cities that "swept about me like dead leaves, brightly colored, torn from branches") could escape the vision of his lost sister. The triumph of *Blue Leaves* and of its performers is that we cannot forget the sorrows that blue spotlights disguise. It is that knowledge that makes Guare not just the older but the wiser brother of tour de farce writers like Christopher Durang. If,

as the successes of *Blue Leaves* and Orton's *Loot* suggest, audiences are now prepared to welcome this darker, zanier humor into the theatrical mainstream, then our theater is fortunate to have ready in the wings not only a master of laughter but a poet of compassion.

Source: Michael Malone. Review of *House of Blue Leaves* in the *Nation,* Vol. 242, no. 22, June 7, 1986, pp. 798–800.

Edith Oliver

Calling the 1986 revival "infinitely better" than the original production of House of Blue Leaves, *Oliver finds this new staging of Guare's play to be "deeper, sadder, more passionate."*

The revival of John Guare's "*The House of Blue Leaves,*" at the Newhouse, in Lincoln Center, is infinitely better than its original production, fifteen years ago—and I had not thought anything could be. The play now seems deeper, sadder, more passionate, and even funnier, if that is conceivable. The actors—and what actors!—make clear much that might have been unnoticed before. "*The House of Blue Leaves,*" in case anyone needs reminding, is a satiric farce about a middle-aged zookeeper, named Artie Shaughnessy, who has a knack for writing imitations of cheap popular songs, and who is the victim of a number of American dreams, which finally destroy him. The place is his living room in Sunnyside, Queens; the time is October 4, 1965, the day Pope Paul VI flew to New York to appear before the United Nations General Assembly to plead for an end to war—perhaps specifically the war in Vietnam (and perhaps, by blessing Artie's sheet music, to ease his way to Hollywood and an Academy Award). Artie lives with his wife, who has recently gone mad and is nicknamed Bananas; he wants to put her in a sanitarium (the house of the title), run off to California with Bunny Flingus, his downstairs neighbor and mistress, who is eagerly abetting him, and then get a job with his best friend, a prominent movie director. Bananas resists the hospital, because she is terrified of shock treatments. As I remarked in my original review, "this play could be considered a whole series of shock treatments, and often I was as horrified at myself for laughing (which I did a lot) as I was at what I heard and saw on the stage." The plot is wild and arbitrary and always outrageous. The other characters are a movie star, deafened by an explosion during the making of her latest picture, who is the director's girlfriend; the Shaughnessys' son, AWOL after twenty-one days in the Army, who arrives with a homemade bomb, his target being the Pope; three goofy nuns, who have been watching the Pope's motorcade from the roof of the Shaughnessys' apartment house; and, finally, the great director himself. The bomb misses the Pope, but it does go off, taking its toll of the assembled company.

Guare's marvellous comic writing, in which every word plays, and his ferocious high spirits glow more than ever in these drab days, but the performance, under the acute, sensitive direction of Jerry Zaks, is what makes most of the difference between the first production and this one. John Mahoney, who appeared as the older man in last year's "Orphans," is Artie Shaughnessy to the life, in all his loony optimism and desperation. But the phenomenal Swoosie Kurtz, as Bananas, in every line and monologue changes what might have been a merely pathetic character into a tragic figure, helpless and loving and demented, and smarter than anyone around her—all this without sacrificing any of the comedy. Stockard Channing is flint-hearted Bunny, and although the caustic tongue of Anne Meara, the original Bunny, is unforgettable, Miss Channing, padded to plumpness, makes the part her own from the moment she enters, stuffing strips of newspaper into her plastic boots against the cold and issuing orders. Christopher Walken, sporting an impeccable Queens accent, is the movie director. Julie Hagerty is the beautiful movie star trying to conceal her deafness from her admirers. Everybody is good. But the true star is John Guare. The play has been well served by the designers: Tony Walton, who conceived that awful apartment; Ann Roth, who created the witty costumes; and Paul Gallo, who devised the lighting.

Source: Edith Oliver. "Old and Improved" in the *New Yorker,* Vol. 62, March 31, 1986, pp. 66–67.

John Simon

Simon reviews a 1986 production and finds that Guare's play retains much of its irreverent and absurdist power. The critic reserves particular praise for the trio of actors essaying the lead roles.

When John Guare's *The House of Blue Leaves* sprouted here in 1971, the theater of the absurd still enjoyed an American afterlife; Guare, moreover, was able to crossbreed American madcap farce with imported absurdism, as if Ionesco had collaborated with George Abbott. And he could introduce bits of true poignance into a blend that, even if it did not

"GUARE'S MARVELLOUS COMIC WRITING, IN WHICH EVERY WORD PLAYS, AND HIS FEROCIOUS HIGH SPIRITS GLOW MORE THAN EVER IN THESE DRAB DAYS"

quite come off, offered, along with withering ironies and wistful clowning, passages of pure whimsy. A fair portion of this survives in the perky revival Jerry Zaks has mounted for the Lincoln Center Theater, although some timeliness, surprise, and bite are, perhaps inevitably, gone.

The basic situation is delightfully painful: A zookeeper, Artie Shaughnessy, pursues his dream of becoming a big Hollywood songwriter. Urging him on is his enthusiastic but silly mistress of two months, Bunny Flingus; holding him back, however passively, is his demented wife, Bananas, whom he can't bring himself to commit. Luring him on is a vague, extorted promise from his school chum Billy Einhorn, now a successful movie director; further enmeshing him is a whole human zoo that stampedes into his modest Queens apartment, notably his violently lunatic son, Ronnie, AWOL from Fort Dix and planning to blow up Pope Paul on his current visit to New York. Zaks's directing, however, is much better with the comedy than with the anguish; with the mad hokum, not the madness that hurts: Corrinna Stroller, Einhorn's mistress, who went deaf from an explosion in the first movie Billy couch-cast her in, was funny and moving as played by Margaret Linn and directed by Mel Shapiro in the original production; here, as performed by the gifted Julie Hagerty, she is only funny.

The comedy routines, though, flourish expectably under Zaks, who gets almost a whole comic act's worth from the mere prologue, in which Artie performs some of his dismal, but not much worse than average, songs at the El Dorado Bar & Grill in Sunnyside. That Artie is played by a superlative actor, John Mahoney, makes the milking of that scene as hilarious as it is harrowing, and casts the right tragicomic shadow over the rest of the play. Throughout, Mahoney inspiredly allows sadness to peep through his comedy and absurdity to puncture his pathos. He is brilliantly flanked by

Swoosie Kurtz, whose Bananas lets you see what a serious business madness is, how heart-rendingly hard a nonfunctional mind must work to little avail, how shattering are the stray truths from the mouths of the cracked; and by Stockard Channing, whose Bunny is as earnestly philosophical as only certain very stupid people can be, and who delivers herself of her practical asininities for an asinine world with a wonderful mixture of modesty and pride.

Though nowhere near this sublime trio, the others will do, even if Ben Stiller makes the hapless Ronnie more one-stringed than called for. Billy Einhorn is an underwritten part, but Christopher Walken, giving one of his more zonked performances, further deflates it. He does, however, sport one of the most satirical hairdos I've ever encountered. Tony Walton's set of a burrow under the Queensboro Bridge, surrounded by bristling urban blight, is smashing, and Ann Roth's costumes and Paul Gallo's lighting are right down there too. Only the final image, the apartment filling up with the blue leaves of insanity, is not brought off as well as the stage direction reads.

Source: John Simon. "Crazed Husbands, Crazy Wives" in *New York,* Vol. 19, no. 13, March 31, 1986, p. 72.

SOURCES

Barnes, Clive. "Theater: John Guare's *House of Blue Leaves* Opens," in *The New York Times,* February 11, 1971, p. 54.

Brustein, Robert. A review of *The House of Blue Leaves,* in *The New Republic,* May 5, 1986, p. 27.

Clurman, Harold. A review of *The House of Blue Leaves,* in *The Nation,* March 1, 1971, p. 285.

Guare, John. *The House of Blue Leaves,* The Viking Press, 1972.

Henry, William A., III. A review of *The House of Blue Leaves,* in *Time,* March 31, 1986, p. 77.

Hewes, Henry. "Under the Rainbow," in *Saturday Review of Literature,* March 20, 1971, p. 10.

Malone, Michael. A review of *The House of Blue Leaves,* in *The New York Times,* June 7, 1986, p. 798.

Novick, Julius. "Very Funny-Or a Long Sick Joke," in *The New York Times,* February 21, 1971, Section 2, p. 9.

Oliver, Edith. A review of *The House of Blue Leaves,* in *The New Yorker,* February 20, 1971, p. 90.

FURTHER READING

Bernstein, Samuel. *The Strands Entwined: A New Direction in American Drama,* Northeastern University Press, 1980, pp. 39-59.
    Bernstein overviews the themes of and critical reaction to Guare's work, including *The House of Blue Leaves.*

Guare, John. A foreword to *The House of Blue Leaves,* Viking Press, 1972, pp. v-xi.
    Guare discusses his inspirations for the play as well as its major themes.

Lyon, Warren. "No More Crying the 'Blue Leaves' Blues," in *The New York Times,* July 25, 1971, pp. 1, 5.
    Chronicles the long process of getting the original production of *The House of Blue Leaves* off the ground. It is written by one of the play's producers.

Martin, Nicholas. "Chaos and Other Muses," in *American Theatre,* April 1, 1999.
    In this interview, Guare discusses his use of language and the inspirations for his plays.

"The Art of Theater IX: John Guare," *Paris Review,* Winter 1992, p. 69.
    This lengthy interview covers the whole of Guare's career including a discussion of *The House of Blue Leaves.*

Peer Gynt

HENRIK IBSEN
1876

Henrik Ibsen wrote *Peer Gynt* in 1867. He never intended that the work be performed on stage; instead, Ibsen envisioned his work as a poetic fantasy to be read. However, *Peer Gynt* quickly became recognized as a masterwork of Scandinavian literature, and in 1876, Ibsen adapted his work for the stage. One reason for the work's popularity derived from Ibsen's use of Norwegian fairy tales, particularly, Asbjornsen's *Norwegian Fairy Tales.* But Ibsen was also poking fun at some of the popular new ideas, including the emerging trends about getting back to nature and simplicity, ideas also popular in the United States since Henry David Thoreau espoused them. Since Ibsen originally intended this work to be read, he had little concern about including Peer's travels or about creating situations or locations that would later prove more difficult to translate to a stage performance. Obviously, he also had little concern about the poem's length, since there are no such restrictions on printed verse. But adapting the lengthy fantasy poem into a play presented some challenges, with Ibsen ultimately forced to cut the work by about one third. Instead of simply removing a large section, such as the adventures that occur in Act IV, Ibsen cut almost every scene by a few lines.

As a play, *Peer Gynt* consists almost entirely as a vehicle for Peer's adventures. He is a character who runs from commitment, and who is completely selfish, having little concern for the sacrifices that others are forced to make in accommodating him.

Ibsen's use of satire and a self-centered protagonist suggests social implications for nineteenth-century society, a topic that always interested Ibsen.

AUTHOR BIOGRAPHY

Ibsen was born March 20, 1828, in Skien, Norway, a lumbering town south of Christiania, now Oslo. He was the second son in a wealthy family that included five other siblings. In 1835, financial problems forced the family to move to a smaller house in Venstop outside Skien. After eight years the family moved back to Skein, and Ibsen moved to Grimstad to study as an apothecary's assistant. He applied to and was rejected at Christiania University. During the winter of 1848, Ibsen wrote his first play, *Catiline,* which was rejected by the Christiania Theatre; it was finally published in 1850 under the pseudonym Brynjolf Bjarme and generated little interest. Ibsen's second play *The Burial Mound* was also written under the pseudonym Brynjolf Bjarme, and became the first Ibsen play to be performed when it was presented on September 26, 1850, at the Christiania Theatre.

In 1851, Ibsen accepted an appointment as an assistant stage manager at the Norwegian Theatre in Bergen. He was also expected to assist the theatre as a dramatic author, and during his tenure at Bergen, Ibsen wrote several plays, including *Lady Inger* (1855) and *Olaf Liljekrans* (1857). These early plays were written in verse and drawn from Norse folklore and myths. In 1857 Ibsen was released from his contract at Bergen and accepted a position at the Norwegian Theatre in Christiania. While there, Ibsen married Suzannah Thoresen (1858). Their only child, Sigurd, was born the following year.

By 1860, Ibsen was under attack in the press for a lack of productivity. When the Christiania Theatre went bankrupt in 1862, Ibsen was left with no regular income, relying on a temporary position as a literary advisor to the reorganized Christiania Theatre for his livelihood. Thanks to a series of small government grants, by 1863 Ibsen was able to travel in Europe and begin what became an intense period of creativity. During this period, Ibsen completed a dramatic epic poem, *Brand,* which achieved critical notice (1866). This was followed by *Peer Gynt* (1867). The first of Ibsen's prose dramas, *The League of Youth* (1869), was the first of his plays to demonstrate a shift from an emphasis on plot to one of interpersonal relationships. This was followed by *Emperor and Galilean* (1873), Ibsen's first work to be translated into English. *A Doll's House* (1879) and *An Enemy of the People* (1882) are among the last plays included in Ibsen's realism period. Ibsen continued to write of modern realistic themes in his next plays, but he also relied increasingly on metaphor and symbolism in *Hedda Gabler* (1890).

A shift from social concerns to the isolation of the individual marks the next phase of Ibsen's work. *The Master Builder* (1892) and *When We Dead Awaken* (1899) all treat the conflicts that arise between art and life, between creativity and social expectations, and between personal contentment and self-deception. Many critics consider these last works to be autobiographical. In 1900, Ibsen suffered his first of several strokes, and his ill health ended his writing career. Ibsen died May 23, 1906.

PLOT SUMMARY

Act I

The play opens with Peer telling his mother, Ase, about the deer hunt he has just returned from. After delivering an exciting story filled with details from the hunt, Peer, who has no deer carcass in sight, admits that he fabricated the whole story. Ase accuses her son of being a lazy liar who is doing nothing to save them from poverty. After she tells him that he might have had a fine dowry if he'd chosen Ingrid as he wife, Peer agrees to marry her. But Ase replies that she is already promised to another, with the wedding scheduled for the next day. Peers states that he intends to stop the marriage, and when Ase protests, he picks her up and places her on a roof. On the way to the wedding, Peer overhears some guests talking and thinks they are speaking of him. He lies on the grass and begins to daydream about how he might be someone grand and important. In the distance, Peer can hear the wedding celebration and music.

Peer arrives at the wedding, but no one will dance with him, and people move away at his approach. Only a young farmer's daughter, Solveig, will speak to him, but she, too, quickly moves away. As a drunken Peer begins telling stories, filled with exaggeration and fancy, many of the young men present begin to make fun of him. When Solveig again appears, she tells Peer that her father has warned her to stay away from Peer. In spite of alternating threats and pleadings, Peer cannot convince her to dance with him. The bridegroom, Mads, who is not very bright, believes the fables and stories that Peer has been telling, and he now asks Peer for help in getting into see the bride, who has locked herself away from him. Sneaking in to see Ingrid is just what Peer has wanted to do and so he agrees to go around back with Mads. As Act I ends, the crowd is in disarray as they see Peer running up the mountain with the bride clutched over his shoulder.

Act II

It is early morning, and Peer is preparing to leave Ingrid. She is still clothed in her wedding finery and begs Peer to take her with him, but he replies that he wants another woman. As the two separate, Ingrid yells threats after Peer, who appears not to care. Meanwhile, Ase, accompanied by Solveig and her parents, is searching for Peer. Ase laments that she had never expected Peer to do such a thing, since he has never done much of anything in the past. Solveig's parents think Ase is as crazy as Peer evidently is, but they continue to help her search for him because it is their Christian duty. But Solveig wants to hear more about Peer and asks Ase to tell her about him. As the men from the village continue to look for Peer, he is given a hiding place by three herdgirls.

Eventually, Peer meets the daughter of the king of the mountain, and after telling her he is a prince, Peer asks her to marry him. The mountain king has several tests for Peer to pass before he is given the king's daughter to marry. The last test, blindness, has no appeal for Peer and he abandons his new bride. Next Peer encounters the Great Boyg, who will not let him pass. Again Peer is offered riddles he must solve, but just when it seems hopeless and Peer sinks to the ground exhausted, the Great Boyg withdraws claiming that Peer has women to help him and the Great Boyg has no power against women. Peer awakens next to his mother's hut, and when he sees the child, Helga, he asks that she bring Solveig to him.

Act III

Peer is an outlaw, hiding from the men of the village. He has built himself a hut in the forest, where he is able to be with Solveig. Meanwhile, Ase has had to pay a harsh fine in her son's name and has been left with nothing. Solveig has also paid a huge price to be with Peer. She has left her family and everyone she loves behind. Peer is safe only while

Henrik Ibsen

he remains in the forest. If he leaves, he becomes fair prey for whoever wants to hunt him down. Peer and Solveig know only a few brief moments of happiness. The mountain king's daughter appears with an ugly malformed child and tells Peer that the child is his. She threatens Peer and promises to haunt him and destroy any happiness he might find with Solveig. Peer remembers from his early religious training that repentance can offer him hope and salvation. Peer tells Solveig to wait in the hut for him, no matter how long it takes. Peer leaves and heads into the village to his mother's hut, where she is dying. Peer tells Ase stories to comfort her and when she is dead he thanks her for all that she has given to him. Peer leaves his mother's body to a neighbor's final care and says that he is leaving for the sea and beyond.

Act IV

This act opens in Morocco. Peer is older and obviously successful, but in many ways he has not changed. As he dines with friends, Peer fills the air with exaggerated stories and complete untruths. Peer also relates that he has made much money in trade, some of it in heathen religious idols and some of it in bibles. Peer also says that he sees himself as a citizen of the world, taking something from each country he visits. Peer is full of bravado, wanting to be emperor of the world. But he alienates those around him and he is robbed of all his goods as his yacht is seized and he is put ashore; but when Peer prays to God for help, the yacht mysteriously blows up with all on board. Peer next moves to the African desert, where he is again robbed. Meanwhile Solveig is still waiting in the hut for Peer to return, although she is quite middle aged now and does not know that Peer has continued in his aimless wanderings.

Act V

Peer is now an old man, and as this act opens he is at sea on a ship headed back toward Norway. But the ship wrecks and Peer barely survives and must push aside the ship's cook who is also trying to stay afloat. When he finally comes ashore, Peer decides that it is time to return home and settle down. Peer meets with the Button Moulder, where he is forced to confront his deeds and account for his life. Peer finally understands that he has been selfish and that his life has been without direction. At that moment, Peer hears Solveig singing and he hurls himself at her feet, begging for her forgiveness. When he would have her cry out his sins, Solveig replies that he has made her life beautiful. Hearing her words, the Button Moulder leaves, but promises that he and Peer will meet again.

CHARACTERS

Ase

Ase is Peer's mother. She loves her son very much and makes many sacrifices for him. But from Peer's words at her death, it is also apparent that she was willing to punish, even beat him, if necessary. Ase wants to believe in Peer, and so, when he tells her his stories, she initially believes him. She pushes Peer to make something of himself, even berating him and calling him lazy when she must. When Peer is banished, she is the one who is fined and who loses everything she has. But in spite of all that she suffers, Ase is happy to see Peer when he appears at her deathbed.

The Button Moulder

The Button Moulder represents Peer's future. In a sense, the Button Moulder is death, who has come to claim Peer. Peer is neither bad enough for hell, nor good enough for heaven. So the Button

Moulder has come for Peer, to melt him in his ladle. Peer is destined to become just one more of the lost souls, indistinguishable from the others who are sent to this nonentity of existence. The Button Moulder is turned away by Solveig whose love for Peer proves that he must be worthy of such devotion.

The Great Boyg

The Great Boyg represents the riddle of existence. He is a shapeless, frightening monster, who cannot be conquered. He blocks Peer's way up the mountain, and he tells him that although he never fights, he is never beaten. When it seems that the Boyg will take Peer, the sound of a woman singing sends him away. The Boyg cannot beat a woman.

Ingrid

Ingrid is the bride kidnapped by Peer. Since she is hiding from her bridegroom at her own wedding, it does not appear too unlikely that Peer is really rescuing her. In fact, when Peer abandons her, Ingrid is very angry, wanting to continue on with him.

Mountain King's Daughter

See Woman in green

Old Man of the Mountain

The father of the woman in green, whom Peer seeks to marry. He has a number of tests that Peer must go through to prove that he can become a troll, and thus, worthy of his daughter.

Peer Gynt

Peer is the central protagonist in this play. When the play opens he has no plans, no future, and no money. He seems not to care about not having these things, and it is his mother who berates him for his lack of ambition. Peer kidnaps Ingrid on her wedding day, but it does not appear to be from love. Instead, he wants her for her dowry, and he really just takes her because he has been denied her. Rather than work for what he wants, Peer simply takes what he thinks he should be given. Peer has many adventures after he abandons Ingrid, but in all of them, he is completely selfish and self-centered, thinking only of what he wants or what will benefit him. Although he finds great wealth, and much of it dishonestly or at least dishonorably, Peer loses what he has several times, and when he finally returns to

Peer (Derek Jacobi, on the left) aboard the ship just before the fateful wreck

his home, he brings no riches home with him. Instead, Peer finds the greatest riches of all, the love of Solveig, which was always there for him to discover.

Solveig

Solveig is a young farmer's daughter who Peer meets at Ingrid's wedding. She is initially interested in Peer, but she is warned off by her father. After Peer runs away with Ingrid, Solveig joins Ase in searching for him. And when Peer is banished, Solveig chooses to leave her sister and parents and join Peer in living an isolated life in the forest. After only a brief time together, Solveig is left alone while Peer, who has left to pick up firewood, leaves for good. She promises to wait for him and she does so, even though the wait has lasted many years. Solveig's love for Peer is far greater than he deserves, but it is her love that saves him and gives meaning to his life.

Woman in green

Believes Peer's lies and agrees to marry him. He abandons her, and later she reappears with a troll-child, whom she identifies as Peer's child. Her threats to destroy Peer's happiness with Solveig cause him to run away.

MEDIA ADAPTATIONS

- An American version of *Peer Gynt* was filmed in 1915.

- *Peer Gynt* was filmed in 1934 by German director Fritz Wendhausen. This film is an adaptation of some of Ibsen's motifs and is not a true version of the play, as Ibsen created, since this film represents Nazi ideology and propaganda and not Ibsen's ideology. Availability of any remaining copies of this film is unknown.

THEMES

Absurdity

Because *Peer Gynt* was conceived of as poetical fantasy, Ibsen had little concern with creating reality. Many of the things that Peer does are unrealistic and absurd, beginning with Act I when the play opens to Peer's inventive and clearly exaggerated story of hunting, a story his mother believes. Another example occurs within a few lines when Peer picks up his mother and sets her atop the roof of her house. Still another sequence that is absurd is Peer's meeting with the trolls in the forest. Peer is willing to become one of the trolls, even wearing a tail and consuming the troll's natural food. Ibsen uses these absurd situations and characters to poke fun at society. The playwright makes clear that the situations Peer is placed in are as absurd as some of the elements within the society where Ibsen lives.

Love

Although Peer kidnaps Ingrid on her wedding day, it is clear that love is not the reason. In fact, Peer is too selfish to really be motivated by love of anything. In his selfishness, Peer wants Ingrid for the dowry she would bring, a dowry that would enable him to escape having to work. However, there is love in this play, and that is the love that motivates Solveig. She sacrifices her family, friends, and home to live with Peer, isolated and ostracized in the forest. And although she can only share his life briefly, Solveig waits patiently for him to return. Peer never tells her when he might return, and in fact, he is gone for many years. But still, Solveig waits, alone in the hut, and when Peer finally returns an old man, she quickly greets him with love and thanks him for having made her life fuller and happier. Solveig offers an example of enduring, committed love for someone who spends much of his life trying to escape any commitment.

Return to Nature

The trolls espousing organic nature mirrors a trend in the 19th century, a back to nature movement and a more natural life that Ibsen was satirizing. The trolls embrace a "simple, homey lifestyle" of natural foods. The food may taste terrible, but the fact that it is "local produce" is more important than taste. The clothing can only be local, nothing imported, which the troll refers to as "Christian clothes." Peer's beliefs are ok, because the trolls care only for outward appearance; if he agrees with the trolls on style, Peer may believe whatever he wants, even if it gives the trolls, "the creeps." Ibsen creates a world where what is natural, regardless of taste or appearance, is more important than ideas or intellect.

Punishment and Revenge

Peer's kidnapping of the bride, Ingrid, results in condemnation and punishment. Much of this is simply revenge, directed toward someone whose bragging and outlandish behavior has flaunted accepted societal rules. The punishment, though, is also shared by Peer's mother, Ase, who loses everything to pay fines leveled toward the only member of Peer's family who is available for punishment, his mother. Ase loses her farm, inheritance, furnishings, everything she owns. She becomes subject to the charity of the town, when she is given a house to live in until her death. Peer can remain free only as long as he remains isolated in the forest. If he should leave the safety of the forest, Peer becomes vulnerable to capture. This means that Solveig, if she wants to share his life, will also have to share Peer's punishment.

Morality

Peer is constantly challenged to explain his moral identity. He quotes William Shakespeare's *Hamlet*, "To thine own self be true," but he lives his life by the troll motto, "Be true to yourself-ish."

When he is an old man, Peer finally recognizes that while he has often quoted the former lines, he has lived the troll's lines. Peer has been selfish and self-centered, thinking only of his own desires and needs. When he is confronted with Solveig's steadfastness and loyalty, he finally recognizes his own moral failure. Humanity, that trait that the trolls wished to eliminate from Peer, is largely defined by man's morality. Without morality, Peer loses much of his humanity and nearly succumbs to the Button Moulder's advances. Only the selflessness of Solveig's love could transform the troll's maxim for life into the adage that Peer needed to embrace for his moral survival—''To thine own self be true.''

Religion

Religion is represented by the allegorical figures of the Great Boyg and the Button Moulder. Both of these figures represent the future that Peer must face as he cannot find a moral compass by which to live his life. The Great Boyg represents the riddle of existence, which must be confronted and answered to live life as a moral human being. The Button Moulder represents Peer's fate when it appears that his life has been without meaning. When Peer lives his life by taking and never giving, he becomes vulnerable to the fate that the Button Moulder offers, a life of nothingness. It is a death worse than an eternity in hell.

STYLE

Act

A major division in a drama. In Greek plays the sections of the drama signified by the appearance of the chorus and were usually divided into five acts. This is the formula for most serious drama from the Greeks to the Romans, and to Elizabethan playwrights like William Shakespeare. The five acts denote the structure of dramatic action. They are exposition, complication, climax, falling action, and catastrophe. The five act structure was followed until the nineteenth century when Ibsen combined some of the acts. Although, *Peer Gynt* is a five act play, Ibsen deviates somewhat from the traditional format. The exposition occurs in the first act when Peer kidnaps Ingrid. The complication occurs in the second act when Peer makes a hasty alliance with the Mountain King's daughter. The climax occurs in

TOPICS FOR FURTHER STUDY

- Discuss the use of Christian allegory in *Peer Gynt*.

- *Peer Gynt* has been described as the national story of Norway. Research the social history of 19th century Norway, and try to explain why you think this play has such appeal.

- *Peer Gynt* is based on myths and fables. Research some Norwegian fables and try to explain how this play might be similar or different from those fables.

- In Act IV, Peer travels extensively and has many adventures, all as he seeks to become wealthy. Do some research into the economic situation in 19th-century Norway. Try to determine what life was like for people without family wealth. Consider what Ibsen might be saying about the relative importance of economic security.

- In *Peer Gynt,* Ase loses everything after she is fined. However, the crime is Peer's. Investigate the legal system in place in 19th-century Norway, and discuss the social implications and options for family members of an accused criminal.

the third act when Peer must flee from the woman in green and the troll child. The fourth act contains the story of Peer's adventures. The falling action occurs in act five when Peer is confronted with his own selfishness and the love of Solveig offers him salvation. There is no catastrophe in this play, since Solveig averts it.

Character

A person in a dramatic work. The actions of each character are what constitute the story. Character can also include the idea of a particular individual's morality. Characters can range from simple stereotypical figures to more complex multi-faceted ones. Characters may also be defined by personality traits, such as the rogue or the damsel in distress.

"Characterization" is the process of creating a life-like person from an author's imagination. To accomplish this the author provides the character with personality traits that help define who she will be and how she will behave in a given situation. For instance, Peer is immediately identified as lazy and a liar. He also is quickly established as selfish and reckless.

Drama

A drama is often defined as any work designed to be presented on the stage. It consists of a story, of actors portraying characters, and of action. But historically, drama can also consist of tragedy, comedy, religious pageant, and spectacle. In modern usage, drama explores serious topics and themes but does not achieve the same level as tragedy.

Genre

Genres are a way of categorizing literature. Genre is a French term that means "kind" or "type." Genre can refer to both the category of literature such as tragedy, comedy, epic, poetry, or pastoral. It can also include modern forms of literature such as drama novels, or short stories. This term can also refer to types of literature such as mystery, science fiction, comedy or romance. *Peer Gynt* is fantasy, written in a mixture of prose and verse.

Plot

This term refers to the pattern of events. Generally plots should have a beginning, a middle, and a conclusion, but they may also sometimes be a series of episodes connected together. Basically, the plot provides the author with the means to explore primary themes. Students are often confused between the two terms; but themes explore ideas, and plots simply relate what happens in a very obvious manner. Thus the plot of *Peer Gynt* is the story of Peer's adventures. But the theme is of how Solveig's love is able to save Peer from the destruction his selfishness has wrought.

Setting

The time, place, and culture in which the action of the play takes place is called the setting. The elements of setting may include geographic location, physical or mental environments, prevailing cultural attitudes, or the historical time in which the action takes place. The locations for *Peer Gynt* include a small village in Norway, a nearby forest, Africa, and a boat at sea. The action begins when Peer is a young man and lasts over many years. During the course of the play, Peer progresses from young man to middle aged man to an old man. Actual ages and a time setting are never provided.

HISTORICAL CONTEXT

Legend has it that when Mark Twain visited London during the Diamond Jubilee celebration of Queen Victoria, he observed that British history had advanced more in the sixty years of her reign than in all of the two thousand years that preceded it. This was certainly true of the whole of Europe, which saw dramatic change occur within the 19th century. With just one invention, the steam engine, the industrial revolution began. Improvements in the steam engine led to faster ships and the easier transport of goods, which led to increased trade, improved economic conditions, and better availability of goods. But the improvements in steam power also led to faster railroad transportation, superior manufacturing looms, more efficient printing presses, and automated farming and agricultural equipment, such as the combine. But industry was not the only area to undergo dramatic change. Education, especially the development of compulsory primary and secondary education, was spreading around throughout the world. At the same time, universities and colleges were spreading quickly, and there was a new emphasis on learning. Meanwhile, newspapers were being founded in major cities around the world, encyclopaedias were being published, and the *World Almanac* was printed for the first time.

The introduction of the telegraph and the intercontinental cable quickly linked the world and made communications easier, as did the invention of the telephone. Other developments also occurred, such as photography, which improved quickly, especially with the ease in which pictures could be taken and developed. Improvements in canning make it easier to process, preserve, and transport previously perishable foods. In addition, the invention of refrigerated rail cars made shipping of food and meat safer and easier. In science, the new study of ecology was invented to describe environmental balance, and the followers of Charles Darwin begin to study the

COMPARE
&
CONTRAST

- 1876: The International Association for the Exploration and Civilization of Africa is founded under the auspices of the Belgian king, Leopold II.

  Today: There are few areas of the earth that remain unexplored, thus the exploration of the space beyond the earth remains a motivating force behind the United States support of NASA.

- 1876: *Robert's Rules for Order* by U.S. Army Engineer Corps Officer Henry Martyn Robert is published. This nonfiction work establishes rules for maintaining order and a democratic procedure for any self-governing association, such as in church or civic organizations.

  Today: The rules that Robert's book established for maintaining order and voting on decisions remains the hallmark of civic, volunteer, and church organizations since its implementation more than one hundred years ago.

- 1876: Although the first typewriters were introduced several years ago, and an improved version is introduced at this year's Philadelphia Centennial Exposition, their expense keeps demand restricted and production is limited. Most people continue to write with pens and pencils.

  Today: The computer had made writing far easier than anyone might have imagined a hundred years ago, and as a result, the typewriter is becoming obsolete.

- 1876: The publication of Englishman Charles Darwin's *Origin of Species* in 1859 has led to an explosion of interest in the new science of anthropology; subsequently, this led to a greater interest in archeology. This new emphasis on science provided Ibsen with material for his new play, *Peer Gynt.*

  Today: The interest in man's past, especially the discoveries available because of archeology, continue to draw the attention of a public seeking answers to the meaning of man's existence.

- 1876: The completion of the Suez Canal in 1869, the completion of the transcontinental railroad in the United States, and the invention of the telephone in 1876 mean that the world has become much smaller.

  Today: Instantaneous communications and satellites have made the world even smaller than it was 120 years ago. People in the developed nations think nothing of flying to destinations that would have taken weeks or months to reach in the 19th century. Nor do people hesitate to complete overseas telephone calls, and with the ease of using internet access, instantaneous communications have become even easier and less expensive to undertake.

---

evolution of man. Advances in medicine identified many of the bacteria that spread disease, while the weapons of war also changed with the invention of the Gatling gun, which made it easier to kill people.

The influence of Darwin in the midst of all this scientific and industrial progress cannot be ignored or underestimated. His books, especially *The Origins of Species,* fed a growing debate about the role of man and religion. Darwin questioned long-standing assumptions about humanity and man's role in the world. His next book, *The Descent of Man,* only

continued to fuel the fire. Religious leaders, who felt that Darwin was attacking a literal interpretation of the bible, were outraged. And the movement to subject the bible to a rigorous scientific examination that it was not designed to withstand, further fueled the debate. The Utilitarian Movement of the mid-nineteenth century also raised questions about the usefulness of religion in man's life. If man's existence was subjected to reason, then religion provided little benefit for men, who should rely more completely on technology, economics, and science for survival. Jeremy Bentham and his followers sought to subject every institution to the light of human reason. However, religion is based on faith, not reason. In many ways, religion was seen as a luxury that modern men did not need for survival. Thus Ibsen's conclusion of *Peer Gynt* appears as almost a rejection of this scientific approach to life. Ibsen is basically arguing that a man's life must have a moral center to have meaning. Society's fear of science, and the loss of humanity that all of this very rapid change had brought, reinforced for many the need to embrace religion if humanity was to endure.

CRITICAL OVERVIEW

In his translation of *Peer Gynt,* Kenneth McLeish states that Ibsen intended his work to be read and not performed on stage. But, McLeish notes, Ibsen's work was quickly recognized as a masterpiece of Scandinavian literature, of equivalent status to Goethe's *Faust* in Germany or Manzoni's *I promessi sposi* in Italy. The reason for this acclaim did not simply lie in the text's brilliance, although many critics did embrace *Peer Gynt*'s poetic narrative. Instead, it was Ibsen's use of Norwegian folklore, especially Peter Christen Asbjorsen's *Norwegian Fairy Tales,* upon which Peer's early adventures are based, that broadened the text's appeal. McLeish also declares that Ibsen's satirizing of several contemporary trends also increased the poem's appeal. Some of these trends, states McLeish, include satire on

> the new 'science' of archeology, of superstition and above all of the 'back to nature' movements of the 1860s: his trolls believe in making their own clothes and eating such 'organic' foods as cowdung and bullpiss, and one of the lunatics fights for the purity of the ancient language, unsullied by importations from foreign tongues—a preoccupation of mid-19th century Norwegian intellectuals.

However, McLeish says that Ibsen was not serious with any of this satire. Purportedly, he intended *Peer Gynt* to be a funny fantasy that would move quickly and hold the reader's attention. As a poem, it largely succeeded.

In 1876, Ibsen adapted his verse poem to the stage. In doing so, he was required to cut sections of the text and make the work shorter in length. Incidental music was added, and McLeish reports that a full orchestra accompanied this first performance. The music helped to fill the time it took to move the sets between scenes. According to McLeish, Ibsen

hated the idea of his verse poem being translated into prose, and so McLeish's translation includes a combination of the verse and prose in an effort to capture more of Ibsen's intent. In contemporary productions, as in the one staged by the National Theatre for which McLeish provided a translation, the largest number of cuts in Ibsen's work occur in the African scenes, which contain much of the 19th century political satire. McLeish points out that these scenes contain much repetition and that many of the ideas would be incomprehensible to modern audiences.

Critics often appreciate satire that pokes fun at society's so-called "sacred cows," and Ibsen's nineteenth-century critics and audience were no different. Although no reviews of the 1876 theatrical production are readily available, Edvard Beyer has provided a compilation of reviews of the printed verse poem when it was published in 1867. These reviews of *Peer Gynt* were mostly positive, although a few critics had serious complaints about the last two acts of the poem. Bjornstjerne Bjornson reviewed Ibsen's new work for his own publication, *Norsk Folkeblad.* Bjornson states that Ibsen's work was "a satire on Norwegian selfishness, narrowchestedness, conceitedness." Beyer points to Bjornson's comments about the Button Moulder scenes, noting that "they serve to bring the tale onto 'Christian ground.'" Bjornson thought that Ibsen intended for the conclusion to demonstrate that Solveig loved Peer because she "loves in us, our image of God," but that Ibsen's conclusion "is unfortunately unclear and by no means carefully worked out." According to Beyer, many of Bjornson's comments concerning the "topicality and validity of the text" are representative of other Norwegian critics of this period. Bjornson notes that Ibsen's poem "includes in its details and as a whole such a grand and bold statement into all our commotion as we have never received before." An unidentified reviewer for *Morgenblader,* says that *Peer Gynt* is

> from beginning to end a veritable torrent of polemic depictions, an adventure drama about egotism, which borrows the licence of folktales in order to give the buoyancy of imagination course for bold symbols, but employs the structure and means of drama in order to impart spontaneous life and vigor to shaping the image of the soul.

This reviewer also says that all the elements of the play are provided and that the reader or audience need not ask additional questions. Beyer notes that this unnamed reviewer offers a review that is "qualified but sympathetic." A strength of the drama is that "by using motifs from folktales" Ibsen "has freed himself from many curbs and restraints, and symbolic allusions have served to bridge gaps." However, this reviewer continues, "the fourth act does not contribute to the progress of the play; nothing changes in a decisive manner until near the end of the fifth act, and the end is no conclusion," but, instead, it leaves more questions. A review in *Aftenbladet,* by Frederik Baetzmann, also finds fault with the final acts, especially the concluding scene with Solveig. Baetzmann points out that having Peer saved "because a woman, Solveig, has remained true to him . . . is of course just as absurd in Christian as in psychological terms." Beyer quotes from several additional reviews of Ibsen's poem, but the essence is that Ibsen's work offers some important and interesting political satire, but the work is flawed by the last two acts, which do not work well with the first three acts. However, in spite of this significant problem, most reviews did recommend Ibsen's newest work.

CRITICISM

Sheri E. Metzger

Metzger is a Ph.D., specializing in literature and drama at the University of New Mexico. In this essay, she discusses the 20th-century use of Peer Gynt *as Nazi propaganda.*

During the period that encompassed the Third Reich, *Peer Gynt* was a favorite production of German theatres, who saw in Henrik Ibsen's work elements that could be manipulated to support Nazi ideology. Ibsen was not a socialist, nor would he have embraced the racism and inhumanity that marked the years of Adolf Hitler's reign. Ibsen was familiar with the need for critics and audiences to attribute a political agenda to his work. Of the claim that *A Doll's House* was a feminist work, Ibsen remarked that he was not a feminist, but instead, he believed in human rights and in exposing social injustice. From this claim, it is easy to see that Ibsen would not have approved of Nazi uses of *Peer Gynt* to support a claim of Aryan superiority. As Martin Esslin notes in his study, *Ibsen and the Theatre: The Dramatist in Production:*

> Ibsen's first and most obvious impact was social and political. His efforts to make drama and the theatre a means to bring into the open the main social and political issues of the age shocked and scandalized a

society who regarded the theatre as a place of shallow amusement.

Thus Ibsen saw the theatre as a place to expose and question social and political issues, not as a place to embrace injustice. Audiences were not shocked by a play that endorsed society; they were shocked by theatre that questioned those conventions. Had Ibsen simply wanted to assert the superiority of social conventions, there would have been no need to write a play about them and no need to move the theatre beyond that of "shallow amusement." But Ibsen had a social conscience, and he would no doubt have been shocked at the use of *Peer Gynt* as a spokesman of the Nazi political machine.

In considering the Nazi-era productions, it is first worthwhile examining a post-World War II German production of Ibsen's play. In this case, *Peer Gynt* still maintains a political ideology, but Aryan superiority is replaced by a fondness or nostalgic effort to recapture an atmosphere reminiscent of nineteenth-century theatre. In his discussion of the 1971 German stage production of *Peer Gynt,* Fritz Paul points out that the German producer, Peter Stein, used eight different actors to play Peer on stage. Paul describes the intention behind this and states that, "through these different emanations and theatrical metamorphoses, Peer loses his individuality and appears simply as a representative of the nineteenth century." Instead, according to Paul, "the modern notion of subjectivity and individuality and all conventional ideas of self and identity are called into question by the change of actors." Or, as Paul argues, "generalization is achieved through individualization." Paul sees this as a stroke of theatrical genius, but in subverting the individual, Stein also recalls the Victorian fear of the individual that was awakened by industrialization and socialist theories. The demand for better wages and living conditions frightened business owners and the aristocracy, and Ibsen's play, with its use of traditional folktales, seemed, on the surface at least, to be recalling a more traditional past, when life was more predictable. In this production of *Peer Gynt,* Stein also recalls that past, when the individual and all the demands that he might make upon society are subordinated to the needs to the general.

When in Act V, Stein has Peer and Solveig reclining in a stylized version of a Pieta, Paul concludes that Stein's stage production includes a non-verbal message for the audience: "In today's world this story from Norway about a man called *Peer Gynt* is also no more than a museum piece. At

WHAT DO I READ NEXT?

- Henrick Ibsen's *Brand* (1866), written the year before *Peer Gynt,* is also written in epic verse. *Brand* is the first of Ibsen's works to achieve both critical and popular attention. This work explores the inhumanity of uncompromising idealism.

- Edmund Spenser's *The Fairie Queene* (1590) is an early verse epic that includes allegorical characters and a fairytale-like motif to explore the meaning of truth.

- *Orlando Furioso* (1532), by Ariosto, is a verse epic that includes love, war, and honor and focuses on man's responsibility to fulfill his duty.

- *Norwegian Folk Tales: From the Collection of Peter Christian Asbjornsen, Jorgen Moe* (reprint 1982), by Peter Christen Asbjorsen, et al., is a collection of fairy tales in contemporary translation. Asbjornsen's stories were the source material for much of *Peer Gynt.*

- Peter Christen Asbjornsen's *East of the Sun and West of the Moon: Twenty-One Norwegian Folk Tales* (reprint 1990) is a collection of folktales; many, if not all, would have been familiar in Ibsen's world.

- *Favorite Folktales From Around the World* (1988), by Jane Yolen, is a collection of more than 160 folk tales from over 40 different cultures and traditions.

---

the same time no judgement is passed on the value of museums and their exhibits in general.'' Although this 1971 production does embrace subtle social and political ideology, it does so in an effort to recall a different era. Stein might have thought he was making a statement about the complexity of modern life in attempting to recall what he considered to be the far simpler life of the nineteenth century, and indeed, there are probably few twentieth-century audiences who would understand the complexity of nineteenth-century life.

A far more political use for *Peer Gynt* is attributed to the many productions during 1933-1944. In an article that explores why Nazi Germany found this play so appealing, Uwe Englert argues that only certain of Ibsen's plays were useful to the Third Reich. Ibsen's social plays, says Englert, were not as useful as the dramas of religion or those with Germanic characters. One of the efforts of the National Socialist cultural policy was to establish new links to Germanic myths. Englert states that during this period in Germany, ''theatre was considered the 'stage of the nation,' which could witness here 'its fortune, its rise and fall, its metamorphosis, its sacrificial offering and the purification of the soul of the nation.''' Thus Germany could use the stage to reinvent itself in whatever reincarnation it chose. There was also a move, according to Englert, to move away from what the National Socialists called ''unheroic bourgeois drama.''

Ibsen fit these initial criteria, but there were several other reasons why this particular playwright became so popular during this period. Englert asserts that the National Socialists ''firmly adhered to German and foreign classics [and] thus National Socialist ideology was firmly imbedded in a great context of tradition and was positively sanctioned by the adoption of great names in theatre literature.'' That the Third Reich considered classical dramas extremely important is not something that should be underestimated, according to Englert. Consequently, the National Socialists undertook an effort to reinvent Ibsen. First, Ibsen's ''Scandinavian origin and his allegedly Germanic appreciation of art were untiringly stressed'' in the popular press. There were also, according to Englert, attempts to link Ibsen to the ideas of the German philosopher, Johann Georg Hamann. Ibsen's genealogy was also traced, and Ibsen was found to have German ancestry through both his mother and father's distant

A Royal Shakespeare Company production of Ibsen's play: Derek Jacobi as Peer Gynt in one of his many incarnations

ancestors. To make all this work, the National Socialists had to concentrate on using Ibsen's earlier works, since these were felt to contain superior links to Fascism, and thus says Englert, "Ibsen was declared an enemy of liberalism and advocate of an order of absolutism."

Peer Gynt was chosen, argues Englert, because Peer sacrifices his humanity as "an embodiment of imperfection and of self-deception, [and] he ostensibly develops into an Americanized money-and-business-man, who does not even hesitate to trade slaves and false idols." In short, Peer becomes the perfect Nazi hero because he embodies all the worst traits of an American. In another example of a stage production of this play, Englert relates a story wherein the Germans met with more resistance than anticipated in their invasion of Norway, and blaming this on Norway's allegiance to England, Peer was depicted as an 'unscrupulous merchant' who embodied the British mercenary spirit of which Ibsen intended his play to be a warning. So popular was *Peer Gynt* that it was performed 1,183 times during 1933-1944. Only William Shakespeare's *Hamlet* was performed more often, states Englert.

IBSEN SAW THE THEATRE
AS A PLACE TO EXPOSE AND
QUESTION SOCIAL AND POLITICAL
ISSUES, NOT AS A PLACE TO
EMBRACE INJUSTICE. AUDIENCES
WERE NOT SHOCKED BY A PLAY
THAT ENDORSED SOCIETY; THEY
WERE SHOCKED BY THEATRE THAT
QUESTIONED THOSE
CONVENTIONS"

Much of this popularity can be traced to Hitler's friend, Dietrich Eckart, who made changes in Ibsen's drama to focus more on an "anti-modern interpretation of Ibsen," an interpretation that rewrites much of the play to create a Peer who rejects materialism and who is able to "overcome the inferior race of the trolls." The trolls, of course, are Jews. In fact, Englert relates that in some performances, the king of the trolls was depicted as Jewish, as he was in a 1938 Munich production.

According to Englert, as a result of Eckart's influence, his version of *Peer Gynt* was the basis for nearly all performances in the following years. Englert concludes that in *Peer Gynt* "the National Socialist cultural politicians saw a literary model that they could use for their propaganda purposes in an unrestrained manner. For this reason, there is hardly another drama which was performed so often in the Third Reich as Henrik Ibsen's *Peer Gynt*. Unfortunately Ibsen's play was also appropriated by other venues, as well.

In 1934, *Peer Gynt* was adapted to film, finding yet another audience in German theatres. In a discussion on the play's transformation onto film, Lilia Popova and Knut Brynhildsvoll state that the film's writer chose to select and stress specific motifs present in the play. While observing that Ibsen's play was well suited to film, since Peer's many adventures and the stories contained within the play are more easily captured by a camera, the authors also note that this film deletes Peer's dream sequences. It is worth considering why the film should delete such an important element of the play, since Ibsen used dream sequences in many of his works, and as Esslin notes, the dream visions are always present, even when suppressed. However, the dream-like Peer would not be in keeping with the Nazi agenda, where hard work is emphasized. Popova and Brynhildsvoll also find that in the film version, even Solveig becomes a propaganda tool, as "a natural woman, who denies her sexuality—at least until Peer's return. By means of her purity and virtue she represents the ideal woman of Fascist ideology."

These authors conclude that this adaptation does not "project the fantastic and utopian ideals of its model." Again, this would not be in keeping with Fascist ideology. As did Englert, Popova and Brynhildsvoll, find that adaptations of this play during this period serve more for propaganda than for an accurate depiction of Ibsen's work. The attempts to use Ibsen's *Peer Gynt* in this manner only serve to indicate the strength of his work. There would be little point in taking the work of an obscure playwright and using it to rewrite history. To use someone of Ibsen's stature to white-wash Nazi ideology was an important goal for the Nazi's, but it was an abomination. Ibsen would have horrified.

Source: Sheri E. Metzger, for *Drama for Students,* Gale, 2000.

John Bemrose

Reviewing a 1989 production staged at the annual Shaw Festival in Canada, Bemrose affirms the lasting power of Ibsen's play and its ability to provoke deep thought "long after the final line has been spoken."

Any theatre that dares to tackle Ibsen's classic 1876 drama, *Peer Gynt,* has its work cut out for it. Not only does the sprawling saga of a Norwegian folk hero run to nearly six hours in performance, but the play demands an emotional range and a level of technical virtuosity—there are over 50 speaking parts—that few companies can muster. All the more credit must go then to the Shaw Festival for its new production of *Peer Gynt* which comes closer than most to what Ibsen had in mind. In some ways, it is surprising that the company in Niagara-on-the-Lake, Ont., took on *Peer* at all. It is better known for mounting dramas of a sunnier, lighter sort, such as its current pleasing interpretation of George Bernard Shaw's 1908 comedy *Getting Married.* But in doing the Ibsen drama, the Festival has successfully stretched itself into new territory. There are rough patches in the production, and the generally worthy text by London, Ont., translator John Lingard contains such awkwardly up-to-date terms as "lifestyle." But there are many moments when the Festival's streamlined version of *Peer*—it has been reduced to three hours—turns into exhilarating theatre.

Among Ibsen's works, *Peer Gynt* is something of an anomaly. The Norwegian playwright is known mostly for such dour, realistic prose-dramas as *Hedda Gabbler* and *The Wild Duck*. But *Peer Gynt*, a much earlier work, is exuberant, frequently humorous and written in lively, highly colored poetry. Its hero, Peer Gynt (Jim Mezon), is one of those figures of world literature who, like Falstaff or Don Quixote, seem even larger than the works that gave them birth. Peer is a Nordic Everyman, who in the course of the play ages from a brawling, fantasy-prone youth to an indomitable old man. During his long life, he suffers the pangs of love, wins and loses power and fortune, and has preposterous adventures with trolls, monkeys and Arabian belly dancers. Those adventures are essentially a dramatization of his spiritual progress—or lack of it. Chronically restless, Peer is usually faithful to only one thing—his desire to run away from himself. In the play, that trait is symbolized by his desertion of Solveig (Gabrielle Rose), the one woman he truly loves.

Peer eventually returns to Solveig, but not before he comes to see that he has wasted his life. The revelation comes from his meeting with a subtly frightening character called the Buttonmoulder (memorably played by Robert Benson), who approaches Peer near the end of the play. It is the Buttonmoulder's job to round up all the souls who are neither bad enough for hell nor good enough for heaven—and melt them down like so many imperfect buttons so they can be used in the making of new souls. He tells Peer that he too must be melted down because, like all the other mediocrities, he has "never been himself." His words set Peer on a last, desperate search to discover what the Buttonmoulder means and to become, if possible, "himself."

Peer is easily one of the most demanding roles in all drama. The actor who plays him is onstage most of the time, the main focus of attention in a story that, in the wrong hands, can seem absurd and tedious. Mezon is by no means a complete Peer: he lacks the resonant sexuality that would make his attractiveness to his various lovers wholly believable. But he displays a physical exuberance that expresses Peer's boundless energy of mind and

> *PEER GYNT* IS EXUBERANT, FREQUENTLY HUMOROUS AND WRITTEN IN LIVELY, HIGHLY COLORED POETRY"

body. In the opening scene, he tells a tall tale to his mother, Aase (given a wry earthiness by Joan Orenstein), about how he has ridden on the back of a stag and fallen off a mountain summit. Mezon acts out Peer's tale with wildly vivid gestures, until he is finally writhing on the floor with the abandon of a three-year-old. And that is the main gift that Mezon brings to his role: he suggests the constant presence of the child within the man.

Indeed, there is a childlike, fairy-tale quality about the entire play. Peer may be lying about the stag, but even more unlikely events happen to him. At one point, he enters the core of a mountain and becomes embroiled with a tribe of trolls. The whole interlude may either be a nightmare or a real event. It is unimportant; the play breaks down the distinction between objective and subjective perceptions and shows that they are equally important. In keeping with that merging of reality and imagination, director Duncan McIntosh has given his production a deep stylistic unity, assisted by Kevin Lamotte's artfully moody lighting. The world they have created for Peer's inward and outward journey is as gloomy and oppressive as the long Norwegian winter, lit by the sudden shafts of Ibsen's poetry.

Most of the 16 actors who play the more than 50 characters whom Peer meets are excellent—and there is something mysteriously satisfying about seeing them in their multiple (sometimes up to seven) roles. Time and again, Peer meets the same faces: Benson appears variously as a man in Peer's native village, a ship's cook and also as the Buttonmoulder. Such repetition symbolizes the fact that, for all his travelling, Peer never gets anywhere: again and again, he is failing to become himself. Near the end of the play, Peer asks the Buttonmoulder what is meant by "becoming oneself." The Buttonmoulder tells him it means "putting yourself to death." That is more than Peer can grasp, but it is a measure of the Shaw Festival's production of *Peer Gynt* that such questions continue to cast a radiance in the mind, long after the final line has been spoken.

Source: John Bemrose. ''A Radiant Revival'' in *Maclean's,* Vol. 102, no. 30, July 24, 1989, p. 50.

John Simon

Simon offers a mixed review of a 1989 production staged by the Hartford Stage Company and starring Richard Thomas (John Boy from television's The Waltons*) in the title role.*

Peer Gynt is one of those very rare plays that see humanity whole. All of man is in it, and most of woman. To look at it is to gaze into an abyss: the abyss of the human soul. Ibsen's hero is artist and wheeler-dealer, dreamer and scrapper, visionary and fool. This eternal adolescent yearns for the heights; this coward needs no banana peel for his pratfalls. Around him are Aase, the overprotective, carping, impossible mother; Ingrid, the Woman in Green, Anitra, three versions of unidealized woman; and Solveig, the ideal beloved-cum-mother figure.

Around Peer, too, are the world and its people; also history, politics, religion, and pusillanimity. It is, like *Lear* and *Faust* and a couple of others, a dramatic summation that encapsulates a universe— in some ways the most inclusive and essential. Certainly it is the last word on man's double nature as questing spirit and wallowing troll. And it squarely confronts the ultimate questions of being and extinction, of the possibilities of God, devil, and mere dissolution. Boldly, it asks what is salvation, if such a thing exists. More boldly yet, it probes deeper and deeper into life with poetic fancy and earthy humor. Boldest of all, it does not stoop to easy answers.

That's why *Peer Gynt* continues to be a fruitful puzzle for successive generations of scholars and critics, theater people and audiences; that is why to produce it and see it remain, after 122 years, thrilling challenges. It is to Mark Lamos's hefty credit to have given us, with his Hartford Stage Company, a two-part, five-hour version that, though judiciously pruned, preserves all the essentials and keeps tickling, stimulating, extending us almost all the way. The difficult madhouse scene is not solved; yet only after the shipwreck scene does invention slacken as Lamos and his gallant band fail to come up with images as lyrical, funny, and daring as have gone before.

One big problem is that Lamos allowed Michael Meyer's *Ibsen* to be his chief guide through the play: that he swallowed whole the misinterpre-

tations Meyer offers especially on page 272 of his book. No, Peer does not die in the lunatic asylum or stormy sea, and the great fifth act is just as really and surreally, psychologically and symbolically, the portrait of a confused, contradictory human being. So as not to give us an allegedly romantic, sentimental, banal protagonist—Meyer's bugbear—Lamos has chosen not to let the hero age and become a figure of pathos; rather, he has him bounce around in youthfully immature vitality all the way. This is a huge mistake: *Gynt* is about life entire, which includes old age, exhaustion, fear of death. The ending of the play can be done perfectly straight without the least danger of banality or sugariness. Correctly understood, it is anything but simple and sentimental; rather, like the rest, funny, absurd, satirical, and sad. Also immensely moving.

Richard Thomas proves such a warm, athletic, intelligent, well-spoken, imaginative, and manifold actor that he could easily have handled that last required dimension: aging. In the supporting cast, Patricia Conolly, Leslie Geraci, and one or two others do handsomely; but some of the other supporting roles, and all the lesser ones, are shortchanged. I admire the courage of the translation by Gerry Bamman and Irene B. Berman, which espouses Ibsen's rhyme and metrics; lacking real poetic powers, however, it falls into a number of pitfalls. Still, it has its good moments and it serves.

There is something anticlimactic about music that is by Grieg, Beethoven, and Mel Marvin. But John Conklin, Merrily Murray-Walsh, and Pat Collins have supplied enough splendid design elements (as well as a few miscarriages) to make this *Peer Gynt* a joyous, unsettling, necessary experience.

Source: John Simon. ''The Way We Don't Live Now'' in *New York,* Vol. 22, no. 17, April 24, 1989, pp. 141–42.

Robert Brustein

While offering a mixed appraisal of the Phoenix theatrical companies production of Peer Gynt, *Brustein has nothing but praise for the power and literary significance of Ibsen's play.*

The intentions of the Phoenix company, which aspires to create a repertory of ''time-honored and modern classics,'' are lofty and honorable, but their productions this year have overwhelmed me with fatigue, impatience, and gloom. My anguished imagination is now subject to a fearful hallucination in

which I see the finest works of the greatest dramatists strewn about the Phoenix stage like so many
violated corpses, while a chorus of newspaper reviewers gleefully sings dirges in the wings. Perhaps
it is unfair to blame anyone but the reviewers
themselves for the absurdities they write about
Aristophanes and Ibsen; certainly, journalists—occupied with exalting the present—have always been
inclined to knock the past. Yet, it cannot be denied
that the Phoenix has provided a generous supply of
corks for this pop-gun fusillade.

For it seems to me that the Phoenix, while
outwardly more deferential toward the past than the
reviewers, is inwardly just as indifferent to it. Instead of letting these plays stand on their own legs,
the company's policy is to hale them into the
twentieth century by the nearest available append-
ages. In *Lysistrata* this resulted in extremely painful
attempts at topicality (as when an assorted collection of pneumatic females chanted ''Sex Almighty,
Aphrodite, rah, rah, rah!'' or an ungainly chorus
carried placards across the stage announcing that
''Athens is a Summer Festival''). In *Peer Gynt,* the
effort is less clumsy but no less obfuscating—a
varnish of ''theatrical values'' is spread thickly over
the surface of the play. The Phoenix production
never betrays the slightest hint that *Peer Gynt* has an
intellectual content, a consistent theme, or, for that
matter, any interest at all beyond a histrionic sweep.
Stuart Vaughan, the director, has staged the mad
scene, for example, as a frenetic phantasmagoria
which is quite chilling in its effect, but one has not
the vaguest idea what such a scene is doing in the
play. With the directorial emphasis on stage effects,
crowd scenes, and occasional ''Method'' touches in
the relations between characters, what was conceived as a masterful play of ideas emerges as just
another stage piece, and a pretty boring one at that.

But *Peer Gynt*'s claim to ''classical'' stature
does not rest on the fact that it provides fat parts for
actors, compelling scenes, or the opportunity for
designers, directors, and technicians to display their
wares; nor is the play particularly distinguished by
any profound psychological insights. Considered
strictly as *theatre* (a word which is coming to mean
the very opposite of drama), the play undoubtedly
has severe defects, especially in form. But like all
great works, *Peer Gynt* survives because it transcends the facile notion of ''theatre,'' because it is
larger than its characters or its effects, and because
what it has to say about the nature of existence
remains both wide and deep.

> *PEER GYNT* IS ONE OF THOSE
> VERY RARE PLAYS THAT SEE
> HUMANITY WHOLE. ALL OF MAN
> IS IN IT, AND MOST OF WOMAN.
> TO LOOK AT IT IS TO GAZE INTO
> AN ABYSS: THE ABYSS OF THE
> HUMAN SOUL''

In fact, *Peer Gynt,* written nearly a hundred
years ago, tells us more about our own condition
than almost anything written in America in recent
times, for Peer's concern with Self is one of the
central problems of our national life. A fanciful
storyteller with a prancing imagination, Peer might
have developed into a great man, but he is too
absorbed in appearances to become anything more
than a great illusionist. As rapist, as honorary troll,
as slave trader, as entrepreneur, as prophet, he is the
incarnation of compromise, the spirit of accommo-
dation, the apotheosis of the middle way. He whirls
giddily around the glove, justifying his absolute
lack of conviction and principle with the protest that
he is being true to himself. The inevitable conclusion to this maniacal egotism is insanity (where the
ego turns in upon itself completely), and it is in the
madhouse that Peer is crowned Emperor. Neither
saint nor sinner, Peer finally learns he has been a
worthless nonentity who existed only in the love of
a faithful wife, and at the end of the play he is
waiting to be melted down, like all useless things,
by the Button Moulder. ''He who forfeits his calling, forfeits his right to live,'' wrote Kierkegaard,
who believed, like Ibsen, that careerist self-absorption and mindless self-seeking are the most monstrous waste of life. Or, as the Button Moulder puts
it: ''To be yourself, you must slay yourself.''

''To be yourself is to kill the worst and therefore to bring out the best in yourself'' is the way the
passage reads in the Phoenix production, which will
give you some idea how easily a profundity can
become a copybook maxim. But although Norman
Ginsbury's doggerel, inaccurate rendering makes
William Archer's Victorian bromides seem sublime
and precise, the adapter is not exclusively to blame
for the general amorphousness of the evening. Stu-

> LIKE ALL GREAT WORKS, *PEER GYNT* SURVIVES BECAUSE IT TRANSCENDS THE FACILE NOTION OF 'THEATRE,' BECAUSE IT IS LARGER THAN ITS CHARACTERS OR ITS EFFECTS, AND BECAUSE WHAT IT HAS TO SAY ABOUT THE NATURE OF EXISTENCE REMAINS BOTH WIDE AND DEEP"

art Vaughan's cutting is almost guaranteed to make the work incomprehensible, and the central roles are all pretty well miscast. If the Phoenix were a true repertory company, Fritz Weaver would have been ideally placed in the part of the Button Moulder; since it is not, he plays the leading role. A heroic actor with a fine gift for irony, Weaver begins to make sense when Peer gets older; but his heavy style is inappropriate to the younger, quicksilver Peer who is turned into an earthbound swain with monotonous speech inflections and a clumsy pair of hooves.

In brief, we must be grateful to the Phoenix for wanting to mount this play, at the same time wondering what the animating impulse was to do so. In the past, the Phoenix had no policy other than to survive; today, its brochure speaks of creating a "new tradition in the theatre." But since the Phoenix has developed no new methods of staging, no new methods of playing, no new interpretative approach, I am puzzled about what this new tradition will be. There seems to be an authentic desire, as yet unrealized, to create a "working, professional group that can grow as a unit," but we have yet to see any sign that the "time-honored and modern classics" will function as anything more than showcases for the company. Alas, the trouble with the Phoenix is the trouble with the American theatre at large; isolated within its theatre walls, it shows no willingness to abandon itself to any purpose higher than its own existence. In this regard, Ibsen's play remains a cogent lesson; for if the American theatre is ever to be a place for art, it must learn to slay itself.

Source: Robert Brustein. ''What's Wrong with the Phoenix?'' in his *Seasons of Discontent: Dramatic Opinions 1959–1965,* Simon & Schuster, 1965, pp. 218–21.

SOURCES

Beyer, Edvard. ''The Reception of Ibsen's *Brand* and *Peer Gynt* in Scandinavia 1866-68,'' in *Contemporary Approaches to Ibsen VIII,* edited by Bjorn Hemmer, Norwegian University Press, 1994, pp. 4-69.

Englert, Uwe. ''Ibsen and Theatre Life in Nazi Germany,'' in *Contemporary Approaches to Ibsen VII,* edited by Bjorn Hemmer, Norwegian University Press, 1991, pp. 85-99.

Esslin, Martin. ''Ibsen and Modern Drama,'' in *Ibsen and the Theatre: The Dramatists in Production,* edited by Errol Durback, New York University Press, 1980, pp. 71-82.

McLeish, Kenneth. *Henrik Ibsen Peer Gynt: A Poetic Fantasy,* translated and adapted by Kenneth McLeish, Nick Hern Books and the Royal national Theatre, 1990.

Paul, Fritz. ''Text-Translation-Performance. Some Observations on Placing Peter Stein's Berlin Production of *Peer Gynt* (1971) within Theatre History,'' in *Contemporary Approaches to Ibsen VII,* edited by Bjorn Hemmer, Norwegian University Press, 1991, pp. 75-83.

Popova, Lilia and Knut Brynhildsvoll. ''Some Aspects of Cinematic Transformation: The 1934 German version of *Peer Gynt,''* in *Contemporary Approaches to Ibsen VII,* edited by Bjorn Hemmer, Norwegian University Press, 1991, pp. 101-111.

FURTHER READING

Gunnarsson, Torsten. *Nordic Landscape Painting in the Nineteenth Century,* translated by Nancy Adler, Yale University Press, 1998.
    Examines the themes and the social and political environment in which Scandinavian painters worked. There is a good representation of the forests and fjords of this area of Europe.

Hanson, Karin Synnove, editor, *Henrik Ibsen, 1828-1978: A Filmography,* Oslo, 1978.
    Contains details about the film productions of Ibsen's work.

Hemmer, Bjorn, editor. *Contemporary Approaches to Ibsen VII,* Norwegian University Press, 1991.
    A collection of essays on Ibsen's work. Of particular note, this volume contains several interesting discussions about Nazi productions of Ibsen's plays.

Hemmer, Bjorn, editor. *Contemporary Approaches to Ibsen VIII,* Norwegian University Press, 1994
    Includes a discussion about the initial production of *Peer Gynt* in 1876.

Lambourne, Lionel. *The Aesthetic Movement,* by Phaidon Press, 1996.

> Presents a discussion of a movement that brought change in architecture, a change that Ibsen refers to in *Peer Gynt.* The motto of this movement, ''art for art's sake,'' created more than just changes in outward beauty; it also resulted in cultural changes that this author explores in this text.

McFarlane, James, editor. *The Cambridge Companion to Ibsen,* Cambridge University Press, 1994.

This book contains 16 chapters that explore different aspects of Ibsen's life and works, including important themes.

Von Franz, Marie Louise. *Psychological meaning of Redemption Motifs in Fairytales,* by Inner City books, 1985.

> This author uses Jungian theories to assign psychological significance to fairytales. This is of interest to students who think that fairytales need to have a significance beyond that of enjoyment.

The Real Thing

TOM STOPPARD

1982

From the overnight sensation of *Rosencrantz and Guildenstern Are Dead* (1966) to the recent success of his script (with Marc Norman) for *Shakespeare in Love* (1998), Tom Stoppard has been acclaimed as one of the most important dramatic writers of the late-twentieth century. *The Real Thing* was first produced in 1982 on London's West End, and the cast included Roger Rees and Felicity Kendal (who subsequently became Stoppard's second wife). Its commercial and critical success was followed two years later by a sell-out production on Broadway in New York, with Glenn Close and Jeremy Irons in the main roles. That production won several Antionette ''Tony'' Perry Awards.

The play focuses upon Henry, who, much like Stoppard, is a successful playwright. Henry is married to an actress, Charlotte, who is playing the lead in his current play; he has fallen in love with another actress, Annie, for whom he soon leaves Charlotte. But is his new love ''the real thing?'' Underlying the major themes of love and adultery are related concerns. Does art influence life? Can life imitate art (the converse of the proverb ''art imitates life'')? Must art have a political and social value, as many people in Britain were then arguing, or can it stand alone, as art for art's sake? Stoppard argues that intellectuals are taking political expression for literature, and he makes a strong case that art should be valued for its aesthetic merits alone.

Audiences in the 1960s and 1970s delighted in Stoppard's wit and cleverness, although they occa-

sionally questioned whether the playwright could apply his genius to real life problems such as love and passion. *The Real Thing* ended such speculation and confirmed Stoppard's reputation for stylistic experimentalism and innovation.

AUTHOR BIOGRAPHY

Tom Stoppard was born Tomas Straussler in Czechoslovakia (now the Czech Republic) on July 3, 1937. His family moved to Singapore in 1939; shortly after, his father, Dr. Eugene Straussler, was killed, and the family moved to India. There, his mother remarried a British army major named Kenneth Stoppard. When the family relocated to England after the War, Stoppard took his stepfather's name. He left high school at seventeen and worked as a journalist on the *Western Daily Press* while writing television and radio plays, short stories, and his only novel, *Lord Malquist and Mr. Moon* (1966).

Stoppard's absurdist play *Rosencrantz and Guildenstern Are Dead* (1966) made him famous. The play was originally produced by the Oxford Theater Group on the Edinborough Festival Fringe; six months later it was bought and produced by the National Theater in London. The widespread acclaim that greeted this play promised great things, and in the past thirty years, Stoppard's reputation as a major contemporary playwright in the English language has grown by leaps and bounds.

Stoppard was first associated with Absurdism, a philosophical movement influenced by philosophers and writers such as Frenchman Albert Camus (*The Plague*), Italian Eugene Ionesco (*The Chairs*), and Irishman Samuel Beckett (*Waiting for Godot*), as well as by a host of Polish and Czech writers who lived in communist regimes. Absurdist writers perceive the world as mysterious and incomprehensible, and this perception often engenders feelings of purposelessness and bafflement. But Absurdism is not a uniformly somber philosophy nor does it produce uniformly serious art; indeed, much of the great Absurdist theater is comedy, or tragi-comedy, and it is in this vein that Stoppard's metaphysical wit and passion for ideas found full expression.

The Real Thing, Stoppard's twentieth play, marked a major departure for the playwright. It was Stoppard's first play to focus upon love. Critics had previously complained that he was all flash and no substance, but *The Real Thing* proved that Stoppard

Tom Stoppard

could address eternal themes such as love and passion with genuine sensitivity and insight. It contains Stoppard's characteristic investigation of an ethical problem—in this case the effects of adultery upon the vulnerable human heart—and his characteristic intervention into contemporary discussions about art—in this case the value of "political art." But when writing *The Real Thing*, Stoppard abandoned Absurdist stage practice for the tenets of realist drama.

Stoppard's life experience has influenced his writing in subtle ways. One of his plays, *Professional Foul* (1977) is set in his birth land, Czechoslovakia, and portrays the plight of dissidents living under a totalitarian regime. *Indian Ink* (1997) is set in India, during the heyday of British Empire (the early-twentieth century), and focuses upon the relationship between a liberal English woman traveler and a young Indian poet. Critics were quick to point out the identical occupation of *The Real Thing*'s protagonist and Stoppard and their common passion for cricket but fortunately chose not to obscure the integrity of the play by making stronger connections between "real" and "fictional" life.

Stoppard's life-long passion for the life and work of William Shakespeare and for Renaissance drama were on display in his screenplay (cowritten with Marc Norman) for the phenomenally successful 1998 film *Shakespeare in Love,* which starred Joseph Fiennes and Gwyenth Paltrow. He continues to write for film and stage and is considered by many to be one of the most important writers of the twentieth century.

PLOT SUMMARY

Act I

Max, an architect, is at home drinking and playing with cards, when his wife, Charlotte, returns home from a trip to Switzerland. Max questions Charlotte about her trip, but his queries are disjointed and digressive. Charlotte is confused. Suddenly he reveals to her that he has found her passport. Charlotte has not in fact been to Switzerland—her present for him, placed in a duty-free bag, is nothing but a clever prop. Max assumes she has been away with a lover. He is devastated but resorts to ironic dialogue to contain his emotion. Charlotte, profoundly alienated from him, yet neither denying nor admitting his accusation, exits.

Scene 2 opens with a hostile exchange between Henry and Charlotte. At first, the audience believes that Henry is her lover. However, the audience soon realizes that they have it all wrong. Scene 1 was actually an extract from Henry's new play *House of Cards.* Charlotte, his wife, is the lead actress in it and Max her co-lead.

Charlotte is far from happy. She feels that she has landed her part in *House of Cards* because she is Henry's wife and not because of her acting ability. She is also resentful about the role she is playing. She complains to Henry that he cannot write female characters, and that she functions as the "feed" for Max's more substantial lines, which also garner better laughs. Charlotte's comments—particularly about the audience's groan following the revelation of her character's adultery—are very pertinent, since the real audience has probably just reacted in such a way.

Max enters, closely followed by his actress wife, Annie. Instead of bringing a bottle of wine, Annie brings a bag of vegetables to the little gathering. As soon as Charlotte and Max have gone into the kitchen, it becomes clear that Annie is having an affair with Henry. When Charlotte and Max reenter,

the dialogue moves into another level: Henry and Annie continue to talk to each other intimately, but to Max and Charlotte, their dialogue appears to be part of the larger conversation. Much of the dialogue has *double entendres* that only the lovers—and the audience—understand.

The scene ends after the socially conscious Annie has talked at length about her latest *cause celebre:* an imprisoned soldier, Brodie, has "bravely" protested against his own army's missiles. Henry is skeptical about the value of such a cause, but Annie, who met Brodie before he was imprisoned, is determined to free him. However, for all her commitment, she reneges on a planned visit to the prison so that she can see Henry later that afternoon.

Scene 3 is a brief reprieve of Scene 1, though in this scene the action is not part of Henry's play and it is enacted between Annie and Max. Max has found Henry's handkerchief in the back seat of the car, where Henry left it after he and Annie made love. This revelation of the affair ends both marriages, and scene 4 finds the lovers together. However, it is clear that there are underlying tensions between them. They clash about Annie's "faithful" devotion to Brodie. Annie is also annoyed when she fails to make Henry jealous about the male actor who is playing opposite her in a new production of *Miss Julie.* Nonetheless, the couple affirm their love for each other. Act I ends with Henry rushing out to pick up his daughter, Debbie, leaving Annie sorting through piles of paper.

Act II

Two years later, Annie and Henry are still living together but they are not living in complete harmony. They continue to have petty disagreements about music, and they continue to disagree about Brodie, who is still imprisoned for his act of protest. Annie is determined to produce a play that Brodie has written. She thinks that it will attract support for his cause. "A writer is harder to ignore. I thought, TV plays get talked about, make some impact. Get his case reopened."

Henry, however, thinks that Brodie cannot write. Henry believes that writing should be valued for its literary and aesthetic worth; but Annie believes that writing should be valued mainly for its political message and its social effect. Henry argues that words are intrinsically "innocent, neutral, precise." If a good writer uses them well, "you can build

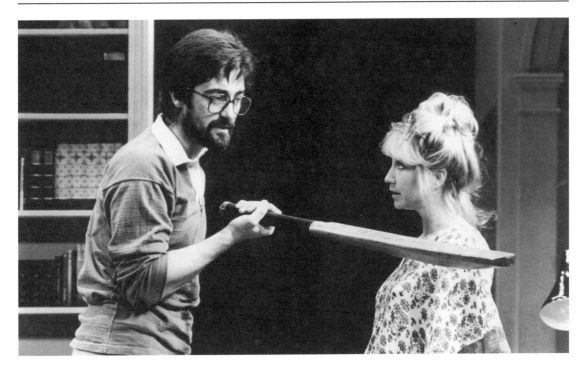

Henry (Roger Rees) and Annie (Felicity Kendal) have an uncomfortable confrontation in a 1982 production of Stoppard's play at the Strand Theatre

bridges across incomprehension and chaos.'' In contrast, Annie argues that if ''you teach a lot of people what to expect from good writing . . . [then] you end up with a lot of people saying you write well.'' Someone like Brodie ''who really has something to write about, something real,'' will therefore be unappreciated.

The audience's reaction to Annie's argument is complicated by the contrast between Brodie and Henry's writing. It is further complicated when the audience learns that Henry has stopped writing literary plays, which he calls ''the real stuff,'' and is instead writing TV science-fiction scripts, in order to finance his current lifestyle with Annie and his alimony payments to Charlotte.

Act II, scene 2 again reprises Henry's play, but with a dire twist: Annie embarks upon an affair with Billy, a fellow actor. Billy has read Brodie's play, and, like Henry, thinks that it is terrible, but he says that he will act in it for Annie. Throughout the scene the two lovers quote from the seventeenth century play *Tis Pity She's a Whore* by John Ford.

In Act II, scene 3, Henry and Charlotte's daughter appears onstage. Debbie has her father's talent for words but appears to be more realistic and pragmat-

ic about love than him. In one telling interchange between them, Henry attempts to express his feelings about love but does so in ironic, elevated language. Debbie cuts through this: ''Don't write it, Fa. Just say it. The first time you fell in love. What?''

Their affectionate interchange is followed by a conversation between Charlotte and Henry. Charlotte, somewhat mellowed, tells her ex-husband some truths about love and commitment.

Scene 4 reveals a glimpse of Annie's growing attachment to Billy. This is followed, in scene 5, by another reprise of Act I, scene 1, this time enacted between Henry and Annie. Henry has discovered that Annie is having an affair with Billy. But the scene is played differently from the earlier versions: neither lover walks out on the other. Instead, they try to negotiate in order to salvage the relationship. Henry is prepared to accept the affair because he still loves Annie and because Annie still loves him.

The complexity—and painfulness—of real life love is further explored in scene 7, in which the couple struggle to integrate the pain of the affair into their relationship. The final scene of the play, between Henry, Annie, and Brodie, suggests that their relationship will endure.

CHARACTERS

Annie

Annie is an actress who is married to Max but is conducting an affair with Henry. She urges Henry to come clean about the affair but is in fact the one who reveals it to Max. In Act II Annie lands the part of August Strindberg's *Miss Julie* in a Glaswegain production of that play and begins an adulterous affair with her co-star Billy.

Annie is politically idealistic, and dedicates herself to the campaign for Brodie's release. She encourages Brodie to write an autobiographical play, believing that it will renew support for the campaign. Brodie's play is so poorly written that Annie enlists Henry to re-write it, refusing, however, to admit to him that it is badly written. Henry at first refuses to cooperate with her but eventually capitulates. In the final scene, Annie turns against Brodie, smashing a bowl of dip into his face. At the same time she appears to give up her affair with Billy and to return to Henry.

Billy

Billy is a young actor who falls in love with Annie. He manages to sweep her off her feet with his enthusiasm and honesty, which she finds a refreshing contrast to Henry's tight-lipped expressions of love.

Brodie

The subject of much discussion and debate throughout the play, Brodie only appears onstage in the final scene. All of Annie's claims about his idealism are finally revealed to be false. When he set fire to the wreath of the Unknown Soldier, Brodie was not seeking to make a political statement; rather, he was seeking to impress Annie, who he had just met. He is also revealed to be ungrateful and chauvinistic.

Charlotte

Charlotte is the lead actress in Henry's new play, *House of Cards*. She is also Henry's wife. Charlotte and Henry do not have a happy relationship. Henry's irony seems to have alienated Charlotte; moreover, she criticizes his writing, complaining that he does not write good female characters. Charlotte is offstage for most of the play but reap-

pears in a crucial scene between Henry and Debbie, during which she reveals to him that she had nine affairs while married to him. More important than the fact of her adultery, however, is her statement on commitment and marriage that she delivers in the same scene.

Debbie

Debbie is Henry and Charlotte's daughter. She appears in the second act, a world-wise seventeen-year-old who has a conversation with her father about sex and love. She claims that sex is not a mystery and that it does not deserve the hyperbole it attracts. Her father admires her skill with words but disagrees with her argument and labels her a sophist. Debbie's pragmatic comments represent a younger generation's view of sex and love.

Henry

Henry, a successful London playwright, is the play's protagonist. Henry is married to Charlotte, the lead actress in his current play *House of Cards*. However, he is estranged from his wife and is having an affair with Annie. Henry and Annie leave their respective spouses and embark on a life together. But when the new couple disagree about Brodie's play, and when Henry learns that Annie is being unfaithful, their relationship is threatened.

Henry's verbal dexterity lands him in trouble as often as it launches him into success. For all his wit and humor, he can be bitingly sarcastic and blisteringly rude; he is also impatient with other people's flawed logic and imprecise expression. Henry is apt to speak as if he was a character in a play, a characteristic that cripples his expression of emotion. He is most eloquent when articulating his belief in the innocence of language and when defending his conception of literature.

Henry undergoes profound change in the course of the play. He is finally able to express love and passion in real language, and his understanding of love also changes.

Max

Max is the lead actor in Henry's new play, *House of Cards*. In *House of Cards* he plays an architect who discovers that his wife is having an adulterous affair. Offstage, Max is Annie's husband.

In the third and last scene in which he appears onstage, Max reenacts his character's discovery of adultery in *House of Cards,* confronting Annie about her affair with Henry. He later tries, unsuccessfully, to win her back with flowers and telephone calls. In the play's final scene, it is revealed that he is in love again and is about to remarry. His joy in his new found love contrasts ironically to Henry's sobered love for Annie.

THEMES

Real Life vs. Art

The title of *The Real Thing* and its subject matter appear to lay bare Stoppard's particular preoccupation in this play: he is characteristically investigating an ethical issue (adultery) and questioning its philosophical partner, the nature of true love. As Richard Corliss stated in a review in *Time,* ''*The Real Thing* announces itself as just that: a real, straightforward play about matters of the heart.'' These are the central preoccupations of *The Real Thing,* but Stoppard's investigation of these issues is broad enough to sweep other topics under his microscope: he also explores the nature of reality and perception.

The play's title describes, firstly, the protagonists' search for ''real love.'' Henry, for all his sarcasm and irony, is at heart an idealist and a romantic, and when he says ''I do'' he means it. But he does not allow for the presence of doubt and insecurity in his loved one's heart and, consequently, does not provide the reassurance that his partners crave. To him, such gestures and words are unnecessary, he sees the desire for them as irrational and incomprehensible. Real love simply exists, it needs no artifice to prop it up.

Henry climbs a learning curve in love when he realizes that the fictions created by the imagination, however false, nonetheless impact the real experience of love—and adultery. Love may be ''knowing and being known,'' but that knowledge depends upon curbing the imagination's sometimes crippling powers of speculation, doubt, and suspicion. As Jack Kroll argued in *Newsweek:* ''For Stoppard, the most human urgency is the need to know, and the highest comedy is the breakdown of this process in an epic bewilderment.''

Deepening the central exploration of Henry's changing understanding of love is Stoppard's exploration of the nature of reality itself. Stoppard unhinges the audience's uncertainty about what is real and fictional in the first two scenes of the play: ''real life'' and representations of real life collapse in the contrast between *House of Cards,* the play-within-a-play, and the ''real'' play, *The Real Thing.* The distinction between reality and art appears to unravel further when Stoppard mixes extracts from plays by his own fictional character Brodie with those by real playwrights John Ford and August Strindberg. These extracts blur the boundaries between reality and art by establishing closer connections between each realm. The extract from *House of Cards,* for instance, alerts the audience to the impending collapse of Henry and Charlotte's marriage, while the extract from Strindberg's *Miss Julie* signals to them that Annie's affair, like Miss Julie's, degrades her.

This blurring of reality and art is intensified by the characters' occupations: they are all paid to create fictions, either onstage or on the page. Charlotte, Max, and Annie are consummate actors, and Annie in particular uses her talents in everyday life, concealing her adultery from Max and then Henry. In a different way, too, Charlotte is aware of the carry-over from her profession into her private life: when Max appears at her home, she complains playfully, ''Don't I get a day off?'' then later, more seriously, complains that she's the ''victim'' of Henry's ''fantasy.'' Henry, of course, is the consummate blurrer of real life and art: he fantasizes in stage dialogue about the possibility of his wife having an affair, but, just as he cannot imagine that possibility in real life, so too in *House of Cards* the imagined affair is revealed to have not taken place. As Charlotte says, ''if Henry caught me out with a lover . . . his sentence structure would go to pot, closely followed by his sphincter.''

Reality, however unpleasant, invariably catches up with those who ignore it, and this is precisely what happens to Henry: art is no longer the receptacle of impossible imaginings but rather the mirror that reflects reality. Stoppard's repetition of certain scenes (Act I, scenes 1 and 3; Act II, scene 5) suggests that life can imitate art in uncanny ways, and confirms, in the play's structure, the overarching theme of Henry's painful realization that art and reality cannot be kept separate from each other.

Language and Meaning

Stoppard believes that language and meaning are open to interpretation. Words in themselves are ''innocent,'' but they can have dangerous effects.

TOPICS FOR FURTHER STUDY

- There are several possible ways to interpret the conclusion of *The Real Thing*. Do you believe that Annie and Henry will be happy together? Or is their relationship, like their first marriages, doomed to failure?

- Describe Henry's beliefs about art and about the relationship of art to society. Then describe Annie's beliefs about the same things. Which set of beliefs do you find more compelling? Why?

- Discuss the relationship between the main play and one or two of the other plays Stoppard refers to in *The Real Thing*. What do these extracts suggest to the audience about Henry and Annie?

- What was your response to the character of Henry? Did you feel alienated by him, or did you empathize with him? Focus your response by discussing two scenes in which he appears and using his behavior in them to illustrate your argument.

- Can a comedy like *The Real Thing* really be a medium for social criticism? Focus your response by discussing two scenes in detail.

- Research the rise of the television and media industry from the 1950s onwards. Has our new communications culture changed the way we think about reality? What position do you think Stoppard takes on this issue?

Both Charlotte and Annie find Henry's incessant word-play oppressive at times, particularly when he becomes sarcastic. His tendency to rely upon irony and sarcasm becomes a mis-use of language when he uses these registers of humor to contain emotion and to create emotional distance—a habit that is exposed by Henry's daughter. Henry's "growth" in the play hinges upon finally being able to express emotions in the everyday language of the heart. As Frank Rich said in the *New York Times,* Henry struggles to "find the language that celebrates love."

Despite the primary focus on matters of the heart, the sub-plot about Brodie's play constitutes the most significant discussion of language and meaning in the play. Stoppard begins this penultimate scene in Act II with an apparently frivolous discussion. Henry says that he cannot distinguish between different classical composers and prefers pop music to opera. Annie is horrified that he does not appreciate Beethoven, but she herself cannot distinguish between the Everly Brothers and the Andrews Sisters. This seemingly inconsequential discussion is actually very telling.

Henry's preference for pop music and Annie's preference for classical music are an ironic contrast to their beliefs about writing. Henry believes that words are sacred. They "build bridges across incomprehension and chaos" and "they deserve respect." Annie, in contrast, is suspicious of attaching any literary or aesthetic value to language. She locates the value of language in its effect upon the world. However, her argument is undercut by the fact that she pleads with Henry to re-write Brodie's crude script. She recognizes, but will not admit, that writing must be well written if it is to have any social or political impact, if it has the power to, in Henry's words, "nudge the world a little."

By placing this discussion at centerstage, Stoppard encourages the audience to make up their own minds about an issue that was and still is very controversial. The audience have experienced the skill and power of Henry's writing and have listened to Henry and Annie's reading of Brodie's play. They can thus evaluate Henry and Annie's arguments. Should people distinguish between "good" and "bad" writing, and if so, how? They can also evaluate Henry and Brodie's *writing.* Which writer is more persuasive and which is more moving? Thus Stoppard intervenes in a controversial discussion about literature and politics while leaving the question unresolved and encouraging the audience to think through the issue themselves.

STYLE

Realism

The Real Thing marks a major departure in style for Stoppard: an abandonment of Absurdist styles for an exploration of Realist technique. Stoppard's move from Absurdism to Realism is apparent in the first scene, when Max speaks at length, and apparently without purpose, about the difference between Japanese and Swiss watches. It is a funny, albeit baffling, speech. A moment later, however, the audience realizes that the digression has real meaning. The "utterly reliable" Swiss watches are losing out to the "snare" and "delusion" of Japanese watches, just as solid, stable marriages are being replaced with no-strings-attached affairs.

Later, when Henry and Annie's embrace is interrupted by the impatient beeping of Henry's wrist-watch, Stoppard humorously reminds the audience of his earlier metaphor—a thoroughly modern one for time's intrusion into love. It is a metaphor that melds modern context with eternal themes.

The characters are concerned with "real life" dramas, such as adultery, money, and family trouble, and the action takes place in living rooms and train carriages, not court yards and throne rooms. Just as the setting is realistic and contemporary, so too is the language. Henry's cricket bat speech, in Act II, scene 1, is a good example of Stoppard's attempt to show his audience the poetry and drama of everyday life in everyday language. "What we're trying to do is write cricket bats, so that we when throw up an idea and give it a little knock, it might . . . travel. . . ."

Perhaps Stoppard's departure from the chaos and incomprehensibility that is characteristic of Absurdism to the making sense of the everyday that is characteristic of Realism is best seen in the character of Henry. His dependence upon humor and word-play suggests that he is alienated from "real" language and incapable of expressing his emotions without being ironic.

This conundrum is most clear in a conversation Henry and Debbie have about love. "Well, I remember, the first time I succumbed to the sensation that the universe was dispensable minus one la-dy—." Debbie, interrupting, tells him that he should "speak" rather than "write": he should be serious rather than ironic, truthful rather than flippant. Unexpectedly, he responds from the heart. "What lovers trust each other with," he tells her, is "knowledge of each other . . . knowledge of self, the real him, the real her, *in extremis,* the mask slipped from the face." Real language, *contemporary* language, can express universal dilemmas as eloquently as elevated Shakespearean verse can, and real life can be as powerful an experience as hyperbolic representations of it in art.

The Play-within-the-Play

In *The Real Thing,* Stoppard uses a favorite theatrical device, the play-within-a-play. His most notable and extensive use of this technique is evident in his landmark *Rosencrantz And Guildenstern Are Dead,* which centers around two minor characters in Shakespeare's *Hamlet* and employs the classic as its backdrop (in this case Stoppard's play is actually the "play within" that is contained within the universe of Shakespeare's "play"). In *The Real Thing,* Stoppard carries this device to a new level. There are not one but four plays-within-the-play: Henry's *House of Cards,* a fictional play; John Ford's *Tis Pity She's A Whore;* August Strindberg's *Miss Julie;* and Brodie's unnamed TV drama, another fictional play. Stoppard's use of them profoundly affects the play's meaning.

The device of the play-within-a-play works to trigger events in the play—the "Mousetrap" in *Hamlet,* for instance—or to comment satirically on events within the play—the figures of Rosencrantz and Guildenstern in *Rosencrantz and Guildenstern Are Dead,* for example. The device also allows the playwright to emphasize certain themes. The opening scene in *The Real Thing,* for instance, prefigures the revelation of Henry's adultery, the disintegration of his marriage, as well as his characteristic over-reliance on irony and wit to control his emotions.

The device of the play-within-a-play in *The Real Thing* has other functions, too, most noticeably the creation of ironic and humorous contrasts. The sophisticated bedroom drama *House of Cards,* and Brodie's crude TV play that book-end *The Real Thing* are qualitatively a gulf apart. Henry's language does not tell, it reveals: Henry's mind is analytic and subtle. Brodie's language not only tells, it hammers home the obvious and destroys any drama in the process: Brodie's thinking is crude and simplistic. The plays demonstrates the difference between the two men's perception of the world and their vision of art. The dramatic works also create a clearer contrast between the two men to whom Annie devotes herself.

Additionally, much of the play's humor derives from the contrast between theatrical representations of life in *The Real Thing* (the extracts from *Miss Julie* and *House of Cards*) and Stoppard's representation of real life in *The Real Thing*. In Act II, scene 2, Billy and Annie rehearse a love scene from *'Tis Pity She's A Whore*. Annie stops rehearsing when Billy becomes "less and less discreet," but he continues to read from the script. The contrast between her colloquial language and his elevated language, between him continuing to rehearse and her ceasing to, intensifies both the humor and the passion of the scene. The device of the play-within-the-play is thus central to the overall development of themes and characters.

HISTORICAL CONTEXT

Britain in the Early-1980s

In the 1970s Britain had been torn apart by industrial action and economic depression. Garbage men went on strike; milkmen went on strike; British Rail employees went on strike. Garbage piled up in the streets, milk was not delivered, and people could not rely upon the trains to arrive at work on time. Due to the OPEC boycott (a western abstention from the oil produced in the Middle East), the price of gas skyrocketed. Compounding all these problems was the undeniable fact that British industry was in decline.

Many of Britain's economic problems in the 1970s had their origins in the Postwar period. After the end of the Second World War, great sections of London had to be re-built and strict food and supply rationing continued well into the 1950s. Although money poured in to Britain to aid the economic recovery, the government channeled much of it into retaining control of the British colonies, the parts of its vast (though soon crumbling) empire. In the long-run, this was a disastrous decision. The British Empire gradually collapsed, and the home economy continued to flounder.

In 1979, after a period of immense social and political turmoil, Prime Minister Margaret Thatcher's conservative Tory party took power in Britain. Mrs.

Thatcher promised to end social disruption and to improve industry profitability. The Tory party retained control of Britain for fifteen years and dramatically altered the fabric of British society.

In 1982, Britain and Argentina's dispute over the Falkland Islands, an obscure island group off the coast of Argentina, escalated into full-scale war. Britain's victory over Argentina seemed puny in the international scheme of things, but the war galvanized nostalgia for British imperial might and encouraged many people to feel, as Thatcher proclaimed, that "Great Britain is great again." Nonetheless, within Britain there was a small, vocal group of people who opposed the war.

In the same year, Prince Charles's wedding to Lady Diana Spencer provided the public with a fairy-tale spectacle that brought the monarchy's popularity to an unprecedented height.

However, not everyone was happy with the direction in which Britain was moving. The eighteen-month long coal-miners' strike in this same period brutally reminded both British and international observers that economic change had come at great social cost. Homelessness became common in Britain's major cities, and the low-cost housing estates in the inner-city that had been built in the Postwar period became notorious poverty traps. Racism, too, was a constant problem, as Britain struggled to integrate recent immigrants into a sometimes hostile society. The period in which Stoppard wrote *The Real Thing* was a mixed bag of goods and attitudes towards the tremendous social and economic change depended very much upon whether one was benefiting or suffering as a result of them.

The British Artistic Tradition of Social Criticism

British artists have a venerable tradition of combining social criticism with artistic innovation, and many people who were unhappy in Thatcher's Britain looked to the theater and to film for critical representations of contemporary society. Film was a popular medium for the British artistic tradition of social criticism. Screenwriter Hanif Kureshi's film *My Beautiful Laundrette* laid bare the racist cancer at the heart of the inner-city, and Richard Attenborough's *Ghandhi* presented the Indian perspective on British colonialism and empire building.

In the dramatic realm, John Osborne protested against middle-class convention and brought work-

COMPARE & CONTRAST

- 1982: The Dow Jones Industrial average, a barometer of stock market activity, tops the 1000 level for the first time.

  Today: In 1999 the Dow Jones Industrial average tops the 10,000 level for the first time, reflecting a booming American economy, record low unemployment, and stable interest rates.

- 1982: President of the Soviet Union Leonid Brezhev, ruler for eighteen years, dies. He is replaced by former KGB chief Yuri Andropov (who dies the following year).

  Today: After the introduction of "peristroika" by President Mikhail Gorbachov, the Soviet Union abandoned communism and centralization in favor of market capitalism and devolution. The current leader of Russia is Boris Yeltsin, whose initially charismatic presidency has since become characterized by erratic behavior and an inability to control economic chaos and endemic corruption.

- 1982: Britain goes to war against Argentina over a territorial dispute involving the Falkland Islands. British forces defeat Argentina after a ten-day battle. Margaret Thatcher declares that "Great Britain was great again." In Argentina, the defeat leads to mass demonstrations and rioting that eventually topples the military government.

  Today: Britain maintains an active military presence in the Falklands. It is also heavily involved in the North Atlantic Treaty Organization's (NATO) military actions in the former Yugoslavia, including Serbia and Kosovo.

---

ing-class characters onto the stage in his decade-defining drama, *Look Back in Anger* (1956). A decade later, Edward Bond, a working-class playwright, attracted enormous controversy with his play *Saved* (1965), a grim depiction of urban violence and social decay in which a baby is stoned to death in its pram. Harold Pinter, in plays such as *The Birthday Party* (1958) and *The Caretaker* (1960), chose not to speak the language of the people but to create his own rhetoric to express the fractured reality he perceived. Stoppard, too, contributed to the British tradition of social criticism with plays such as *Professional Foul* (1977), which is set in Czechoslovakia and focuses on political dissidents living in a totalitarian society, and *Night and Day* (1978), which takes place in a fictionalized Africa and examines the role of the press under a dictatorship.

However, at first glance, *The Real Thing* seems removed from contemporary controversy. But after a more thoughtful examination, it becomes clear that the play takes issue with two pressing social items. In his presentation of Henry and Annie's relationship, Stoppard touches upon the changing status of marriage, and in the sub-plot about Brodie's imprisonment, he attacks segments of the anti-war movement.

Attitudes towards divorce have changed greatly in the second half of the twentieth century. In the 1950s and early-1960s, it was a social taboo to divorce one's spouse. Times have changed, and the play's imagined "society" can accept Henry and Annie's decision to leave their respective spouses with a degree of understanding. But the price of such social change, Stoppard suggests, is that the post-divorce unions are frequently plagued by uncertainty and distrust.

The other important social issue Stoppard explores in *The Real Thing* is the British anti-war movement, which focused upon the presence of American bases on British soil and upon Britain's involvement in the manufacturing and sale of nuclear missiles. One of the most famous anti-war protests during this period was the *permanent* women-only demonstration outside the Greenam Common missile base. The women's movement and the anti-war movement often shared the same umbrella, and it is upon this loose alliance that Stoppard turns his rhetorical guns.

In *The Real Thing,* Annie is active in the anti-missile movement. She meets Brodie, a soldier, when she is on her way to a demonstration. He tries to impress her by lighting a fire on the Cenotaph but is promptly arrested. Annie and Max interpret his action sympathetically: Brodie is "an ordinary soldier using his weekend pass to demonstrate against their bloody missiles." To them, the bases are reprehensible both because they demonstrate society's commitment to war and because they are evidence of American imperialism.

Henry does not agree. To him, Brodie is an ignorant, thoughtless "vandalizer of a national shrine," and his character—and his "cause"—is further damaged by his loutish stupidity and goggle-eyed leering at Annie. Stoppard paints Brodie in the most unsympathetic light. He also does an injustice to the movements that Annie espouses: her quick cancellation of a political appointment for sex with Henry, her championing of Brodie because of his infatuation with her, and her ill-conceived idealism, all suggest that her politics are founded on vanity and egoism more than upon carefully reasoned beliefs. Thus some of the play's central characters, and much of the conflict and the relationships in the play, depend upon Stoppard's depiction of the anti-war movement; not incidentally, Stoppard actively opposed the Falklands War during the period in which the play debuted.

CRITICAL OVERVIEW

When *The Real Thing* first premiered in London in November of 1982, there were two distinctly different reactions to the play— reactions that have come to characterize critical reaction to Stoppard's work. While all reviewers of Stoppard's writing, right from the first ecstatic reaction to *Rosencrantz and Guildenstern Are Dead* in 1966, have exulted in his wit and cleverness, some of them have complained that his writing lacks emotional depth.

Just such a reaction characterized Irving Wardle's hostile review of the premiere of *The Real Thing* in the London *Times.* In "Stoppard's Romance in a Cold Climate," Wardle complained that "the cumulative effect of *The Real Thing* is one of cleverness with its back to the wall." Wardle took a dim view of the debate between Henry and Annie

about Brodie's play. He admitted that it was "a classic statement of the art versus truth debate" but felt that it was part of an over-riding tendency towards "self-laceration" on Stoppard's part. Wardle clearly took Henry as a stand-in for Stoppard, and to an extent he was encouraged to do so by Stoppard himself, who less than a week after he had finished writing the play declared to an American audience that he would read Henry's cricket-bat speech "as though" it were "mine."

In contrast to Wardle's cool review, the *Guardian*'s Michael Billington offered a highly favorable appraisal. Far from criticizing Stoppard for continuing to write "cold" plays, Billington praised the play as "that rare thing . . . an intelligent play about love." Billington acknowledged that the territory Stoppard covered was familiar but argued that the play was worthwhile because of Stoppard's intelligent commentary on ideas connected to the theme of love. Billington's only quibble was that Stoppard had come down too hard on the then-fashionable genre of political drama. He disagreed with Stoppard's assumption that "impassioned political drama is irreconcilable with irony and finesse."

Nonetheless, Billington's review was influential, for it established the dominant interpretation of the play, that by the end of *The Real Thing,* Henry has changed for the better: "pain has transmuted him; and the assumption is that he will be a better writer and a richer man." Much of the later commentary upon *The Real Thing* followed this line of interpretation.

Paul Delaney, writing in *Critical Inquiry* a few years after the initial production, supported Stoppard's response to the then British infatuation with political drama. Delaney suggested that Stoppard "praises art which 'works' aesthetically whether or not it 'works' in terms of social utility." In effect, Delaney identified Stoppard as a cultural conservative: someone who believes that art and literature can be evaluated from a universal standard and that there is a great gulf dividing popular culture like TV, Hollywood films, comic books, and romance novels, from "high" culture like opera, theater, art films, and intellectual novels.

Delaney thus dragged Stoppard into the so-called "Culture Wars." This debate was fought largely within the universities, although it also effected high school curriculum battles, too. The battle was divided between two fronts: on the one hand, people who felt that the curriculum should be more inclusive, and that texts should be read for their social and historical value as well as their aesthetic value; and on the other hand, people who argued that the curriculum should stay as it was, that the "new" writers critics were trying to promote were not good enough and that aesthetic values were all that counted when it came to assessing a novel, poem, or play. Delaney enlisted Stoppard on his own side—the conservatives—although with hindsight, readers might ponder the play's ending, when Henry capitulates and re-writes Brodie's play, and wonder if Delaney was justified in doing so.

More than one critic picked up on the implications of Stoppard's stance against the political value of art. The *New York Times*'s Benedict Nightingale, reviewing the Broadway premiere of the play, pointed out that "every British dramatist seems to be expected to flaunt his social conscience these days." Stoppard's commitments, Nightingale suggested, were only "to be the freedom of the writer to ignore the day's prejudices, choose his own subject-matter, and treat it with all the honesty and artistry he can muster."

Nightingale wrote approvingly of Stoppard's attack on "political correctness," but not everyone was so quick to praise the playwright's representation of the relationship between art and politics. Frank Rich, also writing for the *New York Times,* thought that Stoppard had loaded all his guns and given his opponents only faulty ammunition: "Throughout the play, Henry's ideals about art and language are set against those of a fledgling playwright . . . who writes poorly, but, unlike Henry, champions a social cause. Whatever the relative merits of polemical playwrights versus 'pure' writers, no light is shed here. By painting Brodie as a moral fraud and loutish philistine, Mr. Stoppard lets Henry demolish him without contest—and reduces a complex debate to a smug, loaded dialectic."

Some critics saw Stoppard's sketchy representation of Brodie as yet another example of his inability to create nuanced characters. Leo Sauvage, writing in the *New Leader,* felt that Stoppard put his characters through all sorts of hoops only in order "to find a spur for the changes in Henry." The characterization that most suffers as a result of the playwright's steel-eyed focus on Henry is Annie, whose "bizarre" mixture of "superficial political militancy" is apparently compatible with "her whimsical enthusiasm" and her status as "a sort of updated symbol of *l'eternel feminin.*"

The critical reception of Stoppard's twentieth play was thus fairly positive, although a few prominent critics did express some reservations about the work. Most critics applauded Stoppard's complex exploration of adultery and love and were unanimous in praising his wit and humor. A few argued that the playwright's characteristic prioritization of ideas and technique over emotions and characters weakened the characterizations and the plot development.

CRITICISM

Helena Ifeka

Ifeka is a Ph.D. specializing in American and British literature. In this essay she argues that in The Real Thing *Stoppard takes issue with contemporary pressures to politicize art. Ifeka assesses the persuasiveness of his attack.*

Critics seized upon *The Real Thing* as if it were a rainstorm in a drought, proclaiming that Stoppard had at last written a play with real characters who experienced human emotions. Precisely why they should be so enthusiastic about the playwright's tardy conversion to realism when they once enthusiastically applauded his innovative Absurdism is not clear; nor is it clear why Stoppard has been burdened with the ridiculous smear that his writing was, up until he supposedly proved otherwise in *The Real Thing,* cold and unemotional.

Stoppard had always been a playwright whose intellectual curiosity mirrored his passion for language; he had not been particularly interested in squashing his energy into a realist or naturalist dramatic form but rather had invested time in unpicking the very fabric of such genres. His decision to pick up the realist garment finally and to fit it to his own devices deserves a better response than patronizing applause. It seems unlikely, too, that Stoppard would abandon his passion for the play as a vehicle for ideas, and, indeed, close examination of *The Real Thing* demonstrates that while the dominant theme may well be that of love, Stoppard's underlying concern is with contemporary debates about language and art.

Hillary DeVries was on the right track when, in reviewing the play, she wrote that it covers "familiar Stoppard territory . . . whether our views of art, politics, and emotion have any reality beyond our own perceptions." It is no accident that the play's protagonist is a playwright. By identifying him as such, and by providing an example of his writing,

WHAT DO I READ NEXT?

- John Ford's *Tis Pity She's a Whore* (1633). This passionate seventeenth-century play is the masterpiece of Caroline theater. The dominant theme is as shocking today as it was then: the incestuous love of the siblings Gionvanni and Arabella. Ford delights in exploring the ethical paradoxes created by this love.

- August Strindberg's naturalist drama *Miss Julie* (1888) is now a staple of mainstream theater, but in its own day it was banned by the Danish censor. In the play, Strindberg explores the theme of cross-class love.

- Stoppard's *Arcadia* (1993) is an entertaining play about the Romantic poet Byron's disappearance from Britain in 1809 and other unanswered riddles of Romanticism. It spans two different time periods. *Arcadia* was heralded as Stoppard's most intellectually ambitious play yet.

- Yasmina Reza's *Art* (1997) is a wildly successful French play, translated into English, about three friends' different reactions to a new painting (a black canvas) that one of them has purchased.

- *Shakespeare in Love* by Stoppard and Marc Norman (1998). See this Oscar-winning film to learn more about Stoppard—and about Shakespeare's plays *Romeo and Juliet* and *Twelfth Night*.

- American novelist and essayist Norman Mailer wrote the naturalist novel *The Naked and the Dead* (1948), about the fates of thirteen infantry men who survive the invasion of a Japanese-held island in World War II, as well as the Pulitzer Prize-winning nonfiction work, *The Armies of the Night* (1968) about a pacifist march on the Pentagon in 1967.

- Alan Ayckbourn's *A Chorus of Disapproval* (1984) is a good play to compare to Stoppard's *The Real Thing,* for both plays were written within a few years of each other and both use the device of the play-within-a-play. Ayckbourn's play is set in a small provincial town and is about the antics of an amateur musical society.

Stoppard tells the audience that the key events and developments in the play will hinge upon Henry's gifts as a writer and upon his perception of writing. Henry's profession will determine the play's plot and themes. If this is a play about love, then it is a play about Stoppard's life-long love affair with language.

Stoppard famously tends to be inspired by an idea rather than an image or a story. *The Real Thing* began with an idea or rather a question: could he "structure a play by repeating a given situation—a man in a room with his wife showing up—three times, each differently." Implicit in this question is an understanding of "reality" as something one attains, defines, creates, rather than as a material "given." Stoppard is not interested in peeling away layers of meaning in order to reach, finally, the

kernel of truth but rather in the way language transforms lived experience. It is in language and in all that language can do—the "bridges across chaos" that it can build—that Stoppard is most interested; love—its veracity and its pain—is simply the new season's ball that Stoppard throws through this eternally intriguing hoop.

Bouncing along with this question is one of the most pressing issues in contemporary Britain, that of the relation between art and politics. Henry and Annie's conflict over Brodie's play asks the audience to consider several controversial questions. Should artists use their talent for political purposes? Can art change the "real world" in positive ways? What is the value of art if it has no overt political content? This issue was pressing in Britain for many reasons. Britain had long had a much stronger

A scene from a Donmar Warehouse production of The Real Thing *featuring Jennifer Ehle as Annie and Stephen Dillane as Henry*

support of socially progressive art than America, and British theater has long produced cutting-edge politically conscious drama.

But British liberals were out on a limb in the early-1980s—locked out of political power by Prime Minister Margaret Thatcher's Conservative Party and seeking platforms upon which to voice their concerns. The tremendous social changes of the 1960s and 1970s had radicalized both the theater population and the left wing in general and led to acceptance of the belief that "the personal is political." It naturally followed that this applied not only to how one lived one's life but what one did in one's occupation. Amidst this noisy fray Stoppard dared to wag his finger and say "no."

He uttered that defiant syllable through the conflict between Henry and Annie over their different perceptions of the occupation of writer and the writer's material, language. Ironically, in their different ways they both see language in the same way. Annie believes words are worthless unless tied to politically meaningful freight; Henry believes them to be "innocent" and "neutral" until shaped, carefully and lovingly, into a bridge across chaos. They

> STOPPARD'S INTERVENTION INTO THE MUDDY FORAYS OF BRITISH CULTURAL POLITICS IS A DARING AND A COMMENDABLE ONE: ONE, INDEED, THAT MORE WRITERS IN THE PERIOD SHOULD HAVE HAD THE COURAGE TO FOLLOW HIS LEAD"

do, however, differ about what the motivation of the writer should be. Annie believes that words should be strung together either to lob a hefty bomb at order (the government, the state, the military) or to express a truth that defies those same forces of law and order (oppression of an individual, a person's innocence, group solidarity). Henry, however, has no interest in the relationship between language and society. As far as he is concerned, a relationship, or many relationships, may exist, but what the writer should be concerned about is each word's connection to the next word.

Irving Wardle, in his review of the London premiere of the play, assumed Henry was Stoppard's mouth-piece, a view expressed by Stoppard himself, who less than a week after he had finished writing the play declared to an American audience that he would read Henry's cricket-bat speech "as though" it were "mine." Stoppard's arguments were a welcome change from the pressure to politicize art that dominated British theater and the arts in the 1980s. His arguments remain a strong assertion of the power—and the integrity—of the human imagination, which, after all, should not have to leap through lion's hoops on demand but should instead be free to roam about in whatever territory and with whichever companions it delights in. Be that as it may, there are weaknesses in Stoppard's splendid sophistry.

Henry's arguments fall down when Annie asks him whether he cares in the least about "who wrote it, why he wrote it, *where* he wrote it." To Henry, these considerations simply "don't count." Henry's position is made to seem more reasonable because of the crassness of Brodie's writing and

because Brodie is such an unappealing character. Indeed, if Brodie and Annie are meant to be the wall against which Henry batters his bleeding head, then Stoppard has given his protagonist too many cushions. As Frank Rich remarked in the *New York Times,* "the particular left-wing playwright who arouses Henry's ire proves a straw man—a boorish fraud who's 'a lout with language.' Arguing at length [against] such a pushover of an antagonist" is no difficult feat, and the same might be said of the vehicle through which Henry batters the unseen Brodie, Annie, who is indeed, as Charlotte says, "a feed" for Henry's views. Annie's naivete encourages the audience to ask why her considerations should, indeed, "count."

But count they should, albeit not in the ways that Stoppard suggests. Henry's "bridges across incomprehension and chaos" enable the writer to "nudge the world a little or make a poem which children will speak for you when you're dead." But fame is not every poet's ambition, and the bridges that were created in one lifetime can mean a different thing in another. This is precisely the beauty and wonder of language—that different people in different times and places can look at the bridge and see it in a different light—but it also means that the questions of "who, why, where" are fundamentally important to the reader—if not to the writer.

It is at this point that Stoppard's straw man trips up, because Henry is a writer, not a reader, and Annie is an actress, not an audience member. Each character speaks about language and the profession of a writer from the perspective of the creator and the doer, rather than from the perspective of the listener and the watcher. Both, of course, touch upon these perspectives—Henry in his attempt to create art that will outlast his "mortal coil" and Annie in her hope that her art will also leave its mark upon the world—but their debate is rooted, fundamentally, in their own experience. "Who, why, where," are valuable considerations, for taken together with the art work they can often offer the reader an altogether fresh voice.

Does it help the reader to think about Aphra Behn's identity, and the time in which she was writing, when watching *The Rover?* Does it help the reader to consider August Wilson's background and his relationship to black and white culture when reading *The Piano Lesson?* Undoubtedly, the experience of reading and watching and listening without asking these questions is still a rich one, but holding both birds in one hand makes it richer still.

Stoppard's intervention into the muddy forays of British cultural politics is a daring and a commendable one: one, indeed, that more writers in the period should have had the courage to follow his lead. Ideas, if unquestioned, can be illogical and indeed oppressive, no matter how progressive they appear. Stoppard's essential argument, voiced through the debate between Henry and Annie about the value of the writer and of language, is that language is "sacred" and "innocent" and that its value accrues only in use. It is a logical and a persuasive argument. Its second half, however, that the identity of the writer is meaningless, is less so. Writers should certainly not be valued simply for their identity alone: no one wants to sit through three hours of diatribe if they will not be entertained or moved. But if pursued to its logical endgame, the argument Henry advances would mean that the identity of the writer—their race, their gender, their class, their family circumstances, their relationship to their culture's language—would simply be discounted altogether.

Source: Helena Ifeka, for *Drama for Students,* Gale, 2000.

Robert Brustein

In this favorable appraisal of Stoppard's play, Brustein commends the playwright for turning his dramatic talents to matters of human emotion.

It has sometimes been said of Tom Stoppard, by others besides me, that there is nothing going on beneath the glossy, slippery surface of his bright ideas and arch dialogue. With *The Real Thing* (Plymouth Theater), he has decided to confound his more skeptical critics by chipping a hole in the ice for us to peek through—under the proper conditions, no doubt, suitable also for fishing. You've probably heard by now what's swimming around this chilly pond. The "real thing" is Stoppard's amorous equivalent of the "right stuff"—grace and style in the performance of a difficult task, in this case conducting erotic relationships.

In short, Britain's leading intellectual entertainer is now exhibiting a highly publicized, well-congratulated capacity not just for verbal and literary pyrotechnics but also for feeling, in that his characters can actually experience such human emotions as jealousy, envy, sorrow, and passion. Hearing these exotic emotions expressed, I was reminded of Racine's *Phèdre,* where the lovesick heroine has been assuming all the while that Hippolytus is

> THE 'REAL THING' IS STOPPARD'S AMOROUS EQUIVALENT OF THE 'RIGHT STUFF'—GRACE AND STYLE IN THE PERFORMANCE OF A DIFFICULT TASK, IN THIS CASE CONDUCTING EROTIC RELATIONSHIPS"

frigid, only to discover that he has actually been in love with the young Aricie. "Hippolytus can feel!" says the astonished Phèdre, "but not for me." Mr. Stoppard's aberrational display of sentience left me equally bereft and isolated.

The Real Thing begins with a scene from *House of Cards,* a love triangle written by a successful playwright named Henry, enacted by his actress wife, Charlotte, and his actor friend, Max. Brittle enough to be a genuine piece of Stoppard invention, this is nevertheless not the "real thing" but rather a play-within-a-play (selections from Ford's *'Tis Pity She's a Whore* later form another of these Chinese boxes) about a man exposing his wife's adultery. After Henry's apartment comes in on a revolving turntable, we learn that the "real thing" is actually about the adultery of a husband. Henry has been having it off with Max's wife, Annie, another actress, though one with a bit of social conscience—she has befriended a young soldier arrested for arson at an antimissile demonstration. By the second act, Henry has left Charlotte and moved in with Annie.

When Max learns of Annie's infidelity, he cries. Henry, who finds Max's misery "in not very good taste," also cries when he discovers later that Annie has betrayed him as well with a young actor. Obviously, Hippolytus can feel—but Stoppard is less interested in these lachrymose calisthenics than in demonstrating how it is possible to reveal sentiment without losing one's reputation as a wit. For despite the intermittent weeping, the strongest emotion in the play is a passion for the construction of sentences, and Stoppard (ignoring Max's rebuke that "having all the words is not what life's about") is never more fervid than when Henry is celebrating his own verbal felicity. Defending himself against

Annie's charge that "You only write for people who would like to write like you if only they could write" (note that even his critics speak in carefully polished tropes), Henry replies that language is sacred, even if writers are not, and "If you get the right words in the right order, you can nudge the world a little."

At this point, he has been nudging the world in the direction of quietism by ridiculing soldier Brodie's loutish effort to compose a protest play. Stoppard, whose name was recently used in an ad by British conservatives praising our invasion of Grenada, is as tone deaf before the dissonant inflections of Western political protest as Henry is in the presence of serious music (though he is profoundly sensitive to stirrings of dissent in Eastern Europe). After Annie has rewarded Brodie's bad manners by administering some cocktail dip to his face like a slapstick pie, the play ends with a reconciliatory kiss between husband and wife, Henry writhing to his favorite rock record and Annie entering the bedroom to undress. Thus, love conquers all—even casual adulteries and messy social dissent.

Considering how few people can resist a sophisticated love story, *The Real Thing* is destined to be one of the big hits of the Broadway season, and, when the rights are released, a reigning favorite of middlebrow theater companies. I found it rather coldhearted in its good-natured way, a frozen trifle with little aftertaste. Stoppard has doubtless made some effort to examine his own personal and literary problems, and his writing is rarely defensive or self-serving. But despite the autobiographical yeast leavening the familiar digestible cake mix, *The Real Thing* is just another clever exercise in the Mayfair mode, where all of the characters (the proletarian Brodie excepted) share the same wit, artifice, and ornamental diction. Even Henry's teen-age daughter, at the very moment that she is teasing her father for writing always about "infidelity among the architect class," is fashioning sentences ("Exclusive rights isn't love," she says, "it's colonization") apparently designed for inclusion in a Glossary of Post-Restoration Epigrams. No wonder Stoppard has her refer to herself as "virgo syntacta."

I think I might be less immune to the charms of this admittedly harmless piece of trivia were it not being tarted up everywhere to pass for, well, the real thing. It comes no closer to reality than any of those other adultery plays recently exported from England—and it doesn't even possess the mordancy of Harold Pinter's *Betrayal* or the ingenuity of Peter

Nichols's *Passion.* Born in Czechoslovakia, Stoppard has managed to perfect an expatriate's gift for mimicry—allied to his ear for language is his unique capacity to imitate playwriting styles. But if he began his career impersonating Beckett and Pirandello (*Rosencrantz and Guildenstern Are Dead*) or Bernard Shaw (*Jumpers*) or Joyce and Wilde (*Travesties*), he has recently, along with a large number of contemporaries in the English theater, come entirely under the influence of Noel Coward's witty sangfroid. The question is whether this is a style more appropriate to simulating reality or creating escapism, whether, at this critical point in world history, we are more in need of rhetorical artifice—or poetic truth.

Mike Nichols's production is as beautifully manufactured as the play and, at times, equally contrived. Nichols has always gotten the best out of good actors, and his casting instinct has not failed him here. Still, there is an element of spontaneity occasionally missing from the current production—as if the cast were being corseted in Stoppard's language. Jeremy Irons, looking like a dissipated D'Artagnan, bearded and baggy eyed, has a plummy time with Henry's dialogue, and commands the stage with authentic theatrical grace but Glenn Close, as Annie, tries too hard to charm us out of recognizing that this is one unpleasant lady. An attractive actress with auburn hair and sunken eyes, Miss Close seems at times too easily persuaded of her own radiance. She smiles too much, and she has a habit of hugging herself, which injects a strain of sentimental self-love into these rather hardhearted proceedings (it is also highly unlikely, though this may be a fault of the writing, that she would be playing the young Annabella opposite a considerably younger Giovanni in *'Tis Pity She's a Whore*). As for Christine Baranski as Charlotte and Kenneth Welsh as Max, they, like the rest of the cast—and like Tony Walton's scenery, Tharon Musser's lighting, and Anthea Sylbert's clothes—function as well as possible to fulfill the assigned task, which is to reflect back the showy brilliance of the two leading characters, not to mention the breathtaking contrivances of their author, in his flamboyant exhibition of what it means to be "real."

Source: Robert Brustein. "Hippolytus Can Feel" in the *New Republic,* Vol. 190, no. 4, January 30, 1984, pp. 28–29.

John Simon

Simon offers a mixed review of The Real Thing, *marveling at Stoppard's theatrical skill while la-*

menting the mental gymnastics required to keep pace with the playright's language.

The playwright hero of Noël Coward's story "The Wooden Madonna" has been called by critics "a second Somerset Maugham," "a second Noël Coward," and "a second Oscar Wilde." I am sure that Tom Stoppard has been hailed as all that and more, and with some justification, even though unlike those three he is heterosexual. Surely his new play, *The Real Thing,* is as literate (barring the occasional grammatical lapse), witty, and dizzyingly ingenious as anything you will have seen in a long time, except for *Noises Off,* which, however, is farce rather than high comedy. In fact, Stoppard is as clever a playwright as you can find operating today in the English language. Therein lies his strength and also, I am afraid, his weakness. But do not let anything I am about to say deter you from seeing the play happily, profitably, gratefully.

In Stoppard's novel, *Lord Malquist & Mr. Moon,* there was a question so urgent that it had to be italicized: "*That's what I'd like to know. Who's a genuine what?*" In the intervening seventeen years, things have become more complicated, and the question is not only *who* but also *what* is a genuine what. It is as if *The Real Thing* took place entirely between two facing mirrors, Life and Art, reflecting what they see back and forth to infinity (mirrors playing an endless game of Ping-Pong), except that one cannot be quite sure which mirror is which. And in trying to establish what they are reflecting with any certainty, one is forced to keep turning one's head from one mirror to the other; yet the final answer resides in the last image, the one in infinity, to which neither the dramatis personae nor the audience will ever penetrate. So both have to settle for accepting one uncertainty as a working hypothesis. But which one?

I am giving away an open secret when I say that the play begins with a scene of marriage and infidelity. Or, rather, illusory marriage, for this is a scene from *House of Cards,* a play by Henry Boot, the hero of *The Real Thing*—and illusory infidelity, for the adultery in question, we later learn, was merely putative. The actors are Charlotte, Henry's real-life wife, and Max, their real-life friend, who is married to Annie in real life (I am speaking, of course, as if *The Real Thing* were real life, and as if real life existed), who, however, is in love with Henry, as he is with her. But "real life" is also a house of cards, and soon marriages collapse—

> IN *THE REAL THING,* THE SEMIAUTOBIOGRAPHICAL HENRY BOOT AND, IN LIFE, THE UNAVOIDABLY AUTOBIOGRAPHICAL TOM STOPPARD STATE OR HAVE STATED THEIR INABILITY TO COME TO GRIPS WITH AND WRITE ABOUT LOVE"

painfully for some, happily for others—to re-form in different configurations. Will *they* last?

For example, Annie, likewise an actress as well as a militant pacifist, has, after her marriage to Henry, met on a train from Scotland a simple soldier called Brodie—himself, it seems, an ardent pacifist. Upon setting fire to a wreath on a militaristic monument, he gets six years in jail for arson. To help release him sooner, Annie persuades him to write a play about what happened, a play that, being plain reality, is so bad that the extremely reluctant Henry has to be argued into rewriting it, i.e., putting enough illusion into its bare, rude truth to make it artlike, performable, real. ("I tart up Brodie's unspeakable drivel into speakable drivel," Henry says.) Aside from being debated acrimoniously enough to break up a marriage, this train ride with Brodie will be seen, at least in part, enacted as it might have happened, as Brodie wrote it, as Henry rewrote it, and as, presumably further revised, it was done on TV. And this isn't even the main plot of *The Real Thing,* though it impinges on it, or vice versa. Which mirror are we looking at? The events of life are reflected, somewhat distorted, in art; the events of art, somewhat travestied (or more tragic?), are echoed by life. And, of course, affairs and adulteries and marriages are everywhere, but which, if any, are real? Not necessarily the real ones.

Even the recorded music, classical or popular, that gets played on phonographs or radios extends this state of reflections, echoes, multiple bottoms on and on. A trio from *Cosi fan tutte* comes from an opera about infidelity that proves not infidelity—unless, of course, semblance or intention equals reality. Also there's a bit of *La Traviata* on the radio, about a formerly light woman who now pretends to be unfaithful—actually *is* unfaithful—but only because she believes it will benefit the one man she adores and keeps adoring. All of which comments on the action of the play. And so on. If this makes your head spin, rest assured that in watching *The Real Thing,* the head-spinning is greatly assuaged by spectacle and mitigated by wit—more wit than you can absorb, but what you can is amply sufficient. There is also something from time to time approaching real drama, real feeling, but this is not quite the real thing. Never mind, though; it, too, fascinates.

Yet, undeniably, there is loss. Cleverness, when it is as enormous as Stoppard's, can become a bit of an enormity, especially when it starts taking itself too seriously—either because it is too clever or because it is, after all, not clever enough. Wilde, you see, had the cleverness in *The Importance of Being Earnest* (from which an earlier Stoppard play, *Travesties,* takes off) not to take anything in it remotely in earnest. Congreve, in his differently but scarcely less clever *The Way of the World,* which does have serious overtones, had the good judgment not to make all the characters, situations, and speeches clever or funny. There is genuine dumbness, oafishness, evil in it. Conversely, Pirandello, the grand master of illusion, often isn't being funny at all. But Stoppard's hurtlingly, and sometimes hurtingly, funny cleverness is an avalanche that sweeps away even the chap who started it.

In *The Real Thing,* the semiautobiographical Henry Boot and, in life, the unavoidably autobiographical Tom Stoppard state or have stated their inability to come to grips with and write about love. Yet here, even more than in *Night and Day,* a less successful work, the subject is largely love, and though Stoppard has some pertinent things to say about it, his pertness militates against the pertinence. Take a woman's complaint that so much has been written about the misery of the unrequited lover "but not a word about the utter tedium of the unrequitee," where, as so often here, the very diction undercuts the *cri de coeur,* sometimes, but not always, intentionally. These characters go about their infidelities—really testimonials of love meant to make the other person feel—in a jokey context, with anguish ever ready to melt into epigrams. In *Peter Hall's Diaries,* Sir Peter attends a performance of Shaw's *Pygmalion* with Tom and Miriam Stoppard, and carps that this play is "love without pain." In its more serious moments, *The Real Thing*

seems to be pain without love and, finally, pain without pain.

And remarkable as the wit is, one gasps for respite. Must even a very young girl have adult wit? Must even a common soldier be a laughing philosopher? Must one wife be more clever than the next? And though much of the wit is golden, e.g., "You're beginning to appall me—there's something scary about stupidity made coherent," there is much that is merely silver and tarnishes in the open air. Thus there is rather too much of what I'd call the joke of the displaced or vague referent. For example, a wife says she deplores all this humiliation, and when the husband says he regrets its being humiliating to her, she rejoins, "Humiliating for you, not for me." If her father worries about daughter Debbie's being out late in a part of town where some murders have been committed, Mother quips that Debbie is not likely to kill anyone. The archetypal form of this occurs in: "I'm sorry." "What for?" "I don't know."

Still, it is all civilized and much of it scintillating, even if Stoppard's heart seems mostly in the unfeeling jokes such as the diatribe against digital watches—a long tirade whose every barb works like clockwork—than in the more feeling ones such as "Dignified cuckoldry is a difficult trick, but I try to live with it. Think of it as modern marriage." (I may have got this slightly wrong, but so has Stoppard.) The play has been greatly rewritten since it left London and is, I am told on good authority, much improved here. Certainly the production could scarcely be bettered. Any laugh that Stoppard might have missed, Mike Nichols, the ingenious director, has quietly but dazzlingly slipped in, and Tony Walton's sets are charming and suggestive, and can be changed with a speed that redounds to their glory and the play's efficiency. Anthea Sylbert's costumes look comfortably lived in, and Tharon Musser's hard-edged lighting matches the author's wit.

I have never before liked Jeremy Irons, but here his wimpy personality and windy delivery work wonders for him in creating a Henry who can rattle off jests at breakneck speed, then put on the brakes to achieve heartbreaking slowness. Weakness of aspect and personality become touching, and there is throughout a fine blend of shrewdness and fatuity, irony and vulnerability. Despite his musical illiteracy and assorted pip-squeakeries, this man, in Irons's hands, makes you believe that he is an artist of talent, and that under the flippancies, deep down in his flibbertigibbety soul, he cares about something.

As his two wives, Glenn Close and Christine Baranski are both highly accomplished comediennes, who can get under the skin of comedy as easily as under that of another character. Close's English accent is better, but both look very much like English actresses, which is both apposite and aesthetically unfortunate. As Debbie, Cynthia Nixon manages to be precocious without being obnoxious. Kenneth Welsh is a marvelous Max, wonderfully different on stage and on stage-within-stage. As the young actor Billie, Peter Gallagher slips superbly from difficult accent to accent, and combines pliable ease with solid manliness. In the only somewhat underwritten role of Brodie, Vyto Ruginis nevertheless creates a fully fleshed character.

The one problem with the play is that those two mirrors are so damned clever they can reflect away even with nothing between them. That would make Stoppard another Wilde—not bad. Now how about trying for another Molière?

Source: John Simon. ''All Done with Mirrors'' in *New York,* Vol. 17, no. 3, January 16, 1984, pp. 64–65.

SOURCES

Billington, Michael. ''High Fidelity'' in the *Guardian,* November 17, 1982, p. 9.

Corliss, Richard. ''Stoppard in the Name of Love: *The Real Thing* Brings Romantic Comedy Back to Broadway'' in *Time,* Vol. 123, no. 3, January 16, 1984, pp. 68-9.

Delaney, Paul. ''Cricket Bats and Commitment: The Real Thing in Art and Life'' in *Critical Inquiry,* Vol. 27, no. 1, Spring, 1985, pp. 45-60.

Kroll, Jack. ''Lovers and Strangers'' in *Newsweek,* Vol. CIII, no. 3, January 16, 1984, p. 83.

Nightingale, Benedict. ''Stoppard As We Never Dreamed He Could Be'' in the *New York Times,* January 15, 1984, pp. 5, 26.

Rich, Frank. ''Stoppard's *Real Thing* in London'' in the *New York Times,* June 23, 1983, p. C15.

Rich, Frank. ''Tom Stoppard's *Real Thing:* Love Lost and Found'' in the *New York Times,* January 6, 1984, p. C3.

Sauvage, Leo. ''Where Stoppard Fails'' in the *New Leader,* Vol. LXVII, no. 2, January 23, 1984, pp. 21-22.

Trussler, Simon. *Cambridge Illustrated History of the British Theater,* Cambridge University Press, 1994.

Wardle, Irving. ''Stoppard's Romance in a Cold Climate'' in the London *Times,* November 17, 1982, p. 16.

Zozaya, Pilar. ''Plays-within-Plays in Three Modern Plays: Michael Frayn's *Noises Off,* Tom Stoppard's *The Real Thing,* and Alan Ayckbourn's *A Chorus of Disapproval*'' in *Revista Alicantina de Estudios Ingleses,* November, 1988, pp. 189-201.

FURTHER READING

Billington, Michael. *One Night Stands,* Nick Hern Books, 1993.
   This collection of the *Guardian*'s famous theater critic contains a good selection from two decades of criticism.

Brook, Peter. *The Empty Space,* London, 1968.
   Brook was one of the most influential theater directors in Britain in the Postwar period. He was long associated with the Royal Shakespeare Company. His directorial style showed the influences of Antonin Artaud and Bertolt Brecht. His essay collection analyses the basic problems facing contemporary theater and influenced many British and foreign directors.

Gordon, Robert. *Rosencrantz and Guildenstern Are Dead, Jumpers, and The Real Thing: Text and Performance,* Macmillan, 1991.
   This series focuses upon the plays in performance and is a useful guide to students of performance studies.

Trussler, Simon. *Cambridge Illustrated History of the British Theater,* Cambridge University Press, 1994.
   Trussler's well-informed and forthright history of British theater from the Roman period through to the present is a very readable source book.

Salome

OSCAR WILDE

1893

The story of the princess Salome (pronounced "Sah-loh-may"), stepdaughter of Herod, dates back to the book of Matthew in the Bible. In the original story, Salome dances for Herod's birthday feast, and he is so pleased with her dancing that he offers to give her anything she desires. Urged on by her mother, Salome requests the head of John the Baptist, and so she is responsible for the death of John. Since this first version of the story was written, many writers have retold the story of Salome. One of the most famous versions is the play *Salome* by Oscar Wilde.

Wilde wrote *Salome* in French in 1891, but the play was not produced for five years. In 1892, rehearsals for the play's first planned production began, but they were halted when the licenser of plays for the Lord Chamberlain, the British government official in charge of theater censorship, banned *Salome,* ostensibly because of an old law forbidding the depiction of Biblical characters onstage but probably also because of the play's focus on sexual passion. Wilde was so upset by *Salome*'s censorship that he threatened to leave England and live in France, where he would be granted more artistic freedom.

Wilde remained in England, however, and in 1893, the play was published in French simultaneously in France and England with drawings by the artist Aubrey Beardsley, whose grotesque and even irrelevant illustrations for *Salome* have since become famous in their own right. Upon publication,

the play was hailed by some as a work of genius but dismissed by many others as vulgar and unoriginal. Lord Alfred Douglas, Wilde's lover, translated the play for an English-language edition, but Wilde was so greatly dissatisfied with Douglas's work that he revised the translation extensively (the English translation is now generally considered the work of Wilde). In 1896, with Wilde already in prison, *Salome* was finally produced, but in France, not England. The play did not appear on the English stage until 1905, five years after Wilde's death.

Many critics believe Wilde's inspiration for his version of *Salome* may have been the play *La Princesse Maleine,* written in French by Belgian playwright Maurice Maeterlinck. It is known that Wilde admired Maeterlinck's work; while he was in prison, Wilde asked his friends to bring copies of his work. Like *Salome, La Princesse Maleine* focuses on a strong young woman whose passion leads to her death. Maeterlinck's play is also similar to Wilde's stylistically. *La Princesse Maleine* makes use of the repetition of words and phrases, a method that gives *Salome* its poetic quality.

In the years since Wilde wrote *Salome,* the play has been used as the basis for further work. In 1905, Richard Strauss, retaining Wilde's text, turned the play into an opera, and there have been a number of film versions. In addition, the play itself has been revived many times and continues to be produced today. Once controversial and reviled by many critics, *Salome* is now considered an important symbolic work in modern drama.

AUTHOR BIOGRAPHY

Oscar Fingal O'Flahertie Wills Wilde was born in Dublin, Ireland, on October 16, 1854. His father, Sir William Wilde, was an internationally-known eye and ear surgeon, and his mother, Lady Wilde, born Jane Francesca Elgee, was an Irish Nationalist who published essays, poems, and stories under the name "Speranza," meaning Hope. Wilde had an elder brother, Wills, and a younger sister, Isola, whose death at the age of nine brought Wilde lasting grief.

At ten, Wilde was sent to Portora Royal School in Ulster, where he first developed what became a lifelong love for the art and philosophy of the

Oscar Wilde

Greeks, and where he first became known for his eccentric manner of dress. From there he went to Trinity College, Dublin, and then to Magdalen College, Oxford University, where he continued his study of the classics and was exposed to John Ruskin and Walter Pater's theories of devotion to art. Thus began Wilde's conviction of the importance of Art for Art's sake, rather than for a greater moral purpose, and to the importance of beauty for its own sake as well.

In 1879, Wilde left Oxford for London, where he became known as a witty conversationalist and an aesthete, a person devoted to beauty. Cartoons in the British magazine *Punch* satirized Wilde's outlandish dress and his love of sunflowers and lilies. In 1880, Wilde published his first play *Vera; or the Nihilists,* and in 1881, he published *Poems,* which received mixed reviews. That same year, Wilde was invited to lecture in America, and his tour received enormous publicity. In 1883, he returned to London, then left to live and write in Paris, where he completed a second play, *The Duchess of Padua.*

On May 29, 1884, Wilde married Constance Lloyd, with whom he had two children, Cyril and Vyvyan. In 1890, Wilde published his first major literary work, the novel *The Picture of Dorian Gray.* In 1892, Wilde's comedy *Lady Windermere's Fan* was produced on the London stage; the play was a success with audiences but received a mixed critical reception. An attempt to have *Salome* produced that same year was thwarted by the Lord Chamberlain, who was in charge of theater censorship, ostensibly because of an old law that forbade the depiction of Biblical characters onstage. Wilde continued to write plays, and works such as *A Woman of No Importance* (1893) and *An Ideal Husband* (1895) further enhanced his reputation. *The Importance of Being Earnest* (1895), generally considered Wilde's most brilliant work, met with great success, but Wilde's triumph was soon to be followed by tragedy.

Wilde had been engaging in homosexual relationships, which was against the law in Victorian England. In 1891, Wilde met Lord Alfred Douglas (who was nicknamed Bosie), and the two men became lovers. Wilde became passionately devoted to Douglas, who often acted the spoiled child. Douglas's father, the Marquess of Queensbury, was enraged by the relationship and harassed Wilde. In 1894, Queensbury left a calling card at Wilde's club with the words, "For Oscar Wilde, posing Somdonite," by which Queensbury meant "sodomite" or homosexual. Urged on by Douglas, Wilde sued Queensbury for libel, but at the trial, Queensbury presented evidence of Wilde's sexual relationships with a number of young men.

Wilde dropped his suit but ignored friends' advice to leave the country and was arrested and tried. The jury could not reach a verdict, but Wilde was tried a second time and was convicted and sentenced to two years at hard labor which—because of harsh prison conditions—was a virtual death sentence for a man of Wilde's class.

Wilde suffered terribly in prison, where he irrevocably lost his health. He was released in 1897, but he was bankrupt and, because of the great scandal, was never permitted to see his children again. Wilde left England for France, where he lived under the pseudonym Sebastien Melmoth until his death on November 30, 1900.

PLOT SUMMARY

As *Salome* begins, the Young Syrian, the Page of Herodias, the Cappadocian, the Nubian, and a number of soldiers stand on a great terrace in the palace of Herod. It is night, and the moon is shining. Towards the back of the set, there is a large cistern in which Jokanaan, the prophet is imprisoned. The Young Syrian repeatedly speaks to the Page of how beautiful Salome is, but the Page tells the Syrian that he should not look at Salome so much, that something terrible will happen.

The two also discuss the moon. To the Page, the moon seems like a dead woman. For the Syrian, the moon is a dancing princess. The Cappodocian, the Nubian, and the soldiers discuss various beliefs about the nature of God or the gods. The first soldier says that the Hebrews worship a God that cannot be seen, and the Cappadocian sees no sense in such a belief. In his country, there are no gods left. From the cistern, Jokanaan speaks of the coming of Christ, and there is some discussion of the nature of Jokanaan's prophecies, of whether the prophet is a holy man or is only "saying ridiculous things."

Salome enters, saying she can no longer stay in the banqueting hall with Herod and Herodias. To Salome, the moon is a virgin—"She has never defiled herself." Salome hears the voice of Jokanaan and says she must speak with him, that he must be taken out of the cistern. At first, all say that Jokanaan cannot be removed, but finally the Syrian is persuaded by the princess's charms to bring him forth. Jokanaan is released and begins to speak against Herodias, Salome's mother.

Salome is fascinated by the prophet. At first she tells him that his body is beautiful, but he insults her, calling her the Daughter of Babylon, telling her not to speak to him. She speaks further of his appearance, saying that his hair is terrible but that she desires his mouth. She tells him to let her kiss his mouth. He continues to insult her, and she repeatedly responds, "I will kiss thy mouth." The Syrian begs Salome to stay away from Jokanaan, but she will not listen, and he finally kills himself in despair, falling between them. Jokanaan tells Salome to seek the Son of Man, but when she continues to tell him to let her kiss his mouth, he says she is accursed and goes back into the cistern.

Herod, Herodias, and the rest of the Court enter. Herod slips in the blood of the Syrian. When he is told the Syrian has killed himself, Herod says that he is sorry but that the Syrian looked at Salome too much. Herodias repeatedly says that Herod himself looks at Salome too much. Jokanaan's voice is again heard, prophesying, and Herodias says the prophet constantly insults her and that he must be quiet. Herod says that Jokanaan is a holy man and that he has seen God. Jokanaan says that the Saviour of the World has come. When Herod assumes that the prophet refers to Caesar, two Nazarenes respond that Jokanaan refers to the Messiah, who has come and is working miracles. When told that the so-called Messiah is healing the lepers and the blind and raising the dead, Herod says that the man must be found and told that he cannot raise the dead, that the king will not permit it.

Jokanaan continues to speak against Herodias, and the queen complains to Herod, but Herod says that his marrying Herodias, who was his brother's wife, is the cause of Jokanaan's terrible words. The prophet says a terrible day will come that the moon will turn to blood. At this point Herod asks Salome to dance for him, but she refuses. He tells her that if she dances for him, he will give her anything she asks, even if it is half of his kingdom. Herodias tells Salome not to dance, but the princess says she will dance for Herod. Herod then points out that the moon has become as red as blood, as Jokanaan predicted.

Herodias implores her daughter not to dance, but Salome dances for Herod. After she has finished, Herod asks her what she wants as her reward. Salome answers that she wants the head of Jokanaan.

Herodias approves of Salome's request, but Herod is terrified. He begs Salome to ask for something else. He offers her his great emerald and fifty of his peacocks, but she repeats her request: the head of Jokanaan. Herod tells Salome that Jokanaan is a man of God and that great misfortune will come if he dies, but Salome persists. Herod finally takes the ring of death off of his finger and gives it to a soldier, who hands it to the executioner. The executioner goes down into the cistern.

Salome listens as Jokanaan is killed and wonders why the prophet does not cry out. The executioner brings forth the head of Jokanaan on a silver shield. Salome seizes the head and speaks to it, saying that now she will kiss Jokanaan's mouth; she will "bite it like a ripe fruit." Herod says that Salome has committed a great crime and demands that the torches be put out. He begins to climb the stairs as Salome continues to speak, saying that now she has kissed the mouth of Jokanaan. Herod turns toward Salome, crying, "Kill that woman!" The soldiers crush Salome.

CHARACTERS

A Cappadocian

The Cappadocian briefly discusses the gods with other minor characters at the beginning of the play.

First Soldier

Together with the second soldier, he refuses to bring Jokanaan forth to see. At the end of the play, both obey Herod's orders to kill Salome.

Herod Antipas

Herod Antipas is the Tetrarch of Judaea. He is the husband of Herodias and the stepfather of Salome. He is a powerful man, able to decide which of his subjects will live and which will die. He displays a complicated mix of emotions—cruelty, compassion, fear, and guilt. When the Young Syrian dies, Herod tells Herodias that the Syrian was the son of a king, and that Herod himself drove the Syrian's father from his kingdom and made his queen a slave. Yet, seemingly because of his feelings of guilt, Herod says he considered the Young Syrian a "guest" and made him a captain. Similarly, Herod took his queen Herodias from his own brother; thus Herod's marriage is incestuous. Herod expresses guilt over this, but as with his other abuses of power, Herod does not act on his feelings of remorse, and there is no indication that he will refrain from such wrongdoing in the future. In fact, Herod clearly exhibits incestuous feelings toward Salome, his own stepdaughter.

Herod continually states that he does not kill Jokanaan, although he has imprisoned him, because Jokanaan is a prophet, a man of God, but it is evident that Herod's feelings of guilt and his fear of Jokanaan affect his decision. When Herod's lust for Salome leads him to offer her anything in exchange for her dancing for him, he acts recklessly, and so must have the Prophet killed for Salome. Although it is he who finally orders Jokanaan's death, Herod's guilt turns to rage at Salome, and so he has her killed essentially because of his own actions.

Herodias

Herodias is the wife of Herod and the mother of Salome. She was previously the wife of Herod's brother, and so her marriage to Herod is considered incestuous. Jokanaan continually speaks against her, and she is angry that Herod does nothing to

MEDIA ADAPTATIONS

- *Salome* was adapted as a silent film in 1923. This version was directed by Charles Bryant. It was produced by Alla Nazimova and also starred Nazimova as Salome and Mitchell Lewis as Herod.

- A 1970 Spanish version of *Salome* was directed by Rafael Gassent.

- Another film version was produced and directed by Carmelo Bene in 1972.

- A 1986 film, directed by Claude d'Anna, stars Jo Champa as Salome and Tomas Milian as Herod.

- The 1988 film *Salome's Last Dance,* directed by Ken Russell and produced by Penny Corke, features Nickolas Grace as Oscar Wilde watching a production of his play staged in a brothel by the proprietor. Imogen Millaid-Scott plays Salome as well as a woman named Rose. Stratford Johns plays both Herod and Alfred Taylor. Douglas Hodge plays Jokanaan and Lord Alfred Douglas.

silence the prophet. She also complains that Herod looks at Salome too much and says that Salome should not dance for Herod. When Salome asks for the head of Jokanaan, Herodias believes that Salome does so for love of her mother. Herodias is pleased with Salome's request and pressures Herod to have the prophet executed.

Jews

The Jews argue that Jokanaan is not the prophet Elias and that Jesus is not the Messiah.

Jokanaan

Jokanaan, or John the Baptist, is a Christian prophet. He has been imprisoned by Herod, and, for much of the play, he exists as a disembodied voice coming from the cistern onstage. He speaks continually of the coming of Jesus, whom he believes to be the Messiah, and the punishment awaiting those

who do evil. For Jokanaan, the members of Herod's family are accursed, and he calls Salome the "Daughter of Sodom." Salome wants Jokanaan to see her as a woman and to kiss her, but he speaks only of her evil, thus angering her. Herodias wants Herod to have Jokanaan killed, but Herod believes Jokanaan has seen God, and he fears Jokanaan's terrible prophecies. Jokanaan seems to believe his only purpose in the world is to act as the voice of God, and he seems devoid of human emotion. Even when he is executed, he does not struggle, beg for his life, or even cry out; in fact, he makes no sound at all.

Naaman

Naaman is the executioner who kills Jokanaan and brings his head to Salome on a silver shield.

Nazarenes

The Nazarenes believe that Jokanaan is the prophet Elias and that Jesus is the Messiah. They speak of the miracles Jesus performs.

Nubian

The Nubian discusses the gods with other minor characters at the beginning of the play.

Page

The Page of Herodias is a friend of the Young Syrian and advises him not to look at Salome so much. There is some suggestion that he is in love with the Young Syrian.

Salome

Salome, the title character of the play, is a princess, the daughter of Herodias and the stepdaughter of Herod. She expects to live according to her own desires and is not afraid to disobey Herod. She convinces the Young Syrian to bring her Jokanaan, though Herod has forbidden anyone to see him. She desires Jokanaan sexually and initially speaks admirably of his appearance. When he rebukes her, however, she says that his body is hideous and that his hair is horrible. She still admires, however, the redness of Jokanaan's lips and repeatedly tells him, not that she *wants* to kiss his mouth but that she will, assuming that she will finally have her desires satisfied.

Salome initially refuses to dance for Herod but changes her mind when he says he will give her anything. Upon finishing her dance, she demands the head of Jokanaan, ignoring Herod's plea that she ask for something else. Upon receiving the prophet's head, she kisses his mouth, proving that she has power over Jokanaan, that even though he calls her evil, she can take his life. Her victory, however, is short-lived, for Herod has more power than she and thus can have her killed.

Second Soldier

Together with the first soldier, he refuses to bring Jokanaan forth to see Salome. At the end of the play, both obey Herod's order to kill Salome.

Slave

The slave tells Salome that Herod wishes her to return to the feast.

Tigellinus

Tigellinus is a young Roman. When Jokanaan speaks of the "Saviour of the World," Tigellinus tells Herod that that is one of Caesar's titles

The Young Syrian

The Young Syrian is the Captain of the Guard. He comes from a royal family, but Herod drove his father from his kingdom and made his mother a slave. He seems to be in love with Salome, and it appears that the Page of Herodias may be in love with him. The Young Syrian advises Salome not to speak to the prophet but finally gives in to her demands and brings Jokanaan to speak with her. When Salome insists that she wants to kiss Jokanaan, the Young Syrian kills himself.

THEMES

Religious Beliefs

A number of kinds of religions—pagan, Jewish, and Christian—are represented in *Salome*. From the beginning of the play, the nature of God or the gods is a subject of dispute. The pagans believe in numerous gods, but their gods are dissatisfying to them. The Nubian describes the gods of his country as "fond of blood." His countrymen sacrifice fifty young men and one hundred maidens twice a year, but the Nubian says that even this is not enough for

the gods of his country, whom he describes as "very harsh to us." The Cappodocian says that he has sought the gods of his country in the mountains, where they are said to have been driven by the Romans, but that the gods are not there. The Cappodocian therefore concludes that the gods of his country must be dead. Thus the religions of the pagans in the play are no longer valid for them. Yet they retain their beliefs, and when they are told that the Jews worship a god who cannot be seen, they do not think that the existence of such a god is possible. The Cappadocian describes the beliefs of the Jews as "altogether ridiculous."

While Wilde is not critical of the concept of a God that can't be seen, the religion of the Jews is not satisfactory either. The Jews of the play are a divided people. The second soldier says of the Jews' arguing, "They are always like that. They are disputing their religion." The Pharisees insist that angels exist, while the Sadducees are equally insistent that they do not. One Jew says that no one has seen God since the prophet Elias, while a second argues that even Elias may not have seen God, and a third states that "God is at no time hidden." The Jews agree on only one thing—they want Jokanaan released to them, but the implication is that the Jews will harm Jokanaan, whom most of Wilde's audience would consider a prophet of God.

In considering Wilde's depiction of the Jews, it is important to remember the social context of the play. Wilde wrote at a time when and in a country where Jews were second-class citizens, marginalized in Victorian culture, often hated and feared, and at times called "Christ-killers" because many Christians blamed the Jews for the crucifixion of Jesus. It should also be noted, however, that in the play, Wilde's Jews are not evil and that Wilde is not necessarily critical of the Jewish religion but of those who have turned their religious beliefs into a series of arguments about seemingly trivial issues. In either case, Judaism, as presented in the play, is not a sustaining meaningful religion.

This, of course, leaves Christianity, and it may at first appear that it is this religion, the religion of most of his contemporaries, that Wilde supports. The Nazarenes speak of Jesus healing the lepers and the blind and raising the dead. In addition, the representative of Christianity in the play is Jokanaan, whose prophecies of destruction in the palace of Herod do come true. The Christianity of Jokanaan, however, is angry and hateful. He promises redemption to those who follow Jesus, but most of his

TOPICS FOR FURTHER STUDY

- Research the role of women in Victorian culture. How does *Salome* reflect Victorian beliefs about gender roles?

- Who is the main character in *Salome?* Some critics would answer Salome herself, some would argue Herod, and Wilde himself, though probably in jest, said that the moon is the protagonist of the play. Using evidence from the play, support your point of view.

- Read the story of Salome in the Bible, Matthew 14:1-12. In what ways has Wilde changed the Biblical story? What has he achieved with these changes?

- Read Wilde's play *A Woman of No Importance.* Compare the moral issues raised in this play with those raised in *Salome.* How are the two plays alike? How are they different?

- Discuss Wilde's use of color in *Salome.* What function does the frequent mention of color serve? What might the different colors in the play symbolize?

- Read Sophocles's *Antigone,* a play which also has a strong female character who battles a king and pays with her life. Antigone, however, is generally considered a heroine, while there is some debate about the nature of Salome's character. Compare and contrast these two characters in light of what might be considered ''proper'' roles for women.

---

preaching is of punishment and the evil of those around him.

It is Salome who points out the missing element in Jokanaan's Christianity in a statement that seems to veer away from her previous focus on sexual desire. Speaking to the head of Jokanaan, she says, ''If thou hadst looked at me thou hadst loved me. Well I know that thou wouldst have loved me, and the mystery of love is greater than the mystery of death. Love only should one consider.'' It is Salome, just before her death, who is able to transcend the particulars of various religions, none of which, as presented in Wilde's play, seem to present a meaningful answer to the question of the nature of God.

Sexual Desire

In many Christian traditions, sexual desire is seen as a source of evil. Lust, sexual desire without love, is even one of the seven deadly sins. But Western traditions regarding the evil of sexual desire do not treat male and female desire equally. Historically, female sexual desire has often been seen as more suspect than that of the male. Traditionally, a woman is not really supposed to have sexual desires of her own, but to satisfy the sexual needs of her husband. Women have often been dichotomized as either good girls or bad, virgins or whores. In *Salome,* sexual desire seems to be, at least to some extent, evil, but the sexual desires of the women are treated much more harshly than those of the men.

In the play, Jokanaan is the primary spokesperson against the evil of sexual sin. His focus through most of the play is on Herodias, whom he says will be punished for evil. He describes Herodias as ''she who gave herself to the Captains of Assyria'' and ''she who hath given herself to the young men of Egypt.'' ''Bid her rise up from the bed of her abominations—from the bed of her incestuousness,'' he commands. The marriage of Herodias and Herod, her husband's brother, is indeed considered incestuous, but only Herodias is called to task for the their sexual sin.

In the time period in which the play takes place, women were severely punished for adultery, but their male partners received no such punishment. Such an attitude is reflected in the words of Jokanaan. Herod expresses guilt over his marriage to Herodias,

Stratford Johns as Herod and Glenda Jackson as Herodias in a scene from director Ken Russell's film adaptation of Wilde's play titled Salome's Last Dance

and he is afraid of a supernatural punishment. Yet when Herodias at the end of the play says that she approves of Salome's actions, Herod replies, "There speaks the incestuous wife." Like Jokanaan, he seems to blame Herodias for the evil he believes will come of their marriage.

While Herodias seems to be blamed for her marriage and for other possible sexual indiscretions as well, it is Salome who is truly punished for her sexual desires. Herod and the Young Syrian gaze at Salome to the point that it is noticed by other characters and that does seem unacceptable within the context of the play, but Salome's expression of sexual desire is extremely blatant. She looks at Jokanaan's body and longs to touch his skin, his hair. She says again and again that she will kiss his mouth. The more he rebukes her, the more she seems to desire him.

Salome's intense desire for Jokanaan is unmistakably evil, as she turns to violence to satisfy her needs. After having the object of her desire executed, she says she will not just kiss his mouth but bite it "as one bites a ripe fruit." The play suggests that hidden beneath female sexual desire is the desire to overcome and to destroy. And Wilde, although he often wrote of women who were wrongly ac-

cused of immorality, chose the ultimate punishment for Salome's violent sexual desires. Her insistence on the satisfaction of those desires leads to her destruction.

It is true that Herod and the Young Syrian are both punished for their desire for Salome. Herod suffers the death of Jokanaan, and the Syrian commits suicide when his desire for Salome leads him to give in to her wish to see Jokanaan. But their desire for Salome is portrayed as much more innocuous. Both only gaze at Salome. It even seems as if the Syrian may love her, for he obeys Salome when she says that she may smile at him, beneath her veil, when she passes by. Their desire for her is neither as blatant nor as violent as her desire for Jokanaan, and their punishment is not as severe.

There is a hint of another, possibly sexual, relationship in *Salome,* which does have its basis in love. This is the "friendship" between the Young Syrian and the Page of Herodias. When the Syrian kills himself, the Page's speech about his relationship with the Syrian seems to reveal a deep relationship between the two: "He has slain himself who was my friend. I gave him a little box of perfumes and ear-rings wrought in silver, and now he has killed himself . . . why did I not hide him from the moon?'' Here the Page shows love for the Syrian, but the possible sexual nature of the relationship is unclear.

If Wilde meant the relationship to be homosexual in nature, he could not have made that explicit in the text at the time, so Wilde's purpose here can never be known for sure. It is interesting to note, however, that the one relationship in the text that seems to be based on real love is that between two men. Considering that Wilde was involved in a relationship with Lord Alfred Douglas at the time, it is quite possible that the relationship between the Syrian and the Page reflects that between Douglas and the playwright. In that case, true love is distinctly separate from the evil of female sexual desire.

STYLE

Protagonist

The principal character of a play is called the protagonist. It is he or she around whom the play mostly revolves. Often, readers assume that the protagonist of *Salome* is the princess. She is, after all, the title character, and the play focuses to a great extent on her actions and the results of her actions. Her desire for Jokanaan is central to the story. The identity of the protagonist, however, is not always as clear as one would think. When asked, Wilde himself said, though probably in jest, that the principal character in *Salome* is the moon. It is true that the moon is an important part of the play, and it is not static—the appearance of the moon changes throughout the play, so one could argue that it is not an entirely inanimate object. Still, it seems difficult to offer much support for Wilde's statement. What is certainly worth examination, however, is the possibility that Herod, as some critics have argued, is *Salome's* true protagonist.

In many ways Herod resembles the traditional tragic hero of classical literature, whose fatal flaw, in this case his desire for Salome, leads to his downfall. Herod's character is complex, arguably more so than Salome's, and the large percentage of the lines in the play that are Herod's focus audience attention on him.

But such arguments for Herod as protagonist still do not negate the arguments that could be made

in favor of Salome having that role. The reader of the text of *Salome* could certainly see either character as the protagonist. For a production of *Salome* to work, however, the director would have to make a definite decision as to whether the protagonist is Salome or Herod, and that decision would serve to focus the play's direction. More audience attention could be directed toward one character or the other. If the production were successful, the director's decision about the identity of the protagonist would be clear to the audience.

Lyrical Theater

Salome is often described as a lyrical work, in other words, a play that reads similar to a poem. There are a number of poetic aspects to *Salome*. Perhaps the most obvious is Wilde's use of poetic imagery and language, which is particularly evident in the characters' description of the moon. The Young Syrian says that the moon is ''like a little princess who wears a yellow veil, and whose feet are of silver. . . . You would fancy she was dancing.'' Herod says of the moon, ''The clouds are seeking to hide her nakedness.''

The use of imagery and poetic language is also notable in Salome's description of Jokanaan: ''Thy mouth is like a band of scarlet on a tower of ivory. It is like a pomegranate cut with a knife of ivory.'' Repetition is also common in poetry, whether it be repetition of symbols, as in the recurring descriptions of the moon, or the repetition of words, as when Salome repeatedly says to Jokanaan, ''I will kiss thy mouth.'' In addition, the use of music in a production would contribute to the lyrical nature of the play. Such music could be used throughout, as there are frequent references to the feast offstage, which could certainly involve music. In addition, a production could make much use of music when Salome dances the dance of the seven veils for Herod. The motion of the dance would contribute to the lyrical feel of the play as well.

Symbolism

In literature, a symbol stands for something other than itself. Symbols are used throughout the play, but perhaps the most obvious symbol in *Salome* is the moon. Each character sees the moon as something different. At times it seems to stand for variations of the character's visions of the nature of Salome. The Young Syrian, who admires Salome, sees the moon as a dancing princess. The Page of

Herodias, concerned that the Syrian's desire for Salome will lead to his destruction, says that the moon resembles a dead woman. For Salome herself, the moon is a virgin, undefiled by men. For Herod, who lusts after Salome, the moon is a naked, drunken woman. In addition, the moon is the traditional symbol of the Greek goddess Artemis or Diana, a strong and independent virgin who demanded chastity from both male and female followers. Jokanaan predicts that the moon will turn to blood, and it does turn red, symbolizing the destruction of both Jokanaan and Salome.

Another symbolic element of *Salome* lies in the use of color. The colors red, white, and black are used repeatedly. Red is used for wine, blood, and the mouth of Jokanaan, and seems to indicate a connection between passion and violence. White is used for the feet of Salome and the body of Jokanaan. It can indicate the innocence and purity or be the color of a lifeless body. Black often symbolizes death as well. Jokanaan's hair is black, and at the end of the play, "a great black cloud crosses the moon and conceals it completely." Black, like red, seems to indicate destruction. A number of other colors in the play may be seen as symbolic as well.

In the late-nineteenth century, symbolism came to mean not just the use of single symbols but a particular art form, a reaction against the realism that predominated on stage. Playwright Maurice Maeterlinck, whom Wilde admired and whose work seems to have provided some of the inspiration for *Salome,* is largely credited with bringing symbolism into theater. *Salome* is considered by many critics to be an important symbolist work.

HISTORICAL CONTEXT

The 1890s in Britain were a time of changing values, a time when traditional conceptions of the world were being called into question. One of the major issues of the day revolved around what was called "the woman question"—the debate over a woman's place in society. "The Angel in the House," a popular Victorian poem later made famous in an essay by Virginia Woolf, presented the perfect woman as one who always sacrificed her own comfort for the sake of others, whose major purpose in life was to care for her home and family, who

deferred to her husband at all times, and who had no desires, sexual or otherwise, of her own.

It was also at this time, however, that the term "new woman," probably coined in 1894, came into prominence. The new woman was a member of a more liberated generation. She sought suffrage (the right to vote) for women, which was not achieved in Britain until 1926. She also believed in education for women and the end of the sexual double standard, which allowed men considerable sexual freedom, while insisting that women remain chaste until marriage. Wilde's character Salome could hardly be more directly opposed to the concept of "The Angel in the House." She seeks power over men and has strong sexual desires of her own. Salome, however, is punished for her transgressions with death, and her punishment resembles that of women presented in some Victorian novels, in which virtuous women are rewarded and the putative immoral women are destroyed.

In contemporary society, it is common to assume that such novels are representative of Victorian society as a whole. The Victorian period, however, was in reality much more complicated. Although Wilde's homosexual acts resulted in his imprisonment and almost complete public ostracism, there seem to have also been a fair number of homosexual men who were more successful at concealing the nature of their sexual identities. The 1890s were also the time of the phenomenon of Decadence, an artistic movement began in France and embraced by Wilde as well as other English artists, whose adherents sought to question Victorian respectability with work that was at time overtly sexual and indulged in the depiction of general excess. It should be noted, however, that a backlash against Decadence followed Wilde's trial.

In Victorian England, Christianity predominated. Adherents of other religions, such as Judaism, suffered suspicion and persecution. Nonetheless, Christianity lost some of the influence it had in earlier times. The publication in 1859 of Charles Darwin's *The Origin of Species,* in which he presented his theories of natural selection and evolution, shocked and angered Victorians because it called into question the belief that humans were created by God. For the Victorian, such scientific progress seemed at times to threaten religious beliefs. Fears of such a threat were not entirely unfounded. The late-nineteenth century also saw a rise in agnosticism, a term coined by Thomas Huxley in

COMPARE
&
CONTRAST

- 30 A.D.: Segregation based on gender is rigid. In some cases, wives are little better than slaves. Recent scholarship has uncovered evidence of individual women who did have some power in their society, but such women were rare.

  1893: The status of women is in flux. Some embrace the concept of the perfect submissive woman, while others embrace the idea of the ''new woman,'' educated and more free than her predecessors.

  Today: Women have achieved many opportunities unimaginable by previous generations. Much discrimination against women, previously considered acceptable, has ended through custom or law, though women still face difficulties in many areas.

- 30 A.D.: The Romans allow communities within their empire a modicum of religious freedom, unless said religions threaten the peace of the empire. Numerous religions are represented in Roman society.

  1893: Christianity predominates in Victorian culture, and adherents of other religions are often treated with suspicion. Atheism and agnosticism gain popularity among those seeking alternatives.

  Today: Although there continue to be a large number of people practicing a variety of faiths, many do not see religion as part of their day-to-day lives. Many are agnostics or atheists.

- 30 A.D.: Rules against sexual misconduct are applied unequally. Polygamy is accepted among the wealthy. Adultery by women can be punished with death while adulterous men receive no such punishment.

  1893: Society has rigid rules regarding sexual morality, but many question such rules, acting in opposition to them. Homosexuality is punishable by imprisonment.

  Today: Variations in sexual activity are more acceptable. Homosexuals are not subject to the legal restrictions of former times, but gays still suffer from prejudice and even violence at the hands of others.

1869 to represent the belief that it was impossible to know if God even existed.

Another changing area in Britain at the time involved the structure of the society itself. Previously, the poor and powerless had been blamed for their lot, but some were beginning to see poverty as the result, not of laziness, but of a lack of appropriate employment. The government began to take more responsibility for the problems of the poor. Nonetheless, great gaps between the rich and the poor, the powerful and the powerless, continued to exist.

Salome was written at a time when British culture was undergoing great changes, and in some ways the play seems representative of those changes. *Salome* raises the issues of the status of women, of sexuality and morality, of the meaning of religious belief, of wealth and power. Wilde's portrayal of such issues shocked and angered many of his contemporaries, but others embraced his ideas.

CRITICAL OVERVIEW

From its beginnings, *Salome* was a controversial play, criticized for its perceived immorality. In a sense, the earliest criticism of the play was in the censorship of its first planned production. Rehearsals had begun in June, 1892, at the Palace Theatre in London but were terminated when the government-appointed censor of theatrical productions banned *Salome* from the stage, officially because of an obscure British law forbidding the onstage depiction of Biblical characters—though it is speculated that the play's focus on blatantly sexual issues was another reason. The general public was not exposed to *Salome* until 1892, when the manuscript was published in book form in both London and Paris.

Early critics of the text version of *Salome* were primarily concerned with its perceived immorality. Reflecting widely-held moral ideals of the Victorian period, an anonymous reviewer for the London *Times,* quoted in Karl Beckson's book *Oscar Wilde: The Critical Heritage,* called the play "an arrangement in blood and ferocity, morbid, *bizarre,* repulsive, and very offensive in its adaptation of scriptural phraseology to situations the reverse of sacred." Another anonymous reviewer quoted by Beckson, this one working for the *Pall Mall Gazette,* also argued that the play was offensive, saying of the banning of *Salome* from the British stage, "it would be hard to see how the Examiner of Plays could have acted otherwise" and further noting that "the creeds of an Empire are not toys to be trifled with by any seeker after notoriety."

The reviewer's primary focus, however, was not on the supposed immorality of the play but what he believed to be Wilde's lack of originality. According to this reviewer, *Salome* relies too heavily on the works of other writers. "She is the daughter of too many fathers," he wrote. "Her bones want strength, her flesh wants vitality, her blood is polluted. There is no pulse of passion in her." Wilde, according to this reviewer, "has shown, not for the first time, that he can mimic, where he might have shown—for the first time—that he could create."

In contrast, critic William Archer, also quoted by Beckson, argued that the censorship of *Salome* "was perfectly ridiculous" and also stated that Wilde's play was superior to those of the writers he was accused of mimicking. "There is far more depth in Mr. Wilde's work," Archer wrote. "His characters are men and women, not filmy shapes of mist and moonshine. . . . His palette . . . is infinitely richer."

Salome was not actually produced in England until 1905, five years after Wilde's death. Even then, accusations of immorality continued to dog the play. Of a 1918 production, G. E. Morrison, writing for the *Morning Post* (and quoted by Philip Hoare in *Oscar Wilde's Last Stand*) called *Salome* "a bizarre melodrama of disease," and added, "One may admit its atmosphere though it is an atmosphere people who are healthy and desire to remain so would do well to keep out of." Also quoted by Hoare, Bernard Weller, writing for the *Stage,* described the play as "a very impure work"

and said that *Salome*'s atmosphere was "charged with a sickly voluptuousness." For Weller, the play's supposed immorality could not be separated from its art: "this kind of stuff has no relationship to art." "It is animalism, or worse; for animals have their decencies." But even as art, Weller considered the play a failure and used the review as an opportunity to fault Wilde in general, stating that "the late Oscar Wilde, though an adroit writer of showy, insincere comedies of modern society, had no perception of tragedy."

As moral standards changed in the twentieth century, *Salome*'s "purity" became less of an issue, though some scribes have found the play problematic for other reasons. After discussing the lyrical nature of *Salome,* critic Peter Raby, in his 1988 book *Oscar Wilde,* called *Salome* "a work which attracted vilification, and which almost invites ridicule." The play, according to Raby, is not easy to stage successfully: "It demands a particular style of speech and movement, and an exquisite sensitivity of design." But Raby still considered the play an achievement, especially when one considers the time period in which it was written. "It is remarkable," the critic wrote, "that Wilde . . . could create a truly modern symbolist drama within a theatrical and social context of such pronounced hostility." In a sense, the play was greeted with such harsh criticism because Wilde was a man ahead of his time.

Katherine Worth, in her 1983 book *Oscar Wilde,* seemed to concur, calling *Salome* "the first triumphant demonstration of the symbolist doctrine of total theatre." Like Raby, she saw Wilde as ahead of his time, anticipating a direction that modern theater would take. Many would agree with Worth, who noted that *Salome* "remains Wilde's master work in the symbolic mode."

CRITICISM

Clare Cross

Cross is a Ph.D. candidate specializing in modern drama. In this essay she discusses the connections between love, sexual desire, and power in Wilde's play.

On July 7, 1896, while Wilde was imprisoned in Reading Gaol, thirty-year-old Thomas Wooldridge,

WHAT
DO I READ
NEXT?

- *The Importance of Being Earnest,* a play by Wilde produced in 1895, is generally considered Wilde's best dramatic work. It's cleverness and wit reveal a side of Wilde not as apparent in *Salome.*

- Wilde's plays *A Woman of No Importance* and *Lady Windermere's Fan,* like *Salome,* deal with issues regarding women and sexual morality.

- ''The Angel in the House,'' a 1942 essay by Virginia Woolf, discusses the traditional role of women during Woolf's Victorian childhood and her struggle to overcome that role's limitations.

- *The Awakening* by Kate Chopin, first published in 1899, is an American novel about a woman who casts aside traditional female roles, abandons her family, and seeks fulfillment of her own desires. Like Salome, she is punished for her rebellion.

- Sophocles's play *Antigone,* written in approximately 441 B.C., is, like *Salome,* about a young woman who defies a king and is killed for her rebellion. Unlike Salome, however, Antigone is portrayed as a heroine.

- *Aesthetes and Decadents of the 1890s,* edited by Karl Beckson, is an anthology of British literary work from the period in which Wilde wrote *Salome.* This anthology contains work by Wilde as well as by other authors. It also contains a number of the Aubrey Beardsley illustrations for *Salome,* which appeared in the play's first published edition.

---

a trooper in the Royal Guards, was hanged for the murder of his twenty-three-year-old wife, of whom he was jealous. Wilde was greatly troubled by Wooldridge's death, and the execution became the basis for the poem, ''The Ballad of Reading Gaol,'' in which Wilde proposes that the emotions that led to Wooldridge's crime are, in fact universal:

> Yet each man kills the thing he loves, / By each let this be heard, / Some do it with a bitter look / Some with a flattering word. / The coward does it with a kiss, / The brave man with a sword!

In ''The Ballad of Reading Gaol,'' love is intertwined with violence, inseparable from destruction.

In *Salome,* both Salome and Herod kill the thing they love or desire. Further on in ''The Ballad of Reading Gaol,'' Wilde makes the connection between love and desire clear when he mentions various ways that people kill those they love, one of which seems particularly appropriate to *Salome:* ''Some strangle with the hands of Lust.'' In other words, some kill the thing they love with their desire. Critic Norbert Kohl, in his book, *Oscar Wilde: The Works of a Conformist Rebel,* wrote of such desire in *Salome,* ''Sex is the motivating force behind all the main characters but one,'' and in fact, sexual desire is the most obvious explanation for the behavior of Salome and Herod.

It seems, however, that another motivating factor is at work in the play. When Jokanaan refuses Salome's sexual advances, he is depriving her of much more than the satisfaction of her sexual desires. By rebuking Salome for her desire, he denies her power over him. Similarly, when Salome seems to give in to Herod's passion by dancing for him but then refuses his entreaties to spare Jokanaan's life, she shows that she does not reciprocate Herod's desire, that she only sought to gain something from him, and thus denies him power over her as well. It is this struggle for power, fought on the battlefield of sexual desire, that leads Salome and Herod to kill the thing they love.

From the beginning of the play, Salome is established as a woman who is both desirable and dangerous. The play's first line, in fact, focuses on her appearance, as the Young Syrian remarks, ''How beautiful is the Princess Salome tonight.'' As the play progresses, the Syrian continues to comment on Salome's beauty, and the Page of Herodias becomes alarmed. ''You must not look at her,'' he says. ''Something terrible may happen.'' When Salome comes onstage, she is again established as an object of desire, specifically Herod's desire, as she asks, ''Why does the Tetrarch look at me. . . . It is strange that the husband of my mother looks at me like that.'' Salome is distressed by Herod's gaze, and that seems to be her reason for leaving the feast. ''I will not stay,'' she says. ''I cannot stay.''

By looking at Salome in a sexually suggestive way, Herod has managed to assert some power over her. The only way she can re-establish her own power so far is by avoiding his sight. When Salome hears the voice of Jokanaan, however, she immediately identifies him in regard to the power he holds over Herod, as she asks if Jokanaan is ''He of whom the Tetrarch is afraid.'' It seems to be Jokanaan's power over Herod that first attracts Salome's interest. After hearing Jokanaan's voice, Salome herself asserts her own will over Herod when a slave tells her that the Tetrarch wants her to return to the feast. Salome answers, ''I will not go back.'' When the Syrian tells her, ''If you do not return some misfortune may happen,'' she ignores his statement altogether as she asks more questions about Jokanaan. When she is told that ''the Tetrarch does not wish anyone to speak to [Jokanaan],'' Salome demands to speak to him.

Although the soldier and the Syrian initially refuse to obey Salome, she eventually gains the Syrian's compliance by using his desire for her to overpower him. ''You will do this for me,'' she says, ''and to-morrow when I pass in my litter beneath the gateway of the idol-sellers I will let fall for you a little flower . . . it may be I will smile at you.'' Because the Syrian desires Salome, she easily gains control over him, and so he accedes to her wishes.

When Salome first sees Jokanaan, she steps back, away from him. At first she is repelled by him: ''But he is terrible. . . . It is his eyes above all that are terrible. . . . How wasted he is!'' But as Salome begins to focus on Jokanaan's body, she begins to speak of his appearance more positively, remarking that ''He is like a moonbeam, like a shaft of silver. His flesh must be cool like ivory.'' She becomes intrigued by the prophet and says, ''I must look at him closer.''

> **FOR SALOME, JOKANAAN'S REJECTION OF HER DESIRE RENDERED HER POWERLESS. FOR HEROD, SALOME'S USE OF HIS DESIRE TO ACHIEVE HER OWN ENDS SHOWED HE HAD NO POWER OVER HER. BOTH SALOME AND HEROD RESPONDED TO THIS LACK OF POWER BY KILLING THE THING THEY LOVED''**

But it is only when Jokanaan, who has been decrying Herodias, turns the force of his words upon Salome that she blatantly expresses desire for him. When he calls her the ''Daughter of Babylon'' and admonishes her to ''Come not near the chosen of the Lord,'' instead of responding with anger, she answers him with passion: ''Speak again, Jokanaan. Thy voice is wine to me.'' His refusal to defer to her power seems to inflame her desire. ''Jokanaan,'' she says, ''I am amorous of thy body!. . . Let me touch thy body.'' When he again speaks against Salome, she briefly expresses a confused combination of revulsion and passion: ''Thy body is hideous. . . . It is thy hair that I am enamoured. . . . Thy hair is horrible.''

Desire, however, wins out when she begins to focus on his mouth, saying, ''There is nothing in the world so red as thy mouth. . . . Let me kiss thy mouth.'' At this point, the Syrian, overcome with despair at Salome's desire for Jokanaan, kills himself, but his devotion to Salome has rendered him uninteresting to her. Salome is sure of her power over the Syrian and so she does not acknowledge, or even seem to notice, his death.

Jokanaan, however, continues to reject Salome. ''Cursed be thou,'' he says. ''Daughter of an incestuous mother, be thou accursed!'' Yet, no matter what he says to her, she responds with the same words again and again, ''I will kiss thy mouth, Jokanaan.'' He has made it clear that she has no power over him, and Salome cannot tolerate that, so she repeatedly says, not that she *wants* to kiss him but that she *will* kiss him. She tries to make it clear to him that he must give in to her. Finally, however, he leaves her sight as she left Herod's, but she continues to call after him, ''I will kiss thy mouth.'' His refusal of her advances, in essence, his power over her, makes her more determined. When she insists that she will kiss his mouth, her sexual desire for him is inseparable from her desire for power over him.

As Salome desires Jokanaan, Herod desires Salome. When Herod comes on stage, his first words are ''Where is Salome. . . . Why did she not return to the banquet as I commanded her.'' Thus he expresses his desire to see her as well as his desire for power over her. He is jealous of Salome and says over the Syrian's corpse, ''Truly, I thought he looked too much at [Salome].'' Herod asks Salome to drink wine with him, and she refuses. His sexual desire for her is suggested when he says, ''Salome, come and eat fruit with me. I love to see in a fruit the mark of thy little teeth.'' When she again refuses him, he makes an even more blatant sexual remark: ''Salome, come and sit next to me. I will give thee the throne of thy mother.''

Salome, however, stands fast in her refusal of Herod's advances. Herod expects Salome's obedience as his due and so complains to Herodias, ''You see how you have brought up this daughter of yours.'' Herod first asks, then commands, Salome to dance for him, but even though he is the Tetrarch, she does not obey. As Jokanaan's refusal of Salome gives him power over her, so Salome's refusal of Herod gives her power over him. When Salome will not obey his command, will not acknowledge his power, he tells her that he will give her anything, even half of his kingdom, if she will dance for him. In essence, he says that if she will give in to his passion—and thus give up her power over him—he will offer more power within his kingdom. She need only remain subordinate to him.

At first, Salome's dance seems a submission to the power of Herod. He has first asked, then demanded, then asked again, that she dance, and now she obeys. Herod's passion, however, has put him in a position of vulnerability. When Salome agrees to dance for him, he sees it as submission, but in actuality, her seeming submission gives her greater power over him. Because Herod has such a great desire for Salome, he agrees to submit his will to her. When he says he will give her anything she wants, he grants her almost unlimited power over

him. When Salome then demands the head of Jokanaan, her power over him is complete. He is put into the position of begging her not to demand Jokanaan's head, of offering her the treasures of his kingdom, ''great treasures above all price,'' if she will not exercise her power over him.

At this point Herodias tries to claim that Salome has asked for Jokanaan's head because ''she loves her mother well,'' but Salome will give no one power over her. She says, ''I do not heed my mother. It is for my own pleasure that I ask the head of Jokanaan.'' She makes it clear that she will allow no one power over her.

By appearing to surrender to Herod, Salome finally triumphs over him and, she believes, Jokanaan. When she is given the head of the prophet, Salome speaks to it, emphasizing her own power: ''Ah! thou wouldst not suffer me to kiss thy mouth Jokanaan! Well! I will kiss it now . . . I will bite it with my teeth as one bites a ripe fruit.'' She continues to talk to Jokanaan's head, speaking of her seeming triumph over him: ''Thy head belongs to me. I can do with it what I will. I can throw it to the dogs and the birds of the air.'' Salome believes she has achieved complete control over the man who once rebuked her.

The extent of Salome's real power over Jokanaan, however, is questionable. When he dies, he does not give Salome the satisfaction of showing fear or pain. ''Why does he not cry out, this man?'' she asks. He never acknowledges that she has any power over him. And even though she has taken his life, he has still withheld his love. It is at this point that Salome speaks more of love than desire. I loved thee yet, Jokanaan,'' she says. ''I love thee only . . . I am athirst for thy beauty.'' Because she loves Jokanaan, even though she has killed him, he retains his power over her.

Salome also seems to have lost her control over Herod. His talk of her shows no more desire: ''She is monstrous . . . she is altogether monstrous.'' But she has still deprived him of his power, and so he orders Salome's death as she ordered Jokanaan's. In this way Herod seems to gain control over her, but as with Salome, power, once lost, is not easily regained. Jokanaan is still dead. Herod cannot change that. And so Herod still suffers, and his power is compromised even more because the death of Jokanaan has brought him fear of an even greater power. ''Surely some terrible thing will befall,'' he says. "I began to be afraid." The death of Salome does not change the result of her power over him, power created by his desire.

In "The Ballad of Reading Gaol," Wilde wrote of Wooldridge, "The man had killed the thing he loved, / And so he had to die." Wooldridge's passion for his wife led him to jealousy. Jealousy reveals a sense of powerlessness and a desire for control. The only way Wooldridge could achieve that control was by the murder of his wife. He paid for that murder, however, with his life.

For Salome, Jokanaan's rejection of her desire rendered her powerless. For Herod, Salome's use of his desire to achieve her own ends showed he had no power over her. Both Salome and Herod responded to this lack of power by killing the thing they loved. But the death of Jokanaan did not free Salome from his power over her, and the death of Salome could not fully restore Herod's power to him. Both are ultimately defeated by sexual desire as well as the desire for power.

Source: Clare Cross, for *Drama for Students,* Gale, 2000.

Christopher S. Nassaar

In this essay, Nassaar examines the theme of violence in two of Wilde's works, noting the influence of notorious murderer Jack the Ripper.

In late 1888 a murderer who came to be known as Jack the Ripper terrorized London prostitutes and captured the public's imagination through a series of violent crimes. Not only did he kill prostitutes with a knife but he also ripped and mutilated their bodies, so that the result was quite gruesome. By early 1890, when Oscar Wilde sat down to write *The Picture of Dorian Gray,* the figure of Jack the Ripper was still dominant in the public mind. My thesis here is that the influence of Jack the Ripper is discernible in some of Wilde's writings, specifically *The picture of Dorian Gray* and *Salome.*

In his desire to experience all the sinful pleasure of the world, Dorian Gray in Wilde's novel seeks to go beyond anything the human race has experienced so far. Modeling himself largely on Huysmans's hero Des Esseintes, he seeks to go beyond Des Esseintes. But his relentless pursuit of evil beauty is threatened by Basil Hallward, to whom he reveals his secret. Impulsively, Dorian kills the painter, but he does so in a manner reminiscent of the Jack the Ripper murders:

SALOME IS DEVOID OF ANY MORAL SENSE. HERS IS THE ULTIMATE CRIME. EVEN THE DEPRAVED AND LUSTFUL HEROD, WHO MURDERED HIS OWN BROTHER AND ROBBED HIM OF HIS WIFE, FINDS HER CRIME ABOMINABLE AND ORDERS HER KILLED"

Something glimmered on the top of the painted chest that faced him. His eye fell on it. He knew what it was. It was a knife that he had brought up, some days before, to cut a piece of cord, and had forgotten to take away with him. He moved slowly towards it, passing Hallward as he did so. As soon as he got behind him, he seized it, and turned round. Hallward stirred in his chair as if he was going to rise. He rushed at him, and dug the knife into the great vein that is behind the ear, crushing the man's head down to the table, and stabbing again and again.

There was a stifled groan, and the horrible sound of someone choking with blood. Three times the outstretched arms shot up convulsively, waving grotesque stiff-fingered hands in the air. He stabbed him twice more, but the man did not move. Something began to trickle on the floor. He waited for a moment, still pressing the head down. Then he threw the knife on the table, and listened.

Dorian not only uses a knife on Basil; he stabs again and again, mutilating the body. Nor does the matter end here. Jack the Ripper often disemboweled his victims and removed some inner organs. In like vein, Dorian decides to cut up the body and destroy it completely. Since he does not know how to do this, he resorts to Alan Campbell, who unwillingly performs the task for him and commits suicide as a consequence. Wilde wanted Dorian's act of murder to be seen as an exaggerated plunge into pure evil, and he sought to achieve this effect partly by associating him with Jack the Ripper. His readers in the early 1890s would not have failed to see the similarities between Dorian's act and the crimes of the dreaded Ripper. If anything, Dorian's act is at one level worse than the Ripper's, for he murders not prostitutes but a good man in the act of repentant prayer. Richard Ellmann has argued convincingly and at length that Wilde, after his first homosexual experience in 1886, regarded himself as a criminal and wrote as an artist-criminal. It should come as no surprise, then, that he was very interested in the most famous murderer of his day and sought to echo and reflect his crimes in his literature.

This is not to argue, of course, that Wilde engaged the Jack the Ripper murders in *The Picture of Dorian Gray* in order to interpret them or to add hidden meanings to the text. On the contrary, Wilde often used the environment around him in his literary works. For example, in *The Decay of Lying* the two speakers carry the names of his two sons, Cyril and Vyvyan. In *The Importance of Being Earnest* Jack Worthing's surname is the name of the town Wilde was in when he began the play, the butler is named Lane after his publisher, and Lady Bracknell carries the name of Lady Queensberry's house. There are many other examples of Wilde's use of his environment. In *The Picture of Dorian Gray,* Wilde used Jack the Ripper as a source in presenting the murder Dorian commits. Artistically, this source serves to deepen and intensify the horror of Dorian's act.

Soon afterward, in the autumn of 1891, the desire to write a dark and sinister work of literature caught Wilde's fancy again. *Salome* is a highly complex symbolist play that has many sources, from the Bible to Mallarmé's ''Hérodiade'' and Huysmans's *A Rebours,* but Jack the Ripper is also one of its sources; he quietly occupies a corner in the background of the play and forms a part of its intricate mosaic of multi-layered symbols. There are two reasons to assert that this is the case. The first is that only two dark, serious murders are dramatically portrayed in Wilde's mature *oeuvre:* Dorian's murder of Basil and Salome's killing of John the Baptist, and there are similarities between them. If Wilde used Jack the Ripper as a source for the first murder, it is probable that he also had him in mind for the second. But the second reason is much more compelling. Despite the fact that Salome's crime is an ancient one, it has strong affinities with those of the Ripper. Both criminals, for instance, commit ''sex murders.'' Both are so ferocious in their murders as to horrify people by their sheer savagery. And both mutilate the bodies of their victims in a similar manner. (One of the Ripper's victims was found with her head almost completely severed from her body; also, while the Ripper usually removed some of his victim's inner organs

and took them with him, Salome takes John the Baptist's head.) These similarities would have been noticed in Wilde's day and the inevitable connection would have been made. Thematically, they help to connect the modern and ancient worlds and stress the constancy of human evil. Thus, the influence of the Ripper on *Salome* is more profound than on *Dorian Gray,* if perhaps less obvious.

Another difference is that while Dorian's crime is meant to suggest those of Jack the Ripper, Salome both reflects the Ripper and goes beyond him. Not only does she commit a savage sex murder, but she feasts lustfully on her victim's blood-soaked severed head. And her victim is none other than an exalted Christian saint. In *Dorian Gray* Wilde explored human evil and concluded that human nature is ''gray.'' In *Salome* he wished to confront and explore the absolute blackness of human nature, much like Conrad soon after in *Heart of Darkness.* *Salome* the play goes beyond *The Picture of Dorian Gray* in its exploration of human evil—Dorian has a conscience, Salome has none—and Salome the character, in the crime she commits, goes beyond both Dorian and the Ripper, whose unobtrusive presence in this play, set in a distant land in biblical times, should not be ignored. In his day Jack the Ripper was regarded as the ultimate criminal, a demented slasher with a twisted sense of morality who was the very embodiment of evil. By the end of Wilde's play, however. Salome has exceeded even the Ripper in evil; she emerges as a completely amoral and pleasure-seeking headhuntress:

> SALOME: . . . Tetratch. Tetratch, command your soldiers that they bring me the head of Jokanaan. *A huge black arm, the arm of the* EXECUTIONER, *comes forth from the cistern, bearing on a silver shield the head of* JOKANAAN. SALOME *seizes it.* HEROD *hides his face with his cloak.* HERODIAS *smiles and fans herself. The* NAZARENES *fall on their knees and begin to pray.* SALOME: Ah! thou wouldst not suffer me to kiss thy mouth, Jokanaan. Well! I will kiss it now. I will bite it with my teeth as one bites a ripe fruit. . . . Ah! I have kissed thy mouth, Jokanaan. I have kissed thy mouth. There was a bitter taste on thy lips. Was it the taste of blood. . .? But perchance it is the taste of love.

Salome is devoid of any moral sense. Hers is the ultimate crime. Even the depraved and lustful Herod, who murdered his own brother and robbed him of his wife, finds her crime abominable and orders her killed. In *Salome,* Wilde finally reached the heart of darkness, going beyond Dorian, Huysmans, Paler, Mallarmé, and even Jack the Ripper within the framework of literature.

Source: Christopher S. Nassaar. "Wilde's *The Picture of Dorian Gray* and *Salome*" in the *Explicator* Vol. 53, no. 4, Summer, 1995, pp. 217–20.

Maureen T. Kravec

Kravec discusses the relationship between Wilde's play and the satiric illustrations that were created by Aubrey Beardsley for the published edition of Salome.

Ever since Oscar Wilde first saw them, Aubrey Beardsley's illustrations for *Salomé* have caused controversy. Wilde worried that the drawings, which he believed did not capture the spirit of the play, would reduce the text to the role of "illustrating Aubrey's illustrations." Beardsley's audacious visual objectifications of depravity, looking even more "decadent" than his typical caricatures, may not match the deliberately crafted metaphors of remote, cold beauty that sustain Wilde's tragedy, yet the drawings transcend time and circumstance in much the same way that the dialogue does. Illustrator and author shared a similar sort of satirical vision. Beardsley, eager to translate or illustrate the play, commented that he "thoroughly understood" its spirit, and indeed, his drawings can augment our understanding of the play. The anachronistic drawings, like the text, strike a pose of seriousness while slyly satirizing the human folly of self-centered possessiveness by no means absent in their own society. Herod's court may be seen as a parody of the world of physical voraciousness and moral lethargy in *Dorian Gray* (itself a parody of sorts). Satire by definition involves social criticism, toward which Wilde and Beardsley gravitated, despite their association with "art for art's sake."

Beardsley caricatures Wilde in several illustrations. The resemblance of the chubby face in "The Eyes of Herod," "The Woman in the Moon," and "A Platonic Lament" to the playwright's own has been noticed from the illustrations' very first appearance. In these drawings, Wilde appears in the guise of the monstrous Herod, a central character (not an alter ego but, after all, still a projection from the author's imagination), and as the moon which may be the prime mover or merely a dispassionate observer of the action, depending on one's perspective.

The fullest depiction of Wilde appears in "Enter Herodias," a complex iconographic interpretation of Wilde's craft—and Beardsley's. Herodias, in resplendent hideousness, stands in a doorway; a smug-looking Wilde appears in the foreground, outside of the "frame," gesturing languidly toward his creation. Unlike the roly-poly presence in the other drawings, he is not a caricature, but resembles the Wilde seen in contemporary photographs. The portrait could be called flattering—except that Wilde wears a jester's costume, with an owl cap; while he gestures toward Herodias with one hand, he holds in the other a copy of the play and a curious-looking scepter which resembles nothing so much as the caduceus—the rod entwined with two serpents which the god Mercury carries and which is also a symbol of the medical profession.

This magic wand conjures up a number of associations, all concerning the reconciliation of opposites into a healing synthesis:

> The wings symbolize transcendence; the air; the wand is power, the double serpent is the opposites in dualism, ultimately to be united; they are also the serpents of healing and poison, illness and health; they are hermetic and homeopathic; "nature can overcome nature"; the complementary nature of the two forces operative in the universe and the union of the sexes.

In handing Wilde this symbolic staff, Beardsley portrays him as a godlike jester-alchemist, creating images of folly to convey insight.

Wilde's role as magician appears more clearly in *Salomé* than does his equally important one as physician. The drama's elaborate play of parallel metaphors both profound and absurd traps and bedazzles the characters caught in their own conceits. Salomé's admirers address her in a series of vapid metaphors that shroud her more completely than seven veils; even she cannot penetrate their opacity and find her true identity. A creature of paradox, she resembles both her mother and Iokanaan, a double likeness which Beardsley captures. She is both destroyer and victim. Her request for Iokanaan's head represents for her both epiphany and apocalypse. Wilde points proudly to the elaborate, paradoxical geste he has created.

But Oscar Wilde as a physician of society through this drama? Wilde and Beardsley both had contradictory natures. Both flaunted the conventions of art, propriety, and morality, and yet, did so through the medium of satire, which at least ostensibly attempts to correct. (Even Beardsley's unfinished novel *Under the Hill* has been identified by Linda C. Dowling as a satire on his contemporaries.)

Both men converted to Catholicism later in life. If Beardsley had at this time more than a passing acquaintance with scripture, he might have had in mind the caduceus which Moses makes in Numbers XXI, 4–9, after the Lord sends a plague of serpents to punish the disobedient Jewish people. When Moses appeals to the Lord, he is told to fashion a bronze serpent and mount it on a pole. Whoever looks upon the effigy is healed. This parable might be applied metaphorically to the drama.

Salomé, an inquisitive soul incubated in a decadent society, looks for transcendence but, like the other characters, she fails to find it, refusing to listen to a message she does not want to hear. In the tragic fates of the characters limned by Wilde and Beardsley, the audience might perceive its own illness and draw, if not healing, at least greater self-awareness. Although both playwright and artist probably would have winced at being called "moralists," they consciously placed before their contemporaries a bizarre yet reflective mirror.

Source: Maureen T. Kravec. "Wilde's *Salome*" in the *Explicator,* Vol. 42, no. 1, Fall, 1983, pp. 30–32.

SOURCES

Beckson, Karl. *Oscar Wilde: The Critical Heritage,* Routledge & Kegan Paul, 1970, pp. 133-42.

Kohl, Norbert. *Oscar Wilde: The Works of a Conformist Rebel,* translated by David Henry Wilson, Cambridge University Press, 1980. p. 182

Wilde, Oscar. "The Ballad of Reading Gaol" in *Complete Works of Oscar Wilde,* Harper & Row, 1966.

Worth, Katharine. *Oscar Wilde,* Grove, 1983, p. 73.

FURTHER READING

Briggs, Asa. *A Social History of England,* Weidenfeld and Nicolson, 1994.
This provides information about English society from prehistoric times to the present. It contains a lengthy chapter on the Victorian period.

Ellmann, Richard. *Oscar Wilde,* Vintage Books, 1987.
This book is one of the most recent and complete biographies of Wilde.

Ellmann, Richard. *Oscar Wilde: A Collection of Critical Essays,* Prentice-Hall, 1969.
This book contains a number of essays and poems about Wilde, many written by those who knew him.

Hoare, Philip. *Oscar Wilde's Last Stand: Decadence, Conspiracy, and the Most Outrageous Trial of the Century,* Arcade, 1997.
This book concerns a 1918 production of *Salome* that led to a trial, when Maud Allan, playing Salome, was denounced by a right-wing Member of Parliament, whom she sued for libel. Hoare contends that the trial became a trial of Wilde himself and all he was believed to represent.

Raby, Peter. *Oscar Wilde,* Cambridge University Press, 1988.
This book provides background for many of Wilde's essays, stories, poems, and plays, including a chapter on *Salome.*

Worth, Katherine. *Oscar Wilde,* Grove, 1983.
This is a good basic introduction to Wilde's plays and includes a chapter on *Salome.*

Saved

EDWARD BOND

1965

Saved was first presented on November 3, 1965, at the Royal Court Theatre, London, as a private club production of the English Stage Society. The "club" designation was necessary because the Lord Chamberlain, the head of the Queen's household and the official censor of British theatre, had demanded such substantial alterations to the text before granting a license for performance that the Royal Court had decided to dodge the law in order to present the play as written and without a license. It had long been held that the Lord Chamberlain did not have authority over "private" club productions.

The production caused an uproar. On opening night there were shouts of outrage from the audience and physical violence in the foyers during the intermission and after the show. *Saved* explores the dehumanizing industrial environment and the moral emptiness of the working-class world of South London and the beastliness and brutality that are the result. The scene that most shocked the audience and to which the Lord Chamberlain had objected with no room for compromise involved the murder of a bastard baby in its pram by a group of young working-class louts, including its father. Most of the critics, with such prominent exceptions as Martin Esslin, Penelope Gilliatt, and Alan Brien, "slaughtered" the play. Aroused patrons formed "representative" organizations to fight such "obscene," "sadistic," "filthy," and "unfunny" drama. Leaders of the Royal Court were arrested on a technicality of the law (police officers, who were members of

the English Stage Company, were not required to show their cards when entering the theatre) and there was a court case.

Although the Lord Chamberlain made it clear that he did not intend to challenge the right of private clubs to present plays that had not been approved by his office, the Magistrate's decision stated clearly that the Lord Chamberlain did in fact have jurisdiction over such productions. That closed the door on what had always been seen as an outlet for *avant garde* theatre to be performed free of censorship. The *Saved* case was thus directly instrumental in ending pre-production censorship in England, which officially occurred on September 28, 1968. (*Early Morning,* Bond's next play, was the last play to be banned *in toto* by the Lord Chamberlain.) One of the first results of the demise of the censor was a short repertory season of Bond plays at the Royal Court—*Saved, Narrow Road to the Deep North,* and *Early Morning.* The abolition of the censor by the Theatres Act of 1968 allowed the whole of theatre to deal seriously with contemporary reality in an adult manner.

AUTHOR BIOGRAPHY

Edward Bond was born in 1934 into a working-class family in Holloway, North London. In 1940 he was evacuated to Cornwall and subsequently to his grandparents in Ely, Cambridgeshire. In 1944 he returned to London and attended Crouch End Secondary Modern School, where he was not thought good enough to take the eleven-plus exam, which was necessary in order for him to continue school. He therefore left school at age fifteen, ending his formal education. However, while still in school, he went to see Donald Wolfit's production of *Macbeth,* which had a profound impact on him. He later said in an interview, quoted in *Bond: A Study of His Works:* "for the very first time . . . I met somebody who was actually talking about my problems, the life I'd been living, the political society around me . . . I knew all those people, they were in the street or in the newspapers this (Macbeth) in fact was my world." He also attended the music hall regularly (his sister was a magician's assistant), which taught him theatrical builds and timing.

In 1953 Bond began his two years National Service and while in the army began his first serious writing. In 1958 he submitted two plays to the newly-formed English Stage Company at the Royal

Court Theatre, London, and both were rejected. However, he was invited to join the Writers Group at the Royal Court, under the leadership of the young director William Gaskill, and in 1960 he became a play-reader at the Court. On December 9, 1962, *The Pope's Wedding* was given a single performance in a Sunday night "production without decor" at the Court, the first performance of a play by Bond. By that time, Bond had written five radio plays, two television plays, and seven plays for the theatre, all of which had been rejected. In 1964, *Saved* was accepted for production by the Royal Court, which duly submitted it to the Lord Chamberlain's Office, then charged with the licensing of plays. When the Lord Chamberlain demanded many substantial cuts and changes to the script, the Royal Court declared itself a private club theatre for the production of *Saved,* which opened on November 3, 1965. Bond was finally able to become a full-time writer.

Bond has been a prolific writer. He has written thirty-one plays that have been produced, four screenplays, two books of poems and songs, and adaptations of classics such as Chekhov's *The Three Sisters* and *The Cherry Orchard.* His plays have been translated into twenty-five languages and have had productions throughout the world. In 1977 Edward Bond accepted an Honorary Doctorate from Yale University.

PLOT SUMMARY

Scene One
The play opens in the living-room. Pam has brought Len home for sex. She insists on using the living-room because her bed isn't made. They have just met and when Len asks Pam her name, she says, "Yer ain' arf nosey." They have trouble getting comfortable. Harry, her father, comes in and goes out again. Len is somewhat disconcerted, but Pam doesn't seem to mind the interruption at all. Pam and Len continue their sex play, Harry again puts his head in, and Pam and Len offer him candy (laced with sexual innuendo). Finally, they hear Harry leave the house for work and as Pam undoes Len's belt, Len says, "This is the life."

Scene Two
Scene Two takes place in a park near the flat. Len and Pam are in a boat on an otherwise bare stage. The audience learns that Len is now a boarder

in the flat. They also speak of their relationship, the fact that Harry and Mary haven't spoken in so many years Pam can't remember when the silence started or why, that they had a boy during World War II and that he was killed by a bomb in this park. Fred, the boat handler, calls them in and makes crude sexual jokes. Len jokes back, and it is obvious that Pam is attracted to Fred.

Scene Three

Pete, Barry, Mike, and Colin meet in the park. Pete is dressed in a suit because he is going to the funeral of a boy he killed with his van—intentionally, he says. He openly seeks the admiration of the others and they do admire him for the killing and the fact that he got away with it. They tease Barry and there is lots of low and crude sexual humor. Len comes in and Colin recognizes him from school years before. Mary enters with groceries, Len goes to help her, and there are more crude sexual jokes among the gang.

Scene Four

Scene Four takes place in the living-room. Mary puts food on the table, Len eats, and Harry dozes in the armchair. Pam enters in her slip, turns on the TV and puts on makeup. The TV doesn't work properly and no one knows how to adjust it. The baby starts to cry off-stage and continues to cry throughout the scene. No one does anything to comfort the baby. The only other actions consists of bickering about where Pam should dress and small domestic concerns. Fred arrives and Pam nags him about being late and they leave, Len clears the table and Harry tells Len it is better for him to sleep with his door closed so he won't hear Pam and Fred in her room. The baby continues to scream uncomforted.

Scene Five

Pam is sick in bed and Len tries to comfort her. She is pining for Fred, who has dumped her. Len fetches the baby and Pam wants nothing to do with it; she hasn't looked at it for weeks. (It is worth noting that throughout the play the baby is referred to only as "it" by all the other characters.) Len has bribed Fred with tickets for a football game so he will visit Pam.

Scene Six

The park. Fred is fishing and chatting with Len about his equipment and how to bait a hook—all done with cheap sexual innuendo. Len has been

Edward Bond

fired from his job for staying away from work to care for Pam. Pam comes in with the baby in its pram. She tries to make Fred promise to call on her and he evades her. The baby is drugged with aspirin to keep it quiet and it has had pneumonia once. Pam stamps out in a fit of temper, leaving the baby there, and Len goes after Pam. One by one the rest of the gang wander on talking about sex and making cheap jokes. Barry spots the baby and after violently shoving the pram at Pete, they begin to tease the baby by pinching it. The others, including Fred, join in pinching it, spitting on it, rubbing its face in its own excrement, and finally stoning it to death. After they leave, Pam returns and wheels the pram off without looking into it.

Scene Seven

Fred is in a jail cell and Pam visits him. Fred is outraged because he was attacked by a group of housewives when being brought to jail. Pam feels no animus towards Fred and Fred feels no responsibility for the murder of the baby. He blames Pam for having the baby in the first place and for bringing it to the park. He blames gangs of vandals and even blames the police for not doing their job and stopping the murder. Len brings cigarettes to Fred and, after Pam leaves, tells Fred that he had watched the whole thing.

The center of the controversy surrounding Bond's play: Barry, Pete, Fred, and others stone the baby to death in its carriage

Scene Eight

Harry is ironing clothes in the living-room and chatting with Len. Len has a job again and Pam is still obsessed with Fred. Pam enters drying her hair and immediately accuses Harry and Len of stealing her *Radio Times* magazine. She and Len engage in a silly but verbally violent spat.

Scene Nine

Len is in the living-room cleaning his shoes when Mary enters in her slip and gets ready to go to the movies with a friend. Mary tells Len to feel free to take women to his room. She tears her stocking near the top and asks Len to sew it while she still has it on. While he is sewing them, Harry enters. He watches Len and Mary and then leaves. Len asks Mary to stay in for the evening, but she says she must go.

Scene Ten

Len and Pam are sitting at a table in a cafe waiting for Fred to arrive with his mates for a breakfast to celebrate his release from prison. Pam tries to get Len to leave but he won't go. Fred enters accompanied by the gang and his new girl, Liz. The jokes are still cheaply sexual and stale. Pam at-

tempts to force herself on Fred and is dismissed and humiliated. Liz continually asks Fred what it is like "inside." Len asks Fred what it felt like when he was killing the baby. Finally, the gang and Liz go off and Len tries once more to reconcile with Pam and once more is rebuffed.

Scene Eleven

In the living-room. The table is set for tea. Mary claims the teapot is hers and pours Harry's cup of tea on the floor. They have a verbal fight in which Mary claims most of the things in the house are hers and Harry accuses Mary of being "filthy" with Len. Mary hits him in the head with the teapot. When Harry tells Pam the fight was because Len had Mary's dress up, Len shakes him and Pam cries and blames all her troubles—even the death of the baby—on Len. Len says he will move out.

Scene Twelve

Len is on the floor of his bedroom listening to Pam in the room below. Harry enters dressed in white long underwear and white socks with his head in a skull cap of bandages. Harry has come to say goodnight. Len says he never touched Mary and when he points out that Harry and Mary had a row over it, Harry says, ''She had a row.'' Harry talks of his time in World War II. He remembers it mostly as peace and quiet with a couple of blow-ups. He asks Len not to move out. Harry plans to move out, but when it suits him, not Mary. In the meantime, he will retreat to his room more.

Scene Thirteen

The living-room. Len is fixing a chair, Mary is clearing the table, Pam sits on the couch reading her *Radio Times,* and Harry is filling out his football betting slip. The only dialogue in the scene is when Len asks Pam to fetch his hammer. She does not. Len continues trying to fix the chair and the others continue their empty activities.

CHARACTERS

Barry

Barry, age twenty and described as a little below medium height and fat, is one of the working-class louts who hang around together in South London. There is little to distinguish Barry from his friends, but it is he who leads the assault on the baby in scene six and who throws the last stone at the baby at point blank range.

Colin

Colin, age eighteen, has ''shiny ears, curved featureless face'' and ''shouts to make himself heard.'' He is one of the group of male working-class layabouts centered around Fred.

Fred

Fred, age twenty-one, blond, good looking, and powerfully built, is the man Pam becomes obsessed with and who she claims is the father of her baby. Although he is only one of the gang that murders the baby in the park, Fred is the one who is charged and who goes to jail. Still, Fred feels he is not guilty of a crime because ''It were only a kid.'' Fred, like the others, is never able to see the baby as a human being. Women are very attracted to Fred and he has a new woman, Liz, waiting for him when he is released from jail.

Harry

Harry, Pam's father and Mary's husband, is silent for most of the play. Harry fought in World War II and now holds a non-descript night job. He and Mary have not spoken for years, and when they

do speak it is to engage in a violent row in which Mary breaks a teapot on Harry's head. Near the end of the play, Harry does open up to a certain degree with Len and begs him not to move out of the house.

Len

Len is the central character of the play. He is twenty-one, ''tall, slim, firm, bony,'' and he works at various jobs as a laborer. Pam brings him home to have sex in scene one and he stays as a boarder. Len is good natured and determined to be helpful, even to the extent of trying to reconcile Fred with Pam, even though he is still in love with Pam himself. Len is not a noble character he is a product of his society, which does not allow nobility and he does not rise above the arid culture of his South London working class background. Len does, however, hold on to his human values of compassion and tolerance, and he does refuse to surrender to the bleak spiritual and moral degradation of the other characters.

Liz

Liz, who appears in only one scene, is an empty slut who is awaiting Fred when he is released from prison.

Mary

Mary, Pam's mother, is fifty-three, short with bulky breasts, big thighs, and ''curled gray hair that looks as if it is in a hair-net. Homely.'' She and her husband Harry have not spoken for many years, though neither seems to remember the cause. Mary is not a warm mother-figure, however. She claims to feel pity for the crying baby but does nothing to comfort it; she bashes Harry on the head with a teapot; she partakes in a highly sexual scene with Len. She is as empty of human values as her daughter, Pam.

Mike

Mike is another of the gang of inarticulate louts and is practically indistinguishable from his mates.

Pam

Pam, age twenty-three, is the central female character in the play. She seduces Len in the livingroom of the flat she shares with her parents, Harry and Mary. She is unperturbed when her father comes into the room. Although Len falls in love with her and stays on as a boarder, Pam quickly tires of Len and falls for Fred. She takes Fred to her room for sex, knowing that the rest of the family, including Len, are listening. She has a baby, claiming Fred as the father, but never recognizes it as human. She apparently feels no remorse when the baby is murdered and remains obsessed with Fred. She meets him on his release from prison, offers him her room to stay in, and is rejected. Pam is the epitome of those whom Max Le Blond in the *Dictionary of Literary Biography* says are "condemned to crawl like lice on the underbelly of the welfare state." She ends the play in silence, studying her *Radio Times* and dumbly facing an empty future which she is too inarticulate to contemplate.

Pete

Pete, at age twenty-five, is the oldest of the gang of louts and represents the epitome of their aspirations. His only real distinction is that he has killed a boy with his truck, an act that he claims to have committed deliberately. He seeks admiration from the rest of the group and he receives that admiration. He initiates much of the brutality in the murder of the baby.

THEMES

Alienation and Loneliness

All of the characters in *Saved* suffer alienation from the natural world, from each other, from their work, and from society as a whole; the result is extreme loneliness. The stoning of the baby is only an extreme example of the alienation from all that is natural—the continuation of the species—and humane: no one even recognizes that the baby *is* human. Len is the only character who seems to retain even the *capacity* for compassion, the only one who continues to reach out to others. Nothing illustrates Len's loneliness more than his asking Fred what he has that makes Pam so in love with him. There is slight hope: in his bumbling way Harry does reach out and asks Len not to leave their household. Len is the only human they know and he is needed if the rest are to continue to exist at all.

Anger and Hatred

Anger and hatred are the results of the alienation felt by the characters towards all areas of their lives. These feelings are expressed throughout the play: Pete's killing of the boy; Mary and Harry's long lasting silence and the violence that takes place when that silence is broken; Pam's diatribe over her missing magazine; the stoning of the baby. Perhaps even more frightful than the outbursts is the seeth-

ing fury that the family represses all the time and which is especially evident in the final, silent, scene.

Guilt and Innocence

The murder of the baby, obviously, represents the Biblical Slaughter of the Innocents. Assigning guilt for that act, however, is no simple matter. Fred accepts the penalty, but not out of any sense of guilt: he blames Pam for leaving the baby in the park and for having it in the first place; he blames "roving gangs;" he blames the police for not doing their job. Fred accepts the punishment because that makes him a hero of the criminal class, which he sees operating all around him in all areas of his life. Pete feels no guilt for killing the boy with his van, and he is admired for getting away with it by the others. Harry feels no guilt for killing the soldier in the war and even considers himself "one of the lucky ones" for having had the experience. There is no guilt assigned for the baby, Harry and Mary's son, who was killed by a bomb in the park during the war. Bond places the guilt for the actions of his characters squarely on the society as a whole for having created the inhuman conditions in which they live.

Limitations and Opportunities

There are no opportunities for the characters in *Saved*. They are limited by their births: they were born into the working class of South London; they have very limited education; they have no contact with the larger culture; and they are inarticulate even about their own lives. Len works at two or three different jobs during the course of the play, but they are interchangeable and not worth talking about; Harry goes off to work, but won't talk about it; Fred is in charge of boat rentals; Pete drives a van. Work is something which holds no interest for those who do it and it provides no benefits except small pay. The lack of meaningful work is part of the reason the characters are alienated from their own lives.

Love and Passion

Although *Saved* deals with sexual partnerings, there is little passion and even less love involved. Len and Pam don't even know each others' names when they first start to have sex. They even joke with one another about how many others they have had. Fred uses Pam but never expresses feelings of love or demonstrates passion. Harry and Mary no longer even speak but there never seems to have been a time when they felt love, and Harry talks of sex as something that is "up to the man." Even

Pam's obsession with Fred would be hard to construe as love. Only Len seems to feel love and to express it through a desire to give and to care for others.

Morals and Morality

Morals and morality as an inherent social guide, or even as an abstract guide, do not seem to apply in the society in which *Saved* takes place. Being able to "get away with it" is the criteria for behavior. Pete is admired for killing a boy and not being charged; killing the baby takes place partly because there is no one in authority to see and, as Pete says, "You don't get a chance like this every day." However, Bond is by extension talking about the larger society which condones killing, as Harry did during the war and as his son was killed by a bomb, and which daily kills the spirit of its children.

Science and Technology

Bond sees science and technology, the basis for the industrial society, as the twin evils that have separated mankind from the natural world. There is no longer the satisfaction of creating or even individually contributing for the laborers and factory workers. They have no control over their jobs or how they carry out their work; they never see the end-product as reflecting their efforts. They are forced into regimens that are both physically and psychologically unnatural. Their rewards are material, and even the material is divorced from their understanding and control; i.e., the TV set that they are helpless to adjust. They have become parts of the industrial and technological machine, crowded into an unnatural environment of row houses and government housing that are created to serve the machine; and, the result is that they have lost their humanity. Fred standing in the park with a fishing rod purchased with time payments and fishing in an artificial lake is a powerful image of man's alienation from nature and himself.

Sex

Sex has become an impersonal activity for the characters in *Saved*. Len and Pam use each other in Scene One without even knowing each others' names, and this has apparently happened many times for both of them. Fred uses Pam and then discards her, feeling no responsibility for his actions. The sexual hunt is calculated and impersonal: the church social club and the all-night laundromats are seen as prime hunting grounds. The closest to a humanly warm sexual encounter in *Saved* takes

TOPICS FOR FURTHER STUDY

- How does the British secondary education system differ from that of the United States? Can you think of any changes that might benefit people such as those portrayed in *Saved*?

- What is the "class system" in Britain? Does a class system exist in the United States? Discuss your opinions/ideas.

- Compare *Saved* with a play by other working class writers such as Arnold Wesker or John Osborne (see What Do I Read Next?). Do the characters seem to have the same attributes? Are the worlds they live in the same?

- Edward Bond believes that if people are crowded together, subjected to too much noise, and feel constantly threatened, they will become violent. Do you think there is merit in this? Can you think of areas near you where people live like that? Do you feel constantly threatened

- Edward Bond thinks that the end product of working on an assembly line is dehumanization. Do you agree?

place between Len and Mary when he darns her stocking and becomes aroused. But even there it seems that Mary has calculated just how far she will go and has consciously used Len for her own ego gratification. The alienation of the sexual act from warm human contact is merely one aspect of the dehumanizing lives these people are forced to live.

Violence

Certainly violence occurs in *Saved*. Most of the public outrage was caused by the extreme violence of the baby killing in Scene Six. As Bond says in the introduction to the Methuen edition of *Early Morning*, "I write about violence as naturally as Jane Austin wrote about manners. Violence shapes and obsesses our society . . . It would be immoral not to write about violence." The violence witnessed in Scene Six is sickening, as is the violence regarding the manner in which Pete killed the boy with his van. Violence is the natural result of the depersonalizing aspects of the society in which it takes place, the physical and psychological twisting of the human to fit the work pattern of the industrialized world, the lack of control over their own lives, the crowding together in a sterile environment with no sense of cultural roots.

STYLE

Setting

Saved has thirteen scenes with an intermission suggested after the seventh. Six of the scenes are set in the living-room of the flat in the working-class area of South London that is shared by Harry, his wife Mary, and their daughter Pam—and, after the first scene, Len—and two in an attic bedroom in the same flat; three are in a nearby park; one scene is in a jail cell; and one takes place in a cafe. All of the scenes call for very simple settings. The park is a bare stage (with a boat on it for Scene Two). The interior scenes are also very simply represented: a narrow triangle of flats upstage, giving a very enclosed feeling, with the necessary furniture in front of that for the flat; tables and chairs without the upstage flats for the cafe, and a simple jail-door flat for the jail-cell scene. The settings become more claustrophobic as the lives of the characters become more constricted: all of the park scenes are in the first act and four of the living-room scenes and one of the bedroom scenes are in the second act.

Plot

The plot of *Saved* takes place over a period of about two years. Bond does not show *development* of characters over that time but rather shows *episodes* in the lives of the characters. There is no explanation of what went on during the sometimes considerable time that has elapsed between episodes other than major events: Pam had her baby, Len lost a job, Len got a job, Fred served his time in prison. This lack of detailed accounts of time not shown leads the audience to assume—indeed, to *feel*—that the lives of the characters have continued with the same drab existence. As it accrues, the audience comes to realize that the background is the subject and the episodic actions are only punctuations.

An interesting plot device is the placing of the murder of the baby in the first act. Although the scene is central to the play, by placing it in the first act Bond is able to focus attention on the situation surrounding the murder, rather than focusing on the build-up to the murder. The murder itself is stunningly shocking because it goes against all that society claims to believe: babies are to be protected. But, given the situation, the murder is inevitable and other similar atrocities in the future are also inevitable because no one seems to be seriously affected by it, not even Pam, the baby's mother.

Character Development

With the exception of Len, there is really no character development at all in *Saved* and that is deliberate and part of the point of the play. These characters do not grow, they do not learn from their experiences. Moreover, no explanations are given of their lives or behaviors so that the audience comes to understand their plight. That also is deliberate. As Malcolm Hay and Philip Roberts point out in *Bond: A Study of His Plays,* "Emotive demands for sympathy from the stage can only muddle the issue. Once you sympathize with somebody, you make excuses for them. If you make excuses for that sort of behavior, then you condone it and then you condone what creates the situation." Bond wants his audience to react to his view of society by taking action and changing the society itself, not by simply feeling compassion for the characters trapped in their hopeless situations. Therefore, the audience is shown effects which, individually and cumulatively, are shocking and the audience must then involve themselves to arrive at the causes.

Language

The language in *Saved* is so authentic that the Hill and Wang edition has twenty-seven footnotes to explain the meaning of words or phrases. Some of the English critics, who do not come from the working-class, had trouble understanding some of the language, but all admitted that it certainly sounded natural enough. However, Bond's language is not simple transcription; it is carefully chosen and shaped to convey the play's motivation and themes. Its short, staccato structure, while basically used as aggression or to defend against the aggression of others, or even simply to keep others away, is also highly poetic and frequently comic. As Richard Scharine has pointed out in *The Plays of Edward Bond,* the characters in *Saved* mistrust words and for them "language as a tool functions only to hold others at a distance."

COMPARE
&
CONTRAST

- 1965: As part of the "Welfare State," the government owned and operated all public transportation, telephone, gas, electric, and water utilities, coal, petroleum, and steel industries. The government was by far the largest employer in the nation.

  Today: All the industries listed above, including the utilities, have been privatized—sold to stockholders—to promote efficiency through greater competition.

- 1965: The United Kingdom was a leading trading nation but functioned as a separate entity financially and economically.

  Today: In 1973, the United Kingdom became part of the European Economic Community (now called the European Union). This created the "Common Market" for economic integration of the member countries of Europe with a gradual increase in political integration.

- 1965: As part of the youth movement in popular culture, sexual freedom was being promulgated for both men and women.

  Today: There is a great deal more sexual freedom in society in general and things are talked about and shown in the popular media that could not have been done in 1965.

- 1965: AIDS had not yet occurred at all and other sexually transmitted diseases were easily treated.

  Today: AIDS has brought about a broad recognition that casual sex can lead to death.

- 1965: The British Broadcasting Company (BBC) provided the only television programming in the United Kingdom and operated two channels.

  Today: BBC continues to produce television programming and now operates four television channels, with plans for a fifth. In addition, there are sixteen commercial program companies and, through home satellite television, there are dozens of channels available.

- 1965: Plays had to receive a license from the Lord Chamberlain before they could be produced for the public. He could demand changes or could ban the play *in toto,* and there was no appeal from his decision.

  Today: There is no censorship of theatre. Plays are subject to the same common law provisions against libel and obscenity as are other areas of the media.

HISTORICAL CONTEXT

In 1948, as a result of several acts of Parliament, Great Britain (the United Kingdom of England, Scotland, Wales, and Northern Ireland) became what has become popularly known as a "Welfare State." The intent was to provide a more equitable distribution of the national wealth and to provide the basic needs of food, shelter, health care, and education for all of the country's citizens. Basic services, such as transportation, telephone, electrical, gas, and water utilities were nationalized, as were the steel, coal, and petroleum industries. While extreme by United States standards, the Welfare State remained basically a capitalist economy.

The class hierarchy, ranging from agrarian workers and urban working-class through the various levels of the middle-class to the established levels of the aristocracy remained in place, although, theoretically, it became easier to move up the social and, especially, the economic scale.

The level of education was dependent upon success in examinations taken at various stages. Edward Bond attended the Crouch End Modern School after World War II and was thought not good enough to take the eleven-plus examination, which, if passed, would have allowed him to progress to grammar school (the equivalent of high school in the United States). Thus, his formal education ended at age fifteen, the level at which the majority of British students ended their formal education and entered the work force.

National Service, known in the United States as the "draft," was required of every able-bodied male for a period of two years.

Elsewhere, the United States began bombing North Vietnam as a general policy and the first deployment of U.S. combat troops in Vietnam took place in 1965. Malcolm X was assassinated. Voter registration marchers were attacked by Alabama police and Federalized National Guard troops were sent in to protect them. President Johnson announced programs for a "Great Society" to eliminate poverty in America. "Early Bird," the world's first commercial satellite, was put into orbit and began to relay telephone messages and television programs between the United States and Europe.

The Arts Council of Great Britain had been established immediately following World War II, providing government funds to support all the arts throughout Great Britain. Although support was meager at first, it did have an enormous impact on making the arts available to everyone. Among those receiving support was the English Stage Company at the Royal Court Theatre in London, formed in 1956 to support playwrights whose work had no chance of finding an initial commercial production. It quickly became the inspiration and the national home for new playwriting in Britain. In 1958 the Royal Court formed the "Writer's Group" to work with new writers and Edward Bond, still unproduced, was invited to become part of the group.

In 1965, theatre censorship was still operating under the authority of the Theatres Act of 1843, under which the Lord Chamberlain, head of the Queen's household, was given absolute authority to determine what could and could not be produced on any stage in Great Britain. Plays had to be submitted to his office to receive a license before they could be performed. Stage censorship was an anomaly—a play banned from the stage could be seen by millions on television or heard over the radio. BBC radio and television frequently produced the works of serious playwrights such as Samuel Beckett and Harold Pinter and others who also wrote for theatre.

The Rolling Stones, still playing in pubs the year before, had a huge success with *Satisfaction*. In the United States, the Grateful Dead had its beginning in San Francisco; "op" and "pop" art were fashionable; Congress passed legislation creating the National Endowment of the Arts with an initial grant of $2,500,000.

CRITICAL OVERVIEW

The critical reaction to *Saved* was, for the most part, a slaughter. Irving Wardle of *The Times (London)* said that "The most charitable interpretation of the play would be as a counterblast to theatrical fashion, stripping off the glamour to show that cruelty *is* disgusting and that domestic naturalism *is* boring. But the writing itself, with its self-admiring jokes and gloating approach to moments of brutality and erotic humiliation does not support this view . . . it amounts to a systematic degradation of the human animal." Herbert Kretzmer of the *Daily Express* said, "It is peopled with characters who, almost without exception, are foul-mouthed, dirty-minded, illiterate, and barely to be judged on any recognizable human level at all." J. C. Trewin of *The Illustrated London News* said, "It may not be the feeblest thing I have seen on any stage, but it is certainly the nastiest, and contains perhaps the most horrid scene in the contemporary theatre. (Even as I write that hedging perhaps' I delete it: nobody can hedge about *Saved*.)" B. A. Young, critic for *The Financial Times,* despised the play and said, "if such things are really going on in South London they are properly the concern of the police and the magistrates rather than the audience of theatres, even the Royal Court." Even those reviews that were positive were not geared to bring in the audiences. Penelope Gilliatt of *The Observer* gave a thoughtful and positive review; but it started with "I spent a lot of the first act shaking with claustrophobia and thinking I was going to be sick. The scene where a baby in a pram is pelted to death by a gang is nauseating. The swagger of the sex jokes is almost worse." Alan Brien of *The Sunday Telegraph* was deeply moved and wrote, "It appears that the British audiences and critics can stomach unlimited helpings of torture, sadism, perversion, murder and bestiality when perpetrated by foreigners upon foreigners in the past. . . . But when Edward Bond in *Saved* at the Royal Court shows us London youths, here and now, beating and defiling a bastard baby . . . then a cry goes up to ban and boycott such criminal libels on our national character. . . . *Saved* makes an unsympathetic, disturbing, wearing, sometimes boring evening in the theatre. But I believe it fulfills one of the basic functions of the drama . . . that of making us remember the monster behind the mask on every one of us.''

Although the box office suffered (fifty percent of the seats were sold and 36.7 percent of the possible box office takings were realized during the entire run), the Royal Court kept the play running. And, many of the most influential of the theatre profession rallied to the cause, including Laurence Olivier. Mary McCarthy, the American author, praised the play for its "remarkable delicacy."

Saved had better receptions abroad. Bond was a favorite in Germany and by March, 1968, *Saved* had had more separate productions in Germany than it had had *performances* in England. It received its American premiere at the Yale Repertory Theatre in December, 1968, and shortly after had its Canadian premiere at McGill University in Montreal. A retrospective season of Bond plays, including *Saved,* opened at the Royal Court on February 7, 1969. The critical reactions were very different for this production. Irving Wardle said, "it is now time for the guilty reviewers to queue up and excuse their past arrogance and obtuseness as best they may. As one of the guiltiest, I am glad to acknowledge that my feeling toward the plays has changed, and that if I had originally responded to them as I do now, I should not have applied words like 'half-baked' and 'untalented' to *Saved* and *Early Morning.''*

CRITICISM

Terry W. Browne

Dr. Browne is the author of Playwrights' Theatre: The English Stage Company at the Royal Court Theatre *and* Off Off Broadway: Art and Economics. *In this essay he discusses the power of visual and aural images in Bond's play.*

When *Saved* by Edward Bond opened on November 3, 1965, at the Royal Court Theatre in London, the audience, usually polite in the theatre, shouted abuse at the stage and had physical fights in the lobbies during the intermission and after the play. Among other things, those reactions testify to the power of theatre to make ideas concrete and emotionally gripping.

It is important to remember that reading a play can give only hints at what the power of the play in performance is like. In the theatre the images that are created by the author and brought to physical reality by the director, actors, and designers are experienced by the audience *directly* and immediately without any thought about how they are created or even what they mean. Bond very carefully creates images that cause very powerful responses and, like any powerful experience, linger in the memory.

The image in *Saved* that created the most immediate outrage was, of course, the murder of the baby in its pram. As reported by Hay and Roberts in *Bond: A Study of His Plays,* in the first three drafts of the play Bond had the hoodlums taking the baby out of its pram and tossing it about before murdering it while the baby screamed. As finally performed, the baby is drugged and silent and we never see it. The audience does see the group of thugs torturing the baby or, rather, *reporting* on the torture in a rising frenzy of excitement. Our imaginations provide the details. Moreover, the baby's father, Fred, is lounging downstage at the edge of the "lake." The picture that emerges in the theatre is an almost ritualistic killing punctuated finally by the sounds of the stones smashing into the "baby" in the pram. The fact that we know that a real baby is not in the pram only adds to the feeling of ritual. The audience feels sickened and outraged because they are witnessing not just a random act of violence but an image which speaks of an ongoing savagery toward helpless infants by boys who are little more than children themselves, children of the society of which the audience themselves are a part.

Bond emphasizes the abstract nature of the criminals by calling for them to make "a curious buzzing" like a swarm of insects as they exit. The ritualistic aspect of the scene is further enhanced when Pam returns and coos baby-talk in a "singsong voice, loudly but to herself" in a ritual of motherly care which she never truly displays. It is important to remember that this scene is performed on a bare stage with the location suggested only by the dialogue and the fact that Fred is "fishing" at the opening of the scene. The austerity of the setting further enforces the ritualistic feeling, a ritual in which, as in all ritual, the audience are both observers and, by their very presence, participants. The whole thing is so horrible, so against what we purport to hold most sacred the protection of our children that the reaction is immediate and uncensored and uncontemplated horror.

While the ritualistic murder of the baby caused the most outrage, Scene Nine, in which Len mends Mary's stocking while she is wearing it, placed second. The highly Oedipal inferences of Len having foreplay to sex with his mother-figure was certainly clear. The sight of the middle-aged Mary with her dress pulled up and her leg on a stool while Len kneeled directly in front of her made the audiences "uncomfortable" and caused complaints. When Len turns the lights off and walks to the couch with a handkerchief in his hand, a scene of extreme loneliness, the implication was clear. Again, the reaction was not an intellectualized distaste, but an *immediate* reaction against a scene which breaks one of society's deepest taboos.

Scene Eleven begins with the comedic image of Mary moving the teapot so that Harry cannot reach it, then emptying the tea on the floor all the while childishly claiming that it is hers, not theirs. The comic tone quickly changes, though, when Mary and Harry quarrel, giving vent to years of pent-up rage in a scene that Hay and Roberts find in many respects far more terrible than the killing of the baby because it comes with so many years of hate behind it. Certainly the sight and *sound* of Mary hitting Harry in the head with the full teapot is terrible. Further stage directions call for Harry to wave he bread knife in a gesture misconstrued by Pam as threatening; Pam sprawled on the couch sobbing; Len caught between; and Mary standing and condemning Harry to stay in his room.

Even when violence takes place elsewhere, as with the killing of the boy that is discussed by the gang in Scene Three, the immediate stage image is important. The description of the killing as related by Pete is disgusting, but has nowhere near the power of actually seeing it take place. What the visual stage image does convey is the casual attitude the boys strike while talking about it. It is a scene of cruel, unfeeling braggadocio. The final verbal image we are left with is Pete's suggestion that they should flush the dead boy down the toilet.

Other visual images in *Saved* are also powerful. Critic Penelope Gilliatt wrote of "shaking with claustrophobia." Part of that feeling came from being trapped in a world of casual sex and casual murder; part of the feeling no doubt was also brought on by the setting, which was sparse yet cramped spaces of the interiors, and the blank stage with no hints of nature or horizons in the exterior scenes.

Perhaps the most difficult scene for the reader to imagine with anything like the stage reality is Scene Four. The action is simple: Pam is getting ready to go out with Fred, and Mary, Harry, and Len have supper. The power of this scene comes from the *aural* images: the TV set plays "fairly loud," and the off-stage baby cries without a break throughout the scene approximately eight minutes. One does not react with the intellect to a crying baby; one reacts with the whole body and nervous system. Our almost uncontrollable instinct is to do something to care for the baby, and the people on stage do nothing. Through the sounds the empty sound of the TV, the idle chatter of the people, and the ceaseless crying and screaming of the baby the audience can't help but *feel* the empty desperation of these people.

A subtle visual image is created in Scene Twelve through Harry's costume: long white underwear, pale socks, no shoes, and his head in a skull cap of bandages. Harry comes to Len as a ghost, both of his own past and, perhaps, of Len's future. Again, Bond calls for there to be a knife in this scene, held by Len. It might appear at first that Len would attack Harry, thus carrying out the Oedipal theme of killing his father figure that runs through the play, but that threat quickly disappears. Instead, Harry does his best to reach out to Len and even gives some account of his past.

The final scene is a powerful image that sums up the state of the family, a condition from which there seems to be no rescue. Harry fills out his football betting slip in silence; Mary clears away the dishes from the table, wipes up, and straightens the couch; Pam looks at her *Radio Times* magazine, goes out, comes back; Len tries to fix the chair that was broken when Harry fell on it in Scene Eleven, and he utters the only line "Fetch me ammer" which is ignored. The silence is punctuated by early off-stage sounds of Len pounding on the chair, his on-stage slapping of the chair with his hand, and at one point, after a short silence, Pam "quickly turns over two pages." Amidst the silence, each of these sounds rings out and even the turning of the magazine pages is jolting in the theatre. Each sound and each movement is carefully arranged.

Edward Bond created in *Saved* a play that at first glance seemed to be a naturalistic representation of life in the crowded, working-class area of South London. The world he presents is viscous and empty of humane values. The full effect of his vision, however, can be felt only in the theatre where his carefully constructed visual images and sounds cause the audience to respond viscerally, to *experience* the play. Later the individual audience member will ponder that experience and draw his or her own conclusions about what the life portrayed means. One might even come to understand deeply what Bond means when he says in his introduction to the play, "Clearly the stoning to death of a baby in a London park is a typical English understatement. Compared to the strategic' bombing of German towns it is a negligible atrocity, compared to the cultural and emotional deprivation of most of our children its consequences are insignificant.''

Bert Cardullo

Cardullo examines the religious imagery in Bond's play, noting that, contrary to the title, "no one achieves religious salvation.''

In his ''Author's Note'' to *Saved* (1965) Edward Bond wrote:

> If we are to improve people's behaviour we must first increase their moral understanding, and this means teaching morality to children in a way that they find convincing. Although I suppose that most English people do not consciously disbelieve in the existence of God, not more than a few hundred of them fully believe in his existence. Yet almost all the morality taught to our children is grounded in religion. This in itself makes children morally bewildered—religion has nothing to do with their parents' personal lives, or our economic, industrial and political life, and is contrary to the science and rationalism they are taught at other times. For them religion discredits the morality it is meant to support. . . . If [people] are interested in the welfare of others they should ask ''what is it possible for most people to believe?'' And that means teaching, oddly enough, moral scepticism and analysis, and not faith.

The title of *Saved* is ironic. No one achieves religious salvation in the play. The possibility of achieving it does not seem to exist for the characters: no one prays, even though everyone is in some kind of misery; characters invoke God's name mostly in anger, disgust, or impatience (they say ''Chriss''— a word as close to ''crisis,'' when spoken, as ''Christ''). Fred, in prison for murdering his and Pam's baby, does say ''God 'elp us'' (p. 59), but less because he believes in God than because he wants to comfort the crying Pam, who has come to visit him. Since he is completely unrepentant, his words ring even hollower than they normally would.

Bond teaches moral scepticism and analysis in *Saved*, not faith. He implies that his characters are in crisis in part because ''for them religion [has discredited] the morality it [was] meant to support.'' They are now without religion and some, like Fred,

> BOND TEACHES MORAL SCEPTICISM AND ANALYSIS IN *SAVED*, NOT FAITH. HE IMPLIES THAT HIS CHARACTERS ARE IN CRISIS IN PART BECAUSE 'FOR THEM RELIGION [HAS DISCREDITED] THE MORALITY IT [WAS] MEANT TO SUPPORT''

Pete, Mike, Colin, and Barry, are completely without morality. Children who disbelieve in religion, writes Bond, ''grow up morally illiterate, and cannot understand, because they have not been properly taught, the nature of a moral consideration or the value of disinterested morals at all'' (p. 7). Pete, for example, not only instigates the attack on Pam's baby, he also intentionally runs over another child with his truck. Len, Harry, Mary, and Pam have some morality. They are the main characters, and all four live under one roof. So determined is Harry not to be taken advantage of by Mary, his wife, that he can behave morally toward her only in spite of himself. He ''saves'' Mary at the same time he forsakes her. He asks Len to remain with the family, not only because he likes him and enjoys his company, but also because Len will become a companion to his wife and will possibly help to support her after he, Harry, leaves:

> *Harry* I'd like yer t' stay. If yer can see yer way to. *Len* Why? *Harry* [after a slight pause]. I ain' stayin'. *Len* What? *Harry* Not always. . . . I'll go when I'm ready. When she's on 'er pension. She won't get no one after 'er then. I'll be *out*. Then see 'ow she copes. *Len* Ain't worth it, pop. *Harry* It's only right. When someone carries on like 'er, they 'ave t' pay for it. People can't get away with murder. What'd 'appen then? (p. 93)

Len is the family's savior. He occupies a curious position in their house. He is like a son to Harry and Mary, yet he is not their son (their own boy was killed in a terrorist bombing). He was once their daughter Pam's lover, but isn't anymore; still he has remained her loving friend through all her trials and despite her harsh treatment of him. He nearly becomes Mary's lover at one point; he settles for building her self-esteem rather than satisfying his lust. In Scene 13, the last one in *Saved*, he is still with his adopted family, and we infer that he will be staying: he is repairing a wobbly chair, the one Harry tripped over and damaged in his fight with Mary in Scene 11. Three of the chair's legs are secure, one is loose. Len is the family's fourth leg. He is the outsider who comes in and, through extraordinary sympathy for them and instinctive analysis of their problems, holds the family together. (He says to Pam after Fred deserts her for the last time, ''Can't we try an' get on like before. There's no one else. Yer only live once'' [p. 83].) Len has at once an affection for and an objectivity about Harry, Mary, and Pam that only someone in his position of adopted son-spurned lover could have. His behavior is, from a conventional point of view, eccentric. Nevertheless he is inveterately moral: he helps to convict Fred of murder, then brings hint cigarettes in jail; he is jilted by Pam, yet cares for her child by Fred.

At the end of *Saved*, Len is in the position of savior: of the chair, literally, and of the family, figuratively. He has been having a lot of trouble stabilizing the chair, so he throws his whole body into ''saving'' it. He himself becomes the fourth leg without which the other three cannot be secure; he contorts or sacrifices his body: *Len slips his left arm round the back of the chair. His chest rests against the side edge of the seat. The fingers of his right hand touch the floor. His head lies sideways on the seat*'' (p. 96). The oblique reference to Christ on the cross is, of course, ironic, since Christ has had nothing to do with Len's good works in the play. As Len works on the chair, Pam reads the *Radio Times,* which, she had complained in Scene 8, was always missing when she wanted it—she is now in an emotional state very different from her desperate one at the end of Scene 11, when she said, ''[*crying*]. I'll throw myself somewhere. It's the only way. . . . I can't stand any more. Baby dead. No friends'' (p. 88). The four family members appear to have just had their first supper together in the play—Mary ''collects the plates'' (p. 94) from the table, whereas she had cracked her teapot on Harry's head in Scene 11. Harry fills in the football coupon that he left blank in Scene 9, when he walked in on Len making a pass at Mary. There is not a word of argument in Scene 13; there have been fierce arguments in previous scenes. Indeed, not a word is spoken except by Len: midway in the scene he asks Pam to get him a hammer. She leaves the living room, where they all are, but returns without the hammer. Len says nothing, continuing to work on the chair. It is as if he realizes that it will take a sheer act of will to repair the recalcitrant chair, even as it

has taken one to hold together a family on the verge of disintegration.

Source: ''Bond's *Saved*'' in the *Explicator,* Vol. 44, no. 3, Spring, 1986, pp. 62–64.

William Babula

In this essay, Babula dissects the play's thirteenth scene, which he sees as pivotal in providing both the characters and the audience with the possibility that hope will survive despite the play's dark tone.

In an interview soon after the original production of *Saved,* Edward Bond stated, ''If a problem matters to you, you have a solution or at least you have feelings towards a solution.'' In *Saved* the problem is the survival of hope. The solution, or at least the feeling towards a solution, is suggested by Bond's comment in an author's note on the conclusion of his play, ''Clutching at straws is the only realistic thing to do.'' In Scene Thirteen Edward Bond gives his audience the straw to clutch at as he gives it to his characters on the stage. It is a moment of desperate optimism and a mad pantomime of affirmation. Yet Scene Thirteen gives the title of the drama its significance. Without that closing bit of action it would be almost impossible to find out who or even what is saved. Indeed, it is difficult to do so given Scene Thirteen.

Yet in that scene all the individual actions—coming after the horror of the murder of the baby—do have something in common: all of them are vaguely positive. Pam—assuming the activity is positive—is simply reading. While that may not be much, it is at least a first effort at those ''straws.'' Mary, as the stage directions note, is picking up after the meal: Mary *takes things from the table and goes out.* Later, *She wipes the table top with a damp cloth.* Keeping herself orderly, *She takes off her apron and folds it neatly.* These female actions, which in Mary seem to be almost ritualistic, are barely enough to suggest that the world imaged on the stage has not disintegrated. Yet, they serve to introduce us to the positive activities of the men on stage. While none of the actions can be termed optimistic in the conventional sense of the word—neither those of the men nor those of the women—that is all that Bond allows his audience. In the dramatic world of *Saved,* the positive and meager action of the closing scene imitates the fact of a meager salvation.

The simple actions of Pam and Mary take on a greater significance in the silent movements of

Harry. He comes in, searches through a drawer, finds ink and an envelope, takes out his pen and: *He starts to fill in his football coupon.* Throughout the scene Harry fills out the form, then stamps the envelope, then, in the last action before the curtain falls, Harry *licks the flap on the envelope and closes it quietly.* Harry's activity is one way in which Bond suggests the rather dismal salvation offered. It is the next step from the actions of the women. What could be more desperate and futile than a gamble on a football coupon? At the same time what could be more hopeful or wishful? It is the survival of such desperate hope that allows the odd family collected on stage at the end of the play to survive itself.

Most positive, though also trivial, is the central action of the closing scene: Len's repairing of a chair broken by Harry. As the scene progresses, the audience is suddenly struck by a sharp bang off stage. Perhaps it is a pistol shot, the antithesis of the salvation proposed by the dramatist. But no one on stage reacts. Then another follows and Len carries in the broken chair. On stage the chair and Len become the obvious focus of the audience's attention. Like everyone else in Scene Thirteen Len seems to be acting out a kind of positive ritual. He crouches, he looks under the chair, he inverts it, he tries the loose leg. In fact, Len seems almost to embrace it:

> *He rests his left wrist high on the chair back and his right elbow in the chair seat. His right hand hangs in space. His back is to the audience.*

Finally he speaks the only words spoken in this scene: ''Fetch me 'ammer.'' Once again the audience is faced with the simultaneously positive and trivial. We are all grasping at straws.

But even this straw the dramatist denies to his audience. Len's plea for his hammer goes unanswered. This is no simple vision of people happily at work, surviving through a return to manual labor and commune-like cooperation. Yet Len does not give up; if no one will help he will continue on his own. Perhaps it is in this insistence by Len to go it alone that the audience finds Bond at his most positive. At this point, the stage directions concerning Len read:

> *He has grasped the seat at diagonally opposite corners, so that the diagonal is parallel with the front of his body. He brings the chair sharply down so that the foot furthest from him strikes the floor first.*

The leg is still loose. In an act that appears almost sexual Len once more attempts to fix the broken leg:

IN *SAVED* THE PROBLEM IS

THE SURVIVAL OF HOPE"

> *He bends over the chair so that his stomach or chest rests on the seat. He reaches down with his left hand and pulls the loose rear leg into the socket.*

This time the act is consummated and the leg fixed in the proper place.

Then exhaustion sets in upon Len:

> *Len slips his left arm round the back of the chair. His chest rests against the side edge of the seat. The fingers of his right hand touch the floor. His head lies sideways on the seat.*

His weariness resembles the relaxation after intercourse. Absurd? Certainly. Yet, the action with the chair summarizes all the attempts at some sort of positive activity by Pam, Mary, and Harry. As an audience we see the positive presented together with the mad and the trivial. It is this double sense that allows Scene Thirteen to only be a ''straw.'' The suggestion of sexuality presents the possibility of regeneration at the same time it presents the absurdity of the attempt. His action with the chair is like Harry's with the ticket: it is both desperate and hopeful. Yet each character, even though in isolation from the others—as certainly Len is in his sex act—has contributed some positive action to the total effect of the scene. Ultimately, the chair and the family portrait have been patched up at the close of the play. The audience has before it something both affirmative and absurd. How long can this repaired chair or family survive? The final stage direction: *The curtain falls quickly* suggests that it is better not to ask. It is better rather to go on ''clutching at straws.''

Source: . ''Scene 13 of Bond's *Saved* '' in *Modern Drama,* Vol. XV, no. 1, May, 1972, pp. 147–49.

SOURCES

Bond, Edward. *Saved,* Methuen, 1966, pp. 6, 9-10, 11, 19, 69, 75.

Bond, Edward. *Lear,* Eyre Methuen, 1972, p. 5.

Brien, Alan. *The Sunday Telegraph,* November 7, 1965.

Browne, Terry W. *Playwrights' Theatre,* Pitman Publishing, 1975, pp. 56-57, 62-63, 121.

Gilliatt, Penelope. *The Observer,* November 7, 1965.

Hay, Malcolm, and Roberts, Philip. *Bond; A Study of His Plays,* Eyre Methuen, 1980, pp. 15, 48-49, 54, 62.

Kretzmer, Herbert. *The Daily Express,* November 4, 1965.

LeBlond, Max. "Edward Bond: Criticism," *Dictionary of Literary Biography,* Volume 13: *British Dramatists Since World War II,* Gale, 1982, pp. 83-91.

Scharine, Richard. *The Plays of Edward Bond,* Bucknell University Press, 1976, pp. 54, 69.

Thom, Mary V. "Letters," *Plays and Players,* February, 1966, p. 8.

Trewin, J. C. *The Illustrated London News,* November 13, 1965.

Wardle, Irving. *The Times,* November 4, 1965.

Wardle, Irving. "The Edward Bond View of Life," the London *Times,* March 15, 1970.

Young, B. A. *The Financial Times,* November 4, 1965.

FURTHER READING

Browne, Terry W. *Playwrights' Theatre: The English Stage Company at the Royal Court,* Pitman Publishing, Ltd., 1975.
> Tells the story of the theatre that was primarily responsible for making theatre more socially relevant in post-World War II England. It contains a segment that deals in detail with the first *Saved* production and the ensuing court case.

Cohn, Ruby. *Retreats from Realism in Recent English Drama,* Cambridge University Press, 1991.
> Deals with developments of British Drama since about 1965, including works by Edward Bond. It gives a good overview and covers briefly such critical movements as post-modernism.

Dictionary of Literary Biography, Volumes 13 & 14: *British Dramatists Since World War II,* Gale, 1982.
> This excellent compilation contains entries on every major British dramatist since World War II and also includes articles on the Arts Council of Great Britain and all the major subsidized companies.

Hall, Edward T. *The Hidden Dimension,* Doubleday & Company, Inc., 1966.
> Studies the social and physical pathologies that result from too little physical living space for people.

Hay, Malcolm, and Roberts, Philip. *Bond, A Study of His Plays,* Eyre Methuen, 1980.
> The authors were given unrestricted access to Bond's correspondence, notes, rough drafts, and unpublished plays for their superb study of his work. They have also interviewed directors, designers, and others who worked on productions of his plays.

Hay, Malcolm, editor. *Bond on File,* Methuen, 1985.
> This small volume includes excerpted reviews, performance history, and a selection of Bond's own comments on his work.

Hobson, Harold. *Theatre In Britain, 1920-1983* Phaidon Press Limited, 1984.
> Harold Hobson, for many years the dean of English drama critics, gives an overview of his sixty-three years of attending theatre. This serves as a solid background about what was going on in general, and especially in the commercial theatre, in England during the time Edward Bond and others were developing and writing.

Scharine, Richard. *The Plays of Edward Bond,* Bucknell University Press; Associated University Press, 1976.
> This is an excellent study of Bond's early works, through *The Sea,* 1973. It includes a section on techniques and themes which can be applied to Bond's later works as well.

A Soldier's Play

CHARLES H. FULLER

1981

A Soldier's Play opened November 20, 1981, at the Negro Ensemble Company for the first of 468 performances. Fuller has stated that his play is modeled after Herman Melville's *Billy Budd,* which explores a confrontation between evil and innocence that results in tragedy. While it is about the investigation of a murder, *A Soldier's Play* is not a murder mystery in the strictest sense. The investigation does not consist of policemen unraveling clues or of the simple analysis of physical evidence. Instead, the investigation by a black officer is primarily an exploration into who the slain Waters really was and how racism influences men's behaviors and ideals. The investigator, Captain Davenport, tries to solve this mystery by interviewing the men who served under Waters.

These interviews provide pieces of a puzzle, that when assembled, create a picture of a complex man who often bullied his men but who saw the war as an opportunity for blacks to escape the constraints of segregation. The portrait of Waters reveals a man who has found the only power white men will give to a black man—as a non-commissioned officer in the army during World War II. Critics were enthusiastic about Fuller's play, which won a Pulitzer Prize and the New York Drama Critics Award in 1982, but *A Soldier's Play* also provoked controversy. Where some critics argued that Fuller was forcing audience members to confront their own prejudge, a leading black dramatist, Amiri Baraka, accused

Fuller of working against his own race and of fulfilling the dreams of white power. Fuller's play was never produced on Broadway; rumor has it that Fuller refused to remove the last line of the play, ''you'll get used to it [Negroes being in charge].''

AUTHOR BIOGRAPHY

Charles H. Fuller was born in Philadelphia on March 5, 1939. His father was a printer, and it was while proofreading his father's work that Fuller became interested in literature. While in high school, Fuller and a friend vowed to read every book in the library, but when he realized that there were no books by African Americans, Fuller pledged to fill the shelves. After attending Yiddish theatre, Fuller became focused on drama. Fuller joined the army in 1959 after two years at Villanova University. While in the Army, he served as a petroleum laboratory technician in Korea and Japan. After his time in the army, Fuller attended LaSalle College from 1965 to 1968 and continued to write. Fuller ignores these early efforts, although critics praised his *The Village: A Party* (1968) as showing promise. Fuller's first professionally produced play, *The Brownsville Raid* (1976), drew critical attention. This was followed by *Zooman and the Sign* (1980), which won two Obie Awards. Fuller's next play, *A Soldier's Play* (1981), earned him a Pulitzer Prize for drama, making Fuller only the second black playwright to win this honor. *A Soldier's Play* also garnered the New York Drama Critics Award for best American play and the Outer Circle critics award for best Off-Broadway play in 1982. Fuller's film adaptation of this play earned him an Academy Award nomination for best screenplay adaptation in 1984. Fuller went on to begin work on a collection of plays that dramatizes the black experience during the Civil War. The first of the series of five to six plays was completed in 1988, with the production of *We* for the Negro Ensemble Company. Fuller is also co-founder and co-director of the Afro-American Arts Theatre in Philadelphia (1967-71). In addition, he has been a writer and director of ''The Black Experience'' for WIP-Radio in Philadelphia (1970-71). Fuller has also contributed short stories to anthologies and periodicals and is currently at work on another play.

PLOT SUMMARY

Act I

The play opens with the murder of Sergeant Waters. The audience sees Waters on stage; he is drunk. Immediately there are two shots, but the audience never sees who fires the weapon. In the next scene, five black soldiers are being searched for weapons and they are confined to their barracks, presumably until the risk of a revenge killing ends. Captain Davenport appears on stage and addresses the audience in a monologue that explains why a black lawyer has been sent to a southern army base to investigate a murder. There is immediate conflict when the company captain, Taylor, learns that Davenport is black. Taylor warns Davenport that he will get no cooperation and that no one in authority will allow a black officer to arrest a white man, if the murderer turns out to be white. Taylor also tells Davenport that white officers at the post will not accept a black man of equal rank, and that in his experience, blacks are subordinates without education. Davenport insists on performing his assignment and sets up to interview the men in Waters's company.

The first man interviewed is Wilkie, who tells Davenport that Waters put him in jail and reduced his rank after Wilkie was caught drunk on duty. Wilkie also tells Davenport about the black baseball team and how the black soldiers beat the white soldiers at baseball. From Wilkie, the audience learns that Waters, who thought southern blacks lazy and shiftless, was especially kind to C.J. C.J. was not only good with a baseball bat, but he sang and played the guitar. But the reality is that Waters only pretended to like C.J. In truth, Waters had no use for games or for southern blacks, whom he thought were playing into white stereotypes of black men. Wilkie tries to humanize Waters when he relates the sergeant's hopes for his two children.

The next soldier to be interviewed is Peterson, who tells Davenport that he and Waters came to blows and that Waters beat him after Peterson challenged Waters's authority. In the midst of talking with Peterson, Taylor sends for Davenport. When Davenport reports to Taylor's office, he is told that Taylor has filed papers to stop the investigation. Taylor also reveals that the night Waters was murdered, he has a confrontation with two white officers. One of the officers beat Waters severely before being pulled off by the second man. When Davenport accuses Taylor of covering up a black man's murder by white officers, Taylor replies that both men had faultless alibis. The act ends with Davenport pledging to prove the white officers guilty.

Act II

Act II opens with another monologue by Captain Davenport, who tells the audience that he has gone to Colonel Nivens and received permission to question the two white officers involved. When he finishes this speech, Davenport begins questioning the next man, Henson. Henson relates how C.J. was framed by someone who placed a gun under his bed. When Waters told C.J. that he was under arrest, the young soldier attacked Waters, who then arrested C.J. and charged him with attacking a superior officer during time of war. The men discuss the arrest and decide to go to the captain and tell him that they saw someone sneak into the barracks and plant a gun under C.J.'s bed. When Davenport interviews Cobb, he is told that Cobb visited C.J. in jail and that the young man was severely depressed by the confinement. The day after the visit, C.J. commited suicide. The next interview is with Byrd and Wilcox. Taylor is also present. The atmosphere is filled with tension, but eventually Davenport learns that both Wilcox and Bryd have been cleared when their weapons passed ballistics tests.

At this point, Davenport goes back to interview Wilkie a second time and learns that it was Wilkie who planted the evidence that resulted in C.J.'s arrest. Wilkie also reveals that Waters hated southern blacks and thought they made all blacks look foolish. At that moment, Ellis enters to announce that the company has orders and will be leaving for Europe within 48 hours. Davenport arrests Wilkie and in the next moment learns that Smalls is in the stockade accused of going AWOL. When Davenport confronts Smalls, he confesses that he watched Peterson murder Waters. In a short monologue that follows this revelation, Davenport tells the audience that Peterson was arrested a week later. He also provides a brief follow-up to the men's lives and the audience learns that the entire company was killed during a German advance.

CHARACTERS

Lieutenant Byrd

Byrd is a white, by-the-book military officer. He has a history of confrontation and conflict with black soldiers. The night he is murdered, Byrd beats

Charles Fuller

Waters savagely after he comes upon the sergeant drunk and sick. When questioned by Davenport, Byrd is almost insolent and has to be threaten by Taylor before he will answer.

Corporal Bernard Cobb

Cobb is in his mid to late twenties. He appears to be focused on women—on the women he wants, the ones he has had, the diseases they may have given him. He is closest to C.J. and is almost unmoved by Waters's death.

Captain Richard Davenport

Davenport is an military lawyer, assigned to investigate the murder of Waters. Because he is black, the army really cannot find a place for Davenport and so has assigned him to police black soldiers. He delivers a lengthy monologue when he enters the stage for the first time. This speech tells the audience the background of the story currently being acted on stage. Other officers, most of whom are white, do not know what to make of a black officer, and he is an object of intense curiosity. Davenport is not intimidated by the reception he gets from the white officers. His investigation is thorough, and he quickly is able to delve into the events leading up to Waters's murder.

MEDIA ADAPTATIONS

- In 1984, *A Soldier's Play* was adapted for the screen from Fuller's play as *A Soldier's Story*. The movie starred many of the same actors from the theatrical production, including Adolphe Caesar, Denzel Washington, and Larry Riley. Howard Rollins, Wings Hauser, and David Alan Grier also starred. Norman Jewson directed the film, with a musical score by Herbie Hancock. The film won several awards, including the Edgar Allan Poe Award for Best Screenplay and the Los Angeles Film Critics Association Award for Best Supporting Actor (Adolphe Caesar). Academy Award nominations included Best Adapted Screenplay, Best Picture, and Best Supporting Actor (Caesar). Columbia Tristar Video is the distributor or this 101 minute film.

Corporal Ellis

Ellis is a by-the-book soldier. He is assigned to be Davenport's assistant and his job is to deliver the men to Davenport for questioning.

Private Louis Henson

Henson is in his late twenties. He is nervous and convinced that the Ku Klux Klan is to blame for Waters's murder. Henson is used to being subordinate. He sits back and observes actions but is reluctant to speak up. When questioned by Davenport, Henson has to be ordered to tell his story.

Private C. J. Memphis

Memphis, a young black soldier, was a special favorite of Waters. He entertained with his singing and guitar playing, and he played baseball with the troops as well. Waters likes C.J. initially, but he also sees him as representing everything that blacks need to put behind them—the singing, clowning, and dancing around. C.J. is jailed after he strikes Waters, but Waters had provoked the young soldier and his arrest demoralizes the young man, who had felt

that Waters liked him. C.J.'s death, two months before Waters's, sets in motion the events that follow.

Private First Class Melvin Peterson

Peterson is in his late twenties. He is the neatest of the black troops, shoes polished, his stripe clearly visible, his uniform neatly pressed. Peterson had a history of conflict with Waters, having previously come to blows in a fight with Waters. The area of conflict centered on Peterson's perception that Waters failed to support the men, allowing white soldiers to use the blacks as common laborers and not soldiers. Later when Waters arrests C.J., it is Peterson who insists that the men need to report the truth to the captain. Peterson is aggressive and not intimidated by Waters.

Private Tony Smalls

Smalls is a small man in his late thirties. He is a career soldier and appears genuinely concerned about Waters's murder. Smalls is arrested for going AWOL, and when questioned, he confesses to what he saw the night Waters was murdered.

Captain Charles Taylor

Tayor is a white, West Point educated, officer in his mid to late thirties. When he first meets Davenport, Taylor confesses that he is not comfortable with a black officer. His only experience with blacks is as workmen or subordinates, and he indicates he cannot and does not support Davenport's investigation. He is clearly displeased that Davenport is not subservient or willing to be ordered about by a man of equal rank, who is clearly, in Taylor's mind at least, superior to any blacks. Taylor reluctantly becomes Davenport's ally in the investigation. Taylor, while not believing in equality, also recognizes that blacks deserve to be given justice.

Tech Sergeant Vernon C. Waters

Waters's murder opens the play. Thereafter, his presence on stage is as a voice from the past. He stands slightly off-stage in a pale light and recounts experiences with different individuals. Waters was all military correctness, wanting what was best for his men, but at the same time, hard on them when they disappointed him. Waters had a son for whom he wanted a better future than the one the army offered. He planned to send both his son and daughter to a white man's college so that they would be able to compete with whites and not be left behind. Waters was a complex man who could both praise and attack his men. His goal was to rid the army of southern blacks, who he felt held the entire black community back. But when C.J. commits suicide, Waters is stunned and realizes that he is to blame.

Captain Wilcox

Wilcox is a medical officer who is accused of participating in a beating of Waters on the night he was murdered. Wilcox is the one officer who treats Davenport with respect and who appears to have no bias against blacks.

Private James Wilkie

Wilkie is a career soldier in his early forties. He has recently lost three stripes. He was closest in age to Waters, and in spite of losing rank, pay, and going to jail for ten days, Wilkie claims to have had no hard grudge against Waters. Wilkie was Waters's servant. He ran his errands, managed the ball team, and cleaned his quarters; but when Wilkie got caught drinking, Waters took all his stripes, which had taken him ten years to earn. Then as a bribe to force Wilkie to plant evidence, Waters promises to return his stripes.

THEMES

Alienation

The alienation that black soldiers feel is best demonstrated by the baseball games that are played between white and blacks. The black soldiers view the baseball games as one area where they can prove superiority over white soldiers. The blacks are treated as subservient and subordinate underlings. They are not given the opportunity to be real soldiers; instead they function as little more than servants, handymen, garbage collectors, and gardeners. When these same black soldiers meet white soldiers on the baseball field, the game makes them equal, and when the black team wins, they are superior. Black soldiers emerge from the games knowing that they will be alienated and punished for winning, but their victory makes the alienation more tolerable.

Anger & Hatred

Although he disguises it, Waters really hates what he is—a black man, a black soldier in the army. He is so consumed with self-hatred that he turns it upon the men in his company. Waters is

TOPICS FOR FURTHER STUDY

- Research the role of black soldiers in World War II. Blacks did not fare well after the end of World War I; in view of this experience, what did they hope to change by fighting in this second war?

- Investigate the history of the Ku Klux Klan. Why did it seem to Henson that the Klan must be responsible for Waters's death?

- Compare the film version of *A Soldier's Play*, now titled *A Soldier's Story,* with the theatrical play. How are the characters revealed and the mystery maintained in the film?

- Compare Davenport and Taylor. Each is a captain and each is concerned with justice, but each man has a different plan on how to resolve the murder. How are they alike? How are they different?

- Waters's motive in framing C.J. is to rid the army of those he considers to be southern black fools, who hold back all blacks and prevent their success in a white world. Research the economic status of rural blacks in the 1940s and compare it to that of northern blacks. Is there a large disparity in wages?

given power over other men; it is a power given by whites and largely controlled by whites, but Waters thinks that if he can do the job well, that he can change the white perception of the black man. So he is harder on his men and crueler than a white officer would be, and he tries to eliminate those blacks that he thinks would be unable to compete in a white man's world. Waters sees black survival in becoming white. He hates his own black race and his history, and he turns that hatred upon his men, ultimately being responsible for the death of one of them.

Betrayal

Waters betrays his men, especially C.J., when he plants evidence that implicates the young man in a crime. The sole purpose in framing C.J. is to remove him from the company. But Waters has befriended C.J., praising his singing and playing. The reality is that Waters hates all southern blacks, whom he considers fools who are perpetuating an image of black foolishness with their singing, dancing, and clowning around. C.J. is guilty of all these actions, and in his innocence, he never suspects Waters of betrayal.

Prejudice

Captain Davenport faces prejudice when he arrives at a southern military post to conduct his investigation into Waters's death. When Captain Taylor meets Davenport, the latter is told that the white community will not tolerate a black man investigating whites. But that is not the only reason for Taylor's concern. Taylor admits that in a conversation with other white officers, most admitted they did not want to serve with black officers and could not accept blacks as equals. Indeed, when Davenport finally interviews two white officers, Byrd and Wilcox, Byrd makes clear his distaste for the black captain. Byrd also admits that he beat Waters because the sergeant did not treat him with the respect he deserved as an officer and as a white man.

Racism

Racism is the source for the violence that occurs at this army post. Although there are many black soldiers, they are not welcome in the predominately white community that surrounds the post. When Waters's murder is discovered, initial suspicion falls on the local Ku Klux Klan, who have been responsible for attacks on black soldiers in the past. There is a clear division on the post as well, with the white officers and soldiers aligned against the blacks. The black soldiers feel that if they can only get overseas and into the war, they can prove that they are as good at killing Hitler's men as are the white soldiers. And finally, there is racism within the black community, also. Waters is guilty of racism when he turns on C.J., whose only crime is that he is from the south and represents the type of black man who Waters thinks is holding back other blacks.

Violence

Violence was too often the result of confrontations between whites and blacks. When Waters is murdered, suspicion first falls on white men, nota-

ble the Ku Klux Klan. But violence is also Waters primary way of dealing with difference. Waters identifies rural southern blacks as a hindrance to black advancement. He thinks that their singing and dancing recalls a period of ignorance and subservience that prevents blacks from achieving equality with whites. Rather than look for a way to overcome this problem, Waters seeks a solution in violence. Rather than educate these blacks, Waters has them jailed and placed in a prison population where violence becomes a means of survival; C.J.'s imprisonment leads to his death.

STYLE

Character

A person in a dramatic work. The actions of each character are what constitute the story. Character can also include the idea of a particular individual's morality. Characters can range from simple stereotypical figures to more complex multi-faceted ones. Characters may also be defined by personality traits, such as the rogue or the damsel in distress. "Characterization" is the process of creating a life-like person from an author's imagination. To accomplish this the author provides the character with personality traits that help define who he will be and how he will behave in a given situation. Davenport is a black attorney, who divulges much about himself in the monologues that he uses to update the audience on the action that occurs between scenes. His character is revealed in other ways also, most notably in his confrontations with Taylor.

Drama

A drama is often defined as any work designed to be presented on the stage. It consists of a story, of actors portraying characters, and of action. But historically, drama can also consist of tragedy, comedy, religious pageant, and spectacle. In modern usage, drama explores serious topics and themes but does not achieve the same level as tragedy.

Genre

Genres are a way of categorizing literature. Genre is a French term that means "kind" or "type." Genre can refer to both the category of literature such as tragedy, comedy, epic, poetry, or pastoral. It can also include modern forms of literature such as drama novels, or short stories. This term can also refer to types of literature such as mystery, science fiction, comedy or romance. *A Soldier's Play* is a mystery.

Monologue

A monologue is a speech given by a character and principally addressed to the audience. In a monologue, the character speaking is alone on stage, or thinks he is alone, and thus he speaks the truth. This device is a way for an author to relate to the audience that the speaker really thinks, rather than what he may be telling other characters. A monologue can also be used like a Greek Chorus—to give information about details that occur off stage or between acts or to comments upon action that has occurred. In *A Soldier's Play,* Davenport uses a monologue to tell the audience that has occurred behind the scenes and what he is thinking.

Plot

This term refers to the pattern of events. Generally plots should have a beginning, a middle, and a conclusion, but they may also sometimes be a series of episodes connected together. Basically, the plot provides the author with the means to explore primary themes. Students are often confused between the two terms; but themes explore ideas, and plots simply relate what happens in a very obvious manner. Thus the plot of *A Soldier's Play* is the investigation into who killed Sergeant Waters. But the themes are racism and prejudice.

Setting

The time, place, and culture in which the action of the play takes place is called the setting. The elements of setting may include geographic location, physical or mental environments, prevailing cultural attitudes, or the historical time in which the action takes place. The location for *A Soldier's Play* is an army post in the south. The cultural setting is racism and segregation and the division that occurred within the still segregated military.

HISTORICAL CONTEXT

In 1981, when Charles Fuller wrote *A Soldier's Play,* the United States military was fully integrat-

ed. In fact, the military services have been the largest equal opportunity employer of blacks for many years. But it was not always this way. Historically, blacks have been recruited into the military during wars but unceremoniously returned to civilian life once the war ended. World War II began in much the same way. For many blacks, there was no reason to want to involve themselves in this war. The experience in World War I had taught that once their services were no longer needed that blacks found they had gained nothing by their sacrifice. The freedoms they fought for were not theirs, and the country they defended rejected them. Consequently, many blacks saw World War II as a white man's war, but some, like Sergeant Waters, saw the war as an opportunity to prove that blacks were as brave, as strong, and as accountable as any white soldiers. They reasoned that blacks could shoot a weapon, fly a plane, and kill a German as well as any white man, and they wanted a chance to prove it. They also saw the war as a means to wedge a crack into the segregation that still defined American life. If the military could be integrated, then maybe other areas of American life could be opened up, as well.

During both World War I and II, the army was completely segregated. Blacks were largely restricted to non-combat units, where they were responsible for basic duties that were mostly limited to labor and not combat. In other words, blacks were largely domestics, gardeners, mechanics, and handymen. Only a few blacks were permitted to join artillery units, and these units were also segregated so that blacks fought alongside blacks, and whites fought alongside whites. With the beginning of World War II, black community leaders pressured President Roosevelt to open up aviation schools to blacks. He responded by authorizing an aviation school for blacks, but it took a lawsuit against the War Department before blacks became members of the Army Air Corps. The black unit that was formed became known as the Tuskegee Airmen. Initially no one wanted these black airmen, but eventually they found combat in North Africa and Italy where they distinguished themselves.

Toward the end of the war, black infantry units were sent to Germany, where they participated in the liberation of the concentration camps. It is difficult to imagine what they felt as these victims of American racism liberated the victims of Nazi racism in Europe. But when blacks returned to the United States after the war, they began to demand

COMPARE
&
CONTRAST

- 1944: The cost of living rises almost 30% in one year. For blacks, who already live at or below the poverty line, this inflation makes existence even more difficult.

  1981: Inflation is so great that in an effort to help cut the budget, President Reagan orders that the school lunch program cut back on serving vegetables. In response, the Department of Agriculture declares that ketchup is a vegetable.

  Today: The economy continues to grow, with unemployment low and the Dow Jones tops the 10,000 mark.

- 1944: Women become the backbone of the nations workforce, and the term "Rosie the Riveter" becomes the nickname for women who are now building the machines of war.

  1981: Sandra Day O'Connor becomes the first woman jurist on the U.S. Supreme Court

  Today: While women appear to be equal members of the nations work force, the "glass ceiling" in many companies means that some women still earn only 70% of men's salaries.

- 1944: Prior to the war, blacks had played baseball only in the Negro league. Baseball is curtailed temporarily during the war years; however, women's baseball, The All-American Girls' Baseball League, draws almost a million spectators. After the war ends, Jackie Robinson becomes the first black man to integrate professional baseball

  1981: Baseball is fully integrated, with black players, such as Curt Flood of the St Louis Cardinals, helping to create free agency. However, women are still denied access to professional baseball.

  Today: Some of baseball's biggest stars, including Ken Griffey Jr., are black, but women are still excluded from major league baseball.

- 1944: There has been little opportunity for blacks during the war boom production. Where jobs have been plentiful, conflicts over housing and transportation have caused riots in several major U.S. cities.

  1981: President Reagan's social and economic programs hit blacks especially hard. Many AIDS victims are minorities, especially black drug users, and little effort is being made to fund research while the victims are largely black and Hispanic. Unemployment among blacks is at record levels and will climb to 45% in Los Angeles by the mid 1980s.

  Today: Unemployment is low, but the surplus of jobs is largely in the lower salaried areas; in one area, professional sports, black athletes, such as Carl Lewis, Florence Griffith-Joyner, Michael Jordan, and Tiger Woods prove that blacks can achieve economic benefit from their athletic talents and escape the poverty that holds so many other blacks.

---

greater equality, especially in the military. This demand finally forced President Truman to sign an order that eventually led to the integration of the military, and for the first time ever, blacks would not be cashiered out of the military at war's end. Instead, after the Korean War and Vietnam, blacks became a part of a peace-time military. Prior to World War II, integration had to be forced upon white America. In 1941, President Roosevelt had to order employers and unions to cease all discrimination again blacks. In particular, he emphasized that those companies that were awarded defense contracts must not discriminate. Race riots in 1943 among defense workers signaled that integration would not come easily. It did not come easily in the military either. Although World War II made it easier for blacks to integrate the military, much of that integration led to a greater proportion of black casualties during war. It would take many more years before blacks truly began to achieve a more equitable share of the military effort.

CRITICAL OVERVIEW

In general, *A Soldier's Play* received very favorable reviews when it debuted Off-Broadway in November 1981. Critics were enthusiastic and audiences receptive to Fuller's mystery. For example, Frank Rich's review in *The New York Times,* calls Fuller's play a major breakthrough and "in every way, a mature and accomplished work." *A Soldier's Play* is also "a relentless investigation into the complex, sometimes cryptic pathology of hate." What Rich calls a "skillful portraiture of a dozen characters" creates "a remarkable breadth of social and historical vision." Rich is also enthusiastic about the cast, especially Charles Brown as Davenport, Denzel Washington as Peterson, and Peter Friedman as Taylor, but Rich's greatest praise is for Adolphe Caesar's performance of Waters, a role that is "hateful . . . one moment and a sympathetic, pitiful wreck the next." Referring to Douglas Turner Ward's direction as "superlative," Rich notes that Fuller's play "tirelessly insists on embracing volatile contradictions because that is the way to arrive at the shattering truth." John Beaumont's review for *The Christian Science Monitor* is another emphatic endorsement of Fuller's play. Beaumont calls attention to Fuller's "carefully written, tautly dramatic scenes [which] are filled with racial-psychological insights." But this reviewer also observes Fuller's use of comedic and raunchy material that sounds like the authentic voice of barracks talk. Beaumont also credits an excellent cast and the "admirable staging by Ward for the play's success.

Another endorsement comes from Edwin Wilson at the *The Wall Street Journal.* Wilson's review calls *A Soldier's Play* "a skillfully wrought, thoroughly suspenseful detective story." But Wilson points out that Fuller goes beyond a mystery to create, "one of the most even-handed, penetrating studies of relations among blacks-as well as their relations with whites-that we have yet seen." As is the case with other reviewers, Beaumont also singles out the cast and director as deserving special commendation, and Fuller's "complex web of conflicting attitudes and emotions" as strong elements of the play. Additional ratification for Fuller's play is supplied by Douglas Watt of the *Daily News.*

Calling *A Soldier's Play* "an absorbing, interestingly-layered drama" that could use a bit of tightening, Watt states that an evening at this play is "one of the more satisfying ones in town." While Watt praises Brown and Friedman's performances, he has special kudos for Washington, Caesar, and the other actors who portray the enlisted men; these men, he says, "make up the heart of the play." Watt points to this play as Fuller's "best achievement to date." These words are echoed by Clive Barnes of the *New York Post,* who writes that "Fuller is revealing himself as a playwright of great sensibility . . . [who] must be watched and, even more, cherished." After having complimented Ward's direction and the exceptional work of Caesar and Friedman, Barnes says of Brown, that "he is developing into a consummate actor" whose performance is the best of a fine cast.

Additional praise for Fuller is also provided by Jack Kroll of *Newsweek.* Kroll declares that this latest Fuller play "is a work of great resonance and integrity, bound to be one of the best American plays of this season." The story that Fuller is telling, writes Kroll, is "humanized and dramatized with a deep understanding and a sense of fatality that translate into riveting and revelatory dramatic action." Kroll also has praise for the cast, noting the performances of Brown and Caesar as particularly remarkable. A more mixed review is offered by T.E. Kalem of *Time,* who, while dismissing the investigation as a "dry studies exercise," focuses on the way in which Fuller explores Waters complex character. Of Caesar's performance, Kalem states that Caesar "merits an acting medal of honor" for his portrayal of Waters. Another mixed critique is that of Robert Asahina, whose review appeared in the *Hudson Review.* Asahina singles out the investigation and murder mystery as mere distractions from the more important exploration of how "racism distorts the soul of not just the oppressor but the victim," which Fuller does very well, and for he "is to be commended." Asahina makes the observation that Fuller did not need to set the action in the army during 1944; any war could have provided the same setting for racism, since the attitudes that Fuller expressed are not outdated today.

Fuller's work did stir some controversy. Nearly two years after *A Soldier's Play's* debut, a particularly virulent attack appeared by Amiri Baraka, who was associated with a rival theatrical group. In his article, Baraka begins with what is intended to be a digression on how he always confuses Fuller with another writer whose work is "pretty awful." One source of Baraka's animosity is the ease with which the Negro Ensemble Company is able to raise money from big banks. Baraka is often sarcastic, criticizing both Washington's casting and Brown's acting. His lone voice of opposition, failed to stop the momentum of *A Soldier's Play,* which went on to be made into a successful movie.

CRITICISM

Sheri E. Metzger,

Metzger is a Ph.D., specializing in literature and drama at The University of New Mexico. In this essay, she discusses how Fuller dramatizes the black soldiers' struggle and the two wars that black soldiers fought in World War II.

During World War II, the military finally succumbed to pressure to create black combat battalions. For most of the war, these units were largely for show and had very little role in the war effort, but near the end of the war when the need for more men surfaced, a few of these units were finally mobilized and sent to Europe. Some of these men, who had anticipated they would finally engage in battle, instead helped to liberate concentration camps at Buchenwald, Dachau, and Lambach. What they saw shocked them. These black soldiers, who had come from the segregation of 1940s America, were face to face with the effects of Hitler's racism. But there are other effects of racism, as Charles Fuller proves.

In *A Soldier's Play,* Fuller presents one possible effect of the racism that divides the United States in the 1940s. The black soldiers at this small Louisiana post are anxious to be sent across the ocean to fight Hitler, whom they are confident they can beat as effectively as any white soldiers can. But, as the war drags on, black soldiers sit and wait while whites are sent into battle. This is the racism of exclusion, which breeds hatred and ultimately leads to murder. In his play, Fuller demonstrates that sometimes racism can be turned inward. In *A Soldier's Play,* American racism is juxtaposed against the dark shadow of Hitler's racism. By the time the play ends, Fuller leaves the audience questioning their own prejudices and wondering if racism can be quantitatively judged.

Much of the shock that Americans felt at the end of World War II, derived from Hitler's ghastly extermination of more than 11 million people. This outrage is couched in an awareness that American society could never engage in racism is such an ugly way. But that ignores that effects of systematic racism, which dehumanizes people and consumes them slowly, over time. Sergeant Waters is an example of how racism can destroy a man. Waters readily admits that during World War I he participated in the murder of a young black man. The murder occurred in France when white soldiers took an ''ignorant colored soldier. Paid him to tie a tail to his ass and parade around naked making monkey sounds.'' Waters and other blacks slit the black soldier's throat. He tells Wilkie that blacks must turn their backs on ''fools like C.J.'' who would cheat their own race out of the honor and respect they deserve. Earlier, Waters tells C.J. he has gotten rid of five other soldiers at previous posts. And Waters explains that he did it because he does not want blacks cheated out of the opportunities that he thinks they will derive from fighting in World War II.

This proud admission reveals the hatred that Waters has for his fellow blacks. In his eyes, blacks must meet a higher standard that will help ensure their escape for the oppression of racism. Southern blacks, like C.J., recall stereotypes of black minstrels, who sing, dance, and clown around. Men who look like fools and behave like fools will negate all that a few good blacks can accomplish, according to Waters, who believes that all blacks must be superior to whites if blacks are to become equal to whites. But then C. J. does the unexpected and kills himself, and suddenly Waters is forced to question what he has become. He finally understands that he has willingly destroyed another man and turned his back on his people and has achieved nothing. Whites still do not like him, and they still refuse to accept him as an equal. And the audience must finally admit that they are complicit in this tragedy because they too have tolerated racism.

In constructing this play as a detective story, Fuller seeks to involve the audience in the action on the stage. Suspects are introduced and motives explored in an attempt to keep the audience guessing. In their essay on the detective elements of *A Soldier's Play,* Linda K. Hughes and Howard Faulkner point out that Fuller manages to implicate the audience in the quest to solve the killer's identity and that ''to the degree that we abandon open minds and jump to conclusions about the killer's identity at the outset, we deduce from stereotypes instead of inductively seeking the solution.'' This is because Fuller's red herrings are white officers and the Ku

WHAT DO I READ NEXT?

- Charles Fuller's *The Brownsville Raid* (1976) examines a 1906 incident that resulted in the dishonorable discharge of 167 black soldiers from the 25th Infantry.

- Charles Fuller's *Zooman and the Sign* (1980) is about the quest for justice after a young girl dies and no one in the black community will identify the killer.

- *Taps for a Jim Crow Army: Letters from Black Soldiers in World War II* (1993), edited by Phillip McGuire, provides an authentic voice from black soldiers.

- *The Invisible Soldier: The Experience of the Black Soldier, World War II,* by Mary Motley (1987), consists of a series of interviews with

black officers and enlisted men who served in the military.

- *Liberators: Fighting on Two Fronts in World War II* (1992) by Lou Potter, William Miles, and Nina Rosenblum, relates the experiences of black soldiers who liberated concentration camps of Buchenwald, Dachau, and Lambach. This book is based on a documentary by PBS and is available as a 90 minute video from Direct Cinema Limited in Santa Monica, CA.

- Hondon B. Hargrove's *Buffalo Soldiers in Italy: Black Americans in World War II* (1985) tells the story of the black soldier's experience during World War II.

Klux Klan. The setting is the south, and the audience expects the killer of a black man to be whites.

In that sense, the audience participates in racism. Hughes and Faulkner argue that the audience initially sympathizes with Waters. At the end of the first act, he appears to be sympathetic, but as the second act unfolds, the audience learns that "Waters is, if not a racist himself, one who imposes stereotypes and rigid codes of behavior on fellow blacks." Waters' vision of racial progress does not include fools like C.J. This act of black discriminating against black, just as white can discriminate against black, or white against white is, according to Hughes and Faulkner, suggested by "Them Nazis ain't all crazy," a sentence, they argue, that "reverberates throughout the fabric of the entire play." This sentence, "reminds us that World War II was, in a sense, a racial war, a war to stop Hitler's dream of the Super Race. But black soldiers drafted to fight Hitler first had to confront a racial war of their own in the United States." Thus Waters in both victim and victimizer, according to Hughes and Faulkner, who also point out that the ending of the play tells the audiences that the entire company was wiped

out in that "other racial war in Germany." Thus, the audience is again reminded that both racial wars are connected for the black soldier.

It is worth remembering that Waters is not the only black man to kill another black soldier. The play's conclusion reveals that Peterson is Waters's killer. Both, men, as Hughes and Faulkner note, "double as victimizers impelled by white racism and their own capitulation to imposed stereotypes of 'proper' black behavior. Both [Peterson and Waters] are willing to kill a fellow black to uphold that code, to 'purify' their race; and insofar as they do so, they are also eerie parallels of Hitler, whom Waters partly admires." But racism and prejudice are not limited to Peterson and Waters. Davenport initially thinks Byrd and Wilcox are guilty of the murder. He also assumes, erroneously it turns out, that other white officers are engaged in covering up a white officer's involvement. Later, Taylor, who assumes that blacks are neither intelligent enough nor devious enough to have committed the murder, wants Byrd and Wilcox arrested because he believes the two white officers must be guilty, since, clearly whites must be guilty. There is enough racism and

FULLER ASKS HIS AUDIENCE TO QUESTION THE EFFECTS OF RACISM, TO QUESTION THEIR PREJUDICES. IN *A SOLDIER'S PLAY,* THE EFFECTS OF RACIAL SELF-HATRED LEAD TWO MEN TO MURDER"

prejudice to go around for everyone in the cast to engage in some aspect of this bigotry. Steven Carter's analysis of Davenport's role as detective offers some insight into how Davenport fulfills the traditional role of detective. The traditional skills of the detective, include being able to,

> place reason over emotion, admit past and even current mistakes so that you can find truth in the present, view a situation as a whole rather than be blinded by a part, rid yourself of preconceptions so that you can see reality more clearly. And perhaps hardest and most important of all, acknowledge the destructive elements in your own personality so that you can better understand the destructive side of others.

Carter states that these skills are also effective in counteracting and eliminating racism. That Davenport is able to finally solve the case, according to Carter, "depends largely on his ability to free himself from racist preconceptions of any type." Davenport is able to stay focused on the issue at hand, but, as Carter points out, both Waters and Peterson have become so confused and so involved with in-group bickering that they almost lose sight of their real enemies, white racism at home and Nazi racist imperialism abroad." Self-hatred, the by-product of systematic racism, is responsible for the destruction of both these men. As the play ends, Davenport tells the audience that four men were lost and that "none of their reasons—nothing anyone *said,* or *did,* would have been worth a life to men with larger hearts-men less split by the madness of race in America."

Fuller asks his audience to question the effects of racism, to question their prejudices. In *A Soldier's Play,* the effects of racial self-hatred lead two men to murder, for Waters murders C.J. just as surely as if he had tied the noose. The audience is asked to consider that ordinary men are capable of murder when pushed to extraordinary lengths. William W. Demastes, in an article that questions the role of prejudice in Fuller's play, observes that the typical murder mystery looks to the extreme or atypical conditions that lead to murder, such as the Ku Klux Klan confronting radical blacks. Instead, says Demastes, Fuller "challenges the standard, comfortable assumptions that tensions exist only between such radical elements of both races." The racism that resulted in Nazi concentration camps shocked people, as it should. But Fuller would like his audience to consider that racism that results in blacks murdering blacks is also shocking and deserving of greater thought. When Waters real intent toward C.J. is revealed and when Peterson is disclosed as the murderer, the audience should be dismayed as well as stunned. And they should question their own prejudices.

Source: Sheri E. Metzger, for *Drama for Students,* Gale, 2000.

Robert Asahina

Asahina examines Fuller's play, citing its recent Pulitzer Prize victory as well-deserved. In appraising the racial themes of the drama, the critic credits Fuller with "creating a truly tragic character" in Sergeant Waters.

For a change, this year's Pulitzer Prize actually went to the season's most deserving work: Charles Fuller's *A Soldier's Play,* produced by the Negro Ensemble Company and directed by Douglas Turner Ward. But it deserves criticism as well as praise.

Set in 1944, *A Soldier's Play* could also have been written then; it is a straightforward piece of psychological realism that takes the form of a murder mystery. In the first scene, Vernon C. Waters (Adolph Caesar), a Tech/Sergeant in the 221st Chemical Smoke Generating Company, is killed by two unknown assailants. Waters is black, as are the other noncoms and enlisted men at Fort Neal, Louisiana, in the year before the end of World War II. Suspecting that the killers are white and fearing a racial conflict between the soldiers and the residents of the nearby town of Tynan, the white officers restrict their troops to the base and order an investigation.

A black captain, Richard Davenport (Charles Brown), assigned to the military police, arrives at

Fort Neal to conduct the inquiry (and to narrate the play, which largely consists of flashbacks). Davenport is reluctantly assisted by a white captain, Charles Taylor (Peter Friedman), a West Pointer who makes known his antagonism by aggressively announcing, ''I never saw a Negro until I was twelve or thirteen.'' Still, it is clear to both of them that the investigation is supposed to fail, since everyone assumes that the murderers are white and will thus be impossible to bring to justice in the South. ''Don't take yourself too seriously,'' Taylor warns Davenport, who sardonically acknowledges that ''the matter was given the lowest priority.''

Nonetheless, the black captain persists, eventually daring to cast suspicion on two white officers, Lieutenant Byrd (Sam McMurray) and Captain Wilcox (Stephen Zettler). By this time, Taylor has grudgingly come to respect Davenport's efforts; in fact, he is even more eager than his black colleague to bring charges against his fellow whites. But Davenport has begun to believe that the case is more than an incident of racial violence. His questioning of the black soldiers gradually leads him—and us— to the uncomfortable realization that the murder was committed by someone under Waters' command.

As the captain digs deeper, a complex portrait of the dead sergeant emerges from the flashbacks that spring out of the interrogation sessions around which the play is structured. A veteran of World War I, Waters is a career man and a strict disciplinarian who expects his troops to toe the white man's line as squarely as he does. When he busts Corporal James Wilkie (Steven A. Jones) to the rank of private for being drunk on duty, Waters complains, ''No wonder they treat us like dogs.'' His favorite target for abuse is a Southern black, Private C. J. Memphis (David Alan Grier), who represents everything he despises. Pleasant but slow-witted, Memphis is the star of the company baseball team, as well as a mournful blues guitarist and singer. But to Waters, a Northerner, Memphis is nothing but an embarrassing exemplar of a ''strong black buck.'' ''Niggers aren't like that today,'' the sergeant sneers.

Waters is no simple Uncle Tom, however. ''This country's at war,'' he tells his men, ''and you niggers are soldiers.'' To him, they must be more than good soldiers—they must be the best, for their own sake if not the army's. ''Most niggers just don't care,'' he claims. ''But not havin's no excuse for not gettin'. We got to challenge the man in *his* arena.''

In his twisted way, Waters truly believes that the black race can only advance by following his example—by being better than the white man at his own game. ''Do you know the damage one ignorant Negro can do?'' he asks Memphis. ''The black race can't afford you laughin' and clownin'.''

Davenport soon learns the lengths to which Waters went to ''close our ranks on the chittlins and collard greens style.'' During the year before his death, the company team had been so successful that a game with the Yankees was in the works if the Fort Neal soldiers were to win their conference title. But the better the troops do on the field, the worse they do on the base. ''Every time we beat them at baseball,'' the soldiers complain about their white opponents, ''they get back at us any way they can''—in work details ranging from KP to painting the officers' club. Waters, of course, believes ''these men need all the discipline they can get,'' since he regards their athletic achievements as frivolous, even dangerous, because they reinforce the white man's stereotype of the black.

To his horror, Davenport discovers that Waters found a way of eliminating Memphis while simultaneously sabotaging the team. The sergeant framed the hapless private for a mysterious shooting on the base (''one less fool for the race to be ashamed of''), and when Memphis killed himself in the stockade, the players threw the championship game in protest. But the cost of Waters' demented discipline was a growing desire for vengeance among his troops. As Davenport finally determines, two of them—Private First Class Melvin Peterson (Denzel Washington) and Private Tony Smalls (Brent Jennings)— took matters into their own hands and killed their tormentor. Yet even at the moment of his death, Waters had the last word, or words—the same ones that opened the play. ''You got to be like them,'' he cries in torment. "But the rules are fixed. It doesn't make any difference. They still hate you."

Whatever else can be said about *A Soldier's Play,* Fuller must be credited for creating a truly tragic character for whom those words are an anguished, self-proclaimed epitaph. It is in Waters that the toll of racism is most apparent. To be sure, all the black characters in the drama are representative of different modes of dealing with white oppression: the cautious rationality of Davenport, the self-abasement of Wilkie (brilliantly brought to life by Jones), the unenlightened self-interest of Smalls. Likewise, Memphis embodies the black past, stolid and humble, just as surely as Peterson does the future, or at least one possible future: righteous but also arrogant.

Yet Waters is unique among the men by being both the engineer of his own downfall and the victim of his circumstances; like all genuinely tragic figures, he attains universality because of rather than despite the stubborn reality of his particularity. From the smallest of his affectations—the pompous, gravelly voice, the pipe-smoking, the military carriage, the cultivated disdain for his inferiors—to the enormity of his crimes against his own people in their name, the costs of Waters' unnatural, willful assimilation are painfully apparent. ("Any man don't know where he belongs," says Memphis, "got to be in a lot of pain.") Fuller's resolute writing and Caesar's forceful acting have created a truly unlikeable yet strangely sympathetic character, unpleasant yet unexpectedly revealing of what we fear as the worst accommodationist impulses in ourselves.

Unfortunately, Fuller does not handle the investigation into Waters' violent death as ably as he does the sergeant's tortured life. Somehow the murder mystery comes to dominate the other elements of the play; the larger problems of human behavior in adverse circumstances become secondary to the whodunit questions of motive and opportunity. True, the investigation gives the drama a certain forward momentum, but not enough to disguise the fact that almost everything interesting takes place in the past. The most compelling figure is the victim, whose life is revealed in flashback; the action in the present is, for the most part, structured according to the familiar strategy of revelations leading to further revelations and ultimately to a rather comfortable resolution.

Not too comfortable, mind you; Fuller is to be commended for honestly exposing how racism distorts the soul of not just the oppressor but the victim. For this genuine revelation (as opposed to the convenient revelations that advance the plot) to matter to us, however, it must matter to the character through whose eyes we perceive it. And it is not unreasonable to expect that Davenport's discoveries will change him—somehow. After all, he began his inquiry more or less convinced that the killers were white, and then had to overcome his own prejudices to uncover the truth. He could also see something of himself in Waters. Though younger, the captain must have had to pay the same dues as the sergeant—perhaps even more, to rise to the higher rank.

Yet Davenport maintains an eerie emotional distance throughout (which is underscored by Brown's rather affectless performance; he is so cool that he practically freezes into rigidity). Perhaps Fuller thereby meant to comment on the captain's notion of soldierly conduct, which causes him to be almost color-blind. Indeed, early in the play, Davenport rebuffs Wilkie's presumption of racial familiarity ("You all we got down here," the private claims).

But this sort of irony seems absent elsewhere, particularly from the author's decision to set the play so far in the past. (I do not think the drama required the segregated army, which came to an end after the war; in fact, the play might have been more pointed had it been set after integration. As for the war itself, it could as easily have been Korea or Vietnam—or no war at all, for all the difference it makes to the action.) Did Fuller believe that the attitudes represented by, say, Memphis and Waters would seem outdated today? That Davenport, too, would seem anachronistic, or even Peterson insufficiently militant? Or did he think (or does he recognize) that setting *A Soldier's Play* in 1944 somehow lets all of us—playwright, cast, audience—off the hook? Or was it that he wanted all concerned to consider the drama as art rather than as "relevant" social comment? It is not that I suspect Fuller's motives—it is just that I don't know what they are.

Source: Robert Asahina. "Theatre Chronicle" in the *Hudson Review,* Vol. XXXV, no. 3, Autumn, 1982, pp. 439–42.

Richard Gilman

Calling A Soldier's Play *a "flawed but estimable" work, Gilman offers a mostly favorable re-*

view, noting that Fuller's play is representative of the growth of the Negro Ensemble Company that produced the drama.

After fourteen seasons, the Negro Ensemble Company can no longer be regarded as an exotic enterprise on the fringe. The N.E.C. came into being because the established American theater didn't seem to have any place for the black experience. So the group proceeded to carve such a place for itself, with determination if not always a clear notion of what it was doing. Its stance was either aggressive, that of an adversary, or defensive, which meant insular and self-validating; it stumbled, fell, rose and kept going.

Never quite a true ensemble, in that it frequently brings in performers for particular productions, the company has had difficulty creating an identifiable style, a way of doing things unmistakably its own. If it still has that difficulty, at least its repertory has become much more flexible, so that its socially oriented realism has lost some of the pugnacious, parochial quality that once marred it.

Charles Fuller's *A Soldier's Play,* the opening production of the N.E.C.'s fifteenth season, is exemplary of this change and, as I see it, this growth. A flawed but estimable play, it's about the black experience but is supple enough in its thematic range and social perspectives to treat that experience as part of a complex whole, as part of American reality in its widest sense. To be released from an adversary position may mean a loss of fierceness—it certainly means a reduction in ideological thunder—but it can make for an increase in subtle wisdom and intellectual rigor.

Not that *A Soldier's Play* is a triumph of the dramatic imagination. But it is intelligent and morally various enough to overcome some basic uncertainties and remnants of the N.E.C.'s older confrontational manner, and so commend itself to our attention. Set in a Louisiana army camp in 1944, the play deals with the fatal shooting of a black sergeant (reflecting the times, blacks are called "negroes" or "coloreds"), a martinet who, out of shame at his people's seeming acceptance of their inferior status, is tougher on his own men than are their white officers.

He's far from likable, but when he's killed and the culprits aren't found, the mood turns ugly among

> IN ITS CALM CONCERN FOR PRICKLY TRUTHS AND ITS INTELLECTUAL SOBRIETY, *A SOLDIER'S PLAY* ELICITS THE AUDIENCE'S APPROVAL, IF NOT ITS BOISTEROUS ENTHUSIASM"

the black soldiers. At first, the Klan is suspected, then some white officers, but the brass wants no trouble and the incident is shunted aside. Finally, an investigator is sent from Washington, a black lieutenant with a law degree from Howard University. His relationship with the white captain previously in charge of the case makes up the moral and psychological center of the drama, which on one level proceeds as a moderately absorbing detective story.

The captain, an earnest liberal, is convinced he knows who the killers are but feels his hands are tied, and he grows impatient with the black officer's slow, careful inquiry. The real problem, however, is the dislocation the captain experiences in his abstract good will. "I can't get used to it," he tells the black man, "your uniform, your bars." Still, he comes to accept the investigator, whose mind is much more in tune with reality than his own and who eventually brings the case to a surprising conclusion. Along the way there are some deft perceptions about both political and psychological matters, and a jaunty historical sense: "Look out, Hitler," a soldier says, "the niggers is comin' to get your ass."

The biggest burden the play carries is the direction of Douglas Turner Ward, the N.E.C.'s artistic director, who is also a well-known playwright. Ward manages the many flashbacks, through which the action is propelled, with a heavy hand: lights go up or down with painful slowness, figures from the past *take their places* obediently in the present. There are also some soft spots among the performances and an unpleasant ending, or coda, in which the black officer gratuitously reminds his white colleague of the lessons taught and learned. Yet in its calm concern for prickly truths and its intellectual sobriety, *A Soldier's Play* elicits the audience's approval, if not its boisterous enthusiasm.

Source: Richard Gilman. Review of *A Soldier's Play* in the *Nation,* Vol. 234, no. 3, January 23, 1982, pp. 90–91.

Wilson, Edwin. A review of *A Soldier's Play* in *The Wall Street Journal,* February 26, 1982.

SOURCES

Asahina, Robert. A review of *A Soldier's Play* in *Hudson Review,* Vol. XXXV, No. 3, Autumn, 1982, pp. 439-42.

Baraka, Amiri. "The Descent of Charles Fuller into Pulitzerland and the Need for African-American institutions," in *Black American Literature Forum* Vol. 17, No. 2, Summer, 1983, pp. 51-54.

Barnes, Clive. A review of *A Soldier's Play,* in the *New York Post,* November 23, 1981.

Beaufort, John. A review of *A Soldier's Play,* in *The Christian Science Monitor,* December 1, 1981

Carter, Steven R. "The Detective as Solution: Charles Fuller's *A Soldier's Play*" in *Clues* Vol. 12, No. 1, Spring-Summer, 1991, pp. 33-42.

Demastes, William W. "Charles Fuller and *A Soldier's Play:* Attacking Prejudice, Challenging Form," in *Studies in American Drama* Vol. 2, 1987, pp. 43-56.

Hughes, Linda K. and Howard Faulkner. "The Role of Detection in *A Soldier's Play*" in *Clues* Vol. 7, No. 2 Fall-Winter, 1986, pp. 83-97.

Kalem, T. E. A review of *A Soldier's Play* in *Time,* January 18, 1982.

Kroll, Jack. A review of *A Soldier's Play* in *Newsweek,* December 21, 1981.

Rich, Frank. A review of *A Soldier's Play* in *The New York Times,* November 27, 1981.

Watt, Douglas. A review of *A Soldier's Play* in the *Daily News,* November 25, 1981.

FURTHER READING

Cooper, Michael L. *The Double V Campaign: African Americans and World War II,* Lodestar Books, 1998.
    This book is designed for adolescents, ages 9-12. Cooper describes the problems black soldiers faced as they fought two wars, one against a foreign enemy and one against racism in the United States.

Dryden, Charles W. *A-Train: Memoirs of a Tuskegee Airman,* University of Alabama Press, 1997.
    This is a personal account of Dryden desire to be a pilot during World War II and how his belief in himself helped him to succeed.

Harriott, Esther, ed. *American Voices: Five Contemporary Playwrights in Essays and Interviews,* McFarland & Company, 1988, pp. 112-125.
    In this 1982 interview, Fuller discusses his work and the process of adapting *A Soldier's Play* to film.

Hay, Samuel A. *African American Theatre: A Historical and Critical Analysis,* Cambridge Studies in American Theatre and Drama, Cambridge University Press, 1994.
    Traces the history of Black theatre from its origin as 19th-century social protest.

Sandler, Stanley. *Segregated Skies: All-Black Combat Squadrons of WW II,* Smithsonian History of Aviation Series, Smithsonian Institution Press, 1992.
    This is the story of the Tuskegee Airmen, as told by a military historian, who recounts the story behind the formation of the squadron and their role in the war.

Streamers

DAVID RABE

1976

Although David Rabe has repeatedly denied that *Streamers* was conceived of as such, many commentators view the work as the last piece in a Vietnam War trilogy that also includes *The Basic Training of Pavlo Hummel* (1970) and *Sticks and Bones* (1972). Like most of the playwright's works, *Streamers* had a rather involved composition history from its initial conception to its final form. It started out as a one-act play under the working title ''Frankie'' and was actually begun before Rabe started working on either *Basic Training* or *Sticks and Bones,* but it was not completed and staged until both those works had been produced. According to the dramatist, the one-act ''contained, in an abbreviated form, the first act of *Streamers.*''

Rabe knew the one-act was not ready for production and in 1969 refused an offer for an Off-Broadway staging. Instead, when he went to work as a journalist in New Haven, Connecticut, he developed the play into a full-length work, first by adding the stabbing of Billy and then by expanding the roles of Sergeants Cokes and Rooney. It was finally ready for production at the end of 1975.

The full-length version of the play was premiered at the Long Warf Theater in New Haven, where it opened on January 30, 1976. Under the direction of Mike Nichols, the main players included Michael-Raymond O'Keefe as Martin, Peter Evans as Richie, Joe Fields as Carlyle, John Heard as Billy, Herbert Jefferson, Jr. as Roger, Dolph

Sweet as Cokes, and Kenneth McMillan as Rooney. Nichols also directed the play's restaging in New York at the Mitzi Newhouse Theater, Lincoln Center, where it was produced by Joseph Papp and opened on April 21, 1976. Some of the original cast reprised their roles, but changes included Michael Kell as Martin, Dorian Harewood as Carlyle, Paul Rudd as Billy, and Terry Alexander as Roger. In New York, it ran for over 400 performances and was enthusiastically received by many important critics, including Rex Reed, Christopher Sharp, Edwin Wilson, and Martin Gottfried. A few demurred, including John Beaufort, who, in a review for the *Christian Science Monitor,* argued that the work was too sensational and was devoid of new insights.

Despite its crude content, for many *Streamers* remains Rabe's best work. Its violence and vulgarity may continue to offend some, but the play is certainly the most accomplished part of the so-called trilogy, upon which Rabe's high reputation to some measure still rests. The genius of *Streamers* was clearly recognized when the play was first staged. Among other awards, it was named the Best American Play for 1976 by the New York Drama Critics and received a Drama Desk Award. It is still the most often staged play in Rabe's dramatic canon.

AUTHOR BIOGRAPHY

David William Rabe was born on March 10, 1940, in Dubuque, Iowa, son to William and Ruth McCormick Rabe. His father was a high-school teacher who eventually left teaching to take a job at a meat-packing plant shipping dock, while his mother contributed to the family income by working in a department store. Through their efforts, David was able to attend two Catholic schools in his home town, Loras Academy and Loras College, where, in 1962, he earned a B.A. degree in English.

After graduating from college, Rabe found odd jobs, briefly working as an egg carrier, bellhop, parking-lot attendant, and substitute teacher, but he soon started work on a graduate degree in theater at Villanova University. He dropped out of the program before completing his degree, however, and, in 1965, was drafted into the Army. He spent the next year on a tour of duty in Vietnam, which profoundly affected his subsequent career as a writer. Although he was assigned to a hospital group and was not directly engaged in combat, he was greatly disturbed by the sacrifice of young Americans in what increasingly seemed to be a pointless war.

After returning to the United States, he re-entered Villanova and finished his M.A. degree in theater in 1968. He then started writing about his Vietnam experiences and began working as a journalist, serving as a feature writer for the *New Haven Register* in New Haven, Connecticut. After marrying Elizabeth Pan in 1969, he returned to Villanova University as an assistant professor and playwright in residence. His marriage soon failed, and he did not marry again until 1979, when he wed actress Jill Clayburgh.

In 1971, Rabe gained his commercial success as dramatist when his play *The Basic Training of Pavlo Hummel* was staged by influential producer Joe Papp on Broadway at the Newman Theatre. Although it was Rabe's first New York-produced play in his often dubbed "Vietnam Trilogy," it was the last written. *Sticks and Bones,* which opened in New York later in the same year, had been written and published two years earlier, and *Streamers,* produced in 1976, had begun as a one-act play with the title "Frankie," a work in progress before the playwright even began writing *The Basic Training of Pavlo Hummel.*

Although Rabe has repeatedly disclaimed being an antiwar playwright, throughout his career he has consistently been viewed as an uncompromising, angry, and trenchant critic of misguided or errant public policy shaped in the Vietnam War era. In other major works, including *The Orphan* (1973), *In the Boom Boom Room,* (1974, a revision of the earlier *Boom Boom Room*), *Hurlyburly* (1984), and *A Question of Mercy* (1998), Rabe deals with the deterioration of values both during that War and in its aftermath.

Rabe's drama is noteworthy for its intensity. In his plays, the vulgar and obscene become lyrical, as they do in much of the work of Chicago playwright David Mamet (*Glengarry Glen Ross*). Bordering on the surreal at times, Rabe's work is also rich in symbol and nightmarish violence, and it is also distinctive for accurate rendering of the distinct voices of its diverse characters, which is one of the most significant features of a play like *Streamers,* and for its experimentation with structure and technique. He is a highly regarded dramatist as well as a writer of screenplays and fiction. Although written early in his career, *Streamers* is still singled out as the most polished piece in the playwright's Vietnam

War trilogy if not the most accomplished work Rabe has written for the live stage.

PLOT SUMMARY

Act One

Streamers takes place in a large cadre room in one of the barracks on an unidentified U. S. Army base located in Virginia near Washington, D.C. It is about 1965, during the administration of President Lyndon B. Johnson, and it soon becomes clear that the soldiers quartered in the barracks, some fresh from basic training, are transients awaiting orders that will most likely send them to Vietnam. The cadre room houses three soldiers: Richie, Billy, and Roger.

At rise, Richie is trying to calm down another soldier, Martin, who has made an aborted attempt to kill himself by slitting one of his wrists. Richie is intent on hiding Martin's attempt from the other soldiers, but Martin is distraught and can only talk about how much he hates the Army and how he wants to get out.

The two men are interrupted by Carlyle, a restless black soldier dressed in grease and sweat-stained fatigues. He is looking for Roger, the black barracks mate of Richie and Billy. Martin immediately tells Carlyle of his suicide attempt, much to Richie's dismay, but Carlyle seems completely unfazed by the disclosure and leaves. Billy enters, and Martin also informs him, again explaining how much he hates the Army. After they all leave, Roger enters and starts doing pushups on the floor. Billy returns and talks with Roger about the Army and the "ole sarge," Rooney, a demolitions expert and veteran of World War II who now shakes so badly from alcoholism that he cannot light his own cigar. The two friends banter about the "regular" Army, the "real" Army that Roger wants to be in or be shorn of the military altogether not headed for Vietnam or Disneyland, where the "ole sarge" is going "to be Mickey Mouse." Billy, after asking Roger whether he would rather fight a war in the freezing cold or a place where there were lots of snakes, talks of his experiences at home, before he was drafted.

When Richie comes back in, he tells Roger about what Martin had done. It is soon clear that Richie, openly attempting to establish his homosexuality, enjoys teasing and flirting with Billy,

David Rabe

much to Billy's annoyance. When Richie goes to take a shower, Billy and Roger discuss his effeminate behavior. Roger is convinced that Richie is not really gay, but Billy is not so sure. The friends then prepare to clean the room. Billy goes off to get wax, and Roger opens Richie's locker to look at a pinup hanging inside the door, his proof that Richie is really a heterosexual just putting on an act. Carlyle enters, demanding to know why Roger is looking at a picture of a white woman. He then invites Roger to take a slug from a pint of whiskey he carries and explains why he sought Roger out. The base is, he says, "a little short on soul," and he is looking for a companion, someone who is not "pale" and "boring." Obviously on edge, he tries to talk Roger into going with him to the enlisted men's club or into town, but Roger refuses. Carlyle, who hates the army and all its "jive," is almost frantic at the thought of being shipped off to Vietnam.

When Richie returns from the showers, Carlyle leaves. Billy then comes back and the three men prepare to mop and wax the floor. Billy wants Richie to convince Roger that he actually is gay, and he also wants him to stop his "cute shit," his homosexual flirtations. Roger, somewhat embarrassed, asks Richie if he really has engaged in "fag stuff," and Richie admits that he has. Roger, still not willing to accept Richie as a "screamin' god-damn faggot," talks about his home neighborhood and the murder of a gay man. The three then gab about their common fears their likely combat assignment in Vietnam and the notorious barbarism of the Viet Cong but Roger, still not convinced about Richie's homosexuality, once more asks him if he is "really into it." Richie again explains that he is, but Roger concludes that Richie joined the army to "get away from it," something Richie himself is not sure about.

At this point the "ole sarge," Rooney, and his buddy, Sergeant Cokes, make an inebriated entrance. The two airborne veterans, in their fifties, are loud and boisterous. They are also both sad and funny. They are full of bluster and contempt for the young, inexperienced soldiers, the "buncha shit sacks," but Cokes is also very scared, for he has been diagnosed as having leukemia and is in a kind of drunken denial. Rooney calls Cokes a hero, with jungle boots to prove it. The pair leap around like parachutists preparing for a jump, and Cokes tells two stories, one about a trainee at Fort Bragg who was killed trying to catch a parachute he prematurely released before hitting the ground, and a second about a "gook" in Korea that he trapped in his spider hole by sitting on its lid, then killed by blowing him to bits with a grenade.

Cokes and Rooney next sing "Beautiful Streamer," a song that a man jumping from a plane supposedly sings when he discovers that his parachute is not going to open. Shortly after that, Cokes passes out, and when he regains consciousness, he and Rooney grow angry and bitter, verbally assaulting Billy and the others before turning out the lights and, with arms around each other, slipping out the door.

In the darkened room, Billy tells Roger about a kid named Frankie whom he grew up with, a boy who experimented with homosexual relations and one day found that he was "hooked." Then Carlyle, also drunk, crawls into the room, imitating battle sounds. He explains that he is practicing, getting ready to be killed in Vietnam. He slips to the floor, curls up with his bottle and prepares to go to sleep. The others give him blankets and let him stay. At taps, Roger speculates on the fate of Cokes, betting that he will kill himself. Richie covers Carlyle with another blanket and pats his arm familiarly, earning Billy's disapproval. Roger suggests that Richie does not know why he does such things, which Richie confirms as the act ends.

Act Two, scene one

It is late afternoon, presumably of the next day. Roger convinces Billy, who is vaguely unhappy, to go to the gym to work out, but before leaving their cadre room Billy attempts to explain why he had once thought about becoming a priest. He also talks about getting an off-duty job at a bar and his interest in a girl who works there. The pair also relate how they became friends, then begin doing pushups in preparation for their gym workout. Richie enters and suggests in innuendos that their physical exercise is some sort of ersatz gay sex. Billy, again irritated with Richie's behavior, throws a basketball at him, knocking a bottle of cologne from his hand, and then heads for the door. Richie douses Billy with some cologne as Roger and Billy exit.

Richie, alone, starts to read on his bed, but Carlyle enters and breaks his concentration. Richie informs him that Roger is out and learns that Martin is going to be shipped home. Richie closes the door to the room and offers Carlyle a cigarette. Quite aggressively, Carlyle begins suggesting that Richie, "a punk," wants Carlyle to show him his "rope." Richie, sensing Carlyle's barely repressed violence, begins fending him off, unwilling to get in too deeply. Carlyle becomes alternately abusive and friendly, and he eventually settles down on Richie's bed. However, he is irritated by his perpetual K.P. duty and becomes annoyed with the fact that Richie has never been on K. P. With a final explosive insult, he drives Richie out of the room into the hall.

Billy enters, startled to find Carlyle on Richie's bed. Carlyle asks him if Richie is the "only punk" in the room, but Billy, who is growing physically sick, denies that Richie is gay. Then Richie re-enters and immediately insults Carlyle as "one of them who hasn't come down far out of the trees yet." Carlyle, shifting his mood, attempts to be friendly again. He tells Billy and Richie that he was just "jivin'" when he called Richie a punk.

After Carlyle leaves, Richie asks Billy whether the story he had told about Frankie was really a story about himself, an allegation which infuriates Billy. He tells Richie that his brain is "rancid." The encounter between the two is interrupted by Roger, who enters dressed in civilian clothes. He is planning to go out on the town with Carlyle and wants to borrow some money, which Richie provides. Although he has many reservations about Carlyle and his ideas, when invited by Roger to go along, Billy agrees to accompany them, but Richie declines. They talk of going to a brothel, which Richie finds "disgusting." Carlyle then enters, and informed that Billy is going with him and Roger, finds it "beautiful" because they will all be friends. When Richie asks about his part in the new friendship, the other three stare at him momentarily, then depart, leaving him to his solitude.

Act Two, scene two

It is night. Taps is being played while the four soldiers Billy, Richie, Roger, and Carlyle lounge about the room. Richie tells of his father's desertion of the family when Richie was very young, prompting Carlyle to speak of his father, a butcher who never even acknowledged his paternity. Richie then recalls seeing a television documentary about the homeless in San Francisco, and seeing a "bum" he knew was his father. Carlyle talks of the new friendships, what will become "one big happy family," but almost immediately antagonisms surface. Richie informs Billy that Carlyle is going beat Billy's time with him because Carlyle is decisive. Billy gets furious with Richie, but he lightens up when they all begin talking about school.

Richie, hoping to make Billy jealous, tries to get Roger and Billy to leave so that he can serve Carlyle's desires, but Billy wants no part of providing an opportunity for Carlyle and Richie to engage in sex. He calls Carlyle an animal, and Carlyle pulls out a knife and has to be placated by Roger, who tells Billy that they should just turn away and let Richie and Carlyle do what they want. Both heated and aroused, Carlyle starts ordering Richie to get on his knees and perform oral sex on him. Now convinced of Richie's homosexuality, Roger says that Richie only wants Carlyle as an animal and disgustedly leaves when Carlyle refuses to go outside with Richie.

Carlyle turns out the light, but Billy turns it back on and throws a sneaker at Carlyle and Richie, who is kneeling before Carlyle. Furious, Carlyle goes after Billy with his knife. He orders him to hold out his hand and slashes his palm, annoyed because Billy ruined his "mood." Billy responds by grabbing a razor, but throws it down and begins verbally assaulting both Richie and Carlyle, calling the one a "faggot queer" and the other "Sambo."

Roger returns just before Carlyle knifes Billy again, stabbing him in the gut. First staggering around, bouncing off lockers, Billy finally drops to his knees, mortally wounded, although unaware of it. Roger and Richie are both solicitous of Billy, who begins to panic and sends the hysterical Richie

off to get help, then begins spitting blood as Roger tries to comfort him. Billy, falls to the floor, asks for a blanket, and after covering him with one, Roger runs out shouting for Richie. Carlyle crosses to Billy, who pats his hand and asks him not to stab him again.

Sergeant Rooney then enters, looking for Cokes with whom he has been playing hide-and-seek. He sits on Billy's bed, spots Carlyle, and asks who is, just as Richie rushes into the room and tells Rooney that Carlyle has stabbed Billy. Rooney is at first confused, even slow-witted, but he blocks Carlyle's escape and threatens him with a beer bottle. When Carlyle lunges at Rooney with his knife, Richie runs out again. Rooney screams an eagle yell and breaks the bottle, intending to use it as a weapon, but cuts his hand and just stands dumbfounded as Carlyle stabs him in the belly. Rooney drops to the floor and dies as Carlyle repeatedly hacks at him with his knife.

Roger comes in and pulls Carlyle off Rooney's body, but Carlyle, now whimpering, frees himself. Roger crawls under Billy's bed. Carlyle tells him not to tell anyone what he has done, but when Roger starts talking "weird shit" to him, he flees from the room. Roger then goes to Billy and again tries to comfort him, cradling him in his arms.

A Military Police lieutenant enters and, at gun point, forces Roger to spread eagle against the wall lockers. Then Richie and PFC Hinson, also an M.P., come in. Richie tries to explain that Roger is the wrong man, but the officer just tells him to shut up. Then a third M.P., PFC Clark, enters, shoving Carlyle, handcuffed, before him. Richie immediately accuses the blood-stained Carlyle of the knifings. Another M.P. enters. Hinson checks the bodies of Rooney and Billy and announces that they are both dead.

Carlyle tries to convince the M.P.s that he is covered with chicken blood, but the lieutenant tells the others to sit him down and make him shut up. Richie and Roger then give the officer a breathless account of what happened, after which Carlyle stands up and demands that his cuffs be removed and that they get him a bus ticket home so that he can leave the "jive-time army." The lieutenant again tells him to shut up, but Carlyle says that he has quit the Army. The officer calls in Hinson and Clark and orders them to take Carlyle away.

After the M.P.s have taken the bodies of Billy and Rooney out on stretchers, the officious lieutenant gives Roger and Richie forms to fill out and informs them that they will have to report to his office the next morning. He then marches out. Left alone with Richie, Roger begins to mop up the blood on the floor, much to Richie's horror. He protests that it is Billy's blood, but Roger responds with recriminations, blaming Richie for what happened.

Drunk and very chummy, Cokes enters, carrying a wine bottle. He is looking for Rooney, but Roger tells Cokes that they have not seen him. Cokes sits down on Billy's bed and rambles on about the adventurous day he has spent with Rooney, how they got in four accidents and fights and "got out clean." Then, after moving to sit on Richie's footlocker, he discovers that Richie is sobbing and wants to know why. Roger tells Cokes that it is because Richie is queer. Cokes, explaining that leukemia has given him a new perspective on things, tells Richie that there are worse things than being a homosexual and begins a discursive monologue on life and the "little gook" that he killed in Korea, likening the episode to a Charlie Chaplin movie.

Cokes then asks if he can doze where he sits, and Roger turns out the lights. Roger asks Cokes whether the enemy soldier that Cokes killed was "singing it," meaning "Beautiful Streamer," and Cokes confirms that he was. As the play ends, he begins to sing a mock version of the song in pseudo-Korean, which, by its end, has become a mournful "lullaby, a farewell, a lament."

CHARACTERS

Carlyle

Fresh out of basic training, Carlyle is streetwise black who is both bitter and angry about his situation. Like the other new soldiers, he is awaiting orders that will probably send him to Vietnam. Meanwhile, his aggravation is fed by his demeaning K.P. duties and his isolation. He has carried a lot of racial luggage into the army, and he feels cut off from fellow blacks, those with "soul." He hopes to remedy that by teaming up with Roger.

Carlyle is the most volatile character in the play. He is also a rather complex young man. His moods run from what seems to be gratuitous vio-

lence to contrition and remorse and from innocent charm to assaultive brutality. Also, for all his "jive" and street smarts, he is almost childish. He is, for example, extraordinarily naive, believing at the end that he can cashier himself out of the army and go home, as if his murder of two men has been some sort of game for which he need pay no penalty.

PFC Clark

The other named M.P., he captures Carlyle after he finds him covered with blood and running away from the barracks. He cuffs him and brings him into the cadre room. Like Hinson, he has no developed character.

Sergeant Cokes

Cokes, like Rooney, is a veteran paratrooper in his fifties and a heavy drinker. He has been diagnosed as having leukemia and is trying to come to terms with that knowledge. When he and Rooney first appear in the cadre room, they are raucous and clumsy. They are sentimental and affectionate drunks who stumble around the room, swapping stories and acting out a Screaming Eagle parachute jump while deprecating the younger soldiers.

Cokes tells two significant stories, one about a paratrooper in training who dives to his death when he fails to catch a parachute he releases before reaching the ground and another about an enemy soldier he killed during the Korean War. He trapped the soldier in his spider hole by sitting on its lid, then blew him up with a grenade.

Cokes returns to the barracks at the end of the play, looking for Rooney, with whom he had been playing hide-and-seek after an extraordinary day of mishaps from which the pair had escaped unscathed. Though still drunk, he becomes quieter and more reflective when Roger tells him that Richie is a homosexual. He remains unaware that Rooney has been killed as, at the play's finale, he turns "Beautiful Streamer" into an oddly haunting monody made up of mock-Korean, nonsense words.

Richie Douglas

Richie, barracks mate with Billy Wilson and Roger Moore, is a self-confessed homosexual, though at first he has a difficult time convincing Billy and Roger that his flaunted effeminacy is anything more than an act. Richie seems to have adjusted to army life as well as the other two and certainly a lot better than either Martin or Carlyle. He even tries to protect Martin and help him coverup his failed suicide attempt.

However, it is Richie who sets the violence of the play in motion. He openly flirts with Billy, who becomes annoyed and finally disgusted with him. When Billy does not respond positively to Richie's flirtatious kidding and sexual innuendos, Richie changes tactics. He tries to make him jealous by flirting with the far less benign Carlyle, who is perfectly willing to let Billy perform oral sex on him and, in the last scene, even orders him to do it. When Billy vents his disgust by throwing a sneaker at Richie and Carlyle, Carlyle cuts him with a knife and eventually stabs both Billy and Sergeant Rooney to death.

PFC Hinson

Hinson and Clark, plus one other unnamed enlisted man, are M.P.s under the command of the lieutenant. Hinson is the first enlisted man to follow the officer into the cadre room. He also becomes a stretcher bearer when the bodies of both Billy and Sergeant Rooney are taken out.

Lieutenant

The unnamed M.P. officer is in charge of the enlisted M.P.s who appear on the scene after Carlyle stabs and kills Billy and Sergeant Rooney. He is very officious but somewhat inept in his attempts to discover what has happened. He at first assumes that Roger is the killer, despite Richie's efforts to straighten matters out. His no-nonsense, abrupt manner seems cold and mechanical, sharply contrasting with the bonding affection of the two drunks, Cokes and Rooney. He seems uninterested in the feelings of Roger and Richie, telling them only that they must appear in his office the next morning at 0800 sharp.

Martin

Martin, an enlistee, is a desperately unhappy soldier. When the play opens, it is revealed that he has made a botched effort at suicide by cutting one of his wrists. Richie tries to help him through his confusion and attempts to hide his actions from the others, but Martin is not interested in disguising what he has done and tells both Carlyle and Billy of his suicide attempt. He disappears almost immedi-

MEDIA ADAPTATIONS

- Rabe adapted *Streamers* for film in 1983. Directed by Robert Altman, the work features Matthew Modine as Billy, Michael Wright as Carlyle, Mitchell Lichtenstein as Richie, David Alan Grier as Roger, Guy Boyd as Rooney, George Dzundza as Cokes, and Albert Macklin as Martin. The film is available on videocassette.

ately, and it is later learned that he had been sent home, unfit for military duty.

Roger Moore

The other black soldier in the play, Roger has made a much better adjustment to the Army than Carlyle. He has befriended Billy, and together they share an idealized vision of the Army that does not entirely square with their experience, but they are doing their best to be good soldiers.

Roger is compulsive about keeping the cadre room spotless. He is also neat in person, an obvious contrast to Carlyle, who, when first seen, is covered with grease and sweat. Roger is also concerned with keeping physically fit, thus he expends his restless energy in harmless ways, unlike Carlyle, whose restlessness explodes into violence.

Roger is so compulsive about cleaning up that, after his friend Billy is killed, to Richie's horror, he begins mopping up Billy's blood, cleaning up the mess that he holds Richie responsible for—the deaths of both Billy and Rooney. He obviously bears some guilt himself, for he was very slow to accept the fact that Richie's homosexuality was real, not just some act he was putting on.

Sergeant Rooney

Cokes's drinking buddy and chief non-com in the barracks, Rooney is a World War II veteran who, presumably from alcoholism, has the shakes so badly that he can not light his own cigar. He is a demolitions expert and has received orders that would take him to Vietnam, a place that Roger describes as a "Disneyland" where Rooney, the "ole sarge," will play Mickey Mouse, if he does not blow himself up.

Rooney becomes Carlyle's second victim when he inopportunely appears in the cadre room looking for Cokes after Carlyle has stabbed Billy. He is almost in a drunken stupor, ineffectually waving a bottle around and threatening Carlyle, who kills him by repeatedly stabbing him in the stomach.

Billy Wilson

Billy, like Roger and Richie, is an enlisted man trying his best to adjust to Army life, the reality of which does not measure up to what he and his friend Roger believe should be the ideal. He is the object of Richie's unsolicited homosexual overtures, which greatly annoys him. He repeatedly tries to warn Richie off, often insulting him, but Richie simply deflects the insults and persists.

Billy has the makings of a career Army man. Like the others, he has fears about Vietnam, but, like Roger, he is determined to be a good soldier. The Army has given him a place and an identity that he did not find in his hometown, where he had largely felt isolated and alone. He had wanted to be a priest, with a mission of helping others, and the Army has provided a viable alternative. Although he seems inclined to a chaste life, he goes with Carlyle and Roger to a whorehouse less from desire than to convince Richie once and for all that he is "straight."

Billy eventually becomes victimized by his disgust with Richie when he vents his feelings by throwing his sneaker at Richie and Carlyle when the two are about to engage in sex. The explosive and violent Carlyle responds to Billy's interference by knifing Billy and eventually killing him.

THEMES

Streamers is a work that examines a group of young men of diverse backgrounds who are trying to adjust to life in the U. S. Army; they are acutely aware of the danger that awaits them in Vietnam. The situation is intense and leads to brutal and senseless violence: the seemingly pointless murder of two men.

Alienation and Loneliness

A major focus of *Streamers* is the impact that the army—and war—has on men, its disruptive influence on their lives. Some, like Billy and Roger, are able to make the adjustment, but others, like Martin, and especially Carlyle, cannot.

In Carlyle's case the results are devastating. He is a black man with an angry social consciousness; he feels like an outcast in a world dominated by white authority. When first introduced, he is on a mission to locate another soldier with "soul," that is, another black. He is lonely and jittery, ready to explode, partly to vent his anger at his situation and partly because he knows no other way to cope with his anxiety. Like Martin, Carlyle seems unfit for the Army. Unlike Roger, he has no secure and mature sense of self that will permit him to adjust to the homogenizing demands of military life without feeling like he is surrendering his identity.

Anger and Hatred

Anger is most evident in the complex makeup of Carlyle. It is a non-specific rage that lies close to the surface of his character, ready to erupt at any moment no matter how slight the provocation. His is an impersonal anger, however. He does not target characters as intended victims, making his actions in the course of play seem both arbitrary and almost gratuitous.

Carlyle can not funnel his anger at the impersonal, all powerful bureaucracy of the army. It has taken him from his street world of "jive" and "soul," where he could cope, and put him in an environment where regimentation and authority threaten, metaphorically speaking, to emasculate him, forcing him to surrender that identity. Threatened with such a loss, and under the pressure of the distant war in Vietnam, Carlyle explodes into violence.

Culture Clash

The diverse ethnic and cultural backgrounds of the characters are an essential source of the tension among the soldiers in *Streamers*. The military requires a period of adjustment to its culture, a closed society that neither recognizes nor rewards diversity. Instead, it attempts to impose order, discipline, and a sense of duty that for many of the recruits involves a regimen either too rigorous or too demanding. One of them, Billy, seems to make the adjustment easily, largely because his civilian life had given him no firm self identity. An adjustment is also made by Roger, even by Richie, despite his the social stigma that comes with his homosexuality. This adaptation is not made by Martin, who is driven to attempt suicide, nor, in a more extreme case, by Carlyle.

The Army does promote a comradery, such as that exhibited by the two veterans, Sergeants Rooney and Cokes. Such a comradery seems to be developing between Billy and Roger, whose different cultural backgrounds do not bar their kinship. In sharp contrast to Carlyle, Roger and Billy carry no heavy racial chips on their shoulders, and though both are critical of actual army life, they share a common understanding of its ideals and of good order and discipline.

Death

The murders of both Billy and Rooney seem gratuitous, almost, in fact, pointless. Their deaths are the result of Carlyle's inability to adjust to his situation, one that threatens his fragile identity. In the aftermath of their murders, Carlyle reveals a stupefying immaturity in his apparent belief that army life is some sort of game from which he can somehow walk away when it threatens or no longer amuses him. He simply does not seem to comprehend that there is a penalty attached to killing people. It is that which gives his killings their devastating impact. They awaken no remorse in him, no guilt, no sense of having morally transgressed.

Duty and Responsibility

Military order and discipline have always demanded a sense of duty and responsibility from soldiers, even those enrolled in the ranks through conscription rather than voluntary service. Part of basic training involves inculcating that sense into draftees and recruits, but such indoctrination is not always successful. The army attempts to winnow out those who can not make an adequate adjustment, recruits like Martin, who is discharged after his attempted suicide. A young man incapable of acquiring a mature sense of duty and responsibility may be missed, however, especially a loner like Carlyle, and, as Rabe depicts in his play, the results can be devastating.

Although Carlyle can not be absolved for the murders in *Streamers,* some blame falls on the

TOPICS FOR FURTHER STUDY

- Investigate the Vietnam War situation that existed during the time the play takes place, about 1965, relating your findings to the impressions of the conflict given in *Streamers.*

- Research the use of war in twentieth-century American drama and, on the basis of your discoveries, create a list of ten plays that could be gathered into an anthology of quality works in which war plays a significant role. Justify your choices.

- Investigate the civil rights struggle underway in the United States in the mid-1960s and relate your findings to the racial consciousness of the characters in *Streamers.*

- Read *Sticks and Bones* and *The Basic Training of Pavlo Hummel,* the other two plays in Rabe's Vietnam trilogy and compare their themes, dramatic techniques, and plots with those elements of *Streamers.*

- Restricting your inquiry to the 1960s or 1970s, research the use of the American stage as a medium of social protest, picking a subject like war, civil rights, or women's liberation as a focal issue.

system and the society that sanctions a military and warlike culture. Carlyle is virtually amoral. He has run free all his life, restricted only by the realities of the streets, not by some inner moral compass. The life the military attempts to impose on him is much too restrictive, too suffocating, particularly because he is unable to see the point of it, only its threat. He is unable to develop a sense of duty and responsibility because life has provided him with no meaningful models of such personal qualities.

Friendship

Roger and Billy are the two characters best able to adjust to army life and accept its rigorous demands of good order and discipline. In fact, they approach an ideal in that both are able to think critically but also accept a sense of duty that requires a submerging of their individualism under the surface of military homogeneity. They are not, in short, mindless and robotic recruits, not mere canon fodder. They are also good friends, quietly developing a sense of esprit de corps that is, perhaps, the military's greatest personal reward. They have a common cause, giving them a bond that Carlyle looks for but can not find on the terms expected by military authority.

Identity

Streamers is a play about a crisis of identity in the lives of its major characters. Each, willingly or not, is attempting to adjust to life in the army. Adapting to it requires a sacrifice of some part of self that new soldiers like Martin and Carlyle are unable to make. Roger and Billy have succeeded, however, even Richie, though in his case the situation involves a sort of "outing." He flaunts his homosexuality, not because he wants to escape from the Army but seemingly to prove that his sexual orientation is no impediment to being a good soldier. His need is to maintain an honest identity in the face of traditional attitudes that morally condemned him and other homosexuals and deliberately excluded them from military service.

Race and Racism

As Rabe demonstrates, the army by the time of the Vietnam War had largely become color blind. In fact, it was much more of a melting pot than society at large, in which, despite such civil rights advances as the desegregation of public schools and the market place, people could and did chose to remain socially segregated. The new demands placed on Carlyle are simply too much. He harbors deep resentments towards whites, which, though certainly in large measure justified, gnaw at him as he is forced to comply with what he perceives as white authority. His "safe" world had been the inner-city ghetto streets, despite the crime and violence associated with them. At least there he had an identity, one that the army is forcing him to sacrifice, something, *Streamers* argues, he can not successfully do.

Sex

Part of the intensity of *Streamers* arises from sexual needs. Richie's homosexual desires are directed towards Billy, who grows increasingly angry over Richie's overt flirtations, perhaps because Billy really is not all that secure about his sexual identity. In his disclosure to Roger, he reveals that at one point in his life he had considered becoming a priest, which argues that he was willing to adopt celibacy. In any case, Richie's flirtations include annoying hints that Billy is masking his true sexual preferences, which may be a major reason why Billy accompanies Roger and Carlyle to a bordello, attempting to prove his masculinity and heterosexuality.

Meanwhile, Carlyle, unlike Billy, is willing to use Richie's homosexuality as a way of releasing some of his pent up energy, and perhaps, too, as a way of dominating Richie, a representative of the white race against which he bears angry grudges. For all his brutal directness, Carlyle's motives for his sexual assault on Richie are complex, as is revealed in his emotional lurching between playful affection and violent behavior.

Violence and Cruelty

Violence is endemic in *Streamers*. It principally takes the form of Carlyle's violent reactions, his brutal knifings of Billy and Sergeant Rooney. His actions verge on the inexplicable, which makes them doubly distressing. Carlyle seems to act almost like a cornered animal, enraged and extremely dangerous and unpredictable. Neither Billy nor Rooney does anything to warrant Carlyle's violent responses. On the other hand, Carlyle does not seem to be deliberately cruel. He has no vicious or evil blood lust. His reactions are spontaneous and devoid of anything other than momentary malice, engendered by Billy and Rooney's invasion of his emotional territory.

War and Peace

War lies in the background of *Streamers,* functioning as a kind of catalyst that ups the emotional ante of the play. That the young soldiers may be facing a one-way trip to a distant, Asian "Disneyland" preys on their minds. It is a fact that contributes to the emotional instability of all of them, especially Carlyle, who has a sense of being used by white men to fight in a war in which he has nothing at stake.

The Vietnam War plays no direct part in the action, however. In fact, there are hints of the "guns and butter" sense of it as a distant, aberrant activity occurring in what is really a time of peace at home, where few sacrifices were being made to pursue the

Carlyle (Michael Wright) and Richie (Mitchell Lichenstein) in a scene from director Robert Altman's interpretation of Rabe's play

War with vigor and moral certitude. The pointlessness of the struggle is as destructive of the men's morale as is its threat to their lives.

STYLE

Anti-hero

An anti-hero is a character who contradicts the traditional concepts of heroism; this character type is often employed in realistic literature as a means of satirizing or debunking the hyperbolic, ''can do no wrong'' myth of the hero. Like many ultra-realistic modern works, *Streamers* diminishes the heroic concept to a virtual zero. All of the play's central characters are ordinary humans, at best confused or troubled by their situation. The two veterans, Sergeants Rooney and Cokes, both combat survivors, seem more like drunken clowns than sage role models. Cokes's principal ''heroic'' achievement was to have trapped an enemy soldier in a hole and blown him apart with a hand grenade. Even that rather sordid episode resulted from luck rather than Cokes's courage or cunning. Only in his apparent acceptance of the fact that he has leukemia does Cokes reveal a traditional sense of nobility.

Meanwhile, some of the insecure, untested soldiers are not even able to adjust to what little the Army demands of them. Martin is a minor example, but Carlyle is the main one. His failure has dreadful consequences: the meaningless deaths of two men. In Richie, too, there is a sort of anti-heroic ineptness, revealed, for instance, in his inability to convince Roger that he is gay. Even for Billy and Roger, those who seem able to adjust, the Army seems to involve a pointless routine of busy work, of cleaning the cadre room and latrine. The distant war is merely a kind of grotesquely comic threat that offers neither glory nor honor.

Conflict

Streamers is a play that creates conflict by bringing together and intertwining the lives of men with very diverse backgrounds and needs. These are realistic representatives of the civilian world from which the Army must draw men to mold into soldiers willing and able to adjust to its rules and regulations.

The play's situation is fairly complex. Carlyle and Richie, two focal characters seem on a collision course towards a crude sexual episode, driven by very different motives. The real target of Richie's desire is Billy, but since Billy repeatedly rejects Richie's homosexual advances, Richie tries to arouse some jealousy in him by encouraging Carlyle. Carlyle, who seems perfectly willing to use sex as a way discharging his pent-up fury, also hints that part of his willingness to exploit Richie carnally involves a predatory need to express his power over his real or imagined adversary and persecutor, a white man. Rather than seduction, his sexual aggression towards Richie is savage, more like rape than mere lust. It is from this situation that violence erupts and ends in the deaths of both Billy and Sergeant Rooney.

Empathy

One relationship that is victimized as a result of Carlyle's fury is that between Roger and Billy. These two characters mesh. Despite their disparate background and racial differences, they develop an empathetic relationship and thereby reveal that the military has the promise of providing a context for overcoming such differences. The two work well in tandem, as a team, and are firmly on the way of becoming good friends when Carlyle destroys their bond by killing Billy.

Mood

The mood of *Streamers* is both erratic and explosive, reflective of the troubled and conflicting attitudes of the men, particularly Carlyle, who throughout the play is both angry and unpredictable. His mood swings run through an emotional gamut from savage aggression to child-like bafflement and contrition, making him seem the most complex of the characters.

The distant war in Vietnam has a catalytic effect on the play's mood; it looms like a dark spirit over the play's events. Although the action takes place stateside, the specter of Vietnam is a tangible presence that fuels the men's anxiety, fear, and despair. The men are all aware that the Asian conflict is a threat to their survival, a fact which fans the emotional fire in each of them. All of them are on edge because of it.

Motif

Certain motifs play a significant part in *Streamers*. The dominant symbolic motif is the streamer, the parachute that fails to open and sends it user plummeting to death, which is more fully discussed as a symbol. Also important is the nearly obsessive need of Roger and Billy to clean and polish their surroundings. They are the best adjusted soldiers, willing to engage in routines that reflect two of the Army's guiding principles: that order and discipline must control the soldier's habits and that the habits must be so deeply ingrained in the soldier as to become almost instinctive. The personal hygiene of Billy and Roger contrasts sharply with the slovenliness of Carlyle, whose greasy and stained fatigues seem to blatantly signal his dangerous maladjustment to Army life.

Naturalism

Although it is hardly documentary in method, *Streamers* has a ''slice of life'' quality to it. Like life, it does not seem shaped to fit the needs of a dominate theme, and it lacks the clear causality of the typical thesis play in the realistic tradition. Its characters, largely anti-heroic, do not line up on some side of an ethical dilemma. In fact, there is no central figure, no consistent protagonist. It is impossible to say exactly whose play it is, although it is clear that Carlyle comes closest to serving as the dominant plot driver.

Naturalism tends to examine life clinically, particularly life in its lowest forms. It comes closer to replicating life rather than merely imitating it. While Rabe's play is not about society's dregs, it does unmask some unsavory qualities in fairly average people, the savage and crude needs of Carlyle, for example. No ''polite'' restraints bar its honest portrayal of its characters' needs, no matter how seamy. Nor is there any restraint on their vulgarity.

Setting

The barracks cadre room in which all of the action of *Streamers* takes place, though large enough, is a very confining space psychologically. It plays an important part in creating the claustrophobic, ''no exit'' atmosphere of the drama, the sense of entrapment that is particularly unsettling for those characters unable to adjust to Army life, notably Carlyle. It is also a space that can be interpreted as a microcosmic representation of the larger world beyond, an American society that at the time was wracked by such stressful and discordant problems as racial unrest and the anti-war movement.

Beyond the cadre room and the unidentified Army base, there is the Vietnam War, what Roger and Billy cynically refer to as "Disneyland," a nightmarish and extremely dangerous fantasy world where Sergeant Rooney will be playing "Mickey Mouse." It threatens each of the characters. Billy, for example, fears its jungle setting because he is terrified of snakes. For all, the War is an intrusive presence that for the soldiers seems to lie just outside, like a lion at the gates.

Slang

One of the most compelling features of *Streamers* is its frank language. It is a cauldron of jarring voices that reflect the different heritages and personal histories of its characters. Much of the dialogue is crude and slangy, full of obscenities and inarticulate verbal ravings that come perilously close to leaving clear sense behind though not the emotional mood of the speaker.

Sharp distinctions are made between the speech characteristics of the different soldiers, of Richie and Carlyle, for example. The former's talk is generally quieter and more coherent. It is also more bookish, grammatically "correct" and rational. The latter's is much more energetic, far less rational and controlled, and loaded with "jive" slang and sudden mood shifting that make it at times seem barely under mental control; Carlyle's explosive speech patterns are a clear representation of his anguished, enraged psyche.

Symbol

Much has been made of the symbolic import of the titular reference of *Streamers*. In their inebriated antics, Sergeants Rooney and Cokes put on a mock airborne exercise, a parachute drop, and doing it sing what may be viewed as the play's coda, "Beautiful Streamer" (sung to the tune of Stephen Foster's "Beautiful Dreamer"). A streamer is a parachute that does not open correctly and plummets its victim to death. At the end of play, in a mock oriental threnody, Cokes sings the song again.

Symbolically, the parachutist may be perceived as a kind of everyman. If his chute opens, he survives the fall to earth, but if it does not, he perishes. There is a terrible arbitrariness to the jumper's fate, outside his ability to control. Similarly, the young soldiers are "dropped" into a situation that they can not control. They may or may not land softly on their feet, making the adjustment necessary to survive Army life.

HISTORICAL CONTEXT

Although *Streamers* was not staged until 1976, it was started several years earlier, in 1969, when the Vietnam War was still in progress. The period of Rabe's own service (1965-1967) is the referent time, a point at which the country was being divided over the efficacy and morality of that war. Lyndon Johnson was then president, having succeeded John F. Kennedy, who was assassinated on November 22, 1963.

The 1960s were an exciting decade, a period of great turbulence and change, some of it violent. Advances in civil rights were undertaken by Johnson and a compliant Congress, completing programs begun by Kennedy to create what became known as the Great Society. Arising at the same time was a movement known as the Counter Culture, prompted by such gurus as Timothy Leary, who advised America's youth to use mind-expanding drugs like LSD and to "turn on, tune in, and drop out." The Counter Culture was also comprised of people motivated by ecological concerns, the antiwar movement, and ideals that contradicted the 1950s concept of the American Dream, which focused on homogeneity and status quo.

Violence in America took acute forms in the 1960s, including assassinations, race riots, and brutal murders. Leaders felled by assassins included President Kennedy, his brother Senator Robert Kennedy, civil rights leader Dr. Martin Luther King, Jr., and militant black leader Malcolm X. Racial tensions in the South escalated as the federal government began enforcing desegregation of schools and other public institutions, leading to riots such as that in Birmingham, Alabama, in 1963. Violence would erupt in northern cities as well, notably in the wake of the murder of Dr. King. The worst outbreak occurred in the Watts area of Los Angeles over a five-day period in 1965. Less clearly motivated by racial tensions were other notable crimes of violence, like the 1969 Polanski-Tate murders committed by Charles Manson and his "family."

At the beginning of the 1960s, the "Baby Boomers" (the many children born during the economic boon following World War II) had come of age. In that year, four million of them were matriculating at American colleges and universities. Only some took Leary's advice, trekking to the drug-

COMPARE
&
CONTRAST

- 1960s: Fidel Castro's rule in Cuba reminds Americans that communism is "only 90 miles away." President Kennedy and Soviet premier Nikita Kruschev spar over the missiles in Cuba, averting open hostilities only when Kruschev orders the removal of the weapons from that island nation.

  Today: Although Castro remains in power, and the U.S. sanctions against him are still in effect, the fall of Russia's communist government effectively ended the Cold War. Cuba is no longer considered a threat to the United States.

- 1960s: In 1962, Rachel Carson publishes *The Silent Spring,* the seminal work in the environmental movement. The federal government begins taking steps to protect the environment from further damage. The first landmark legislation is the Clean Air Act of 1963.

  Today: Environmental concerns have grown considerably since the 1960s. Most recent studies concern global warming and the population explosion. Bleak predictions about future inability to prevent such disasters as mass starvation, the destruction of the ozone layer, and the depletion of natural resources are often in the news, despite efforts of nay-sayers to minimize them.

- 1960s: Perhaps the greatest single "happening" symbolizing the new consciousness of the 1960s is the rock festival held at Woodstock, New York, in 1969. There, to celebrate the new tuned-in culture and protest civil wrongs and the Vietnam War, thousands gather for "three days of peace, love, and music."

  Today: In 1999, in an effort to tap into nostalgia, promoters stage a new Woodstock festival that will be remembered not as a love-in but an embarrassing commercial flop that led to minor rioting when greedy concessionaires gouged attendees for food and drink after prohibiting the concert goers from bringing their own supplies into the festival area.

- 1960s: The United States is just beginning to enter the "Informational Age." Computers are large and extremely costly devices designed for large organizations rather than home use. By mid-decade communication satellites are in orbit and new fiber optic cables greatly expand communication channels.

  Today: In the post-industrial society it is common for many homes to have personal computers. Communication with virtually any place in the world is now possible via computers and satellite links, and the Internet is rapidly becoming a virtual library, making information retrieval quick, cheap, and easy.

culture Mecca, the Haight-Ashbury district of San Francisco, or other flower-children Edens. Most reconciled themselves to the values of the older generation, despite some necessary soul searching prompted by the war in Vietnam and the civil rights movement at home. Some were caught up in different kinds of revolutionary change, from such cultural phenomena as the Beatles to exciting advances in technology, which, by the end of the decade, landed American astronauts on the moon, less than a decade after John Glenn took the first American space craft into the earth's orbit. It was during the 1960s that the time-sharing computer was invented, the "pill" or oral contraceptive was introduced, and communication satellites, in effect, began a much more rapid shrinkage of an already shrinking world.

And there were other changes that would have an equally significant impact on America, including the striking down of anti-abortion laws by the Supreme Court and the growing militancy of the feminist movement, which in 1968 began taking a graphic form in its bra-burning demonstrations against the Miss America contest, a pageant that feminists felt objectified women and reduced female merit to superficial appearance.

The decade of the 1960s was both an exciting and unsettling time. It ushered in a new permissiveness suggested by the catch phrase ''doing your own thing.'' Authority was openly challenged, not just over the war in Vietnam but also over such things as student rights. In the arts, among other things, permissiveness took the form of beating down the barricades of censorship. Throughout the decade, films like *Midnight Cowboy, Easy Rider, Bob and Carol and Ted and Alice,* and *Who's Afraid of Virginia Woolf* openly and graphically dealt with issues and themes that a decade earlier would have been taboo. By 1968, when the ''tribal-love rock'' musical, *Hair,* used a nude production number and ''dirty'' language, hardly anybody even seemed shocked. It was a decade of rapid and extraordinary change, the consequences of which are still being debated.

CRITICAL OVERVIEW

Streamers is the third and last play of what has been termed Rabe's ''Vietnam trilogy.'' By the time it was first staged at the Long Wharf Theatre in New Haven, Connecticut, on January 30, 1976, the playwright's reputation as a harsh and uncompromising critic of the War was already well established. At the time the play opened, the War had already been over for three years; in a sense, the work seemed like a painful post mortem. However, *Streamers* is not really about the War per se; it is about men trying to adjust to life in the Army at a time when that adjustment is exacerbated by the certainty that the country is going to put their lives on the line in Southeast Asia. The War is like an unseen presence, a threat that increases the stakes for each of the principal characters and makes the situation extremely unstable.

In light of the fact that much of America was trying to bind up the War's wounds and relegate the ''conflict'' to the past as an unnecessary, shameful, misguided, and divisive policy blunder, the play's success seems almost extraordinary. The New York production of the work ran for over 400 performances and was greeted with several enthusiastic reviews. It also garnered for Rabe important awards, including a Best American Play citation from the New York Drama Critics in 1976. Most critics recognized that the play had much less to do with the War than with the interrelationships of young, citizen soldiers, and that, in fact, it imposed serious

questions about the efficacy of military discipline and order in a democracy that by the time of the Vietnam engagement had extended individual freedom to lengths previously unknown in American history. As *Newsweek*'s Jack Kroll noted in his review of the New Haven staging of the play, the cadre room in which all the action occurs is ''a microcosm for some of the most explosive tensions in today's society racial, sexual, social.''

That idea, that the barracks room is a small-world, partial replica of American society under duress is repeatedly sounded in the commentaries on *Streamers,* even in reviews and interpretations by hostile critics like Stanley Kauffmann in the *New Republic,* who found the work badly flawed and its world not so cunningly made. Kauffmann, one of Rabe's detractors, argued that ''two stories of homosexual tension, of black disquiet are arbitrarily pushed together, as if there were some real relation between psychosexual drama and racial bitterness,'' and further complained that they ''are hurriedly married at the end by a sheerly insane violent act, unfounded in character.''

Yet most of the play's early critics recognized that it is precisely the dangerous and arbitrary commingling of psychologically unsteady and barely mature men that military service occasions, providing a heated crucible for dramatic tension and violent energy. As Kauffmann himself pointed out, that the action occurs during war time is what is important, not the specific conflict involved. The situation develops into what Harold Clurman referred to in the *Nation* as a '''universal' inference,'' a world depicting humanity as ''poor forked animals caught in a trap of which they can never understand the exact identity or the way out.''

For some critics, Rabe was sort of an *enfant terrible* (defined as a person who stirs up controversy in an unconventional manner) in the American theater, crude but unrelentingly honest, a writer unwilling to compromise his art for the more delicate ears and stomachs in his audience. His language is raw, often obscene, and highly charged with emotion, and his action is sometimes savage. Some critics found the savagery and frank sexuality excessive, and even very favorable reviewers like the *Saturday Review*'s Henry Hewes warned that ''many in the audience may find the unpleasant combination of overt homosexual activity and gory violence too strong to take.''

Few could fault Rabe for his honesty, however, a quality for which most critics praised him. And despite the rawness of the play's language and its crude violence, many critics agreed with Hewes that *Streamers* was "the most beautiful play" that Rabe had by that time written.

Hewes's assessment may seem odd given the content of *Streamers,* but it is a judgment not about the themes and overt violence of the play but rather the artful qualities of the work. It sums up the long-standing judgment of most critics, that *Streamers* is the best of the three plays in the Vietnam trilogy and possibly the best play that to date Rabe has written. It is certainly the work for which he remains best known.

CRITICISM

John W. Fiero

Fiero is a Ph. D., now retired, who taught drama and playwriting at the University of South-western Louisiana and is now a freelance writer and consultant. In this essay he examines the inter-play of characters in the drama and the work's paradoxical theme.

David Rabe's *Streamers* is a play without a hero, even, perhaps, without a protagonist in any classic sense of that term. Of a play it is usually a helpful question to ask "whose play is it?" But in the case of *Streamers,* there is certainly no ready answer. Normally, the protagonist is also the plot driver, the character who has the most at stake and propels the action towards a climax and resolution. More than a character, it is the situation in Rabe's play that seems to move things on, a situation that is entirely outside the abilities of the characters either to direct or control but only to respond to as personal needs and desires direct.

Somewhat like the characters in Jean Paul Sartre's *No Exit,* the characters in *Streamers* are placed in a confining space and proceed to torment each other because their needs and personal histories are out of sync and at critical moments antagonistic. Beyond the walls defining their space there is a powerful force in control of their lives, a force that is impersonal and demanding, a force that to some degree strips each of them of their former identities. All of the young recruits are its victims, even the predatory Carlyle, whose personal history and sense of identity make him more an outsider than the rest. For him, the Army can not become a home, as it seems to be becoming for Billy and Roger and had

long ago become for Sergeants Rooney and Cokes. Even Richie is trying to make it his home, although he is clearly trying to do it partly on his own terms. He parades his homosexuality and openly flirts with Billy with a troubling and ill-fated insouciance that the U. S. military then as now would not tolerate once it is discovered. Richie, consciously or not, is a candidate for a "Section 8," an article of the military code that mandated the discharge of homosexuals, the mentally ill, and others deemed unfit for service.

The major characters most at odds with what the Army demands and expects are Carlyle and Richie. Billy and Roger, on the other hand, are having far less trouble adjusting to military life. Although they are critical of the Army and fearful of their fate, of being sent into Vietnam, they know what it means to be "standin' tall"—to be neat, orderly, and proud of their soldiering. It becomes almost an obsession for both of them, as is evident near the end of the play, when, much to Richie's horror, Roger begins swabbing up the murdered Billy's blood.

Although Roger remains sensitive to his ethnic heritage, in Billy he has found a companion who has made him see that friendship can transcend racial barriers. He tells the belligerent Carlyle when he first meets him that some whites "got little bit of soul," that there are a "couple real good boys around this way." The white authority that gnaws at Carlyle's innards does not bother Roger. He points out to Carlyle that the first sergeant is black, calmly hinting that things, albeit slowly, are changing for the better.

Carlyle, however, has no patience. He profoundly resents the Army's intrusion into his psychological and emotional space, and he is almost frantic in his need to escape its claustrophobic pressures. He is desperate to find another black to identify with, another man with soul, one who shares his views and his desire to be free, someone with whom he can talk the talk with empathetic understanding . He is both extremely unstable and dangerous, a man without an adequate emotional safety valve. Outwardly, he may be predatory and savage, but inwardly he is a very frightened and bewildered young man whose sense of identity is quickly eroding. He is, as Henry Hewes says, "a confused, unhappy ghetto animal caught in a bad scene."

Sometimes Carlyle's inner fear breaks through his savage exterior, taking the form of a child-like

WHAT DO I READ NEXT?

- Rabe edited a collection of plays entitled *Coming to Terms: American Plays and the Vietnam War* (1985). In addition to *Streamers,* the anthology includes Tom Cole's *Medal of Honor Rag,* Amlin Gray's *How I Got That Story,* Emily Mann's *Still Life,* Terrence McNally's *Botticelli,* Stephen Metcalf's *Strange Snow,* and Michael Weller's *Moonchildren.*

- Among other plays providing an interesting contrast to Rabe's work are Megan Terry's *Viet Rock* (1967), Christopher Durang's *The Vietnamization of New Jersey* (1978), Arthur Kopit's *Indians* (1968), Lanford Wilson's *The Fifth of July* (1979), Ronald Ribman's *The Burial of Esposito* (1971), Robert Patrick's *Kennedy's Children* (1976), and David Berry's *G. R. Point* (1980).

- Among the important nonfiction written on the Vietnam War is the work of Tim O'Brien, notably *If I Die in a Combat Zone Box Me Up and Ship Me Home* (1973), *Going after Cacciato* (1978), and *The Things They Carried* (1990); Joe Haldeman's *War Year* (1972); Philip Caputo's *A Rumor of War* (1977); Neil Sheehan's *A Bright Shining Lie* (1988); Michael Herr's *Dispatches* (1968); and Ron Kovic's *Born on the Fourth of July* (1976).

- Poetry written by Vietnam veterans was anthologized in *Winning Hearts and Minds* (1972).

---

contrition and even confusion over what is real and what is merely a game, a kind of naivety that sharply contrasts with his abusive speech and behavior. However, more than hatred of his real or imagined persecutors, it is that very inner fear that explains his brutal and violent responses to Billy and Sergeant Rooney and even to Richie, towards whom he is alternately playfully if roughly affectionate and savagely cruel.

In commenting on what happens in the play, more than one critic has complained that the murder of Billy seems inadequately motivated. For the *New Republic*'s Stanley Kauffmann, Carlyle's stabbing of him is a "sheerly insane violent act, unfounded in character, only prefigured by the playwright *outside* these characters," i.e., in the blood of the cut wrist of Martin, who disappears from the play before the end of the first act. Kauffmann argued that the "two stories of homosexual tension, of black disquiet are arbitrarily pushed together, as if there were some real relation between psychosexual drama and racial bitterness." Perhaps, however, there is, at least in Carlyle's distraught mind. Rabe chooses not to probe that mind terribly deeply. He does not, for example, allow Carlyle to reflect on his life at any

great length, whereas, in their reminiscences, the other characters disclose significant facts about themselves, thereby giving helpful clues to their psychological makeup.

For example, from Billy's account of his teenage years, it may be deduced that he hides uncertainties about his own sexual propensities, which in turn explains his anger towards Richie, who is trying to break through Billy's "straight" facade. It may not be that Billy is in fact bisexual, but it may be that he fears he is. His trip to the black bordello in the company of Roger and Carlyle is a rite of passage that confirms his heterosexuality and allows him to parade it before Richie.

Carlyle, though, remains a very perplexing character, partly because the contents of his mental and emotional suitcase are not put on public view. He tells little about himself, other than the fact that his father would not even acknowledge his paternity. Even some of the most admiring critics of *Streamers* treat him as an unfathomable psychopath, one who has no rational motives for his violence. But Carlyle is in one sense most emblematic of what is wrong. There is something missing for all of the men awaiting a transfer overseas. None

Carlyle's slovenly attire and lazy demeanor symbolize his disaffection with the discipline and decorum required for military life

of them considers the war necessary for some just and rational purpose such as making the world safe for democracy. Rather, though dangerous and life threatening, it is a senseless absurdity, exhibiting all the irrationality of the cartoon world of Disney. The men do not talk about ridding the world of monsters like Hitler or Mussolini; they talk instead of the faceless Vietcong, an enemy that is savage and brutal, an enemy waiting to impale them on sharp stakes anointed with elephant excrement.

Faced with such a possible fate, it is hardly any wonder that Carlyle and even Rooney spend their waking hours tugging on bottles of whiskey or beer. Carlyle even practices creeping through the jungle, trying to learn how to evade a senseless and inglorious death. Cokes joins Rooney in a drunken rampage, not because he is to be sent into the jungles of Asia but because he has been diagnosed as having leukemia, a blood cancer that to him is as inexplicable, arbitrary, and irrational as anything that might be encountered in a Vietnam combat zone.

Carlyle's mental Chinese boxes are very different from those of any other character in the play. For him, the Army itself is a staging area for Vietnam, an area in which he has already encountered the enemy and is in a kind of mortal combat with him.

His enemy is the white man who has a long history of wronging the black man and whose authority has forced him to learn ghetto survival strategies—his verbal taunting, his swaggering, and his reflexive knife-wielding response to invasions of his turf— whether it is Billy's interference with his sexual encounter with Richie or Rooney's inept attempt to prevent his escape from the cadre room. He feels caged and threatened, in a situation that is analogous to being in the jungle or rice paddies of Southeast Asia. His violence is certainly understandable, although, certainly in Billy's case, it is tragically misdirected. Both Billy and Rooney pay the ultimate price for the social injustices of their fellow whites.

Although the Army provides a context for senseless violence, it also provides the opportunity for putting an end to some of it. That is the paradox of *Streamers.* At one level it is an anti-war play, or at least an anti-Vietnam War play. However, it does not condemn military life per se. After all, it is not really the Army that victimizes Carlyle; it is an American society that in the 1960s was deeply involved in another struggle, that over civil rights and wrongs. In fact, the Army provides a means for advancing racial integration in social and workplace conditions that, for example, the ghetto in Carlyle's experiences outside had simply denied him. It was not until drafted into the Army that Carlyle faced having to give his white enemies a personal identity or begin to confront their potential as friends. He seems, for example, both amused and partly baffled by the fact that Billy wants to accompany him and Roger on their excursion into town.

What Rabe captures in *Streamers* is an encapsulated sense of the social changes underway in American society during the Vietnam War. In Carlyle's case, the dream deferred does not dry up like a raisin in the sun, it explodes into racial violence, like it did in the Watts section of Los Angeles, California, in 1965. He is not insane, but he is enraged and incapable of controlling his anger and fear. To use the central metaphor of the play, Carlyle's parachute is too tightly bound by racial injustice to open and land him safely on his feet. He is outfitted with a streamer.

Against the main action line, the drunken antics of Sergeants Rooney and Cokes serve as a kind of choric counterpoint, at first comic but in the end soulful and sad. Despite their seediness, they have an affectionate, brotherly bond, a comradery made possible because they share something the younger soldiers, the "shit sacks," have yet to experience: a battlefield baptism by fire. They act childishly, like a pair of aging drunks attempting to recapture their lost youth in juvenile games, but like circus clowns or the great comedian, Charlie Chaplin, they are not just funny; they are also full of pathos.

At the end, Sergeant Cokes, left unaware that Rooney has been stabbed to death, but aware that he himself is sick and dying, begins reflecting both on his friendship with Rooney and the irrational nature of life, on how he and Rooney had been in four accidents and fights and escaped without harm. He also reveals that his sickness has given him a new perspective on life. When Roger tells him that Richie is a homosexual, and Richie confirms it, Cokes tells him that it is not so bad, then reflects on things he would change if he had a second chance. He confesses that he can not forget the Korean soldier, the "funny little guy" he blew up with a grenade, and how he would now let that soldier go unharmed.

Cokes's nostalgic monologue seems to serve as a halting but eloquent commentary on what the play is finally all about the inexplicable and arbitrary nature of life. There is no way that he or anyone else

> LIKE THE CHARACTERS IN JEAN PAUL SARTRE'S *NO EXIT*, THE CHARACTERS IN *STREAMERS* ARE PLACED IN A CONFINING SPACE AND PROCEED TO TORMENT EACH OTHER BECAUSE THEIR NEEDS AND PERSONAL HISTORIES ARE OUT OF SYNC AND AT CRITICAL MOMENTS ANTAGONISTIC"

is going to "figure it out." Like Cokes, the most one can do is display some courage in the face of it.

Source: John W. Fiero, for *Drama for Students,* Gale, 2000.

Philip C. Kolin

Kolin is a noted authority on the Vietnam War. In this essay, he evaluates Rabe's play, the final in a trilogy. Kolin finds Streamers *to be "a brutal and realistic portrait of young men coming of age."*

The last play in his Viet Nam trilogy, David Rabe's *Streamers* (1976) explores an archetypical theme— the rite of passage into manhood—in the lives of four young soldiers (Billy, Roger, Richie, Carlyle) who are in a period of transition from stateside Army life to Viet Nam combat. The testing ground for these young men is a barracks frequently described as "a home," "my house," or a "happy family" where they are to learn the "obligations" of soldiering. An essential character in their drama of manhood is the father (or father figure); and multiple examples in *Streamers* underscore Rabe's message about the failure of fatherhood for a Viet Nam generation. The sons in the barracks are abused, betrayed, and deserted by fathers who are alcoholic, diseased, self-destructive, and malicious. (Ironically, LBJ is likened to Hitler [page 31] in leading the American fatherland.) Appropriately, *Streamers* may rival any other American play in its blatant use of phallic symbols; but the symbolic phalli in *Streamers*—liquor bottles, knives, stakes, and the streamers (or unopened parachutes—the "Big icicle" [page 41]) which lend their metaphoric name to the title—are stage metaphors of an ignoble manhood.

"*STREAMERS* IS A BRUTAL AND
RITUALISTIC PORTRAIT OF YOUNG
MEN COMING OF AGE—BEING
GROOMED FOR MANHOOD AND
DEATH"

The most glaring examples of destructive father figures are Rooney and Cokes, veteran sergeants who recommend themselves as heroes for the boys to emulate. Both men transmit a latent death wish by singing a song (to the lullaby tune of "Beautiful Dreamer") that "a man sings" (page 42) about parachutes that fail to open. Rooney, the platoon sergeant, lives down the hall and visits his boys nightly to make sure they are asleep; they fear and obey him as they would an ogre father— "We're good boys," says Billy Wilson (a willing son). As if baptizing Roger (page 62), Rooney sprinkles him with whiskey from his bottle. Ironically, a "chill" (page 62) emanates from Rooney's room, for he has just received his papers for Viet Nam. There he will play "Mickey Mouse" in "Disneyland" (page 10), the macabre playground of death for many young men. The boys recognize Rooney as a bungler—"the poor ole bastard who cannot light his own cigar for shakin' is supposed to go over there blowin' up bridges" (page 10). His cigar—a phallic symbol suggesting heat and power—becomes an instrument of self-destruction. In fact, Rooney is powerless to protect his boys from the pathological fury of Carlyle, a "new boy," who repeatedly stabs Billy (and later Rooney) full of holes.

Sergeant Cokes, Rooney's friend, is equally ineffective and doomed (he has leukemia). Always swilling or swinging a liquor bottle (his phallic emblem), he has trouble navigating despite the fact that he can wear special combat boots that let the water (life?) out. At play's end, he and Rooney go through a foolish game of hide and seek with tragic results (car accidents, near deaths, and the loss of friends). The play ends ominously with Cokes singing the streamers lullaby in "a makeshift language imitating Korean" (page 109) to boys soon to confront death on oriental shores.

Rabe reinforces his message about Viet Nam fathers through domestic parallels of paternal crimes.

Richie's father leaves the family when the boy was six—"sneaking out" and pushing his son in the grass (page 76). The father was thus possibly responsible for Richie's homosexual fantasies and desire for punishment gladly inflicted by Carlyle. Himself a victim of father desertion, Carlyle sardonically recounts how his daddy abandoned the family but still worked "in the butcher shop two blocks up the street" (page 79). Both location and occupation—nearby father turned butcher—psychologically maim the son. In fact, daddy denies he has a son at all. Ironically, Billy likes his father, but Billy too has been scared by memories of other father figures who have seduced—and destroyed—youth. His friend Frankie "got his ass hooked" on homosexuality (page 49) by one of those "old guys" who "were hurting and happy as hell to have us" (page 48). Rabe offers an ironic parallel here: young men are ensnared by old homosexuals the same way they are trapped by Army fathers like Cokes and Rooney.

Streamers is a brutal and ritualistic portrait of young men coming of age—being groomed for manhood and death. America's sons suffer at the hands of irresponsible Army fathers who are degenerate and degenerating. But, as Rabe shows, Army fathers are not essentially different from their civilian counterparts.

Source: Philip C. Kolin. "Rabe's *Streamers*" in the *Explicator,* Vol. 45, no. 1, Fall, 1986, pp. 63–64.

Alan Rich

Rich reviews Rabe's play, assessing it as the culmination of the author's previous efforts and a work of riveting theatricality.

Streamers is the great play that has been trying—in several guises and with several degrees of success—to burst out of David Rabe in the five or so years he has been on the scene. It is at the Mitzi Newhouse now, in a stunning production directed by Mike Nichols; neither author nor director has come close to this level of accomplishment in the past, and I urge you to share with me the keen pleasure of having your faith restored in the power of American drama to make important and worthwhile sense.

Rabe's play may (or may not; it isn't important) form a trilogy with his two other works about the Vietnam war (*Sticks and Bones* and *Pavlo Hummel*).

On its own, it is a harrowing study, set among some kids in a Virginia army camp in 1965, of lives torn apart by the shadow of war or imminent death. The kids are vulnerable and decent, but their uprooting from predictable, protective life-styles has both intensified and warped their ability to connect to one another. When they have made a tentative beginning at reaching each other, an intruder further upsets this uneasy balance, and the climax is one of shattering, wasteful, but thoroughly motivated violence. Two elderly, drunken career soldiers weave a path through their life like a discordant cantus firmus, a sort of updated Quirt and Flagg underscoring that today there is No Price Glory.

The play is superbly performed, notably by Paul Rudd as an earnest, uncomprehending, Midwestern square, Peter Evans as a troubled but reasonably self-contained homosexual, and Dorian Harewood as a lower-class soldier desperately trying to cope with his place in life. The pace and tone are masterfully modulated by Mr. Nichols, and the entirety makes you realize that sometimes sitting on the edge of your seat is more than an idle theatrical catch-phrase.

Source: Alan Rich. "Hank Cing and Hank Sunk" in *New York*, Vol. 9, no. 19, May 10, 1976, p. 78.

Edith Oliver

Oliver offers a highly favorable review of Streamers, *calling the play "almost literally stunning."*

David Rabe's almost literally stunning "Streamers"—a New York Shakespeare Festival production at the Newhouse which originally opened at Long Wharf, in New Haven—is the final play of his trilogy about Vietnam; the two others are "*The Basic Training of Pavlo Hummel*" and "*Sticks and Bones*." All the action of "*Streamers*" takes place in one room in an Army barracks in Virginia in 1965, when the worst of the war still lies ahead. The room itself seems an oasis of civilization. The three young enlisted men who live in it get along well. They are Billy, a sympathetic, rather innocent fellow from Wisconsin; Roger, a black soldier who seems far more realistic and mature than the others and is a close friend of Billy's; and Richie, a well-to-do homosexual from Manhattan. Billy teases Richie some about his effeminacy, and Richie teases back; Roger does not quite believe it or take it very seriously. None of his business anyway. But the inevitable brutality and pain and violence of the Army and the war (along with loyalty and under-

" *STREAMERS* IS A HARROWING STUDY, SET AMONG SOME KIDS IN A VIRGINIA ARMY CAMP IN 1965, OF LIVES TORN APART BY THE SHADOW OF WAR OR IMMINENT DEATH"

standing and surprising tenderness) cannot be kept at bay. Their old sergeant in Korea, Cokes is back from Vietnam and is dying of leukemia. Both are drunk and appallingly reminiscent. Cokes, laughing heartily, tells an anecdote about a soldier whose parachute didn't open, and he sings a song to go with it—"Beautiful Streamer," to the tune of "Beautiful Dreamer." A more important intruder is a black soldier named Carlyle, a far rougher type than Roger, and half out of his mind with anger and frustration after three months on K.P. He never lets up on Richie, and it is he who precipitates the terrible, bloody climax of the play. This climax almost seems gratuitous, yet it is integral to the story; nothing in the play is done purely for effect. At the end, two of the young soldiers are sobbing on their cots, and the dying old sergeant again sings "Beautiful Streamer," but as softly as Stephen Foster might have wanted it, and in Vietnamese.

Mr. Rabe is a strong dramatist, and as capable of comedy—much of the soldiers' talk is funny—as he is of tragedy. The plot is filled with mood and incident, and every line rings true. To a certain extent, "*Streamers*" lacks the originality—the totally persuasive illusion of firsthand observation and inevitability—that helped make "*Pavlo Hummel*" the masterpiece it is. (Why another black with a knife? Why another homosexual as whipping boy?) Even so, it is very good. The performance, under Mike Nichols' direction, could not be better. The actors, some of them familiar to me, some not, all seem new, so inseparable are they from their roles. The principals, in order of appearance, are Peter Evans (Richie), Dorian Harewood (Carlyle), Paul Rudd (Billy), Terry Alexander (Roger), and Kenneth McMillan and Dolph Sweet as the two old sergeants. The spare, clear setting is by Tony Walton.

Source: Edith Oliver. Review of *Streamers* in the *New Yorker*, Vol. LII, no. 11, May 3, 1976, pp. 76–77.

SOURCES

Clurman, Harold. "Theatre" in the *Nation,* May 8, 1976, p. 574.

Hewes, Henry. "To 'Disneyland' and Back" in the *Saturday Review,* April 17, 1976, p. 48.

Kauffmann, Stanley. "Molehills" in the *New Republic,* June 12, 1976, p. 20.

Kroll, Jack. "Three Cuts to the Quick" in *Newsweek,* February 23, 1976, p. 89.

Rabe, David. "Afterword: 1992" in *The Vietnam Plays,* Grove Press, 1993, p. 181.

FURTHER READING

Asahina, Robert. "The Basic Training of American Playwrights: Theatre and the Vietnam War" in *Theatre,* Vol. 9, Spring, 1978, pp. 30-37.
    Asahina argues that Rabe, despite his flaws, is the only dramatist focusing on the Vietnam conflict "concerned with the art of the theater." He considers *Streamers* Rabe's best work and separates characters into those who, like parachutists, "will float" and those who "will plunge" to their fate.

Beidler, Phillip D. *American Literature and the Experience of Vietnam,* University of Georgia Press, 1982.
    Beidler credits Rabe with producing the most important Vietnam War plays in the 1970s. *Streamers* is discussed as a play dealing with the brutal influence on soldiers who have yet to go to Southeast Asia, and argues that the character of Carlyle evokes "the dark latencies" in the other major characters.

Hertzbach, Janet S. "The Plays of David Rabe: A World of Streamers" in *Essays on Contemporary American Drama,* edited by Hedwig Bock and Albert Wertheim, Hueber, 1981, pp. 173-86.
    Hertzbach examines the metaphors, basic themes, and topical allusions in Rabe's plays and concludes that *Streamers* is the most direct, structurally coherent, and "persuasive" of the playwright's works.

Hurrell, Barbara. "American Self-Image in David Rabe's Vietnam Trilogy" in *Journal of American Culture,* Vol. 4, 1981, pp. 95-107.
    Hurrell discusses the deleterious effect of the Vietnam War on the conscience of America as seen in Rabe's "trilogy," which depicts struggles between conflicting and "incompatible" images of one's self and those of antagonistic forces, including, in *Streamers,* fellow soldiers with diverse backgrounds.

Kolin, Philip C. "David Rabe's *Streamers*" in the *Explicator,* Vol. 45, Fall, 1986, pp. 63-64.
    Kolin discusses the archetypical rite of passage theme evoked in Rabe's play and the important role of the "destructive father figures" whose crimes against the young soldiers lead to the barracks violence.

Kolin, Philip C. *David Rabe: A Stage History and a Primary and Secondary Bibliography,* Garland, 1988.
    A major research tool for further Rabe study, Kolin's book includes an exhaustive bibliography through the 1980s and a thorough stage history of Rabe's plays, including *Streamers.*

Marrance, Bonnie. "David Rabe's Viet Nam Trilogy" in *Canadian Theatre Review,* Vol. 14, Spring, 1977, pp. 86-92.
    Marrance argues that Rabe's so-called "trilogy" is not anti-war per se but is rather concerned with the effects of Vietnam conflict on his ordinary characters. The author claims that *Streamers,* a modern "well-made play," chronicles those effects with "documentary realism."

Rosen, Carol Cynthia. *Plays of Impasse: Contemporary Drama Set in Confining Institutions,* Princeton University Press, 1983.
    On pages 236-250 of her study, Rosen identifies both *The Basic Training of Pavlo Hummel* and *Streamers* as "impasse" plays. *Streamers* presents a "no-exit situation" that, in "entropic" fashion, deteriorates into violence, the only possible response in a "system which promises nothing."

Werner, Craig. "Primal Screams and Nonsense Rhymes: David Rabe's Revolt" in *Educational Theatre Journal,* Vol. 30, December, 1978, pp. 517-29.
    Werner argues that language problems lie the heart of Rabe's war plays. In *Streamers* it is the "collapse of metaphor" that leads to an inescapable "concrete reality" resulting in death.

Three Tall Women

EDWARD ALBEE

1991

Critics have noted autobiographical elements in several of Albee's plays, particularly *Who's Afraid of Virginia Woolf* (1962) and *A Delicate Balance* (1966). By his own admission, however, *Three Tall Women* is Albee's most intentionally autobiographical work to date.

The protagonist of the play, a compelling woman of more than ninety years old, reflects on her life with a mixture of shame, pleasure, regret, and satisfaction. She recalls the fun of her childhood and her marriage, when she had an overwhelming optimism for her future. Yet she bitterly recalls the negative events that resulted in regret: her husband's extramarital affairs, the death of her husband, and the estrangement of her gay son.

The woman's relationship with her son is the clearest indication that Albee was working through some troubled memories of his own in *Three Tall Women*. The playwright was raised by conservative New England foster parents who disproved of his homosexuality. Like the son in his play, he left home at eighteen. Albee admitted to the *Economist* that the play ''was a kind of exorcism. And I didn't end up any more fond of the woman after I finished it than when I started it.''

Besides exorcising some personal demons with the play, Albee regained some respect among New York theater critics. Many critics despaired that the playwright, who showed such promise during the 1960s and 1970s, had dried up creatively. In fact,

Three Tall Women was awarded the Pulitzer Prize for Drama in 1994, as well as the Drama Critics Circle, Lucille Lortel, and Outer Critics Circle awards for best play.

AUTHOR BIOGRAPHY

Born in 1928, Albee was adopted by Reed and Frances Albee, a wealthy couple involved in the theater. He was a precocious writer, composing poetry at the age of six and a play at twelve. As a teenager, he left home when his parents disapproved of his sexual preference; this confrontation would appear later in his plays, in particular *Three Tall Women.*

Albee's first one-act play, *The Zoo Story,* (1958), garnered comparisons with the works of Tennessee Williams and Eugene Ionesco. Subsequent works such as *The Death of Bessie Smith* (1960), *The Sandbox* (1960), and *The American Dream* (1962) earned Albee a place among the top avant-garde writers of the day.

Without doubt, Albee's best-known work is *Who's Afraid of Virginia Woolf* (1962). In this three-act drama, a middle-aged, hard-drinking couple argues and complains about their miserable lives. Critics suggested autobiographical motives in Albee's depiction of George and Martha, the feuding husband and wife, and welcomed the play as an invigorating exploration of the troubled lives of American families. The play was turned into a film starring Richard Burton and Elizabeth Taylor in 1966. That same year, Albee earned the first of three Pulitzer Prizes for *A Delicate Balance.*

During the 1970s and 1980s, he produced a string of notable failures that included *Box* and *Quotations from Mao Tse-Tung* (1969), *All Over* (1971), and *The Lady from Dubuque* (1980). The only play during this period that received a generally favorable response was *Seascape,* for which he won a second Pulitzer Prize in 1975.

While his plays remained popular on university stages and in regional theaters around the country, Albee seemed like a professional outcast. During this time he continued to write, and taught the craft of playwriting at the University of Houston in Texas. Then, in the early 1990s, he earned his third Pulitzer Prize as well as widespread critical and popular acclaim for *Three Tall Women.* In 1993 the Signature Theatre in Manhattan devoted an entire season to Albee's plays.

In 1996, President Bill Clinton awarded him the National Medal of the Arts for his distinguished career. Critic Robert Brustein noted in *The New Republic,* "His late career is beginning to resemble O'Neill's, another dramatist who wrote his greatest plays after having been rejected and abandoned by the culture. Happily, unlike O'Neill, he may not have to wait for death to rehabilitate him."

PLOT SUMMARY

Act I

At the beginning of *Three Tall Women,* three ladies—generically named A, B, and C—are sitting around a wealthy, extravagantly decorated bedroom.

A is an elderly woman who insists that she is ninety-one years old. A young, bright woman, C is the lawyer for A's estate. She disagrees, and claims that A is actually ninety-two. B, who seems to be A's caretaker, is fifty-two years old and attempts to mediate the dispute. These are the three tall women of the play's title.

In spite of B's objections and A's protestations, C will not relent. She can't understand why A would lie about one year of her life. "I can imagine taking off ten—or *trying* to," C admits. "Though more probably seven, or five—good and tricky—but *one!?* Taking off *one year?* What kind of vanity is *that?* Their dispute is the beginning of a complicated gap between age and experience that grows wider, and more poignant, as the play progresses.

B accompanies A to the bathroom, then returns to the room to talk with C alone. B explains how difficult A's life has become. She can no longer control some of her bodily functions. For example, she wets the bed; yet, stubborn as she is, A refuses to wear a diaper or take other precautions. B is philosophical regarding A's predicament. "It's downhill from sixteen on! For all of us!" she reminds C.

A returns from the bathroom, cranky and demanding. She takes her favorite chair back from C, asks for her pillows, and makes herself comfortable. Then she begins what may be a daily routine: she reminisces about her life when she was young, pretty, and popular. This continues for the remainder of Act I—A recalls stories from her youth, while B and C listen, comment, and learn from her experience.

As A chronicles her life as a young girl she is occasionally confused, but her demeanor remains dignified. Initially, C needles her for her petty prejudices and forgetfulness, but the women seem to bond during the conversation.

Just as A begins to tell B and C about an affair she once had as a young lady, she realizes she must go to the bathroom again. B helps her off, then returns to the room alone to talk with C about A's declining health. A broke her arm when she fell, and as a result of the break, the bone is disintegrating. The doctors want to remove it, but A will not let them.

The sound of crashing glass from the bathroom disturbs their conversation. Apparently A occasionally plays foolish pranks. On a whim, she has broken a glass in the bathroom sink, and B must now play the stern disciplinarian. She scolds A for her childish behavior. A returns to the bedroom.

C is trying to straighten out A's bank account and get all her bills paid, but A misplaces important paperwork and forgets to sign checks. C realizes that A is mistrustful of everyone around her.

Occasionally, A complains that ''he never comes to see me.'' B explains to C that she is referring to her son, who visits infrequently. A rails that her son doesn't love her but ''he loves his boys, those boys he has,'' suggesting the reason her son is not around is that he is gay, and his mother's intolerance has driven him away.

As A prepares for her nap, she remembers taking care of her own mother when she was dying. In the middle of her story, she freezes suddenly. C thinks she has died, but B recognizes that the old woman has had a stroke. They exit to call A's son and her doctor.

Act II

At the beginning of Act II, A is on her deathbed. B and C are nearby, discussing her condition. Then another A enters, looking perfectly healthy, without even a sling on her arm.

''Any change?'' she asks. ''Ho, we're . . . just as we were; no change.'' With B's response, it becomes obvious that, in an odd turn of events, A,

Edward Albee

B, and C are now aspects of the same person, at different times of life. While A is the elderly version of this eccentric, anonymous woman, B is the same woman at fifty-two, and C is the protagonist at twenty-six.

Act II is comprised of a series of monologues from these three versions of the protagonist at three different stages of her life. As each woman speaks in turn, she provides different perspectives and descriptions of key events in her life.

Whatever the event, each aspect of this woman views it differently because of her age and experience. C seems more innocent and adventurous, while B is a bit stodgy and unforgiving. A has the perspective of age, and no longer worries much about the opinion of others. At no time are the differences among these characters more pronounced than when their son—known as The Boy—actually appears, visiting his sick mother on her deathbed.

The Boy appears just as he was the day he ran away. When he arrives, B is enraged and screams at him to leave.

Since the three versions of the tall woman exist only as figments of the old women's imagination, however, The Boy cannot see nor hear the three women, only his mother on her deathbed.

Meanwhile, C is amazed at the sight of her future child, while A is touched he has come back to see her, even though it is almost too late.

As The Boy sits near his dying mother's bed, A, B, and C continue their rambling personal history. She chronicles the death of her husband from prostate cancer. None of the individual aspects of this unique woman seem to fit together; none of the versions like each other. A resents C's youth, B thinks A and C are foolish, and C can't stand the thought of becoming A or B.

Near the end, each woman focuses on the happiest time of her life. C assumes the best is yet to come. She is very optimistic about her future.

B enjoys her time of life, with "half of being adult done, the rest ahead of me. Old enough to be a *little* wise, past being *really* dumb."

A believes the same thing. "The happiest moment? Coming to the end of it, I think," says A. For her, the final detachment from life—right before death—signals maturity, comfort and peace. "That's the happiest moment," A insists in the final lines of the play, "When it's all done. When we can stop."

CHARACTERS

A

A is the "tall woman" of the play's title. As the elder version of B and C, A is an intriguing blend of contradictions. In the first act, while she is being cared for by B and C, she is alternately childish and dignified, panic-stricken and stoic.

A's narrative is punctuated by crude, bigoted comments. The Italian man her sister married was "a wop." The domestic servants she knew as a girl "knew their place; they were polite, and well-behaved; none of those uppity niggers, the city ones."

A's intolerance has proven especially harmful in her relationship with her homosexual son. She found his lifestyle and sexual preferences abhorrent, and he left home because of her attitude. For twenty years they did not see one another, and she ultimately regrets it.

In the second act, Albee provides sympathetic glimpses of A. As she watches herself dying, she interacts with her two younger selves and earns at least grudging respect and admiration for her long life. Through her character, Albee seems to suggest that old age provides unique insight into the human condition, and prepares us for death. "That's the happiest moment," says A in the final words of the play. "When it's all done. When we can stop. When we can stop."

B

B turns out to be two different characters. During the first act, she is A's live-in caretaker. In this role, she is a servant to the older woman, helping her eat, dress, move around, and go to the bathroom. She also functions as a buffer between A and C, the youngest of the women. While C finds A's antics pathetic and ridiculous, B is more sympathetic.

In the second act, B is the "tall woman" at fifty-two years old. She is able to reflect on the first half of her life with some measure of objectivity. She urges C to accept life's vicissitudes and unfairness. While C is idealistic and A is resigned, B is cynical. For instance, although her marriage is an unhappy one, she is pragmatic; she settles for the financial security in lieu of sexual fidelity.

In spite of her problems, however, she insists middle-age is the best age to be. "This must be the happiest time," she tells A, C and the audience, "half of being adult done, the rest ahead of me. Old enough to be a *little* wise, past being *really* dumb."

The Boy

The Boy is the "tall woman's" estranged son. He is discussed during the first act, but doesn't appear until the second act. Even then, it is only for a short time; he sits at her bedside after her stroke and never says a word.

From A and B, the audience learns that the boy is gay, and his mother did not approve of his sexuality or his lifestyle. During an argument while he was still a teenager, his mother threatened to throw him out of the house. Feeling rejected and betrayed, he left on his own accord. The two were estranged for twenty years.

C

In the first act, C functions as a representative of A's lawyer, visiting on business. It seems that A has not been signing all her checks and paying all her bills, and C has come to put her accounts in proper order.

Despite her professional role, she is harshly critical of A's personality. She argues with A about her real age, mocks her for her faulty memory, and is offended by her bigoted remarks.

By the end of the first act, though, she begins to change her tone. Watching A struggle with simple tasks, such as going to the bathroom, inspires sympathy for her situation. When A has her stroke, C seems genuinely concerned for her.

In the second act, C is the "tall woman" in the prime of her youth. She is young and quite idealistic. She does not want to accept her future as told by A and B; she cannot believe she would marry a man she does not love and drive away her son.

While A is the voice of experience and B is a cynic, C is Hope personified. Despite all she is told about the dangers that lie ahead for her, she insists, "I *know* my best times . . . haven't happened yet. They're to *come*. Aren't they?"

THEMES

Aging

The characters in *Three Tall Women* provide insights into a universal theme: the human aging process. By depicting a woman at three different stages of her life, Albee cleverly juxtaposes three very different experiences and perspectives.

C is twenty-six and represents youth. Idealistic and free-spirited, C refuses to believe her two older aspects when they tell her what her life has in store for her. She can not believe she will one day marry a man she doesn't love, cheat on him, and drive her only son out of the house. Even near the end she insists, "I *know* my best times . . . haven't happened yet. They're to *come*."

B represents middle age, halfway between her carefree youth and the decrepitude of old age. At her age, she has gained some perspective on her life, but has become a bit jaded in the process. Still, she considers her age as the best time of her life. "This must be the happiest time," she says, "half of being adult done, the rest ahead of me. Old enough to be a *little* wise, past being *really* dumb."

A represents the final years of life. In the first act she displays dignity despite her obvious physical and mental hardships. She exhibits prejudice and pettiness. She enjoys reminiscing about her life, yet is sometimes confused and frustrated by her inability to recall the details of some things. By the time she suffers a stroke while talking about the death of her mother, her affliction seems like an act of mercy.

The second act of the play provides a different perspective of A. As she walks around her own deathbed, musing about her life and her present condition, she is still old, but now healthy. Also, her confusion has disappeared. She reflects on a full life, a mix of joy and tragedy, successes and failures.

Gender Differences

Three Tall Women is somewhat unique in its presentation of gender differences. It is an honest, sympathetic play about women. Women in the play are multi-faceted creatures, capable of both petty jealousies and noble gestures.

The absence of male characters in the play is conspicuous. Men are only talked about, and the single male character that appears on stage, the "tall woman's" son, never speaks a word. Yet the woman's relationship with men, in particular her husband and her son, have profoundly affected her life.

Each version of the woman has a different perspective on relationships with men. C fondly remembers the handsome boy who took her virginity, and fantasizes about her future husband. She is fascinated by the sight of The Boy, her future son. Too young to realize her opinion about him will change when she gets older, she is shocked at the furious reaction of B to his appearance.

B has already met and married the man of her dreams. She affectionately calls him "the penguin," and he has taught her some hard lessons about relationships. "Men cheat; men cheat a *lot*," she informs her younger self. "We cheat *less*, and we cheat because we're lonely; men cheat because they're men." The penguin never appears to defend himself, so the impression of men he leaves behind is a distinctly unfavorable one.

As the eldest of the trio, A has long since forgiven her husband and recovered from the death of her father. She even regrets her estrangement from her son. In the course of more than ninety years, she was a daughter, a wife, a mother, and a widow. From these experiences, she has gained a more tolerant and balanced perspective of the men in her life.

TOPICS FOR FURTHER STUDY

- One of the strongest themes in *Three Tall Women* is the way an individual's perspective on aging *changes* as he or she gets older. This theme is often found in poetry as well, particularly in the work of the English Romantic poets of the early nineteenth century. Read William Wordsworth's "Ode: Intimations of Immortality" (1804) or selections from William Blake's collection of poetry, *Songs of Innocence and of Experience* (1794). Contrast the portrayal of childhood and adulthood expressed by Albee, Wordsworth and Blake. In what ways are they different? How has the passage of time affected the way people view age and experience?

- The protagonist's life was largely shaped by her childhood in the early part of the century. Research the "Jazz Age" of America in the 1920s. Describe what life was like for the wealthy in the larger cities on the East Coast and compare it with today. Also, compare the opportunities available to women at that time with today. How have things changed for women?

- When C learns how her life has turned out, she is very surprised. Write an outline of your personal goals in life. Where do you see yourself in five years? In ten? In fifty? Try to include as many details as you can. Then write a completely different plan that would make you just as happy. Change your career, your relationships, and your lifestyle. How can you accomplish each of your two projected lives? What elements of your plans are things you can control, and which are those you cannot?

- How are men portrayed in the play? Consider her first love, her husband, and her son. Are these portrayals fair? Give reasons for your answer.

- The "tall woman" and her son have a confrontation about his friends, his sexual orientation, and his lifestyle. As a result, they do not speak to each other for twenty years. What could they have done differently to avoid this estrangement? Write a scene in which the two characters meet again after twenty years.

STYLE

Point of View

One of the greatest accomplishments of *Three Tall Women,* according to critics, is its creative use of the narrative *point of view.* A story is always told from someone's perspective, whether that person is the protagonist in the plot, an innocent bystander, a relative relating family history, or an omniscient narrator.

Rarely, however, is the narrator of a story able to confront her younger selves on the same stage at the same time. This is the clever feat of *Three Tall Women.*

Essentially, the play is bifurcated—it is two plays in one. The first act presents A, an elderly woman in declining health, being tended by B, her middle-aged caretaker, and C, a representative from her attorney's office. In the second act, the three women are revealed to be on woman—the protagonist—at different stages of her life. Separately, the narrative voices of these women, representing youth, middle, and old age, are compelling and lyrical. In concert, their combined points of view sound a symphony of poignant, and universal, human experience.

Thematic Construction

Most plays are built around a plot, or a *story.* Typically a hero, the play's *protagonist,* struggles against overwhelming odds to achieve some goal—a lover or a kingdom, for example. These plays are filled with conflict, with *action.*

There is no real *action* to the plot of *Three Tall Women.* Instead Albee provides the play with a

Samantha Bond, Sara Kestelman, and Maggie Smith as the three different versions of the same woman depicted in Albee's play

collection of *themes,* ideas his characters express that provide a context for the discussion and debate that is the real structure of the play. Each scene is driven by one of these ideas, until that idea leads into another.

At the beginning of the play, for example, *age* and *aging* are established as important ideas immediately, and the earliest discussion among the play's "three tall women" is about the aging process. C argues with A over her proper age. ("You're nine-ty-*two*," C insists.)

Once this situation is established it becomes the background setting for a host of other ideas in the play, and the "plot" progresses to the next theme: youth. There is no greater contrast to A's struggles with age than her fond reminiscences of her youth. Though all of her memories come back to her in bits and pieces, she remembers her girlhood, riding horses, winning ribbons and prizes at shows, and her close relationship with her sister and mother.

Soon, another theme emerges: marriage. A reminisces about meeting her husband, his infideli-ties, and the fun they had together. Each of A's memories provides a piece of the patchwork that is the *thematic construction* of *Three Tall Women.*

HISTORICAL CONTEXT

Edward Albee's plays, like his own life, have been shaped by the changing nature of American *families.* Albee himself was adopted at an early age by wealthy New England parents, shuffled around to various private schools until he was eighteen. Like the son in *Three Tall Women,* he quarreled with his mother over his homosexuality and left home; he then attended college briefly, living off a trust fund in Greenwich Village until he began his successful career as a professional playwright.

By the time he wrote *Three Tall Women* in 1991, he had been in a longstanding relationship with the same man for more than twenty years. Albee did not experience the "typical" American family life, but then, judging by the evolution of American families during his career, neither had many of his audience members.

From 1970 to 1990, the marriage age of men went from 22.5 to nearly 26 years old. At the same time, the median age for women to marry climbed from 20.6 to 24 years old. Besides marrying older, many Americans were choosing not to marry at all. During those two decades, the annual marriage rate per 1000 people in the population decreased from 10.8 to 9.1.

To further complicate and change the cherished notion of wedlock, the "no-fault" divorce reforms of the 1970s made divorce faster and easier. During the 1980s, one in every three marriages ended in divorce. By 1995, just over 25% of the 34.3 million families were led by single parents. In fact, more than one of every four children had divorced parents.

Moreover, the number of unmarried couples living together nearly tripled between 1970-1980, up to 1.6 million. By 1995 that number had skyrocketed to 3.7 million, and unmarried births, which accounted for only 11% of all births in America in 1970, accounted for 31% of births in 1993.

A number of explanations have been offered for the decline of the "nuclear family" (i.e. mother, father, sister and brother, all related and living in the same house). For one, more women than ever before were choosing to enter the workforce, and build careers before, or instead of, building families.

Also, wider acceptance of divorce also led to an increased expectation from marriage. If a man or woman was not happy in a relationship, he or she became more likely to seek divorce in order to find a more suitable match.

Variations on the nuclear family became the norm in the nineties. Single parent families, stepfamilies, childless families, communal families, and families with same sex parents became more common.

The proliferation of same sex parents were a result of more tolerant adoption laws. Still, while acceptance of homosexual lifestyles was increasing, widespread tolerance was a long way off.

While many large companies, such as IBM, acknowledge unmarried couples who live together (including homosexual and lesbian couples) by extending to them the same benefits shared by married employees, many rights and privileges were not sanctioned. No states allowed homosexual couples to legally marry, and some states had legislation that prevented homosexual couples from adopting a child who was not the biological offspring of one of the partners.

The 1990s were also the years of "Don't ask, don't tell." While the United States military still forbids homosexuality in its ranks, the application forms for military service were changed to avoid asking about sexual preference. Recruits were encouraged to be discreet about sexual matters, particularly if they were gay.

CRITICAL OVERVIEW

Most of the critics who reviewed *Three Tall Women* when it appeared in Off-Broadway in 1994 were enthusiastic about the play. Moreover, they seemed relieved that he had finally produced another play that had wide popular and critical appeal. As a writer for the *Economist* declared, "after a long dry spell for American drama, relieved by successful imports from London, New York has a good, homemade play at last."

Several reviewers, including the *New Republic*'s Robert Brustein, noted Albee's personal stake in the play. "*Three Tall Women* is a mature piece of writing," Brustein judged, "clearly autobiographical, in which Albee seems to be coming to terms not only with a socialite foster parent he once satirized in past plays, but with his own advancing age.''

William A. Henry III concurred. In a review in *Time,* ''Albee is exorcising his own demons in having the dowager deny her homosexual son.''

In the *New Yorker,* John Lahr contended, ''The last great gift a parent gives to a child is his or her own death, and the energy underneath *Three Tall Women* is the exhilaration of a writer calling it quits with the past.''

Critics maintained that much of this Pulitzer Prize-winning play's appeal seems to lie in the unique interaction as three separate aspects of the same woman. ''Albee's plays have always walked a line between heightened realism and dark comedy,'' Jack Helbig wrote in *Booklist.* Even his most surreal works are populated with characters who wouldn't seem out of place in real life.'' In *Three Tall Women,* Helbig continued, the trio of characters are able to provide unique insight into one woman's life because of their separate perspectives—a feat that can't be accomplished in simple, realistic drama.

The character of A is the focal point of the play. As Tim Apello suggested in the *Nation,* ''Albee has this little problem as a dramatist: He abhors plots. But just as one realizes, with mounting irritation, that A's colorful fragmented vignettes will never cohere into a single structured picture—nobody cracks Albee's mosaic code—the author saves the play with a big switch in the second act. The three actresses fuse into one contrapuntally evoked character, A through the ages.''

Still, A is an unlikely dramatic hero, and as Brustein pointed out, it took a feat of adept artistic skill to make her sympathetic. ''A is an entirely vicious old wretch,'' Brustein asserted, ''with a volatile tongue and a narrow mind, but it is a tribute to the writing and the acting that she gradually wins our affections. Although prejudiced against 'kikes,' 'niggers,' 'wops' and 'fairies' (among them her own son), she is a model of vitality and directness when compared with the humor-impaired liberal C, who protests her intolerance.''

Albee's writing in *Three Tall Women* drew comparisons to a wide variety of other authors. Appelo observed, ''*Three Tall Women* cops a bit of the puckish bleakness of Beckett (the sole dramatist Albee has claimed utterly to admire), and a bit of *Long Day's Journey Into Night,* but the grief and affection seem distant, glimpsed through the wrong end of a telescope. It's O'Neill without guild, and with much less galumphing verbal rhythms.''

In addition, Brustein suggested that the characters in the play suggest ''a Beckett influence, though on the surface the play appears to be a drawing-room comedy in the style of A. R. Gurney.''

In spite of the play's insight into the human condition, its autobiographical perspective, and roundly recognized appeal, a handful of reviewers took exception with the relentlessness with which Albee pursues his themes. ''*Three Tall Women . . .* is by no means an entirely successful play,'' Ben Brantley wrote in the *New York Times.* ''It makes its points so blatantly and repeats them so often that one perversely longs for a bit more of the cryptic obliquity that is Mr. Albee's signature.''

Another *Times* critic, Vincent Canby, maintained: ''*Three Tall Women* initially seems to be about the process of dying and death itself, though that's not the full story. It's more about the inevitable changes effected by time and circumstances, about the accumulation of events that can shape a character and that are so many they eventually become meaningless. It doesn't help that at no one of her three ages is A a very interesting woman. She's bossy and gauche as young C, bitter and tired as B and self-absorbed as old A.''

A few disgruntled critics took an historical approach to criticizing the playwright, and wondered aloud where his talents had been hidden for so long. ''Whatever happened to Edward Albee?'' Stefan Kanfer sarcastically asked in the *New Leader.*

Kanfer actually found several things to praise about Albee's play, but in the final analysis asserted: ''If this were 1962, *Three Tall Women* would herald the arrival of a playwright as promising as David Ives. One could hardly wait to see his next production. But we have been through all that with Albee, and this elegant minor effort gives very little reason to cheer. After years of commercial and esthetic disappointments, Edward Albee is once again Off-Off-Broadway. Like so many of his characters through the decades, he is going out the way he came in.''

CRITICISM

Lane A. Glenn

Lane A. Glenn is a Ph.D. specializing in theatre history and literature. In this essay he examines how Edward Albee combines elements of absurdist drama with realism in Three Tall Women.

As much as anything else, the popular success of Edward Albee's 1994 Pulitzer Prize-winning drama *Three Tall Women* can be attributed to the fickleness of American scholars and theater reviewers. As numerous articles and interviews pointed out during the show's lengthy New York run, Albee was once the darling of the American Theater scene. In the early 1960s he was hailed as the next Eugene O'Neill and was considered a literary genius of the age.

He quickly fell out of favor, however, and for more than twenty years his plays received only lukewarm, or even hostile response from New York reviewers. Albee found work teaching and directing, while he continued to write plays.

What changed? What great cultural upheaval or fundamental shift in Albee's writing style suddenly made *Three Tall Women* more palatable than two decades of near misses? The playwright himself was hesitant to hazard a guess.

"*Three Tall Women* is the first play [of mine] that has gotten almost unanimously favorable press in the United States," Albee told *American Theatre,* But I didn't expect it to, necessarily. I think of my plays as a continuing pattern of me writing. I don't think I've written a bad play or a good play; I don't think in those terms."

It is precisely Albee's unwillingness to think in conventional terms, to create a "good" play or a "bad" play based on current cultural standards, that has set him at loggerheads with American critics. Ironically, it is also his insistence on defining his own terms that has led him to be one of the most influential (though not most produced) American playwrights of the twentieth century.

While fickle reviewers like Stefan Kanfer in the *New Leader* asked, "Whatever happened to Edward Albee?" artistic allies like Lawrence Sacharow, the director of the American premiere of *Three Tall Women,* insist the playwright has been toiling away at the same kind of work—his own—throughout his career, whether it was popular or not. "There's a

perfectly logical through-line from *The Zoo Story* to here," Sacharow told the *Dallas Morning News.*

That through-line, which is quite apparent in *Three Tall Women,* is a combination of styles: Albee's unique blend of absurdist elements and American realism, mixed with characters, themes and dialogue that are distinctly "Albee-esque."

In a 1962 essay for *New York Times Magazine* titled "Which Theatre is the Absurd One?" Albee defended his style of writing plays, insisting that "The avant-garde theatre is fun; it is free-swinging, bold, iconoclastic and often wildly, wildly funny. If you will approach it with childlike innocence-putting your standard responses aside . . . if you will approach it on its own terms, I think you will be in for a liberating surprise."

He was reacting to reviewers who already, so early in his professional career, had begun categorizing and criticizing him according to how well his plays fit in with typical Broadway fare, which for most of the twentieth century has meant *realism* in every aspect of production.

While many of America's best-known playwrights have experimented with form and style, by and large their most popular plays have contained plots, characters, settings and themes that are realistic. Eugene O'Neill penned Expressionistic dramas like *The Emperor Jones* and *The Hairy Ape,* but he is mainly remembered for his realistic plays like *Desire Under the Elms* and *Long Day's Journey Into Night.*

Likewise, Tennessee Williams and Arthur Miller dabbled in experimental styles of writing, but both achieved their greatest successes with more recognizably realistic plays like *Cat on a Hot Tin Roof* and *Death of a Salesman.*

Albee, on the other hand, found his initial success *Off*-Broadway with short, quirky one-acts like *The Zoo Story* (1959) and *The American Dream* (1961). Thereafter, despite plays like *Who's Afraid of Virginia Woolf* (1962) that stylistically approached the realism of O'Neill, Williams, and Miller, Albee's work was conveniently associated with writers of a new non-realistic movement, "absurdism."

Critic Martin Esslin popularized "absurdism" as a label in his 1961 study *The Theatre of the Absurd.* Esslin used the term to describe experimental plays produced mainly by European authors from the mid-1940s to the early 1960s. These

WHAT DO I READ NEXT?

- In a career spanning four decades, Edward Albee has written more than twenty plays. Two of his most popular remain the 1958 one-act play *The Zoo Story,* and the award-winning *Who's Afraid of Virginia Woolf,* (1962) which also became a film starring Elizabeth Taylor and Richard Burton.

- *The Great Gatsby* is F. Scott Fitzgerald's famous 1922 portrait of America's Jazz Age. The novel's protagonist, the self-made millionaire Jay Gatsby, is considered the embodiment of American ambition in the early part of this century.

- Tennessee Williams's *The Glass Menagerie* (1944) is a "dream play" featuring the character of Amanda Wingfield, a woman who lives in a St. Louis tenement with her two children: Laura, a shy young woman; and her brother Tom, a poet who supports the family by working in a warehouse.

- Longer life expectancy, health issues, age discrimination, and retirement concerns are just a few of the topics discussed in *Aging and Old Age* (1996) by Richard A. Posner or *Aging America* (1992) by Karen A. Conner.

---

writers—Samuel Beckett, Eugene Ionesco and Jean Genet among them—were influenced by the existential philosophy of artists like Jean Paul Sartre, who famously argued that human beings are "condemned to be free." They sought to show their audiences how irrational and unjust the world could be.

To achieve their goals, absurdists produced plays that consciously countered traditional expectations of plot, character, language, and logic through a variety of anti-realistic techniques. For example, time and place were often unimportant and unknown. Plots in these plays did not necessarily develop through a series of cause-and-effect events. Instead, actions and dialogue often centered around *themes* or a particular *mood.* This thematic construction is often *circular,* with plots ending where they began.

Since communication through language was viewed as a rational tool (in an irrational world), absurdists often parodied language, and demonstrated how inadequate it was when actually trying to describe the human experience. Any attempts to improve the human condition in absurdist drama typically prove futile, or even comical in a dark way.

Some of the most famous absurdist plays include Genet's *The Balcony* (1956), Ionesco's *The Chairs* (1952) and Beckett's *Waiting for Godot,* which is credited with introducing the absurdist movement to America in 1953.

Albee has employed the characteristics of absurdism throughout his career. As Jack Helbig noted in a review of *Three Tall Women* for *Booklist,* "Albee's best plays have always walked a line between heightened realism and dark comedy. Even his most surreal works are populated with characters who wouldn't seem out of place in real life." This is certainly true of *Three Tall Women,* a play that contains many of the techniques of absurdism.

The "plot" of *Three Tall Women,* for example, does not arise out of a series of cause-and-effect actions. There is, in fact, no clear "protagonist" seeking some kind of realistic goal. There is only an old woman, dying and attended by her caretaker and attorney, who later transform into aspects of her younger self. Instead of actions, the story centers on themes—youth and age, innocence and experience, sex, love, and disillusionment.

Like the absurdists, Albee also experiments with language as a means of revealing deeper, hidden meanings, and suggesting the irrationality of existence. With the character of A, he is able to blend realism with theatricality. A's mental faculties are deteriorating along with her physical func-

THE SUCCESS OF *THREE TALL WOMEN* MAY SIGNAL A PLAY THAT HAS MANAGED TO CHANGE OUR PERCEPTIONS AND BROADEN THE SCOPE OF OUR DRAMA"

tions, so she might be expected to act unexpectedly. Her sound is the sound of "half-naturalistic, wholly calculated incipient-Alzheimer's talk," as Tim Appelo pointed out in the *Nation*.

On a realistic level, this provides a reasonable excuse for A's overt bigotry and childish pranks. Stylistically, it also allows for the play's many monologues, soliloquies, and moments when the characters directly address the audience.

One of the most recognizable traits of absurdist writing is its nebulous treatment of character identities, time, and place, all of which are elusive in *Three Tall Women.* Ionesco's plays are peopled with vague characters like "The Professor," "The Pupil," and "The Maid." Beckett chose to christen his characters with nonsense names like "Hamm," "Clov," and "Nagg."

Albee, who has included figures as generic as "The Man" and "The Woman" in other plays, achieved an even more basic cast of characters in *Three Tall Women* by dubbing the ladies, simply, "A," "B," and "C." Decisions such as this, however, cannot be made lightly, or without thought for the larger concerns of the play.

As Albee told a group of his students at the University of Houston (reported in the *Texas Monthly*), "Lack of resolution is not necessarily good. The difference between interesting ambiguity and unintentional ambiguity is very important. Ambiguity demands as much control as anything else does."

Just as ambiguous in *Three Tall Women* is the time and place of the play's action. There is a specific location—a "wealthy" bedroom—reproduced on the stage, but the world outside is a mystery. The larger "place" of the play is never known, nor is it particularly important.

Most of the play, after all, takes place in the past, and is *described* rather than portrayed by the

"three tall women" of the play's title. Time becomes even more malleable in the hands of the characters themselves.

At the beginning of the play, A cannot decide if she is ninety-one or ninety-two years old. As she lays on her deathbed throughout the second act, B and C become separate aspects of A at different points in her life, and through the imagination of a dying woman nearly a century of experience is viewed simultaneously, through three separate prisms of experience.

Drawing a parallel to his absurdist predecessors, Robert Brustein noted in the *New Republic,* "Beckett was the first dramatist to condense the past and present lives of a character into a single dramatic action, and *Krapp's Last Tape* is a play to which *Three Tall Women* owes a deep spiritual debt . . . Beckett compressed youth and age through the device of a tape recorder, Albee uses doppelgangers; but both plays evoke the same kind of existential poignance."

An "existential poignance" is what has driven some reviewers and theatergoers away from absurdist drama. Many found the approach of the absurdists to be unnecessarily depressing, and wondered (often aloud) why someone would go to such lengths to even *write* about such feelings. Esslin, however, found a very different motive at work. In *The Theatre of the Absurd* he suggests:

> Ultimately, a phenomenon like the Theatre of the Absurd does not reflect despair or a return to dark irrational forces but expresses modern man's endeavor to come to terms with the world in which he lives. It attempts to make him face up to the human condition as it really is, to free him from illusions that are bound to cause constant maladjustment and disappointment. . . Today, when death and old age are increasingly concealed behind euphemisms and comforting baby talk, and life is threatened with being smothered in the mass consumption of hypnotic mechanized vulgarity, the need to confront man with the reality of his situation is greater than ever. For the dignity of man lies in his ability to face reality in all its senselessness; to accept it freely, without fear, without illusions— and to laugh at it."

Albee agrees. In an interview with *The Progressive,* he told Richard Farr, "I've found that any play which isn't close to laughter in the dark is very tedious. And conversely, even the purest comedy, if it isn't just telling jokes, has got to be tied to reality in some way. I think a play should do one of two things, and ideally both: It should change our perceptions about ourselves and about consciousness, and it should also broaden the possibilities of drama. If it can do both, that's wonderful. But it's certainly got to do one of the two.''

The success of *Three Tall Women* may signal a play that has managed to do both—change our perceptions and broaden the scope of our drama. By combining traditionally absurdist techniques with a realistic situation, and infusing the whole with his own unique approach to language and age-old themes, Albee managed to convince his reviewers and audiences to once again approach him on his own terms, which is the only way he will write.

''You learn from people who've come before you and who have done wonderful things,'' Albee admits, ''The trick is to take the influences and make them so completely you that nobody realizes that you're doing anything else but your own work.''

Source: Lane A. Glenn, for *Drama for Students,* Gale, 2000.

Tim Appelo

Calling Three Tall Women *a return to form, Appelo praises the playwright for being ''back in tune with his times.''*

Photos reveal Edward Albee to be stricken with the Dick Clark Syndrome: an inexplicable imperviousness to physical decay. Instead, time has taken its toll on his festering reputation.

But I'm thrilled to report that Albee the artist lives. The Vineyard Theater production of his 1991 play *Three Tall Women,* his first big New York premiere in over a decade, should help reverse his audience's exodus. No more the noisy young shockmeister pop star, now Albee plays unplugged, still singing, softly, his bitter old themes of domestic-*cum*-cosmic discord. Rod Stewart unplugged is a lazy disgrace, Clapton a drab craftsman, but Albee is more like Neil Young: chastened by age, sad where once he soared, yet still quavering on.

Three Tall Women is largely a portrait of Albee's late, very estranged adoptive mother at 92, though the character querulously insists she's 91. (In a 1966 *Paris Review* interview, Albee querulously insisted he was 37; the interviewer reminded him he'd be 38 when the piece was published.) James Noone's set neatly conveys the old woman's luxe past and funereal future: A central floral painting is flanked by floral wallpaper, floral prints, floral lace curtains, a bed with floral pillows and a blighted floral rug worn down to atoms.

So is the wraithlike heroine, but there's a death dance of semisenescent reminiscence left in the old

> ''MUCH OF THE VALUE OF *THREE TALL WOMEN* IS THE LIGHT IT SHEDS ON ALBEE'S LIFE AND OTHER WORK''

gal yet. Myra Carter is, as the young people say, *awesome* in the role of A, the nonagenarian mom. Her phrasing of Albee's half-naturalistic, wholly calculated incipient-Alzheimer's talk is impeccable; her voice dwindles to an Edith Evans warble, ascends to a helium keening, erupts abruptly into lacerating sobs as required. Her moods, too, are musical—her memories lark and plunge. We're eager and grateful for each vivid bit of that past recaptured: her debutante milieu; her runty, randy groom; horseback riding; riding her horse's groom in the stables as she screams in sexual triumph. (Some of these memories are voiced by other actors, whom I'll introduce shortly.) *Three Tall Women* cops a bit of the puckish bleakness of Beckett (the sole dramatist Albee has claimed utterly to admire), and a bit of *Long Day's Journey Into Night,* but the grief and affection seem distant, glimpsed through the wrong end of a telescope. It's O'Neill without guilt, and with much less galumphing verbal rhythms. ''Eventually he lets me talk about when he was a little boy,'' says A of her son's visits—Michael Rhodes plays the wordless role well enough—''but he never has an opinion on that; he doesn't seem to have an opinion on much of anything that has to do with us, with me.'' Creepily remote, Albee has predicted that he won't think much about his mom now that he's devoted a play to explicating her life. But I'll bet he didn't keep mum with Ma in real life: This is the guy of whom Richard Burton wrote, ''A week with him would be a lifetime.''

Old A is reproved by young C (Jordan Baker), a B-school type trying to get A's finances in order. The role is as thin as the pinstripes on C's suit, and Baker is way the hell the spindliest actor in the show. Twenty-six-year-old C is reproved by B (Marian Seldes), A's 52-year-old caretaker. As dazzling a talent as Carter, Seldes is earthy and spectral, not by turns but at once. Hunched like a sardonic question mark, she moderates the conflict between the old and young women, but she's openly on the old bat's side. She's like Mrs. Danvers on Prozac—

still mean and weird, but detached, sourly entertained by life as if watching it from beyond, a well-adjusted shade. Her sly arched-brow amusement reminds me of Ian McKellen; her marvelously odd hand gestures remind me of Thai opera, except that I can't comprehend Thai opera, while her gestures clearly underline the dialogue. Many lovely ensemble moments seem centered on her hands, as if she were conducting. (Though Lawrence Sacharow's direction must have been superb, Ingmar Bergman was probably right to say that Albee's best plays can do without a director, just as chamber music doesn't require a dictatorial baton. The man is a composer, just as he wanted to be at age 11.)

Albee has this little problem as a dramatist: He abhors plots. But just as one realizes, with mounting irritation, that A's colorful fragmented vignettes will never cohere into a single structured picture—nobody cracks Albee's mosaic code—the author saves the play with a big switch in the second act. The three actresses fuse into one contrapuntally evoked character, A through the ages. It's played wonderfully (even Baker gets better), like a close basketball game going down to the wire. While the finale is a characteristic letdown (Albee favors inconclusive conclusions), by then the play has wandered around A's life long enough to give us a satisfying sense of her.

Mysteriously, we get very little sense of her relationship with her son, just a sketchy recounted encounter or two. I wanted more on this relationship, and fewer of the life lessons the play overbearingly urges upon us: "It's downhill from 16 on for all of us . . . stroke, cancer . . . walking off a curb into a 60-mile-an-hour wall . . . slit your throat. . . . All that blood on the Chinese rug. My, my." You can get deeper philosophical insights from Dionne Warwick's Psychic Friends Network. Yet even when Albee says something stupid, he says it in cadences of great and practiced beauty. The wisdom that eludes him in platitudes ("[Women] cheat because we're lonely; men cheat because they're men") he expresses better in drama: the anecdote of the pricey bracelet A's fellatio-craving husband proffers upon his angry penis is funny and scary, a lightning glimpse of a nightmare marriage.

I freely admit that much of the value of *Three Tall Women* is the light it sheds on Albee's life and other work. He has described *TTW* as an "exorcism." The original title of *Who's Afraid of Virginia Woolf?* was *The Exorcism,* which was retained as the title of the third act, and *TTW* makes me wonder

whether critics haven't been misinterpreting his masterpiece all these years, focusing on George and Martha as archetypal man and wife (or, in a popular interpretation that infuriates Albee, as a gay couple in hetero drag. I don't see what difference it makes, nor why Albee sternly forbids all-male productions of the show). What gets exorcised—killed off—in *Woolf* is the imaginary kid. In *TTW,* the kid kills off the memory of his mom. What if George and Martha are "really" Edward and his ever-bickering mother, who needled him cruelly about his adoption and never forgave his desertion? In any case, the heroine A of *TTW* is a kind of combination of the Liz Taylor and Sandy Dennis characters in *Woolf:* alternately a snarly and simpering, sickly fake mother, yet admirably defiant of the unmitigated insult of old age. From the first-act debate about a classic actress (Bette Davis in the case of *Woolf,* Norma Shearer in *TTW*) to the last act's rather heavy-handed stripping away of bourgeois illusions (who has them anymore?), the plays seem parallel, sister dramas reaching out to each other across the intervening wastes and oases of Albee's career.

Why is such a self-conscious iconoclast so annoyingly moralistic? Albee is the third-generation namesake of a top vaudeville impresario who got started with a revolting attraction: a twenty-four-ounce preemie advertised as "small enough to fit in a milk bottle." The child's name was Baby Alice. Does this have something to do with his reviled abstract play *Tiny Alice?* Edward Albee I ran a theatrical enterprise so bluenosed it blacklisted the actors it ruthlessly enslaved if they so much as uttered the words "son of a gun" on any of its nationwide stages. Having authored five "son of a bitch's" in *Woolf* alone, Edward Albee III was the Tom Paine of the dirty-speech movement in American theater, though he was more besides. Maybe there's an in-joke in his *Alice,* and a secret triumph in its commercial oblivion: the horribly lowest-common-denominator entertainment answered by a work of arrogant mandarin incomprehensibility, spurned by the ignorant masses.

With the entirely intelligible *Three Tall Women,* Albee is evidently mature enough not to crave our hatred. Maybe he doesn't even hate his mother anymore. What's more, he's back in tune with his times. In the three tall women's last-ditch attempt to define the nature of happiness, Seldes's B muses that her position at 52 is ideal: "Enough shit gone through to have a sense of the shit that's ahead, but way past sitting and *playing* in it. This *has* to be the happiest time." Shit happens—in a day when the nation's leading dramatic characters are Beavis and Butthead, what moral could be more modish than that?

Source: Tim Appelo. Review of *Three Tall Women* in the *Nation,* March 14, 1994, pp. 355–56.

Jeane Luere

While critical of the playwright's neglect in the area of plot, Luere praises Albee's play as his strongest in years.

Receptive audiences at Vienna's English Theatre, which in the past has been host to Tennessee Williams, Harold Pinter, Lanford Wilson, are hailing the new Edward Albee offering, giving the play's three-in-one heroine emotional precedence over men and women in his previous dramas. In stirring anecdotes, the eldest third of Albee's strong composite heroine, a ninety-year-old with a prodigal son, divulges her prejudices, her attitudes and insights on the lack of substance in the upper crust into which she has married. The two other onstage characters, materializations of her self before childbirth and at middle age, hear the older component bemoan her husband's and friends' lack of backbone or moral fibre. Regrettably, her disillusion has led her to replace the legendary milkman or back seat of a car with the family's groom and stable.

As in previous plays, the author is more concerned with characters and situations than with problems and their trite resolution. Albee's power to generate real characters is legendary; and his delicate drawing of this newest one, a tall mother whose indiscretions alienate her son, may show the author's intellectual sympathy for her, quelling critics' sporadic hints at anti-female strains in earlier work. However, Albee's mother-image in *Three Tall Women,* drawn with wit and truth, is itself more palatable than the insight into life which the play dramatizes. Albee's new work warns that in a land where the populace is obsessed with self-fulfillment and determined to be happy, what must cease at once is our perpetuation of our offsprings' notion that in life we get what we want, that parents and the world at large are perfect caregivers—or even caregivers at all. Rather, in the words of Albee's aged mother-composite, we must prepare the world's young for the actualities of a life in which "surcease or a series of surceases" is our only joy. Truth is our only salvation. So long as we hide from our children the sad truth of our imperfections and our mutability, we must expect the tragic splits that rend mothers and children.

> " IN *THREE TALL WOMEN* ALBEE MOVES FROM HIS DEMONS TOWARD JOY, SURCEASE, AND DEATH"

Officiously, critics in the 1970s and 1980s often chided Edward Albee for drawing homosexual characters, like those in his *Tiny Alice,* too subtly, forming them implicitly rather than explicitly. With *Three Tall Women,* the upbraiders may be silenced. Albee's newest male character, a defiant son who, in his forties, returns to kiss his bedfast mother's hands and face—and who materializes on the stage as the youth who had packed his "attitudes" and left twenty years earlier—is strikingly portrayed by Howard Weatherall. The nature of the son evolves in frank phrases from the lips of his mother, delivered with chagrin by Myra Carter, who refers to her son and his friends as "he and his boys" and who laments, "He doesn't love me, he loves those boys he has!" Yet, in the mother's dotage, the son brings special gifts of candied orange peel and freesia and sees to happy outings for her.

New York critics who in 1983 misinterpreted the talentless former freak in Albee's *Man Who Had Three Arms* as an intimate revelation of the author's self may infer the present drama to be another little masochistic exercise, making amends for his "attitudes" as a teenager. If the play's authorial intention is a coming to terms with self, Weatherall's sincerity in the role of the son makes viewers long for their own second chance to reconcile with an aged parent as honestly as this character does.

The play's form is as convoluted as one expects from Albee. Here he intrigues us with the work's structure, forces us to figure out which of two worlds he is drawing us into—the totally naturalistic world of Act One, whose three tall women are a law clerk, a ninety-year-old mother and her nurse, or the presentationally-staged world of act two where a maternal, mystical identity falls to each actress.

The playwright's penchant for puzzles unsettles even deeply-moved audiences who crowd the sold-out theatre. Rapt viewers may lose the beauty and tension of Albee's language for those precious minutes they need to solve the problem of which world confronts them on stage. Yet critics' complaints about structure are not so indicative of a play's merit as the sentiment (as opposed to sentimentality) that an audience credits in the play. Albee's long-time obsession with the orchestration of emotions and with theatrical effectiveness culminates here. Audiences applaud how effectively the playwright has rendered the mother's guilt for infidelities and for failing to remain the pedestal-figure her son perceived her to be in his babyhood. Even so, the play's structure may need a touch of the author's clever directorial hand before moving from Vienna—a site Albee has called "off-off-Broadway"—to New York.

The cast's delivery of the emotion in Albee's language and in his subtext is cuttingly valid, particularly in act 2 when the actresses unfold the life of the mother at ages 26, 52, and 90. Carter is an electric presence on stage as the oldest maternal figure, and voices each bit of Albee's dialogue so piquantly that what might have been, with a lesser actress, rambly and senile chatter about a lecherous father-in-law, a frigid sister, and deceased friends, instead etches the mother's character just as finely as brush strokes create an amorphous WOLS leaf. Thus we feel the tension of the mother-character who suffers from her own infirmities. She won't admit that she can no longer manage her finances, or that she is partner to her son's long disaffection. Her resentment of male infidelity, her isolation by friends' deaths, her guilt at indiscretions—each is a theme from earlier Albee works like his miniature American tragedy, *The Sandbox,* or his Pulitzer prize drama *Delicate Balance,* themes broadened and surging with life in *Three Tall Women.*

Representing the demanding and expectant youth of the mother, Cynthia Bassham is at once innocent and sophisticated. Bassham, who last year made indelible the naivete of Honey in *Who's Afraid of Virginia Woolf?,* sashays in a sleek gown as a Bergdorf-Goodman fashion model who climbs the social ladder when she marries into wealth. Later, Bassham's character, with haunted voice and mein, recoils at the prospect of living her life without joy. The actress's expressive face is proud and stubborn in act 2 as she innocently balks at hints of what may be slated for her life; and her face is livid in act 2 when she sees the actualities descend upon her.

Kathleen Butler, who triumphed in Albee's 1987's *Marriage Play* as a disenchanted wife who would rather be hit than left, now creates a more put-upon figure as the shrewder, middle span of Albee's composite mother. With humour the actress conveys the play's authorial discernments on the sad consistency of life—that with a doctor's firm slap and a hard first breath a baby comes in, and at the end, with a harder breath goes out. With strength and gravity, Butler demonstrates that a son's sulks and attitudes may freeze mother-love for a spell no matter how desperately she wants to forgive him. Later, with conviction, Butler shines as her mid-life character announces that, though her life has been crammed with hurt, she has now climbed the hill from which one can look back halfway and ahead halfway—in Albee's phrase, "the only time we have a three hundred and sixty degree view!"

After a painful search for serenity with the materialized components of her selves, Albee's ultimate mother-image realizes that joy lies not in the events of our lives but in surcease when each of her conflicts ends. Alone, at the mercy of caregivers and her own infirmities, she rejoices in the surcease of anxiety over real or imagined results of her actions or misjudgments of the past. In *Three Tall Women* Albee moves from his demons toward joy, surcease, and death; perhaps now he will write for us of love instead of disillusion.

Source: Jeane Luere. Review of *Three Tall Women* in *Theatre Journal,* Vol. 44, no. 2, May, 1992, pp. 251–52.

SOURCES

Albee, Edward. "Which Theatre is the Absurd One?" in *New York Times Magazine,* February 25, 1962, pp. 30-1, 64, 66.

Appelo, Tim. A review of *Three Tall Women* in the *Nation,* March 14, 1994, p. 355.

Bigsby, C. W. E., editor. *Edward Albee: A Collection of Critical Essays,* Prentice-Hall, 1975.

Brantley, Ben. A review of *Three Tall Women* in the *New York Times,* April 13, 1994.

Brustein, Robert. A review of *Three Tall Women* in the *New Republic,* April 4, 1994, p. 26.

Canby, Vincent. A review of *Three Tall Women* in the *New York Times,* February 20, 1994.

A review of *Three Tall Women* in the *Economist,* April 23, 1994, p. 91.

Esslin, Martin. *The Theatre of the Absurd,* Anchor Books, 1961, p. 316.

Farr, Richard. An interview with Edward Albee in *The Progressive,* August, 1996, p. 39.

Helbig, Jack. A review of *Three Tall Women* in *Booklist*, April 1, 1995, p. 1372.

Henry III, William A. A review of *Three Tall Women* in *Time*, February 21, 1994, p. 64.

Kanfer, Stefan. A review of *Three Tall Women* in the *New Leader*, February 14, 1994, p. 23.

Lahr, John. A review of *Three Tall Women* in the *New Yorker*, May 16, 1994.

Samuels, Steven. An interview with Edward Albee in *American Theatre*, September, 1994, p. 38.

Taitte, Lawson. A review of *Three Tall Women* in the *Dallas Morning News*, September 8, 1996.

Yoffe, Emily. A profile of Edward Albee in *Texas Monthly*, May, 1993, p. 98.

FURTHER READING

Amacher, Richard E. *Edward Albee*, Twayne Publishers, Inc., 1969.
    Amacher explains the playwright's relationship to the Theatre of the Absurd, and attempts to establish his place in American theater during the first decade of his career.

Bigsby, C. W. E. *A Critical Introduction to Twentieth Century American Drama*, Cambridge University Press, 1982.
    In the second volume in this series, Edward Albee's work is discussed alongside profiles of such American artistic notables as Arthur Miller and Tennessee Williams.

Bloom, Harold, editor. *Edward Albee*, Chelsea House Publishers, 1987.
    This collection includes a dozen critical essays covering such topics as language in Albee's plays, influences on the playwright, and the psychology of character in Albee's work.

Esslin, Martin. *The Theatre of the Absurd*, Doubleday, 1969.
    Esslin's treatise provided the context for a whole new genre within American drama. Albee's work is placed in context with Samuel Beckett, Eugene Ionesco, and Jean Genet.

Kolin, Philip C. *Conversations with Edward Albee*, University Press of Mississippi, 1988.
    This is a wide-ranging collection of interviews with the playwright, conducted by notable playwrights, critics and actors.

Roudane, Matthew Charles. *Understanding Edward Albee*, University of South Carolina Press, 1987.
    Part of the *Understanding Contemporary American Literature* series, Roudane's study analyzes Albee's artistic output from *The Zoo Story* through *The Man Who Had Three Arms*.

Trifles

SUSAN GLASPELL

1916

Susan Glaspell's one-act play, *Trifles,* is based on actual events that occurred in Iowa at the turn of the century. From 1899-1901 Glaspell worked as a reporter for the *Des Moines News,* where she covered the murder trial of a farmer's wife, Margaret Hossack, in Indianola, Iowa. Hossack was accused of killing her husband, John, by striking him twice in the head with an ax while he slept.

Initially it was assumed that burglars had murdered the farmer, but a subsequent sheriff's investigation turned up evidence suggesting Mrs. Hossack was unhappy in her marriage. Ultimately, she was charged with and found guilty of the crime and sentenced to life in prison.

Over the course of sixteen months, Glaspell wrote twenty-six articles covering the case, from the announcement of the murder until Hossack's conviction. The author found herself feeling more and more sympathy for the accused, in spite of the grisly nature of the crime.

Years later, Glaspell and her husband, George Cook, along with some friends, founded the Provincetown Players, an amateur theatrical company on Cape Cod, Massachusetts. In 1916 the group presented a summertime series of plays that included Eugene O'Neill's *Bound East for Cardiff.* In need of a new play to end the season, Cook suggested Glaspell should write a one-act for the company. Her memory of the Hossack trial inspired *Trifles.*

Trifles is a murder mystery that explores gender relationships, power between the sexes, and the nature of truth. In the play, the farmer and his wife never actually appear; instead, the story focuses on the prosecutor, George Henderson, who has been called in to investigate the murder; Henry Peters, the local sheriff; Lewis Hale, a neighboring farmer who discovered Wright's body; and Mrs. Peters and Mrs. Hale, wives to the two local men.

While the men bluster and tramp around the farmhouse searching for clues, the women discover bits of evidence in the "trifles" of a farmer's wife—her baking, cleaning and sewing. Because the men virtually ignore the women's world, they remain blind to the truth before their eyes.

AUTHOR BIOGRAPHY

On July 1, 1882, Susan Glaspell was born in Davenport, Iowa. She excelled in academics as a student, studying Latin and journalism. After graduation from high school, she worked as a newspaper reporter for the *Davenport Morning Republican,* then as the society editor for the *Weekly Outlook.* From 1897-1899 she attended Drake University and received a Ph.D. in Philosophy.

Immediately after college she resumed her career as a journalist, writing for the *Des Moines News.* In 1900 she was assigned to cover the trial of Margaret Hossack, an Iowa farmer's wife accused of murdering her husband while he slept. The trial would later become the basis for Glaspell's short story "A Jury of Her Peers" and one-act play *Trifles.*

Glaspell traveled the world from 1901-1915, working as a freelance author. She spent time in Chicago, New York, Colorado, and Paris, while contributing articles to the *Chicago Daily Review,* as well as national magazines like *Harper's, Leslie's,* and *Munsey's.* In 1913 she married George Cram Cook, a longtime friend who had recently divorced his second wife. The couple settled in New York and spent summers in Provincetown, on Cape Cod, Massachusetts.

Glaspell made quite an impression on the American literary scene in the first few decades of the

Susan Glaspell in 1948

twentieth century. Along with Cook, and the legendary playwright Eugene O'Neill, she helped found the Provincetown Players, an amateur theatre company that was partly responsible for launching the "little theatre" movement across America, and helped define American dramatic literature in the modern era. Eleven of her plays were first produced by the Provincetown Players, including *Trifles, The People, The Outside, Woman's Honor, Bernice, Inheritors,* and *The Verge.*

In 1931 she was awarded the Pulitzer Prize for her play, *Alison's House.* In the full-length drama, the family of a dead poet reflect on her life and writing and discover a greater understanding of love and each other.

Glaspell was a prolific writer. At the time of her death in 1948, she had written fifty short stories, nine novels, and fourteen plays; most of these works feature strong female protagonists and stories that focus on the experiences of women. Perhaps not surprisingly, her work faded from public interest during the conservative 1950s, and practically disappeared from bookshelves and the stages of amateur theatres. Yet in the past few decades, her work is being reexamined and celebrated by a new group of critics and audiences.

PLOT SUMMARY

The setting for *Trifles,* a bleak, untidy kitchen in an abandoned rural farmhouse, quickly establishes the claustrophobic mood of the play. While a cold winter wind blows outside, the characters file in one at a time to investigate a violent murder: the farm's owner, John Wright, was apparently strangled to death while he slept, and his wife, Minnie, has been taken into custody as a suspect in the crime.

The sheriff, Henry Peters, is the first to enter the farmhouse, followed by George Henderson, the attorney prosecuting the case. Lewis Hale, a neighbor, is next to enter. The men cluster around a stove to get warm while they prepare for their investigation.

Mrs. Peters and Mrs. Hale follow the men into the kitchen; yet, they hesitate just inside the door. They are obviously quite disturbed by what has happened in the house and proceed with more care than their husbands.

In a play filled with minor details (trifles) that take on major significance, the entrance of the characters is very revealing. There is an obvious divide—social, psychological, and physical—separating the men from the women, a fact that takes on a larger significance as the play progresses.

The investigation begins with Henderson questioning Lewis, who discovered the murder the day before. Lewis explains that he was on his way into town with a load of potatoes and stopped at the Wright farmhouse to see if John and Minnie wanted to share a telephone line with him, since they were neighbors. The farmer admits that he didn't think John would be interested, since he didn't like to talk much and didn't seem to care about what his wife might want.

When he appeared at the Wright's door early in the morning, he found Minnie rocking nervously in a chair, pleating her apron. When he asked to see her husband, she quietly told Lewis that he was lying upstairs with a rope around his neck, dead.

Lewis summoned his partner, Harry, to check the grisly scene. The two men found John just as his wife described him. Minnie claimed someone strangled him in the middle of the night without disturbing her. "I sleep sound," she explained to her shocked neighbor.

Henderson suggests the men should look around the house for clues, beginning with the bedroom

upstairs and the barn outside. Henry casually dismisses the room where Minnie sat, suggesting there is "nothing here but kitchen things."

It is those very kitchen things, however, which prove to be the most telling clues about what really happened in the Wright farmhouse. Climbing up on a chair to view the top shelf of a cupboard closet, Henderson finds some broken jars of fruit preserves. Mrs. Peters asserts that Minnie was afraid those jars would freeze and break while she was away. "Well, can you beat the woman!" Henry scoffs, "Held for murder and worryin' about her preserves." Lewis chimes in, "Well, women are used to worrying over trifles."

This callous exchange highlights one of Glaspell's most important themes in the play—differences between the sexes—and propels the plot forward into its next stage, the real detective work accomplished by Mrs. Peters and Mrs. Hale.

The men go upstairs to continue their investigation, giving the two women a chance to talk privately for the first time. As they gather things to take to Minnie—a change of clothes, her shawl, and her familiar apron—Mrs. Hale remembers her friend from years ago, before she married John. "She used to wear pretty clothes and be lively, when she was Minnie Foster, one of the town girls singing in the choir," Mrs. Hale recalls.

Minnie married John, who moved her to a lonesome farmhouse at the bottom of a hill. John was, by all accounts, a taciturn man with a violent temper. Under his roof, Minnie no longer socialized, and her gay party attire turned to drab, functional house clothes.

What the men are seeking, Mrs. Peters notes, is evidence of a specific incident that must have sparked the murder. What the women are finding, however, are small signs of detachment and frustration everywhere—a loaf of bread left outside a breadbox, a table partly cleaned, and a piece of quilt with frantic, uneven stitching.

The men return and pass through the kitchen in time to hear the women discussing whether Minnie was going to quilt or knot the sewing project. To them, the question is frivolous, just the sort of thing women use to occupy their time.

While their husbands search for evidence outside the house, Mrs. Peters and Mrs. Hale discover the final, essential clues to the mystery in the kitchen. While looking for some paper and string to wrap Minnie's things, Mrs. Peters discovers an empty birdcage with a broken door in a cupboard.

Neither woman can recall whether she actually had a bird, but Mrs. Hale remembers that Minnie did have a beautiful singing voice when she was younger. Their find takes on tragic significance, however, when Mrs. Hale opens Minnie's sewing box and discovers a small canary wrapped in a piece of silk—with a broken neck.

Suddenly, the men return. Instinctively, Mrs. Hale hides the sewing box under the pieces of quilt. When Henderson notices the cage and asks about the bird, Mrs. Peters joins Mrs. Hale in hiding evidence. ''We think the—cat got it,'' she lies.

The men decide to take one final look around upstairs, leaving the women alone to decide their course of action. Neither will say what is on their minds out loud, but both show understanding and sympathy for the plight of Mrs. Wright.

As a girl, Mrs. Peters remembers a boy killing her kitten with a hatchet, which brings back her feelings of rage and helplessness. She also recalls years of loneliness and desolation, when she and her husband were homesteading in the Dakota plains, and her baby died, leaving her alone in the house.

For her part, Mrs. Hale has vivid memories of Minnie Foster when she was happy and outgoing, before she became Mrs. Wright, imprisoned in this bleak farmhouse, cut off from the world.

The women consider their alternatives: disclose what they know, or cover up the clues that suggest a motive to the crime. Mrs. Peters finds the answer in the men's patronizing treatment. ''My, it's a good thing the men couldn't hear us,'' she says half-jokingly. ''Wouldn't they just laugh! Getting all stirred up over a little thing like a—dead canary.'' Without admitting it aloud, this is the only excuse the women need to keep Minnie's private agony a secret.

The men return once again. Henderson glances quickly at the items Mrs. Peters has collected to take to Minnie, not noticing the sewing box with the dead bird.

While the men take one last look around to examine the windows of the house, Mrs. Peters frantically tries to hide the box in her handbag. It won't fit and she begins to panic. Just as the doorknob turns and the men start back into the room Mrs. Hale finds room for the box in her coat. The trifles are safely hidden.

CHARACTERS

Lewis Hale

Lewis Hale is a farmer and neighbor of the Wright family. A straightforward, honest man, Hale is a bit rough around the edges from the harsh life of a rural farmer.

Hale was the first to discover John's murder when he stopped by the Wright's farmhouse to interest them in sharing a telephone line. He is slow to judgment and hesitant to suggest that Minnie may have been involved somehow.

Mrs. Hale

Mrs. Hale is the wife of Lewis. At first timid, she eventually commits what she thinks is a justifiable crime: a conspiracy to conceal evidence from a murder investigation.

Mrs. Hale accompanies her husband to the crime scene to gather items for the imprisoned Minnie. As the men search the house for clues, however, Mrs. Hale gets frustrated with their patronizing attitude; she understands and empathizes with Minnie's isolation and alienation. In their youth, she was friends with Minnie, who was then a vivacious and interesting girl. She knew Minnie was isolated and probably lonely after her marriage; moreover, she noticed her change into a drab, quiet woman as the years passed.

Of the two women in the play, Mrs. Hale seems to be the more observant and more prone to action. It is she who notices most of the clues first—the bread left outside the box, the hasty quilt stitching, and the dead canary in Mrs. Wright's sewing kit. She is the one who suggests that John was an unhappy, abusive man who may have deserved his fate.

Ultimately, it is Mrs. Hale who hides the dead canary—evidence suggesting a motive for the crime—in her coat pocket to prevent the men from finding it.

George Henderson

George Henderson is the attorney that will eventually prosecute Minnie. He is younger than the other characters; accordingly, he is more brash, sarcastic, and foolish. When questioning Hale about John's murder he misses important details.

Unlike Hale and Peters, Henderson is quick to make judgments. At the end of the play, he mocks

MEDIA ADAPTATIONS

- *Trifles* is based on a Glaspell short story entitled "A Jury of Her Peers." A short film version of *A Jury of Her Peers* was produced in 1981 by Texture Films. The program aired on PBS in 1987.

- Another film adaptation of *A Jury of Her Peers,* entitled *An Eye for an Eye,* was created by Diana Maddox for the Canadian Broadcasting Corporation's "Guest Stage" television series in 1956.

- The Canadian Broadcasting Corporation aired a radio drama version of *Trifles,* directed by Denis Johnston, in February, 1999.

Mrs. Hale and Mrs. Peters for their interest in whether Minnie was going to quilt or knot her sewing project, not realizing the answer was actually one of the clues he was seeking.

Henry Peters

As sheriff in the small, rural town, Henry Peters plays a surprisingly small part in the investigation of John's murder. He visited the farmhouse the day before, found John's body, arrested Minnie, and secured the premises.

The morning of the investigation, Peters sent one of his men out to build a fire and warm the house. Now, he has turned the investigation over to Henderson, and says very little himself.

Mrs. Peters

In some ways, Mrs. Peters is an outsider in this bleak, rural community. Unlike Mrs. Hale, she did not know Minnie as a young woman, and therefore doesn't see the toll living with John had taken on her.

However, she does understand the loneliness and rage Minnie felt. As a child, she watched angrily and helplessly as a boy viciously killed her kitten with a hatchet. Later in life, while she and her husband were living in the Dakota countryside, her two-year-old baby died.

Mrs. Peters begins the play as the cautionary voice of reason, warning Mrs. Hale, "I don't think we ought to touch things." By the end, however, she empathizes with Minnie's actions and helps Mrs. Hale conceal evidence.

THEMES

Gender Differences

Perhaps the single most important theme in *Trifles* is the difference between men and women. The two sexes are distinguished by the roles they play in society, their physicality, their methods of communication and—vital to the plot of the play—their powers of observation.

In simple terms, *Trifles* suggests that men tend to be aggressive, brash, rough, analytical and self-centered; in contrast, women are more circumspect, deliberative, intuitive, and sensitive to the needs of others. It is these differences that allows Mrs. Peters and Mrs. Hale to find the clues needed to solve the crime, while their husbands miss the same clues.

Glaspell differentiates between her male and female antagonists as they enter the Wright farmhouse at the beginning of the play. The men stomp through the door first, and head purposefully toward the stove for warmth. They are the leaders of the community—the sheriff, the local prosecutor, and a neighboring farmer. They get to business immediately, discussing the facts of the case.

Meanwhile the women, perhaps sensing the gloom and terror in the house, enter timidly and stand close to each other just inside the door. They are partly identified by the roles their husbands play. An important detail is they are always referred to by their married names only, and no first names are used.

As the investigation commences, the men seek obvious clues that might suggest a motive for the crime—perhaps indications of alcoholism or physical abuse. Henderson overlooks the small, but significant, clues that tell the real story. He ignores Lewis, who tells him that John never seemed to care what his wife wanted, and dismisses the mess in the kitchen as the result of shoddy housekeeping. When the women rise to Minnie's defense, he even mocks them for simply trying to be "loyal to your sex."

When the men leave the room to examine other parts of the house, the real detective work begins.

TOPICS FOR FURTHER STUDY

- Read John Millington Synge's famous one-act play *Riders to the Sea* and compare it to Glaspell's *Trifles*. How does each play employ symbolism and local color? How is the one-act format important to each work?

- One of the most important characters in *Trifles* is Mrs. Wright, yet she never appears on the stage. Why did Glaspell leave her out of the play? How does her absence impact Mrs. Hale and Mrs. Peters? Discuss the ways the play would be different if Mrs. Wright was present.

- Research the lives of women in rural American communities at the turn of the century. What were typical tasks assigned to women? How did the requirements of frontier life determine the role women played in the family? Explore how the frontier experience affected the decisions made by Mrs. Peters and Mrs. Hale in the play.

- *Trifles* contains several important *symbols*. In literature, a symbol is something that represents something else, and is often used to communicate deeper levels of meaning. What are some of the important symbols in *Trifles?* How does Glaspell use these symbols to propel the plot, and convey deeper levels of meaning about her characters or themes?

The women discuss Minnie as she used to be—a happy, young girl in pretty clothes who sang in the town choir. Because their lives are also focused on the home, Mrs. Peters and Mrs. Hale are able to interpret some of the silent cries for help that the men were unable to see or hear.

By the time they find the damaged birdcage and the dead canary, Mrs. Peters and Mrs. Hale know the truth: John Wright drove his wife to murder him by isolating her from her friends and depriving her of beauty and song. The "trifles" of the play embody the possessive, patronizing attitude men sometimes have toward the lives of women.

Isolation

The devastating effects of isolation—especially on women—is another theme of the play. The men seem better suited to the loneliness and isolation of rural farming. John Wright, for example, is described as a hard-working farmer who kept to himself. He did not share a telephone line, and no one other than his wife knew him very well.

The women, on the other hand, are deeply affected by isolation. Mrs. Peters remembers with dread when she and her husband were homesteading in the Dakota countryside and her only child died,

leaving her alone in the house all day while her husband was out working the farm. Mrs. Hale, who has several children of her own, imagines how terrible it would be to have to live in an empty house, like Minnie, with nothing but a canary and a taciturn man for company.

For Minnie, isolation drove her to murder. Remembered by Mrs. Hale as a happy, outgoing young girl in pretty clothes, Minnie Foster's whole life changed when she married John. They lived in a gloomy farmhouse "down in a hollow" where Minnie couldn't even see the road. No one came to visit, and she did not go out. The couple was childless, and John killed the only other life in the house: the canary his wife bought to sing to her and ease her lonely mind.

STYLE

One-Act Play

The *structure* of a play affects all of its most important elements—the plot, characters, and themes. An episodic play, such as William Shakespeare's *Hamlet,* requires many twists and turns of plot, numerous characters and locations, and great stretches of time in order for the story to unfold. A climactic play, such as Sophocles's famous tragedy *Oedipus Rex,* typically presents only a handful of characters involved in a single plot, which builds toward a climax—the most important moment in the play.

One of the most restrictive forms is the one-act play, a style favored by *Trifles* author Susan Glaspell. In every respect the one-act play is more tightly compressed than a full-length climactic Greek tragedy. Because one-acts are typically short, with playing times of fifteen to forty-five minutes, the number of characters introduced must be limited, and their personalities must be developed quickly.

Glaspell takes full advantage of this limitation in *Trifles.* The men in the play are stereotypical characters. Their actions and words immediately suggest personalities that are condescending, egotistical, and self-important. The women, meanwhile, begin the play timidly, allowing their husbands to blunder about the crime scene. Then, given the chance to be alone, they open up to each other and show a strong sense of female intuition that allows them to solve the play's mystery very quickly.

Because of the limited time frame, the one-act format also tends to focus on a single location and a tight plot. Each of these aspects holds true for *Trifles.* There is a single setting, the Wright farmhouse, which is located in the countryside and set back from the road, a lonely, desolate place. The plot involves seeking clues to suggest a motive for the murder of John Wright. Furthermore, there are no unimportant words or actions. Everything that is said and done, from the way the characters enter Mrs. Wright's kitchen to the discovery of her dead canary, relates in some way to the mystery at hand.

Local Color

In the late nineteenth century, a popular style of writing known as ''local color'' emerged, a style characterized by its vivid description of some of the more idiosyncratic communities in the American landscape. Writers such as Bret Harte, Mark Twain, and Nathaniel Hawthorne created characters whose speech and attitudes reflected the deep South, the western frontier, or New England Puritanism. Their short stories and novels particularly appealed to people in larger cities, who found these descriptions of faraway places exotic and entertaining.

Susan Glaspell began writing during this age of regionalism, and *Trifles* incorporates many of the elements of local color: regional dialect, appropri-ate costuming, and characters influenced by a specific locale.

Trifles is filled with a strong sense of *place.* The characters in the play are deeply rooted in their rural environment. Lewis Hale was on his way into town with a load of potatoes when he stopped by the Wright's house to see about sharing a party line telephone, a common way for people in small communities to afford phone service during the first few decades of the century. The lives of the women seem to consist of housekeeping chores, food preparation, sewing, and raising children, with little time left for socializing.

The characters' manner of speech reveals their limited education and rural, Midwestern environment. They use a colloquial grammar peppered with country slang. ''I don't think a place'd be any cheerfuller for John Wright's being in it,'' Mrs. Hale tells Henderson. Their lives, too, have been deeply affected by their regional experiences. While homesteading in the Dakota countryside, Mrs. Peter's two-year-old baby died, leaving her alone in the house while her husband was away.

Still, at the same time that she provides these carefully crafted details of country life, Glaspell provides her audience with ideas that transcend local color. The struggle between the sexes, loneliness, and the elusive nature of truth are all experiences shared by people across cultures and boundaries of geography.

HISTORICAL CONTEXT

Women's Issues

In many ways, Susan Glaspell's success at the turn of the century signaled a new age for women, and *Trifles,* still her best-known play, represents the struggles women of her era faced. Born in 1876, Glaspell's grandparents were some of the pioneers who settled her hometown of Davenport, Iowa.

In an age when few women went to college, and even fewer actually sought careers beyond menial labor outside the home, Glaspell did both, graduating from Drake University with a Ph.D. in Philosophy in 1899, and immediately embarking on a lifetime of freelance journalism, playwriting, and fiction writing.

In 1916, the year Glaspell wrote *Trifles* for the Provincetown Players, some of the important issues

COMPARE
&
CONTRAST

- 1916: In the United States, the women's rights movement began in earnest in the nineteenth century. Margaret Sanger opens the first birth control clinic in 1916. In 1920 the 19th Amendment gives women the right to vote. The average life expectancy for men is 53.5 years; for women it is 55 years.

    Today: Women have made great strides worldwide, and their average life expectancy remains 2-3 years longer than that of men (both are expected to live well past age seventy). The Supreme Court's decision in *Roe v. Wade* (1973) gives women the right to choose an abortion during the first few months of pregnancy.

- 1916: In cities, dance halls are popular places for young men women. "Ragtime" music moves into mainstream America in 1911 when Irving Berlin writes a syncopated dance tune called "Alexander's Ragtime Band." The sheet music to the song sells more than a million copies.

    Today: Rap is a very popular musical genre in America. Like the ragtime music at the turn of the century, rap has its roots in black American culture, but has fans in all segments of society. While overall music sales increase a mere 9%, rap music boasts a 31% gain.

- 1916: Alcohol abuse is deemed one of the biggest problems faced by Americans. As a result, twenty-three states have anti-saloon laws in 1916. By 1919, the 18th Amendment to the Constitution is passed, prohibiting the "manufacture, sale, or transportation of intoxicating liquors." Prohibition begins in 1920. Thirteen years later the "experiment" is considered an economic and social disaster, and Prohibition is repealed in 1933.

    Today: America's "War on Drugs" is often thought of as the new Prohibition. Between 1980-1995 the U.S. government spends over $300 billion trying to rid the country of illegal drugs, particularly marijuana and cocaine. As a result of the drug trade in America's inner cities, minorities are particularly affected by drug convictions. Many groups across the country are calling for legalization of various controlled substances, particularly marijuana.

- 1916: Movies are a very popular genre of entertainment. Each week, nearly thirty million Americans see black-and-white film comedies, documentaries, or full-length features. A film studio might gross as much as $3 million in a year, while top stars might receive weekly salaries of $3,000.

    Today: Entertainment, particularly movies and music, is America's second leading export product behind the aerospace industry, grossing billions of dollars each year. A major motion picture might cost over $100 million to film and market, and its leading stars might receive salaries of $10-20 million or more. The most expensive film in Hollywood history is made in 1997. *Titanic* is a financial gamble at over $200 million but earns nearly $400 million in gross sales.

- 1916: In 1912 there are 900,000 automobiles registered in the United States. With the advent of the production innovations-in particular, the assembly line-automobile production increases drastically. By 1919 the number of cars registered soars to 6.7 million. The Model T is the most popular automobile, priced at $850 and available in a single color: black.

    Today: The assembly of cars has become more complicated as automotive technology has grown more complex. In response to environmental protection laws, General Motors introduces the first all-electric car, the EV1, in 1996. Capable of traveling only a hundred miles between charges, and accelerating to only about 55 miles per hour, the cars are not immediately successful.

of the day were women's suffrage, birth control, socialism, union organizing, and the psychological theories of Sigmund Freud. Women had not yet achieved the right to vote, and in most states women could not sit on juries. It wasn't until 1920 that the 19th Amendment granted women the right to vote.

Only a year after she was jailed for writing *Family Limitation,* the first book on birth control, Margaret Sanger opened America's first birth control clinic in Brooklyn, New York. Charged with "maintaining a public nuisance," she was once again arrested, and served thirty days in the Queens County Penitentiary. It wasn't until 1973 that the Supreme Court's *Roe v. Wade* decision gave women the right to choose an abortion during the first few months of pregnancy.

Life in America's industrial cities was harsh. Manufacturing jobs paid only a few dollars a day for 10-12 hours of work, and children under fourteen constituted a sizable portion of America's workforce. The factory system created wage-earning opportunities for women, leading to a chance for financial independence.

Yet women earned significantly less than their male counterparts, and most were relegated to jobs in domestic service, textile factories, or offices. Unfortunate women often found themselves working in "sweatshops," small factories that forced employees to spend long hours in a dirty, unsafe environment for substandard wages.

Life for rural women, as shown by Mrs. Peters and Mrs. Hale in *Trifles,* was not much better. A large portion of America's population was still scattered in rural towns, ranches, and farmsteads across the country at the turn of the century. Women were largely responsible for the maintenance of the family, including cleaning, laundry, food preparation, and childcare. They often had to make clothes and bedding for families.

Farming could be lonely life for women. In *Trifles,* Mrs. Peters, whose husband is now the sheriff of their small community, remembers when she and her family were homesteaders in the Dakota territory, and her first baby died, leaving her alone in the house most of the day while her husband worked outside. Another character, Minnie, is driven to kill her husband as a result of the hopelessness and desperation she feels from her isolated and joyless life.

In dramatizing the lives of these rural women, Glaspell captured an intimate portrait of American history on the stage. She also contributed to a significant literary and artistic event: America's "Little Theatre Movement." *Trifles* was produced by the Provincetown Players, an amateur, experimental group of actors, designers, and playwrights Glaspell and her husband, George Cook, had assembled at their vacation home on Cape Cod, Massachusetts.

The goal of the Provincetown Players was to present plays by new American writers, relying on innovative scenery and staging techniques. The group moved to Greenwich Village in New York City in the fall of 1916 and remained active until 1929, helping to launch the careers of such notable authors as Eugene O'Neill, e. e. cummings, Edna Ferber, and Edna St. Vincent Millay.

At the same time that the Provincetown Players were finding success in New York, similar "little theatres" began springing up around the country. The Toy Theatre in Boston and the Chicago Little Theatre opened in 1912; and the Detroit Arts and Crafts Theatre opened in 1916. By 1917, nearly fifty such organizations were producing plays in what would become, by the end of the century, a diverse network of regional theaters across America, offering quality alternatives to community theaters and standard Broadway fare.

CRITICAL OVERVIEW

Unfortunately, there has never been a high-profile performance of *Trifles* in a major, mainstream theatrical venue, so production reviews are scarce and tend to describe performances at regional, amateur theaters, and colleges across the country. Most critical commentary has focused on the *published* literary work and its contributions to feminist thought and literature.

In a preface to a collection of essays, *Susan Glaspell: Essays on Her Theater and Fiction,* contemporary playwright Megan Terry lauded Glaspell's work. She maintained:

> I admire the control, the precision and the power of *Trifles.* It never tires. It seems to be a perfect play and accomplishes all the playwright's intentions. It is a model of subtlety and understatement. I marvel at its compactness and perfection, and the satisfaction it conveys to the reader or audience in the sure achievement of its creator. The play is more than an inspiration, it's a quiet, firm and constant standard to match. The wry warmth of her mind, the compassion of her heart combine with the architecture of her play to give

you a total feeling of these Mid-West people. The work is suffused with the sense of justice, wit, and fairness Glaspell must have possessed as a person.

This sentiment is echoed in the work of other critics. In an essay from the same collection of essays, Linda Ben-Zvi was encouraged by the playwright's portrayal of women in *Trifles,* particularly in the actions of Mrs. Peters and Mrs. Hale at the end of the play. "Glaspell does not actually present the victimization of women or the violent acts such treatment may engender," Ben-Zvi noted, "instead, she stages the potential for female action and the usurpation of power. By having the women assume the central positions and conduct the investigation and the trial, she actualizes an empowerment that suggests that there are options short of murder that can be imagined for women."

Ben-Zvi examined the Hossack murder trial that inspired Glaspell to write *Trifles.* She also explored the role of women at the turn of the century and found parallels with the lives of women in the present day.

She asserted: "It is either a testament to the skill with which Glaspell constructed *Trifles* and "A Jury of Her Peers" or proof of how little women's lives have changed since 1916 that contemporary feminist critics still use the play and story as palimpsests for their own readings of contemporary feminist issues, and these readings still point to some of the dilemmas that faced Glaspell and her personae in 1901 and 1916."

Elaine Hedges, in an essay titled "Small Things Reconsidered: 'A Jury of Her Peers'," agreed that the most important theme of the story is the role of women in society—then or now—and praises Glaspell's mastery of local color. "Women's role, or 'place,' in society, their confinement and isolation, the psychic violence wrought against them, their power or powerlessness vis-à-vis men, are not concerns restricted to Glaspell's time and place," Hedges asserted, "But these concerns achieve their imaginative force and conviction in her story by being firmly rooted in, and organically emerging from, the carefully observed, small details of a localized way of life."

From the baking shelf in Minnie's kitchen, to her apron, shawl, and pieces of quilt, it is the rural environment and the tiny details of life on a Midwestern farm that speak volumes about the plight of women on the American frontier.

Liza Maeve Nelligan maintained that those same details reinforce the idea of women as mere household objects. In "The Haunting Beauty from the Life We've Left: A Contextual Reading of *Trifles* and *The Verge*," Nelligan suggested, "*Trifles* neatly encapsulates what historians have named the 'cult of domesticity' of the nineteenth century." Accordingly, women were "pious, gentle, instinctive and submissive than men," and therefore suited to creating and maintaining a nurturing home environment.

While on the surface this may sound condescending and limiting, in practice, Nelligan contended, it may also have provided women a stronger common bond and purer sense of propriety and justice. "Clearly," Nelligan wrote, "Glaspell intended to show that women in the domestic sphere were vulnerable to the brutality of men like John Wright, but she also dramatizes the powerful sense of solidarity women shared and assumes that this solidarity was somehow responsible for superior female morality."

The same culture that largely confined women to the home, also excluded them from the ballot box and the courtroom. Karen Alkalay-Gut explored the *legal* issues of a play that presents the inconsistency of America's legal system at the turn of the century, when women could be tried for crimes, but were forbidden to vote for judges or sit on juries themselves. "The objective plot of Glaspell's most successful play, *Trifles,* is very much at odds with the triviality of the title," Alkalay-Gut asserted.

To her, the conundrum of the female characters in the play is no trifling matter. She contended: "Women, in the context of *Trifles* and even more in the story "Jury of Her Peers," are trapped by a social system that may lead them into crime and punish them when they are forced to commit it. It is this situation of the double bind with which the women of the play identify and which readers and audiences continue to explore."

CRITICISM

Lane A. Glenn
Lane A. Glenn is a Ph.D. specializing in theatre history and literature. In this essay he explores the dubious moral message of Susan Glaspell's Trifles.

Susan Glaspell's *Trifles* concerns a woman who was once young, pretty, and outgoing until she found herself in a loveless marriage with a stern,

WHAT DO I READ NEXT?

- *Trifles* is an adaptation of "A Jury of Her Peers," a short story based on an actual trial Glaspell covered as a reporter in Des Moines, Iowa.

- Other Glaspell plays include *The Outside, The Verge, Inheritors,* and *Alison's House,* which earned her the Pulitzer Prize in 1931.

- John Millington Synge's *Riders to the Sea* is a well-written one-act mystery play. In Synge's play, the women of the Aran Islands watch helplessly as their husbands and sons sacrifice their lives to the sea as fishermen.

- *Fried Green Tomatoes at the Whistle Stop Cafe* by Fannie Flagg, is a novel chronicling the story of Idgie and Ruth, two women who fight sexism and racism in a small Alabama town in the 1930s.

- Eugene O'Neill is one of the most recognized names in American drama, and certainly the most famous playwright to emerge from the Provincetown Players, the small amateur theater company Glaspell helped create in 1915. Like Glaspell, O'Neill wrote several one-act, "slice of life" plays that were first performed in Provincetown, including *Bound East for Cardiff, In the Zone, The Long Voyage Home,* and *The Moon of the Caribbees.*

- Sandra Dallas's *The Diary of Mattie Spenser* is the fictional account, told in diary form, of an Iowa woman who weds in 1865. After her marriage, she travels with her husband to the Colorado Territories, builds a sod house, raises children, and encounters all the hazards of the nineteenth-century American wilderness.

---

anti-social farmer. Her isolation, the gloom of her surroundings, and her husband's dispassion slowly drove her to the brink of insanity. She tried to fend off her depression with bits of gaiety—brightly colored quilting and a caged songbird—but when her husband, in a sudden act of aggression, broke the cage and killed the bird and its singing, she was driven over the edge.

In the middle of the night, she slipped a noose around her husband's neck, and strangled him in his sleep. When the county prosecutor arrives with the town's sheriff and a local farmer to investigate the scene, their wives quickly discover the miserable life Mrs. Wright led, and choose to hide the evidence of her crime.

For all its protestations about the treatment of women in rural America at the turn of the century, and in spite of the nearly unanimous approval of the play's final outcome among feminist literary critics, there is something unsavory about the resolution of *Trifles.* The most shocking and irresponsible act in the play is not John Wright's mental abuse of his wife, Minnie, nor is it even the murder itself, which happened before the play actually begins.

The most shocking act is the deliberate cover-up of Mrs. Wright's heinous act by two well intentioned but ultimately criminal conspirators. Their decision to cloak Mrs. Wright from the prying, but bumbling, eyes of the men in the play suggests a dubious sense of morality, and poses a frightening model of vigilante justice that, if widely adopted by those who felt neglected or marginalized, would seriously undermine the efforts of any judicial system.

Everything about *Trifles,* from its harsh treatment of its two-dimensional male characters to the play's final words, Mrs. Hale's clever, sarcastic remark, "We call it—knot it, Mr. Henderson," suggests the audience should endorse, even applaud these women for their shrewdness and loyalty to their sex.

Yet what, really, is their accomplishment? In rationalizing and justifying Minnie Wright's actions, then concealing evidence from her investigators, these formerly innocent, law-abiding Midwestern farm wives have become accomplices to a grisly murder. In seeking retribution for perceived oppression, and in trying to *reform* society, they have actually denigrated the moral fiber of their world.

Interestingly, in the years since *Trifles* was first produced, many scholars have found reason after reason to condone the actions of Mrs. Peters and Mrs. Hale. Intentionally or not, Glaspell has encouraged successive generations of critical scofflaws.

Feminist critics in particular have suggested a variety of people to blame for the crime of murder, other than Minnie Wright. According to these sympathetic scholars, John Wright, her difficult husband, Mrs. Peters, Mrs. Hale, and the town that abandoned her all contributed to the inevitable tragedy.

In an essay entitled ''A Map for Rereading: Or, Gender and the Interpretation of Literary Texts,'' Annette Kolodny suggests, ''The essential crime in the story, we come to realize, has been the husband's inexorable strangulation, over the years, of Minnie Foster's spirit and personality; and the culpable criminality is the complicity of the women who had permitted the isolation and the loneliness to dominate Minnie Foster's existence. . . .''

Kolodny employs one of the most important ruses of creative defense attorneys: create sympathy for the defendant, and cast the blame somewhere else. She even goes so far as to propose that ''the ending is a happy one: Minnie Foster is to be set free, no motive having been discovered by which to prosecute her.''

Karen F. Stein echoes Kolodny's judgment in ''The Women's World of Glaspell's *Trifles*.'' She observes, ''The lack of a telephone, the shabby furniture, the much-mended clothing, and a canary with a broken neck bear mute but telling witness to the harsh meanness and cruelty of John Wright. Considering Minnie her husband's victim (like her symbolic analogue, the strangled songbird), the women conspire to hide the evidence they discover.'' Taking her simple description of the play's action and symbolism a step further, Stein explains, ''Through the women's identification with her, we understand Minnie's desperate loneliness, which drove her to do away with her brutal husband.''

In her introduction to *Trifles* in *Images of Women in Literature,* Mary Anne Ferguson congratulates Mrs. Peters and Mrs. Hale for their service to women everywhere. ''Through their concern for another woman and their decision to aid her, the

> IN THE NINETEENTH CENTURY, WOMEN WERE WIDELY CONSIDERED TO BE NATURALLY MORALLY SUPERIOR TO MEN—A CONDITION THAT DID NOT EARN THEM MORE RIGHTS OR PRIVILEGES BUT RAISED EXPECTATIONS OF THEIR BEHAVIOR IN DOMESTIC SETTINGS"

women in Susan Glaspell's *Trifles* rise above male perceptions of them as ludicrously inferior,'' Ferguson contends. ''Their awareness comes through shared anger at the men's views, and their actions invalidate the stereotype of women as 'fuzzy' thinkers concerned only with trifles. . . . The play shows that 'sisterhood is powerful' by belying the conception that women are catty among other women.''

Perhaps it should not be surprising that the clearly immoral acts of Mrs. Peters and Mrs. Hale elicit sympathy, and even applause, from many critics and readers of *Trifles*. Glaspell has, after all, created a decidedly slanted, one-sided murder mystery out of a relationship that must have been more complex than the carefully scattered, symbolic clues it left behind.

The playwright builds support for the undeniably guilty Minnie Wright slowly and deliberately, one clue at a time, in order to allow resentment against the real victim of this crime—the murdered Mr. Wright—to fester in the minds of the audience.

By the time all the evidence has been assembled—the lonely location of the Wright farmhouse, Mr. Wright's gruff personality, his wife's shabby clothes, and the strangulation of a canary—Minnie Wright has been built up as a martyr for victimized women everywhere. Her husband, on the other hand, has become an icon of aggression, cruelty, and masculine oppression. With no one to speak for him in front of ''a jury of her peers,'' Mrs. Wright's husband never stood a chance.

The absence of Minnie Wright from the action of the play is another shrewd manipulation of emotion by Glaspell. Without her presence on the stage, the audience must construct its own impression of her character from the comments of the other women and the clues as they are found. Given this one-sided information, she becomes a sort of ''Everywoman,'' an amalgamation of all women who have ever been lonely, in loveless marriages, or perhaps even abused by men.

In actuality, though, how far removed is Mrs. Wright from the ax-wielding Lizzie Borden, who murdered her parents in their sleep one night in 1892, then was acquitted of her crime because no one could believe a woman was capable of such an atrocity?

The guilt or innocence of the women of *Trifles* is not the central issue for every critic of the play. Linda Ben-Zvi, editor of *Susan Glaspell: Essays on Her Theater and Fiction,* and author of an essay titled, '''Murder, She Wrote': The Genesis of Susan Glaspell's *Trifles*,'' chose the middle ground. In her essay, which compares Glaspell's play to the actual events it is based on, she asserts that Glaspell was not seeking to either convict or pardon Minnie Wright, but to perform a much greater service for women everywhere by reminding them of the state of gender relations:

> Whether Margaret Hossack or Minnie Wright committed murder is moot; what is incontrovertible is the brutality of their lives, the lack of options they had to redress grievances or to escape abusive husbands, and the complete disregard of their plight by the courts and by society. Instead of arguing their innocence, Glaspell concretizes the conditions under which these women live and the circumstances that might cause them to kill.

Ben-Zvi casts a long shadow of blame across a society that would push these women to such an act of desperation. She, like many critics before her, attempts to construct a defense that relies on extenuating circumstances—justifiable homicide prompted by neglect and misery.

In so doing, she excuses the relative immorality of the play itself. ''By having Mrs. Peters and Mrs. Hale unequivocally assume Minnie's guilt and also assume justification for her act,'' Ben Zvi continues, ''Glaspell presents her audience/jury with a defense that forces it to confront the central issues of female powerlessness and disenfranchisement and the need for laws to address such issues.'' In other words, because the play serves a higher purpose—the enlightenment of disenfranchised women everywhere—its crimes should be excused.

The problem underlying the behavior of the women in *Trifles* is the inherent contradictions in their actions. They claim the moral high ground, and indeed, until they actually commit the crime of hiding evidence in a murder investigation, they are probably guiltless people. But their unfortunate choice to commit the crime pulls them down from the height of moral purity to the depths of criminal depravity. They become no better than the murderess herself.

In the nineteenth century, women were widely considered to be naturally morally superior to men—a condition that did not earn them more rights or privileges but raised expectations of their behavior in domestic settings. In ''Gender Ideology and Dramatic Convention in Progressive Era Plays, 1890-1920,'' Judith L. Stephens suggests that a play like *Trifles* ironically defeats its own goal of liberating women from oppressive male stereotypes because it assumes some of the very stereotypes of women that were promoted by a male-dominated society.

In other words, by depicting the men in the play off as foolish and crude, and elevating the women to the status of clever sleuths, charged with defending one of their own against an unjustly oppressive male-dominated world, the play inadvertently promotes that which it seeks to undermine. Women are not morally superior to men, any more than men are intellectually superior to women, simply by virtue of their gender.

Stephens finds it regrettable that, by allowing the women in *Trifles* to subvert conventional law, Glaspell perpetuates the idea that men and women exist in separate spheres, forever isolated by uncontrollable differences. ''By finding and concealing the incriminating evidence,'' Stephens insists, ''the women win their own individual victory, but the system continues intact.'' Like the murderer Minnie Wright, they may have won the battle, but they have ultimately lost the war.

Source: Lane A. Glenn, for *Drama for Students*, Gale, 2000.

Judith Kay Russell

In this essay, Russell compares the three female characters in Glaspell's play to female characters of Greek mythology. The critic cites numerous examples from the text that support her thesis.

On the surface, Susan Glaspell's one-act play *Trifles* focuses on the death of an oppressive husband at the hands of his emotionally abused wife in an isolated and remote farm in the midwest. Beneath the surface, the collective behaviors of Mrs. Hale, Mrs. Peters, and Mrs. Wright in Glaspell's play bear strong resemblance to those of the Fates (Clotho the Spinner, Lachesis the Disposer of Lots, and Atropos the Cutter of the Thread) in Greek mythology. Although Glaspell brings new vigor to the myth, the attention given to Mrs. Hale's resewing the quilt, the change in Mrs. Peters's perspective on law and justice, and the rope placed by Mrs. Wright around her husband's neck are nonetheless grounded in the story of the Three Sisters who control the fate of men.

Mrs. Hale embodies the qualities of Clotho the Spinner, the sister who spins the thread of life. Mrs. Hale subtly suggests that Mrs. Wright is not the sole agent in the death of Mr. Wright. On the surface, Mrs. Hale's ungrammatical reference to that event, ''when they was slipping the rope under his neck'' (79), can be attributed to improper subject and verb agreement, which is not uncommon in certain regional dialects. However, the use of the plural pronoun and singular verb subtly suggests the involvement of more than one in a single outcome, and it foreshadows the conspiracy of the three women and their efforts to control the outcome or the fate of all characters. Furthermore, the information concerning the domestic life of the Wrights is supplied, or spun, mainly by Mrs. Hale; she describes Mr. Wright as ''a hard man'' and, with her recollections of the young Minnie Foster (now Mrs. Wright) as ''kind of like a bird'' (82), she establishes the connection of Mr. Wright's involvement in the physical death of the canary and spiritual death of his wife. The condescending manner in which the men joke about the women's concern regarding Mrs. Wright's intention ''to quilt or just knot'' the quilt evokes a defensive remark from Mrs. Hale in which she hints that it is unwise to tempt fate; she asserts, ''I don't see as it's anything to laugh about'' (79–80). Finally, by ''just pulling out a stitch or two that's not sewed very good'' and replacing it with her own stitching (80), Mrs. Hale symbolically claims her position as the person who spins the thread of life.

The second member of the Three Sisters, Lachesis the Disposer of Lots, is personified by Mrs. Peters. The viability of the thread spun by Mrs. Hale depends on the actions and reactions of Mrs. Peters. To claim her position as the member of the Fates responsible for assigning destiny, she must abandon objectivity and move toward subjectivity. Her objectivity is exemplified by her assertion that ''the law is the law'' and her view on physical

> ALTHOUGH SOME BELIEVE THAT THE POWER OF THE THREE SISTERS RIVALS THAT OF ZEUS, GLASPELL REMINDS HER AUDIENCE THAT, REGARDLESS OF MYTH OR TWENTIETH-CENTURY LAW, IT STILL TAKES THREE WOMEN TO EQUAL ONE MAN. THAT IS THE INEQUALITY ON WHICH SHE FOCUSES''

evidence as she informs Mrs. Hale, ''I don't think we ought to touch things'' (79–80). The sight of the dead canary and the recognition that ''somebody—wrung—its—neck'' marks Mrs. Peters's initiation into subjectivity and the sisterhood (83). The discovery of the dead bird awakens Mrs. Peters's suppressed childhood memories of rage toward the ''boy [who] took a hatchet'' and brutally killed her kitten (83). In her mind, the kitten, Mrs. Wright, and the bird become enmeshed. Mrs. Peters realizes that the dead bird will be used to stereotype Mrs. Wright as a madwoman who overreacts to ''trifles.'' At this point, Mrs. Peters emerges from the shadow of her role as the sheriff's wife and becomes ''married to the law'' (85). Her new concept of law subjectively favors justice over procedure. She claims her position as the sister who dispenses the lots in life when she moves to hide the bird and thus denies the men ''something to make a story about'' (85).

Mrs. Wright represents Atropos the Cutter of the Thread. Symbolically, Mrs. Wright is first linked to Atropos in Mr. Hale's description of her ''rockin' back and forth'' (73), a motion similar to that made by cutting with scissors. The connection to Atropos is further established when Mrs. Peters discovers the dead bird in Mrs. Wright's sewing box and exclaims, ''Why, this isn't her scissors'' (83). Ironically, the dead canary takes the place of the scissors: The death of the bird is directly tied to the fate of Mr. Wright. In addition, Mrs. Wright assumes mythical status through her spiritual presence and physical absence from the stage. Mr. Hale relates that in his questioning of Mrs. Wright, she admits that her husband ''died of a rope round his neck,'' but she doesn't know how it happened because she "didn't wake up"; she is a sound sleeper (74–75). Mrs. Wright denies personal involvement in the death of her husband, yet she acknowledges that he died while she slept beside him in the bed. Mrs. Wright says, "I was on the inside" (75). Although she may be referring to her routine "inside" position of sleep behind her husband in the bed placed along the wall, Mrs. Wright's statement suggests a movement from the outside (her individual consciousness) to the inside (the collective consciousness of the Fates). Her involvement with the rope of death is the equivalent of severing the thread of life. She did not spin the thread, nor did she assign the lot; she merely contributed a part to the whole, and that collective whole becomes greater than the sum of its parts. For this reason, Mrs. Wright is correct in denying individual knowledge or responsibility in the death of her husband.

In *Trifles,* Mrs. Hale weaves the story or describes the circumstances, Mrs. Peters weighs the evidence and determines the direction of justice, and Mrs. Wright carries out the verdict; although the procedure is somewhat reversed, the mythic ritual is performed nevertheless. Susan Glaspell's use of the Fates, or the Three Sisters, does not weaken her dramatization of women who are oppressed by men. Although some believe that the power of the Three Sisters rivals that of Zeus, Glaspell reminds her audience that, regardless of myth or twentieth-century law, it still takes three women to equal one man. That is the inequality on which she focuses.

Source: Judith Kay Russell. "Glaspell's *Trifles* in the *Explicator,* Vol. 55, no. 2, Winter, 1997, pp. 88–90.

Phyllis Mael

Mael examines Glaspell's play and a recent film adaptation by Sally Heckel within the context of feminist writings; the critic notes Glaspell's prescient accuracy in charting feminist doctrines.

In 1916 Susan Glaspell wrote "*Trifles,*" a one-act play to complete the bill at the Wharf Theatre (the other play was *Bound East for Cardiff* by Eugene O'Neill). One commentator on Glaspell's work believes the play was originally intended as a short story, but, according to Glaspell, "the stage took it for its own." In 1917, however, Glaspell rewrote the work as a short story, "Jury of Her Peers," which appeared in *Best Short Stories of 1917.* That work was adapted by Sally Heckel in 1981 for her Academy-Award nominated film.

The setting for all three works is the same: a gloomy farmhouse kitchen belonging to John Wright, recently strangled, and his wife Minnie, now being held in prison for the crime. Three men enter the set: one, the neighboring farmer who discovered the body; another the district attorney; and a third, the sheriff. Two women accompany them: Mrs. Hale, the farmer's wife and childhood friend of Minnie and Mrs. Peters, the sheriff's wife. While the men search the bedroom and barn for clues to a possible motive for the murder, the women move about the kitchen, reconstructing Minnie's dismal life. Through their attentiveness to the "trifles" in her life, the kitchen things considered insignificant by the men, the two women piece together, like patches in a quilt, the events which may have led to the murder. And because they empathize with the missing woman, having lived similar though different lives, they make a moral decision to hide potentially incriminating evidence.

It is unlikely that had either woman been alone, she would have had sufficient understanding or courage to make the vital decision, but as the trifles reveal the arduousness of Minnie's life (and by implication of their own), a web of sisterhood is woven which connects the lives of all three enabling Mrs. Hale and Peters to counter patriarchal law, a decision particularly weighty for Mrs. Peters, who, as she is reminded by the district attorney, is "married to the law."

Having taught both play and short story in my "Images of Women in Literature" classes, I am continually amazed at the power of Glaspell's feminist understanding of the difficult decision with which the two early twentieth century rural women struggle. The volatile discussions which accompany class readings of these works, the questioning of the legality and morality of the women's choice, attest to the relevance of the issues Glaspell raises.

Current feminist research in developmental psychology can help increase our admiration for Glaspell's challenging presentation of the moral dilemma and the way in which Minnie's trifles raise the consciousness of both women, especially Mrs. Peters, moving them from awareness to anger to action. This research can also help us better appreciate Sally Heckel's recent adaptation of these issues to the medium of film, more specifically her use of close-up and composition within the frame, to provide a cinematic equivalent of Glaspell's statements in drama and prose.

Freud would not have been surprised by the decision taken by Mrs. Hale and Peters for in 1925 he wrote that women's superego was never ''so inexorable, so impersonal, so independent of its emotional origins as we require it to be in men . . . for women the level of what is ethically normal is different from what it is in men . . . women show less sense of justice than men . . . they are less ready to submit to the great exigencies of life . . . they are more often influenced in their judgment by feelings of affection or hostility.'' Freud's use of value-laden terms such as ''less'' emerges from a vision of moral development based upon a male model which tends ''to regard male behavior as the 'norm' and female behavior as some kind of deviation from that norm.''

Freud's model of mature moral development as ''inexorable . . . impersonal . . . independent of emotional origins'' reappears in the 1960s as the sixth or post-conventional stage of Lawrence Kohlberg's six stages of moral development. Not surprisingly, when women are given Kohlberg's test, they rarely attain the sixth stage where decisions are based upon universal ethical principles but typically are stuck at the third and fourth (or conventional) levels where decisions are based upon contextual concerns.

But Kohlberg's moral scale in turn relies upon a model of human development such as Erik Erikson's ''expansion of Freud'' where separation, not relationship, becomes the model and measure of growth. Freud, Erickson, and Kohlberg, although recognizing that women's development is different from men's, present their model, based upon male experience, as universal.

Recent feminist research in developmental psychology challenges the sexual asymmetry of the patriarchal view in which male development is the norm and women's development is perceived (as with Freud) as ''less.'' Of particular value for a discussion of Glaspell's and Heckel's works are Nancy Chodorow's writings on gender development and Carol Gilligan's on moral development.

According to Chodorow, the ''process of becoming a male or female someone in the world begins in infancy with a sense of 'oneness,' a 'primary identification' . . . with the person responsible for early care. Emerging from this phase, every child faces the challenge of separation: distinguishing *self* from *other*. . . . Because women are the primary caretakers of children, that first 'other' is almost without exception female; consequently, boys and girls experience individuation and relationship

FIFTY YEARS BEFORE THE CURRENT WOMEN'S MOVEMENT, SUSAN GLASPELL UNDERSTOOD HOW CONSCIOUSNESS RAISING COULD EMPOWER WOMEN TO TAKE ACTIONS TOGETHER WHICH THEY COULD NOT TAKE AS INDIVIDUALS, HOW AS WOMEN SHARE THEIR EXPERIENCES, THEY COULD ACT OUT OF A NEW RESPECT FOR THE VALUE OF THEIR LIVES AS WOMEN, DIFFERENT FROM, BUT CERTAINLY EQUAL TO, THE WORLD OF MEN''

differently. For boys, the typical development is more emphatic individuation and firmer ego boundaries, i.e., in order to become male, boys experience more strongly a sense of being ''not female.'' For girls, because the primary parent (or other) is of the same sex,'' a basis for 'empathy' [is] built into their primary definition of self.'' They ''come to experience themselves as less differentiated than boys, as more continuous with and related to the external object-world. . . . The basic feminine sense of self is connected to the world, the basic masculine sense of self is separate.''

This distinction in itself carries no value judgment and merely describes a difference. But because theories of psychological development (e.g., Freud's and Erikson's)'' focus on individuation . . . and maturity is equated with personal autonomy, concern with relationships appears as a weakness of women rather than as a human strength.''

If we turn from gender to moral development, a similar pattern emerges. Because women ''define themselves in a context of human relationship,'' their moral decisions differ from those of men. For women, typically, moral problems arise ''from conflicting responsibilities rather than from competing rights,'' require for their ''resolution a mode of thinking that is contextual rather than . . . abstract,'' are concerned more with relationships than rules.

Since Kohlberg perceives the expansion of moral understanding moving from the preconventional (or individual) through the conventional (or societal) to the post-conventional (or universal), women, who see the self and other as interdependent, whose moral judgments are more closely tied to feelings of empathy and compassion, who see moral problems as problems of responsibility in relationship, are more closely aligned with the conventional, a less mature stage of development. Gilligan, however, insists the relational bias in women's thinking is not a developmental deficiency as traditionally seen by psychologists but a different social and moral understanding. What we have are "two modes of judging, two different constructions of the moral domain—one traditionally associated with masculinity and the public world of social power, the other with femininity and the privacy of domestic interchange."

With this theoretical basis, we can now turn to Glaspell's works and more fully appreciate her astute depiction of these two different modes of judging: the post-conventional revealed through the words and actions of all three men and by Mrs. Peters early in each work, the conventional mode voiced by Mrs. Hale and by Mrs. Peters at the end of each work as her consciousness has been raised through the demeaning remarks made by the men and, more significantly, through her exposure to the trifles of Minnie's life.

From the moment the men enter the kitchen, they begin to judge the absent Minnie according to abstract rules and rights. For example, dirty towels suggest to them that Minnie "was not much of a housekeeper." To Mrs. Hale, however, responding from within a specific context, dirty towels imply that either "there's a great deal of work to be done on a farm" or "towels get dirty awful quick. Men's hands aren't always as clean as they might be." As the men continue to criticize or trivialize the domestic sphere (e.g., laughing at the women's concern for broken jars of preserves or their curiosity as to whether Minnie was going to "knot or quilt" her sewing), the stage directions indicate: "the two women move a little closer together."

Their moral "moving closer together" does not occur, however, until Mrs. Peters empathically understands Minnie's situation. For initially, Mrs. Peters parrots the male judgmental mode, demonstrating Glaspell's keen understanding of women's acquiescence to patriarchal law. When Mrs. Hale reproaches the men for disparaging remarks about

Minnie's housekeeping, Mrs. Peters timidly responds: "It's no more than their duty." As Mrs. Hale restitches Minnie's erratic sewing on a piece of quilting, Mrs. Peters nervously suggests: "I don't think we ought to touch things." And when Mrs. Hale objects to the men searching and "trying to get Minnie's own house to turn against her." Mrs. Peters replies: "But, Mrs. Hale, the law is the law." Her concern with "duty" and what one "ought to do" support a post-conventional view, corroborating the district attorney's trust in Mrs. Peters as "one of us."

Mrs. Hale, on the contrary, supports Minnie from the outset (although it's not clear that she could or would have taken the final action on her own). She responds to Mrs. Peter's comment that "the law is the law" with "and a bad stove is a bad stove"—implying the need to re-interpret abstract law within a particular context. When Mrs. Peters declares: "The law has got to punish crime," Mrs. Hale urges a redefinition of one's notion of crime. Reflecting on Minnie's drab and lonely life, she cries: "I wish I'd come over here once in a while! . . . That was a crime! Who's going to punish that?"

As Mrs. Peters listens to Mrs. Hale's recollections of Minnie's past and comes into physical contact with Minnie's present, "It was as if something within her, not herself had spoken, and it found in Mrs. Peters something she did not know as herself." Minnie's lonely life evokes memories of the stillness when Mrs. Peter's first baby died while she was homesteading in the Dakotas. Minnie's violent response to the killing of her pet canary recalls murderous feelings in Mrs. Peters when her pet kitten had been brutally slain. Sharing her memories with Mrs. Hale, Mrs. Peters recognizes her connection with other women and, consequently, is capable of moving from a typically male to a more typically female mode of judgment.

In filming the Glaspell works, Sally Heckel utilizes the visual and aural resources of cinema to highlight each trifle, create context, and reinforce relationships. Through close-up (e.g., a jar of preserves, a piece of quilting), the supposedly insignificant kitchen things assume larger-than-life proportions—emphasizing the significance of the domestic sphere. Through a combination of off-screen dialogue and closeup, Heckel creates the context necessary for the women's final decision. For example, when the district attorney is heard to state, "We need a motive," the camera provides a close-up of sugar spilt on a counter (evidence of interrupted work). Another man will state: ''We need some definite thing to build a story around,'' and Heckel offers a close-up of Mrs. Hale's hand on the quilt piece, under which is hidden the dead canary. Thus, while the men speak abstractly off-screen, on-screen, Heckel depicts the particulars, the specific context from which the women will make their moral choice.

A third visual device, composition within the frame, creates relationships, and Heckel will use this to visually unite the women and/or objects. In one frame, she links the remaining jar of preserves, the broken bird cage, and the now-restitched piece of quilt—a visual equivalent of the connections that lead Mrs. Hale and Peters to their joint decision.

Heckel's powerful contemporary film of Glaspell's earlier works attest to the vitality of Glaspell's vision. Fifty years before the current women's movement, Susan Glaspell understood how consciousness raising could empower women to take actions together which they could not take as individuals, how as women share their experiences, they could act out of a new respect for the value of their lives as women, different from, but certainly equal to, the world of men.

Source: Phyllis Mael. ''*Trifles:* The Path to Sisterhood'' in *Literature/Film Quarterly,* Vol. 17, no. 4, 1989, pp. 281–84.

SOURCES

Alkalay-Gut, Karen. ''Murder and Marriage: Another Look at *Trifles*,'' in *Susan Glaspell: Essays on Her Theater and Fiction,* University of Michigan Press, 1995, pp. 71-81.

Ben-Zvi, Linda, editor. *Susan Glaspell: Essays on Her Theater and Fiction,* University of Michigan Press, 1995.

Ferguson, Mary Anne. *Images of Women in Literature,* Houghton Mifflin Company, 1977, p. 390.

Hedges, Elaine. ''Small Things Reconsidered: 'A Jury of Her Peers','' in *Susan Glaspell: Essays on Her Theater and Fiction,* University of Michigan Press, 1995, pp. 49-69.

Kolodny, Annette. ''A Map for Rereading: Or, Gender and the Interpretation of Literary Texts,'' in *New Literary History,* University of Virginia, Spring, 1980, p. 451-67.

Nelligan, Lisa Maeve. ''The Haunting Beauty from the Life We've Left: A Contextual Reading of *Trifles* and *The Verge,*''

in *Susan Glaspell: Essays on Her Theater and Fiction,* University of Michigan Press, 1995, pp. 85-104.

Stein, Karen F. ''The Women's World of Glaspell's *Trifles,*'' in *Women in American Theatre,* Crown Publishers, Inc., 1981, p. 251-54.

Stephens, Judith. ''Gender Ideology and Dramatic Convention in Progressive Era Plays, 1890-1920,'' in *Performing Feminisms: Feminist Critical Theory and Theatre,* Johns Hopkins University Press, 1990, p. 283-93.

FURTHER READING

Ben-Zvi, Linda, editor. *Susan Glaspell: Essays on Her Theater and Fiction,* University of Michigan Press, 1995.
    This useful collection includes sixteen essays examining several of Glaspell's plays and short stories. Four separate articles consider *Trifles* and ''A Jury of Her Peers.''

Egan, Leona Rust. *Provincetown as a Stage: Provincetown, the Provincetown Players, and the Discovery of Eugene O'Neill,* Parnassus Imprints, 1994.
    Egan's account of the Provincetown Players. Chronicles the group's production of plays by some of the most famous American playwrights of the early ''little theatre'' movement, including Glaspell and Eugene O'Neill.

Jones-Eddy, Julie. *Homesteading Women: An Oral History of Colorado, 1890-1950,* Macmillan, 1992.
    The author interviewed several women for this account of the American West seen through the eyes of frontier women who raised families, built and kept homes, and survived the harsh rural life of the Colorado Territories.

Riley, Glenda and Richard W. Etulain, editors. *By Grit and Grace: Eleven Women Who Shaped the American West,* Fulcrum, 1997.
    This collection of biographical essays includes profiles of well-known figures such as Annie Oakley and Calamity Jane, as well as civil rights activist Mary Ellen Pleasant and women's suffrage leader Abigail Scott Duniway.

Waterman, Arthur E. *Susan Glaspell,* Twayne Publishers, 1966.
    A biography that chronicles Glaspell's early life as a Iowa reporter through her career as a playwright and novelist in New York and Massachusetts.

Trouble in Mind

ALICE CHILDRESS

1955

Trouble in Mind is the first professionally produced play written by Alice Childress, a pioneering African-American playwright. Childress directed the first production of the play, which debuted on November 5, 1955, in Greenwich Mews Theatre, New York City, and ran for 91 performances. For *Trouble in Mind,* Childress was awarded an Obie Award in 1956 for best original Off-Broadway production, making her the first African-American woman to win an Obie. Though *Trouble in Mind* was award-winning and a hit with critics and audiences at the time, the production was plagued with problems, including a clash between the original director and cast that prompted Childress to take his place. This is ironic considering *Trouble in Mind* is about the troubled production of a fictional, anti-lynching Broadway play, *Chaos in Belleville.* Wiletta Mayer, the African-American lead of the *Chaos,* as well as the other black actors, must deal with the condescending attitude of their white director, Al Manners. Wiletta stands up to Manners and reveals his racist attitudes but faces severe consequences as a result. *Trouble in Mind* also had script problems.

The original production was also a three-act play with a relatively happy ending, while the published version, discussed in this entry, has only two acts and an ambiguous, though downbeat, close. Childress has said that she was not satisfied with either ending. Childress had a chance to take *Trouble in Mind* to Broadway, but the producers demanded too many changes that Childress felt would

have compromised the play. Though *Trouble in Mind* was not seen on Broadway, critics have acknowledged its power. As John O. Killens writes in his essay, "The Literary Genius of Alice Childress," "In this play Childress demonstrated a talent and ability to write humor that had social impact. Even though one laughed throughout the entire presentation, there was, inescapably, the understanding that although one was having an undeniably emotional and profoundly intellectual experience, it was also political."

AUTHOR BIOGRAPHY

Childress was born on October 12, 1920 (some sources say 1916), in Charleston, South Carolina. When she was about five years old, her parents separated, and she was sent to live in New York City with her maternal grandmother, Eliza White. Reared in Harlem, White encouraged her granddaughter's creative side. As a child, Childress improvised plays with friends and was a voracious reader. Childress's education ended after her second year of high school when she was forced to support herself upon the deaths of both White and her mother.

In 1941, Childress became involved with the American Negro Theater. Though technically an amateur group, Childress learned every aspect of the theater, from set building to directing, acting, and writing, in her 11 years of involvement. During this time period, Childress held many menial jobs, including an salesperson and domestic, to provide for herself and her daughter, Jean, from her first marriage. These experiences played into her later work, especially her writing.

Childress's first success was as an actress, including an appearance in the original Broadway company of *Anna Lucasta*. In 1949, Childress wrote her first produced play, a one-act entitled *Florence*. Three years later, Childress wrote *Gold Through the Trees,* the first play by an African-American woman to be professionally produced on the American stage. Childress directed the Off-Broadway production of her play *Trouble in Mind* in 1955. These plays led to Childress's growing reputation as a writer, though she continued to act in theater, television, and film for several decades.

In 1957, Childress married her second husband, Nathan Woodward, a musician and music educator. She co-wrote several musical plays with him, in-

Alice Childress

cluding *Young Martin Luther King.* Childress concentrated on theatrical writing in the 1960s, including a two-year appointment at the Radcliffe Institute for Independent Study. There she wrote what became her best known play, *The Wedding Band: A Love/Hate Story in Black and White.* The play explores an interracial romance set in Charleston during World War I. *The Wedding Band* was presented by the New York Shakespeare Festival in 1972.

While Childress continued to write plays, she also tried her hand at fiction in the 1970s and 1980s. Childress's best known fiction work was her 1973 juvenile novel, *A Hero Ain't Nothing But a Sandwich.* Critics have pointed to this book as the first child's novel to deal with urban realism: the 13-year-old main character struggles with heroin addiction. Though the novel earned numerous awards, including the Best Young Adult Novel citation from the American Library Association, it was controversial at the time. Childress also authored the screenplay for the 1977 movie version. Childress wrote another acclaimed juvenile novel in 1982, *Rainbow Jordan,* following her first adult novel *A Short Walk* (1981). The latter explores African-American experience from the turn of the century to the Civil Rights movement.

Over the course of her life, Childress received numerous awards for her many contributions to the arts, including the Harlem School of the Arts Humanitarian Award in 1987. She died of cancer in New York City on August 14, 1994, leaving behind an unfinished novel about two of her great-grandmothers.

PLOT SUMMARY

Act I

Trouble in Mind opens inside the entrance of a Broadway theater in New York City. Wiletta Mayer, a middle-aged, African-American actress, bangs on the door and finally lets herself in. She scolds the elderly doorman, Henry, for not letting her in out of the cold, until she sees the stage. While she is enraptured by the sight of the theater, Henry recognizes her from when he was an electrician on a show twenty years ago. When Henry leaves, John Nevins, a young African-American actor, enters. He tries to hide his nervousness. In talking to him, Wiletta realizes that they come from the same place and that she knows his parents. Wiletta gives him career advice about how black people are perceived by white directors and others who run the show. She tells him that he should lie and say he was in the last revival of *Porgy and Bess,* even though it is untrue. John is skeptical of her counsel.

Millie, another African-American actress, enters. Soon, a young white actress, Judith Sears, and an elderly African-American actor, Sheldon Forrestor, join the conversation. John tries to approach Judy several times, but the other actors prevent him, talking about this play and previous productions they have been in. Judy reveals that this is her first play, and she hopes it will educate their audience. The other actors do not disagree outright. Their conversation is interrupted by the appearance of the play's director, Manners, his assistant, Eddie, and Henry. After greetings are exchanged, Manners shows them the sketches for the production's scenic design. He compliments each member of the cast, especially Wiletta, who worked on a movie with him some time ago.

Manners tells the cast about the play and how the production came to be. He say that it is ahead of its time in its depiction of race. The cast has questions about their parts, but Manners insists that they read a scene in the middle of act one. Judy gets up to read, but she is nervous and forgets where down-

stage is. Manners yells at her. Manners tries to make Wiletta act naturally, but it comes off wrong, and he seems racist. Wiletta becomes very cautious around him. The cast continues with the read. The black actors question words and situations they object to. Manners tries to smooth things over, but does not concede such things are objectional. He has them read from the beginning of act one.

Henry shows up with coffee and doughnuts. Manners becomes angry when Henry does not bring him the proper pastry. His anger and condescending attitude increase when Eddie informs Manners that his ex-wife is on the phone. Manners takes the call while Wiletta tries to make Eddie more comfortable. Judy invites the cast to visit her family's home in Bridgeport. Wiletta and Millie tell her she better ask them before she makes such an invitation because they might not want them there.

Manners turns the conversation to the script. He asks the cast to explain to him what is going on. When they do, he has Wiletta sing the song at the end of act one. She knows the song and performs it well. Manners demands to know what she is thinking about. She tells him that she knows what he wants, but he is not satisfied with this answer. Manners makes her play a word association game that makes Wiletta uncomfortable. Manners leads Judy offstage to take about her role. Immediately, the black cast members tell John to not get too close to Judy. While talking about racial topics, they say accusatory things to each other. John, Sheldon, and Millie leave, and Wiletta is left alone. Henry comes in and tries to comfort her. He is still mad about what Manners did to him earlier. As Henry talks about Ireland and the problems there, he grows increasingly indignant. Wiletta shares his anger. She says she will be an actress no matter what is thrown in her path.

Act II

Three mornings later, Manners and Eddie are rehearsing with a new addition, white actor Bill O'Wray. O'Wray plays Renard, the father figure in the play, and is passionately reading a long-winded speech from the play. When he is done, Bill seems unsure of himself. Bill offers suggestions to Manners about the play. Manners goes on about his personal problems, then asks a favor of Bill. He tells Bill to stop leaving at lunch hour because it looks like he does not want to eat with the black members of the cast. Bill tells Manners that he does not want to eat with them, not because he is prejudice, but because he does not want people to stare at him.

Wiletta enters. She tries to tell Manners about problems she has with the script. Manners is dismissive of her concerns. He compliments her everytime she tries to say something. Wiletta finally gets out that she thinks the third act might not seem a natural outcome after the first, but Manners tells her not to think. When the rest of the cast joins them, Judy looks more sophisticated and John acts more like Manners. Manners starts rehearsal at the beginning of act three. Wiletta has a hard time focusing on her lines. The play soon reaches a dramatic climax, as John's character goes out to be lynched and Wiletta's character lets him go. Manners acts like the consummate director.

When they reach the end of the scene, Sheldon reveals that he has not read the whole play, just the parts that he is in. Manners fills him in on the ending. He also compliments all the actors on their work, except Wiletta. Manners asks her if she will let him help her. Wiletta tells him that he will not listen to her suggestions, though he does pay attention to the others' thoughts. Manners explains that she must lose herself in the part by relating, but Wiletta does not understand why Job, John's character, does not get away. John tries to intercede, but he acts just like Manners. Manners will not listen to Wiletta, and the cast falls into a bit of infighting.

Manners attempts to control his cast. He asks them to imagine a lynching. He is surprised when Sheldon says that he has seen one. Sheldon relates the story. Manners and Bill are affected by the story, and the former calls for lunch. The cast decides to go together. Wiletta still tries to make her point about the script, but Manners dismisses her concerns again. Some of the cast leaves, and Wiletta says she will catch up them later.

Lights flicker to indicate the passage of time, and when the lights come up again, the stage is empty. The cast, save Wiletta, enters. To one side, Manners and Eddie chide Bill for making what could be seen as a racist joke. Wiletta arrives just as Manners begins rehearsal. She tells him she wants to talk to him after rehearsal, but Manners is noncommittal. They begin to read act three. Wiletta ignores Manners's order to keep John on his knees. She challenges Manners about the play: she does not believe her character would send her son out to a lynch mob. Though others try to silence her, she asks Manners if he would do it to his son. He ignores the question and justifies his position. Wiletta accuses him of prejudice and keeps trying to ask him her question. Manners finally answers her in an

angry outburst. He says that he and his son could not be compared to her and John's character.

Manners and Eddie quickly leave, and the cast is in disarray. The cast is both accusatory and supportive of what Wiletta said. Sheldon is on her side, but he tells her to apologize to in an effort to keep their jobs. Wiletta is firm in her conviction that the play is a lie. Judy and Bill are resentful of what the black actors say about whites. Finally, Eddie comes in and informs that rehearsal is over. He will call them about tomorrow's rehearsal. The cast, except Wiletta, leave. Henry sees that Wiletta is upset and tries to calm her. She says that she will show up at rehearsal tomorrow, no matter what, so that Manners has to fire her in person. At Henry's urging, she recites something on stage: Psalm 133.

CHARACTERS

Millie Davis

Millie is a thirty-five-year-old African-American actress. She is married and says she does not need to work. She displays more wealth than the other African-American characters; she wears a mink coat and an expensive watch. Like Wiletta, she is conscious of how she acts and what she says around whites, and she tries to guide John's behavior. Millie also does not like the kind of roles she must play because of her race. She says at one point that she did not tell her relatives about the last production because she repeated but one stereotypical line over and over again. Though Millie expresses her objections about a couple of things, she is not willing to put her job on the line for such matters.

Sheldon Forrester

Sheldon is an elderly African-American character actor and aspiring songwriter. Like Millie and Wiletta, he is conscious about how he acts and what he says around the white people involved in the production. He also tries to advise John about his interactions with whites, especially Judy. Sheldon, more than Millie and Wiletta, wants everyone to get along and not fight amongst themselves. But he also questions certain aspects of *Chaos in Belleville* in a non-confrontational manner. Sheldon is the only character to have really seen a lynching, a central event in the play. When Wiletta speaks out, Sheldon is only somewhat supportive of her.

MEDIA ADAPTATIONS

- *Trouble in Mind* was filmed by the BBC as a television movie.

Henry

Of Irish descent, Henry is the 78-year-old doorman at the theater where the rehearsals are taking place. Henry knows Wiletta from when he worked as an electrician at shows, and obviously admires her talent. He has hearing problems, which lead to a misunderstanding with Manners, but Henry always tries to fix problems. Henry is fully supportive of Wiletta at the end of each act when she tries to deal with her situation. He relates the oppression of the Irish by the English to Wiletta's dilemmas. Henry is Wiletta's only consistent ally.

Al Manners

Manners, who is white, is the director of *Chaos in Belleville.* He wants to remain in control of the production at all times, but he is callous toward the feelings and beliefs of all the actors, especially Wiletta. Manners's self-assuredness is shaken several times, until he finally bursts out in anger when Wiletta compares herself to him. Though Manners will probably continue to direct the production, he has lost the trust of those who work for him.

Wiletta Mayer

Wiletta is the central character in *Trouble in Mind.* She is a middle-aged African-American actress, and she plays the lead in the play, *Chaos in Belleville.* Wiletta was a singer at one time in her career, and Henry, the doorman, knows her from a production he worked on 20 years earlier; Wiletta also appeared in a movie directed by Manners some time ago. Though Wiletta loves acting, she knows that whites, especially directors and producers, have certain expectations of blacks as actors. She tries to advise John at the beginning of the play on how best to get along, though he does not really want to believe her. By the middle of *Trouble in Mind,*

Wiletta has not taken her own advice. She speaks out against what she perceives as racist problems with the script, and later, the director's demeaning attitude towards her. Wiletta realizes that she has lost her job by her actions at the end of the play. However, these actions lead to the revelation that Manners is racist, despite his claims to the contrary.

John Nevins

John is an idealistic young African-American actor, making his Broadway debut in *Chaos in Belleville.* Though he and Wiletta come from the same hometown, Newport News, Virginia, John is more educated than Wiletta, and usually feels superior to her. He does not like most of the advice she gives him about how to act around whites in show business, though the other, more experienced black actors echo what Wiletta has said. John seems somewhat attracted to Judy, and the other African-American actors try to keep them separated. Instead of listening to the counsel of his elders, by Act II, John is imitating Manners in speech and mannerisms. However, when Manners reveals that he does not think of blacks and whites as comparable, John realizes the error of his ways and supports Wiletta.

Bill O'Wray

Bill is a middle-aged white actor. He is perpetually worried when he is not acting, but delivers his lines in the play with power. Bill does not want to lunch with the African-American actors because he says the stares they draw makes it hard for him to eat. Bill says several additional things that could be interpreted as racist and is defensive about his actions.

Judy Sears

Judy is a young white actress. Though she is a graduate of the Yale School of Drama, she is naive, and *Chaos in Belleville* is her first job. Judy often speaks lovingly of her mother and father, who live in Bridgeport, Connecticut, and invites the whole cast to visit them there. She believes doing this play will be educational and hopes that it will help ease racism, but she also is conscious of how her character seems smug. When the African-American actors feel resentment and anger, Judy tries to be supportive, but she feels as though they are lashing out at her personally. A sensitive woman, Judy espouses the belief that people are all the same and that racism is wrong.

THEMES

Race and Racism

Every aspect of *Trouble in Mind* is touched by race and/or racism. Each African-American character discusses his or her experience as a black actor in a business dominated by whites. In the beginning, Millie, Wiletta, and Sheldon try to guide John, the neophyte, about how to behave around their white counterparts. Sheldon and Millie advocate getting along and not getting too close Wiletta does as well, until the end of the play when she can no longer tolerate the condescending attitude of the white director, Manners. But in their collective advice, the actors also reveal their true feelings about the play they are rehearsing for, *Chaos on Belleville.* As with many of the productions they have appeared in, they feel their roles are stereotypical and the script awful. Yet they take these jobs because they need the work.

For their part, the white people involved with the production vary in their reactions to the black actors. Bill O'Wray, an actor, says he is not prejudiced, but he does not want to eat lunch with them. Judy, the young actress, is idealistic about race relations and believes the performance will play a positive role in addressing racial concerns. Yet when the black actors discuss the problems they have dealing with whites, Judy resents what they are saying. Manners also claims to not be racist, but he will not listen to Wiletta's concerns about the plays. He also treats his black actors differently than his white actors. When Wiletta finally pushes Manners too far, he reveals in an outburst that she should not compare herself to him, presumably because of her race. The complexities of race and racism drive the plot and define characters in *Trouble in Mind.*

Sexism

While racism is explored in an explicit manner, sexism is much more implicit in the text of *Trouble in Mind.* In the beginning of the play, for example, John is not completely comfortable with the advice Wiletta gives him. It is partially due to racial concerns, but also because of what she is telling him. Most of the sexism, however, is focused on the character of Manners, the white director. He treats the female cast members differently than their male counterparts. For example, Manners invades Judy's space moments after meeting her in a way that makes her uncomfortable. He does not do the same

TOPICS FOR FURTHER STUDY

- Compare and contrast Wiletta in *Trouble in Mind* to Jackie "Moms" Mabley in Childress's 1987 play *Moms: A Praise Play for a Black Comedienne.* Both characters are black actresses, though Moms was a real person. Discuss Childress's depiction of their professional lives and the choices they made.

- Research the social conditions surrounding African Americans in the United States in the mid-1950s. How does *Trouble in Mind* reflect these conditions? How does Childress depict them within the play?

- Explore the themes of *Trouble in Mind* via the song of the same name and Psalm 133.

- Research the psychology of groups. How does your research explain the African-American actors' struggle between presenting a united front and their infighting in *Trouble in Mind*?

thing with any of the male characters. Similarly, when Manners finds out Judy attended drama school at Yale, he calls her names when he wants to put her in her place. This shows his discomfort with her being perhaps better educated than him.

Manners is more demeaning in his actions towards Wiletta. When he throws a piece of paper on the ground, he makes her pick it up. He will not let Judy, John, nor Sheldon do it. Manners tells the cast that he did this as a trick to get them thinking about acting, though Wiletta does not see it that way. Further, Manners never lets Wiletta express her opinion. Each time she tries to raise a concern about the script, he tells her not to think or compliments her to change the subject or says the problem is with her, not the script. Manners also does the same thing to Millie. When Wiletta finally forces the issue, Manners reveals his true feelings about her: in his mind, she cannot be compared to him. As a black woman, Manners cannot see Wiletta as his equal.

Peer Pressure

The African-American characters in *Trouble in Mind* put pressure on each other to act in certain ways. From the beginning, Wiletta, Millie, and Sheldon try to curb John's behavior so that they can all get along with the white director and actors. Sheldon and Millie physically keep him from Judy when she is first introduced. Sheldon also repeatedly says that he wants peace and harmony among the black actors in front of the others. He believes this will help them keep their jobs now and get jobs in the future. Before the situation with Wiletta and Manners blows up completely, Sheldon does his part to maintain such an amity. The other black actors also jump in on occasion. Even after the blow-up, Sheldon wants Wiletta to apologize to Manners. He believes such an apology will smooth things over. Wiletta will not bow to such pressure to conform, and she is left alone with Henry at the end of the play.

STYLE

Setting

Trouble in Mind takes place in New York City in fall of 1957. By the author's own estimation, the play is a drama-comedy. All of the action is confined to the stage of a Broadway theater where the rehearsals for *Chaos in Belleville* take place. The stage is littered with props from previous productions, including tables and benches where the characters sit. Because the play is set in a Broadway theater, some of the black actors, especially Sheldon, feel that they must act the way they believe white people want them to. It is clearly a white man's theater.

Play within a Play

Trouble in Mind focuses on the rehearsals for a Broadway play, *Chaos in Belleville*. In *Chaos*, Job (played by John) is a young man living in the South who has been called up for military service. He wants to vote, and his actions in this matter lead to a lynch mob coming after him. His family work as sharecroppers. His mother Ruby (played by Wiletta) sends him to his death, believing a lynch mob will show him mercy. Sheldon plays Job's father, Sam, while Millie's character is named Petunia. Some members of this family work for the white Renard (played by Bill O'Wray) and his daughter Carrie (played by Judy). Renard and his daughter treat the blacks as lessers, like children who need the guid-

ance of whites. Renard offers to house Job in jail to protect him, and Ruby lets him go, which ultimately leads to Job's death. Though ostensibly an anti-lynching play, the racist undertones of *Chaos* offend the black actors. Because they need the work, however, they quietly put up with things like the demeaning language and action, until Wiletta cannot take it anymore and speaks her mind. The white characters, especially Judy and Manners, believe *Chaos* will do good and hopefully change their audience's feelings about race. The divergent attitudes towards the play within the play show how far apart both sides really are.

Stereotypes

Stereotypes are used in several different ways in *Trouble in Mind*. Many of the black actors feel that the characters they portray in *Chaos in Belleville* are stereotypical. These characters are naive and child-like, wearing cheap clothes and using cliched language. Sheldon's character Sam just sits and whittles a stick in several scenes. Ruby does not protect her son but listens to the advice of Renard and his daughter. Only Job seems strong and more original, but he is murdered by the end of *Chaos*. The white characters in *Chaos* are also cliched. Bill's character Renard is the benevolent father and guardian of the sharecroppers. Judy's Carrie tries to be their friend and help them. She puts herself at some risk by doing this, but no harm comes to her.

On several occasions in *Trouble in Mind*, the black actors accuse each of other of being stereotypical "Uncle Toms" and "Jemimas." Early in the play, for example, Wiletta advises John to always laugh and pretend to be happy in front of the white director. When John says that this behavior seems "Tommish," Wiletta admits it is, but that being a "yes man" is necessary for survival. Indeed, for much of the play, most of the black actors act this way. Critics have also noted that Childress's characterizations of whites are somewhat stereotypical. They especially point to Judy, as a stereotypical idealistic young white Northern liberal.

HISTORICAL CONTEXT

In the mid-1950s, the United States was a world leader on several fronts. Home to many scientific and technological innovations, America was also one of the principal players in the high stakes arms race with the Soviet Union. The so-called Cold War

COMPARE
&
CONTRAST

- **1955:** Marian Anderson is the first black singer to appear with the Metropolitan Opera.

  Today: There are many black opera singers appearing on stages across America. One of the most famous is Jessye Norman.

- **1955:** The first woman is admitted to the Harvard School of Divinity.

  Today: The first woman graduates from one of the last gender segregated institutions, the Citadel.

- **1954:** The Supreme Court rules in Brown v. Board of Education that public schools should be integrated. To follow this order, many schools resort to bussing students.

  Today: There is a movement away from bussing

students and letting them attend their neighborhood schools. This sometimes means that schools are racially segregated once again.

- **1955:** While riding a bus, Rosa Parks refuses to give up her seat to a white person. This leads to the Montgomery, Alabama, bus boycott and a firestorm of controversy.

  Today: Rosa Parks is still regarded as a hero of the Civil Rights Movement. She is often lauded for her courageous act, which is considered by many to have been one of the primary catalysts of one of the most important social movements in American history.

---

with the Soviets and their allies continued to escalate throughout the decade. This war deeply affected the American people. Many feared atomic bombs would be used and that there would be world-wide annihilation. Some went as far as to build fall-out shelters in their backyards. Americans also feared Communists and Communism. People like Senator Joseph McCarthy made careers out of accusing people of being Communist spies.

The United States was also the world's economic leader. American consumer demand increased rapidly after World War II, leading to a strong economy and the growth of labor unions. Though labor unions thrived gaining new benefits for their members they were also suspected by some as harboring communists. To feed the growing economy, American industries spent a significant amount of money on research and development for the first time. One industry that exploded in the 1950s was television. At the beginning of the 1950s, less than 20% of American households had televisions, but by 1960, they were found in 90% of American homes. These televisions were black and white, as were nearly all broadcasts by the burgeoning networks. Color television sets were not available until

1954 and were very expensive. The growing economy also led to the expansion of suburbs, a cheap, safe place to live, primarily for white families.

Despite such prosperity and international leadership, the United States was still racially segregated in many facets of society, especially in the South. For the most part, African Americans did not benefit from the consumer boom. The so-called "Jim Crow" laws found in parts of the South dictated that blacks were separated from whites in fundamental ways. There were separate drinking fountains, restaurants, hotels, churches, and seats on the bus. An African American attempting to cross racial lines and eat in a white restaurant could be prosecuted and sent to jail.

By the mid-1950s, these laws were being challenged and the modern civil rights movement was born. Two significant related events occurred in 1955. In Montgomery, Alabama, Rosa Parks was fined for refusing to give up her seat to a white passenger. A bus boycott was organized, and by 1956, Alabama's segregation laws were ruled unconstitutional. The events in Montgomery led to bus boycotts in other cities in the South. Even more controversial was the desegregation of public schools. Throughout the 1950s, there were a series of law suits that forced the integration of schools from the elementary to the university level. Until this time, the schools that students in many areas attended were based on race. Black schools were almost always poorer than their white counterparts. Indeed, in this time period, all schools faced problems because of a shortage of teachers, an increase in the number of students attending school, and the pressure to turn out better educated students to compete with the Soviets.

The most significant law suit was 1954's Brown v. The Board of Education of Topeka, Kansas. The Supreme Court ruled that school segregation was unconstitutional, and schools were ordered to integrate. The actual implementation took nearly 20 years because of the huge public debate and sometimes violent resistance, especially in the South. To ensure its ruling was followed, the Supreme Court and other government officials had to step in repeatedly to force change. African Americans were not the only ones suffering from racial discrimination. In New York City, there were charges that public schools discriminated against Italians and Puerto Ricans.

CRITICAL OVERVIEW

Critics of the original production of *Trouble in Mind* found much to praise. Harry Raymond of *The Daily Worker* wrote, "*Trouble in Mind* is a play with an important point of view about the problems of Negro actors in the theatre. She has written about it with a brightness and compassion that sends the audience home with some sound thoughts on one of the major social problems in the field of American culture." The critic of the *New York Times* agreed with Raymond's sentiment, arguing that "Miss Childress has some witty and penetrating things to say about the dearth of roles for Negro actors in the contemporary theatre, the cut-throat competition for these parts, and the fact that Negro actors often find themselves playing stereotyped roles in which they cannot being themselves to believe." Subsequent critics, like Helen Keyssar in her 1984 essay "Foothills: Precursors of Feminist Drama," take the idea one step further. Keyssar believes that "While *Trouble in Mind* is most immediately a black social protest play whose context and inspiration is the racial integration movement of the fifties,

it is also a play *about* roles in which female stereotypes are acknowledged and jarred."

Many critics note that Childress's female characters, especially Wiletta, are keys to the success of *Trouble in Mind*. Others found Wiletta and her stand inspiring. Keyssar writes in "Foothills," that "*Trouble in Mind* is unabashed in its evocation of empathy for its protagonist Wiletta Mayer." Gayle Austin, in her essay "Black Woman Playwright as Feminist Critic," describes the limited views of African-American women on stage, then points out that Childress has created new images for them. She writes, "Childress, in writing the roles of Wiletta and Millie, has provided some alternative images of black women, three dimensional characters with weaknesses and strengths."

Austin believes the characters are still "fresh" today, though other critics have mixed feelings on the subject. Claire Messud of the *Times Literary Supplement* reviewed a 1992 London production of *Trouble in Mind;* she writes, "*Trouble in Mind* cannot help, in some ways, feeling dated: stereotypes, both black and white, have changed more in the past thirty-five years than in the entire century before that. But, transmogrified, they have not disappeared, and the play is not without resonances and relevance today." Other critics believe *Trouble in Mind* did transcend time other ways. Sally R. Sommer, writing about the play in a 1979 *Village Voice* article argues, "Twenty-three years later we can look at the play and see its double cutting edge: It predicts not only the course of social history but the course of black playwriting. The best parts of the play, its multi-leveled language and seething, funny role-re-enactments, prefigure the tough black style of the '60s plays naturalistic dramas that hit hard, inset with sermon-like arias for solo performers."

Yet some critics criticized the play for those very aspects. Doris E. Abramson, in her book *Negro Playwrights in the American Theatre 1925-59,* finds much to praise about the play, but she also argues "*Trouble in Mind* has interesting characters and dialogue, though both tend to ring false whenever they are saturated with sermonizing." Other critics find the plot of the play to be rather thin. Abramson also faults Childress on several other fronts. She writes, "A reader of the script is very much aware of the author pulling strings, putting her own words into a number of mouths. This is not, however, to deny the theatrical effectiveness of the play in production." Later in the book, Abramson argues that "It would be better if she did not assault race prejudice at every turn, for she sometimes sacrifices depth of character in the process.'' Not all critics agree with Abramson's criticisms. Austin believes that the play is complex and works on a number of levels. ''Her play-within-a-play structure allows her to demonstrate the way male images portray black women and show both the actor's true and false feelings about the image.''

CRITICISM

A. Petrusso

Petrusso explores how the play being rehearsed in Trouble in Mind, *entitled* Chaos in Belleville, *reflects* Trouble's *tensions and characters, especially Wiletta.*

In Alice Childress's *Trouble in Mind* a racially mixed group of actors and a white director and writer are rehearsing a Broadway play that is ostensibly anti-racism and anti-lynching. The white actors and director believe that *Chaos in Belleville* will impart a positive message of racial tolerance to its audience; they believe they are doing good work. Most of the black actors do not believe that this is true. These actors play the same kind of stereotypical servant roles in which they are always cast. They took these roles because they needed the work, not because they believe they are imparting any great social message. By looking at the parts of *Chaos in Belleville* being rehearsed, it becomes obvious that, in many ways, the world depicted in *Chaos* is not much different than *Trouble.* Only Wiletta's rebellion and the strength she draws from her defiance is a significant divergence.

The first part of *Chaos in Belleville* rehearsed is Act One, Scene Two, on page 15. This reading begins in *Trouble in Mind* in the middle of act one. When this scene opens, Carrie (played by Judy) asks her father, Renard (read by Eddie for the moment), if their black servants can have a barn dance to celebrate the birthday of Petunia (played by Millie). Renard does not want to have the dance now because there is an election at hand. He asks another black servant, Ruby (played by Wiletta) if she thinks they should. Ruby replies, ''Lord, have mercy, Mr. Renard, don't ask me 'cause I don't know nothin'.'' Carrie begs her father. Her father dismisses Ruby and Petunia to the porch while he talks to his daughter. Carrie pleads with him again, pointing out that she gave her word. Renard finally

concedes, not without hesitation, and Carrie informs the women. Carrie goes to lay out her organdy dress, but Ruby insists on doing it for her. Carrie then decides to take a nap, and Petunia gives her blessing.

This scene has several striking parallels to *Trouble in Mind.* Renard controls the lives of his servants just as Al Manners, the director of *Chaos,* believes he knows what is right for his cast. The Judge has the last say, like Manners. Both do not get straight answers out of their African-American servants/cast because the men do not really want to hear what they have to say. Renard and Manners are convinced of their superiority, and act accordingly. However, both men are completely out of touch with the reality of the servants/cast. Similarly, Renard's daughter Carrie and Judy both need affirmation and act like naive children to get it. Though Judy fears Manners a bit, she needs attention and to be told what to do. She also wants to do what is right even if it seems racist.

There is more going on beneath the surface for the African-American characters. Millie does not like playing the servant role and tries to undermine Judy at every turn during the reading. Ironically, her character says to Carrie, ''you just one of God's golden-haired angels.'' Millie does not believe this. Also ironic in some ways is the striking parallel is between Wiletta at this stage of *Trouble* and her character. When Ruby is asked by Renard for her opinion, she denies having one. A few lines later, Manners looks to Wiletta for an opinion on whether ''darkies'' is an acceptable phrase considering the context. Like Renard, he does not really want her true opinion on this subject. She tells Manners, ''Lord, have mercy, don't ask me, 'cause I don't know.'' This is the exact line from the script. This causes Wiletta much anxiety and is the beginning of her rebellion against Manners. Indeed, Wiletta's desire to express an opinion on the play is the primary source of dramatic tension by act two.

From this scene, Manners immediately jumps back to the beginning of *Chaos* in act one, page three. Many of the attitudes and themes of the previous scene are reinforced. It opens with Ruby shelling beans on the back porch and her husband, Sam, played by Sheldon, sitting next to her. Their son, Job, played by John, enters. Job informs his mother that he is going to vote. Sam tries to discourage him, telling him that Renard has said to stay away from that. Job argues that he has been drafted and that another black man told him that ''when that

WHAT DO I READ NEXT?

- *For Colored Girls Who Have Considered Suicide/When the Rainbow is Enuf,* a play by Notozake Shange published in 1977. The play concerns African-American women who are fighting for their integrity and self-respect.

- *Florence,* a play by Childress which was first produced in 1949. The play explores racism in the South under Jim Crow laws. The title character is an actress who lives in New York City and has a hard time finding work.

- *The First Black Actors On the Great White Way* is a nonfiction book written by Susan Curtis in

1998. It is a history of black actors in New York City.

- *A Raisin in the Sun,* a play by Lorraine Hansberry first produced on Broadway in 1959. The play focuses on the life of a strong black woman.

- *Like One of the Family Conversations from a Domestic's Life* (1956) is a collection of monologues written by Childress. The primary character, an African-American domestic named Mildred Johnson, comments on working for white people as well as her life as a single woman.

---

happens, a man's sposed to vote and things.'' Job goes despite his parents' protests and feeble attempts to stop him. Carrie and Renard come out to see what is happening. Renard comments on how black people are worthless, while Carrie says she feels sorry for them. Before the reading ends, Carrie says, ''If we're superior we should prove it by our actions.''

Like the servants in the play, who blindly follow what their white employer says without thinking for themselves, the older black actors advise John, the young, inexperienced actor, to agree with everything the white director and actors say, no matter what he really thinks. Wiletta especially believes it is the best way to get along, at least at the beginning of the play. But, unlike their *Chaos* counterparts, Wiletta, Sheldon, and Millie do express their discontent, however subtle. During this reading, Millie's coldness and reactions disturb Judy so much that she cries Carrie would also cry over such a reaction. Like Carrie, Judy is sensitive and empathetic, but does not fully understand what the black actors feel reading this play. Judy and Carrie also ape their parents' attitudes, with no real comprehension. Throughout the play, Judy talks about her close relationship to her parents and their beliefs. She says that her mother believes in integrated education. The Judge, like Manners, is full of

himself and sure of his attitudes. This affects what Carrie thinks and says, since she does not display many thoughts that seem original.

The next discussion of *Chaos in Belleville* is not a full rehearsal but a description of the larger story. Some of the local African-American population will vote for the first time, and there is opposition from whites as well as blacks. In this atmosphere, the Judge does not want to have the barn dance. He, Sam, and Ruby believe that Job is headed for trouble. The focus turns to Ruby for a moment. Her anxieties over her son compel her to sing a well-known song. Wiletta knows the song and gives a moving rendition. It is not enough for Manners that she aced the song and understood what he wanted as a director; he wants to know what she was thinking, so he proceeds to humiliate her while playing a word association game. She sings the song again, and it is a bit better. Manners takes full credit for her ''transformation'' and dismisses the first effort entirely. Like the Judge, he wants to control everything. Such an attitude flames Wiletta's discontent.

Act two of *Trouble in Mind* opens with a monologue from *Chaos.* It is a thundering speech given by Renard, played by the previously absent actor Bill O'Wray. In the speech, directed at other white citizens, Renard advocates a superficial "moderation" and "tolerance" for their black counterparts. He believes that this will ease tensions over voting and demonstrate their superior nature. Just as telling as this speech are the events that take place while it is being given. Eddie, Manners's assistant, is supposed to play applause at key moments. He misses one cue, and at the end of the monologue, Manners tells Eddie that "Inattention aggravates the hell out of me!" Yet, in act two especially, Manners does not pay any attention to Wiletta's concerns about the play or her need to talk about them.

The next piece of *Chaos in Belleville* rehearsed is the beginning of act three. Menial tasks are attended to while the air is filled with tension. Ruby irons clothes. Petunia anxiously looks out of the window. Sam sits in the corner and whittles a stick. Carrie cries. They all hear an angry lynch mob and wonder if Job is dead or alive. Fearing for her safety Ruby tries to send Carrie home, but Carrie will not hear of it. Instead, Carrie is determined to save Job's life by getting her father and a judge to intercede. Sheldon says a prayer and Job shows up. Ruby tells him he should not have been so adamant about his right to vote. Job says he has done nothing wrong and he will run. Ruby believes he should give himself up to the mob and tell them he has done nothing wrong. Carrie wants to put him in the county jail for safekeeping. Renard shows up and offers his protection; Job takes it with his parents' encouragement. Renard also makes Job admit that he has made a mistake. Job does so indirectly.

The only person capable of action in this scene is Renard. He is the benevolent superior who, while helpful, also wants to ensure his power is absolute. Carrie's determination means nothing because she does nothing. Ruby, Petunia, and Sam are stereotypical, domestic characters, who rely solely on Renard's judgement. Ruby is portrayed as incredibly naive in thinking that the mob would not kill her son because he is innocent, just as she would be supported by her friends. Job also believes he will be safe with the white man, though he will not be. He dies anyway, as revealed when the plot is further summarized for Sheldon who has not read the whole script. Unlike Renard, however, Manners cannot control every one. He cannot get Wiletta under control because he refuses to acknowledge her ideas and her need to express herself. To accomplish this goal, though, Manners does things like "playfully" threatening to spank her when she tries to talk to him. Still, Job goes along with Renard, just as John stops associating with the black actors and

> THE WHITE ACTORS AND DIRECTOR BELIEVE THAT *CHAOS IN BELLEVILLE* WILL IMPART A POSITIVE MESSAGE OF RACIAL TOLERANCE TO ITS AUDIENCE; THEY BELIEVE THEY ARE DOING GOOD WORK. MOST OF THE BLACK ACTORS DO NOT BELIEVE THAT THIS IS TRUE"

starts to act like Manners. Sam and Millie also vocalize their superficial support as well.

After a break for lunch, the cast returns and they back through parts of act three of *Chaos*. Job says he will still vote. Ruby wants to follow Carrie's suggestion and have Job put in jail for safekeeping. Ruby directs Job to fall on his knees where she prays over him. This is the last moment of *Chaos* depicted before all hell breaks loose. At this point, Wiletta tries to deliver Ruby's lines, but the sight of John on his knees upsets her. She keeps trying to get him to stand up, which angers Manners greatly. Wiletta seizes this opportunity to tell Manners that she does not believe that Ruby would send her son to the lynch mob. She says that it makes Ruby look like the villain, more than anyone else. The white audience would be superior because they know what the right course of action should be. This leads to a bitter discussion that reveals Manners to be racist and insensitive. The lesson from Job's death is not the one the white playwright intended.

Unlike the other characters and actors, Wiletta undergoes a big transformation in *Trouble in Mind* because of *Chaos in Belleville*. She begins the play as a Ruby, bowing, at least on the surface, to Manners's status as unquestionable leader. But ultimately, she is Job. She faces Manners's wrath for daring to question him, as Job dares to vote. Job dies by the end of *Chaos* while Wiletta is probably out of a job. Wiletta is not dead, however, and vows to continue to fight. She will show up the next day so that Manners has to fire her to her face. Like Job, Wiletta's actions are not fully supported by her peers. Sheldon wants Wiletta to apologize to Manners, which could be compared to Job being sent to the lynch mob by his mother. Wiletta chooses to be alone at the end of *Trouble in Mind* unlike anyone in *Chaos in Belleville* because she is stronger. The job, while important, does not compare to her victory.

Source: A. Petrusso, for *Drama for Students,* Gale, 2000.

Claire Messud

Messud reviews a revival production of Childress's play. While noting that many of the playwright's themes seem dated, "the play is not without resonances and relevance today."

"Any upheaval in the universe is terrifying because it so profoundly attacks one's sense of reality . . . the black man has functioned in the white man's world as a fixed star, as an immovable pillar: and as he moves out of his place, heaven and earth are shaken to their foundations." Thus wrote James Baldwin in 1963, in an open letter to his nephew on the Hundredth Anniversary of the Emancipation. But he could have been summarizing the theme of Alice Childress's 1956 play, *Trouble in Mind,* currently enjoying a belated British premiere at London's Tricycle Theatre.

The play takes as its universe a theatre where rehearsals are under way for *Chaos in Belleville,* itself a play about the South after the Civil War. The characters in the play-within-a-play are familiar stereotypes: the white plantation owner; his liberal but misguided daughter; the faithful mammy; the maid; the good-for-nothing Uncle Tom, whittling a stick; and the rebel son. The storyline of *Chaos* purports to be a cry against injustice—whites recognizing the error of their ways when the rebel black youth is killed—but it is the plantation owner who takes credit for the change, so as to keep white reality intact.

Curiously, the actors who play the roles are themselves stereotypes, mid-twentieth-century versions of the characters they portray. There is the older white actor who refuses to eat with the black cast; the wealthy blonde Barbie doll; the conciliatory older actress and the younger, more spirited one; the toadying yes-man actor; and the bright young man, just out of college, looking for and expecting a better life. Their director, the aptly named Al Manners, admirably played by Maurice Roëves, is a white man who believes, "in principle", in black equality, but who fears disruption. "Social change", he argues, "takes time and tact."

The catalyst for discussion about social change is Wiletta Mayer (Carmen Munroe), a woman who,

throughout her theatrical career, has toed the line, conformed to type ("Whatever you say", she repeats, and "Don't ask me 'cos I don't know"), but who ultimately refuses to do so when playing the role of the black mammy: demanded by the script to turn her son over to the white authorities, Wiletta refuses the act, the lines, and the part in *Chaos in Belleville,* if need be. And, as Baldwin warns, heaven and earth shake. The monologue Childress has written for Wiletta is rousing, but it is above all the fire and passion of Munroe's splendid performance that make the production really worth seeing.

The script is strong and involving throughout, with only one truly mawkish moment (when Judy, the well-meaning white girl, turns to John, the young man, and cries, "You are a puppet with strings on. And so am I. Everyone's a stranger and I'm the strangest of all!" before rushing from the stage); and the fine cast do it justice. It cannot be easy to play humanized stereotypes, as most of them are called upon to do; but, under the direction of Nicolas Kent, they succeed far better than do their characters in *Chaos in Belleville.*

Trouble in Mind cannot help, in some ways, feeling dated: stereotypes, both black and white, have changed more in the past thirty-five years than in the entire century before that. But, transmogrified, they have not disappeared, and the play is not without resonances and relevance today.

Source: Claire Messud. "Roles of Thunder" in *Times Literary Supplement,* no. 4673, October 23, 1992, p. 18.

Elizabeth Brown-Guillory

Brown-Guillory discusses Childress's play in this excerpt, touching on the Trouble in Mind,*'s history and stage technique.*

The theme of rejecting stereotypes and of not compromising one's integrity is further explored in Childress' *Trouble in Mind,* which was produced at the Greenwich Mews Theatre in New York in 1955. Running for ninety-one performances, *Trouble in Mind* won for Childress the Obie Award for the best original off-Broadway play of the 1955–1956 season and was subsequently produced twice in 1964 by the BBC in London. When offered a Broadway option, Childress refused because the producer wanted her to make radical script changes. Alice Childress says of her rejection of the Broadway offer, "Most of our problems have not seen the light of day in our works, and much has been pruned from our manuscripts before the public has been allowed a glimpse of a finished work. It is ironical that those who oppose us are in a position to dictate the quality of our contributions'' [Abramson].

Childress' *Trouble in Mind* needed ''pruning'' because it is a satiric drama about white writers, producers, and directors who, because they are ignorant of blacks, support or defend inaccurate portraits. Childress insists in this drama that blacks must maintain their integrity and identity in the theater, refusing to accept roles that characterize them as exotic or half-human creatures, regardless of the monetary losses.

Making use of the play-within-a-play, *Trouble in Mind* is set on a Broadway stage where the characters rehearse *Chaos in Belleville,* a play written by a white about blacks. Wiletta Mayer, a veteran black actress, offends the sensibilities of the white director when she asserts that no black mother, as in *Chaos in Belleville,* would tell her son to give himself up to be lynched, regardless of his innocence or guilt. Appalled by other untruths, Wiletta announces that she will not perform unless some changes are made in the script. Because of her frankness, she is summarily dropped from the cast.

Trouble in Mind, Childress' first professionally produced play outside of Harlem, received glowing reviews. Loften Mitchell, in *Black Drama* [1967], commented, ''Now the professional theatre saw her outside of her native Harlem, writing with swift stabs of humor, her perception and her consummate dramatic gifts.'' Equally laudatory is the assessment made by Arthur Gelb of the *New York Times* [5 November 1955], who says that Childress has ''some witty and penetrating things to say about the dearth of roles for Negro actors in contemporary theatre, the cut-throat competition for these parts and the fact that Negro actors often find themselves playing stereotyped roles in which they cannot bring themselves to believe.''

Source: Elizabeth Brown-Guillory. ''Alice Childress, Lorraine Hansberry, Ntozake Shange: Carving a Place for Themselves on the American Stage'' in *Their Place on the Stage: Black Women Playwrights in America,* Greenwood, 1988, pp. 25–49.

> CHILDRESS INSISTS IN THIS DRAMA THAT BLACKS MUST MAINTAIN THEIR INTEGRITY AND IDENTITY IN THE THEATER, REFUSING TO ACCEPT ROLES THAT CHARACTERIZE THEM AS EXOTIC OR HALF-HUMAN CREATURES, REGARDLESS OF THE MONETARY LOSSES''

Austin, Gayle. ''Alice Childress: Black Woman Playwright as Feminist Critic,'' *Southern Quarterly,* Spring 1987, pp. 53-62.

Childress, Alice. ''*Trouble in Mind*'' in *Black Theater: A 20th Century Collection of the Work of Its Best Playwrights,* Dodd, Mead & Company, 1971, pp. 135-74.

Keyssar, Helen. ''Foothills: Precursors of Feminist Drama,'' in *Feminist Theatre: An Introduction to Plays of Contemporary British and American Women,* Macmillian, 1984, pp. 22-52.

Killens, John O. ''The Literary Genius of Alice Childress,'' in *Black Women Writers (1950-80): A Critical Evaluation,* Anchor Books, 1984, p. 128.

Messud, Claire. ''Roles of Thunder,'' *Times Literary Supplement,* October 23, 1992, p. 18.

Raymond, Harry. ''Alice Childress Play at 'Mews' Sparkling, Witty Social Satire,'' *Daily Worker,* November 8, 1955, p. 7.

A review of *Trouble in Mind* in *The New York Times,* November 5, 1955, p. 23.

Sommer, Sally R. ''Black Figures, White Shadows'' in *The Village Voice,* January 15, 1979, p. 91.

FURTHER READING

Brown-Guillory, Elizabeth. ''Alice Childress: A Pioneering Spirit'' in *Sage,* Spring 1987, pp. 66-68.
An interview with Childress which focuses primarily on biographical information and professional inspiration.

SOURCES

Abramson, Doris E. *Negro Playwrights in the American Theatre, 1925-1959,* Columbia University Press, 1969, pp. 188- 205.

Brown-Guillory, Elizabeth. *Their Place on the Stage: Black Women Playwrights in America,* Greenwood Press, 1988, pp. 28-34.

 Discusses many playwrights, including Childress. The analysis of Childress includes a discussion of *Trouble in Mind.*

Bryer, Jackson R., editor. ''Alice Childress,'' in *The Playwright's Art: Conversations with Contemporary American Dramatists,* Rutgers University Press, 1995, p. 48.

 This interview, which took place about a year before Childress's death, covers her life and career.

Dugan, Olga. ''Telling the Truth: Alice Childress as Theorist and Playwright,'' *The Journal of Negro History,* Annual 1996, pp. 123-37.

 This essay discusses Childress's theories about drama and African Americans in her essays as well as some basic biographical information.

Jennings, La Vinia Delois. *Alice Childress,* Twayne, 1995.

 This book considers Childress's entire literary career, including *Trouble in Mind.* Some biographical information is also included.

Ubu Roi

ALFRED JARRY
1896

The plays of Alfred Jarry are considered by many to be the first dramatic works of the theatre of the absurd. They are credited with a great number of literary innovations and are seen as major influences of the dada and symbolist movements in art. *Ubu Roi* (translated as *King Ubu* and *King Turd*) is Jarry's most famous work. *Ubu Roi* eliminates the dramatic action from its Shakespearean antecedents and uses scatological humor and farce to present Jarry's views on art, literature, politics, the ruling classes, and current events.

Ubu Roi first saw life as schoolboy farce, a parody of Felix Hebert, one of Jarry's teachers. Co-authored with his friend, Henri Morin, the skit was transformed into a marionette play through several versions. In 1891, Jarry published a story, ''Guignol,'' reminiscent of the Punch and Judy performances popular throughout Europe, which showcased a vile and murderous Pere Ubu. A two-act version of *Ubu Roi* with songs for marionettes, *Ubu sur la Batte,* appeared in print in 1906.

The opening night of December 11, 1896, caused quite a stir according to Roger Shattuck in his work *The Banquet Years.* Actor Firmin Gernier stepped forward to speak the opening line—''Merdre!'' (translated as ''Shitter!''). The audience erupted in pandemonium. It took nearly fifteen minutes to silence the house and continue the play. Several people walked out without hearing any more. Fist fights broke out in the orchestra. Jarry supporters

shouted, "You wouldn't understand Shakespeare either!" Those who did not appreciate Jarry's attack on theatrical realism replied with variations of *le mot Ubu.*

The stage manager startled the audience into silence by turning up the house lights and catching several screaming patrons standing on their seats and shaking their upraised fists. Gernier improvised a dance and the audience settled back down long enough for the action to proceed to the next "merdre," when the audience exploded once again. The interruptions continued throughout the play until the curtain fell. One audience member, a stunned and saddened William Butler Yeats, remarked "[W]hat more is possible? After us the Savage God."

In his book *Jarry: Ubu Roi,* Keith Beaumont detailed three accusations that were made against *Ubu Roi* by spectators and critics in the aftermath of the outrageous performance. The first focused on the play's "alleged" vulgarity and obscenity. Secondly, perhaps in view of the political atmosphere of the time, critics condemned the play and its performance as the theatrical equivalent of an "anarchist" bomb attack and as an act of political subversion. The third accusation leveled against the play and its performance was that they in no way constituted a "serious" piece of literature or of theater but rather a gigantic hoax.

AUTHOR BIOGRAPHY

Alfred Jarry, considered by some to be the father of the theater of the absurd, was born in Laval, France, on September 8, 1873. His father, Anselme, represented a wool factory as a traveling salesman, and his mother (nee Caroline Quernest) was the daughter of a judge. As a youth, Jarry won scholastic prizes in foreign languages and science. But the rebellious spirit and biting wit that marked his adult life were already making themselves known. With his school friends, Jarry mounted productions that made fun of his physics teacher, Felix Herbert. These parodies of Herbert were rewritten as *Ubu Roi* (1896; translated as *King Turd* in 1953).

The Ubu saga continued with *Ubu enchaine* (1900; translated as *King Enslaved* in 1953) and *Ubu cocu* (1944; translated as *King Cuckolded*). Jarry also wrote two novels. *Le Surmale: Roman moderne* (1902; translated as *The Supermale: A Modern Novel* [1968]) tells the story of a man who has a love making contest with a machine. The other novel, *Gestes et opinions du Docteur Faustroll, pataphysicien* (1911; translated as *The Exploits and Opinions of Dr. Faustroll, Pataphysician* [1965]) defined "pataphysics" as the science of imaginary solutions.

In his later years, Jarry demonstrated outrageous behavior; he mimicked the monotonous speech and the jerky walk of Pere Ubu; his abuse of ether and alcohol distorted his ability to distinguish himself from the characters he had created. Jarry died in a charity hospital in Paris on November 1, 1907. He was just thirty-four years of age.

PLOT SUMMARY

Act I

Pere Ubu, along with Mere Ubu and Captain Bordure, plot the killing of the King of Poland. Pere Ubu poisons Bordure's men, who have assembled at a sumptuous feast, by providing an excrement covered toilet brush for all to taste. The act ends with Pere Ubu demanding that Mere Ubu, Captain Bordure, and the other conspirators "swear to kill the king properly."

Act II

Pere Ubu attacks and kills King Venceslas of Poland. Queen Rosemonde and her youngest son, Bougrelas, escape to a mountain cave, but the Queen dies. The dead ancestors appear to Bougrelas and demand vengeance, giving him a large sword.

After some prompting from Mere Ubu about sharing some of his newly ill gotten wealth, Pere Ubu throws gold coins to the crowd. Several are trampled in the mad rush. Pere Ubu's response is to provide more gold as a prize to whoever wins a footrace. Afterwards, Pere Ubu invites the assembled multitude to an orgy at the palace.

Act III

Pere Ubu and Mere Ubu discuss what to do now that they are the sovereigns of Poland. Pere Ubu has decided, now that he no longer has any need of Captain Bordure, not to elevate him to the rank of Duke of Lithuania. Bordure ends up in Pere Ubu's dungeon but escapes to ally himself with Czar Alexis. Meanwhile, Pere Ubu executes all of Poland's nobles so that he can then lay claim to their properties. Then, he follows suit with the magistrates and the financiers, claiming a reform in both the law and financial dealings of the government. When he realizes that all of the government workers have been killed, Ubu shrugs and simply says that he himself will go door to door to collect the taxes.

Bordure sends Ubu a letter in which he reveals his plans to invade Poland and re-establish Bougrelas as the rightful King. Ubu weeps and sobs in fear until Mere Ubu suggests they go to war. Pere Ubu agrees but refuses to "pay out one sou" for its expense. With the cardboard cutout of a horse's head around his neck, Ubu leads his army off to battle against Bordure, Czar Alexis, and Bougrelas.

Act IV

Mere Ubu searches the crypt that holds the remains of the former Kings of Poland for the Polish treasure. She discovers it among the bones of the dead kings but cannot carry it all out at once. When she says that she'll come back tomorrow for the rest of the treasure, a voice from one of the tombs shouts, "never, Mere Ubu." Bougrelas advances to Warsaw and wins the first battle. Mere Ubu escapes amid rifle shots and a hail of stones. Meanwhile, Pere Ubu and the czar do battle in the Ukraine. The tide shifts, first one way, then another. Finally, Pere Ubu and his army are bested. They escape to a cave in Lithuania. A bear attacks while Ubu is in the cave with two of his soldiers; Ubu climbs to safety on a rock, and, when asked for help, responds by mumbling a Pater Noster ("Our Father, who art in heaven . . ."). After the soldiers kill the bear, Ubu falls asleep, and the two men decide to escape while they have the opportunity.

Act V

After crossing Poland in four days to escape Bougrelas and his army, Mere Ubu arrives at the cave where Pere Ubu is sleeping fitfully. Unseen by her husband, Mere Ubu pretends to be a supernatural apparition to make Pere Ubu ask forgiveness for his "bit of pilfering." Instead, Mere Ubu is treated to a litany of her faults. When he discovers that it is Mere Ubu in the cave, Pere Ubu throws the dead bear on top of her. Not taking any chances that it might still be alive, Pere Ubu climbs up on the rock and begins the Pater Noster routine again. Angered that Mere Ubu laughs at him, Pere Ubu begins to tear her to pieces. But, before he can do much damage, Bougrelas and his army arrive and soundly beat the Ubus, who just manage to escape to a ship on the Baltic Sea. Pere Ubu plans to get himself

A portrait of Alfred Jarry done in 1897 by F. A. Cazalz

nominated Minister of Finances in Paris so that the whole sordid series of events can begin again.

CHARACTERS

Captain Bordure

Bourdure kills King Venceslas of Poland, paving the way for Pere Ubu to become the king. Later, Bordure abandons Ubu, goes over to the Russians, and plots the death of Pere Ubu and the reclamation of the Polish throne by Bougrelas with the czar. Pere Ubu recognizes Bordure in the middle of the battle, and, the stage directions indicate, tears him to pieces.

Bougrelas

Bougrelas is the sole surviving son of King Venceslas and Queen Rosemonde. He escapes from the battle with Pere Ubu, receives a visit from all his dead ancestors demanding vengeance, and eventually defeats Pere Ubu and regains the crown.

Queen Rosemonde

Queen Rosemonde tries to warn King Venceslas by recounting one of her dreams. In the dream, Ubu

MEDIA ADAPTATIONS

- The Gertrude Stein Repertory Theatre has plans to present UBU WEDNESDAYS, "an exciting new multi-media look of the creation of the innovative UBU PROJECT. Collaborating with artists in Japan and Russia, GSRT is developing new theatre for the twenty-first century by integrating traditional stage-bound techniques with the limitless space of the World Wide Web." The UBU PROJECT is the GSRT's original, full-length adaptation of Alfred Jarry's 1896 work, *Ubu Roi.* The project features live actors present in the performance space, projected characters via video-conferencing, and "Digital Puppets" derived from the Japanese performance traditions of *bunraku* and *ningyo buri.* More information can be found on the World Wide Web at http://www.gertstein.org/details/pro-ubu.htm.

- The American Repertory Theatre presented *Ubu Rock* by Shelley Berc and Andrei Belgrader based upon *Ubu Roi.* Music and lyrics by Rusty Magee, directed by Andrei Belgrader. A special return engagement was sponsored by the Boston Phoenix and WFNX-FM. This performance closed March 23, 1996, at the Loeb Drama Center.

kills Venceslas and becomes King of Poland. During the battle, the queen escapes down the secret stairway with her son, Bougrelas, but dies shortly after in a cave in the mountains.

Mere Ubu

Other than her outrageous husband, Mere Ubu is the only character in the play who exhibits more than two or three basic character traits. That is not to say, however, that Mere Ubu is a fully rounded, complex character in the play. On the contrary, she is merely a watered down version of her pompous husband. She does act like Lady Macbeth early in the play by suggesting that Pere Ubu slaughter the entire Polish royal family and ascend to the throne.

After that, she makes no additional contribution to the plot of the drama.

Pere Ubu

Pere Ubu is less than a "king," even lesser than a traditional dramatic character. He kills the royal family of Poland in order to gain the throne, plunders their wealth, and steals whatever and whenever he desires. When threatened by the Polish king's surviving son, Ubu runs and hides. And, through everything, he stuffs himself with food and drink and shouts obscenities. Jarry uses the perverse behaviors of Pere Ubu—greed, ambition, tyrannical behavior, absolute stupidity—to satirize the middle class life he hated.

The original character of Pere Ubu was first seen as a marionette. The clipped speech and robot-like movements of the play's Pere Ubu derive from this earlier incarnation. Jarry wanted Ubu to be played masked, but the actor who portrayed the character in its outrageous performance at the Theatre de l'Oeuvre, Firmin Gernier, refused. However, the rapid speech, the jerky stylized movements, and the bulging pear-shaped costume were maintained.

Unlike characters in more conventional plays, Pere Ubu is free from the restraints of good and evil. He experiences his own perversity with a sick joy, a bombastic attitude, and a foul tongue. It has been suggested that the character of Ubu is played "in life itself" rather than dreamed or written. Pere Ubu lives on, not so much because of the play that bears his name, but because of Jarry's transformation into his own creation.

King Venceslas

Venceslas is King of Poland. He raises Pere Ubu to the rank of Count of Sandomir. Venceslas ignores the warning of his wife and goes to the "Review" without a sword. There, the army of Pere Ubu, led by Captain Bordure, kills the King. The ghost of King Venceslas visits his sole surviving son, Bougrelas, as part of the assembled dead who demand vengeance.

THEMES

Absurdity

As a philosophical term, absurdity describes the lack of reasonableness and coherence in human existence. As a literary term, absurdity seems to have been coined especially for Pere Ubu. Throughout the play, Pere Ubu appears to be unaware of what is happening around him. Murder, dismemberment, the trampling of a townsperson when Pere Ubu distributes gold—none of these atrocities faze Ubu. The character of Pere Ubu is absurd in another way: his reason for living seems to be to kill everyone; his actions that lead up to these killings can be described as "irrefutably logical." Logic equals killing everyone.

Art and Experience

Alfred Jarry's view of a new theater centered on two conditions: the need to "create new life" in the theater by creating a new type of character and the need to transcend the "things that happen all the time to the common man."

Pere Ubu fulfills the definition of the new type of character—as did Jarry himself. Jarry not only wrote the adventures of Pere Ubu, he lived them. He walked like Ubu; he talked in the clipped robotic speech of Ubu. Novelist Andre Gide wrote that Jarry showed no human characteristics. "A nutcracker, if it could talk, would do no differently. He asserted himself without the least reticence and in perfect disdain of good manners." Jarry fished for his neighbors' chickens from a tree and drove waiters crazy by gorging himself on meals ordered, and eaten, in reverse order, dessert first. In time, Jarry became known to his friends as Pere Ubu.

As for the need to transcend everyday actions and situations, Jarry advanced a type of "shock treatment." Ubu's opening line ("Merdre!") accomplished that rather handily. Jarry's admitted intention was to stir up the passive audiences pandered to by the realistic theater. Stock characters and slapstick action, the staple of Punch and Judy marionette performances, could express universal concerns and escape the narrow confines of the "lived reality" of the realistic theater.

Dadaism

Ubu Roi predates the official founding of Dadaism by about ten years. Nevertheless, Pere Ubu and his alter ego Alfred Jarry seem worthy ancestors to this literary and artistic movement. Dadaism was devoted to the negation of all traditional values in philosophy and the arts. The *Dada* review pro-

TOPICS FOR FURTHER STUDY

- Playwright Eugene Ionesco has written that his plays are not exercises in absurdity but denunciations of our decaying language. How might *Ubu Roi* fall into that description?

- Many critics have said that *Ubu Roi* satirizes the bourgeois values of turn of the century European society. Show how the actions and character of Pere Ubu accomplish this satire.

- Scholars have frequently remarked on the allusions to Shakespeare found in *Ubu Roi*. Find and explain specific references to *Hamlet, Julius Caesar,* and *Macbeth* in this play and comment on their effectiveness as a dramatic tool.

- The first public performance of *Ubu Roi* caused a riot in the Theatre de l'Oeuvre. Research this opening performance and observe not only what happened but how some of the eyewitnesses reacted to this. Compare these reactions to those that accompanied the opening of "controversial" plays such as Edward Albee's *Who's Afraid of Virginia Woolf?* or *Hair* by Gerome Ragni, James Rado, and Galt McDermot.

claimed its intention to replace logic and reason with deliberate madness and to substitute intentionally discordant chaos for established notions of beauty or harmony in the arts.

Ubermensch ("Superman")

The term Ubermensch comes from Nietzsche's *Thus Spake Zarathustra.* It is used to designate the goal of human existence. Humans should commit themselves to earthly goals. They should sacrifice their lives for these goals and out of the destruction that would result from such sacrifice would rise the "Ubermensch."

Out of the destruction in *Ubu Roi,* Pere Ubu rises, though more like a "Stupidman." Ubu is the antithesis of Nietzsche's Superman, although he is

An example of Jarry's absurdity, as reflected in the odd costuming of his lead characters

an individual process of self-creation, unique and undefinable, and, like his creator Alfred Jarry, forever unfinished.

STYLE

Jarry had definite ideas, not only about the staging for *Ubu Roi,* but for the theater in general. In an essay, translated by Barbara Wright as "Of the Futility of the Theatrical," Jarry discusses "a few things which are particularly horrifying and incomprehensible . . . and which clutter up the stage to no purpose."

It would be dangerous, says Jarry, for the writer to impose the *decor* [stage setting] that he himself would imagine and conceive. For "a public of artists" (as opposed to the general public), each audience member should be able to see a play in a *decor* that does not "clash with his own view of it." The general public, on the other hand, can be shown any "artistic" *decor* because "the masses do not understand anything by themselves, but wait to be

told how to see things." A colorless background, an unpainted backdrop or the reverse side of a set, can allow the spectator to "conjure up for himself the background he requires." Better still, Jarry continues in this essay, "the spectator can imagine, by a process of exosmosis [the passage of gases or liquids through membranes], that what he sees on the stage is the real *decor.*

The actor in a play should use a mask to cover his head, argues Jarry, and replace it with the "effigy of the CHARACTER." The masks should not be a copy of the ancient Greek dramatic masks— one for tears, one for laughter—but should somehow indicate "the nature of the character: the Miser, the Waverer, the Covetous Man." Six main positions (and six in profile) are enough for every expression. Jarry uses the example of a puppet showing bewilderment by "starting back violently and hitting its head against a flat" to illustrate his point (*Ubu Roi* made one its first appearances as a marionette drama.)

Another important element for Jarry is that the actor have a "special voice." The voice must be "appropriate to the part, as if the cavity forming the mouth of the mask were incapable of uttering anything other than what the mask would say." The whole play, Jarry concludes, ''should be spoken in a monotone.''

HISTORICAL CONTEXT

The New Wave of Arts and Letters

''We want to demolish museums and librar-ies!'' These fighting words come not from the mouth of a fanatic or a terrorist but rather from the pen of Italian poet Emilio Marietti. He, along with other artists and writers, wanted to destroy all that preserved traditional art and learning in Western Europe. These ''futurists,'' who spurned the value of tradition, wanted to break completely free from the past. They wanted to fashion an entirely new civilization that would divorce itself from the seri-ous moral and cultural crises of the late-nineteenth century.

Jarry's Europe was preoccupied with change. Developments in the sciences brought into question the role of a divine creator (particularly the work of Charles Darwin, which presented validation of the theory of evolution). Changes in communication (the telephone, the ''wireless'') and in transporta-tion (the bicycle, the automobile) skewed tradition-al understandings of time and space. The introduc-tion of moving pictures and X-rays redefined the ways in which people saw the world around them. What had once been the province of magic became reality in the waning years of the nineteenth century.

Liberation from the past and all of its traditions could only be achieved through acceptance of and immersion in these rapid changes. Painter Umberto Boccioni stated the goal: ''Let's turn everything upside down. . . . Let's split open our figures and place the environment inside them.'' Another futur-ist proclaimed, ''A speeding automobile is more beautiful than *The Victory of Samothrace*''; con-temporary achievement, rather than an ancient Greek statue, reigned supreme.

Fin de Siecle Political Turmoil

Two major events before World War I that transformed political life in France were the Boulanger Affair and the Dreyfus Affair. General Boulanger attempted to seize power in France in the 1880s. Molded by a carefully orchestrated publicity campaign, Boulanger appeared as the ''messiah,'' the proverbial knight in shining armor who would save France's honor at all costs. His play for power

failed, however, and Boulanger left France in dis-grace amid allegations of treason.

Accused of selling military secrets to the Ger-mans, Army Captain Alfred Dreyfus, on the other hand, sparked debate between those who were con-vinced of his innocence and expected the Republic to uphold the ideals of justice and freedom and those associated with the traditional institutions—the Church, the army—who considered themselves to be upholding and defending the honor of France. Intellectuals organized themselves and pressed for the exoneration of Dreyfus. Novelist Emile Zola, in his famous front page letter to the editor *J'Accuse,* demonstrated the power of the written word in changing governmental decisions.

Jarry's written words would not bring political change, though they would, with the production of *Ubu Roi,* change the way in which a pompous caricature could impact the literary consciousness of an age.

CRITICAL OVERVIEW

When actor Firmin Gernier stepped forward and spoke his opening line as Pere Ubu—''Merdre!'' (often translated as ''Shitter!'')—the audience erupt-ed. Some would say the controversy still rages. What those who study late-nineteenth century thea-ter do agree on is that Jarry attacked theatrical realism head-on and things just haven't been the same since.

Brian E. Rainey in an essay in the *Wascana Review* noted that ''*Ubu* is at once a commentary on and a revolt against the world in which Jarry lived.'' Anarchy, greed, corruption, and cowardice all play prominent roles in *Ubu Roi*. Pere Ubu seeks to destroy everything; he holds nothing sacred. Jarry provided the prototype for much of what would come to be known in the future as a Brechtian or ''alienation effect.'' Pere Ubu may speak *en Francais,* but his vices are not exclusively French. He has achieved real universality.

Many critics have dismissed *Ubu Roi* as imma-ture and childish. G. E. Wellwarth in his article ''Alfred Jarry: The Seeds of Avant-Garde Drama'' argued that the ''superficial childishness of the *Ubu* plays should not prevent the reader from taking them seriously. The fact that Jarry's mind remained in many essentials that of a child in no way dimin-ishes his importance as the originator of a scream of

COMPARE & CONTRAST

- Late-1800s: In the Franco-Prussian War (1870-71) France loses the Alsace and Lorraine regions. It is the end of the French monarchy. The war, however, does not slow industrial expansion, which continues at a rapid pace. The artistic and cultural scene flourishes and witnesses the Impressionists, Art Nouveau, and the novels of Flaubert and Zola.

  Today: With the collapse of the Berlin Wall and the Soviet Union, the Cold War ends. The U.S. economy thrives, even in the face of "mini-wars" with Iraq and Serbia. The Impressionists still draw a crowd as museums sell out shows of Monet.

- Late-1800s: The Industrial Revolution changes the face of England, the Continent, and the United States. Factories are churning out goods at an unprecedented rate.

Today: The Industrial Revolution has moved to other countries where consumer goods, like electronic equipment and clothing, can be manufactured for less. Charges of "sweatshop labor" are leveled against many prominent American companies.

- Late-1800s: Pere Ubu shocks the Paris theatre going audience and causes rioting in the seats when the first word he utters is considered profanity.

Today: Cable television brings profanity in film to living rooms while the internet makes other unsavory forms of content—such as hate propaganda and child pornography—available.

---

protest which Antonin Artaud later decreed as the official theme of avant-garde drama.''

Ubu Roi presents Jarry's warped version of a naive childish fantasy—the good king killed by an evil person who wants the throne, the young and virtuous heir to the throne avenging his father, battles resembling those fought with toy soldiers, eerie (but not too scary) "supernatural" events, a fight with a pretend bear, and so on.

"If Pere Ubu exerted a profound influence on the young intellectuals of the period," stated Dan M. Church in *Drama Survey,* "it was not because they had seen him on the stage or had read about him in a book; it was because they saw him and knew him through his flesh-and-blood incarnation: Alfred Jarry." The nihilism of Ubu appealed to the young late nineteenth-century intellectuals. The foul-mouthed, rotund comic figure and the nascent revolutionaries stood side by side. But, argued Church, with two World Wars and the rise of dictators, Pere Ubu has changed from the symbol of the revolutionary to the embodiment of all that they are revolting

against: the shining emblem of totalitarianism, the perfect representation of bourgeois bureaucracy, and the poster boy for the insanity of war and mass murder.

CRITICISM

William P. Wiles,

In this essay, Wiles examines Jarry's play as a ground breaking work, what is considered by many to be the first drama in the Theatre of the Absurd.

It is highly doubtful that Alfred Jarry's *Ubu Roi* will be performed on a high school stage any time soon. Why then subject it to academic scrutiny in a reference work aimed at the high school audience? The answer, quite simply enough, is because it was the first. In art, establishing a precedent is most important. Once Pere Ubu waddled to the middle of the stage and uttered his scandalous, foul-mouthed opening line, the theater could never be the same

WHAT DO I READ NEXT?

- Two works by French author Albert Camus explore the concept of the absurd in modern literature. *The Myth of Sisyphus* and *The Stranger* emphasize the psychological implications of the absurd.

- *Waiting for Godot*, a play written in French by Irish born playwright Samuel Beckett, is a tragicomedy in which nothing happens except conversations that suggest the meaninglessness of life. Although bleak and austere, the drama is humorous, making a statement about the will to live and the ability to hope when hope is lost.

- According to *The Reader's Encyclopedia,* the plays of Eugene Ionesco are characterized by deliberate *non sequiturs,* the logic of nightmares, and strange metamorphoses. These farces are essentially comic, however, because Ionesco is sympathetic to any human attempt, inadequate or otherwise, at communication and love. Two of his better-known works are *The Chairs* and *Rhinoceros.*

- *The Maids* and *The Balcony* by French dramatist and novelist Jean Genet reveal a deep concern with the illusory nature of reality, particularly with the definitions of good and evil by a society that exhibits duplicity and hypocrisy.

---

again. The entire dramatic experience had been fashioned into something new and different. Jarry opened a Pandora's box and neglected to close the lid.

Jarry rebelled, not only against the prevailing traditions and conventions of *fin de siecle* (''end of the century'') drama, but against absolutely everything. He rejected the world of reality and the world of ideas and constructed his own world detailed in his *Pataphysics.* For example, Jarry's refusal to use ''realistic'' stage props is built on the idea that these artificial trappings prevent the audience from seeing its own personal vision of the setting in which the action (or non-action) occurs. The raising and lowering of the curtain, then, disrupts the creative relationship between the audience and the drama. The elaborate recreation of a room or an outdoor location would be the vision of the set designer and not the audience.

Instead, Jarry used descriptive placards and representational devices (a single actor for a parade of soldiers; wicker mannequins for the nobles) to shock his blockhead audience ''so that we can tell from their bear-like grunts where they are—and also how they stand.''

Nearly every anti-realist artistic movement of the twentieth century used Jarry's confrontational dramatic format as a model. Todd London explained in his essay ''My Ubu, Myself'' that the Dadaists took inspiration from Jarry's chaos, while the Symbolists emulated Jarry's emphasis on image over action. The description of the *Ubu* set illustrates a rough, contradictory beauty: ''You will see doors open on fields of snow under blue skies, fireplaces furnished with clocks and swinging wide to serve as doors, and palm trees growing at the foot of a bed so that little elephants standing on bookshelves can browse on them.'' The Surrealists admired Jarry's unwillingness to distinguish art from life, especially as he came more and more to embody his creation—Pere Ubu—in his public life. As Andre Breton explained in *Free Rein,* ''Beginning with Jarry . . . the differentiation long considered necessary between art and life has been challenged, to wind up annihilated as a principle.''

It is odd that so much attention has been paid to a play that has not been performed that many times since its debut in 1896. Rather, it is the transformation of Alfred Jarry into his character Pere Ubu that garners the notice of scholars. The shift from Jarry to Ubu did not happen all at once but occurred progressively as the distinctions between the life and the work of art blurred and fused into a unique continuity. Roger Shattuck stated in *The Banquet*

A scene from a contemporary (1998) interpretation of Jarry's work, featuring Luis Alberto Soto as Pere Ubu and Christine Entwistle as Mere Ubu

Years that this living creation was Jarry's attempt to abandon himself to "the hallucinatory world of dreams. . . . Jarry converted himself in a new person physically and mentally devoted to an artistic goal. . . . He had found his Other, the flesh of his hallucination."

In late-nineteenth century France, farces and well-mannered plays with polite plots controlled the mainstream theater. Pere Ubu's explosive opening line disrupted this veneer of civility and established the rules for the avant-garde of the new century. The rules, of course, were there were no rules. Jarry not

only put "the word" on the stage, he also brought "the object" in the form of a toilet brush which Pere Ubu serves as one of the courses at a banquet. With this new level of tastelessness (the guests lick the brush and are poisoned), Jarry illustrates the satirical qualities of scatology to degradation and violence.

John Updike, quoted in *Twentieth Century Literary Criticism,* provided an excellent summation:

How are we to judge Alfred Jarry? Apollinaire expressed the hope that his weird words will be the foundation of a new realism which will perhaps not be inferior to that so poetic and learned realism of ancient

Greece. Gabriel Brunet explained him by saying, ''Every man is capable of showing his contempt for the cruelty and stupidity of the universe by making his own life a poem of incoherent absurdity.'' I think the second estimate more plausible; Jarry's life, as a defiant gesture, matters more that his works, which are largely pranks and propaganda of a rarefied sort. Compared to Jarry, most of today's so-called Black Humorists seem merely ex-admen working off their grudges in sloppy travesties of a society whose tame creatures hey remain still. Though we cannot grant him the comprehensive sanity and the reverent submission to reality that produce lasting art, we must admire his soldier's courage and his fanatic's will.

Jarry turned the theater upside-down and inside-out. He took reality and placed it into a magician's top hat. With a wave of his wand and a magic word or two, he produced not a loveable furry white rabbit but the grotesque and foul-mouthed Pere Ubu. People have not been able to look at drama in the same way since.

Source: William P. Wiles, for *Drama for Students,* Gale, 2000.

Donald Gilman

In the following essay, Gilman provides an overview of Jarry's play, explaining the plays concepts and themes.

In this five-act satirical farce, Jarry adapts the serious story of seizure of power to the comic aims of ridicule and relief. Mère Ubu, playing upon her husband's bestial instincts, urges him to overthrow Wenceslas, King of Poland. After enlisting Bordure's assistance, Ubu usurps the throne in the second act, murdering the ruler and his two sons. Bourgelas, one of the King's sons, escapes with his mother. Meanwhile, in order to placate the Poles and satisfy his greed, Ubu offers the people gold that he reclaims through taxation. In the third act, Ubu assumes authority, liquidating the nobility and magistrates and confiscating national wealth. He also condemns Bordure who, taking refuge in Russia, requests Czar Alexis to help restore order and justice. Alexis attacks, and Mère convinces Ubu of the necessary recourse to war.

In Act IV, while Ubu battles against the Russians, his wife plunders the treasures of Poland. Ubu kills Bordure, but the decimation of his army compels him and his two Palotins to retreat. In fending off a rapacious bear, the Palotins perceive their leader's cowardice and abandon him. In the final act, Ubu's wife flees Bourgelas's avenging army, arriving at the cave where Ubu is sleeping. Darkness enables her to impersonate the angel Gabriel

> THROUGH THE HUMOR, RESULTING FROM FANTASY AND FOOLISHNESS, JARRY ATTACKS THE MATERIALISM, EGOCENTRICISM, AND SUPERFICIALITIES WHICH, EMBODIED BY UBU, REFLECT BOURGEOIS AIMS AND ATTITUDES"

which, in turn, impels him to confess his wrongdoings. The light of daybreak, though, reveals her identity, and Ubu reverts to his former ways. Bourgelas attacks, and the Ubus, along with the Palotins who return, sail home with nostalgia for Poland.

Ubu's grotesqueness evokes caricature and disbelief. His rotund body and pear-shaped head seem ludicrous and fantastical, and the opening trite insults between Mère and Père suggest a slapstick show or a puppet-play. Like the closing scenes in farce, a comic resolution dispels danger as husband and wife return home, physically secure and morally unchanged. Lack of development of character excludes introspection: throughout the play, Ubu remains stupid, indolent, and totally egocentric; his wife stays avaricious, complaining, and domineering. Through incongruities and inversions, Jarry employs irony to elicit surprise and to induce absurdity. Besides his ridiculous appearance, Ubu swears meaningless oaths (''by my green candle'', ''shitter''), exaggerates the ordinary (his feast becomes a two-day orgy), and misconstrues reality (a bear is a ''little bow-wow''). By exploiting the unexpected, Jarry has this Falstaff-like personage debunk the solemn and dignify the preposterous: his stepping on Wenceslas's toe incites revolution; unlike the agile Czar, he jumps over a trench; and, seated safely on a rock, he recites a *paternoster* during the Palotins' struggle with the bear. Jarry also uses dramatic parody: like Macbeth urged to depose Duncan, Ubu yields to his wife's goadings, but his clumsiness, moral blindness, and inanities turn potential pathos into rollicking burlesque. Disparities of language and action heighten the ridiculous. During deliberations and battles, Ubu blends religious and literary references with nonsensical statements, thereby reducing the serious and dignified to the trivial and foolish. And, in the dream-sequence that recalls epic conventions, medieval allegories, and Renaissance romances, Mère convinces Père that her ugliness is comparable to Aphrodite's beauty and her depravities to saintly accomplishments.

The deceptions and distortions, though, present a superficial enjoyment that obscures the horrors of human bestiality and bourgeois shallowness. Ubu's self-absorption and obsession with material wealth and sensual gratification explain his callous disregard and vicious abuse of others; and, prodded by his unbridled instincts, he acts irrationally and erratically. In depicting this primal nature devoid of reason and discipline, Jarry converts innocuous horseplay into actions provoking appalling disgust. For example, Ubu's attack on his guests with bison-ribs provokes amusement; but his subsequent serving of human excrement at table replaces laughter with repugnance. Mère's duplicity punctures pleasure. By injecting false courage into Ubu's cowardly character, she yields to her insatiable greed for wealth and power, manipulating her husband to commit pillage and genocide.

As caricatures, they resemble cartoon animations; but their self-interest, insensitiveness, and indignities reflect the values and evils in bourgeois society. Exemplifying the ethos of this post-Darwinian era, Ubu disregards spiritual values; religion lacks belief, and Ubu facilely recites prayers to escape danger and death. He is a survivor whose instincts endure, and whose bestial superiorities destroy the weak and unfortunate. If Ubu is Everyman, he is also, paradoxically, Nobody, with his prosperity encasing a spiritual void. Instead, Ubu's obesity suggests a material gluttony that assures an aggression necessary for success and stature.

In neglecting the unities of time, place, and action, Jarry constructs a series of scenes resembling a montage of inconsistent happenings and absurd characterizations. Ubu's ludicrous appearance, irrational behavior, and vile words demonstrate a rejection of the established principles of verisimilitude and decorum; and at the first performance, the audience, expecting entertaining farce, was stunned and outraged. But by shattering the illusions that often, paradoxically, define reality, Jarry reveals the potential evils inherent in the subconscious. Through the humor, resulting from fantasy and foolishness, Jarry attacks the material-ism, egocentricism, and superficialities which, embodied by Ubu, reflect bourgeois aims and attitudes. Ubu's jokes are meaningless, insensitive utterances, and his unscrupulous deeds become unconscionable crimes. Satire, moreover, evolves into a probing of the dynamics of human impulses. Time and place dissolve, and Ubu emerges as an emblem of man's primal nature. Futility and absurdity characterize Ubu's endeavors: his actions end at the beginning; speech is claptrap; his uncontrolled affections and merciless, unrelenting aggressions destroy order and civilization. Jarry goes beyond a renunciation of conventional dramatic practice and accepted social standards. By creating a drama that suggests the later theories and plays of Artaud, Beckett, Genet, and Ionesco, he forces the spectator to confront, through Ubu, the savagery, isolation, and pain of human existence.

Source: Donald Gilman. *"Ubu Roi"* in *The International Dictionary of Theatre,* Vol. 1: *Plays,* edited by Mark Hawkins-Dady, St. James Press, 1992, pp. 847–49.

Michael Zelenak

Zelenak reviews a revival production of Jarry's play, one that takes considerable liberties with the playwright's text. The critic opines that by placing an emphasis on slapstick and scatological humor—as well as adding modern pop culture references—the Irondale production company captures the essence of Jarry's play while making it accessible to modern audiences.

Few dramatic works have attained the iconographic status of Alfred Jarry's *Ubu roi.* Its original two-performance production by Lugne-Poe in 1896 caused the greatest sensation in the French theater since Hugo's *Hernani* sixty years earlier. Jarry's play took only one word—the infamous *merdre*—to cause a near riot. Amidst the hysterical audience demonstrations, fist-fights and shower of missiles, the actors found themselves spectators to a theatrical event that dwarfed the one on stage. Although *Ubu* remains central to the avant-garde tradition, one might wonder: "Why revive *Ubu?*" And if one answers that question, a larger one looms: How to do *Ubu* ninety years later?

The Irondale Ensemble's New York production of *Ubu Roi* (1984–87) put itself in an active relationship to the text, using it simply as a starting point, a "pre-text" for a performance. They approached *Ubu* as a comedy-parody of the bourgeois world spirit, an ironic celebration of its endless adaptability and will to survive. Furthermore, they had fun with *Ubu*. The Irondale's *Ubu Roi* in some ways resembles a series of cabaret or burlesque skits. Just as much of *Ubu* is cartoon Shakespeare, the Irondale's is a cartoon *Ubu*. Very little of the actual Jarry text is used, but it follows the plot and incidents of the play fairly closely. The production is irreverent from its opening moment, which finds Ubu enthroned on the toilet, grumbling "Shit!" Taking the cue from Jarry, the scatological metaphor is sustained throughout. When Ubu has to think hard or soliloquize, he retreats to his toilet seat; the cue for the beginning of Ubu's coup d'etat is the password "shit." Pa Ubu (Josh Broder) is not a fully realized "character," but a grab-bag of comic techniques, most often the comic straight man or the deadpan stand-up comic. Pa Ubu is dim-witted and gross. He picks his nose, substitutes turds for meat at a state dinner to save money. He is an Aristophanic creation, operating from the basest, bottom-line human instincts, *viz.* food, sex and money. Ma Ubu (Molly Hickcock) is heavily camped, sometimes *a la* Mae West. The production is filled with low comedy, one liners, gags and intricate "bits" perhaps similar to the *commedia dell'arte's lazzi*. Its success is not due to any particularly brilliant comic moments but rather to the cumulative effect of the rapid succession of gags and routines and the almost endless invention of the company.

The level of humor ranges widely from slapstick and crude farce to literate satire. Irondale borrows from Shakespeare almost as much as Jarry did. Wenceslas is possibly even costumed to look like Duncan, and Ma Ubu's exhortations to her husband more than a little resemble Lady Macbeth. Wenceslas' wife has prophetic dreams very similar to those of Caesar's wife. A bear right out of *The Winter's Tale* eats most of Ubu's army near the end. In a parody of the parade of ghostly apparitions in Act V of *Richard III,* Pa Ubu has a similar vision. "Why have you come?" he questions the shades of his victims. "Because the show is going badly" they respond. It is surprising that the production holds together, since the audience is addressed directly so often. One scene is stopped halfway through because Ubu remembers that two scenes have been skipped. The humor is free-wheeling, at times reminding me of the old Firesign Theater. When the old Nobility beg King Ubu to spare their lives, he gives them a chance by presenting a mock "game show" where the category is "Reagan Fuck-ups." The nobility are executed for the wrong answer. Likewise, the "Financial advisors," an

JARRY'S PLAY IS A REBELLION AGAINST BOURGEOIS VALUES, ETHICS AND 'GOOD TASTE'"

identically costumed chorus of moustached, cigar-chomping Groucho Marxes who move in unison, get a similar opportunity to play charades for their lives. They get the right answer. but are executed for not getting a laugh. There are references to everything from *My Favorite Martian* and "Eggo Waffles" to Ferdinand and Imelda Marcos, evoked by Ma and Pa Ubu in the last scene as they sneak out of Poland and sail into the sunset.

The Jarry plot is the basic scene-by-scene scenario for Irondale's *Ubu.* The hen-pecked Pa Ubu is pushed by his wife into leading a coup to topple King Wenceslas of Poland and seize the crown for himself. He is aided, in the Irondale production, by Manure, Duke of Lithuania. Ubu redistributes the wealth ("Ninety per cent of the wealth for me!"), doublecrosses everyone and is transformed from "a skinny little runt" to a bloated hedonist with pillows padding his belly. But Ubu remains the Master of Ceremonies, the clown controlling the action, also doubling as narrator and interpreter. He is constantly improvising one-liners and slipping quick jokes to the audience. Each sequence or scene is like a Saturday Night Live version of the Jarry original. The play becomes a pretext for the company to hang its jokes on. When the conspirators plan the murder of Wenceslas, Manure (Paul Lazar), Duke of Lithuania, gets a little carried away in his enthusiasm:

> MANURE. My plan . . . is to take my stiff, hard, gleaming sword out of its sheath and shove it into his parted flesh and start to thrust, thrust, thrust (getting excited).

> UBU. Cut through the hormones, Manure!

Later, when Manure gets similarly excited by the prospect of total war against the anti-Ubu armies, Pa Ubu cuts him off with: "That's fine for you, you're into that quasi-homosexual ritualistic behavior." Ubu continuously switches from character to actor to clown. He taunts the chained and manacled Manure with:

> UBU. This is it. You're no getting out of here. You're gonna die. You ain't ever gonna be in Shakespeare in

the Park, you're never gonna do that Dr. Pepper commercial, never be on David Letterman.

The most interesting incorporation of the audience into the performance is a series of abrupt interruptions of the play's action, modeled on the Aristophanic *parabasis.* Sometimes Ubu steps out of the play to explain some aspect of improvisational theater or the company's work. At one point Ubu paces through the audience and muses:

> Those of you who've seen our plays before know that we're a political company. You may be wondering why is this political company doing a play about shit? Not only about shit, but shit for shit's sake.

Ubu promises that the play will get more political. Later, General Lasky, Commander of the pro-Ubu armies, marches out and tells the audience that the company has been heavily criticized by "textual purists" for mutilating Jarry's text. In an effort to be more faithful to the original script, a simultaneous French reading of the text will now be given so that the critics can check for accuracy. He then introduces Sven, a Swedish-born graduate of the Sorbonne, who proceeds to translate everything being said into French (with a noticeable Swedish lilt). The situation becomes hilarious as Sven tries to "take over the play," getting in the way of the actors and turning even commonplace exchanges into wildly funny sequences. In effect, we are following several different levels of action or "texts within a text:" the text of Jarry's *Ubu,* the Irondale's commentary on that text, and another "text" created by the improvisation and dialogue with the audience.

Despite the numerous contemporary references, the production is not overtly or obviously political. The specific political references, jokes and parallels all seem part of the overall comedic momentum, not its point. But Ma and Pa Ubu perhaps represent a more insidious attack on middle class values, habits and ethics. Pa Ubu is so likeable ("the Santa Claus of the Atomic Age" as one critic has put it) not because he is a negation of bourgeois values, but their apotheosis. Ubu knows no moderation—he is bourgeois values writ large, taken to extremes. He is the ultimate glutton, miser, sadist and egomaniac. Ubu is cold, raw bourgeois instinct with bad manners and without tact. He has no pretenses and the Ubu Administration has no P.R. director. Ubu is the bourgeoisie seen from the belly down. Appropriately, the distinguishing mark of the pro-Ubu armies is their stomachs: the Ubu Loyalists all have padded paunches like their leader.

The production attempts to move to a political level through the use of nonspecific and non-verbal techniques. The play begins with the company singing "I'm so happy to be an American" and ends with a flag-waving rendition of "It's a Grand Old Flag." Beginning with the anti-Ubu Revolution, led by Buggerless, son (played by a woman) of the executed King, the purely physical, mimed aspect of the production increases. When Ubu exhorts his troops into war frenzy, a loud electronic metronome starts. The actors begin a sequence which I can only describe as a "biomechanical gestus of war ritual." This is repeated during battle sequences. In the middle of the rousing flag-waving finale, the electronic cue comes again; the actors almost robot-like respond frantically to the cue. The metronome beats faster and faster as the lights fade while the gestus of war continues.

The Irondale's eclectic techniques, their ability to bring a contemporary feel to the imagination of the performance and, above all, the intense and dynamic audience-actor bond created by the improvisational nature of the performance, puts the audience in a very active relationship to the text and the theatrical event. The Irondale's work is always "in progress;" a play is rehearsed and performed over a period of years. The rehearsal process never stops, and the company stresses that performances are actually "shared rehearsals." The Irondale's commitment to improvisational performance encourages the actors to experiment and make changes during performance, so that no two performances are the same. The performance text continues to evolve with parts being added or dropped. What we have is a very close parallel to the textual/performance process of the classical age of *commedia dell'arte.* Actors can discover a specific *burla* or "running gag" that works for this specific audience, or try to see how far the audience will go in a specific vein. They are also free to comment broadly on anything from current events to the performance and the audience. Rather than attempting to create any type of consistent or conventional characterization, the *Ubu* company is a company of clowns that seems to be making-up the characters as they go along, employing anything from song-and-dance, stand-up comedy, acrobatics, to low farce and mime.

Most theater seeks to render the audience passive; the result is the deadening feel to so many contemporary productions. It seeks to bludgeon us into a lethargic loss of individuality, to surrender up our consciousness so that our experience can be shaped and manipulated by the production. This technique is not without its social ramifications. Brecht was quick to realize that although this model can be made to work for Shakespeare and Ibsen, it also worked for Goebbels and Hitler—something about this "fascist" theater experience can effect our reactions to situations and events outside the theater. Interestingly, the theories of Wagner, Appia and Craig reached their zenith not at Bayreuth but at Nuremburg.

The Irondale's *Ubu roi* employs another model of consciousness. Its production lives, moment-to-moment, only by the direct, active involvement of its audience. There is no pre-determined terminal point when the production is "finished" or ready. It is a commonplace that comedy is subversive. The "low comedy" technique that marks clowning is perhaps anti-authoritarian by its very nature, and this type of satire is itself an act of rebellion. Clearly, Jarry's play is a rebellion against bourgeois values, ethics and "good taste." The Irondale Ensemble attempts to extend this revolt further not simply by rebelling against Jarry's text but by the company's revolt against the notion of the fixed text and their refusal to accept the authoritarian restraints imposed upon conventional theater performance.

Source: Michael Zelenak. "Ubu Rides Again: The Irondale Project and the Politics of Clowning" in *Theatre,* Vol. XVII, no. 3, Summer/Fall, 1987, pp. 43–45.

SOURCES

Beaumont, Keith. *Jarry: Ubu Roi,* Grant & Cutler Ltd., 1987.

Bell, David F. *Romance Notes,* Spring, 1975.

Breton, Andre. "Alfred Jarry as Precursor and Initiator" in *Free Rein,* University of Nebraska Press, 1996.

Church, Dan M. "Pere Ubu: The Creation of a Literary Type" in *Drama Survey,* Winter, 1965, pp. 233-43.

Goddard, Stephen. "Alfred Jarry (French, 1873-1907)" on http://www.ukans.edu/~sma/jarry/jarrytxt.htm.

Grossman, Manual L. "Alfred Jarry and the Theater of his Time" in *Modern Drama,* May, 1970, pp. 10-21.

Lindsey, Heather. "'Merdre!' Most Foul: Scatology on Stage" on http://www.fas.harvard.edu/~art/merdre.html.

London, Todd. "My Ubu, Myself: The Singular Hallucination of Alfred Jarry" on http://www.fas.harvard.edu/~art/myself.html.

"Projects: The Gertrude Stein Repertory Theater: UBU" on http://www.gertstein.org/details/pro-ubu.htm.

Twentieth Century Literary Criticism, Vol. 14, Gale, 1984, pp. 266-77.

Wellworth, G. E. "Alfred Jarry: The Seed of Avant-Garde Drama" in *Criticism,* Vol. 4, no. 1, Winter, 1962, pp. 108-19.

FURTHER READING

http://hamp.hampshire.edu/~ngzF92/jarrypub/commence.html.
　　This site has a brief biography of Jarry, as well as links to other Jarry sites. The Bibliography of English Translations link may prove especially helpful.

http://www.fas.harvard.edu/~art/ubu.html.
　　This site for a production of *Ubu Rock* also contains an interesting set of links to online articles concerning *Ubu Roi.* The article on the play's opening night in December of 1896 may prove particularly illuminating.

Shattuck, Roger. *The Banquet Years: The Origins of the Avant Garde in France, 1885 to World War I: Alfred Jarry, Henry Rousseau, Erik Satie and Guillaume Apollinair,* Random House, 1979.
　　This influential volume examines the cultural upheaval brought about by such turn-of-the-century artists as Jarry and Composer Erik Satie. Shattuck discusses how the arts were driven into a period of renewal and accomplishment and how the ground-work for Dadaism and Surrealism was laid.

Glossary of Literary Terms

A

Abstract: Used as a noun, the term refers to a short summary or outline of a longer work. As an adjective applied to writing or literary works, abstract refers to words or phrases that name things not knowable through the five senses. Examples of abstracts include the *Cliffs Notes* summaries of major literary works. Examples of abstract terms or concepts include ''idea,'' ''guilt'' ''honesty,'' and ''loyalty.''

Absurd, Theater of the: See *Theater of the Absurd*

Absurdism: See *Theater of the Absurd*

Act: A major section of a play. Acts are divided into varying numbers of shorter scenes. From ancient times to the nineteenth century plays were generally constructed of five acts, but modern works typically consist of one, two, or three acts. Examples of five-act plays include the works of Sophocles and Shakespeare, while the plays of Arthur Miller commonly have a three-act structure.

Acto: A one-act Chicano theater piece developed out of collective improvisation. *Actos* were performed by members of Luis Valdez's Teatro Campesino in California during the mid-1960s.

Aestheticism: A literary and artistic movement of the nineteenth century. Followers of the movement believed that art should not be mixed with social, political, or moral teaching. The statement ''art for art's sake'' is a good summary of aestheticism. The movement had its roots in France, but it gained widespread importance in England in the last half of the nineteenth century, where it helped change the Victorian practice of including moral lessons in literature. Oscar Wilde is one of the best-known ''aesthetes'' of the late nineteenth century.

Age of Johnson: The period in English literature between 1750 and 1798, named after the most prominent literary figure of the age, Samuel Johnson. Works written during this time are noted for their emphasis on ''sensibility,'' or emotional quality. These works formed a transition between the rational works of the Age of Reason, or Neoclassical period, and the emphasis on individual feelings and responses of the Romantic period. Significant writers during the Age of Johnson included the novelists Ann Radcliffe and Henry Mackenzie, dramatists Richard Sheridan and Oliver Goldsmith, and poets William Collins and Thomas Gray. Also known as Age of Sensibility

Age of Reason: See *Neoclassicism*

Age of Sensibility: See *Age of Johnson*

Alexandrine Meter: See *Meter*

Allegory: A narrative technique in which characters representing things or abstract ideas are used to convey a message or teach a lesson. Allegory is typically used to teach moral, ethical, or religious lessons but is sometimes used for satiric or political purposes. Examples of allegorical works include Edmund Spenser's *The Faerie Queene* and John Bunyan's *The Pilgrim's Progress.*

Allusion: A reference to a familiar literary or historical person or event, used to make an idea more easily understood. For example, describing someone as a ''Romeo'' makes an allusion to William Shakespeare's famous young lover in *Romeo and Juliet.*

Amerind Literature: The writing and oral traditions of Native Americans. Native American literature was originally passed on by word of mouth, so it consisted largely of stories and events that were easily memorized. Amerind prose is often rhythmic like poetry because it was recited to the beat of a ceremonial drum. Examples of Amerind literature include the autobiographical *Black Elk Speaks,* the works of N. Scott Momaday, James Welch, and Craig Lee Strete, and the poetry of Luci Tapahonso.

Analogy: A comparison of two things made to explain something unfamiliar through its similarities to something familiar, or to prove one point based on the acceptedness of another. Similes and metaphors are types of analogies. Analogies often take the form of an extended simile, as in William Blake's aphorism: ''As the caterpillar chooses the fairest leaves to lay her eggs on, so the priest lays his curse on the fairest joys.''

Angry Young Men: A group of British writers of the 1950s whose work expressed bitterness and disillusionment with society. Common to their work is an anti-hero who rebels against a corrupt social order and strives for personal integrity. The term has been used to describe Kingsley Amis, John Osborne, Colin Wilson, John Wain, and others.

Antagonist: The major character in a narrative or drama who works against the hero or protagonist. An example of an evil antagonist is Richard Lovelace in Samuel Richardson's *Clarissa,* while a virtuous antagonist is Macduff in William Shakespeare's *Macbeth.*

Anthropomorphism: The presentation of animals or objects in human shape or with human characteristics. The term is derived from the Greek word for ''human form.'' The fables of Aesop, the animated films of Walt Disney, and Richard Adams's *Watership Down* feature anthropomorphic characters.

Anti-hero: A central character in a work of literature who lacks traditional heroic qualities such as courage, physical prowess, and fortitude. Anti-heros

typically distrust conventional values and are unable to commit themselves to any ideals. They generally feel helpless in a world over which they have no control. Anti-heroes usually accept, and often celebrate, their positions as social outcasts. A well-known anti-hero is Yossarian in Joseph Heller's novel *Catch-22.*

Antimasque: See *Masque*

Antithesis: The antithesis of something is its direct opposite. In literature, the use of antithesis as a figure of speech results in two statements that show a contrast through the balancing of two opposite ideas. Technically, it is the second portion of the statement that is defined as the ''antithesis''; the first portion is the ''thesis.'' An example of antithesis is found in the following portion of Abraham Lincoln's ''Gettysburg Address''; notice the opposition between the verbs ''remember'' and ''forget'' and the phrases ''what we say'' and ''what they did'': ''The world will little note nor long remember what we say here, but it can never forget what they did here.''

Apocrypha: Writings tentatively attributed to an author but not proven or universally accepted to be their works. The term was originally applied to certain books of the Bible that were not considered inspired and so were not included in the ''sacred canon.'' Geoffrey Chaucer, William Shakespeare, Thomas Kyd, Thomas Middleton, and John Marston all have apocrypha. Apocryphal books of the Bible include the Old Testament's Book of Enoch and New Testament's Gospel of Peter.

Apollonian and Dionysian: The two impulses believed to guide authors of dramatic tragedy. The Apollonian impulse is named after Apollo, the Greek god of light and beauty and the symbol of intellectual order. The Dionysian impulse is named after Dionysus, the Greek god of wine and the symbol of the unrestrained forces of nature. The Apollonian impulse is to create a rational, harmonious world, while the Dionysian is to express the irrational forces of personality. Friedrich Nietzche uses these terms in *The Birth of Tragedy* to designate contrasting elements in Greek tragedy.

Apostrophe: A statement, question, or request addressed to an inanimate object or concept or to a nonexistent or absent person. Requests for inspiration from the muses in poetry are examples of apostrophe, as is Marc Antony's address to Caesar's corpse in William Shakespeare's *Julius Caesar*: ''O, pardon me, thou bleeding piece of earth, That I am meek and gentle with these butchers!. . . Woe to the hand that shed this costly blood!. . .''

Archetype: The word archetype is commonly used to describe an original pattern or model from which all other things of the same kind are made. This term was introduced to literary criticism from the psychology of Carl Jung. It expresses Jung's theory that behind every person's ''unconscious,'' or repressed memories of the past, lies the ''collective unconscious'' of the human race: memories of the countless typical experiences of our ancestors. These memories are said to prompt illogical associations that trigger powerful emotions in the reader. Often, the emotional process is primitive, even primordial. Archetypes are the literary images that grow out of the ''collective unconscious.'' They appear in literature as incidents and plots that repeat basic patterns of life. They may also appear as stereotyped characters. Examples of literary archetypes include themes such as birth and death and characters such as the Earth Mother.

Argument: The argument of a work is the author's subject matter or principal idea. Examples of defined ''argument'' portions of works include John Milton's *Arguments* to each of the books of *Paradise Lost* and the ''Argument'' to Robert Herrick's *Hesperides.*

Aristotelian Criticism: Specifically, the method of evaluating and analyzing tragedy formulated by the Greek philosopher Aristotle in his *Poetics.* More generally, the term indicates any form of criticism that follows Aristotle's views. Aristotelian criticism focuses on the form and logical structure of a work, apart from its historical or social context, in contrast to ''Platonic Criticism,'' which stresses the usefulness of art. Adherents of New Criticism including John Crowe Ransom and Cleanth Brooks utilize and value the basic ideas of Aristotelian criticism for textual analysis.

Art for Art's Sake: See *Aestheticism*

Aside: A comment made by a stage performer that is intended to be heard by the audience but supposedly not by other characters. Eugene O'Neill's *Strange Interlude* is an extended use of the aside in modern theater.

Audience: The people for whom a piece of literature is written. Authors usually write with a certain audience in mind, for example, children, members of a religious or ethnic group, or colleagues in a professional field. The term ''audience'' also applies to the people who gather to see or hear any performance, including plays, poetry readings, speeches, and concerts. Jane Austen's parody of the gothic novel, *Northanger Abbey,* was originally intended for (and also pokes fun at) an audience of young and avid female gothic novel readers.

Avant-garde: A French term meaning ''vanguard.'' It is used in literary criticism to describe new writing that rejects traditional approaches to literature in favor of innovations in style or content. Twentieth-century examples of the literary *avant-garde* include the Black Mountain School of poets, the Bloomsbury Group, and the Beat Movement.

B

Ballad: A short poem that tells a simple story and has a repeated refrain. Ballads were originally intended to be sung. Early ballads, known as folk ballads, were passed down through generations, so their authors are often unknown. Later ballads composed by known authors are called literary ballads. An example of an anonymous folk ballad is ''Edward,'' which dates from the Middle Ages. Samuel Taylor Coleridge's ''The Rime of the Ancient Mariner'' and John Keats's ''La Belle Dame sans Merci'' are examples of literary ballads.

Baroque: A term used in literary criticism to describe literature that is complex or ornate in style or diction. Baroque works typically express tension, anxiety, and violent emotion. The term ''Baroque Age'' designates a period in Western European literature beginning in the late sixteenth century and ending about one hundred years later. Works of this period often mirror the qualities of works more generally associated with the label ''baroque'' and sometimes feature elaborate conceits. Examples of Baroque works include John Lyly's *Euphues: The Anatomy of Wit,* Luis de Gongora's *Soledads,* and William Shakespeare's *As You Like It.*

Baroque Age: See *Baroque*

Baroque Period: See *Baroque*

Beat Generation: See *Beat Movement*

Beat Movement: A period featuring a group of American poets and novelists of the 1950s and 1960s—including Jack Kerouac, Allen Ginsberg, Gregory Corso, William S. Burroughs, and Lawrence Ferlinghetti—who rejected established social and literary values. Using such techniques as stream of consciousness writing and jazz-influenced free verse and focusing on unusual or abnormal states of mind—generated by religious ecstasy or the use of drugs—the Beat writers aimed to create works that were unconventional in both form and subject matter. Kerouac's *On the Road* is perhaps the best-known example of a Beat Generation novel, and Ginsberg's *Howl* is a famous collection of Beat poetry.

Black Aesthetic Movement: A period of artistic and literary development among African Americans in the 1960s and early 1970s. This was the first major African-American artistic movement since the Harlem Renaissance and was closely paralleled by the civil rights and black power movements. The black aesthetic writers attempted to produce works of art that would be meaningful to the black masses. Key figures in black aesthetics included one of its founders, poet and playwright Amiri Baraka, formerly known as LeRoi Jones; poet and essayist Haki R. Madhubuti, formerly Don L. Lee; poet and playwright Sonia Sanchez; and dramatist Ed Bullins. Works representative of the Black Aesthetic Movement include Amiri Baraka's play *Dutchman,* a 1964 Obie award-winner; *Black Fire: An Anthology of Afro-American Writing,* edited by Baraka and playwright Larry Neal and published in 1968; and Sonia Sanchez's poetry collection *We a BaddDDD People,* published in 1970. Also known as Black Arts Movement.

Black Arts Movement: See *Black Aesthetic Movement*

Black Comedy: See *Black Humor*

Black Humor: Writing that places grotesque elements side by side with humorous ones in an attempt to shock the reader, forcing him or her to laugh at the horrifying reality of a disordered world. Joseph Heller's novel *Catch-22* is considered a superb example of the use of black humor. Other well-known authors who use black humor include Kurt Vonnegut, Edward Albee, Eugene Ionesco, and Harold Pinter. Also known as Black Comedy.

Blank Verse: Loosely, any unrhymed poetry, but more generally, unrhymed iambic pentameter verse (composed of lines of five two-syllable feet with the first syllable accented, the second unaccented). Blank verse has been used by poets since the Renaissance for its flexibility and its graceful, dignified tone. John Milton's *Paradise Lost* is in blank verse, as are most of William Shakespeare's plays.

Bloomsbury Group: A group of English writers, artists, and intellectuals who held informal artistic and philosophical discussions in Bloomsbury, a district of London, from around 1907 to the early

1930s. The Bloomsbury Group held no uniform philosophical beliefs but did commonly express an aversion to moral prudery and a desire for greater social tolerance. At various times the circle included Virginia Woolf, E. M. Forster, Clive Bell, Lytton Strachey, and John Maynard Keynes.

Bon Mot: A French term meaning "good word." A *bon mot* is a witty remark or clever observation. Charles Lamb and Oscar Wilde are celebrated for their witty *bon mots.* Two examples by Oscar Wilde stand out: (1) "All women become their mothers. That is their tragedy. No man does. That's his." (2) "A man cannot be too careful in the choice of his enemies."

Breath Verse: See *Projective Verse*

Burlesque: Any literary work that uses exaggeration to make its subject appear ridiculous, either by treating a trivial subject with profound seriousness or by treating a dignified subject frivolously. The word "burlesque" may also be used as an adjective, as in "burlesque show," to mean "striptease act." Examples of literary burlesque include the comedies of Aristophanes, Miguel de Cervantes's *Don Quixote,*, Samuel Butler's poem "Hudibras," and John Gay's play *The Beggar's Opera.*

C

Cadence: The natural rhythm of language caused by the alternation of accented and unaccented syllables. Much modern poetry—notably free verse—deliberately manipulates cadence to create complex rhythmic effects. James Macpherson's "Ossian poems" are richly cadenced, as is the poetry of the Symbolists, Walt Whitman, and Amy Lowell.

Caesura: A pause in a line of poetry, usually occurring near the middle. It typically corresponds to a break in the natural rhythm or sense of the line but is sometimes shifted to create special meanings or rhythmic effects. The opening line of Edgar Allan Poe's "The Raven" contains a caesura following "dreary": "Once upon a midnight dreary, while I pondered weak and weary. . . ."

Canzone: A short Italian or Provencal lyric poem, commonly about love and often set to music. The *canzone* has no set form but typically contains five or six stanzas made up of seven to twenty lines of eleven syllables each. A shorter, five- to ten-line "envoy," or concluding stanza, completes the poem. Masters of the *canzone* form include

Petrarch, Dante Alighieri, Torquato Tasso, and Guido Cavalcanti.

Carpe Diem: A Latin term meaning ''seize the day.'' This is a traditional theme of poetry, especially lyrics. A *carpe diem* poem advises the reader or the person it addresses to live for today and enjoy the pleasures of the moment. Two celebrated *carpe diem* poems are Andrew Marvell's ''To His Coy Mistress'' and Robert Herrick's poem beginning ''Gather ye rosebuds while ye may. . . .''

Catharsis: The release or purging of unwanted emotions— specifically fear and pity—brought about by exposure to art. The term was first used by the Greek philosopher Aristotle in his *Poetics* to refer to the desired effect of tragedy on spectators. A famous example of catharsis is realized in Sophocles' *Oedipus Rex,* when Oedipus discovers that his wife, Jacosta, is his own mother and that the stranger he killed on the road was his own father.

Celtic Renaissance: A period of Irish literary and cultural history at the end of the nineteenth century. Followers of the movement aimed to create a romantic vision of Celtic myth and legend. The most significant works of the Celtic Renaissance typically present a dreamy, unreal world, usually in reaction against the reality of contemporary problems. William Butler Yeats's *The Wanderings of Oisin* is among the most significant works of the Celtic Renaissance. Also known as Celtic Twilight.

Celtic Twilight: See *Celtic Renaissance*

Character: Broadly speaking, a person in a literary work. The actions of characters are what constitute the plot of a story, novel, or poem. There are numerous types of characters, ranging from simple, stereotypical figures to intricate, multifaceted ones. In the techniques of anthropomorphism and personification, animals—and even places or things— can assume aspects of character. ''Characterization'' is the process by which an author creates vivid, believable characters in a work of art. This may be done in a variety of ways, including (1) direct description of the character by the narrator; (2) the direct presentation of the speech, thoughts, or actions of the character; and (3) the responses of other characters to the character. The term ''character'' also refers to a form originated by the ancient Greek writer Theophrastus that later became popular in the seventeenth and eighteenth centuries. It is a short essay or sketch of a person who prominently displays a specific attribute or quality, such as miserliness or ambition. Notable characters in lit-erature include Oedipus Rex, Don Quixote de la Mancha, Macbeth, Candide, Hester Prynne, Ebenezer Scrooge, Huckleberry Finn, Jay Gatsby, Scarlett O'Hara, James Bond, and Kunta Kinte.

Characterization: See *Character*

Chorus: In ancient Greek drama, a group of actors who commented on and interpreted the unfolding action on the stage. Initially the chorus was a major component of the presentation, but over time it became less significant, with its numbers reduced and its role eventually limited to commentary between acts. By the sixteenth century the chorus—if employed at all—was typically a single person who provided a prologue and an epilogue and occasionally appeared between acts to introduce or underscore an important event. The chorus in William Shakespeare's *Henry V* functions in this way. Modern dramas rarely feature a chorus, but T. S. Eliot's *Murder in the Cathedral* and Arthur Miller's *A View from the Bridge* are notable exceptions. The Stage Manager in Thornton Wilder's *Our Town* performs a role similar to that of the chorus.

Chronicle: A record of events presented in chronological order. Although the scope and level of detail provided varies greatly among the chronicles surviving from ancient times, some, such as the *Anglo-Saxon Chronicle,* feature vivid descriptions and a lively recounting of events. During the Elizabethan Age, many dramas— appropriately called ''chronicle plays''—were based on material from chronicles. Many of William Shakespeare's dramas of English history as well as Christopher Marlowe's *Edward II* are based in part on Raphael Holinshead's *Chronicles of England, Scotland, and Ireland.*

Classical: In its strictest definition in literary criticism, classicism refers to works of ancient Greek or Roman literature. The term may also be used to describe a literary work of recognized importance (a ''classic'') from any time period or literature that exhibits the traits of classicism. Classical authors from ancient Greek and Roman times include Juvenal and Homer. Examples of later works and authors now described as classical include French literature of the seventeenth century, Western novels of the nineteenth century, and American fiction of the mid-nineteenth century such as that written by James Fenimore Cooper and Mark Twain.

Classicism: A term used in literary criticism to describe critical doctrines that have their roots in ancient Greek and Roman literature, philosophy, and art. Works associated with classicism typically exhibit restraint on the part of the author, unity of design and purpose, clarity, simplicity, logical organization, and respect for tradition. Examples of literary classicism include Cicero's prose, the dramas of Pierre Corneille and Jean Racine, the poetry of John Dryden and Alexander Pope, and the writings of J. W. von Goethe, G. E. Lessing, and T. S. Eliot.

Climax: The turning point in a narrative, the moment when the conflict is at its most intense. Typically, the structure of stories, novels, and plays is one of rising action, in which tension builds to the climax, followed by falling action, in which tension lessens as the story moves to its conclusion. The climax in James Fenimore Cooper's *The Last of the Mohicans* occurs when Magua and his captive Cora are pursued to the edge of a cliff by Uncas. Magua kills Uncas but is subsequently killed by Hawkeye.

Colloquialism: A word, phrase, or form of pronunciation that is acceptable in casual conversation but not in formal, written communication. It is considered more acceptable than slang. An example of colloquialism can be found in Rudyard Kipling's *Barrack-room Ballads:* When 'Omer smote 'is bloomin' lyre He'd 'eard men sing by land and sea; An' what he thought 'e might require 'E went an' took—the same as me!

Comedy: One of two major types of drama, the other being tragedy. Its aim is to amuse, and it typically ends happily. Comedy assumes many forms, such as farce and burlesque, and uses a variety of techniques, from parody to satire. In a restricted sense the term comedy refers only to dramatic presentations, but in general usage it is commonly applied to nondramatic works as well. Examples of comedies range from the plays of Aristophanes, Terrence, and Plautus, Dante Alighieri's *The Divine Comedy,* Francois Rabelais's *Pantagruel* and *Gargantua,* and some of Geoffrey Chaucer's tales and William Shakespeare's plays to Noel Coward's play *Private Lives* and James Thurber's short story ''The Secret Life of Walter Mitty.''

Comedy of Manners: A play about the manners and conventions of an aristocratic, highly sophisticated society. The characters are usually types rather than individualized personalities, and plot is less important than atmosphere. Such plays were an important aspect of late seventeenth-century English comedy. The comedy of manners was revived in the eighteenth century by Oliver Goldsmith and Richard Brinsley Sheridan, enjoyed a second revival in the late nineteenth century, and has endured into the twentieth century. Examples of comedies of manners include William Congreve's *The Way of the World* in the late seventeenth century, Oliver Goldsmith's *She Stoops to Conquer* and Richard Brinsley Sheridan's *The School for Scandal* in the eighteenth century, Oscar Wilde's *The Importance of Being Earnest* in the nineteenth century, and W. Somerset Maugham's *The Circle* in the twentieth century.

Comic Relief: The use of humor to lighten the mood of a serious or tragic story, especially in plays. The technique is very common in Elizabethan works, and can be an integral part of the plot or simply a brief event designed to break the tension of the scene. The Gravediggers' scene in William Shakespeare's *Hamlet* is a frequently cited example of comic relief.

Commedia dell'arte: An Italian term meaning ''the comedy of guilds'' or ''the comedy of professional actors.'' This form of dramatic comedy was popular in Italy during the sixteenth century. Actors were assigned stock roles (such as Pulcinella, the stupid servant, or Pantalone, the old merchant) and given a basic plot to follow, but all dialogue was improvised. The roles were rigidly typed and the plots were formulaic, usually revolving around young lovers who thwarted their elders and attained wealth and happiness. A rigid convention of the *commedia dell'arte* is the periodic intrusion of Harlequin, who interrupts the play with low buffoonery. Peppino de Filippo's *Metamorphoses of a Wandering Minstrel* gave modern audiences an idea of what *commedia dell'arte* may have been like. Various scenarios for *commedia dell'arte* were compiled in Petraccone's *La commedia dell'arte, storia, technica, scenari,* published in 1927.

Complaint: A lyric poem, popular in the Renaissance, in which the speaker expresses sorrow about his or her condition. Typically, the speaker's sadness is caused by an unresponsive lover, but some complaints cite other sources of unhappiness, such as poverty or fate. A commonly cited example is ''A Complaint by Night of the Lover Not Beloved'' by Henry Howard, Earl of Surrey. Thomas Sackville's ''Complaint of Henry, Duke of Buckingham'' traces the duke's unhappiness to his ruthless ambition.

Conceit: A clever and fanciful metaphor, usually expressed through elaborate and extended comparison, that presents a striking parallel between two seemingly dissimilar things—for example, elaborately comparing a beautiful woman to an object like a garden or the sun. The conceit was a popular device throughout the Elizabethan Age and Baroque Age and was the principal technique of the seventeenth-century English metaphysical poets. This usage of the word conceit is unrelated to the best-known definition of conceit as an arrogant attitude or behavior. The conceit figures prominently in the works of John Donne, Emily Dickinson, and T. S. Eliot.

Concrete: Concrete is the opposite of abstract, and refers to a thing that actually exists or a description that allows the reader to experience an object or concept with the senses. Henry David Thoreau's *Walden* contains much concrete description of nature and wildlife.

Concrete Poetry: Poetry in which visual elements play a large part in the poetic effect. Punctuation marks, letters, or words are arranged on a page to form a visual design: a cross, for example, or a bumblebee. Max Bill and Eugene Gomringer were among the early practitioners of concrete poetry; Haroldo de Campos and Augusto de Campos are among contemporary authors of concrete poetry.

Confessional Poetry: A form of poetry in which the poet reveals very personal, intimate, sometimes shocking information about himself or herself. Anne Sexton, Sylvia Plath, Robert Lowell, and John Berryman wrote poetry in the confessional vein.

Conflict: The conflict in a work of fiction is the issue to be resolved in the story. It usually occurs between two characters, the protagonist and the antagonist, or between the protagonist and society or the protagonist and himself or herself. Conflict in Theodore Dreiser's novel *Sister Carrie* comes as a result of urban society, while Jack London's short story "To Build a Fire" concerns the protagonist's battle against the cold and himself.

Connotation: The impression that a word gives beyond its defined meaning. Connotations may be universally understood or may be significant only to a certain group. Both "horse" and "steed" denote the same animal, but "steed" has a different connotation, deriving from the chivalrous or romantic narratives in which the word was once often used.

Consonance: Consonance occurs in poetry when words appearing at the ends of two or more verses have similar final consonant sounds but have final vowel sounds that differ, as with "stuff" and "off." Consonance is found in "The curfew tolls the knells of parting day" from Thomas Grey's "An Elegy Written in a Country Church Yard." Also known as Half Rhyme or Slant Rhyme.

Convention: Any widely accepted literary device, style, or form. A soliloquy, in which a character reveals to the audience his or her private thoughts, is an example of a dramatic convention.

Corrido: A Mexican ballad. Examples of *corridos* include "Muerte del afamado Bilito," "La voz de mi conciencia," "Lucio Perez," "La juida," and "Los presos."

Couplet: Two lines of poetry with the same rhyme and meter, often expressing a complete and self-contained thought. The following couplet is from Alexander Pope's "Elegy to the Memory of an Unfortunate Lady": 'Tis Use alone that sanctifies Expense, And Splendour borrows all her rays from Sense.

Criticism: The systematic study and evaluation of literary works, usually based on a specific method or set of principles. An important part of literary studies since ancient times, the practice of criticism has given rise to numerous theories, methods, and "schools," sometimes producing conflicting, even contradictory, interpretations of literature in general as well as of individual works. Even such basic issues as what constitutes a poem or a novel have been the subject of much criticism over the centuries. Seminal texts of literary criticism include Plato's *Republic,* Aristotle's *Poetics,* Sir Philip Sidney's *The Defence of Poesie,* John Dryden's *Of Dramatic Poesie,* and William Wordsworth's "Preface" to the second edition of his *Lyrical Ballads.* Contemporary schools of criticism include deconstruction, feminist, psychoanalytic, poststructuralist, new historicist, postcolonialist, and reader- response.

D

Dactyl: See *Foot*

Dadaism: A protest movement in art and literature founded by Tristan Tzara in 1916. Followers of the movement expressed their outrage at the destruction brought about by World War I by revolting against numerous forms of social convention. The Dadaists presented works marked by calculated madness and flamboyant nonsense. They stressed total freedom of expression, commonly through primitive displays of emotion and illogical, often senseless, poetry. The movement ended shortly after the war, when it was replaced by surrealism. Proponents of Dadaism include Andre Breton, Louis Aragon, Philippe Soupault, and Paul Eluard.

Decadent: See *Decadents*

Decadents: The followers of a nineteenth-century literary movement that had its beginnings in French aestheticism. Decadent literature displays a fascination with perverse and morbid states; a search for novelty and sensation—the ''new thrill''; a preoccupation with mysticism; and a belief in the senselessness of human existence. The movement is closely associated with the doctrine Art for Art's Sake. The term ''decadence'' is sometimes used to denote a decline in the quality of art or literature following a period of greatness. Major French decadents are Charles Baudelaire and Arthur Rimbaud. English decadents include Oscar Wilde, Ernest Dowson, and Frank Harris.

Deconstruction: A method of literary criticism developed by Jacques Derrida and characterized by multiple conflicting interpretations of a given work. Deconstructionists consider the impact of the language of a work and suggest that the true meaning of the work is not necessarily the meaning that the author intended. Jacques Derrida's *De la grammatologie* is the seminal text on deconstructive strategies; among American practitioners of this method of criticism are Paul de Man and J. Hillis Miller.

Deduction: The process of reaching a conclusion through reasoning from general premises to a specific premise. An example of deduction is present in the following syllogism: Premise: All mammals are animals. Premise: All whales are mammals. Conclusion: Therefore, all whales are animals.

Denotation: The definition of a word, apart from the impressions or feelings it creates in the reader. The word ''apartheid'' denotes a political and economic policy of segregation by race, but its connotations— oppression, slavery, inequality—are numerous.

Denouement: A French word meaning ''the unknotting.'' In literary criticism, it denotes the resolution of conflict in fiction or drama. The *denouement* follows the climax and provides an outcome to the primary plot situation as well as an explanation of secondary plot complications. The *denouement* often involves a character's recognition of his or her state of mind or moral condition. A well-known example of *denouement* is the last scene of the play *As You Like It* by William Shakespeare, in which couples are married, an evildoer repents, the identities of two disguised characters are revealed, and a ruler is restored to power. Also known as Falling Action.

Description: Descriptive writing is intended to allow a reader to picture the scene or setting in which the action of a story takes place. The form this description takes often evokes an intended emotional response—a dark, spooky graveyard will evoke fear, and a peaceful, sunny meadow will evoke calmness. An example of a descriptive story is Edgar Allan Poe's *Landor's Cottage*, which offers a detailed depiction of a New York country estate.

Detective Story: A narrative about the solution of a mystery or the identification of a criminal. The conventions of the detective story include the detective's scrupulous use of logic in solving the mystery; incompetent or ineffectual police; a suspect who appears guilty at first but is later proved innocent; and the detective's friend or confidant— often the narrator—whose slowness in interpreting clues emphasizes by contrast the detective's brilliance. Edgar Allan Poe's ''Murders in the Rue Morgue'' is commonly regarded as the earliest example of this type of story. With this work, Poe established many of the conventions of the detective story genre, which are still in practice. Other practitioners of this vast and extremely popular genre include Arthur Conan Doyle, Dashiell Hammett, and Agatha Christie.

Deus ex machina: A Latin term meaning ''god out of a machine.'' In Greek drama, a god was often lowered onto the stage by a mechanism of some kind to rescue the hero or untangle the plot. By extension, the term refers to any artificial device or coincidence used to bring about a convenient and simple solution to a plot. This is a common device in melodramas and includes such fortunate circumstances as the sudden receipt of a legacy to save the family farm or a last-minute stay of execution. The *deus ex machina* invariably rewards the virtuous and punishes evildoers. Examples of *deus ex machina* include King Louis XIV in Jean-Baptiste Moliere's *Tartuffe* and Queen Victoria in *The Pirates of Penzance* by William Gilbert and Arthur Sullivan. Bertolt Brecht parodies the abuse of such devices in the conclusion of his *Threepenny Opera.*

Dialogue: In its widest sense, dialogue is simply conversation between people in a literary work; in its most restricted sense, it refers specifically to the speech of characters in a drama. As a specific literary genre, a ''dialogue'' is a composition in which characters debate an issue or idea. The Greek philosopher Plato frequently expounded his theories in the form of dialogues.

Diction: The selection and arrangement of words in a literary work. Either or both may vary depending on the desired effect. There are four general types of diction: ''formal,'' used in scholarly or lofty writing; ''informal,'' used in relaxed but educated conversation; ''colloquial,'' used in everyday speech; and ''slang,'' containing newly coined words and other terms not accepted in formal usage.

Didactic: A term used to describe works of literature that aim to teach some moral, religious, political, or practical lesson. Although didactic elements are often found in artistically pleasing works, the term ''didactic'' usually refers to literature in which the message is more important than the form. The term may also be used to criticize a work that the critic finds ''overly didactic,'' that is, heavy-handed in its delivery of a lesson. Examples of didactic literature include John Bunyan's *Pilgrim's Progress,* Alexander Pope's *Essay on Criticism,* Jean-Jacques Rousseau's *Emile,* and Elizabeth Inchbald's *Simple Story.*

Dimeter: See *Meter*

Dionysian: See *Apollonian and Dionysian*

Discordia concours: A Latin phrase meaning ''discord in harmony.'' The term was coined by the eighteenth-century English writer Samuel Johnson to describe ''a combination of dissimilar images or discovery of occult resemblances in things apparently unlike.'' Johnson created the expression by reversing a phrase by the Latin poet Horace. The metaphysical poetry of John Donne, Richard Crashaw, Abraham Cowley, George Herbert, and Edward Taylor among others, contains many examples of *discordia concours.* In Donne's ''A Valediction: Forbidding Mourning,'' the poet compares the union of himself with his lover to a draftsman's compass: If they be two, they are two so, As stiff twin compasses are two: Thy soul, the fixed foot, makes no show To move, but doth, if the other do; And though it in the center sit, Yet when the other far doth roam, It leans, and hearkens after it, And grows erect, as that comes home.

Dissonance: A combination of harsh or jarring sounds, especially in poetry. Although such combinations may be accidental, poets sometimes intentionally make them to achieve particular effects. Dissonance is also sometimes used to refer to close but not identical rhymes. When this is the case, the word functions as a synonym for consonance. Robert Browning, Gerard Manley Hopkins, and many other poets have made deliberate use of dissonance.

Doppelganger: A literary technique by which a character is duplicated (usually in the form of an alter ego, though sometimes as a ghostly counterpart) or divided into two distinct, usually opposite personalities. The use of this character device is widespread in nineteenth- and twentieth- century literature, and indicates a growing awareness among authors that the ''self'' is really a composite of many ''selves.'' A well-known story containing a *doppelganger* character is Robert Louis Stevenson's *Dr. Jekyll and Mr. Hyde,* which dramatizes an internal struggle between good and evil. Also known as The Double.

Double Entendre: A corruption of a French phrase meaning ''double meaning.'' The term is used to indicate a word or phrase that is deliberately ambiguous, especially when one of the meanings is risque or improper. An example of a *double entendre* is the Elizabethan usage of the verb ''die,'' which refers both to death and to orgasm.

Double, The: See *Doppelganger*

Draft: Any preliminary version of a written work. An author may write dozens of drafts which are revised to form the final work, or he or she may write only one, with few or no revisions. Dorothy Parker's observation that ''I can't write five words but that I change seven'' humorously indicates the purpose of the draft.

Drama: In its widest sense, a drama is any work designed to be presented by actors on a stage. Similarly, ''drama'' denotes a broad literary genre that includes a variety of forms, from pageant and spectacle to tragedy and comedy, as well as countless types and subtypes. More commonly in modern usage, however, a drama is a work that treats serious subjects and themes but does not aim at the grandeur of tragedy. This use of the term originated with the eighteenth-century French writer Denis Diderot, who used the word *drame* to designate his plays about middle- class life; thus ''drama'' typically features characters of a less exalted stature than those of tragedy. Examples of classical dramas include Menander's comedy *Dyscolus* and Sophocles' tragedy *Oedipus Rex.* Contemporary dramas include Eugene O'Neill's *The Iceman Cometh,* Lillian Hellman's *Little Foxes,* and August Wilson's *Ma Rainey's Black Bottom.*

Dramatic Irony: Occurs when the audience of a play or the reader of a work of literature knows something that a character in the work itself does not know. The irony is in the contrast between the intended meaning of the statements or actions of a character and the additional information understood by the audience. A celebrated example of dramatic irony is in Act V of William Shakespeare's *Romeo and Juliet,* where two young lovers meet their end as a result of a tragic misunderstanding. Here, the audience has full knowledge that Juliet's apparent ''death'' is merely temporary; she will regain her senses when the mysterious ''sleeping potion'' she has taken wears off. But Romeo, mistaking Juliet's drug-induced trance for true death, kills himself in grief. Upon awakening, Juliet discovers Romeo's corpse and, in despair, slays herself.

Dramatic Monologue: See *Monologue*

Dramatic Poetry: Any lyric work that employs elements of drama such as dialogue, conflict, or characterization, but excluding works that are intended for stage presentation. A monologue is a form of dramatic poetry.

Dramatis . ersonae: The characters in a work of literature, particularly a drama. The list of characters printed before the main text of a play or in the program is the *dramatis personae.*

Dream Allegory: See *Dream Vision*

Dream Vision: A literary convention, chiefly of the Middle Ages. In a dream vision a story is presented as a literal dream of the narrator. This device was commonly used to teach moral and religious lessons. Important works of this type are *The Divine Comedy* by Dante Alighieri, *Piers Plowman* by William Langland, and *The Pilgrim's Progress* by John Bunyan. Also known as Dream Allegory.

Dystopia: An imaginary place in a work of fiction where the characters lead dehumanized, fearful lives. Jack London's *The Iron Heel,* Yevgeny Zamyatin's *My,* Aldous Huxley's *Brave New World,* George Orwell's *Nineteen Eighty-four,* and Margaret Atwood's *Handmaid's Tale* portray versions of dystopia.

E

Eclogue: In classical literature, a poem featuring rural themes and structured as a dialogue among shepherds. Eclogues often took specific poetic forms, such as elegies or love poems. Some were written as the soliloquy of a shepherd. In later centuries, ''eclogue'' came to refer to any poem that was in the pastoral tradition or that had a dialogue or mono-

logue structure. A classical example of an eclogue is Virgil's *Eclogues,* also known as *Bucolics.* Giovanni Boccaccio, Edmund Spenser, Andrew Marvell, Jonathan Swift, and Louis MacNeice also wrote eclogues.

Edwardian: Describes cultural conventions identified with the period of the reign of Edward VII of England (1901-1910). Writers of the Edwardian Age typically displayed a strong reaction against the propriety and conservatism of the Victorian Age. Their work often exhibits distrust of authority in religion, politics, and art and expresses strong doubts about the soundness of conventional values. Writers of this era include George Bernard Shaw, H. G. Wells, and Joseph Conrad.

Edwardian Age: See *Edwardian*

Electra Complex: A daughter's amorous obsession with her father. The term Electra complex comes from the plays of Euripides and Sophocles entitled *Electra,* in which the character Electra drives her brother Orestes to kill their mother and her lover in revenge for the murder of their father.

Elegy: A lyric poem that laments the death of a person or the eventual death of all people. In a conventional elegy, set in a classical world, the poet and subject are spoken of as shepherds. In modern criticism, the word elegy is often used to refer to a poem that is melancholy or mournfully contemplative. John Milton's ''Lycidas'' and Percy Bysshe Shelley's ''Adonais'' are two examples of this form.

Elizabethan Age: A period of great economic growth, religious controversy, and nationalism closely associated with the reign of Elizabeth I of England (1558-1603). The Elizabethan Age is considered a part of the general renaissance—that is, the flowering of arts and literature—that took place in Europe during the fourteenth through sixteenth centuries. The era is considered the golden age of English literature. The most important dramas in English and a great deal of lyric poetry were produced during this period, and modern English criticism began around this time. The notable authors of the period—Philip Sidney, Edmund Spenser, Christopher Marlowe, William Shakespeare, Ben Jonson, Francis Bacon, and John Donne—are among the best in all of English literature.

Elizabethan Drama: English comic and tragic plays produced during the Renaissance, or more narrowly, those plays written during the last years of and few years after Queen Elizabeth's reign. William Shakespeare is considered an Elizabethan dramatist in the broader sense, although most of his work was produced during the reign of James I. Examples of Elizabethan comedies include John Lyly's *The Woman in the Moone,* Thomas Dekker's *The Roaring Girl, or, Moll Cut Purse,* and William Shakespeare's *Twelfth Night.* Examples of Elizabethan tragedies include William Shakespeare's *Antony and Cleopatra,* Thomas Kyd's *The Spanish Tragedy,* and John Webster's *The Tragedy of the Duchess of Malfi.*

Empathy: A sense of shared experience, including emotional and physical feelings, with someone or something other than oneself. Empathy is often used to describe the response of a reader to a literary character. An example of an empathic passage is William Shakespeare's description in his narrative poem *Venus and Adonis* of: the snail, whose tender horns being hit, Shrinks backward in his shelly cave with pain. Readers of Gerard Manley Hopkins's *The Windhover* may experience some of the physical sensations evoked in the description of the movement of the falcon.

English Sonnet: See *Sonnet*

Enjambment: The running over of the sense and structure of a line of verse or a couplet into the following verse or couplet. Andrew Marvell's "To His Coy Mistress" is structured as a series of enjambments, as in lines 11-12: "My vegetable love should grow/Vaster than empires and more slow."

Enlightenment, The: An eighteenth-century philosophical movement. It began in France but had a wide impact throughout Europe and America. Thinkers of the Enlightenment valued reason and believed that both the individual and society could achieve a state of perfection. Corresponding to this essentially humanist vision was a resistance to religious authority. Important figures of the Enlightenment were Denis Diderot and Voltaire in France, Edward Gibbon and David Hume in England, and Thomas Paine and Thomas Jefferson in the United States.

Epic: A long narrative poem about the adventures of a hero of great historic or legendary importance. The setting is vast and the action is often given cosmic significance through the intervention of supernatural forces such as gods, angels, or demons. Epics are typically written in a classical style of grand simplicity with elaborate metaphors and allusions that enhance the symbolic importance of a hero's adventures. Some well-known epics are Homer's *Iliad* and *Odyssey,* Virgil's *Aeneid,* and John Milton's *Paradise Lost.*

Epic Simile: See *Homeric Simile*

Epic Theater: A theory of theatrical presentation developed by twentieth-century German playwright Bertolt Brecht. Brecht created a type of drama that the audience could view with complete detachment. He used what he termed "alienation effects" to create an emotional distance between the audience and the action on stage. Among these effects are: short, self-contained scenes that keep the play from building to a cathartic climax; songs that comment on the action; and techniques of acting that prevent the actor from developing an emotional identity with his role. Besides the plays of Bertolt Brecht, other plays that utilize epic theater conventions include those of Georg Buchner, Frank Wedekind, Erwin Piscator, and Leopold Jessner.

Epigram: A saying that makes the speaker's point quickly and concisely. Samuel Taylor Coleridge wrote an epigram that neatly sums up the form: What is an Epigram? A Dwarfish whole, Its body brevity, and wit its soul.

Epilogue: A concluding statement or section of a literary work. In dramas, particularly those of the seventeenth and eighteenth centuries, the epilogue is a closing speech, often in verse, delivered by an actor at the end of a play and spoken directly to the audience. A famous epilogue is Puck's speech at the end of William Shakespeare's *A Midsummer Night's Dream.*

Epiphany: A sudden revelation of truth inspired by a seemingly trivial incident. The term was widely used by James Joyce in his critical writings, and the stories in Joyce's *Dubliners* are commonly called "epiphanies."

Episode: An incident that forms part of a story and is significantly related to it. Episodes may be either self-contained narratives or events that depend on a larger context for their sense and importance. Examples of episodes include the founding of Wilmington, Delaware in Charles Reade's *The Disinherited Heir* and the individual events comprising the picaresque novels and medieval romances.

Episodic Plot: See *Plot*

Epitaph: An inscription on a tomb or tombstone, or a verse written on the occasion of a person's death. Epitaphs may be serious or humorous. Dorothy Parker's epitaph reads, "I told you I was sick."

Epithalamion: A song or poem written to honor and commemorate a marriage ceremony. Famous examples include Edmund Spenser's

"Epithalamion" and e. e. cummings's "Epithalamion." Also spelled Epithalamium.

Epithalamium: See *Epithalamion*

Epithet: A word or phrase, often disparaging or abusive, that expresses a character trait of someone or something. "The Napoleon of crime" is an epithet applied to Professor Moriarty, arch-rival of Sherlock Holmes in Arthur Conan Doyle's series of detective stories.

Exempla: See *Exemplum*

Exemplum: A tale with a moral message. This form of literary sermonizing flourished during the Middle Ages, when *exempla* appeared in collections known as "example-books." The works of Geoffrey Chaucer are full of *exempla*.

Existentialism: A predominantly twentieth-century philosophy concerned with the nature and perception of human existence. There are two major strains of existentialist thought: atheistic and Christian. Followers of atheistic existentialism believe that the individual is alone in a godless universe and that the basic human condition is one of suffering and loneliness. Nevertheless, because there are no fixed values, individuals can create their own characters—indeed, they can shape themselves—through the exercise of free will. The atheistic strain culminates in and is popularly associated with the works of Jean-Paul Sartre. The Christian existentialists, on the other hand, believe that only in God may people find freedom from life's anguish. The two strains hold certain beliefs in common: that existence cannot be fully understood or described through empirical effort; that anguish is a universal element of life; that individuals must bear responsibility for their actions; and that there is no common standard of behavior or perception for religious and ethical matters. Existentialist thought figures prominently in the works of such authors as Eugene Ionesco, Franz Kafka, Fyodor Dostoyevsky, Simone de Beauvoir, Samuel Beckett, and Albert Camus.

Expatriates: See *Expatriatism*

Expatriatism: The practice of leaving one's country to live for an extended period in another country. Literary expatriates include English poets Percy Bysshe Shelley and John Keats in Italy, Polish novelist Joseph Conrad in England, American writers Richard Wright, James Baldwin, Gertrude Stein, and Ernest Hemingway in France, and Trinidadian author Neil Bissondath in Canada.

Exposition: Writing intended to explain the nature of an idea, thing, or theme. Expository writing is often combined with description, narration, or argument. In dramatic writing, the exposition is the introductory material which presents the characters, setting, and tone of the play. An example of dramatic exposition occurs in many nineteenth-century drawing-room comedies in which the butler and the maid open the play with relevant talk about their master and mistress; in composition, exposition relays factual information, as in encyclopedia entries.

Expressionism: An indistinct literary term, originally used to describe an early twentieth-century school of German painting. The term applies to almost any mode of unconventional, highly subjective writing that distorts reality in some way. Advocates of Expressionism include dramatists George Kaiser, Ernst Toller, Luigi Pirandello, Federico Garcia Lorca, Eugene O'Neill, and Elmer Rice; poets George Heym, Ernst Stadler, August Stramm, Gottfried Benn, and Georg Trakl; and novelists Franz Kafka and James Joyce.

Extended Monologue: See *Monologue*

F

Fable: A prose or verse narrative intended to convey a moral. Animals or inanimate objects with human characteristics often serve as characters in fables. A famous fable is Aesop's "The Tortoise and the Hare."

Fairy Tales: Short narratives featuring mythical beings such as fairies, elves, and sprites. These tales originally belonged to the folklore of a particular nation or region, such as those collected in Germany by Jacob and Wilhelm Grimm. Two other celebrated writers of fairy tales are Hans Christian Andersen and Rudyard Kipling.

Falling Action: See *Denouement*

Fantasy: A literary form related to mythology and folklore. Fantasy literature is typically set in nonexistent realms and features supernatural beings. Notable examples of fantasy literature are *The Lord of the Rings* by J. R. R. Tolkien and the Gormenghast trilogy by Mervyn Peake.

Farce: A type of comedy characterized by broad humor, outlandish incidents, and often vulgar subject matter. Much of the "comedy" in film and television could more accurately be described as farce.

Feet: See *Foot*

Feminine Rhyme: See *Rhyme*

Femme fatale: A French phrase with the literal translation "fatal woman." A *femme fatale* is a sensuous, alluring woman who often leads men into danger or trouble. A classic example of the *femme fatale* is the nameless character in Billy Wilder's *The Seven Year Itch,* portrayed by Marilyn Monroe in the film adaptation.

Fiction: Any story that is the product of imagination rather than a documentation of fact. characters and events in such narratives may be based in real life but their ultimate form and configuration is a creation of the author. Geoffrey Chaucer's *The Canterbury Tales,* Laurence Sterne's *Tristram Shandy,* and Margaret Mitchell's *Gone with the Wind* are examples of fiction.

Figurative Language: A technique in writing in which the author temporarily interrupts the order, construction, or meaning of the writing for a particular effect. This interruption takes the form of one or more figures of speech such as hyperbole, irony, or simile. Figurative language is the opposite of literal language, in which every word is truthful, accurate, and free of exaggeration or embellishment. Examples of figurative language are tropes such as metaphor and rhetorical figures such as apostrophe.

Figures of Speech: Writing that differs from customary conventions for construction, meaning, order, or significance for the purpose of a special meaning or effect. There are two major types of figures of speech: rhetorical figures, which do not make changes in the meaning of the words, and tropes, which do. Types of figures of speech include simile, hyperbole, alliteration, and pun, among many others.

Fin de siecle: A French term meaning "end of the century." The term is used to denote the last decade of the nineteenth century, a transition period when writers and other artists abandoned old conventions and looked for new techniques and objectives. Two writers commonly associated with the *fin de siecle* mindset are Oscar Wilde and George Bernard Shaw.

First Person: See *Point of View*

Flashback: A device used in literature to present action that occurred before the beginning of the story. Flashbacks are often introduced as the dreams or recollections of one or more characters. Flashback techniques are often used in films, where they are typically set off by a gradual changing of one picture to another.

Foil: A character in a work of literature whose physical or psychological qualities contrast strongly with, and therefore highlight, the corresponding qualities of another character. In his Sherlock Holmes stories, Arthur Conan Doyle portrayed Dr. Watson as a man of normal habits and intelligence, making him a foil for the eccentric and wonderfully perceptive Sherlock Holmes.

Folk Ballad: See *Ballad*

Folklore: Traditions and myths preserved in a culture or group of people. Typically, these are passed on by word of mouth in various forms—such as legends, songs, and proverbs— or preserved in customs and ceremonies. This term was first used by W. J. Thoms in 1846. Sir James Frazer's *The Golden Bough* is the record of English folklore; myths about the frontier and the Old South exemplify American folklore.

Folktale: A story originating in oral tradition. Folktales fall into a variety of categories, including legends, ghost stories, fairy tales, fables, and anecdotes based on historical figures and events. Examples of folktales include Giambattista Basile's *The Pentamerone,* which contains the tales of Puss in Boots, Rapunzel, Cinderella, and Beauty and the Beast, and Joel Chandler Harris's Uncle Remus stories, which represent transplanted African folktales and American tales about the characters Mike Fink, Johnny Appleseed, Paul Bunyan, and Pecos Bill.

Foot: The smallest unit of rhythm in a line of poetry. In English-language poetry, a foot is typically one accented syllable combined with one or two unaccented syllables. There are many different types of feet. When the accent is on the second syllable of a two syllable word (con- *tort*), the foot is an "iamb"; the reverse accentual pattern (*tor* -ture) is a "trochee." Other feet that commonly occur in poetry in English are "anapest", two unaccented syllables followed by an accented syllable as in inter-*cept*, and "dactyl", an accented syllable followed by two unaccented syllables as in *su*-i- cide.

Foreshadowing: A device used in literature to create expectation or to set up an explanation of later developments. In Charles Dickens's *Great Expectations,* the graveyard encounter at the beginning of the novel between Pip and the escaped convict Magwitch foreshadows the baleful atmosphere and events that comprise much of the narrative.

Form: The pattern or construction of a work which identifies its genre and distinguishes it from other genres. Examples of forms include the different genres, such as the lyric form or the short story form, and various patterns for poetry, such as the verse form or the stanza form.

Formalism: In literary criticism, the belief that literature should follow prescribed rules of construction, such as those that govern the sonnet form. Examples of formalism are found in the work of the New Critics and structuralists.

Fourteener Meter: See *Meter*

Free Verse: Poetry that lacks regular metrical and rhyme patterns but that tries to capture the cadences of everyday speech. The form allows a poet to exploit a variety of rhythmical effects within a single poem. Free-verse techniques have been widely used in the twentieth century by such writers as Ezra Pound, T. S. Eliot, Carl Sandburg, and William Carlos Williams. Also known as *Vers libre*.

Futurism: A flamboyant literary and artistic movement that developed in France, Italy, and Russia from 1908 through the 1920s. Futurist theater and poetry abandoned traditional literary forms. In their place, followers of the movement attempted to achieve total freedom of expression through bizarre imagery and deformed or newly invented words. The Futurists were self-consciously modern artists who attempted to incorporate the appearances and sounds of modern life into their work. Futurist writers include Filippo Tommaso Marinetti, Wyndham Lewis, Guillaume Apollinaire, Velimir Khlebnikov, and Vladimir Mayakovsky.

G

Genre: A category of literary work. In critical theory, genre may refer to both the content of a given work—tragedy, comedy, pastoral—and to its form, such as poetry, novel, or drama. This term also refers to types of popular literature, as in the genres of science fiction or the detective story.

Genteel Tradition: A term coined by critic George Santayana to describe the literary practice of certain late nineteenth- century American writers, especially New Englanders. Followers of the Genteel Tradition emphasized conventionality in social, religious, moral, and literary standards. Some of the best-known writers of the Genteel Tradition are R. H. Stoddard and Bayard Taylor.

Gilded Age: A period in American history during the 1870s characterized by political corruption and materialism. A number of important novels of social and political criticism were written during this time. Examples of Gilded Age literature include Henry Adams's *Democracy* and F. Marion Crawford's *An American Politician.*

Gothic: See *Gothicism*

Gothicism: In literary criticism, works characterized by a taste for the medieval or morbidly attractive. A gothic novel prominently features elements of horror, the supernatural, gloom, and violence: clanking chains, terror, charnel houses, ghosts, medieval castles, and mysteriously slamming doors. The term ''gothic novel'' is also applied to novels that lack elements of the traditional Gothic setting but that create a similar atmosphere of terror or dread. Mary Shelley's *Frankenstein* is perhaps the best-known English work of this kind.

Gothic Novel: See *Gothicism*

Great Chain of Being: The belief that all things and creatures in nature are organized in a hierarchy from inanimate objects at the bottom to God at the top. This system of belief was popular in the seventeenth and eighteenth centuries. A summary of the concept of the great chain of being can be found in the first epistle of Alexander Pope's *An Essay on Man,* and more recently in Arthur O. Lovejoy's *The Great Chain of Being: A Study of the History of an Idea.*

Grotesque: In literary criticism, the subject matter of a work or a style of expression characterized by exaggeration, deformity, freakishness, and disorder. The grotesque often includes an element of comic absurdity. Early examples of literary grotesque include Francois Rabelais's *Pantagruel* and *Gargantua* and Thomas Nashe's *The Unfortunate Traveller,* while more recent examples can be found in the works of Edgar Allan Poe, Evelyn Waugh, Eudora Welty, Flannery O'Connor, Eugene Ionesco, Gunter Grass, Thomas Mann, Mervyn Peake, and Joseph Heller, among many others.

H

Haiku: The shortest form of Japanese poetry, constructed in three lines of five, seven, and five syllables respectively. The message of a *haiku* poem usually centers on some aspect of spirituality and provokes an emotional response in the reader. Early masters of *haiku* include Basho, Buson,

Kobayashi Issa, and Masaoka Shiki. English writers of *haiku* include the Imagists, notably Ezra Pound, H. D., Amy Lowell, Carl Sandburg, and William Carlos Williams. Also known as *Hokku.*

Half Rhyme: See *Consonance*

Hamartia: In tragedy, the event or act that leads to the hero's or heroine's downfall. This term is often incorrectly used as a synonym for tragic flaw. In Richard Wright's *Native Son,* the act that seals Bigger Thomas's fate is his first impulsive murder.

Harlem Renaissance: The Harlem Renaissance of the 1920s is generally considered the first significant movement of black writers and artists in the United States. During this period, new and established black writers published more fiction and poetry than ever before, the first influential black literary journals were established, and black authors and artists received their first widespread recognition and serious critical appraisal. Among the major writers associated with this period are Claude McKay, Jean Toomer, Countee Cullen, Langston Hughes, Arna Bontemps, Nella Larsen, and Zora Neale Hurston. Works representative of the Harlem Renaissance include Arna Bontemps's poems ''The Return'' and ''Golgotha Is a Mountain,'' Claude McKay's novel *Home to Harlem,* Nella Larsen's novel *Passing,* Langston Hughes's poem ''The Negro Speaks of Rivers,'' and the journals *Crisis* and *Opportunity,* both founded during this period. Also known as Negro Renaissance and New Negro Movement.

Harlequin: A stock character of the *commedia dell'arte* who occasionally interrupted the action with silly antics. Harlequin first appeared on the English stage in John Day's *The Travailes of the Three English Brothers.* The San Francisco Mime Troupe is one of the few modern groups to adapt Harlequin to the needs of contemporary satire.

Hellenism: Imitation of ancient Greek thought or styles. Also, an approach to life that focuses on the growth and development of the intellect. ''Hellenism'' is sometimes used to refer to the belief that reason can be applied to examine all human experience. A cogent discussion of Hellenism can be found in Matthew Arnold's *Culture and Anarchy.*

Heptameter: See *Meter*

Hero/Heroine: The principal sympathetic character (male or female) in a literary work. Heroes and heroines typically exhibit admirable traits: ideal-ism, courage, and integrity, for example. Famous heroes and heroines include Pip in Charles Dickens's *Great Expectations,* the anonymous narrator in Ralph Ellison's *Invisible Man,* and Sethe in Toni Morrison's *Beloved.*

Heroic Couplet: A rhyming couplet written in iambic pentameter (a verse with five iambic feet). The following lines by Alexander Pope are an example: ''Truth guards the Poet, sanctifies the line,/ And makes Immortal, Verse as mean as mine.''

Heroic Line: The meter and length of a line of verse in epic or heroic poetry. This varies by language and time period. For example, in English poetry, the heroic line is iambic pentameter (a verse with five iambic feet); in French, the alexandrine (a verse with six iambic feet); in classical literature, dactylic hexameter (a verse with six dactylic feet).

Heroine: See *Hero/Heroine*

Hexameter: See *Meter*

Historical Criticism: The study of a work based on its impact on the world of the time period in which it was written. Examples of postmodern historical criticism can be found in the work of Michel Foucault, Hayden White, Stephen Greenblatt, and Jonathan Goldberg.

Hokku: See *Haiku*

Holocaust: See *Holocaust Literature*

Holocaust Literature: Literature influenced by or written about the Holocaust of World War II. Such literature includes true stories of survival in concentration camps, escape, and life after the war, as well as fictional works and poetry. Representative works of Holocaust literature include Saul Bellow's *Mr. Sammler's Planet,* Anne Frank's *The Diary of a Young Girl,* Jerzy Kosinski's *The Painted Bird,* Arthur Miller's *Incident at Vichy,* Czeslaw Milosz's *Collected Poems,* William Styron's *Sophie's Choice,* and Art Spiegelman's *Maus.*

Homeric Simile: An elaborate, detailed comparison written as a simile many lines in length. An example of an epic simile from John Milton's *Paradise Lost* follows: Angel Forms, who lay entranced Thick as autumnal leaves that strow the brooks In Vallombrosa, where the Etrurian shades High over-arched embower; or scattered sedge Afloat, when with fierce winds Orion armed Hath vexed the Red-Sea coast, whose waves o'erthrew Busiris and his Memphian chivalry, While with perfidious hatred they pursued The sojourners of

Goshen, who beheld From the safe shore their floating carcasses And broken chariot-wheels. Also known as Epic Simile.

Horatian Satire: See *Satire*

Humanism: A philosophy that places faith in the dignity of humankind and rejects the medieval perception of the individual as a weak, fallen creature. "Humanists" typically believe in the perfectibility of human nature and view reason and education as the means to that end. Humanist thought is represented in the works of Marsilio Ficino, Ludovico Castelvetro, Edmund Spenser, John Milton, Dean John Colet, Desiderius Erasmus, John Dryden, Alexander Pope, Matthew Arnold, and Irving Babbitt.

Humors: Mentions of the humors refer to the ancient Greek theory that a person's health and personality were determined by the balance of four basic fluids in the body: blood, phlegm, yellow bile, and black bile. A dominance of any fluid would cause extremes in behavior. An excess of blood created a sanguine person who was joyful, aggressive, and passionate; a phlegmatic person was shy, fearful, and sluggish; too much yellow bile led to a choleric temperament characterized by impatience, anger, bitterness, and stubbornness; and excessive black bile created melancholy, a state of laziness, gluttony, and lack of motivation. Literary treatment of the humors is exemplified by several characters in Ben Jonson's plays *Every Man in His Humour* and *Every Man out of His Humour*. Also spelled Humours.

Humours: See *Humors*

Hyperbole: In literary criticism, deliberate exaggeration used to achieve an effect. In William Shakespeare's *Macbeth*, Lady Macbeth hyperbolizes when she says, "All the perfumes of Arabia could not sweeten this little hand."

I

Iamb: See *Foot*

Idiom: A word construction or verbal expression closely associated with a given language. For example, in colloquial English the construction "how come" can be used instead of "why" to introduce a question. Similarly, "a piece of cake" is sometimes used to describe a task that is easily done.

Image: A concrete representation of an object or sensory experience. Typically, such a representation helps evoke the feelings associated with the object or experience itself. Images are either "literal" or "figurative." Literal images are especially concrete and involve little or no extension of the obvious meaning of the words used to express them. Figurative images do not follow the literal meaning of the words exactly. Images in literature are usually visual, but the term "image" can also refer to the representation of any sensory experience. In his poem "The Shepherd's Hour," Paul Verlaine presents the following image: "The Moon is red through horizon's fog;/ In a dancing mist the hazy meadow sleeps." The first line is broadly literal, while the second line involves turns of meaning associated with dancing and sleeping.

Imagery: The array of images in a literary work. Also, figurative language. William Butler Yeats's "The Second Coming" offers a powerful image of encroaching anarchy: Turning and turning in the widening gyre The falcon cannot hear the falconer; Things fall apart. . . .

Imagism: An English and American poetry movement that flourished between 1908 and 1917. The Imagists used precise, clearly presented images in their works. They also used common, everyday speech and aimed for conciseness, concrete imagery, and the creation of new rhythms. Participants in the Imagist movement included Ezra Pound, H. D. (Hilda Doolittle), and Amy Lowell, among others.

In medias res: A Latin term meaning "in the middle of things." It refers to the technique of beginning a story at its midpoint and then using various flashback devices to reveal previous action. This technique originated in such epics as Virgil's *Aeneid*.

Induction: The process of reaching a conclusion by reasoning from specific premises to form a general premise. Also, an introductory portion of a work of literature, especially a play. Geoffrey Chaucer's "Prologue" to the *Canterbury Tales*, Thomas Sackville's "Induction" to *The Mirror of Magistrates*, and the opening scene in William Shakespeare's *The Taming of the Shrew* are examples of inductions to literary works.

Intentional Fallacy: The belief that judgments of a literary work based solely on an author's stated or implied intentions are false and misleading. Critics who believe in the concept of the intentional fallacy typically argue that the work itself is sufficient matter for interpretation, even though they may concede that an author's statement of purpose can be useful. Analysis of William Wordsworth's *Lyri-*

cal Ballads based on the observations about poetry he makes in his "Preface" to the second edition of that work is an example of the intentional fallacy.

Interior Monologue: A narrative technique in which characters' thoughts are revealed in a way that appears to be uncontrolled by the author. The interior monologue typically aims to reveal the inner self of a character. It portrays emotional experiences as they occur at both a conscious and unconscious level. images are often used to represent sensations or emotions. One of the best-known interior monologues in English is the Molly Bloom section at the close of James Joyce's *Ulysses*. The interior monologue is also common in the works of Virginia Woolf.

Internal Rhyme: Rhyme that occurs within a single line of verse. An example is in the opening line of Edgar Allan Poe's "The Raven": "Once upon a midnight dreary, while I pondered weak and weary." Here, "dreary" and "weary" make an internal rhyme.

Irish Literary Renaissance: A late nineteenth- and early twentieth-century movement in Irish literature. Members of the movement aimed to reduce the influence of British culture in Ireland and create an Irish national literature. William Butler Yeats, George Moore, and Sean O'Casey are three of the best-known figures of the movement.

Irony: In literary criticism, the effect of language in which the intended meaning is the opposite of what is stated. The title of Jonathan Swift's "A Modest Proposal" is ironic because what Swift proposes in this essay is cannibalism—hardly "modest."

Italian Sonnet: See *Sonnet*

J

Jacobean Age: The period of the reign of James I of England (1603-1625). The early literature of this period reflected the worldview of the Elizabethan Age, but a darker, more cynical attitude steadily grew in the art and literature of the Jacobean Age. This was an important time for English drama and poetry. Milestones include William Shakespeare's tragedies, tragi-comedies, and sonnets; Ben Jonson's various dramas; and John Donne's metaphysical poetry.

Jargon: Language that is used or understood only by a select group of people. Jargon may refer to terminology used in a certain profession, such as computer jargon, or it may refer to any nonsensical

language that is not understood by most people. Literary examples of jargon are Francois Villon's *Ballades en jargon*, which is composed in the secret language of the *coquillards*, and Anthony Burgess's *A Clockwork Orange*, narrated in the fictional characters' language of "Nadsat."

Juvenalian Satire: See *Satire*

K

Knickerbocker Group: A somewhat indistinct group of New York writers of the first half of the nineteenth century. Members of the group were linked only by location and a common theme: New York life. Two famous members of the Knickerbocker Group were Washington Irving and William Cullen Bryant. The group's name derives from Irving's *Knickerbocker's History of New York.*

L

Lais: See *Lay*

Lay: A song or simple narrative poem. The form originated in medieval France. Early French *lais* were often based on the Celtic legends and other tales sung by Breton minstrels—thus the name of the "Breton lay." In fourteenth-century England, the term "lay" was used to describe short narratives written in imitation of the Breton lays. The most notable of these is Geoffrey Chaucer's "The Minstrel's Tale."

Leitmotiv: See *Motif*

Literal Language: An author uses literal language when he or she writes without exaggerating or embellishing the subject matter and without any tools of figurative language. To say "He ran very quickly down the street" is to use literal language, whereas to say "He ran like a hare down the street" would be using figurative language.

Literary Ballad: See *Ballad*

Literature: Literature is broadly defined as any written or spoken material, but the term most often refers to creative works. Literature includes poetry, drama, fiction, and many kinds of nonfiction writing, as well as oral, dramatic, and broadcast compositions not necessarily preserved in a written format, such as films and television programs.

Lost Generation: A term first used by Gertrude Stein to describe the post-World War I generation of American writers: men and women haunted by a sense of betrayal and emptiness brought about by the destructiveness of the war. The term is commonly applied to Hart Crane, Ernest Hemingway, F. Scott Fitzgerald, and others.

Lyric Poetry: A poem expressing the subjective feelings and personal emotions of the poet. Such poetry is melodic, since it was originally accompanied by a lyre in recitals. Most Western poetry in the twentieth century may be classified as lyrical. Examples of lyric poetry include A. E. Housman's elegy "To an Athlete Dying Young," the odes of Pindar and Horace, Thomas Gray and William Collins, the sonnets of Sir Thomas Wyatt and Sir Philip Sidney, Elizabeth Barrett Browning and Rainer Maria Rilke, and a host of other forms in the poetry of William Blake and Christina Rossetti, among many others.

M

Mannerism: Exaggerated, artificial adherence to a literary manner or style. Also, a popular style of the visual arts of late sixteenth-century Europe that was marked by elongation of the human form and by intentional spatial distortion. Literary works that are self-consciously high-toned and artistic are often said to be "mannered." Authors of such works include Henry James and Gertrude Stein.

Masculine Rhyme: See *Rhyme*

Masque: A lavish and elaborate form of entertainment, often performed in royal courts, that emphasizes song, dance, and costumery. The Renaissance form of the masque grew out of the spectacles of masked figures common in medieval England and Europe. The masque reached its peak of popularity and development in seventeenth-century England, during the reigns of James I and, especially, of Charles I. Ben Jonson, the most significant masque writer, also created the "antimasque," which incorporates elements of humor and the grotesque into the traditional masque and achieved greater dramatic quality. Masque-like interludes appear in Edmund Spenser's *The Faerie Queene* and in William Shakespeare's *The Tempest*. One of the best-known English masques is John Milton's *Comus*.

Measure: The foot, verse, or time sequence used in a literary work, especially a poem. Measure is often used somewhat incorrectly as a synonym for meter.

Melodrama: A play in which the typical plot is a conflict between characters who personify extreme good and evil. Melodramas usually end happily and emphasize sensationalism. Other literary forms that use the same techniques are often labeled "melodramatic." The term was formerly used to describe a combination of drama and music; as such, it was synonymous with "opera." Augustin Daly's *Under the Gaslight* and Dion Boucicault's *The Octoroon, The Colleen Bawn,* and *The Poor of New York* are examples of melodramas. The most popular media for twentieth-century melodramas are motion pictures and television.

Metaphor: A figure of speech that expresses an idea through the image of another object. Metaphors suggest the essence of the first object by identifying it with certain qualities of the second object. An example is "But soft, what light through yonder window breaks?/ It is the east, and Juliet is the sun" in William Shakespeare's *Romeo and Juliet*. Here, Juliet, the first object, is identified with qualities of the second object, the sun.

Metaphysical Conceit: See *Conceit*

Metaphysical Poetry: The body of poetry produced by a group of seventeenth-century English writers called the "Metaphysical Poets." The group includes John Donne and Andrew Marvell. The Metaphysical Poets made use of everyday speech, intellectual analysis, and unique imagery. They aimed to portray the ordinary conflicts and contradictions of life. Their poems often took the form of an argument, and many of them emphasize physical and religious love as well as the fleeting nature of life. Elaborate conceits are typical in metaphysical poetry. Marvell's "To His Coy Mistress" is a well-known example of a metaphysical poem.

Metaphysical Poets: See *Metaphysical Poetry*

Meter: In literary criticism, the repetition of sound patterns that creates a rhythm in poetry. The patterns are based on the number of syllables and the presence and absence of accents. The unit of rhythm in a line is called a foot. Types of meter are classified according to the number of feet in a line. These are the standard English lines: Monometer, one foot; Dimeter, two feet; Trimeter, three feet; Tetrameter, four feet; Pentameter, five feet; Hexameter, six feet (also called the Alexandrine); Heptameter, seven feet (also called the "Fourteener" when the feet are iambic). The most common English meter is the iambic pentameter, in which each line contains ten syllables, or five iambic feet, which individually are composed of an unstressed syllable followed by an accented syllable. Both of the following lines from Alfred, Lord Tennyson's

"Ulysses" are written in iambic pentameter: Made weak by time and fate, but strong in will To strive, to seek, to find, and not to yield.

Mise en scene: The costumes, scenery, and other properties of a drama. Herbert Beerbohm Tree was renowned for the elaborate *mises en scene* of his lavish Shakespearean productions at His Majesty's Theatre between 1897 and 1915.

Modernism: Modern literary practices. Also, the principles of a literary school that lasted from roughly the beginning of the twentieth century until the end of World War II. Modernism is defined by its rejection of the literary conventions of the nineteenth century and by its opposition to conventional morality, taste, traditions, and economic values. Many writers are associated with the concepts of Modernism, including Albert Camus, Marcel Proust, D. H. Lawrence, W. H. Auden, Ernest Hemingway, William Faulkner, William Butler Yeats, Thomas Mann, Tennessee Williams, Eugene O'Neill, and James Joyce.

Monologue: A composition, written or oral, by a single individual. More specifically, a speech given by a single individual in a drama or other public entertainment. It has no set length, although it is usually several or more lines long. An example of an "extended monologue"—that is, a monologue of great length and seriousness—occurs in the one-act, one-character play *The Stronger* by August Strindberg.

Monometer: See *Meter*

Mood: The prevailing emotions of a work or of the author in his or her creation of the work. The mood of a work is not always what might be expected based on its subject matter. The poem "Dover Beach" by Matthew Arnold offers examples of two different moods originating from the same experience: watching the ocean at night. The mood of the first three lines— The sea is calm tonight The tide is full, the moon lies fair Upon the straights. . . . is in sharp contrast to the mood of the last three lines— And we are here as on a darkling plain Swept with confused alarms of struggle and flight, Where ignorant armies clash by night.

Motif: A theme, character type, image, metaphor, or other verbal element that recurs throughout a single work of literature or occurs in a number of different works over a period of time. For example, the various manifestations of the color white in Herman

Melville's *Moby Dick* is a "specific" *motif,* while the trials of star-crossed lovers is a "conventional" *motif* from the literature of all periods. Also known as *Motiv* or *Leitmotiv.*

Motiv: See *Motif*

Muckrakers: An early twentieth-century group of American writers. Typically, their works exposed the wrongdoings of big business and government in the United States. Upton Sinclair's *The Jungle* exemplifies the muckraking novel.

Muses: Nine Greek mythological goddesses, the daughters of Zeus and Mnemosyne (Memory). Each muse patronized a specific area of the liberal arts and sciences. Calliope presided over epic poetry, Clio over history, Erato over love poetry, Euterpe over music or lyric poetry, Melpomene over tragedy, Polyhymnia over hymns to the gods, Terpsichore over dance, Thalia over comedy, and Urania over astronomy. Poets and writers traditionally made appeals to the Muses for inspiration in their work. John Milton invokes the aid of a muse at the beginning of the first book of his *Paradise Lost:* Of Man's First disobedience, and the Fruit of the Forbidden Tree, whose mortal taste Brought Death into the World, and all our woe, With loss of Eden, till one greater Man Restore us, and regain the blissful Seat, Sing Heav'nly Muse, that on the secret top of Oreb, or of Sinai, didst inspire That Shepherd, who first taught the chosen Seed, In the Beginning how the Heav'ns and Earth Rose out of Chaos. . . .

Mystery: See *Suspense*

Myth: An anonymous tale emerging from the traditional beliefs of a culture or social unit. Myths use supernatural explanations for natural phenomena. They may also explain cosmic issues like creation and death. Collections of myths, known as mythologies, are common to all cultures and nations, but the best-known myths belong to the Norse, Roman, and Greek mythologies. A famous myth is the story of Arachne, an arrogant young girl who challenged a goddess, Athena, to a weaving contest; when the girl won, Athena was enraged and turned Arachne into a spider, thus explaining the existence of spiders.

N

Narration: The telling of a series of events, real or invented. A narration may be either a simple narrative, in which the events are recounted chronologically, or a narrative with a plot, in which the account is given in a style reflecting the author's artistic concept of the story. Narration is sometimes used as a synonym for ''storyline.'' The recounting of scary stories around a campfire is a form of narration.

Narrative: A verse or prose accounting of an event or sequence of events, real or invented. The term is also used as an adjective in the sense ''method of narration.'' For example, in literary criticism, the expression ''narrative technique'' usually refers to the way the author structures and presents his or her story. Narratives range from the shortest accounts of events, as in Julius Caesar's remark, ''I came, I saw, I conquered,'' to the longest historical or biographical works, as in Edward Gibbon's *The Decline and Fall of the Roman Empire,* as well as diaries, travelogues, novels, ballads, epics, short stories, and other fictional forms.

Narrative Poetry: A nondramatic poem in which the author tells a story. Such poems may be of any length or level of complexity. Epics such as *Beowulf* and ballads are forms of narrative poetry.

Narrator: The teller of a story. The narrator may be the author or a character in the story through whom the author speaks. Huckleberry Finn is the narrator of Mark Twain's *The Adventures of Huckleberry Finn.*

Naturalism: A literary movement of the late nineteenth and early twentieth centuries. The movement's major theorist, French novelist Emile Zola, envisioned a type of fiction that would examine human life with the objectivity of scientific inquiry. The Naturalists typically viewed human beings as either the products of ''biological determinism,'' ruled by hereditary instincts and engaged in an endless struggle for survival, or as the products of ''socioeconomic determinism,'' ruled by social and economic forces beyond their control. In their works, the Naturalists generally ignored the highest levels of society and focused on degradation: poverty, alcoholism, prostitution, insanity, and disease. Naturalism influenced authors throughout the world, including Henrik Ibsen and Thomas Hardy. In the United States, in particular, Naturalism had a profound impact. Among the authors who embraced its principles are Theodore Dreiser, Eugene O'Neill, Stephen Crane, Jack London, and Frank Norris.

Negritude: A literary movement based on the concept of a shared cultural bond on the part of black Africans, wherever they may be in the world. It traces its origins to the former French colonies of Africa and the Caribbean. Negritude poets, novelists, and essayists generally stress four points in their writings: One, black alienation from traditional African culture can lead to feelings of inferiority. Two, European colonialism and Western education should be resisted. Three, black Africans should seek to affirm and define their own identity. Four, African culture can and should be reclaimed. Many Negritude writers also claim that blacks can make unique contributions to the world, based on a heightened appreciation of nature, rhythm, and human emotions—aspects of life they say are not so highly valued in the materialistic and rationalistic West. Examples of Negritude literature include the poetry of both Senegalese Leopold Senghor in *Hosties noires* and Martiniquais Aime-Fernand Cesaire in *Return to My Native Land.*

Negro Renaissance: See *Harlem Renaissance*

Neoclassical Period: See *Neoclassicism*

Neoclassicism: In literary criticism, this term refers to the revival of the attitudes and styles of expression of classical literature. It is generally used to describe a period in European history beginning in the late seventeenth century and lasting until about 1800. In its purest form, Neoclassicism marked a return to order, proportion, restraint, logic, accuracy, and decorum. In England, where Neoclassicism perhaps was most popular, it reflected the influence of seventeenth- century French writers, especially dramatists. Neoclassical writers typically reacted against the intensity and enthusiasm of the Renaissance period. They wrote works that appealed to the intellect, using elevated language and classical literary forms such as satire and the ode. Neoclassical works were often governed by the classical goal of instruction. English neoclassicists included Alexander Pope, Jonathan Swift, Joseph Addison, Sir Richard Steele, John Gay, and Matthew Prior; French neoclassicists included Pierre Corneille and Jean-Baptiste Moliere. Also known as Age of Reason.

Neoclassicists: See *Neoclassicism*

New Criticism: A movement in literary criticism, dating from the late 1920s, that stressed close textual analysis in the interpretation of works of literature. The New Critics saw little merit in historical and biographical analysis. Rather, they aimed to examine the text alone, free from the question of how external events—biographical or otherwise—may have helped shape it. This predominantly American school was named ''New Criticism'' by one of its practitioners, John Crowe Ransom. Other important New Critics included Allen Tate, R. P. Blackmur, Robert Penn Warren, and Cleanth Brooks.

New Negro Movement: See *Harlem Renaissance*

Noble Savage: The idea that primitive man is noble and good but becomes evil and corrupted as he becomes civilized. The concept of the noble savage originated in the Renaissance period but is more closely identified with such later writers as Jean-Jacques Rousseau and Aphra Behn. First described in John Dryden's play *The Conquest of Granada,* the noble savage is portrayed by the various Native Americans in James Fenimore Cooper's ''Leatherstocking Tales,'' by Queequeg, Daggoo, and Tashtego in Herman Melville's *Moby Dick,* and by John the Savage in Aldous Huxley's *Brave New World.*

O

Objective Correlative: An outward set of objects, a situation, or a chain of events corresponding to an inward experience and evoking this experience in the reader. The term frequently appears in modern criticism in discussions of authors' intended effects on the emotional responses of readers. This term was originally used by T. S. Eliot in his 1919 essay ''Hamlet.''

Objectivity: A quality in writing characterized by the absence of the author's opinion or feeling about the subject matter. Objectivity is an important factor in criticism. The novels of Henry James and, to a certain extent, the poems of John Larkin demonstrate objectivity, and it is central to John Keats's concept of ''negative capability.'' Critical and journalistic writing usually are or attempt to be objective.

Occasional Verse: poetry written on the occasion of a significant historical or personal event. *Vers de societe* is sometimes called occasional verse although it is of a less serious nature. Famous examples of occasional verse include Andrew Marvell's ''Horatian Ode upon Cromwell's Return from England,'' Walt Whitman's ''When Lilacs Last in the Dooryard Bloom'd''— written upon the death of Abraham Lincoln—and Edmund Spenser's commemoration of his wedding, ''Epithalamion.''

Octave: A poem or stanza composed of eight lines. The term octave most often represents the first eight lines of a Petrarchan sonnet. An example of an octave is taken from a translation of a Petrarchan sonnet by Sir Thomas Wyatt: The pillar perisht is whereto I leant, The strongest stay of mine unquiet mind; The like of it no man again can find, From East to West Still seeking though he went. To mind unhap! for hap away hath rent Of all my joy the very

bark and rind; And I, alas, by chance am thus assigned Daily to mourn till death do it relent.

Ode: Name given to an extended lyric poem characterized by exalted emotion and dignified style. An ode usually concerns a single, serious theme. Most odes, but not all, are addressed to an object or individual. Odes are distinguished from other lyric poetic forms by their complex rhythmic and stanzaic patterns. An example of this form is John Keats's ''Ode to a Nightingale.''

Oedipus Complex: A son's amorous obsession with his mother. The phrase is derived from the story of the ancient Theban hero Oedipus, who unknowingly killed his father and married his mother. Literary occurrences of the Oedipus complex include Andre Gide's *Oedipe* and Jean Cocteau's *La Machine infernale,* as well as the most famous, Sophocles' *Oedipus Rex.*

Omniscience: See *Point of View*

Onomatopoeia: The use of words whose sounds express or suggest their meaning. In its simplest sense, onomatopoeia may be represented by words that mimic the sounds they denote such as ''hiss'' or ''meow.'' At a more subtle level, the pattern and rhythm of sounds and rhymes of a line or poem may be onomatopoeic. A celebrated example of onomatopoeia is the repetition of the word ''bells'' in Edgar Allan Poe's poem ''The Bells.''

Opera: A type of stage performance, usually a drama, in which the dialogue is sung. Classic examples of opera include Giuseppi Verdi's *La traviata,* Giacomo Puccini's *La Boheme,* and Richard Wagner's *Tristan und Isolde.* Major twentieth- century contributors to the form include Richard Strauss and Alban Berg.

Operetta: A usually romantic comic opera. John Gay's *The Beggar's Opera,* Richard Sheridan's *The Duenna,* and numerous works by William Gilbert and Arthur Sullivan are examples of operettas.

Oral Tradition: See *Oral Transmission*

Oral Transmission: A process by which songs, ballads, folklore, and other material are transmitted by word of mouth. The tradition of oral transmission predates the written record systems of literate society. Oral transmission preserves material sometimes over generations, although often with variations. Memory plays a large part in the recitation and preservation of orally transmitted material. Breton lays, French *fabliaux,* national epics (including the Anglo- Saxon *Beowulf,* the Spanish *El Cid,* and the Finnish *Kalevala*), Native American myths and legends, and African folktales told by plantation slaves are examples of orally transmitted literature.

Oration: Formal speaking intended to motivate the listeners to some action or feeling. Such public speaking was much more common before the development of timely printed communication such as newspapers. Famous examples of oration include Abraham Lincoln's "Gettysburg Address" and Dr. Martin Luther King Jr.'s "I Have a Dream" speech.

Ottava Rima: An eight-line stanza of poetry composed in iambic pentameter (a five-foot line in which each foot consists of an unaccented syllable followed by an accented syllable), following the abababcc rhyme scheme. This form has been prominently used by such important English writers as Lord Byron, Henry Wadsworth Longfellow, and W. B. Yeats.

Oxymoron: A phrase combining two contradictory terms. Oxymorons may be intentional or unintentional. The following speech from William Shakespeare's *Romeo and Juliet* uses several oxymorons: Why, then, O brawling love! O loving hate! O anything, of nothing first create! O heavy lightness! serious vanity! Mis-shapen chaos of well-seeming forms! Feather of lead, bright smoke, cold fire, sick health! This love feel I, that feel no love in this.

P

Pantheism: The idea that all things are both a manifestation or revelation of God and a part of God at the same time. Pantheism was a common attitude in the early societies of Egypt, India, and Greece— the term derives from the Greek *pan* meaning "all" and *theos* meaning "deity." It later became a significant part of the Christian faith. William Wordsworth and Ralph Waldo Emerson are among the many writers who have expressed the pantheistic attitude in their works.

Parable: A story intended to teach a moral lesson or answer an ethical question. In the West, the best examples of parables are those of Jesus Christ in the New Testament, notably "The Prodigal Son," but parables also are used in Sufism, rabbinic literature, Hasidism, and Zen Buddhism.

Paradox: A statement that appears illogical or contradictory at first, but may actually point to an underlying truth. "Less is more" is an example of a paradox. Literary examples include Francis Ba-

con's statement, "The most corrected copies are commonly the least correct," and "All animals are equal, but some animals are more equal than others" from George Orwell's *Animal Farm.*

Parallelism: A method of comparison of two ideas in which each is developed in the same grammatical structure. Ralph Waldo Emerson's "Civilization" contains this example of parallelism: Raphael paints wisdom; Handel sings it, Phidias carves it, Shakespeare writes it, Wren builds it, Columbus sails it, Luther preaches it, Washington arms it, Watt mechanizes it.

Parnassianism: A mid nineteenth-century movement in French literature. Followers of the movement stressed adherence to well-defined artistic forms as a reaction against the often chaotic expression of the artist's ego that dominated the work of the Romantics. The Parnassians also rejected the moral, ethical, and social themes exhibited in the works of French Romantics such as Victor Hugo. The aesthetic doctrines of the Parnassians strongly influenced the later symbolist and decadent movements. Members of the Parnassian school include Leconte de Lisle, Sully Prudhomme, Albert Glatigny, Francois Coppee, and Theodore de Banville.

Parody: In literary criticism, this term refers to an imitation of a serious literary work or the signature style of a particular author in a ridiculous manner. A typical parody adopts the style of the original and applies it to an inappropriate subject for humorous effect. Parody is a form of satire and could be considered the literary equivalent of a caricature or cartoon. Henry Fielding's *Shamela* is a parody of Samuel Richardson's *Pamela.*

Pastoral: A term derived from the Latin word "pastor," meaning shepherd. A pastoral is a literary composition on a rural theme. The conventions of the pastoral were originated by the third-century Greek poet Theocritus, who wrote about the experiences, love affairs, and pastimes of Sicilian shepherds. In a pastoral, characters and language of a courtly nature are often placed in a simple setting. The term pastoral is also used to classify dramas, elegies, and lyrics that exhibit the use of country settings and shepherd characters. Percy Bysshe Shelley's "Adonais" and John Milton's "Lycidas" are two famous examples of pastorals.

Pastorela: The Spanish name for the shepherds play, a folk drama reenacted during the Christmas season. Examples of *pastorelas* include Gomez

Manrique's *Representacion del nacimiento* and the dramas of Lucas Fernandez and Juan del Encina.

Pathetic Fallacy: A term coined by English critic John Ruskin to identify writing that falsely endows nonhuman things with human intentions and feelings, such as "angry clouds" and "sad trees." The pathetic fallacy is a required convention in the classical poetic form of the pastoral elegy, and it is used in the modern poetry of T. S. Eliot, Ezra Pound, and the Imagists. Also known as Poetic Fallacy.

Pelado: Literally the "skinned one" or shirtless one, he was the stock underdog, sharp-witted picaresque character of Mexican vaudeville and tent shows. The *pelado* is found in such works as Don Catarino's *Los effectos de la crisis* and *Regreso a mi tierra.*

Pen Name: See *Pseudonym*

Pentameter: See *Meter*

Persona: A Latin term meaning "mask." *Personae* are the characters in a fictional work of literature. The *persona* generally functions as a mask through which the author tells a story in a voice other than his or her own. A *persona* is usually either a character in a story who acts as a narrator or an "implied author," a voice created by the author to act as the narrator for himself or herself. *Personae* include the narrator of Geoffrey Chaucer's *Canterbury Tales* and Marlow in Joseph Conrad's *Heart of Darkness.*

Personae: See *Persona*

Personal Point of View: See *Point of View*

Personification: A figure of speech that gives human qualities to abstract ideas, animals, and inanimate objects. William Shakespeare used personification in *Romeo and Juliet* in the lines "Arise, fair sun, and kill the envious moon,/ Who is already sick and pale with grief." Here, the moon is portrayed as being envious, sick, and pale with grief—all markedly human qualities. Also known as *Prosopopoeia.*

Petrarchan Sonnet: See *Sonnet*

Phenomenology: A method of literary criticism based on the belief that things have no existence outside of human consciousness or awareness. Proponents of this theory believe that art is a process that takes place in the mind of the observer as he or she contemplates an object rather than a quality of the object itself. Among phenomenological critics

are Edmund Husserl, George Poulet, Marcel Raymond, and Roman Ingarden.

Picaresque Novel: Episodic fiction depicting the adventures of a roguish central character ("picaro" is Spanish for "rogue"). The picaresque hero is commonly a low-born but clever individual who wanders into and out of various affairs of love, danger, and farcical intrigue. These involvements may take place at all social levels and typically present a humorous and wide-ranging satire of a given society. Prominent examples of the picaresque novel are *Don Quixote* by Miguel de Cervantes, *Tom Jones* by Henry Fielding, and *Moll Flanders* by Daniel Defoe.

Plagiarism: Claiming another person's written material as one's own. Plagiarism can take the form of direct, word-for- word copying or the theft of the substance or idea of the work. A student who copies an encyclopedia entry and turns it in as a report for school is guilty of plagiarism.

Platonic Criticism: A form of criticism that stresses an artistic work's usefulness as an agent of social engineering rather than any quality or value of the work itself. Platonic criticism takes as its starting point the ancient Greek philosopher Plato's comments on art in his *Republic.*

Platonism: The embracing of the doctrines of the philosopher Plato, popular among the poets of the Renaissance and the Romantic period. Platonism is more flexible than Aristotelian Criticism and places more emphasis on the supernatural and unknown aspects of life. Platonism is expressed in the love poetry of the Renaissance, the fourth book of Baldassare Castiglione's *The Book of the Courtier,* and the poetry of William Blake, William Wordsworth, Percy Bysshe Shelley, Friedrich Holderlin, William Butler Yeats, and Wallace Stevens.

Play: See *Drama*

Plot: In literary criticism, this term refers to the pattern of events in a narrative or drama. In its simplest sense, the plot guides the author in composing the work and helps the reader follow the work. Typically, plots exhibit causality and unity and have a beginning, a middle, and an end. Sometimes, however, a plot may consist of a series of disconnected events, in which case it is known as an "episodic plot." In his *Aspects of the Novel,* E. M. Forster distinguishes between a story, defined as a "narrative of events arranged in their time- sequence," and plot, which organizes the events to a "sense of causality." This definition closely mirrors Aristotle's discussion of plot in his *Poetics.*

Poem: In its broadest sense, a composition utilizing rhyme, meter, concrete detail, and expressive language to create a literary experience with emotional and aesthetic appeal. Typical poems include sonnets, odes, elegies, *haiku,* ballads, and free verse.

Poet: An author who writes poetry or verse. The term is also used to refer to an artist or writer who has an exceptional gift for expression, imagination, and energy in the making of art in any form. Well-known poets include Horace, Basho, Sir Philip Sidney, Sir Edmund Spenser, John Donne, Andrew Marvell, Alexander Pope, Jonathan Swift, George Gordon, Lord Byron, John Keats, Christina Rossetti, W. H. Auden, Stevie Smith, and Sylvia Plath.

Poetic Fallacy: See *Pathetic Fallacy*

Poetic Justice: An outcome in a literary work, not necessarily a poem, in which the good are rewarded and the evil are punished, especially in ways that particularly fit their virtues or crimes. For example, a murderer may himself be murdered, or a thief will find himself penniless.

Poetic License: Distortions of fact and literary convention made by a writer—not always a poet—for the sake of the effect gained. Poetic license is closely related to the concept of "artistic freedom." An author exercises poetic license by saying that a pile of money "reaches as high as a mountain" when the pile is actually only a foot or two high.

Poetics: This term has two closely related meanings. It denotes (1) an aesthetic theory in literary criticism about the essence of poetry or (2) rules prescribing the proper methods, content, style, or diction of poetry. The term poetics may also refer to theories about literature in general, not just poetry.

Poetry: In its broadest sense, writing that aims to present ideas and evoke an emotional experience in the reader through the use of meter, imagery, connotative and concrete words, and a carefully constructed structure based on rhythmic patterns. Poetry typically relies on words and expressions that have several layers of meaning. It also makes use of the effects of regular rhythm on the ear and may make a strong appeal to the senses through the use of imagery. Edgar Allan Poe's "Annabel Lee" and Walt Whitman's *Leaves of Grass* are famous examples of poetry.

Point of View: The narrative perspective from which a literary work is presented to the reader.

There are four traditional points of view. The "third person omniscient" gives the reader a "godlike" perspective, unrestricted by time or place, from which to see actions and look into the minds of characters. This allows the author to comment openly on characters and events in the work. The "third person" point of view presents the events of the story from outside of any single character's perception, much like the omniscient point of view, but the reader must understand the action as it takes place and without any special insight into characters' minds or motivations. The "first person" or "personal" point of view relates events as they are perceived by a single character. The main character "tells" the story and may offer opinions about the action and characters which differ from those of the author. Much less common than omniscient, third person, and first person is the "second person" point of view, wherein the author tells the story as if it is happening to the reader. James Thurber employs the omniscient point of view in his short story "The Secret Life of Walter Mitty." Ernest Hemingway's "A Clean, Well-Lighted Place" is a short story told from the third person point of view. Mark Twain's novel *Huck Finn* is presented from the first person viewpoint. Jay McInerney's *Bright Lights, Big City* is an example of a novel which uses the second person point of view.

Polemic: A work in which the author takes a stand on a controversial subject, such as abortion or religion. Such works are often extremely argumentative or provocative. Classic examples of polemics include John Milton's *Aeropagitica* and Thomas Paine's *The American Crisis.*

Pornography: Writing intended to provoke feelings of lust in the reader. Such works are often condemned by critics and teachers, but those which can be shown to have literary value are viewed less harshly. Literary works that have been described as pornographic include Ovid's *The Art of Love,* Margaret of Angouleme's *Heptameron,* John Cleland's *Memoirs of a Woman of Pleasure; or, the Life of Fanny Hill,* the anonymous *My Secret Life,* D. H. Lawrence's *Lady Chatterley's Lover,* and Vladimir Nabokov's *Lolita.*

Post-Aesthetic Movement: An artistic response made by African Americans to the black aesthetic movement of the 1960s and early '70s. Writers since that time have adopted a somewhat different tone in their work, with less emphasis placed on the disparity between black and white in the United States. In the words of post-aesthetic authors such as Toni Morrison, John Edgar Wideman, and Kristin Hunter, African Americans are portrayed as looking inward for answers to their own questions, rather than always looking to the outside world. Two well-known examples of works produced as part of the post-aesthetic movement are the Pulitzer Prize-winning novels *The Color Purple* by Alice Walker and *Beloved* by Toni Morrison.

Postmodernism: Writing from the 1960s forward characterized by experimentation and continuing to apply some of the fundamentals of modernism, which included existentialism and alienation. Postmodernists have gone a step further in the rejection of tradition begun with the modernists by also rejecting traditional forms, preferring the anti-novel over the novel and the anti-hero over the hero. Postmodern writers include Alain Robbe-Grillet, Thomas Pynchon, Margaret Drabble, John Fowles, Adolfo Bioy-Casares, and Gabriel Garcia Marquez.

Pre-Raphaelites: A circle of writers and artists in mid nineteenth-century England. Valuing the pre-Renaissance artistic qualities of religious symbolism, lavish pictorialism, and natural sensuousness, the Pre-Raphaelites cultivated a sense of mystery and melancholy that influenced later writers associated with the Symbolist and Decadent movements. The major members of the group include Dante Gabriel Rossetti, Christina Rossetti, Algernon Swinburne, and Walter Pater.

Primitivism: The belief that primitive peoples were nobler and less flawed than civilized peoples because they had not been subjected to the tainting influence of society. Examples of literature espousing primitivism include Aphra Behn's *Oroonoko: Or, The History of the Royal Slave,* Jean-Jacques Rousseau's *Julie ou la Nouvelle Heloise,* Oliver Goldsmith's *The Deserted Village,* the poems of Robert Burns, Herman Melville's stories *Typee, Omoo,* and *Mardi,* many poems of William Butler Yeats and Robert Frost, and William Golding's novel *Lord of the Flies.*

Projective Verse: A form of free verse in which the poet's breathing pattern determines the lines of the poem. Poets who advocate projective verse are against all formal structures in writing, including meter and form. Besides its creators, Robert Creeley, Robert Duncan, and Charles Olson, two other well-known projective verse poets are Denise Levertov and LeRoi Jones (Amiri Baraka). Also known as Breath Verse.

Prologue: An introductory section of a literary work. It often contains information establishing the situation of the characters or presents information about the setting, time period, or action. In drama, the prologue is spoken by a chorus or by one of the principal characters. In the "General Prologue" of *The Canterbury Tales,* Geoffrey Chaucer describes the main characters and establishes the setting and purpose of the work.

Prose: A literary medium that attempts to mirror the language of everyday speech. It is distinguished from poetry by its use of unmetered, unrhymed language consisting of logically related sentences. Prose is usually grouped into paragraphs that form a cohesive whole such as an essay or a novel. Recognized masters of English prose writing include Sir Thomas Malory, William Caxton, Raphael Holinshed, Joseph Addison, Mark Twain, and Ernest Hemingway.

Prosopopoeia: See *Personification*

Protagonist: The central character of a story who serves as a focus for its themes and incidents and as the principal rationale for its development. The protagonist is sometimes referred to in discussions of modern literature as the hero or anti-hero. Well-known protagonists are Hamlet in William Shakespeare's *Hamlet* and Jay Gatsby in F. Scott Fitzgerald's *The Great Gatsby.*

Protest Fiction: Protest fiction has as its primary purpose the protesting of some social injustice, such as racism or discrimination. One example of protest fiction is a series of five novels by Chester Himes, beginning in 1945 with *If He Hollers Let Him Go* and ending in 1955 with *The Primitive.* These works depict the destructive effects of race and gender stereotyping in the context of interracial relationships. Another African American author whose works often revolve around themes of social protest is John Oliver Killens. James Baldwin's essay "Everybody's Protest Novel" generated controversy by attacking the authors of protest fiction.

Proverb: A brief, sage saying that expresses a truth about life in a striking manner. "They are not all cooks who carry long knives" is an example of a proverb.

Pseudonym: A name assumed by a writer, most often intended to prevent his or her identification as the author of a work. Two or more authors may work together under one pseudonym, or an author may use a different name for each genre he or she publishes in. Some publishing companies maintain ''house pseudonyms,'' under which any number of authors may write installations in a series. Some authors also choose a pseudonym over their real names the way an actor may use a stage name. Examples of pseudonyms (with the author's real name in parentheses) include Voltaire (Francois-Marie Arouet), Novalis (Friedrich von Hardenberg), Currer Bell (Charlotte Bronte), Ellis Bell (Emily Bronte), George Eliot (Maryann Evans), Honorio Bustos Donmecq (Adolfo Bioy-Casares and Jorge Luis Borges), and Richard Bachman (Stephen King).

Pun: A play on words that have similar sounds but different meanings. A serious example of the pun is from John Donne's ''A Hymne to God the Father'': Sweare by thyself, that at my death thy sonne Shall shine as he shines now, and hereto fore; And, having done that, Thou haste done; I fear no more.

Pure Poetry: poetry written without instructional intent or moral purpose that aims only to please a reader by its imagery or musical flow. The term pure poetry is used as the antonym of the term ''didacticism.'' The poetry of Edgar Allan Poe, Stephane Mallarme, Paul Verlaine, Paul Valery, Juan Ramoz Jimenez, and Jorge Guillen offer examples of pure poetry.

Q

Quatrain: A four-line stanza of a poem or an entire poem consisting of four lines. The following quatrain is from Robert Herrick's ''To Live Merrily, and to Trust to Good Verses'': Round, round, the root do's run; And being ravisht thus, Come, I will drink a Tun To my *Propertius.*

R

Raisonneur: A character in a drama who functions as a spokesperson for the dramatist's views. The *raisonneur* typically observes the play without becoming central to its action. *Raisonneurs* were very common in plays of the nineteenth century.

Realism: A nineteenth-century European literary movement that sought to portray familiar characters, situations, and settings in a realistic manner. This was done primarily by using an objective narrative point of view and through the buildup of accurate detail. The standard for success of any realistic work depends on how faithfully it transfers common experience into fictional forms. The realistic method may be altered or extended, as in stream of consciousness writing, to record highly subjec-

tive experience. Seminal authors in the tradition of Realism include Honore de Balzac, Gustave Flaubert, and Henry James.

Refrain: A phrase repeated at intervals throughout a poem. A refrain may appear at the end of each stanza or at less regular intervals. It may be altered slightly at each appearance. Some refrains are nonsense expressions—as with ''Nevermore'' in Edgar Allan Poe's ''The Raven''—that seem to take on a different significance with each use.

Renaissance: The period in European history that marked the end of the Middle Ages. It began in Italy in the late fourteenth century. In broad terms, it is usually seen as spanning the fourteenth, fifteenth, and sixteenth centuries, although it did not reach Great Britain, for example, until the 1480s or so. The Renaissance saw an awakening in almost every sphere of human activity, especially science, philosophy, and the arts. The period is best defined by the emergence of a general philosophy that emphasized the importance of the intellect, the individual, and world affairs. It contrasts strongly with the medieval worldview, characterized by the dominant concerns of faith, the social collective, and spiritual salvation. Prominent writers during the Renaissance include Niccolo Machiavelli and Baldassare Castiglione in Italy, Miguel de Cervantes and Lope de Vega in Spain, Jean Froissart and Francois Rabelais in France, Sir Thomas More and Sir Philip Sidney in England, and Desiderius Erasmus in Holland.

Repartee: Conversation featuring snappy retorts and witticisms. Masters of *repartee* include Sydney Smith, Charles Lamb, and Oscar Wilde. An example is recorded in the meeting of ''Beau'' Nash and John Wesley: Nash said, ''I never make way for a fool,'' to which Wesley responded, ''Don't you? I always do,'' and stepped aside.

Resolution: The portion of a story following the climax, in which the conflict is resolved. The resolution of Jane Austen's *Northanger Abbey* is neatly summed up in the following sentence: ''Henry and Catherine were married, the bells rang and everybody smiled.''

Restoration: See *Restoration Age*

Restoration Age: A period in English literature beginning with the crowning of Charles II in 1660 and running to about 1700. The era, which was characterized by a reaction against Puritanism, was the first great age of the comedy of manners. The finest literature of the era is typically witty and urbane, and often lewd. Prominent Restoration Age writers include William Congreve, Samuel Pepys, John Dryden, and John Milton.

Revenge Tragedy: A dramatic form popular during the Elizabethan Age, in which the protagonist, directed by the ghost of his murdered father or son, inflicts retaliation upon a powerful villain. Notable features of the revenge tragedy include violence, bizarre criminal acts, intrigue, insanity, a hesitant protagonist, and the use of soliloquy. Thomas Kyd's *Spanish Tragedy* is the first example of revenge tragedy in English, and William Shakespeare's *Hamlet* is perhaps the best. Extreme examples of revenge tragedy, such as John Webster's *The Duchess of Malfi,* are labeled "tragedies of blood." Also known as Tragedy of Blood.

Revista: The Spanish term for a vaudeville musical revue. Examples of *revistas* include Antonio Guzman Aguilera's *Mexico para los mexicanos,* Daniel Vanegas's *Maldito jazz,* and Don Catarino's *Whiskey, morfina y marihuana* and *El desterrado.*

Rhetoric: In literary criticism, this term denotes the art of ethical persuasion. In its strictest sense, rhetoric adheres to various principles developed since classical times for arranging facts and ideas in a clear, persuasive, appealing manner. The term is also used to refer to effective prose in general and theories of or methods for composing effective prose. Classical examples of rhetorics include *The Rhetoric of Aristotle,* Quintillian's *Institutio Oratoria,* and Cicero's *Ad Herennium.*

Rhetorical Question: A question intended to provoke thought, but not an expressed answer, in the reader. It is most commonly used in oratory and other persuasive genres. The following lines from Thomas Gray's "Elegy Written in a Country Churchyard" ask rhetorical questions: Can storied urn or animated bust Back to its mansion call the fleeting breath? Can Honour's voice provoke the silent dust, Or Flattery soothe the dull cold ear of Death?

Rhyme: When used as a noun in literary criticism, this term generally refers to a poem in which words sound identical or very similar and appear in parallel positions in two or more lines. Rhymes are classified into different types according to where they fall in a line or stanza or according to the degree of similarity they exhibit in their spellings and sounds. Some major types of rhyme are "masculine" rhyme, "feminine" rhyme, and "triple" rhyme. In a masculine rhyme, the rhyming sound falls in a single accented syllable, as with "heat" and "eat." Feminine rhyme is a rhyme of two syllables, one stressed and one unstressed, as with "merry" and "tarry." Triple rhyme matches the sound of the accented syllable and the two unaccented syllables that follow: "narrative" and "declarative." Robert Browning alternates feminine and masculine rhymes in his "Soliloquy of the Spanish Cloister": Gr-r-r—there go, my heart's abhorrence! Water your damned flower-pots, do! If hate killed men, Brother Lawrence, God's blood, would not mine kill you! What? Your myrtle-bush wants trimming? Oh, that rose has prior claims— Needs its leaden vase filled brimming? Hell dry you up with flames! Triple rhymes can be found in Thomas Hood's "Bridge of Sighs," George Gordon Byron's satirical verse, and Ogden Nash's comic poems.

Rhyme Royal: A stanza of seven lines composed in iambic pentameter and rhymed *ababbcc.* The name is said to be a tribute to King James I of Scotland, who made much use of the form in his poetry. Examples of rhyme royal include Geoffrey Chaucer's *The Parlement of Foules,* William Shakespeare's *The Rape of Lucrece,* William Morris's *The Early Paradise,* and John Masefield's *The Widow in the Bye Street.*

Rhyme Scheme: See *Rhyme*

Rhythm: A regular pattern of sound, time intervals, or events occurring in writing, most often and most discernably in poetry. Regular, reliable rhythm is known to be soothing to humans, while interrupted, unpredictable, or rapidly changing rhythm is disturbing. These effects are known to authors, who use them to produce a desired reaction in the reader. An example of a form of irregular rhythm is sprung rhythm poetry; quantitative verse, on the other hand, is very regular in its rhythm.

Rising Action: The part of a drama where the plot becomes increasingly complicated. Rising action leads up to the climax, or turning point, of a drama. The final "chase scene" of an action film is generally the rising action which culminates in the film's climax.

Rococo: A style of European architecture that flourished in the eighteenth century, especially in France. The most notable features of *rococo* are its extensive use of ornamentation and its themes of lightness, gaiety, and intimacy. In literary criticism, the term is often used disparagingly to refer to a decadent or over-ornamental style. Alexander Pope's "The Rape of the Lock" is an example of literary *rococo.*

Roman a clef: A French phrase meaning "novel with a key." It refers to a narrative in which real persons are portrayed under fictitious names. Jack Kerouac, for example, portrayed various real-life beat generation figures under fictitious names in his *On the Road.*

Romance: A broad term, usually denoting a narrative with exotic, exaggerated, often idealized characters, scenes, and themes. Nathaniel Hawthorne called his *The House of the Seven Gables* and *The Marble Faun* romances in order to distinguish them from clearly realistic works.

Romantic Age: See *Romanticism*

Romanticism: This term has two widely accepted meanings. In historical criticism, it refers to a European intellectual and artistic movement of the late eighteenth and early nineteenth centuries that sought greater freedom of personal expression than that allowed by the strict rules of literary form and logic of the eighteenth-century neoclassicists. The Romantics preferred emotional and imaginative expression to rational analysis. They considered the individual to be at the center of all experience and so placed him or her at the center of their art. The Romantics believed that the creative imagination reveals nobler truths—unique feelings and attitudes—than those that could be discovered by logic or by scientific examination. Both the natural world and the state of childhood were important sources for revelations of "eternal truths." "Romanticism" is also used as a general term to refer to a type of sensibility found in all periods of literary history and usually considered to be in opposition to the principles of classicism. In this sense, Romanticism signifies any work or philosophy in which the exotic or dreamlike figure strongly, or that is devoted to individualistic expression, self-analysis, or a pursuit of a higher realm of knowledge than can be discovered by human reason. Prominent Romantics include Jean-Jacques Rousseau, William Wordsworth, John Keats, Lord Byron, and Johann Wolfgang von Goethe.

Romantics: See *Romanticism*

Russian Symbolism: A Russian poetic movement, derived from French symbolism, that flourished between 1894 and 1910. While some Russian Symbolists continued in the French tradition, stressing aestheticism and the importance of suggestion above didactic intent, others saw their craft as a form of mystical worship, and themselves as mediators between the supernatural and the mundane. Russian symbolists include Aleksandr Blok, Vyacheslav Ivanovich Ivanov, Fyodor Sologub, Andrey Bely, Nikolay Gumilyov, and Vladimir Sergeyevich Solovyov.

S

Satire: A work that uses ridicule, humor, and wit to criticize and provoke change in human nature and institutions. There are two major types of satire: "formal" or "direct" satire speaks directly to the reader or to a character in the work; "indirect" satire relies upon the ridiculous behavior of its characters to make its point. Formal satire is further divided into two manners: the "Horatian," which ridicules gently, and the "Juvenalian," which derides its subjects harshly and bitterly. Voltaire's novella *Candide* is an indirect satire. Jonathan Swift's essay "A Modest Proposal" is a Juvenalian satire.

Scansion: The analysis or "scanning" of a poem to determine its meter and often its rhyme scheme. The most common system of scansion uses accents (slanted lines drawn above syllables) to show stressed syllables, breves (curved lines drawn above syllables) to show unstressed syllables, and vertical lines to separate each foot. In the first line of John Keats's *Endymion,* "A thing of beauty is a joy forever:" the word "thing," the first syllable of "beauty," the word "joy," and the second syllable of "forever" are stressed, while the words "A" and "of," the second syllable of "beauty," the word "a," and the first and third syllables of "forever" are unstressed. In the second line: "Its loveliness increases; it will never" a pair of vertical lines separate the foot ending with "increases" and the one beginning with "it."

Scene: A subdivision of an act of a drama, consisting of continuous action taking place at a single time and in a single location. The beginnings and endings of scenes may be indicated by clearing the stage of actors and props or by the entrances and exits of important characters. The first act of William Shakespeare's *Winter's Tale* is comprised of two scenes.

Science Fiction: A type of narrative about or based upon real or imagined scientific theories and technology. Science fiction is often peopled with alien creatures and set on other planets or in different dimensions. Karel Capek's *R.U.R.* is a major work of science fiction.

Second Person: See *Point of View*

Semiotics: The study of how literary forms and conventions affect the meaning of language. Semioticians include Ferdinand de Saussure, Charles Sanders Pierce, Claude Levi-Strauss, Jacques Lacan, Michel Foucault, Jacques Derrida, Roland Barthes, and Julia Kristeva.

Sestet: Any six-line poem or stanza. Examples of the sestet include the last six lines of the Petrarchan sonnet form, the stanza form of Robert Burns's ''A Poet's Welcome to his love-begotten Daughter,'' and the sestina form in W. H. Auden's ''Paysage Moralise.''

Setting: The time, place, and culture in which the action of a narrative takes place. The elements of setting may include geographic location, characters' physical and mental environments, prevailing cultural attitudes, or the historical time in which the action takes place. Examples of settings include the romanticized Scotland in Sir Walter Scott's ''Waverley'' novels, the French provincial setting in Gustave Flaubert's *Madame Bovary,* the fictional Wessex country of Thomas Hardy's novels, and the small towns of southern Ontario in Alice Munro's short stories.

Shakespearean Sonnet: See *Sonnet*

Signifying Monkey: A popular trickster figure in black folklore, with hundreds of tales about this character documented since the 19th century. Henry Louis Gates Jr. examines the history of the signifying monkey in *The Signifying Monkey: Towards a Theory of Afro-American Literary Criticism,* published in 1988.

Simile: A comparison, usually using ''like'' or ''as'', of two essentially dissimilar things, as in ''coffee as cold as ice'' or ''He sounded like a broken record.'' The title of Ernest Hemingway's ''Hills Like White Elephants'' contains a simile.

Slang: A type of informal verbal communication that is generally unacceptable for formal writing. Slang words and phrases are often colorful exaggerations used to emphasize the speaker's point; they may also be shortened versions of an often-used word or phrase. Examples of American slang from the 1990s include ''yuppie'' (an acronym for Young Urban Professional), ''awesome'' (for ''excellent''), wired (for ''nervous'' or ''excited''), and ''chill out'' (for relax).

Slant Rhyme: See *Consonance*

Slave Narrative: Autobiographical accounts of American slave life as told by escaped slaves. These works first appeared during the abolition movement of the 1830s through the 1850s. Olaudah Equiano's *The Interesting Narrative of Olaudah Equiano, or Gustavus Vassa, The African* and Harriet Ann Jacobs's *Incidents in the Life of a Slave Girl* are examples of the slave narrative.

Social Realism: See *Socialist Realism*

Socialist Realism: The Socialist Realism school of literary theory was proposed by Maxim Gorky and established as a dogma by the first Soviet Congress of Writers. It demanded adherence to a communist worldview in works of literature. Its doctrines required an objective viewpoint comprehensible to the working classes and themes of social struggle featuring strong proletarian heroes. A successful work of socialist realism is Nikolay Ostrovsky's *Kak zakalyalas stal* (*How the Steel Was Tempered*). Also known as Social Realism.

Soliloquy: A monologue in a drama used to give the audience information and to develop the speaker's character. It is typically a projection of the speaker's innermost thoughts. Usually delivered while the speaker is alone on stage, a soliloquy is intended to present an illusion of unspoken reflection. A celebrated soliloquy is Hamlet's ''To be or not to be'' speech in William Shakespeare's *Hamlet.*

Sonnet: A fourteen-line poem, usually composed in iambic pentameter, employing one of several rhyme schemes. There are three major types of sonnets, upon which all other variations of the form are based: the ''Petrarchan'' or ''Italian'' sonnet, the ''Shakespearean'' or ''English'' sonnet, and the ''Spenserian'' sonnet. A Petrarchan sonnet consists of an octave rhymed *abbaabba* and a ''sestet'' rhymed either *cdecde, cdccdc,* or *cdedce.* The octave poses a question or problem, relates a narrative, or puts forth a proposition; the sestet presents a solution to the problem, comments upon the narrative, or applies the proposition put forth in the octave. The Shakespearean sonnet is divided into three quatrains and a couplet rhymed *abab cdcd efef gg.* The couplet provides an epigrammatic comment on the narrative or problem put forth in the quatrains. The Spenserian sonnet uses three quatrains and a couplet like the Shakespearean, but links their three rhyme schemes in this way: *abab bcbc cdcd ee.* The Spenserian sonnet develops its theme in two parts like the Petrarchan, its final six lines resolving a problem, analyzing a narrative, or applying a proposition put forth in its first eight lines. Examples of sonnets can be found in Petrarch's *Canzoniere,* Edmund Spenser's *Amoretti,* Elizabeth Barrett

Browning's *Sonnets from the Portuguese,* Rainer Maria Rilke's *Sonnets to Orpheus,* and Adrienne Rich's poem "The Insusceptibles."

Spenserian Sonnet: See *Sonnet*

Spenserian Stanza: A nine-line stanza having eight verses in iambic pentameter, its ninth verse in iambic hexameter, and the rhyme scheme ababbcbcc. This stanza form was first used by Edmund Spenser in his allegorical poem *The Faerie Queene.*

Spondee: In poetry meter, a foot consisting of two long or stressed syllables occurring together. This form is quite rare in English verse, and is usually composed of two monosyllabic words. The first foot in the following line from Robert Burns's "Green Grow the Rashes" is an example of a spondee: Green grow the rashes, O

Sprung Rhythm: Versification using a specific number of accented syllables per line but disregarding the number of unaccented syllables that fall in each line, producing an irregular rhythm in the poem. Gerard Manley Hopkins, who coined the term "sprung rhythm," is the most notable practitioner of this technique.

Stanza: A subdivision of a poem consisting of lines grouped together, often in recurring patterns of rhyme, line length, and meter. Stanzas may also serve as units of thought in a poem much like paragraphs in prose. Examples of stanza forms include the quatrain, *terza rima, ottava rima,* Spenserian, and the so-called *In Memoriam* stanza from Alfred, Lord Tennyson's poem by that title. The following is an example of the latter form: Love is and was my lord and king, And in his presence I attend To hear the tidings of my friend, Which every hour his couriers bring.

Stereotype: A stereotype was originally the name for a duplication made during the printing process; this led to its modern definition as a person or thing that is (or is assumed to be) the same as all others of its type. Common stereotypical characters include the absent- minded professor, the nagging wife, the troublemaking teenager, and the kindhearted grandmother.

Stream of Consciousness: A narrative technique for rendering the inward experience of a character. This technique is designed to give the impression of an ever-changing series of thoughts, emotions, images, and memories in the spontaneous and seemingly illogical order that they occur in life. The

textbook example of stream of consciousness is the last section of James Joyce's *Ulysses.*

Structuralism: A twentieth-century movement in literary criticism that examines how literary texts arrive at their meanings, rather than the meanings themselves. There are two major types of structuralist analysis: one examines the way patterns of linguistic structures unify a specific text and emphasize certain elements of that text, and the other interprets the way literary forms and conventions affect the meaning of language itself. Prominent structuralists include Michel Foucault, Roman Jakobson, and Roland Barthes.

Structure: The form taken by a piece of literature. The structure may be made obvious for ease of understanding, as in nonfiction works, or may be obscured for artistic purposes, as in some poetry or seemingly "unstructured" prose. Examples of common literary structures include the plot of a narrative, the acts and scenes of a drama, and such poetic forms as the Shakespearean sonnet and the Pindaric ode.

Sturm und Drang: A German term meaning "storm and stress." It refers to a German literary movement of the 1770s and 1780s that reacted against the order and rationalism of the enlightenment, focusing instead on the intense experience of extraordinary individuals. Highly romantic, works of this movement, such as Johann Wolfgang von Goethe's *Gotz von Berlichingen,* are typified by realism, rebelliousness, and intense emotionalism.

Style: A writer's distinctive manner of arranging words to suit his or her ideas and purpose in writing. The unique imprint of the author's personality upon his or her writing, style is the product of an author's way of arranging ideas and his or her use of diction, different sentence structures, rhythm, figures of speech, rhetorical principles, and other elements of composition. Styles may be classified according to period (Metaphysical, Augustan, Georgian), individual authors (Chaucerian, Miltonic, Jamesian), level (grand, middle, low, plain), or language (scientific, expository, poetic, journalistic).

Subject: The person, event, or theme at the center of a work of literature. A work may have one or more subjects of each type, with shorter works tending to have fewer and longer works tending to have more. The subjects of James Baldwin's novel *Go Tell It on the Mountain* include the themes of father-son relationships, religious conversion, black life, and sexuality. The subjects of Anne Frank's

Diary of a Young Girl include Anne and her family members as well as World War II, the Holocaust, and the themes of war, isolation, injustice, and racism.

Subjectivity: Writing that expresses the author's personal feelings about his subject, and which may or may not include factual information about the subject. Subjectivity is demonstrated in James Joyce's *Portrait of the Artist as a Young Man,* Samuel Butler's *The Way of All Flesh,* and Thomas Wolfe's *Look Homeward, Angel.*

Subplot: A secondary story in a narrative. A subplot may serve as a motivating or complicating force for the main plot of the work, or it may provide emphasis for, or relief from, the main plot. The conflict between the Capulets and the Montagues in William Shakespeare's *Romeo and Juliet* is an example of a subplot.

Surrealism: A term introduced to criticism by Guillaume Apollinaire and later adopted by Andre Breton. It refers to a French literary and artistic movement founded in the 1920s. The Surrealists sought to express unconscious thoughts and feelings in their works. The best-known technique used for achieving this aim was automatic writing—transcriptions of spontaneous outpourings from the unconscious. The Surrealists proposed to unify the contrary levels of conscious and unconscious, dream and reality, objectivity and subjectivity into a new level of "super-realism." Surrealism can be found in the poetry of Paul Eluard, Pierre Reverdy, and Louis Aragon, among others.

Suspense: A literary device in which the author maintains the audience's attention through the build-up of events, the outcome of which will soon be revealed. Suspense in William Shakespeare's *Hamlet* is sustained throughout by the question of whether or not the Prince will achieve what he has been instructed to do and of what he intends to do.

Syllogism: A method of presenting a logical argument. In its most basic form, the syllogism consists of a major premise, a minor premise, and a conclusion. An example of a syllogism is: Major premise: When it snows, the streets get wet. Minor premise: It is snowing. Conclusion: The streets are wet.

Symbol: Something that suggests or stands for something else without losing its original identity. In literature, symbols combine their literal meaning with the suggestion of an abstract concept. Literary symbols are of two types: those that carry complex associations of meaning no matter what their con-

texts, and those that derive their suggestive meaning from their functions in specific literary works. Examples of symbols are sunshine suggesting happiness, rain suggesting sorrow, and storm clouds suggesting despair.

Symbolism: This term has two widely accepted meanings. In historical criticism, it denotes an early modernist literary movement initiated in France during the nineteenth century that reacted against the prevailing standards of realism. Writers in this movement aimed to evoke, indirectly and symbolically, an order of being beyond the material world of the five senses. Poetic expression of personal emotion figured strongly in the movement, typically by means of a private set of symbols uniquely identifiable with the individual poet. The principal aim of the Symbolists was to express in words the highly complex feelings that grew out of everyday contact with the world. In a broader sense, the term "symbolism" refers to the use of one object to represent another. Early members of the Symbolist movement included the French authors Charles Baudelaire and Arthur Rimbaud; William Butler Yeats, James Joyce, and T. S. Eliot were influenced as the movement moved to Ireland, England, and the United States. Examples of the concept of symbolism include a flag that stands for a nation or movement, or an empty cupboard used to suggest hopelessness, poverty, and despair.

Symbolist: See *Symbolism*

Symbolist Movement: See *Symbolism*

Sympathetic Fallacy: See *Affective Fallacy*

T

Tale: A story told by a narrator with a simple plot and little character development. Tales are usually relatively short and often carry a simple message. Examples of tales can be found in the work of Rudyard Kipling, Somerset Maugham, Saki, Anton Chekhov, Guy de Maupassant, and Armistead Maupin.

Tall Tale: A humorous tale told in a straightforward, credible tone but relating absolutely impossible events or feats of the characters. Such tales were commonly told of frontier adventures during the settlement of the west in the United States. Tall tales have been spun around such legendary heroes as Mike Fink, Paul Bunyan, Davy Crockett, Johnny Appleseed, and Captain Stormalong as well as the real-life William F. Cody and Annie Oakley. Literary use of tall tales can be found in Washington Irving's *History of New York,* Mark Twain's *Life on the Mississippi,* and in the German R. F. Raspe's *Baron Munchausen's Narratives of His Marvellous Travels and Campaigns in Russia.*

Tanka: A form of Japanese poetry similar to *haiku.* A *tanka* is five lines long, with the lines containing five, seven, five, seven, and seven syllables respectively. Skilled *tanka* authors include Ishikawa Takuboku, Masaoka Shiki, Amy Lowell, and Adelaide Crapsey.

Teatro Grottesco: See *Theater of the Grotesque*

Terza Rima: A three-line stanza form in poetry in which the rhymes are made on the last word of each line in the following manner: the first and third lines of the first stanza, then the second line of the first stanza and the first and third lines of the second stanza, and so on with the middle line of any stanza rhyming with the first and third lines of the following stanza. An example of *terza rima* is Percy Bysshe Shelley's ''The Triumph of Love'': As in that trance of wondrous thought I lay This was the tenour of my waking dream. Methought I sate beside a public way Thick strewn with summer dust, and a great stream Of people there was hurrying to and fro Numerous as gnats upon the evening gleam,. . .

Tetrameter: See *Meter*

Textual Criticism: A branch of literary criticism that seeks to establish the authoritative text of a literary work. Textual critics typically compare all known manuscripts or printings of a single work in order to assess the meanings of differences and revisions. This procedure allows them to arrive at a definitive version that (supposedly) corresponds to the author's original intention. Textual criticism was applied during the Renaissance to salvage the classical texts of Greece and Rome, and modern works have been studied, for instance, to undo deliberate correction or censorship, as in the case of novels by Stephen Crane and Theodore Dreiser.

Theater of Cruelty: Term used to denote a group of theatrical techniques designed to eliminate the psychological and emotional distance between actors and audience. This concept, introduced in the 1930s in France, was intended to inspire a more intense theatrical experience than conventional theater allowed. The ''cruelty'' of this dramatic theory signified not sadism but heightened actor/audience involvement in the dramatic event. The theater of cruelty was theorized by Antonin Artaud in his *Le Theatre et son double* (*The Theatre and Its Double*), and also appears in the work of Jerzy Grotowski, Jean Genet, Jean Vilar, and Arthur Adamov, among others.

Theater of the Absurd: A post-World War II dramatic trend characterized by radical theatrical innovations. In works influenced by the Theater of the absurd, nontraditional, sometimes grotesque characterizations, plots, and stage sets reveal a meaningless universe in which human values are irrelevant. Existentialist themes of estrangement, absurdity, and futility link many of the works of this movement. The principal writers of the Theater of the Absurd are Samuel Beckett, Eugene Ionesco, Jean Genet, and Harold Pinter.

Theater of the Grotesque: An Italian theatrical movement characterized by plays written around the ironic and macabre aspects of daily life in the World War I era. Theater of the Grotesque was named after the play *The Mask and the Face* by Luigi Chiarelli, which was described as ''a grotesque in three acts.'' The movement influenced the work of Italian dramatist Luigi Pirandello, author of *Right You Are, If You Think You Are.* Also known as *Teatro Grottesco.*

Theme: The main point of a work of literature. The term is used interchangeably with thesis. The theme of William Shakespeare's *Othello*—jealousy—is a common one.

Thesis: A thesis is both an essay and the point argued in the essay. Thesis novels and thesis plays share the quality of containing a thesis which is supported through the action of the story. A master's thesis and a doctoral dissertation are two theses required of graduate students.

Thesis Play: See *Thesis*

Three Unities: See *Unities*

Tone: The author's attitude toward his or her audience may be deduced from the tone of the work. A formal tone may create distance or convey politeness, while an informal tone may encourage a friendly, intimate, or intrusive feeling in the reader. The author's attitude toward his or her subject matter may also be deduced from the tone of the words he or she uses in discussing it. The tone of John F. Kennedy's speech which included the appeal to ''ask not what your country can do for you'' was intended to instill feelings of camaraderie and national pride in listeners.

Tragedy: A drama in prose or poetry about a noble, courageous hero of excellent character who, because of some tragic character flaw or *hamartia*, brings ruin upon him- or herself. Tragedy treats its subjects in a dignified and serious manner, using poetic language to help evoke pity and fear and bring about catharsis, a purging of these emotions. The tragic form was practiced extensively by the ancient Greeks. In the Middle Ages, when classical works were virtually unknown, tragedy came to denote any works about the fall of persons from exalted to low conditions due to any reason: fate, vice, weakness, etc. According to the classical definition of tragedy, such works present the ''pathetic''—that which evokes pity—rather than the tragic. The classical form of tragedy was revived in the sixteenth century; it flourished especially on the Elizabethan stage. In modern times, dramatists have attempted to adapt the form to the needs of modern society by drawing their heroes from the ranks of ordinary men and women and defining the nobility of these heroes in terms of spirit rather than exalted social standing. The greatest classical example of tragedy is Sophocles' *Oedipus Rex*. The ''pathetic'' derivation is exemplified in ''The Monk's Tale'' in Geoffrey Chaucer's *Canterbury Tales*. Notable works produced during the sixteenth century revival include William Shakespeare's *Hamlet, Othello,* and *King Lear*. Modern dramatists working in the tragic tradition include Henrik Ibsen, Arthur Miller, and Eugene O'Neill.

Tragedy of Blood: See *Revenge Tragedy*

Tragic Flaw: In a tragedy, the quality within the hero or heroine which leads to his or her downfall. Examples of the tragic flaw include Othello's jealousy and Hamlet's indecisiveness, although most great tragedies defy such simple interpretation.

Transcendentalism: An American philosophical and religious movement, based in New England from around 1835 until the Civil War. Transcendentalism was a form of American romanticism that had its roots abroad in the works of Thomas Carlyle, Samuel Coleridge, and Johann Wolfgang von Goethe. The Transcendentalists stressed the importance of intuition and subjective experience in communication with God. They rejected religious dogma and texts in favor of mysticism and scientific naturalism. They pursued truths that lie beyond the ''colorless'' realms perceived by reason and the senses and were active social reformers in public education,

women's rights, and the abolition of slavery. Prominent members of the group include Ralph Waldo Emerson and Henry David Thoreau.

Trickster: A character or figure common in Native American and African literature who uses his ingenuity to defeat enemies and escape difficult situations. Tricksters are most often animals, such as the spider, hare, or coyote, although they may take the form of humans as well. Examples of trickster tales include Thomas King's *A Coyote Columbus Story,* Ashley F. Bryan's *The Dancing Granny* and Ishmael Reed's *The Last Days of Louisiana Red.*

Trimeter: See *Meter*

Triple Rhyme: See *Rhyme*

Trochee: See *Foot*

U

Understatement: See *Irony*

Unities: Strict rules of dramatic structure, formulated by Italian and French critics of the Renaissance and based loosely on the principles of drama discussed by Aristotle in his *Poetics*. Foremost among these rules were the three unities of action, time, and place that compelled a dramatist to: (1) construct a single plot with a beginning, middle, and end that details the causal relationships of action and character; (2) restrict the action to the events of a single day; and (3) limit the scene to a single place or city. The unities were observed faithfully by continental European writers until the Romantic Age, but they were never regularly observed in English drama. Modern dramatists are typically more concerned with a unity of impression or emotional effect than with any of the classical unities. The unities are observed in Pierre Corneille's tragedy *Polyeuctes* and Jean-Baptiste Racine's *Phedre*. Also known as Three Unities.

Urban Realism: A branch of realist writing that attempts to accurately reflect the often harsh facts of modern urban existence. Some works by Stephen Crane, Theodore Dreiser, Charles Dickens, Fyodor Dostoyevsky, Emile Zola, Abraham Cahan, and Henry Fuller feature urban realism. Modern examples include Claude Brown's *Manchild in the Promised Land* and Ron Milner's *What the Wine Sellers Buy.*

Utopia: A fictional perfect place, such as ''paradise'' or ''heaven.'' Early literary utopias were included in Plato's *Republic* and Sir Thomas More's

Utopia, while more modern utopias can be found in Samuel Butler's *Erewhon,* Theodor Herzka's *A Visit to Freeland,* and H. G. Wells' *A Modern Utopia.*

Utopian: See *Utopia*

Utopianism: See *Utopia*

V

Verisimilitude: Literally, the appearance of truth. In literary criticism, the term refers to aspects of a work of literature that seem true to the reader. Verisimilitude is achieved in the work of Honore de Balzac, Gustave Flaubert, and Henry James, among other late nineteenth-century realist writers.

Vers de societe: See *Occasional Verse*

Vers libre: See *Free Verse*

Verse: A line of metered language, a line of a poem, or any work written in verse. The following line of verse is from the epic poem *Don Juan* by Lord Byron: ''My way is to begin with the beginning.''

Versification: The writing of verse. Versification may also refer to the meter, rhyme, and other mechanical components of a poem. Composition of a ''Roses are red, violets are blue'' poem to suit an occasion is a common form of versification practiced by students.

Victorian: Refers broadly to the reign of Queen Victoria of England (1837-1901) and to anything with qualities typical of that era. For example, the qualities of smug narrowmindedness, bourgeois materialism, faith in social progress, and priggish morality are often considered Victorian. This stereotype is contradicted by such dramatic intellectual developments as the theories of Charles Darwin, Karl Marx, and Sigmund Freud (which stirred strong debates in England) and the critical attitudes of serious Victorian writers like Charles Dickens and George Eliot. In literature, the Victorian Period was the great age of the English novel, and the latter part of the era saw the rise of movements such as decadence and symbolism. Works of Victorian literature include the poetry of Robert Browning and Alfred, Lord Tennyson, the criticism of Matthew Arnold and John Ruskin, and the novels of Emily Bronte, William Makepeace Thackeray, and Thomas Hardy. Also known as Victorian Age and Victorian Period.

Victorian Age: See *Victorian*

Victorian Period: See *Victorian*

W

Weltanschauung: A German term referring to a person's worldview or philosophy. Examples of *weltanschauung* include Thomas Hardy's view of the human being as the victim of fate, destiny, or impersonal forces and circumstances, and the disillusioned and laconic cynicism expressed by such poets of the 1930s as W. H. Auden, Sir Stephen Spender, and Sir William Empson.

Weltschmerz: A German term meaning ''world pain.'' It describes a sense of anguish about the nature of existence, usually associated with a melancholy, pessimistic attitude. *Weltschmerz* was expressed in England by George Gordon, Lord Byron in his *Manfred* and *Childe Harold's Pilgrimage,* in France by Viscount de Chateaubriand, Alfred de Vigny, and Alfred de Musset, in Russia by Aleksandr Pushkin and Mikhail Lermontov, in Poland by Juliusz Slowacki, and in America by Nathaniel Hawthorne.

Z

Zarzuela: A type of Spanish operetta. Writers of *zarzuelas* include Lope de Vega and Pedro Calderon.

Zeitgeist: A German term meaning ''spirit of the time.'' It refers to the moral and intellectual trends of a given era. Examples of *zeitgeist* include the preoccupation with the more morbid aspects of dying and death in some Jacobean literature, especially in the works of dramatists Cyril Tourneur and John Webster, and the decadence of the French Symbolists.

Cumulative Author/Title Index

Nationality/Ethnicity Index

African American

Baraka, Amiri
  Dutchman: V3
Childress, Alice
  Trouble in Mind: V8
  The Wedding Band: V2
Fuller, Charles H.
  A Soldier's Play: V8
Hansberry, Lorraine
  A Raisin in the Sun: V2
Hughes, Langston
  Mule Bone: V6
Hurston, Zora Neale
  Mule Bone: V6
Shange, Ntozake
  for colored girls who have
    considered suicide/when the
    rainbow is enuf: V2
Smith, Anna Deavere
  Twilight: Los Angeles, 1992: V2
Wilson, August
  Fences: V3
  The Piano Lesson: V7

American

Albee, Edward
  Three Tall Women: V8
  Who's Afraid of Virginia
    Woolf?: V3
  The Zoo Story: V2
Baraka, Amiri
  Dutchman: V3
Childress, Alice
  Trouble in Mind: V8
  The Wedding Band: V2

Eliot, T. S.
  Murder in the Cathedral: V4
Fierstein, Harvey
  Torch Song Trilogy: V6
Fuller, Charles H.
  A Soldier's Play: V8
Gibson, William
  The Miracle Worker: V2
Glaspell, Susan
  Trifles: V8
Guare, John
  The House of Blue Leaves: V8
Hammerstein, Oscar
  The King and I: V1
Hansberry, Lorraine
  A Raisin in the Sun: V2
Hart, Moss
  You Can't Take It with You: V1
Hellman, Lillian
  The Children's Hour: V3
  The Little Foxes: V1
Henley, Beth
  Crimes of the Heart: V2
Hurston, Zora Neale
  Mule Bone: V6
Inge, William
  Bus Stop: V8
  Come Back, Little Sheba: V3
  Picnic: V5
Kaufman, George S.
  You Can't Take It with You: V1
Kopit, Arthur
  Oh Dad, Poor Dad, Mamma's
    Hung You in the Closet and
    I'm Feelin' So Sad: V7
Kushner, Tony
  Angels in America: V5

Lawrence, Jerome
  Inherit the Wind: V2
Lee, Robert E.
  Inherit the Wind: V2
Mamet, David
  American Buffalo: V3
  Glengarry Glen Ross: V2
  Speed-the-Plow: V6
McCullers, Carson
  The Member of the Wedding: V5
Medoff, Mark
  Children of a Lesser God: V4
Miller, Arthur
  All My Sons: V8
  The Crucible: V3
  Death of a Salesman: V1
Norman, Marsha
  'night, Mother: V2
Odets, Clifford
  Waiting for Lefty: V3
O'Neill, Eugene
  The Emperor Jones: V6
  The Hairy Ape: V4
  The Iceman Cometh: V5
  Long Day's Journey into
    Night: V2
Rabe, David
  The Basic Training of Pavlo
    Hummel: V3
  Streamers: V8
Rodgers, Richard
  The King and I: V1
Shange, Ntozake
  for colored girls who have
    considered suicide/when the
    rainbow is enuf: V2

Shepard, Sam
    Buried Child: V6
    Fool for Love: V7
    True West: V3
Shue, Larry
    The Foreigner: V7
Simon, Neil
    Brighton Beach Memoirs: V6
    The Odd Couple: V2
Smith, Anna Deavere
    Twilight: Los Angeles, 1992: V2
Stein, Joseph
    Fiddler on the Roof: V7
Valdez, Luis
    Zoot Suit: V5
Vidal, Gore
    Visit to a Small Planet: V2
Wasserstein, Wendy
    The Heidi Chronicles: V5
Wilder, Thornton
    Our Town: V1
    The Skin of Our Teeth: V4
Williams, Tennessee
    Cat on a Hot Tin Roof: V3
    The Glass Menagerie: V1
    The Night of the Iguana: V7
    A Streetcar Named Desire: V1
Wilson, August
    Fences: V3
    The Piano Lesson: V7
Wilson, Lanford
    Burn This: V4

Argentinian

Dorfman, Ariel
    Death and the Maiden: V4

Canadian

Highway, Tomson
    The Rez Sisters: V2
Pollock, Sharon
    Blood Relations: V3

Chilean

Dorfman, Ariel
    Death and the Maiden: V4

Czechoslovakian

Capek, Karel
    R.U.R.: V7

English

Ayckbourn, Alan
    A Chorus of Disapproval: V7
Barnes, Peter
    The Ruling Class: V6

Bolt, Robert
    A Man for All Seasons: V2
Bond, Edward
    Lear: V3
    Saved: V8
Christie, Agatha
    The Mousetrap: V2
Coward, Noel
    Hay Fever: V6
    Private Lives: V3
Delaney, Shelagh
    A Taste of Honey: V7
Ford, John
    'Tis Pity She's a Whore: V7
Goldsmith, Oliver
    She Stoops to Conquer: V1
Hare, David
    Blue Room: V7
    Plenty: V4
Jonson, Ben(jamin)
    The Alchemist: V4
Marlowe, Christopher
    Doctor Faustus: V1
    Edward II: V5
Orton, Joe
    Entertaining Mr. Sloane: V3
    What the Butler Saw: V6
Osborne, John
    Look Back in Anger: V4
Pinter, Harold
    The Birthday Party: V5
    The Caretaker: V7
    The Homecoming: V3
Rattigan, Terence
    The Browning Version: V8
Rice, Tim
    Jesus Christ Superstar: V7
Shaffer, Peter
    Equus: V5
Stoppard, Tom
    Arcadia: V5
    The Real Thing: V8
    Rosencrantz and Guildenstern Are Dead: V2
Webber, Andrew Lloyd
    Jesus Christ Superstar: V7

French

Jarry, Alfred
    Ubu Roi: V8
Rostand, Edmond
    Cyrano de Bergerac: V1
Sartre, Jean-Paul
    No Exit: V5

German

Brecht, Bertolt
    Mother Courage and Her Children: V5
    The Threepenny Opera: V4
Weiss, Peter
    Marat/Sade: V3

Greek

Aeschylus
    Prometheus Bound: V5
Euripides
    The Bacchae: V6
    Iphigenia in Taurus: V4
    Medea: V1
Sophocles
    Ajax: V8
    Antigone: V1
    Electra: V4
    Oedipus Rex: V1

Hispanic

Valdez, Luis
    Zoot Suit: V5

Irish

Beckett, Samuel
    Krapp's Last Tape: V7
    Waiting for Godot: V2
Behan, Brendan
    The Hostage: V7
Shaw, George Bernard
    Major Barbara: V3
    Man and Superman: V6
    Pygmalion: V1
Sheridan, Richard Brinsley
    School for Scandal: V4
Wilde, Oscar
    The Importance of Being Earnest: V4
    Salome: V8

Italian

Pirandello, Luigi
    Six Characters in Search of an Author: V4

Mexican

Carballido, Emilio
    I, Too, Speak of the Rose: V4

Native Canadian

Highway, Tomson
    The Rez Sisters: V2

Norwegian

Ibsen, Henrik
    A Doll's House: V1

Subject/Theme Index

Humor
    The House of Blue Leaves:
        71, 77, 79
    The Real Thing: 112-114, 117
    Saved: 147-148, 152, 154
    Ubu Roi: 249, 253, 256

I

Identity
    Streamers: 186
Imagery and Symbolism
    Salome: 127, 134-135
    Streamers: 188-190
Imagination
    Peer Gynt: 87, 92, 94, 96
Insanity
    The House of Blue Leaves:
        73, 77, 79-80
Irony
    The House of Blue Leaves: 77, 80
    The Real Thing: 108-109,
        112-113
Isolation
    Trifles: 221

J

Judaism
    Salome: 128, 131, 135

K

Killers and Killing
    Ajax: 2, 6
    All My Sons: 19, 27
    Salome: 128-129, 133-134,
        139-141
    Saved: 147, 150-152
    A Soldier's Play: 161, 163,
        167, 170-171
    Streamers: 180-182
    Trifles: 224, 226, 228
    Trouble in Mind: 241
    Ubu Roi: 250-251, 256

L

Landscape
    Peer Gynt: 89-90, 93-94
Language and Meaning
    The Real Thing: 111
Law and Order
    Ajax: 3, 9
    All My Sons: 19-20, 26-28
    Salome: 128, 136
    Saved: 145-147, 152-155
    A Soldier's Play: 162-163,
        167-168
    Trifles: 217-218, 223-228
    Trouble in Mind: 241-242
Limitations and Opportunities
    Saved: 150

Loneliness
    Bus Stop: 59
Loneliness
    Bus Stop: 56, 59-60
    Trifles: 221-222, 225-228
Love
    Peer Gynt: 92
Love and Passion
    Saved: 150
Love and Passion
    All My Sons: 19-20, 26
    The Browning Version: 42, 45-47
    Bus Stop: 56-57, 60, 63-65
    Peer Gynt: 92-94
    The Real Thing: 107-109, 112-
        114, 117-118
    Salome: 127-129, 133-135,
        138-141
    Saved: 151

M

Marriage
    All My Sons: 19-20
    Bus Stop: 63-64
    Peer Gynt: 89, 92
    The Real Thing: 111, 113-115
    Salome: 133, 135-136
    Three Tall Women: 205-206
Mental Instability
    The House of Blue Leaves: 75-76
Middle East
    All My Sons: 27
    The Browning Version: 47
Monarchy
    All My Sons: 29-32
    Peer Gynt: 89, 93, 95
    Salome: 126, 128-129, 139-140
    Ubu Roi: 251, 256
Money and Economics
    All My Sons: 23-24, 28
    The House of Blue Leaves:
        74, 77-79
    The Real Thing: 113-115
    Saved: 151-153
Monologue
    A Soldier's Play: 162-163, 167
Mood
    Streamers: 180-181, 189
Moral Corruption
    Bus Stop: 59
Morality
    Peer Gynt: 92
Morals and Morality
    Saved: 151
Morals and Morality
    All My Sons: 23-24, 28-31
    The House of Blue Leaves: 75-77
    Peer Gynt: 93, 96
    Salome: 135-137
    Saved: 151
    Streamers: 185, 187-190
    Trifles: 227-228

    Ubu Roi: 255-256
Murder
    Ajax: 2, 5, 7
    Saved: 145, 147, 150, 152, 154
    A Soldier's Play: 161-163,
        169-172
    Streamers: 184-185
    Trifles: 216-218, 222, 225-228
    Trouble in Mind: 237, 240
Music
    Bus Stop: 55-57, 62
    The House of Blue Leaves: 71-76
    Peer Gynt: 88, 90, 96
    The Real Thing: 108, 112, 116
    Salome: 127, 134
    A Soldier's Play: 162, 166
    Streamers: 180, 182, 189-191
    Trifles: 219, 221, 223
    Trouble in Mind: 236, 241
Mystery and Intrigue
    A Soldier's Play: 161, 167, 169
Myths and Legends
    Ajax: 1-3, 6-12
    Peer Gynt: 93-94

N

Narration
    Three Tall Women: 204
Nature
    Peer Gynt: 87, 92, 94, 96
    Salome: 128, 131-132, 135, 137
Nietzschean Philosophy
    Ubu Roi: 253
North America
    The House of Blue Leaves:
        73, 75, 78
    Saved: 153-154
Nuclear War
    All My Sons: 27

O

Oedipus Complex
    All My Sons: 29-32
Old Age
    Three Tall Women: 200-201, 204

P

Peer Pressure
    Trouble in Mind: 240
Persecution
    All My Sons: 27
    A Soldier's Play: 167-169
    Streamers: 184, 188-189, 193-194
Personal Identity
    Streamers: 184-186
Personality Traits
    Bus Stop: 60
    Peer Gynt: 93-94

W

War and Peace
   Streamers: 186
War, the Military, and Soldier Life
   Ajax: 2-3, 7-9
   All My Sons: 20, 23-27
   The House of Blue Leaves: 77-79

The Real Thing: 114-116
Salome: 129, 131
Saved: 150-151
A Soldier's Play: 161-163,
   166-171
Streamers: 179-182, 185-195
Ubu Roi: 255-256

Wildlife
   Streamers: 179, 181, 186,
      189, 191
World War II
   All My Sons: 18, 26-27
   Saved: 149, 153-154
   A Soldier's Play: 166-168, 171